The UK Space
Resources, Environment and the Future
Third Edition

Edited by

J.W. House
Halford Mackinder Professor of Geography,
University of Oxford

Weidenfeld and Nicolson

London

ISBN 0 297 78182 0 cased
ISBN 0 297 78183 9 paperback

George Weidenfeld and Nicolson Ltd
91 Clapham High Street, London SW4 7TA

Text set in 10/11 pt IBM Press Roman, printed and bound
in Great Britain at The Pitman Press, Bath

Contributors

Chapter 1
> J.W. House, *M.A., D.Litt. (Oxon.)*
> *Halford Mackinder Professor of Geography, University of Oxford*

Chapter 2
> R. Lawton, *M.A. (Liverpool)*
> *Professor of Geography, University of Liverpool*

Chapter 3
> L.W. Hanna, *M.Sc., Ph.D. (Belfast)*
> *Senior Lecturer in Geography, University of Newcastle upon Tyne*

Chapter 4
> G. Humphrys, *B.A. (Bristol), M.A. (McGill), Ph.D. (Wales)*
> *Senior Lecturer in Geography, University College of Swansea*

Chapter 5
> B. Fullerton, *M.A. (London)*
> *Senior Lecturer in Geography, University of Newcastle upon Tyne*

Chapter 6
> D.R. Diamond, *M.A. (Oxon.), M.Sc. (Northwestern)*
> *Reader in Regional Planning, London School of Economics and Political
>   Science*

Chapter 7
> The Contributors

Contents

Figures

Page

Tables

Preface to the Third Edition

During even the short period of three editions (1973, 1977, 1982), the economic, social and political geography of the UK has experienced almost unparalleled change, following upon three decades of unprecedented capitalist expansion. What began as a national stock-taking, an evaluation of resources, both natural and human, became a commentary and interpretation of dramatic and rapidly shifting trends. Which trends represent a secular and permanent realignment, leading to structural as well as spatial transformations of the society and economy of the UK, it is still too early to assess. This makes it even more important to monitor and evaluate the kaleidoscopic changes taking place. The great debate has shifted in focus, from growth to stabilization or the counteracting of decline, from environmental enhancement to its protection, from regional equilibrium to regional economic survival, from devolution to resisting the centralizing power of the State, and from full employment to the consequences of mass unemployment.

The geographical perspective reflects a sensitivity to the differences, trends and problems arising from both the short- and long-term characteristics of people and places. These are interpreted within the framework of changes over the past few decades and their related processes of policy-making and decision-taking, both public and private. In other words, a set of detailed considered judgements is offered on a mosaic of change in the UK Space, rather than an opening out of new research frontiers. Towards these, the full bibliographies to each chapter are intended as a signpost. Some consideration is given to theories and models which help to explain change, and also to the political forces which increasingly disturb and distort an economic and social interpretation of events.

Particular thanks are due to all who prepared diagrams, typed the manuscript and aided the proof-reading and index compilation. To my secretary, Ms Pauline Linières, I owe an especial debt of gratitude.

University of Oxford   J W HOUSE
February 1982

1

The Regional Perspective

1   THE UK AT THE CROSSROADS

I.1   The Short and the Longer Term

Traditionally, geographical interpretation has adopted a longer-term view, discounting short-term fluctuations in economy, society or polity. The characteristics, location and pattern of all resources, including people, have been studied over time, using both systematic (or sector) and regional methods of analysis (Dury 1968; Smith 1949; Stamp and Beaver 1971; Watson and Sissons 1964). The 1980s are a very problematical period, however, since three decades of hitherto unparalleled capitalist expansion have been followed by the UK's deepest depression since the 1930s. It is too early to say if this downturn is merely cyclical or presages a redefinition of Britain's role and standing, struggling to adjust to slow growth or economic stagnation. The post-industrial society was to have been affluent, if not hedonistic, and certainly conscious of material achievements and escalating demands for goods, for space and for leisure. The leisure is there, but for the unemployed; the service economy has arrived, but accompanied by de-industrialization; greater affluence is present, but in a more sharply polarized society.

Nevertheless, UK economic and social growth since World War II has been considerable, though slower and more fitful than among our European neighbours or major industrial competitors. A GDP of £114.9 billions in 1979 represented a fifty per cent rise in real terms on the 1961 figure. Little wonder that Rostow could speak of the high mass consumption society in the UK or that living standards have improved for the majority. Yet progress has been uneven, in space and time, and markedly so among different groups in society. Successive governments, variably committed to welfare, have sought to mitigate adverse changes on both people and places. Differentials between the more affluent and the less so began to narrow and there was some convergence between the fortunes of regions until the early 1970s, but both gains have since been eroded.

Explanations of the downturn in the British economy and prescriptions for the ailing patient are legion, but both internal conditions and externalities must share the blame. A complex, urban industrial society in the mature, some would say late, stages of capitalist development inevitably finds it difficult to adjust to a less competitive position in the world economy. Shortcomings of labour vie with those of management as prime scapegoats, multinational firms and governments are not immune from severe criticism, and the unstable world trading and monetary systems have not been insignificant influences. After the decline of world multilateral trading, British entry to the EEC in the early 1970s was seen by some as an essential safeguard for a more prosperous long-term future. Unfortunately, it coincided with the onset of world depression and, in spite of impressive short-term achievements, the case has yet to be proven.

I.2   De-industrialization and the Post-Industrial Society

The value of gross industrial output accelerated during the 1960s, even taking
inflation into account, whilst the index of power consumed tells a similar story.
The working population (ch. 2.IV) has not increased in like ratio, and, even before
the current recession, male employment was falling, though female jobs and activity
rates had been rising for some time. Over the past two decades there has been an
improvement in real income per capita, with earnings growing faster than prices.
Living standards for the great majority have risen, as indicated by an increase in the
volume of domestic consumption at about 2% per annum.

Yet the seeds of industrial transformation and decline had been sown much
earlier. Probably since at least 1870 the UK had been slow to adopt new technology
or keep ahead in innovation, had built up non-competitive manning levels and
lagged behind in technical education (Kilpatrick and Lawson 1980, 100). Social
factors, too, contributed to holding back British productivity rates. Countervailing
trends have thus been at work, pointing in one direction to the post-industrial
society of greater affluence, an enriched and expanded services sector and a lower
but more remunerative level of employment in manufacturing, with a higher
technological status and more concentration on growth branches (table 1.1).
Though there was movement towards the post-industrial society, the recessions of
the 1970s have reversed the optimistic trends and shown more starkly the
vulnerability of the UK economy to a reduced world trading status. Manufacturing
decline has been accompanied by high and rising unemployment. Between 1965

TABLE 1.1

Industrial Production, UK, 1954–79

Index change, ± national mean, 6 ranked lead and lag sectors (1954–79), output by value					
> *5% over national mean*	1954–60	1960–7	1963–70	1970–5	1975–9
Chemicals	+24.9	+38.2	+33.8	+12.1	+17.2
Electrical engineering	+24.2	+26.4	+24.4	+12.3	+13.6*
Other manufactures	+14.0	+21.3	+21.5	+2.1	+17.6
Gas, water, electricity	+12.8	+23.0	+19.7	+19.4	+16.7
Glass, etc.	–	+15.3	+11.1	+19.8	+1.3
Mechanical engineering	–	+16.2	+10.8	+1.1	–8.4
> *5% below national mean*					
Mining and quarrying	–31.2	–47.9	–45.8	–14.7	+194.7[†]
Shipbuilding	–28.4	–59.5	–38.0	+2.4	–21.9
Leather, etc.	–31.1	–44.2	–31.2	–8.5	–8.4
Clothing/footwear	–	–10.9	–21.0	+9.8	+6.5
Timber/furniture	–17.1	–9.1	–10.5	+9.2	+3.4
Metals	–	–15.5	–9.3	–22.4	+3.1

* computers +139.2; radio/electronic comp. +40.5
[†] coal –11.0; oil/nat. gas +3,013.0

Source: Central Statistical Office data

and 1981 1.6 million manufacturing jobs were lost (nearly 30% of the total) and by 1981 only 29% were engaged in manufacturing, compared to 37% in 1965. Service employment had risen by 1.95 million jobs over the same period, in the public and private sectors combined, employing 59.3% of the workforce in 1980 compared with 48.8% in the earlier year (Keeble 1981, 459). The loss of manufacturing jobs in the UK had been more serious than among her competitors and more serious too than the general economic downturn in the economy. Though overmanning had been reduced, it was an uneven, enforced process. Manufacturing output had held up better until the stagnation induced by the depressions of the 1970s. This was de-industrialization caused by economic malaise (Blackaby 1979, Sheriff 1979), not the confident harbinger of the post-industrial age (fig. 1.1).

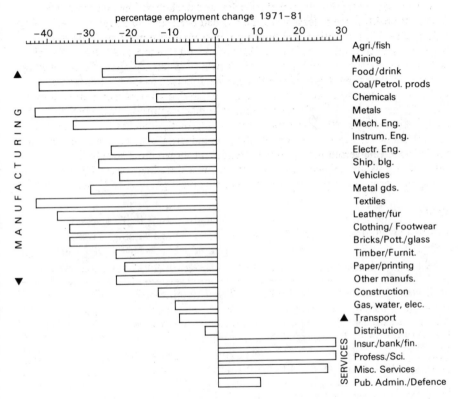

Figure 1.1   The UK post-industrial society

Not every commentator saw slow economic growth as an unmitigated evil (Beckerman 1979), though it impacted seriously on poverty. Nor was there agreement on the causes of de-industrialization or on what should be done in terms of public policy. Moore and Rhodes (1976, 40) postulated that the UK industrial economy had priced itself out of world markets, that it had been deprived by the expansion of the public sector, and, perhaps most of all, there was the impact of cumulative causation, involving low productivity, slow growth of demand, balance of payments problems, low investment rates and slow adaptation to change. Stout

(1979, 173) pointed out that explanations 'have broken into one of a number of chains of cause and effect, highlighting some feature or stage of a circular process, which is as much a symptom as it is a cause'. The policy implications were clearer — 'unless there is a radical shift in policy full employment will become a never-to-return feature like cockfighting and the tram' (Sheriff 1979, 17).

Unemployment (ch. 2.IV.4) had indeed become the spectre haunting all governments in the 1980s. In one year alone, unemployment had risen by one million, standing in August 1981 at 2.9 millions or 12.2% of the workforce, compared with 4.1% as an annual average in 1975. Unemployment in the regions (August 1981) varied from 18.9% (23.1% for males) in Northern Ireland, down to 8.8% (10.5% for males) in Greater London. Levels of 36% out of work in Strabane, 26% in Consett, 22% in Corby or 21% in Ebbw Vale conjured back visions of the 1930s (Townsend 1980). Even though structural unemployment may be little more than one-half the regional total (Hannah 1981), the social problems were severe and cures, both short and long term, hard to find (Layard 1981). With a stricken economy it was highly unlikely that expansion of services, with a developed export role, could spearhead economic recovery (Harris and Taylor 1978). Nor has it been by any means clear that the benefits of North Sea oil have been wisely used or that they could provide the engine-room for renewed economic growth (Quinlan 1981, Mason 1979, Lewis and McNicoll 1978).

I.3   Social Change

From the austerity, rationing and limited choice of imported goods in the early 1950s, to the years of 'never had it so good', the swinging sixties and the inflation, high unemployment and the energy crisis of the 1970s, there has been a moderate but progressive improvement in well-being for most people in the UK (Toland 1980, 13—14). At constant prices, average weekly male manual earnings have risen steadily (1951 £31, 1977 £54), though household incomes have varied according to the number of wage-earners, the elderly or the single-income families. Class divisions have become blurred and earning power has to some extent replaced life-style or habits as the prime means of class differentiation; in particular, manual/non-manual differences are much less apparent. The housing stock has visibly improved, with a greater balance of higher quality and an owner-occupation rate over 50% by 1978. By that same year more than 50% also had some form of central heating, more than 90% had television (50% had colour). Yet, ironically, soaring house prices (Nellis and Longbottom 1981) put property-owning beyond the reach of an increasing number of young couples and singles. Drudgery for the housewife has been greatly reduced and ownership of consumer durables is remarkably widespread. Moreover, standards of nutrition are now high and still rising.

Educational provision has greatly increased, comprehensive schools have been widely accepted, and the university population has almost trebled since 1951. In 1977 81% of manual workers took an annual holiday of three weeks or more, compared to the 2% who did so in 1961. Sensitivity to environmental problems, their management and improvement, became a watchword in the late 1960s, although for the under-privileged minorities the quality of life, expressed in urban ghettoes, inadequate housing, congestion, noise and squalor, has deteriorated further. This in spite of an increasing commitment, until 1980, of public expenditure on housing, social security, the health service and education. On the distaff side the poor have become poorer and society to that extent more polarized. The rising figures for juvenile delinquency and in offences known to the police speak for themselves. Quite apart from the urban social tensions, expressed in rioting, polarization has also become more generally apparent in British political life (Butler and Sloman 1980). At the 1979 election the entrenchment of the Labour party in the North and the Conservatives in the South was strongly underlined, whilst in 1981 the grip of Labour on the majority of metropolitan counties was perceptibly tightened.

Mobility, too, is a sign of spreading affluence, in spite of the steady withdrawal or attenuation of public transport services. The boom in motor vehicles has been dramatic, even traumatic, whilst the virtual completion of the motorway net, an improved truck road system, and more internal air routes (ch. 5) are other striking features. Commuting has become a way of life for hundreds of thousands. Mental images and perceptions of space have widened and there has been a rising demand for more personal space and access to more public recreational space. Inter-regional gross migration flows (ch. 2.II.5) have been building-up, though in the 1970s there had been shifts in direction, volume and regional incidence. Mobility has also been enforced upon those out of work, or seeking a lower cost of living (Cebula 1980). Yet the paradox of preference for immobility in less privileged areas is perhaps a surprising tribute to the strength of community feeling, even in an age of greater movement potential. The facilities for greater mobility and the technological changes in transport are the subject-matter of chapter 5.

I.4 Land

Change and flux in economy and society inevitably have repercussions on the land, its use and misuse (Best 1959; Best and Coppock 1962; Stamp 1962; Champion 1974). Of the 24.0 million ha of UK land (1970) the 2.0 million ha built-upon are the most valuable, congested (ch. 6), and in striking contrast to no less than 6.7 million ha under rough grazings. With a population density over 309 per km^2 and a loss of farmland running at about 15,600 ha per annum in the period 1961–75, it is not surprising that there is widespread concern for conservation and careful husbanding of land (table 1.2). With agriculture doubling its output since the war, whilst using no more labour and even suffering a reduction of the improved land surface, this concern may at first sight seem misplaced (Wibberley 1981, 13). That it is not so, is well indicated by the mounting pressures for alternative or multiple uses of land and the uniquely high priority rightly given to land-use allocation in postwar economic and social planning in the UK, though the very high rate of increase in land values since the 1960s has threatened to imperil these achievements.

Potential land-use conflicts, severe in the urban cores (Fordham 1974), around the business district perimeter, where town meets country, and in major estuarine tracts, are spreading to even the remoter rural areas, where there may be a need to harmonize farming, forestry, tourism, water policies and access for the townsman. With perhaps the most sophisticated town and country planning mechanism in operation anywhere, the UK (ch. 6.IV) still lacks the comprehensive, inter-related central programmes for space allocations at the *regional* level, with appropriate priorities assigned to what have all too often seemed to be conflicting strands of public policies. For example, Green Belt land is subject to the slow but persistent

TABLE 1.2

Land Use Change, UK, 1950–2000

1,000 ha	1950	1965	1950–65 change	% change pa	est. 2000	1965–2000 est. change	% change pa
Agricultural	20,254	19,623	−631	−0.2	18,122	−1,502	−0.2
Forest	1,532	1,816	+284	+1.2	2,617	+800	+1.2
Urban	1,773	2,043	+270	+1.0	2,745	+702	+1.0
Other	532	608	+76	+0.9	608	0	0
Total land	24,092	24,092	0	0	24,092	0	0

Source: Champion (1974)

growth of non-conforming uses, eroding 600 ha per annum in the Metropolitan Green Belt alone — about 2% per decade (Munton 1981, 17). Proposals in all current structure plans would increase Green Belts by up to one-third, but 1979 policy changes returned the situation to the *status quo*, accepted 80,000 new houses bordering Greater London and became more permissive on industrial siting (Elson 1981, 20). Chapter 3.I surveys land use and land classification. Chapter 6.II.2 discusses the patterning and structure of urban land use.

I.5   Decisions and Policies

Because governments now spend the most sizeable part of GNP it is logical to give precedence to public policy objectives as these affect the UK space. Certainly the spatial perspective in UK policy-making is the least developed, hitherto poorly-esteemed and neglected. Yet almost all economic and social policies necessarily have, and have had, a spatial outcome, not infrequently without clearly defined spatial intentions. Among the principal public policy objectives since the war which have had important spatial implications, the following might be listed:

(a) *maximization of sustained national economic growth without an unacceptable level of inflation*, success in which continues to prove elusive. The role of regional or spatial policies in meeting this objective is contested but it seems clear that successive inflationary bouts have been escalated by the scarcities of land and labour in affluent areas, with differentially higher costs there, whilst untapped or under-utilized resources continue to characterize the North, Wales, Scotland and N Ireland. The diminishing of this contrast in living standards and opportunities would thus contribute to the goals of social justice and, as the ill-fated *National Plan* (1964) recognized, might also have added significantly to the solution of national economic growth with least inflation.

(b) *balance as between the regions*, sometimes referred to as 'the need to rectify imbalance' and interpreted to refer to equality of living environment, adequacy and choice of employment, equitable dissemination of growth, prosperity and the full realization of economic potential. This objective logically relates to that above but, in view of the disparity of resources, both human and natural, the uneven way in which these have been developed through time, and the varied regional legacies of problems which have resulted, true equalization seems to be totally impracticable. A reduction in the present inequality, on the other hand, seems both feasible and desirable. Until the late 1970s there had been some convergence in levels of regional unemployment, female activity rates, migration flows and per capita earnings (Keeble 1981, 459). This improvement was set sharply into reverse during the economic recession of the early 1980s.

The objective of regional balance and equilibrium is the opposite of centre-periphery polarization, to whose diminution so much thinking on regional policy in France was devoted during the 1960s. It may also be related to the search for greater political devolution (ch. 1.IV.2), the accommodation or even the neutralization of regionalist or nationalist sentiments, which gained widespread momentum briefly during the 1970s.

(c) *social justice*, including the full-employment policy, relief of unemployment and improvement of the activity rate, spread of welfare particularly to the lower-paid and under-privileged, income and wealth redistribution, and equality of access to education, health and housing opportunities. Problems of racial minority groups are particularly pressing.

(d) *improvement in the balance of payments*, to provide the basis for and reinforcement of economic growth in the UK, and to strengthen participation in world economy, society and polity.

(e) increasingly since the late 1960s, the consciousness of the imperative need for *conservation* of scarce national assets in the landscape and townscape heritage, and the safeguarding of threatened aspects of the quality of life.

Among this amalgam of policies, whose mix and priorities have varied with the political complexion of governments, deliberate priority for coordinated action at regional, area or locality level remained rare, though economic first-aid policies have been perhaps the most effective for the Assisted Areas. The block grant financing for local authorities has increasing, if still inadequate, regard for local problems and needs, whilst acceptance of regional priorities may be detected in a rising number of key central decisions on communications, major new industrial projects or the decentralization of some government or nationalized industry establishments. It was only during the 1970s, however, that governments showed concern for longer-term and coherent analysis, forecasting and strategy formulation at the regional level. This coincided with, but in larger measure also stimulated, the flow of research and the development of relevant analytical techniques by social scientists and geographers, joined by regional economists, sociologists and political scientists (Chisholm and Manners 1971; House 1973).

As yet regional analysis, forecasting and programming is scarcely beyond its infancy in the UK and, not least, the complex nature of development itself remains imperfectly understood. Policies by central or local government must be examined alongside the decision-taking of countless entrepreneurs, firms and corporations, whilst the actions and intentions of multifarious groups and key individuals may also need to be taken into account. All or some of these non-public actions may work in directions or at a tempo contrary to the intentions of public policy. Through the complex interactions which result, the UK space is further differentiated, the characteristics of regions or sub-systems evolve and change, their inter-relationships are modified. It is difficult indeed to measure, much less predict, the spatial outcome of public policies and they are in turn variously susceptible to change by events, constraints of the times, new political controls or management thinking. This process of change has accelerated during the postwar years, threatening even basic interpretations of the regional economic and social geography of the UK. The next step must thus be to look at the changing identity, and the role of the variegated and variously-defined regions making up the national space (Manners *et al* 1980).

II   REGIONS: IDENTITY, SIGNIFICANCE AND FUNCTIONS

II.1   A Perspective on Regions

To many Americans the notion of a regional breakdown of so small a unit as the UK might seem absurd, even for the purposes of an analysis, much less as the basis for more effective overall planning. To many citizens of the UK, on the other hand, if the evidence of the Redcliffe-Maud Report (Roy. Commn on Local Government in England 1969) is to be accepted, even the provincial level of regionalism is an unfamiliar, perhaps unwelcome extension of their concept of home area. This is characteristically and parochially expressed as a parish or an urban ward. For some economists, regional identities are impediments to more effective use of national resources and space, but for most geographers, at least until recently, regions in their infinite diversity have been both a key tool of analysis and the prime means of interpreting the use of resources and space. More importantly, the spatial organization of economy and society expresses itself in discernible and inter-related, if complex, entities. In a practical sense governments, both central and local, work through networks of units, not always the same territorial entities for all purposes, and by this means help to reinforce the identities of particular areas.

Though few today are likely to accept that the UK space may be unambiguously divided into universal-type regions which will command widespread acceptance, there is likely to be greater coincidence of views on the first-stage, or national/provincial, level of identity. In reviewing regions, the many types, their utility and validity, may first be considered briefly; then the region-forming or disintegrating forces; the flows and inter-regional linkages, of which presently so little is ascertainable; the hierarchy, network or sub-system aspects of regions; and, finally, the significance of regions within the organization of the national space. All this is an essential prelude to a consideration of the current de facto regions, the eight former economic planning regions of England, together with Wales, Scotland and N Ireland, their differentiation, problems and prospects. The criteria for regional identity include: some dominant or inter-related set of attributes; utility in terms of economy, efficiency or convenience; administrative role, popular recognition or representation; and, in a practical sense, the extent to which the area identified may serve effectively as the territorial basis for understanding or promoting economic and social advancement.

II.2   Types of Region

Given a potential infinity of regions, in scale, level or characteristics, some priority ordering is necessary. Conventionally, geographers have identified sets of systematic regions, starting with those derived from the physical environment, followed by those with historical, economic, social or politically dominant attributes. Thereafter regrouping of regions to multi-factor identities in space has been the prelude to a regionalization of the total UK space, as near universal in character as possible. The weaknesses of such an approach are allegedly that subjectivity creeps in early, there is unacceptable abstraction from reality in the process, and that the end-product risks being no more than academic. It may have neither practical utility nor reflect the long-felt territorial loyalties of the people.

It cannot be gainsaid that the traditional divisions of the UK space into uplands and lowlands, with as complex a differentiation according to geological history, morphological character and present surface or drainage characteristics, as in any area of comparable size in the world, remain an essential prelude to further regional differentiation. Likewise climatic, soil and vegetation characteristics diversify the physiographic units, are as fundamental as ever to an understanding of land quality and potential, and establish a framework for the range, flexibility and profitability of its uses (fig. 3.1). Yet even in an increasingly environmentally-conscious age, the physical nature of the UK is always likely to take second place, in official eyes, to regionalization derived from economic, social or political attributes.

Determination of priorities as between economic, social or political regional nets is likely to vary with the analyst and the purpose. It involves basically a choice between dominant or spatially inter-related forms of production, incomes, consumption or marketing in the case of economic issues; the spatial structure of society, regional, urban and local life-styles, class, mobility or social pathology, among social criteria; effective political voice, democratic representation, national and sub-national recognition, or efficiency of government, in political terms (Robertson 1965; House 1969). All such factors tend to be inextricably inter-related and it may be that the nearest approach to collective identity is that of regional units with a common problem-mix, a related social or cultural identity and a sufficiently coherent and forceful political voice to seek redress or to power improvements.

From a planning point of view, since the war there has been some priority for identifying and studying urban regions (Wise 1966; Grieve and Robertson 1964; Senior 1966), or town-country relationships expressed in space, with special emphasis on circulation or activity spaces; mobility evidence, including journey to work, shopping, entertainments and so forth, affords the prime data. The provincial level of region has consistently been favoured by geographers, (Fawcett 1919; Gilbert 1939) but has variably and rarely found an echo in local government reform proposals (ch. 1.IV.3).

II.3   Region-forming/Region-disintegrating Forces

The seemingly well-defined, if not entirely static, regions beloved of geographers in this and other European countries earlier in this century, are less acceptable today. If planning is to work in the direction of fulfilling regionalist aspirations in economy, society or polity, it is important to interpret, guide and work with the forces for change, not all of which are likely to be within planning control and many of which are at times in conflict with each other. Regional identities by some criteria are dissolving, but in others being steadily reinforced. Overall, the possibility exists for fashioning and developing new kinds of identity suited to a wider range of aspirations over the next few decades.·

Among the balance of forces operating on the differentiation of regions, at present the centrifugal or disintegrating tendencies may be thought to be in the ascendant, though very unevenly over the UK space. Moreover, the process has very far to go before identities are lost. Such fluidity of change is not new, but has been greatly accelerated in recent times by: concentration of decision-taking, both political and economic, at or near the metropolis; economies of scale in production, concentrating upon fewer, larger, more nodal sites, whether these be for factories, farms, ports or profitable rail lines; urbanization, trending persistently towards larger-scale units, concentration within national growth areas and away from the less privileged regions or, within those regions, away from the sparsely settled hinterlands. These urbanizing tendencies (ch. 6) have been counteracted, but only partially, by suburban and commuting spread and sprawl; the basic contrast of polarization from larger regional tracts remains (Wibberley 1954). Rising inter-regional mobility of population, culminating in the peak net southward flows in the depression years of the early 1930s, supplies the most dramatic evidence, offset but only in limited measure by the regional aid policies of successive governments to the present time.

Less apparent than the mass flows of people in search of betterment but equally indicative of some loss of regional differentiation is the spread of common urban life-styles and aspirations, matched by consumer demand, and the uniformity fostered by advertising and the media. Yet against the dictates of such standardization or gravity model economics, there has been a marked, perhaps rising reaction. Apart from the Royal Commission evidence that people think in terms of a very localized, not to say parochial 'home area', there is mounting and widespread evidence of a built-in reluctance to migrate in search of opportunity, even though greater means of mobility and better knowledge of the market make this possible. The strength of Welsh, Scottish or Ulster feelings on the matter of political devolution from Whitehall is a nationalist expression, weighted by sizeable populations, resources and problems, which finds echoes in less dramatic but equally heartfelt ways in the less privileged regions of England. Furthermore, to some extent the greater mobility of the townsman, allied with aspirations of the countryman, is reducing urban/rural distinctions and the gradient in living standards and attitudes between the two milieux. To the extent that policies of economic balance between the regions progress, the provincial metropoli can help stabilize their hinterlands and act as the political, economic or social foci of either freshly-defined or reinforced regional identities.

It is appropriate to add that effective regional planning may be the most powerful of forces for stabilizing and developing new forms of regionalism. To be effective such planning needs to be applied to base populations and resources of adequate, even optimal size. Currently a population of around three millions is thought desirable for regional economic planning, whilst one of not less than 250,000 persons is thought preferable for any first-tier local government unit in the future. Likewise for New Towns, target populations have been progressively revised upwards to 250,000 and beyond for the latest generation (ch. 2.IV.6, ch. 6.IV.1). These norms have become somewhat academic at a time of major economic recession and the shift in emphasis from growth to stabilization, from the regions back to the centre, and from the New Towns to an emphasis on the inner city.

II.4   Flows and Linkages

The study of these cardinal region-forming and disintegrating forces has hitherto been greatly limited by lack of adequate data and the absence of a sufficient framework of inter-regional accounts (Woodward and Bowers 1970; Brown 1972;

Kemp-Smith and Hartley 1976). These shortcomings have led some to interpret regions as more clear-cut or self-contained than is justifiable. Strategies for individual planning regions often failed to take account of proposals formulated in adjacent regions. As a result there never emerged a coherent national strategy for the space-economy.

Migration of population, both in gross flows and in the net interchange over a period of time, is probably the most useful general-purpose indicator of regional differences in job prospects and living environment (ch. 2). Though net flows may be only a small proportion of total resident population, there is a trend towards increased gross mobility either as an outcome of rising affluence or as a result of the explosive forces of the search for work. If the Assisted Areas are to build up their populations, they will need to do this by attracting residents of other areas as well as by seeking to retain more of their own citizens.

Flows of passenger or freight traffic by the various transport media, including the interchange of telecommunications, further indicate both the state of inter-regional linkages, but also the sinews upon which further growth is likely to be generated (ch. 5). The traditional importance of the radial network of roads and railways based upon London has been reinforced in the motorway and air ages. The lack of adequate alternative axial routeways not only gave rise, between the wars, to the Great Industrial Belt or axial zone (Hobson 1951) from Yorkshire—Lancashire through the Midlands to the metropolis, but has also ensured that the national economic skeleton has changed so little since that time. The completion of the M4 London—S Wales, M62 Lancashire—Yorkshire and M8 Clyde—Forth motorway is, however, creating potentially powerful cross-flows. Chisholm (1971) indicates that freight costs are not such a significant charge on production in a wide diversity of manufacturing that plants are tied to a restricted range of locations. That there is so little voluntary movement of plants and firms, least of all to the Assisted Areas, has much to do with the immobilities engendered by earlier location decisions, allied with strong adverse perceptions of the risks or inconvenience that added distance might create.

In spite of considerable advances in regional economics in recent years the formulation of *model frameworks* for inter-regional accounts or transaction flows remains a subject fraught with conceptual difficulties and lacking in adequate data sources. An interesting practical step (Brown 1972, 72 *et seq*) has been to define the degree of 'openness' of regions, that is the relationship between the trade external to the region and the regional GDP. The measure is imprecise and the relationship is apt to be distorted by variable areas or population size of regions, each of which tends to increase the volume of intra-regional compared to inter-regional or international trading. Nevertheless, 'openness' is a vital concept when the principles of regional policies are under review. To the extent that regions are open and thus more effectively interlinked it is increasingly likely that nationally-based policies for economic growth and its diffusion will be successful, rather than individual regional variations of such policies. In reality the trade/GDP ratio highlights strongly the categories of UK economic region: the peripheral or Development regions have a lesser degree of openness, though it is in all cases greater than for comparable sovereign states of equal size; the Intermediate regions, the regions of mixed trends and the growth regions have more varied degrees of greater openness. The most 'open' region is the E Midlands, athwart the major national communications arteries, followed by E Anglia, almost an economic dependency of the SE. The SE itself ranks low in openness, sharing bottom place with Scotland, though differentiated by being almost at the opposite end of the spectrum of quantum GDP. In other words, by virtue of its size and complexity, the SE has a very high intra-regional trade, as well as high ranking in inter-regional and international trading flows.

Clearly the study of both flows and linkages between regions, of people, commodities, wealth and investment, should have a high priority among operational planners and social scientists. Of these topics that of linkages is likely to prove the most difficult. On a correct evaluation of essential economic and social linkages between regions (Archibald 1967), not only at the analysis stage but, more formatively, at the subsequent stages of monitoring and management of regional change, ultimately rests the entire regional planning process. A further important consideration is the multiplier effects of regional linkages (Archibald 1967; Wilson 1968), both in the diffusion of economic growth or the contraction through the impact of backwash. The deliberate creation of interlinked industrial growth complexes on the French or socialist world models has remained foreign to UK economic planners, though the short-lived MIDAs programme for three selected estuaries was something of a step in that direction.

II.5   Regional Context

The interpretation of flows and linkages leads logically to the identification of scale-order relationships between units within the framework of the UK space. Techniques for the analysis of these relationships are still in active evolution and most work so far has been confined to urban hierarchies (ch. 6.III.2) and to circulation space. Somewhat surprisingly, there is no substantive analytical work on the efficiency of alternative nets of regions and their component sub-regions. Officialdom still creates units for administrative purposes, on occasion almost arbitrarily, and then studies their characteristics and problems, rather than the more creative reverse process.

Early work on the urban hierarchy by Smailes (1947) during the immediate postwar years identified indicators of the economic and social status of settlements, mapping their hinterlands and describing the resultant hierarchy of inter-relationships. This was followed up by Green (1950, 1952) in pioneering work on the pattern of urban hinterlands through an analysis of public bus services, again a useful general-purpose barometer of individual and collective needs for circulation space. Carruthers (1957, 1962) studied service centres in Greater London and in England and Wales, and both his work and that by Smith (1968) established a more sophisticated urban hierarchy. Moser and Scott (1961) and Grove and Roberts (1980) made a comprehensive statistical analysis of British towns, whilst Hall (1971, 1973) made a novel interpretation of city regions and standard metropolitan labour areas (SMLAs).

A clearer understanding of the way in which units of various types relate to one another and nest within units of larger size, to make up a network or hierarchy, or a functioning sub-system, within the UK space, is obviously very important in regional planning. Yet there is little indication that this type of research is being given adequate priority. For the lack of such knowledge many sub-regional plans necessarily have to be formulated for ill-defined units, and the outcome risks lacking wider context or applicability.

II.6 Some Theoretical Considerations

The past few decades have seen the rapid development of regional science and a spatial perspective previously lacking in economics. New theories and models have been formulated (Wilson 1974), others adapted to the study of patterns, flows, networks and inter-relationships in space. In particular, the regional and sub-regional levels of interpretation have been emphasized, but applications in regional planning or resource management have lagged behind.

The objectives of regional theory are clear: to model regional behaviour at the intra- and inter-regional scales, and that for several purposes. First, to analyse changes in space with a view to fuller understanding of the dynamics of the situation, and thus to contribute to judgements upon change. Secondly, to enable conditional predictions to be made, within many practical constraints, upon a clear, longer-term view of alternative futures. Thirdly, to contribute to the planning, programming and monitoring of change, and thus to a more effective spatial allocation of public, and for that matter private, investment.

The theories most commonly drawn upon are those concerned with determination of regional incomes, inter-regional income exchange, regional growth and regional policy- or decision-making. The fundamentals of these theories are derived from economics, at both the macro (national/regional) and the micro (firm, city, human group) scales. To avoid confusion among geographers it is important to realize that an economist's use of the term 'region', whether homogeneous or nodal, is in essence a space-less or point connotation. The transposition to the geographer's finite and variegated patterning of space is not too difficult, but there evaporates a good deal of theoretical elegance in the process.

Useful theories include those concerned with regional growth (Brown 1972, 84); the supply-based interpretation of the neoclassical production function; demand-related theories, once more than one product is being considered, with industrial functions taken as given and different; and the Harrod-Domar macro-economic model based upon the concept of a closed economy. Export-base theory, with its extensions in the evolution of multiplier effects, analyses the relationship between regional prosperity and levels of regional export activity (Brook and Hay 1974). This leads on to more complex input-output analysis, based upon as complete as possible a matrix of spatial transactions and accounts. The more complex the analysis, the more the deficiencies of the regional or sub-regional data base become quickly apparent in the UK, and the more the computational problems mount with a sharp marginal upturn at each stage of expanding the relevant model.

The relationship between the course of growth and change, and the relevant policy objectives is bridged either by classical equilibrium theories or cumulative causation theories such as those of Myrdal (1957) or Hirschman (1958). In classical economic theory, factor flows between regions are considerable, but through time work in the direction of an equalization of conditions and the elimination of differences between regions. In the cumulative causation model, on the other hand, it is postulated by Myrdal, but modified by Hirschman, that regions become less equal with time. In the centre-periphery concept, essentially a gravity model formulation of considerable complexity, the centre (prosperous region, metropolis, central place) enjoys cumulative advantages, generates capital and attracts labour from the periphery. As in classical theory, the equalizing-return flows of capital seeking cheaper investment opportunities and the improvement of labour supply by outmigration from the poorer region are admitted. These are the beneficial 'spread' effects, but according to Myrdal they are more than offset by the adverse 'backwash' effects, through the further cumulative impoverishment of the poorer region in terms of labour, investment or entrepreneurial skills; conversely, the more prosperous region continues to attract capital, wages rise and inflation is promoted. The truth of regional differences in the UK since the war lies more with the implications of the Myrdal view of the cumulative causation model than with the neoclassical equilibrium model.

In reality, regional theories and their applications through models currently represent an imperfect art. An adequate data base is only slowly being created; the complexity of models even on a two-region basis are considerable, and the inputs are often restricted to trade variables or inter-industry transactions. The problems of incorporating time into the models is formidable, whilst the cross-correlation between econometric sectoral (Renton 1974) and spatial models poses very serious problems. The formulation of planning models is a further operational dimension and perhaps the most difficult of all to achieve, and once achieved, to sustain and update for the purposes of monitoring and feedback.

Decision models based upon linear programming, with certain constraints built in, are thus very partial and necessarily somewhat abstract at the present time. The formulation of an optimal allocation of activities among regions is an even more theoretical construct, with or without a transport-cost variable built in to the equilibrium analysis of the traditional input-output models (Saigal 1965). In addition to the work of Brown (1972) mentioned above, some important practical achievements include the structural model of the Welsh economy (Nevin *et al* 1966), based on an input-output analysis of inter-industry flows, with some capacity to afford conditional predictions. The *Strategic Plan for the SE* (SE Jt Planning Team 1970) studied ten potential employment-population distributions for that region, but it proved possible to model and investigate fully only two of these spatial strategies. The *Strategic Plan for the North West* (DoE 1974), however, did not take such methodology further, and the preferred spatial options seem to have been based as much on judgement as upon the objective findings of the modelled processes of change. The latest E Anglia strategy (E Anglia Reg. Strategy Team 1974) employed simulation techniques for the study of population, employment and resource potential, but stopped far short of attempting a full-scale regional model. Finally, the sub-regional models for Leicester and Leicestershire (Leicester Cy Coun. and CC 1969), Coventry—Solihull—Warwickshire (Coventry C Coun. 1971), and Nottinghamshire and Derbyshire (Notts—Derby Sub-regional Planning Unit 1969) illustrate more deliberately spatial options for the allocation of population and employment growth.

It may be that the next decade will produce an effective range of complex operational regional models and that these will become standard in each planning authority, to match the existing national econometric models in the universities of Cambridge, London (LSE) and Southampton (Renton 1974). It is at least as likely that such models will remain beyond immediate reach and, furthermore, it may well be that in the efficiency-equity 'trade-off' in regional planning the demands for greater social and spatial justice will produce some powerful political inputs to disturb the objective symmetry and elegance of even the existing models.

II.7 Regional Balance

Wide subscription to a doctrine of promoting greater regional balance implies that there are undesirable (or politically inconvenient) inequalities, even distortions, in the UK space, which might be reduced or removed by effective public action through urban and regional planning (McCrone 1969). A simple centre-periphery model (e.g. fig. 4.11) is inappropriate to explain the differentiation of these islands, but there are nevertheless markedly differing economic and social conditions and problems between the regions. There is sufficient concentration of affluence in parts of the Midlands and the South East to provide a sharp and coherent contrast to the less favoured regions in the North, Wales, Scotland and N Ireland, at the opposite end of the scale. Characteristically the less favoured areas are located on the outer margins of the UK space but they also have common problems arising from an industrial structure related to the use of coal, steam-power and the establishment of a range of traditional nineteenth-century manufactures. These have been increasingly affected during this century by competition from other products or from new centres of production in other countries. The tribulations of coal-mining, the heavy metallurgical industries or textiles lie at the heart of problems of industrial restructuring in the Assisted Areas of the UK, but in what proportion their regional problems are an outcome of unfavourable location as against outdated or narrow industrial structure remains a matter for conjecture. Both conditions illustrate marginality (House 1966) and point up the need to overcome a dual adversity, a task which cannot but be made more problematical as the UK develops within Europe and its outer areas may risk becoming even more peripheral within a European context.

Doubt might well be cast on the reality of creating ultimate balance or equilibrium between the economic regions of the UK, if such a state is to mean effective equalization of job opportunity, living standards, or environmental conditions. The fundamental diversities of the UK preclude such an achievement, no matter the aggregate cost to public funds or the distortion of logical investment decisions which may prove acceptable. An intermediate, realizable and worthwhile target, however, is to move towards the earliest possible achievement of self-sustaining economic growth in the less favoured regions, adjusting, by any necessary public action, growth pressures in other regions of the UK space in the interim. A firmer economic base might thereby be implanted and developed in the Assisted Areas, their resources of manpower, land and social capital more fully utilized. With a growth-oriented strategy the Assisted Areas might then move to a more competitive status within the EEC as well as within the UK. This would build upon the most logical economic growth localities and employment sectors, whilst accepting, even programming for, decline in the least favoured places (House 1976).

II.8 Economic Health and Deprivation

Figure 1.2 shows the volume and structure of employment in 1973, before the onset of major economic depression. It allows quick assessment of the relationship between regional space and the quantum of its labourforce, the absolute numbers in any industry group in any one region and its relative importance compared with other regions, the degree of diversification and, in particular, a comparison of the numbers in service industries (orders XX–XXVII, 1968 Standard Industrial Classification) with those in manufacturing or extractive occupations. It further

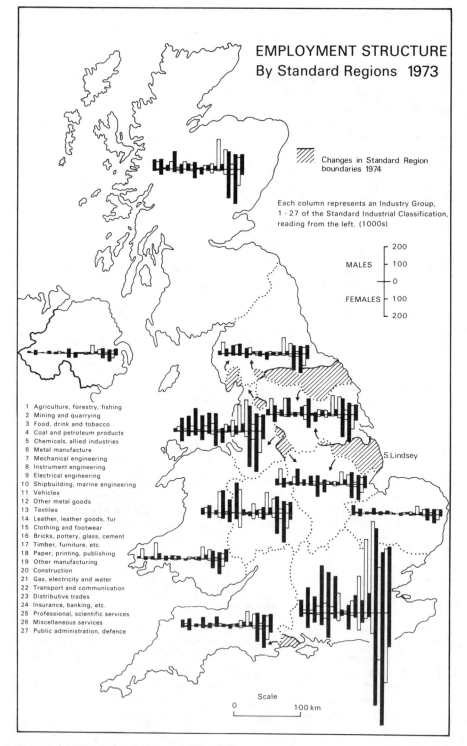

EMPLOYMENT STRUCTURE
By Standard Regions 1973

Changes in Standard Region
boundaries 1974

Each column represents an Industry Group,
1 - 27 of the Standard Industrial Classification,
reading from the left. (1000s)

200

MALES   100

0

FEMALES   100

200

S.Lindsey

1 Agriculture, forestry, fishing
2 Mining and quarrying
3 Food, drink and tobacco
4 Coal and petroleum products
5 Chemicals, allied industries
6 Metal manufacture
7 Mechanical engineering
8 Instrument engineering
9 Electrical engineering
10 Shipbuilding, marine engineering
11 Vehicles
12 Other metal goods
13 Textiles
14 Leather, leather goods, fur
15 Clothing and footwear
16 Bricks, pottery, glass, cement
17 Timber, furniture, etc.
18 Paper, printing, publishing
19 Other manufacturing
20 Construction
21 Gas, electricity and water
22 Transport and communication
23 Distributive trades
24 Insurance, banking, etc.
25 Professional, scientific services
26 Miscellaneous services
27 Public administration, defence

Scale

0   1·00 km

Figure 1.2   Employment structure, UK, 1973

graphically illustrates the proportionate and absolute importance of male and female contributions to the labourforce in each region. In essence the contrast, more fully developed later, between *four zones* is hinted at: the least-favoured regions: the North, Scotland, Wales and Ulster (Self 1965); the less-favoured regions: Yorks. and Humberside, the NW; the zones of mixed trends: the SW and E Anglia; and the hitherto more affluent, diversified and balanced regions of the E and W Midlands and the SE. During the 1970s the W Midlands developed some characteristics of the least-favoured regions.

Indicators of economic health or social deprivation reinforce these essential regional contrasts (Dennis and Clout 1980). The least-favoured regions have had a higher proportion of jobs in fast-decline industries, with an above-average ratio of unskilled male manual workers and lower activity rates. However, average weekly earnings of males over 21 in full-time employment no longer show the sharp contrasts of earlier days (e.g. 1979 Northern Region £99.9, Scotland £101.2, Wales £97.6, N Ireland £93.4, in comparison with GB £101.4). Yet indirect evidence, on retail turnover or household expenditure, confirms the lower living standards of peripheral regions. Their greater social *malaise* is highlighted by lower ratios of pupils staying on at school beyond 16 years (UK 27, North 19, N Ireland 23%; but note Wales 28 and Scotland 37%, indicating different educational traditions), the volume of sickness benefit, higher mortality rates, and higher levels of the needs element of Rate Support Grants (RSG).

The situation in the traditionally more prosperous areas is not quite a mirror image, though positive and favourable aspects emerge on almost all counts. Remedial action by government (Short 1978, 1981) has redressed the regional imbalance, in some measure, by differential expenditure, particularly through infrastructure and public works, including industrial building.

Since the early 1970s the measurement and assessment of *spatial disparities in social conditions and well-being* have emerged as a major research field for geographers in the UK. Studies have been at different scale levels: the national/ regional (Coates and Rawstron 1971; Knox 1974, 1975) and the intra-urban. Such research has been powerfully motivated by social concern and has been directed towards more committed and more effective policy-making by public authority. Research methods have sought social indicators to define degree and extent of well-being or deprivation. A great mass of data has had to be processed, commonly using principal components or factor analysis, to bring to light the key groupings of social variables and their distribution through the national space.

Coates and Rawstron interpreted the distributional patterns of employment, income, housing, health and education. Knox defined ten constituents of level of living, including housing, health and education. He then refined these to a set of indicants (e.g. university places as one indicant of education) and expressed these in turn as variables, measured on an interval scale (e.g. that part of the population 'at risk' for any indicant). Fifty-three variables were established and, from an analysis of these, four diagnostic variables were found to be the most significant: persons per room; per cent of households without fixed bath; per cent unemployed; per cent persons over sixty years. The distributional pattern of the combined four diagnostic variables (Knox 1975, 39) showed a clear correspondence, in England and Wales, between high deprivation and the Development Areas (DAs); conversely, the most favoured conditions occurred in a broad belt from the Kent coast through the Home Counties to the Midlands. Inner urban areas, especially central London

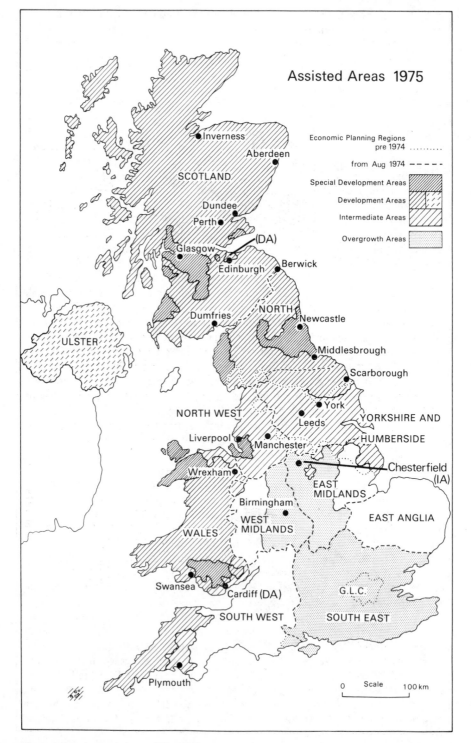

Figure 1.3   Assisted Areas, UK, 1975

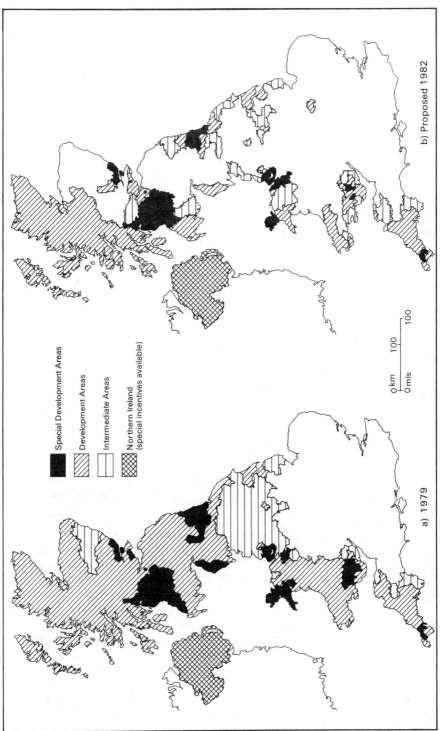

Figure 1.4   Assisted Areas, UK, 1979 and 1982

(Eversley 1973), and the heart of the conurbations were islands of low levels of living. Less expected perhaps were the unfavourable scores for Norfolk and much of Lancashire, whilst Yorkshire N Riding and Westmorland stood out when compared with the greater deprivation around them.

Chapter 2, sections III.3, 4 and 5 discuss social structure, housing, personal incomes and education achievement.

Figure 1.3 shows the pattern of Assisted Areas in 1975, referred to in the next section and analysed in chapter 4 in terms of the impact on manufactures and services. Suffice it for the moment to comment on the striking, but not surprising, coincidence between the Assisted Areas and those already seen to be suffering the most pronounced economic and social hardships. In the Assisted Areas (AAs), the Special Development Areas (SDAs), created in 1967, formed a hard core of localities with severe problems, set within Development Areas (DAs) which covered the North, Scotland, most of Wales, Ulster and much of Cornwall. The Intermediate Areas (IAs) (1969) are well represented in the former economic planning regions on the southern or eastern borders of the DAs. In 1979 the new Conservative Government announced a reduction in the financial and geographical basis for regional aid to industry, to be phased in three stages and completed by 1982 (fig. 1.4). This 'rolling back of the regional aid map' reflects a more selective and localized approach through government intervention, attempting to 'treat different parts of the country more consistently and fairly'. From covering 40% of the employed population there is a reduction to cover only 25% (1982). The SDAs survive with little change and still cover more than half N Region and Scottish workers (Townsend 1980, 10). The former regional extent of DAs are broken up, leaving the Scottish Highlands and much of Cornwall as the most coherent areas. It is, however, the former IAs which have been most sharply truncated, both in reductions of aid and in the contraction of the areas covered.

III   PUBLIC POLICIES ON THE REGIONS

III.1 An Outline Assessment

General public policy objectives with spatial implications were mentioned in section 1.1. Since the 1940s the need for such policies has varied with the state of the national economy, and both the policy mix and the extent of its enforcement have shifted according to the economic, social and political objectives of successive governments (McCrone 1969, 1972; Chisholm 1974; Holland 1976; Maclennan *et al* 1979; Law 1980; Moore, Rhodes and Tyler 1980). Nevertheless, there has been a general political consensus on the continuing importance of full employment, industrial location policy, regional aid, the extension of welfare through the social services, population redistribution measures, the improvement of both the national infrastructure, particularly communications and housing, the total living environment and the need for local government reform. Priorities within all these policies have characteristically been given to distressed or Development (Assisted) areas or districts, under a wide range of changing definitions and locations through time. Political differences between the parties have related to the extent of public involvement, the balance between inducements and controls, the definition, range and degree of enforcement of particular policies. Such policies for the UK space have required a regional planning mechanism, in the economic and social fields, and in physical terms for town and country, the latter of great diversity and complexity, more wide-ranging in its nature than for any other Western country.

The interim verdict must be that though public policies have proliferated they have rarely been consistently applied for long enough and have been insufficiently related, with a particular gap between the objectives and achievements respectively of physical, economic and social aspects of planning, at either national or regional level. Cumulatively, however, the effects have been considerable in terms of industry, both manufacturing and services; other key economic sectors, including coal, electricity, gas, oil and natural gas; communications, rail, road, air, ports and telecommunications; the conurbations, cities and towns; and on the definition of local government units or functions and the status of the national groups within the UK. At times governments have acted directly through particular policies and institutions, but almost as frequently influence has been indirect, often hard to trace. For this reason it is difficult here to make more than a general assessment of the impact of such policies on the UK space; that collectively and cumulatively these effects have been significant, even dramatic, there can be no doubt (McCallum 1979).

III.2 Pre-1960
(for references to all Acts see 'Public General Acts', pp. 505–7)

The mounting depression and severe unemployment of the early 1930s led to government intervention in S Wales, NE England, Cumberland and Clydeside, designated Special Areas under the 1934 Act of that name (Pitfield 1978). Though powers were few and the effects very limited, only 4% of factories established in GB 1934–8 going to the Special Areas, the prewar years saw the introduction of trading (later called industrial) estates, with powers to build and lease factories. Policy was directed towards relief of unemployment *in situ* but, uniquely for regional policy in the UK, there was also some attempt at planned inter-regional transfer and resettlement. However, only 30,000 families were moved in six years, at high cost, and the experiment was never repeated.

Rearmament and the upturn of the trade cycle achieved much more than the Special Areas policy, though unemployment relief has remained in the forefront among objectives ever since. In 1940 the *Royal Commission on the Distribution of the Industrial Population* (Barlow Report) drew attention to the marked disparity in economic growth trends, in favour of the South East and the Midlands (the axial zone) and at the expense of the North, Wales and Scotland. The report called for national action on distribution of industry and population, recommended decentralization from congested urban areas, the redevelopment of older regions and the introduction of balance and diversification into their regional economies. Creation of garden cities and satellite towns was proposed, together with the expansion of rural towns. These far-reaching recommendations necessitated a new central organization for planning and in 1943 the Ministry of Town and Country Planning was born. A further view by the Commission was that there should be strategic dispersal of industries, to avoid the risks inherent in major vulnerable concentrations. This objective was in fact considerably furthered during the war through the policies of the Board of Trade, creating large ordnance factories and influencing the location of much new engineering, aircraft and vehicle production towards the peripheral and less exposed industrial regions of the north and west. Some of the major ordnance factories were available for conversion to trading (industrial) estates after the war, as at Aycliffe and Spennymoor in the North East, or Hirwaun and Bridgend in S Wales. Furthermore a pool of skilled labour, especially women, had been created in the Special Areas, capable of retraining for postwar industry, management had had the experience of operating successfully in the areas and their general communications had been improved. By 1945 unemployment in the Special Areas had fallen to the record low level of 1.5%.

Almost equally formative in changes in the UK space during the post-1945 period were the *Distribution of Industry Act* (1945) and the *Town and Country Planning Act* (1947). Though the former was responsible for industrial location controls and inducements, and was vigorously prosecuted in the early postwar years, whilst the latter was concerned with development control, monitoring and programming changes in land use, the two objectives overlapped. Until 1954 there was also government control of building through a system of licences.

The Development Areas designated under the 1945 Act were more extensive, covering a population of 6.5 millions (13.5% of the nation), in comparison with the 4 million people in the prewar Special Areas. In territorial terms they were extensions of the Special Areas, to include major towns which had previously been excluded. As the agent for location policy, the Board of Trade had powers to build factories and buy land, make loans to trading estate companies, finance basic public services, make loans and grants to firms, and to reclaim derelict land. In addition, under the 1947 *Town and Country Planning Act* all applications to build factories or factory extensions of 465 m^2 or more had to have an industrial development certificate (IDC) issued by the BoT. In issuing such certificates the Board sought to ensure the 'proper' distribution of industry, a loose and flexible objective, but one which was used, with varying insistence, to the advantage of the Development Areas (DAs). As far as a common objective can be established it seems to have been the need to diversify the industrial structure of the DAs by the introduction and stimulation of new growth elements. A geographical outcome of this policy was a threefold division of the UK into: 'overgrowth' areas, mainly in the Midlands and SE England, in which manufacturing growth was discouraged; the DAs; and the remainder of the UK, commonly referred to as 'grey' areas, in which neither encouragement nor discouragement was officially applied to those seeking industrial growth. Northern Ireland had similar legislation and effectively, though not in name, DA status. Further DAs were later added to the original four: Wigan and St Helens (1946); Merseyside, and parts of the Scottish Highlands (1949); NE Lancashire (1953).

In the years 1945–51 the DA policy showed dramatic results, no less than two-thirds of all recorded moves in manufacturing going to DAs. There was at that time plenty of mobile industry seeking new or additional factory space, the inducements in the DAs were substantial, not least in the availability of modern or converted wartime factories for rental, plus a skilled or semi-skilled labourforce on the spot. The early momentum was soon lost, however, and priority for exporters, many of whom sought to expand existing operations or develop new capacity in the more affluent areas, coupled with declining unemployment in the DAs, led to the relaxation of regional policy on industrial location. As an indication of this, no 'advance factories' – the spearhead of economic aid to the dispersed, less attractive sites in DAs – were built in the entire period 1947–59. Additionally, during the

1950s, the New Towns created under the 1946 Act were beginning to develop as powerful magnets for some of the light industries which might otherwise have been persuaded to move to DA sites.

The nationalization of the rail services, electricity generation and supply, the gas and coal industries, together with the alternating public and private control of the steel industry, permitted unusual coherence of central decisions, forward planning and rationalization of these key sectors. Although the collective outcome of decisions in these and other infrastructural sectors such as roads and ports, might thus have reinforced the regional and spatial policy objectives on industrial location or use of land, the opportunities were not fully taken. Indeed rationalization in the sense of taking high-cost or less profitable production units or links out of the industrial or communications networks threatened to have a precisely contrary effect. It is of course possible to argue that such a coordinated overview of spatial decision-taking would have been foreign to any postwar political climate in the UK, a verdict somewhat confirmed in due course by the demise of the ill-fated *National Plan* of 1964. The lack of such inter-related policy-making in the 1950s, in part the result of the independence rather than interdependence in the formulation and prosecution of policies by individual ministries, was undoubtedly costly and frustrating to any thoughts of coherent regional planning. Concurrently the development plans by the counties and boroughs under the 1947 Act were being conceived and implemented without proper national context or allocation of resources, somewhat independent even of adjacent areas, and there continued that bugbear of planning in the UK, the lack of adequate inter-relationship between economic, social and land-use aspects of planning policies concerned with space.

During the late 1950s, however, economic conditions deteriorated, unemployment rose again, becoming particularly severe in localized pockets, and official thoughts turned once again to the need for a more effective spatial, if still not a regional, policy. The DA policy had been largely allowed to lapse and was revived, somewhat in piecemeal form, in amended legislation in 1958 (*Distribution of Industry, Industrial Finance Act*), recognizing the special needs of the pockets of more severe unemployment within the larger, but virtually defunct DAs. The decline in the fortunes of coal from 1957 onwards (ch. 4.I.2) foreshadowed the emergence of many problem localities where pits closed in rising numbers during the following decade. The steel industry similarly felt a recession and the capital goods industries, whose postwar revival had so effectively buttressed the economies of the major DAs, showed disturbing tendencies to instability and downturn once more. The *Cotton Industry Act* (1959) involved public funds in a major reorganization and re-equipment operation for one of Britain's traditional staple industries, a practice which was to become characteristic and widespread among UK industry during the 1970s.

III.3 1960–72

During the 1960s public policies on the UK space widened, became more coherent and inter-related, with emergence for the first time of regional economic planning. There was recognition that relief of unemployment and social justice remained the priority objectives for the least favoured areas, and that this might lead at times to inefficient public investments, in 'lame ducks' or localities. Yet there was a more fundamental need, on a continuing basis, to examine, plan, programme and monitor the economic and social change in the major regions of the UK. To do this effectively required the appropriate planning mechanisms at national and regional level. It also implied that all major investment decisions, even by private entrepreneurs, needed to be reviewed and approved since they were likely to have regional or local repercussions, multiplier or 'spin-off' effects. The point that the social costs of the development of firms or industry are often borne by the community was well taken, justifying close and prior review of the locational intentions of any leader firm or key industry. Similarly, the role and significance of key decisions on major infrastructural improvements, such as roads, harbours, airports, housing or office space were now more fully understood. They could be, though regrettably not always were, taken into account in the context of regional development. In short, the regional development process became more comprehensively studied, its ingredients more fully appraised and the relationships between manufacturing and services, in particular, more effectively understood. Belatedly, but importantly, the necessity of bringing local government units and functions more into line with the requirements of the times was also appreciated. Finally, the reducing of inequalities over the UK space was thought likely to satisfy demands for fuller and more diverse employment, social justice, regionalist aspirations or the wish for improved living environments in less favoured areas. In its own right it should make a significant contribution to overall national development.

Under the *Local Employment Acts* (1960 and 1963) the spatially-coherent DAs were abandoned in favour of more rapidly changing and highly localized Development Districts (DDs). These were identified initially by an unemployment level double the national average over a period of six months; in time 4.5% became a general yardstick for this, and imminent unemployment was also accepted as a justification for the scheduling of districts. Some of the grant and loan powers of the Board of Trade were extended, Industrial Estates Corporations were established for England, Wales and Scotland (though some estates now fall outside the scheduled districts) and the IDC system was widened to include conversion of non-industrial buildings. Yet the policy was negative: the scheduled districts were fragmented and transitory, being descheduled when the employment situation rose above the statutory unemployment threshold; and the districts variously included rural areas, localities of mining decline, or coastal holiday resorts with off-season unemployment, outmigration and lack of alternative work. In 1961 12.5% of the national population was covered by Development Districts, in 1963 7.2%, in 1966 16.8%. Scheduling bore no relation to a district's potential for development. Indeed, often the converse was true, and competition between districts, as for example between Merseyside and Snowdonia, was very uneven. Industrialists lacked confidence in the continuity of scheduling, the growth potential, and the adequacy and skills of any labourforce available in or near these pockets of heavy unemployment.

1963 was a very formative year in the emergence of regional planning, with the production of White Papers on C Scotland (Scott. Dev. Dept 1963) and NE England (Sec. State Trade, Ind. and Reg. Devel. 1963). These recognized that economic first aid to a dispersed and changing set of limited locations would not solve even the basic problems of DDs, and might well be at the expense of the economic health of wider regions, that larger and more coherent regions would need to be designated, and that within these the concentration of public investment at *growth points* or *growth zones* would be the most effective means of promoting regional development. Infrastructure was to have a high priority in regional programmes for the two areas, the living environment should be improved, but diversification of the industrial structure and relief of unemployment remained enduring priorities.

In quite different spheres 1963 also saw the creation of the government-sponsored Location of Offices Bureau, part of the policy of persuading office development to move out of C London (1,976 firms and 139,326 jobs moved in 1963–76, but mostly to other locations within the SE) (Rhodes and Khan 1971; LOB 1972); the Beeching Report on the rail system (MoT 1963); and the *Water Resources Act* of the same year. All contributed to the new thinking on how to achieve economic growth by fuller use of resources, balanced development for all economic regions and the recognition that such development might increasingly come from redistribution of services (Marquand 1978) as much as from changes in location of new manufacturing. Nevertheless, in several key decisions in the early 1960s the government showed itself alive to the need to influence location of new car-assembly plants (at Linwood and Bathgate in C Scotland, or three plants on Merseyside), aluminium smelters (Invergordon, Lynemouth in Northumberland, and Anglesey) or major greenfield steel plants (Ravenscraig on Clydeside and Newport–Llanwern in S Wales).

There followed quickly the creation under the short-lived Department of Economic Affairs (DEA) of the eight economic planning regions of England (1965), each with its Council of lay members and its Board comprising senior representatives of the relevant Ministries at regional level (Turnbull 1967). Although consultative and advisory, the Councils and Boards came to represent the regional interest upwards to central government, downwards to their constituent local authorities. They had counterparts in the Welsh Office, the Scottish Development Department and, until recently, in the Economic Council for N Ireland. The greater part of section 1.IV below is concerned with examining the economic and social problems faced at regional level, the strategies and courses of action recommended and the impacts of the first decade of this rudimentary beginning of true regional planning. Outline or interim strategies were published for all regions, but only the SE (SE Joint Planning Team 1970), the NW (DoE 1974) and the W Midlands (1971) reached the stage of a definitive strategy, accepted by the government as the framework for future structure planning in those regions under the *Town and Country Planning Act* (1968). In 1974 the E Anglian EPC published its definitive strategy, (E Anglia Regional Strategy Team 1974), and that for Yorkshire and Humberside came out in spring 1976 (Yorks. and Humberside EPC 1976).

Meanwhile control over the location of services as well as manufacturing continued to be the spearhead of policies for regional balance, relief of unemployment or social justice in less favoured areas. The introduction of Selective Employment Tax (1965) had a differential effect on the regions; in the DAs, with an already lower ratio in service occupations, the effect was less than in more affluent areas. In 1966 a new *Industrial Development Act* abolished DDs and re-created coherent DAs, covering virtually all the N Region, large parts of SW England and virtually all Scotland and Wales; N Ireland had similar status, but under its own legislation. These were the largest and most coherent development areas hitherto, with 40% of the UK space and 20% of the UK population. There has since been some conflict of interest between those favouring an economic

growth and investment concentration policy for these areas, and others who
continued to stress the merits of discriminatory, at times dispersing, policies of
relief to unemployment in or as near as possible to the localities afflicted.

The 'teeth' of the location policies were strengthened, the threshold for IDC
exemptions was raised, with industrial development in the Midlands and SE more
positively restricted. Financial inducements to industrialists to move to DAs were
also increased. Investment grants were provided in DAs at double the national rate,
no longer limited in relation to jobs created, and in 1967 a Regional Employment
Premium (doubled in 1974, but cancelled in 1977) was introduced, helping to
reduce labour costs there (Mackay 1976). Also in 1967 localized Special
Development Areas (SDAs) were defined within DAs, largely in response to the
severe local unemployment being created by coal-mining rundown. The SDAs
enjoyed additional advantages of higher grants on new buildings, rent-free
government factories for periods up to five years and assistance to cover operating
costs. These measures led to a sharp rise in industrial moves to the DAs and in jobs
created there.

In 1970–1 policies on industrial location were revised and investment grants
were replaced by depreciation allowances on plant and machinery. In DAs a system
of free depreciation was introduced and assistance under the *Local Employment
Act* (1970) was strengthened. The general feeling in the areas was that the new
measures would diminish the inflow of mobile industry, particularly the capital-
intensive projects, and that it would be important to make the inducements to
immigrant firms equally available to established industry.

The very success of the 1966 measures led to marked reaction in the regions
bordering the DAs, whose problems were neither so wide-ranging nor so severe,
least of all in the fashionable indicator of unemployment levels, and yet whose
economic growth rates were scarcely more favourable. This led to an investigation
into the problems of the so-called 'grey' or 'intermediate' areas (Sec. State
Economic Affairs 1969). The main conclusion reached was that such areas were
diverse in character, strongly represented in Yorks. and Humberside, in the NW, in
certain coalfields of the Midlands, on the borders of Wales, at Plymouth and at
Edinburgh–Leith. There was some evidence that parts of these areas were suffering
economically from being within the shadow of adjacent DAs and were receiving few
benefits in return. Though the recommendations of the Hunt Committee for the
scheduling of wide intermediate areas (IAs) were not accepted (1969), and
incidentally a proposal to deschedule Merseyside as a DA was refused, an
intermediate level of regional aid was granted to more restricted scheduled IAs.
In the *White Paper* (DTI 1972) a wider definition of IAs was proposed, embracing
most of Yorks. and Humberside, together with the NW (outside Merseyside),
Wrexham, the south-east borders of Wales, the Plymouth hinterland and
Edinburgh–Leith; to this list of scheduled areas parts of Derbyshire, N Lincolnshire
and Nottinghamshire were added later. The UK then had no less than *five
gradations* of economic and social aid to scheduled areas, on a descending scale of
priorities and an ascending scale of interdictions, as follows: SDAs; DAs; IAs; non-
scheduled areas; and overgrowth areas. Such sophistication may have been ideal for
allocation and channelling growth when the national growth momentum was high
and sustained. It was somewhat illusory in the slow, fitful growth of the UK during
the 1970s.

In support of the policies on new or expanded manufacturing location, the

Location of Offices Bureau policy was strengthened during 1965 and had notable success in influencing intra-regional dispersal within the SE or within the W Midlands. In spite of steady growth in modern office accommodation and lower rentals in the DAs, however, it was the planned dispersal of government rather than private offices which had the most marked effect on the inflow of such service jobs to the North, Scotland or Wales. Government-sponsored moves accounted for about 3,000 per annum in the 1960s, whilst some 41% of government jobs planned for dispersal were to go to the DAs during the 1970s (Hardman Report, Civil Service Dept 1973). Though the dispersal programme was partially realized there was considerable opposition from many who were to be moved (Ashcroft *et al* 1979).

In terms of infrastructure, regional allocations in the later 1960s came to reflect more effectively the needs and priorities of regional development, though it is less clear that the motorway programme had this intended effect. Widespread and mounting concern for conservation of both urban and rural environments also played its part in the eventual negative decision on the third London airport and in discussions on the proposed London Motorway Box.

Feasibility studies, 1969–71, probed the possibilities of fast economic and population growth in Humberside, Tayside and Severnside for later in the century, though specifically without intended detriment to the priorities for the DAs up to 1981. The government later decided that none of the fast-growth areas would be needed, and that controlled growth in existing urban areas or New Towns would more than cope with the extra population by the end of the century. For the extensive agricultural and recreational components of the UK space the 1966 *Agriculture Act* and the 1968 *Countryside Act* were especially formative, whilst the 1968 and 1971 *Town and Country Planning Acts* instituted a more flexible planning system. There was potential for better integration between economic and social planning at national level, reflected through the economic regional strategies, and physical or land-use planning at the level of a new pattern of local government units.

III.4 Post-1972

Regional aid policies since 1972 have had mounting economic depression as a backcloth. The *Industry Acts* of the early 1970s (1972, 1975) substantially increased inducements for firms to move or to develop within the Assisted Areas. IDCs were no longer required in SDAs or DAs and Regional Development Grants (RDGs) were instituted, to stimulate expansion or modernization of industry. RDGs were to be available to both native and incoming firms, and creation of new jobs was no longer an essential requirement.

Section A of the 1972 Act established the National Enterprise Board, to promote growth and restructuring at the level of firms and industries. Section 7 permitted regional selective financial assistance for improving job prospects in the Assisted Areas either by new job provision or by safeguarding existing jobs. In the mid-1970s, these powers for Scotland and Wales were transferred to Development Agencies, intended to promote industrial growth, provide factories and industrial estates, improve infrastructure, clear derelict land and, in particular, promote indigenous manufacturing by smaller Welsh or Scottish companies. Under Section 8, applicable to the whole country, selective financial aid was to be available for restructuring particular firms or industries. The clothing, ferrous foundry, machine tool, motor vehicle and wool textile industries were early beneficiaries. Loans and grants under the *Local Employment Act* (1972) were run down as the new policy developed.

RDGs were the heart of the policy. In the SDAs the grant was 22% for plant and machinery, for new buildings and works. DAs had 20% for plant and machinery and, in common with IAs, 20% for buildings and works. Table 1.3 shows the sum total by Assisted Area of RDGs 1972–3 to 1980–1.

TABLE 1.3

Regional Development Grants, UK, 1972–3 to 1980–1 (£m)

	Plant and Machinery			Building and Works					Grand total
	SDA	DA	Total	SDA	DA	IA	DLCA	Total	
Scotland	276	270	547	82	66	2	NIL	151	698
Wales	100	268	369	18	50	16	NIL	84	453
Northern	282	443	725	66	75	NIL	NIL	142	868
Yorks. and H.	NIL	36	36	NIL	15	117	NIL	132	169
E Midlands	NIL	0.2	0.2	NIL	NIL	12	3	16	16
S West	0.4	30	30	0.3	8	4	NIL	13	43
W Midlands	NIL	NIL	NIL	NIL	NIL	0.5	2	2	2
N West	232	55	287	48	7	94	NIL	150	438
	891	1,105	1,997	216	223	249	5	694	2,692

Source: House of Commons (1981A), *Industry Act 1972*, Annual Rept.

The map of regional aid was progressively widened and deepened. Merseyside (1974), parts of N Wales (1977), additional areas of Scotland (1977) and Falmouth (1979) became SDAs; Edinburgh and Cardiff (1974), Humberside and Shotton (1977) became DAs; Chesterfield (1974) became an IA, whilst parts of N Yorks. were downgraded to IA status. At its maximum extent the Assisted Area cover included 43% of the labourforce.

In 1979 the new Conservative government began a phased reduction in the areas aided and in the levels of aid given. This recognized that preceding policies had been declining in effectiveness, that the nature of the regional problem was changing to a sharper focus on the inner cities and older industrial conurbations, and that, politically, market forces should be released from such tight constraints. The new policy retained the three levels of aid: SDAs, DAs and IAs, but over a transitional period of three years the coverage was diminished to only 25% of the employed population (fig. 1.4). The claim was that by a more selective policy the more seriously affected Assisted Areas (Townsend 1980) would be more effectively aided and different parts of the country would be treated more consistently and fairly. Rates of grant in the SDAs remained the same, but in the DAs were reduced from 20 to 15% and the 20% building and works grant in IAs was phased out. Regional selective assistance under Sections 7 and 8 was tightened up and focussed on limited areas of highest unemployment. IDC exemption thresholds were raised to 4,645 m² and permission for extensions was at least as liberally treated. Section 8 funds were to be used mainly to attract mobile international investment. Special assistance to the shipbuilding industry continued under Pt II of the 1972 Act. The creation of Enterprise Zones (EZs) in the heart of stricken localities – Belfast, Clydebank, Hartlepool, Salford, Merseyside (Speke), Newcastle/Gateshead, Wakefield, Dudley and the Lower Swansea Valley (1981) – promised a fresh but controversial element in spatial discrimination policy. In 1982 the Isle of Dogs (London) was added to the list. In each EZ there is to be a 10-year holiday from rates, and some taxes, and from a wide range of planning controls, offered to both industrial and commercial development.

III.5 The Regional Debate

There has been a long-continuing and unresolved argument on the merits and demerits of regional policy in its implications for national economic growth (Robertson 1965; McCrone 1969; Moore and Rhodes 1973, 1976; Cameron 1974; Chisholm 1974, 1976; Diamond 1974; Sant 1975; Holland 1976; Buck and Atkins 1976). One school of thought, reinforced by DEA thinking at the time of the abortive National Plan of 1964, sees sound economic merit in a strong regional policy. Whilst there are under-utilized resources of labour, land and plant in the AAs, it will be in the overall national interest to bring these more fully into use, rather than add to the already inflationary pressures by allowing growth in the congested (non-assisted) areas. Furthermore, social capital will be more effectively used thereby and workers will no longer be compelled to migrate in search of employment or betterment. In spite of the seemingly peripheral location of AAs it has not been established that spatial variations in transport costs are likely to be constraints upon such a regional policy, and indeed it is further argued that there are no significant variations in profitability in similar operations according to region (Chisholm 1974, 223). Finally, branch plants in the AAs have generally performed well and in more recent times have not fulfilled dire predictions of vulnerability to closure at the first whiff of depression.

The counter-arguments rest upon the proposition that preferential regional policies may well have been at the expense of aggregate national growth momentum (Chisholm 1974). Policies favouring regions could be justified only if they contributed to self-reliant, self-sustaining growth (Segal 1979). Furthermore, if regional policies are to be continued as a form of social and spatial justice, 'a faster rate of national growth is a necessary precondition' (Sec. State Trade and Industry 1972, 1). To achieve such national growth must be the first priority, and since 1945 it has proved to be remarkably elusive. If the regional problem is but the more severe variant of a national problem, it is national remedies which must be sought: freedom of choice for firms to locate and to develop *in situ* wherever that may be; promotion of retraining, redeployment and greater mobility of labour, both sectorally and spatially; more flexible use of housing policy to promote expansion in the more logical economic-growth points or zones. Much growth takes place outside regional policy in any case and it should not be artificially constrained. Expansion of service industries is linked particularly to variations in regional affluence, and this cannot readily and logically be diffused by regional policies. Finally, the effects of interdiction through refusal of IDCs in the non-assisted areas may have frustrated growth potential. Similarly, the constraints of Office Development Permits (ODPs) in Greater London have greatly contributed to inflationary rentals and distorted the market pattern.

In the late 1970s the regional debate was intensified (House of Commons 1981B). Evidence that there had been some convergence on indices of economic performance among AAs and non-AAs (Keeble 1977, 4) was held to demonstrate the cumulative beneficial effects of regional policies. To others, the same evidence illustrated the downturn in previously more prosperous industrial areas (Massey 1979, 241), and though there had been convergence in relative terms, the absolute differences in unemployment levels among regions remained as great as ever (Marquand 1980, iii). In clear contradiction to Keeble's neoclassical economic interpretation stood the neo-Marxist structuralist arguments that the issue of spatial inequality and its persistence was the outcome of capitalist social formation (Dunford *et al* 1981, 377). Regional inequality was seen not as 'a frictional or abnormal outcome of capitalist production' but as a state of affairs 'positively useful for unplanned private production for profit' (Massey 1979, 242). Holland (1976) stressed that 'the free working of the market will initiate further cumulative imbalance [among regions] unless monitored and offset by government policy'. Regional policy was an attempt to intervene in the centralization and the centripetal forces of capitalist accumulation, a process in which meso-level multinational firms had the dominant role.

To the notion that the regional problem might not be one primarily of quantitative change on the spatial surface (Massey 1979, 233), but rather of forms and levels of the processes of production, was added the thought that the problem might not even be regional at all. Frictions and imperfections over space were less a matter of the Standard Regions but rather to be interpreted through 'towns and cities at different levels in the urban hierarchy' (Goddard 1981, 47). The rapid rate of population and job loss highlighted the inner city focus on problems of unemployment and deprivation (Eversley 1973). The 1976 Labour government commitment to revitalize the decaying inner cities, if necessary at the expense of continuing dispersal policies to New Towns or overspill areas, was supplemented by the creation of Enterprise Zones to bring back jobs to the inner city.

The counterpart of inner city decay was the vigorous population and industrial growth in non-conurbation sub-regions during the 1970s. Keeble (1980) showed that in 1966–71 changes in manufacturing employment by sub-region were closely associated with AA status, but that for 1971–6 the degree of urbanization was the dominant factor in loss of industrial jobs at county level. Using a shift-share analysis for 1952–71, Fothergill and Gudgin (1978) found that between 1959 and 1971 industrial jobs declined proportionately most in London, followed by the conurbations. In other sub-regions manufacturing increased: the more rural the sub-region the greater the relative increase. The largest increases were found in industrial non-city sub-regions and in free-standing cities. Such urban-based differentiation suggests that management of economic change in the urban network should be at least a counterpart for more regionally designed policies. Hughes (1979, 173) indicated that the treatment of such urban network problems falls into a 'policy-gap' caused by the separation of industrial (economic) from physical (land-use) planning. The basis for an urban policy, like that for the early regional policies, should be derived from the 'imperfections in the operation of land markets to secure an optimal distribution of economic activity over space'. The basic truth must remain that regional (or sub-regional) and urban patterns, and thus policy requirements, are inextricably intertwined. Some might argue, falsely, that regional policies have been responsible for the decline in industrial jobs in the cities. Even if this had partly been the case, an urban policy would need different ingredients (Massey and Meegan 1978, 287), capable of being effective on a much more detailed scale.

Academic evaluations of the virtual half-century of regional policies concentrate upon employment change as a general barometer of success, even though such policies have been oriented to investment rather than directly towards job provision, or indirectly to the relief of unemployment (Marquand 1980, 4). A general verdict is that 'there is no methodology for assessing the effects of regional policy that is unequivocally defensible and robust' (Marquand 1980, x). The general improvement in the status of AAs in the 1960s and 1970s is undeniable, but how much was directly to be attributed to regional policies remains in some doubt (Ashcroft 1978; Brownrigg and Greig 1980). Moore, Rhodes and Tyler (1977) estimated that from 1960–76, including the shipbuilding policies and all multiplier effects, there had been a net creation of 540,000 jobs in the AAs. The 8th Report of the Expenditure Committee (House of Commons) referred to the creation of 56,000 new jobs and the safeguarding of a further 35,000 jobs in 1976–7, whilst the Department of Industry contended that under the provisions of the *Industry Act* (1972), between 1974 and 1978 366,000 jobs had been either created or saved.

Such aggregate figures of achievement cannot be taken simply at face value. First, it is difficult to evaluate the counter-factual situation, i.e. what would have happened in the absence of a regional policy (Schofield 1979). Secondly, there is the difficulty of measuring diversion of jobs from more prosperous areas to the AAs against the net creation of additional activity. Sir Keith Joseph (House of Commons, 1979) described the offsets to AA employment gains: sheer loss of investment because of higher levels of taxation or borrowing to provide RDGs; diversion of investment and jobs from other regions; displacement of investment and jobs elsewhere by unfair, subsidized AA competition; and displacement when a subsidized project pre-empts scarce labour (ironic in the early 1980s!). Another problem is the choice of a startpoint for a 'policy-off' platform; conventionally this has been the period 1951–8.

Regional policies may be assessed from three perspectives (Schofield 1979, 251): impact on regional distribution of economic activity, aggregate efficiency effect on the economy, and their financial impact on the national Treasury (net Exchequer costs). Regional changes in economic activity have been analysed by simple statistical methods (time-series studies, cross-section studies), shift-share analysis and regression methods. Regression studies (Schofield 1979, 263) have proved the most revealing, confirming the positive influence of regional policies in the 1960s, with an indication that IDC controls (possibly lagged one year) may have been stronger than aids to capital and those more powerful than other measures. Assessments on the aggregate efficiency effect or net Exchequer impact are more difficult to evaluate. Examination of resource and opportunity costs gave no indication that 'the diversionary effects of regional policy have led in general to any inefficient use of real resources' (Marquand 1980, 110). Neither can it be concluded that 'alternative uses of the fiscal resources devoted to regional incentives would have led to any better overall economic position'.

In the early 1980s the regional debate is widening. New potentials for regional development are being advocated: innovation processes and entrepreneurship (Thwaites 1978; Swales 1979; Goddard 1981); or, for example, the age and quality of regional capital, as a proxy for the introduction of new products and processes, variations in management strategies, or labour transfer and training (Mackay 1979, 282). Increasingly, the whole field of public expenditure in the regions needs to be reviewed in relation to their contribution to national revenues (Wilson 1979, 84). Normal inter-regional fiscal transfers and public expenditures on goods and services, whether or not weighted for equity, are an important contributor to regional prosperity. Major infrastructure decisions, the course and net outcome of North Sea oil exploitation, the EEC, and even the domestic tide of regionalism will be other significant parameters, suggesting that regional policies as such may decline in significance through the 1980s, in favour of nationwide macro-economic policies, e.g. the national *Industrial Strategy* (Dept Industry 1975; Cameron 1979).

III.6 Some EEC Implications

There is much to hope for but also something to fear in the prospects for Britain's regions within the EEC of the Nine (House 1976; Maclennan 1979). Economic opinion is divided upon the gains and losses and the time over which these may become evident. Nevin (1972) took the optimistic view that 'peripheral regions in the UK may enjoy a marginal profit after entry into the EEC' but he felt that this would be 'largely as a result of increased growth momentum in the national economy'. In this view he appeared to be siding with those who see the regional problem as capable of alleviation only within a national context. He was careful to stress that existing British regional policy should not be weakened in the interim and foresaw that the government might have to take additional protective measures for the AAs as other national governments had already consistently done. Brown (1972) was less sanguine and thought that the development areas would 'presumably suffer more [in Europe] from positions peripheral to their market areas than they do now'. He thought that the regional problem in the EEC would continue to grow especially since international factor movements did not have the built-in economic stabilizers which national governments can provide for their regions.

Keeble (1976, 281) took a more optimistic view, encouraged by the vigour of industrial growth in the UK AAs after 1965. British firms would no longer need to locate in Europe to avoid tariffs; AAs suffered no significant transport cost disadvantage; and in world trading terms ports in peripheral regions should be equally competitive. Furthermore, common language would attract European plants of US firms rather to the UK; the available labour in the AAs was a unique asset; EEC regional policy would supplement the AAs policy; and, additionally, the general momentum of EEC growth would diffuse to even the peripheral areas of the UK. Against these optimistic points must be set: the lack of equally competitive transport organization, by road or rail, in the peripheral areas, and the quoting of 'special' rates for more isolated firms in sub-regions; the lack of regular cargo-liner sailings and the limited development of container bases; the need to break bulk or transfer transport media by sea passage to Europe and the time factor involved as a marginal extra; the continuing perceptions of cost disadvantage by many industrialists in respect of AA location; the lack of skills, adaptability and productivity among those to be drawn from the unemployed; unemployment or even activity rates no reliable indicator of labour availability or quality.

Planners in the AAs (Northern EPC 1972, Welsh Council 1971, Yorks. and

Humberside EPC 1972) emphasized that the impact of EEC membership will be neither dramatic, for good or ill, nor quickly felt. On the contrary the impact will be highly selective, upon particular industry groups, or even industrial firms, rather than upon regional economies as a whole, and its effects will often be indirect. For example, in the N Region it was estimated that almost one-half of the labourforce would be scarcely affected, one-quarter should benefit and one-quarter would suffer adverse effects.

In 1975 the EEC established the *Regional Development Fund*, with an annual allocation to the UK government in step with national expenditure on the projects concerned. The allocations were thus to supplement rather than supplant nationally-based regional aids. Ceilings of national aid to particular regions were set. Only N Ireland came into the highest category for aid, but the EEC was to be notified of all proposed aids with more than 35% net grant equivalent. The British SDAs and DAs fell into the second category with a 30% grant ceiling, whilst the IAs were classed with non-AAs and limited to a 20% maximum (House 1976). About two-thirds of ERDF grants were for infrastructure and these were transmitted via the UK government in full to the local or other public authorities concerned. Table 1.4 shows the regional allocations of ERDF grants for the years 1975—81.

IV   NEW PATTERNS FOR DEMOCRACY

IV.1   The Political Variable
(for references to all Acts, see Public General Acts, pp. 505—7)

In giving primacy to economic or administrative principles of efficiency or convenience, studies of regional conditions have traditionally discounted political forces and processes. Planners at all levels have been similarly neglectful, ignoring or underestimating the need for effective public participation in, and acceptance of, proposals for change. It has, however, become dramatically apparent that both politicians and the people they represent intend to be more fully and directly involved in all decisions affecting popular well-being, expectations and aspirations, whether these be well-founded or not. The pursuit of social justice has also come to have an important spatial dimension, in the clamour for the redress of deprivation or perceived wrongs, and the demand for greater identity, self-expression and direct control over decision-making and destiny.

Political ferment occurs at different territorial scales, from the national pressures for devolution of government to N Ireland, Scotland and Wales, to the claims of English regionalists; or the sturdy political pressures from interest groups in town or countryside. Such ferment is channelled in the first instance through voting, in whose changing patterns and structures there are intriguing geographical variations (Busteed 1975; Taylor and Gudgin 1976; Gudgin and Taylor 1979). Secondly, the legislative programmes of governments seek to adjust the delicate balance of powers, functions, or territorial units, but satisfaction with any particular outcome is all too elusive and equilibrium remains unstable. Likewise in planning, the encouragement of public participation has been tardy (Sewell and Coppock 1977) and not without many pitfalls, in another aspect of the search for a new balance between equity and operational efficiency. Such a search inevitably ends in a compromise between the general and the particular interests involved. If the nature of the compromise is to be an improvement it must satisfy the wish for decentralization of power with least dislocation to the overall affairs of the nation. Such a desirable state of affairs is difficult enough to formulate, even more so to enact.

The complex skein of wishes for decentralization may be rationalized along a spectrum from local government reform, with modest claims for redistribution of powers, functions and units, to more far-reaching demands for increasing degrees of autonomy for constituent nations of the UK. In more extreme forms the nationalist aspirations in Scotland, and perhaps in N Ireland also, are for national status within a UK federation or even ultimately sovereign independence. It is convenient to assess the case and the provision for devolution, at the level of the nations, separately from the enacted and completed local government reform in all four nations of the UK.

IV.2 Devolution

Before discussing the proposals for devolution (Peacock 1977; Bogdanor 1979) it is important to appreciate the existing differences between Scotland, Wales and N Ireland in terms of the extent of devolved powers, the varied dates of such devolution and the contrasting historical, social, cultural and economic background to claims for further devolution. Since these great differences do exist it is unlikely that a similar prescription for devolution will be equally applicable or acceptable to all three nations.

Scotland has had a Secretary of State since 1885, and from 1939 the Scottish Office has been the focus for a wide measure of administrative devolution (H of C 1974). As a member of the UK government the Secretary of State has a major responsibility for formulation and execution of policy on agriculture and fisheries; education; local government and environmental services; social work, health and housing; roads and certain aspects of shipping and road transport. He is also responsible for a range of other functions from police and fire services to sport and tourism. The UK government administrative functions are carried out in five Scottish Departments based in Edinburgh. For most of the subjects there is separate legislation, a right preserved under the Act of Union of 1707, handled by the Scottish Grand Committee (all 71 Scottish MPs). The Secretary of State also has a major role in the planning and development of the Scottish economy.

The first Minister for *Welsh* affairs was appointed in 1951 and most important measures of devolution took place between 1964 (creation of the first Sec. of State for Wales and the Welsh Office) and 1975. The Welsh Office now has responsibility for housing, health, the social services, primary and secondary education, child care, town and country planning, forestry and agriculture. The Secretary of State has a general responsibility for economic development and for the coordination of government action to promote welfare in Wales. Welsh interests are further represented by the 36 Welsh MPs who sit on the Welsh Grand Committee, a forum for discussion and debate rather than for decision.

The devolution of powers to the parliament of *N Ireland (Govt of Ireland Act 1920)* had been substantial and had continued until the dissolution of Stormont in March 1972 (Arthur 1977). A bicameral parliament had been set up (52 members in a House of Commons, plus 26 members of a Senate) with considerable internal powers over economic and social affairs, but limited in its authority to tax or retain customs revenue; the armed forces and international matters were also reserved to

reform had only just been completed; health and water authorities had scarcely settled in; it was not clear that either more democratic participation or greater efficiency would ensue from the creation of any kind of regional institution. The number of regions, their boundaries and financing (Lord Pres. Council 1977) might also pose controversial problems.

The *Scotland and Wales Bill* (1976) introduced the concept of a referendum in each country after the passing of the Acts (1978), with a binding clause that 40% of the electorate must be in favour in each country (Balsom and McAllister 1979). In the event 51.6% voted in favour in Scotland, but this was only 32.8% of the adjusted electorate. Six Scottish regions voted Yes: Strathclyde, Central, Fife, the Lothians, together with the Highlands and the Western Isles. Shetland voted No in sizeable proportions (Gronnenberg 1978). In Wales the proposals were defeated nearly 4 to 1: on a 60% turnout only 11.9% of the adjusted electorate voted in favour. Even in the Welsh heartland, Gwynedd and Dyfed, only 34.4 and 28.1% respectively voted Yes.

The SNP sought to have the legislation repealed to give effect to the absolute majority in the Scots referendum. Refused this, the SNP combined with the Conservatives to bring down the Labour Government (1979) but at the ensuing election the SNP suffered a severe electoral setback. Nothing was thus solved and devolution ferments have faded for the moment in the face of severe economic recession. It seems inescapable that the issue will be raised again, the questions put differently and some re-apportionment of powers granted, to take account of both equity and legitimate regional political aspirations.

IV.3 Local Government Reform

In a democratic society it is not surprising to find that local government units are diverse in size, character and resources, that many were established early and there has been persistent reluctance to accept change in either boundaries or in functions (Dearlove 1979). For the more limited purposes for which they were designed, the counties or boroughs served well enough and many have had a continued existence since early times. The *Local Government Acts* of 1888 and 1894 confirmed the existence of many such units, but it is universally accepted that during the present century the pattern of units has proved increasingly unsatisfactory, not least because their functions have been increased. Major changes in economy and society have taken place and the relationships between central and local government have become more complex. Nevertheless, there remains a widespread feeling that in local government the least change is the best change, and it is equally clear that in defining and seeking acceptance of any new pattern of units or redistribution of functions the British penchant for compromise is always needed (Smith 1964–5; Freeman 1968). Compromise is needed in several respects: on the balance of powers and the extent of devolution from the centre to the constituent nations, regions, cities, counties or districts; on the size of units for various kinds of function, and the pattern and nesting of such units within a nation-wide administrative hierarchy, particularly having regard for the important relationships between town and hinterland. The 'viability of local democracy' has more than once been a priority principle in official reports on local government reform. The difficulty is to preserve this without doing violence to the economy, efficiency, convenience or choice which people have come to expect in an increasingly mobile and sophisticated urban society. With the grafting of a wide range of planning functions on to local government since the 1947 Act and the rise of regional planning in the 1960s the search for new patterns became increasingly urgent.

Successive attempts at local government reform since the 1940s foundered less at the stage of principle than when new boundaries or new units were proposed to take the place of counties, boroughs or districts, in whose 'iconography' so many have believed for so long (Gilbert 1939, 1948; Thomas 1952; Mackintosh 1968). Yet the need for reform became steadily more pressing and the advantages to be derived more clearly seen. This led finally to major investigations in the late 1960s in all the national units of the UK (RC Local Govt England 1969; RC Local Govt Greater London 1960; RC Local Govt Scotland 1969; Welsh Office 1970; Govt N Ireland 1967, 1969). These enquiries were made more urgent by a rising tide of regionalism in England and a renewed sense of national identity, even of grievance, in Scotland, Wales and N Ireland. During the same period the *Royal Commission on the Constitution* (see Kilbrandon Report 1973) was set up to provide an essential link in the problem of redistributing at least administrative powers between centre, the nations and the regions.

England
The Redcliffe-Maud Report (Roy. Commn Local Govt in England 1969) was voluminous, innovating and controversial, surely the most substantively researched document ever likely to appear on local government reform. Even here there were two clearly conflicting schools of thought, respectively in the majority report and in the memorandum of dissent by Senior. Both were limited by their terms of reference, to report 'within existing functions' of local government. The majority report proposed 61 new local government areas, each covering town and country; in 58 of them, termed unitary areas, none less in size than 250,000, none larger than 1,000,000 people, a single authority would group all personal and social services with no lower second tier, whilst in the other three, the metropolitan areas around Birmingham, Liverpool and Manchester, as already for London (1960), there was to be a second tier of metropolitan districts. Counties and boroughs were to disappear and the economic planning regions to be replaced by provinces, each with a provincial council of undefined powers. The memorandum of dissent declined to accept the unitary area principle, seeing in it a violation of both the facts of social geography and the principles of democracy, which required more local ties than the large unitary authorities might permit. A two-tier system was preferred by Senior, based on city-regions, with directly elected authorities, and a second order of town districts, below which there should be common councils at community level.

The proposals aroused discussion and controversy in academic (James, House and Hall 1970; Thomas *et al* 1969) and political circles. There was general agreement among geographers on the importance of the provincial level in any new patterns for planning or democracy, but a division of opinion on the merits of the unitary as compared with the two-tier system, and a good deal of criticism about the nature of specific units or boundaries. The unitary principle had much to recommend it, in its cleaner break with the past, the designation of units large enough for effective planning, the coherence of functions and the possibility of capitalizing upon the rising mobility and enlarging space perceptions of the population. Such a fresh system of units would have required new concepts of community, but offered the prospect of abandoning the parochialisms which for so

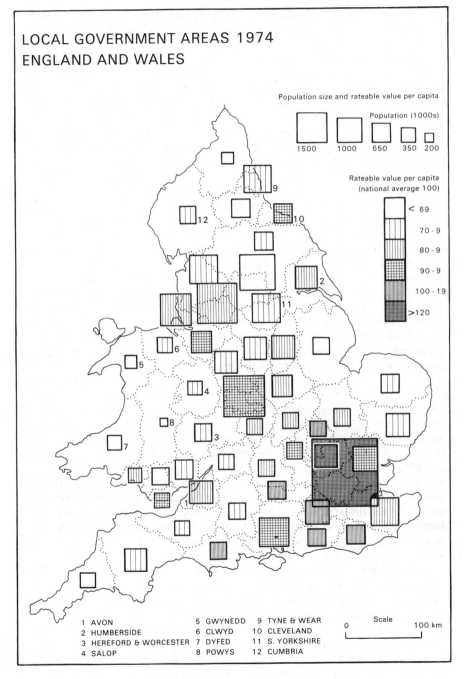

LOCAL GOVERNMENT AREAS 1974
ENGLAND AND WALES

Population size and rateable value per capita

Population (1000s)

1500 1000 650 350 200

Rateable value per capita
(national average 100)

< 69

70 - 9

80 - 9

90 - 9

100 - 19

>120

1 AVON	5 GWYNEDD	9 TYNE & WEAR
2 HUMBERSIDE	6 CLWYD	10 CLEVELAND
3 HEREFORD & WORCESTER	7 DYFED	11 S. YORKSHIRE
4 SALOP	8 POWYS	12 CUMBRIA

Scale

0   100 km

Figure 1.5   Local Government areas, England and Wales, 1974

long have bedevilled planning in the UK, even as high as the level of large towns or counties.

Though the majority report proposals were acceptable to the government of the day they did not find the same favour with its successor. The *Local Government Act* (1972), operational from 1 April 1974, recognized two forms of authority, counties and districts, with a two-tier metropolitan-type structure for Merseyside, SE Lancashire—NE Cheshire (SELNEC), the W Midlands, W Yorkshire, S Yorkshire and the Tyne-Wear area. These metropolitan authorities had boundaries which most commentators have regarded as too tightly-drawn, thus infringing the city-hinterland principle. They relied for their effectiveness upon the right planning decisions being taken at the strategic regional level, denied when the EPCs were abolished in 1979. The pattern of local government areas adopted is seen on fig. 1.5. The considerable disparity in size and rateable value per capita among the first-order units is clear, underlining the point that, together with the problems arising from economic restructuring and unfavourable location, the DAs had poorer, and at times larger, local government units for the most part. During the passage of the legislation through Parliament amendments to the units were vigorously pressed, as on Teesside (Cleveland County), Herefordshire—Worcestershire and the NE borders of Essex. Larger cities which became county districts under the new scheme campaigned strongly and with success for greater devolution of planning powers to the second-tier authorities. The definition and longer-term revision of second-tier units was undertaken by the Local Government Boundary Commission for England. The districts correspond as far as possible with pre-existing county districts, lie within or close to the preferred population range of 75,000 to 100,000, and are claimed to be acceptable in large measure to the local populations concerned.

Scotland

The *Wheatley Commission* (Roy. Commn Local Govt in Scotland 1969) rejected the unitary principle as unworkable for Scotland, believing that a single-tier solution would result neither in efficient planning and administration of the major services, nor in satisfactory democratic representation (Page 1978). On the other hand, a regional level of administration already existed in Scotland since regions had been established for planning purposes, and Scotland itself had a measure of economic and social powers devolved from Whitehall. The second tier in Scotland might best be represented by 37 'shires' and a third level, if required, could be made up of 'localities', typically a small town plus hinterland; of these there might be between 100 and 250 according to the criteria for definition. In the event the Commission settled for the 37 shires for local services and allocated personal services to the region; community councils were recommended for the localities. The *White Paper* (Scottish Office 1971) accepted the Wheatley proposals in principle, but changed the pattern of units, first by abandoning attempts at uniformity throughout Scotland and secondly by increasing the number of the new authorities.

Under the *Local Government (Scotland) Act* (1973) 430 Authorities (4 cities, 21 large burghs, 176 small burghs, 33 counties and 196 districts) were replaced by 65 Authorities (9 regions, 53 districts and 3 all-purpose island councils). The new units were a more deliberate attempt to establish logical economic and social entities in both city region and countryside. 9 regions were defined rather than the 7 regions of the Wheatley Report; Fife was re-established and the identity of the Borders was accepted. There is great size variation among the regions. Strathclyde has half the population of Scotland and the greatest concentration of urban economic and social problems. The Highlands, on the other hand, have only 8% of the population spread over a vast rural hinterland. The Scottish regions now have strategic planning, transportation, education and some social responsibilities. The districts have housing and local planning powers, but there is divided authority over social provision. Water and drainage are local government functions, at regional level in Scotland, unlike England. Furthermore, community councils have been established as forums of social opinion in each community. Regional reports on planning for each new region have served as a basis for corporate policy-making.

Wales

Local government reform in Wales has created 8 county councils, 5 of which bear historic Welsh named (fig. 1.7), and 36 district councils to replace 13 counties, 4 county boroughs and 164 district councils. Most of the new county councils have populations over 200,000 but Powys has no more than 100,000, spread over 500,000 ha of rural territory. Glamorgan has been split into three rather than two, to avoid the creation of an E Glamorgan which would have had over 900,000 people. The two-tier system is similar in division of functions to that in England, with the county councils responsible for highways and traffic, education and personal social services. District councils deal with housing, refuse collection, public cleansing, clean air and the prevention of nuisances. Town and country planning is shared between county and district councils.

The variety of area or population size among the new local government units for both Scotland and Wales recognizes that, in remote rural or mountainous areas, there is justification for special treatment. Furthermore, the diversity reflects traditional community ties and loyalties and thus gives expression to the overriding principle of 'preserving or fostering a viable local democracy'.

Northern Ireland

The first UK nation to complete the 1970s local government reorganization was N Ireland. Since the creation of the Stormont Parliament in 1922 local government had been carried on through 73 directly elected units, 27 of them with populations of less than 10,000. These units had the characteristic two-tier structure of counties and county boroughs, with dependent urban or rural districts. The local government franchise had been restricted, and generally biased against minority groups. There have also been persisting complaints about gerrymandering of constituencies. Reform proposals in 1969 favoured a reduction from 73 to 17 single-tier local government units, with strengthening of the powers of Stormont as a central upper tier of authority. The principle behind definition of the new units was alleged to be town-hinterland relationships, or everyday circulation spaces. With the exception of Fermanagh there was a clean break with previous territorial units.

The proposals encountered widespread opposition and in 1970 new proposals emerged from an independent review body. These confirmed that the local government functions of Stormont should be increased, to include all 'regional' services, whilst 'district' services should be devolved to 26 districts, each based on a town with its immediate hinterland; Londonderry and Belfast were to remain county boroughs but with transfer of some powers to Stormont. Johnson (1970) believed that the increase of powers to an upper-tier provincial authority might well be justified, in terms of area, size of population, or rateable value when the province is compared with larger English county or city authorities.

In 1973 the 26 District Councils, elected by proportional representation, became responsible for local environmental services. Regional services came directly under the Ministry of Development, whilst Area Boards administered locally education, public libraries, health and personal services. Belfast and Londonderry are the largest districts, but have no additional powers.

V   ECONOMIC REGIONS AND NATIONS

V.1   Regional Strategies

The formulation of regional strategies was one of the principal tasks assigned to the Economic Planning Councils. The process was uneven, lacking in adequate guidelines (Carter *et al* 1978) and the outcome by the time of the dissolution of the EPCs (1979) had been very varied. The SE (SE Jt Planning Team 1970), the W Midlands (1971) and the NW (DoE 1974) had been approved in principle by the minister and should thus have become the framework for County Structure Plans under the 1968 *Town and Country Planning Act*. Other regions were still engaged in the third tripartite phase of strategy formulation when they ceased to exist. The last strategy, for the Northern Region, was received but no ministerial benediction was pronounced.

With the passing away of the regional level of planning, the responsibility passed to consortia of county authorities, as in the W Midlands or, alternatively and more commonly, to direct bilateral links between the county as a structure plan authority and the central government ministries. Structure plans (Barras 1978) are: (a) to state and justify the authority's policies and proposals for the development and use of land, (b) to interpret regional and national policies in terms of physical and environmental planning, and (c) to provide the framework and statutory basis for local plans. In practice, delay in preparation and approval of third-stage regional strategies meant that formulation of structure plans went ahead independently. Even so, many structure plans have been delayed and local plans have often been drawn up and put into effect, lacking context in a wider framework. In the SE, for example, the Greater London Development Plan (1969) was submitted one year ahead of the Strategic Plan for the SE. In the absence of an approved GLC plan London boroughs proposed local plans almost independently.

The following regional interpretations evaluate problems and the policies and plans advanced since the 1960s for tackling them. Provisional regional accounts 1966–78 (Godley 1980) provide a statistical background, for reference purposes. Since the regional strategy concept has been statutorily denied since 1979 the critique has become somewhat more academic. In the hope, if not the certainty, that regional planning will come back into favour in due course the evaluation of the diversity of methods and achievements during the years 1965–79 lays a groundwork for future prospects.

V.2   The Least Favoured Regions

Of the four regions identified, three (Scotland, Wales and N Ireland) have a national identity and already enjoy a measure of administrative devolution. Only the N

TABLE 1.4

Economic Regions and Nations, 1981

	Popn 1981 (000s)	% change 1971–81	Density per km² (1979)	% in metro counties (1981)	Employment change 1963–73* % in fast growth¹/fast decline² sectors		1971–81 % change manufs	GDP per capita (1979) UK=100†	EEC Regional Fund % allocn 1975–81 Indus. Tourism	Infra-structure
Least favoured										
Northern	3,097	−1.4	200	37	27	14	−15.4	93.0	18.3	21.4
Scotland	5,116	−2.0	67		30	12	−17.8	96.6	19.5	27.4
Wales	2,790	2.2	133	NIL	32	11	−11.1	88.4	15.1	16.6
N Ireland	1,543**	0.1	109	NIL	34	19	−38.0	77.5	17.5	12.5
Less favoured										
Yorks. and H.	4,854	−0.1	316	42	28	15	−15.3	95.4	2.0	8.2
N West	6,406	−2.9	883	64	28	10	−17.6	95.9	25.8	8.9
Mixed trends										
S West	4,326	6.0	181	NIL	32	9	−4.8	91.6	1.2	3.3
E Anglia	1,865	11.7	148	NIL	28	10	+1.6	94.0	NIL	NIL
'Growth'										
E Midlands	3,807	4.8	240	NIL	25	20	−8.1	98.6	0.5	1.3
W Midlands	5,136	0.5	395	51	32	5	−17.3	96.4	NIL	0.4
S East	16,729	−1.2	619	40	32	4	−18.5	113.4	NIL	NIL
Greater London	6,696	−10.1	4,355	100	–		–	–	NIL	NIL

¹ > 100 Metal goods; timber; other manufs; financial, professional, scientific services; catering and hotels; national and local govt
² < 85 Agriculture; mining and quarrying; shipbuilding; textiles; leather; clothing
* before economic recession set in
† less Continental Shelf
** 1979 estimate

Source: Census 1981, Prelim. Repts; Reg. Trends 1981; Dept Employment

Region of England lacks this degree of independence in regional decision-taking.
All four are characterized by certain common problems, though their incidence and
mix vary, and there are differences too in the policies adopted and the extent of
their success. The problems include: higher and persistent unemployment rates;
a narrow industrial base, with a higher ratio of fast-decline industries, not adequately
compensated for by new post-1945 growth elements; lower median incomes;
persistent out-migration, particularly of the young and more able; peripheral
location in the UK space, and according to some (Brown 1972) even more marginal
in an enlarged Common Market economy; and a less favourable living environment
for the majority, especially in the cities. The least favoured regions, on the other
hand, have been, and continue to be, the main beneficiaries of the regional and
industrial location policies of successive governments. Some degree of economic
and social convergence there had been during the 1970s, but largely due to the
relative decline in prosperity elsewhere.

TABLE 1.5

Manufacturing Starts, Least Favoured Regions, 1966–77

	No.	1966–71 Employment (000s)	No.	1972–7 Employment (000s)	RDGs 1972–March 1980 £m	£s per cap. employees in manufs 1980
UK	5,854	452.7	5,390	280.5	(GB) 2201	324
Northern	330	45.9	247	17.0	751	1,727
Scotland	576	51.7	618	32.9	585	954
Wales	384	38.1	342	17.1	350	1,136
					Indus. and Invest. Grants 1975–80	
N Ireland	112	16.8	35	3.2	260	1,368

Source: Reg. Trends 1981, Tables 10.5, 10.6, 10.7

Northern Region (fig. 1.6)

In the nature, range and severity of its economic and social problems the N Region
is a microcosm of the least-favoured regions (Bowden 1965; House 1969). For this
reason, perhaps, it has consistently been used as a pilot-area for the application of
government location policies, from the *Special Areas Act* (1934) to the present
day. Much of the earlier legislation was remedial in character, with relief of
unemployment as a perennially and continuing high priority. In the *1963 White
Paper* (Sec.Trade and Industry 1963), however, for the first time the emphasis was
briefly laid on economic growth by diversification, improvement of the infrastructure and the living environment and, most significantly, on the concentration
of future public investment into a designated 'growth zone'. These more
comprehensive objectives were followed up and codified in the first-stage strategy
document, entitled *Challenge of the Changing North* (NEPC 1966). Three years
later an *Outline Strategy for the North* was published (NEPC 1969), one of only a
small number of second-stage strategies to have as strong a spatial as a sectoral
perspective in its recommendations. Perhaps for this reason the sub-regional
proposals did not find favour with the local planning authorities and the document
was looked upon by the optimists as falling short of legitimate regional aspirations.

Others regarded the diagnosis and recommendations as both realistic and practical, though not acceptable to local politicians. The third stage of definitive strategy took place in 1973–6 (NRST 1976) but its findings had no echo in government circles. The Economic Planning Council published reports on key sectors, such as housing, education and ports (NEPC 1969, 1970, 1971). The local authority-sponsored North of England Development Council concurrently undertook successfully the major task of promoting the NE and Cumbria, aiding more official efforts to attract industry and improve regional living conditions.

It is fair to ask how far all these reports and all this activity has solved or mitigated the basic problems affecting the N Region. The verdict must be more cautious than commendatory. For all the fluctuations in unemployment levels in the UK since the war, the N Region level has obstinately remained between one and a half and twice the national figure and it is difficult to envisage secular, long-term improvement based on present policies. Until the recession of the late 1970s, industrial restructuring had made significant progress: the growth-decline mix in employment improved markedly.

Diversification of the labour market increased and until the late 1960s there was a significant number of industrial moves into the region, particularly from the SE to a lesser extent from Yorks. and Humberside (NRST 1975; Nunn 1980). On the positive side, the government-sponsored industrial estates and the intermittent advance-factory programme had proved major attractions. IDC approvals were freely granted and the region benefited from their restriction in the growth regions. The well-known proliferation of branch plants took place, with few HQ or R and D units coming into the North (Thwaites 1978). A higher ratio of the new jobs were for women and girls, though the increasingly desperate regional need was for male employment (Johnson 1978). Linkages with indigenous firms within the North were few (NRST 1976A) and, indeed, there was some weakening of the internal manufacturing structure by external takeovers (Smith 1979). Indigenous firms constantly complained that they were disadvantaged in comparison with 'subsidized' in-migrant firms and that they were unable to benefit to the same degree from government incentives.

Indeed, the structural problems of the regional economy arose directly from the dominance of mining and industries in secular employment decline and, indeed, in many cases also from technological or managerial backwardness. Coal-mining, steel, shipbuilding, agriculture and transport were the major job-loss sectors. In 1973–8 46,000 further manufacturing jobs were lost, even before the onset of the deepest part of the economic depression. Restructuring of the economy by replacement of manufacturing jobs could not hope to match the rate of loss. The hallmarks have thus long been high levels of unemployment, low activity rates and a persistent net outmigration of the younger and more able (House 1964–72).

Diversification is not solely a matter of manufacturing. The service industry in the North has been traditionally underrepresented (Fullerton 1960, 1966; NRST 1976B; James 1978). Government incentives were lacking to attract office developments from London or the Midlands (NRST 1976C). To become more competitive the N Region required both closer, cheaper, faster integration into the national communications network and an uplift for the urban environment. To some extent both these often-mentioned handicaps were psychological rather than real in the eyes of either locals or would-be immigrants. The M6, A1(M) Durham motorway, the HST inter-city rail link, regional airports at Newcastle and Teesside

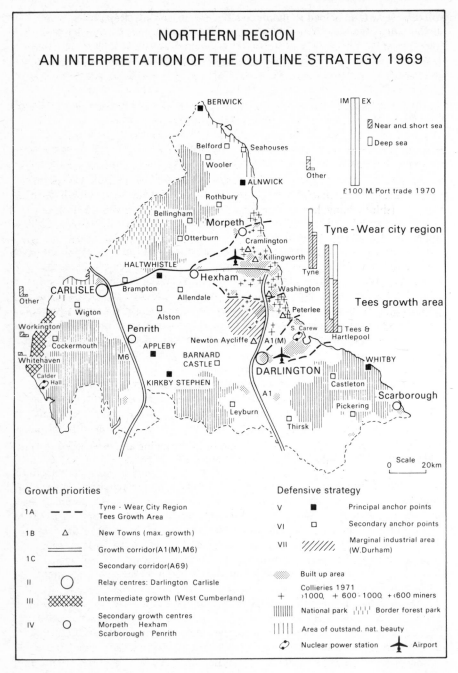

NORTHERN REGION
AN INTERPRETATION OF THE OUTLINE STRATEGY 1969

BERWICK

IM   EX

◩ Near and short sea

▢ Deep sea

Belford □   Seahouses

□ Wooler

Other

■ ALNWICK

£100 M. Port trade 1970

Rothbury

Bellingham

Morpeth

Otterburn

Cramlington

Tyne - Wear city region

HALTWHISTLE

Killingworth

Tyne

Hexham

CARLISLE   Brampton

Washington

Other

Allendale

Tees growth area

Wigton

Alston

Peterlee

Workington

S Carew

Penrith

Cockermouth

Newton Aycliffe   A1(M)

Tees & Hartlepool

Whitehaven   M6

APPLEBY

WHITBY

Calder Hall

BARNARD CASTLE □

DARLINGTON

KIRKBY STEPHEN

Castleton

Scarborough

A1

Pickering

Leyburn

Thirsk

Scale

0   20km

Growth priorities

1A   – – –   Tyne - Wear City Region / Tees Growth Area

1B   △   New Towns (max. growth)

1C   ═══   Growth corridor(A1(M),M6)
      ───   Secondary corridor(A69)

II   ◯   Relay centres: Darlington Carlisle

III   ⨯⨯⨯   Intermediate growth (West Cumberland)

IV   ◯   Secondary growth centres / Morpeth Hexham / Scarborough Penrith

Defensive strategy

V   ■   Principal anchor points

VI   □   Secondary anchor points

VII   ////   Marginal industrial area (W.Durham)

▒ Built up area

+ Collieries 1971 / >1000, + 600 - 1000, + <600 miners

‖‖‖ National park ¦¦¦ Border forest park

‖‖‖ Area of outstand. nat. beauty

⌀ Nuclear power station   ✈ Airport

Figure 1.6   Northern Region, 1969 Outline Strategy

and at Teesport, all helped to modernized communications. Replanning of city centres, slum clearance, housing improvement areas, CRAs and re-zoning transformed the Industrial Revolution city landscapes (NRST 1977A). Improved education facilities and provision for recreation added to a living environment which at the coast and in the countryside more than matched the best any other region could offer.

The 1969 *Outline Strategy* was a short-lived but innovating document (fig. 1.6). Now that a selective urban network management policy is being canvassed (Goddard 1981), its principles may return to favour. Influenced by French planning practice it postulated a spatially-defined and inter-related growth hierarchy of settlements and sub-regions. Appropriate defensive elements were proposed for areas in decline or in remoter, less competitive locations. Priorities for investment were assigned, with a first priority for restructuring the Tyne-Wear urban-industrial economy (shipbuilding, heavy engineering, more developed services, industrial estates) and developing its linkages with the complementary structure of Teesside (chemicals, oil refining, iron and steel). Unfortunately, the serious further decline of shipbuilding, the dramatic round (1980–1) of steel closures (Consett, –4,000 jobs) and the low labour levels of capital-intensive chemical and petrochemical production set such an optimistic restructuring into reverse.

Both Tyne-Wear and Teesside are flanked by the coalfield, which has been running down its workforce since the late 1950s. Many redundant men have been re-employed at other pits, but there have been residual welfare and social problems in many scattered former pit villages. Durham CC classified all its villages, from A (growth) to D (no further public investment). The designation of many pit villages as category D, after closure of the local mine, aroused the most determined (and successful) opposition at community level. The New Towns at Peterlee, Newton Aycliffe and Washington, together with the CC developments at Killingworth and Cramlington, have implanted growth and a new living environment in the coalfield (NRST 1977B), aided by the SDA policy since 1967. Not all decaying settlements have a perpetual birthright to continue, and both retraining and outmigration seem inescapable. West Cumberland faces problems similar to those of marginal W Durham. Only one coal-mine was working in 1981 and steelmaking at Workington was threatened. Government AA policy helped soften the industrial restructuring, aided by a remarkable community spirit.

Other novel elements in the *Outline Strategy* were the proposals for corridor growth at nodes, along the main south-north motorways and rail links, east and west of the Pennines. The corridor concept through Durham aroused memories of earlier thinking on a prospective Tyne-Tees linear city. For the vast rural hinterland it was accepted that growth at the most logical centres in conurbation or cities would increase gradients in living standards, to the disadvantage of the countryside, and lead to accelerated rural depopulation. To stabilize the rural areas and indeed to build up jobs in both industry and services, to support the primary agricultural population, rural 'anchor point' settlements were to be designated. The *Outline Strategy* (Northern EPC 1969) was indicative, a discussion basis, and was lacking in precision as to space allocations, timings or priorities.

The *Northern Region Strategy* (NRST 1977) was an entirely different kind of document, sectoral rather than spatial in character. Unlike any other regional strategy, it analyzed intersectoral allocation of public expenditure and was concerned to generate improvements positively rather than merely seeking to control or divert pressures for development. As a tripartite document it was somewhat constrained by local authority interests. The sector objectives included: rapid movement to self-sustaining economic growth, in the long term, without the need for special government assistance; greater variety of choice in employment; greater equity in distribution of benefits; and improvement and protection of the environment. Industry within the region should be given particular stimulus to growth, and in time less reliance on 'mobile' industry should be envisaged. SDA status should be limited, since it afforded few additional benefits, but assistance should be more selectively concentrated.

Spatial options were: continuance of present policies; urban rehabilitation; concentration; growth zones; and market forces. For rural areas (NRST 1976D), market forces, centralization or balanced development were posed as alternative courses for policy. It was decided after consultation that no single alternative would be appropriate for the region, and also that different choices, or combinations of choices, would be appropriate in different parts of the region. As in 1969 this was a politically judicious conclusion.

The Strategy was pioneering in its attempt to make explicit the public expenditure implications of the recommendations, but was criticized for inadequate justification of the new policies (House *et al* 1978). It was innovating in being concerned with the processes of economic regeneration rather than focussing upon spatial issues. Sadly, it was the last in the line of regional strategies, but a very fitting monument to the passing of regional planning.

Scotland (fig. 1.7)

The basic regional development problems of Scotland have much in common with those of N England, but there are differences of significance, both in degree and in kind. The differences in degree arise from the greater territorial size and population of Scotland, a more marked degree of concentration of that population in the industrial C Lowlands, with a vast, thinly-peopled rural hinterland, and an even more peripheral location in respect of the major economic growth areas of the Midlands and SE England (Robertson 1975). Differences in kind arise from the degree of autonomy exercised by representatives of the Scottish nation, the distinctive problems posed by slow population growth, the need to decongest and distribute massive overspill from the Clydeside conurbation, the sharp contrast offered by major rural problem areas, and a particular sequence of stages in regional planning. The massive potential of North Sea oil is a further differentiator.

Perhaps the most important factor of all lies in the economic, social and political identity of Scotland, giving coherence and purpose to its planning and strengthening its independent voice in UK affairs. This identity was referred to by Cairncross (1954), speaking of the Border as 'not a barrier between two economic systems but a line between two segments of a single economy'. He further added 'yet the segment lying north of the Border is a distinct society with a unity and cohesion of its own', and he was in no doubt that the Scottish economy functioned as a unit and had an independent momentum. Later writers have confirmed this diagnosis (McCrone 1969; Mackay and Mackay 1974; Scottish Council 1974; Moore and Rhodes 1974; Firn 1975; Mackay 1979), which is indeed derived from the facts of geography, with the concentrated urban population of C Scotland well away from the southern borders and 160 km from the nearest industrial region of England, on Tyne-Wear.

Already in the Special Areas programme of the early 1930s Scotland had a Secretary of State, compared with only commissioners in other areas. This degree of continuing autonomy and independence in economic and social decision-taking or planning had been advantageous in two ways: clearer formulation of the problems, through the availability of Scottish statistics, and coherence in the design or application of policies. The ability to measure national income and to calibrate and monitor economic change proved particularly valuable during the 1960s when UK regional policies shifted in emphasis from unemployment relief towards achievement of balanced economic growth. Scotland had faced the same restructuring problems as other least-favoured regions in postwar years, but her legacy from past industrial revolutions had been less constraining. Moreover, the resulting secular unemployment in declining industries such as coal-mining, mechanical engineering or shipbuilding was highly concentrated in and around Clydeside and in Lanarkshire, affecting the economic health of sizeable, congested populations. In industrial restructuring shipbuilding was uniquely hard hit, culminating in the failure of Upper Clyde Shipbuilders; the Dundee jute industry passed through particularly difficult times, whilst employment in the primary industries fell sharply. On the credit side the electronics industry had a sharp rise in employment in the period 1961–75 and United States investment in Scotland has been striking. Furthermore, in contrast to the overall decline of manufacturing jobs, mostly for males, there had been increases in professional and scientific services, and in insurance, banking and finance. These new jobs, however, employed mainly women and not a few of those part-time only.

Yet the overall verdict must be similar to that for N England: the massive rundown in male jobs in basic industries has not been fully compensated for by the growth of new forms of employment or a marked rise in jobs for women in manufacturing (Turnock 1979). Rates of growth in service employment have lagged behind UK levels and, as in N England, there is the same clamour for more R and D units, more head-offices and a more forceful decentralization of central government establishments, to add to the Savings Bank and the headquarters of the British National Oil Corporation established in Glasgow.

Regional planning had an early start in Scotland and its effectiveness has proved a valuable aid both to economic development policies generally and to the formulation of sub-regional proposals within an overall Scottish programme. The *Clyde Valley Regional Plan* (Abercrombie and Matthews 1946) appeared at a time when the government was particularly active in steering industry under the *Distribution of Industry Act* (1945). Though undue concentration of such industrial moves into Clydeside helped to diversify industry there, it was at the expense of balance in the Central Lowlands or, indeed, over Scotland as a whole. Scottish economists and planners were early on alive to the need for balanced distribution of growth and equally emphatic in both the Cairncross Committee (1952) and the Toothill Report (1961) that this objective would not be realized by the 'worst-first' policy of priority for relief of unemployment where it was most severe. Indeed, Toothill spoke deliberately of the need to build up industrial complexes and centres which offered the best prospect of becoming zones of growth. This found an echo in the White Paper of the following year (SDD 1963), which designated nine growth areas (fig. 1.6). These included the then four New Towns of C Scotland (SDD 1978), together with Irvine (later designated a New Town) and the Grangemouth/Falkirk area, the latter with considerable potential for

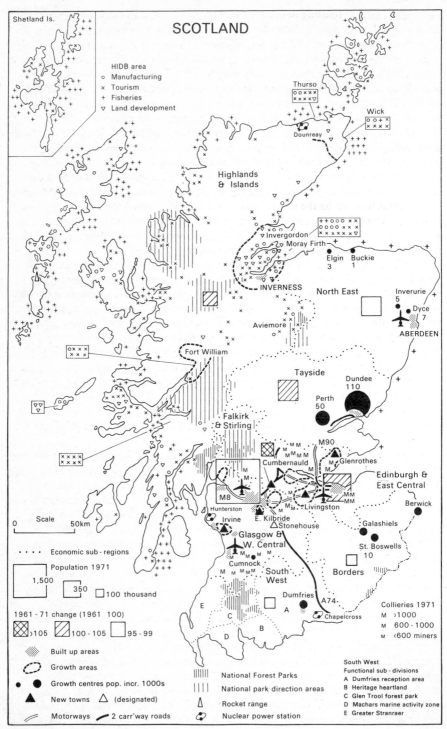

Figure 1.7   Scotland

both industrial and housing development. Other growth areas were older industrial tracts like N Lanarkshire, C Fife, the Lothians around Livingston and the Vale of Leven, which had land and labour but where social capital was run down.

Though the *Industrial Development Act* (1966) defined the greater part of Scotland as a DA and thus temporarily annulled the 'growth area' concept, the philosophy of concentrating growth at designated nuclei has proved remarkably persistent, cropping up in all the later sub-regional studies. Since Scotland was the proving ground it is interesting to note the comments of Cameron and Reid (1966). They concluded that from an industrial location point of view C Scotland was too small and well-developed for small growth areas to have particular advantages in terms of external economies. Growth areas were really the means of integrating various strands of economic and social policy, with an emphasis on potential for substantial population growth. From the White Paper, however, it is clear that the growth areas were to be the most ready and effective channel for attracting industrial investment and creating locally new living environments. The benefits of this would be diffused through their labour hinterlands and would link up with the development proposed in Glasgow and Edinburgh.

Equally innovating, the publication of a plan for expansion of the Scottish economy 1965–70 (Scottish Office 1966) sought to speed up the evolution of a modern industrial structure in Scotland, to make the fullest use of manpower and to cut the net out-migration rate of 40,000 per annum in the 1960s. It provided a planning framework, both in sectoral terms and in respect of sub-regional patterns of growth and expansion. Between 1965 and 1971 initial strategies had been prepared for seven of the eight planning regions of Scotland (McGuiness 1968, Self *et al* 1967) and two major transportation studies had been achieved, for Greater Glasgow and Perth. Physical planning, so active in English regions during the same period, lagged behind sub-regional plan formulation in Scotland. This put Scotland in a better position to develop structure plans within a set of existing sub-regional strategies and within the overall context of a short-term Scottish Plan (McDonald 1977).

In the strategies the regional development problems of Scotland emerged as of three types: those of the peripheral rural regions (Knox and Cottam 1981) – sizeable, diverse but over-dependent on primary industries and with severe infrastructural deficiencies, notably in public transport; the decaying industrial tracts in need of diversification, rehabilitation and an improvement in living environment; and, thirdly, the problems of an over-developed, congested conurbation on Clydeside. It is the last, with an almost stagnant population of about two millions, which uniquely dominated the Scottish planning scene and has overshadowed all other sub-regions since the war.

Clydeside Decisions on the future shape, structure and size of the Strathclyde conurbation have been and remain the key to the prospects for dispersal of population and the dissemination of growth throughout Scotland (Minay 1965). With the preparation of the last of the regional strategies, the *West Central Scotland Plan* (1974), the dimensions and prospects for the Clydeside economy became clearer. The short-term problems there are only too tragically apparent, and it now seems highly improbable that indigenous economic growth can be generated on the scale necessary to permit the massive redistribution of people and work which many think essential. The dilemma may be posed thus: Clydeside is too congested and its industrial structure cannot adequately be transformed within

its borders, yet the large-scale redistribution of overspill population has not been
adequately matched by attraction of industry out of Clydeside. The overspill plan
for Glasgow envisaged a movement of 383,000 out of the conurbation by 1980.
No fewer than 54 local authorities have had overspill agreements with Glasgow, plus
the five New Towns, but planned overspill for the 66 schemes over long distances
has been difficult to achieve. Most industrial firms leaving Clydeside (Henderson
1973) have preferred sites within 48 km, whilst the 'growth areas' of C Scotland
attracted no less than 60% of overspill families and three-quarters of industrial
moves to overspill areas. West Central Scotland (Strathclyde) continues to have the
unfavourable hallmarks of two-thirds of Scots unemployment and a continuing net
population loss.

The risk that the solution to Clydeside's problems would be at the expense of
the rest of C Scotland seemed to have been diminished by the possibility of creating
a major fast-growth sub-region based on Tayside (Campbell and Lyddon 1970), the
open end of industrial Scotland, and also by the vigour of other sub-regional
planning proposals (Robertson, Johnson-Marshall and Matthew 1966, 1968). A
further intriguing prospect for revitalizing the role of C Scotland is the Oceanspan
proposal (1970) for creating a 'land bridge' with rapid transit systems between the
Atlantic and the North Sea. Vital to the concept is the development of Hunterston
on the Clyde as the prime site for an integrated post-industrial complex, with
903 ha zoned for industry (ch. 5.V). In the adverse economic climate of the
1980s the Tayside, Oceanspan and Hunterston schemes must remain little more
than relics of a vanished age of growth optimism.

Scottish marginal regions There is a contrast between the Highlands and Islands,
with NE Scotland, on the one hand, and the Borders and SW on the other. The case
for the diversion of investment to the Highlands and Islands, in the face of overall
Scottish priorities is not universally accepted, and indeed there are those who argue
that even north of the C Lowlands there is a better case for investing in the
modernized agrarian structure, manufacturing base and growth prospects of NE
Scotland (Mackay and Buxton 1965; Gaskin 1968). Certainly the *Gaskin Report*
cautiously confirms the 'substantial assets for further development' in the North
East, but saw an important ingredient in the solution of the problems of that
region in the redistribution of overspill from the Aberdeen city region to two main
growth zones: the lower Don valley and, on a smaller scale, the lowlands of
Banffshire and W Morayshire.

Redevelopment and growth in the Highlands and Islands is almost an 'act of
faith' for many Scots (Thomson and Grimble 1968) and it is impossible to ignore
the substantial achievements of the Development Board created for that region in
1965. These have been equally impressive whether one considers the many
disseminated improvements in fisheries, tourism, manufacturing and land
development, or the larger-scale proposals to create growth areas: on the Moray
Firth (HIDB 1968), in the Wick—Thurso region or around Lochaber (Fort William).
Increasingly, a policy of concentration and urbanization seems called for (Turnock
1970) and the eastern littoral is likely to prove a powerful magnet for major new
developments.

By contrast, the strategy proposals for the C Borders (SDD 1968) and the South
West (SDD 1970) may be seen as programmes for arresting decline and out-
migration. By the careful promotion of a regional community as an inter-related
and regrouped pattern of small towns, with St Boswells and Berwick as growth

centres, the Borders plan seeks to exploit intermediate location of the area, whilst seeking new industries and developing Galashiels as a commercial centre. The strategy for the SW is couched more in sectoral terms with proposals for new job creation and relief of unemployment, attraction of industry and improvement of communications. The tourist plan for Galloway (Scottish Tourist Board 1968) touches on one of the most promising prospects, with detailed proposals for the sub-regions shown on fig. 1.7.

During the early 1980s the uneven impact of recession within Scotland was most marked. In sharp contrast to the economic stagnation on Clydeside, the NE flourished from the impact of North Sea oil development (Gaskin and Mackay 1978; SEPD 1978; Parsler and Shapiro 1980). There is a general drift of labour NE and substantial public and private investments have been made in roads, harbours, housing, drilling rigs and platform sites. Nicoll (1973) spoke of the need for a new axis Aberdeen to Ayr along which growth nodes might be created. Hunterston–Irvine–Kilmarnock might be one such node, but the economic climate of the 1980s makes such growth-allocating strategies more than somewhat academic.

Wales (fig. 1.8)
By comparison with Scotland, Wales (Thomas 1977) is smaller, lacking in economic coherence, and its three economic sub-regions are increasingly interdependent with adjacent areas of the English economy. The M4, the HST rail service and establishment of English-owned branch plants have reinforced this dependency. As a senior Welsh geographer put it (Bowen 1957), 'we certainly cannot accept that what is now Wales in a political sense represents a unity of any kind', though he was quick to point out the cultural identity of a smaller Welsh heartland redoubt. The Welsh Council (created 1968) is responsible for economic strategy proposals, and there are many institutions at national level to reinforce the Welsh cultural personality (Lloyd and Thomason 1963). On the whole, however, Wales lacks the Scottish degree of self-sufficiency or economic independence (Nevin, Rose and Round 1966) and until recently the devolution of decision-taking to Wales had been more apparent than real. Like all least favoured regions Wales is a net recipient of funds from the rest of the UK (Tomkins 1971), though the creation of three new Welsh economic bodies in 1976 gave her a stronger voice in her own affairs: the Welsh Development Agency, for industrial expansion, investment and land reclamation; the Development Board for Rural Wales; and the Land Authority (under the Community Land Act), since lapsed.

Wales passed through the characteristic stages of the development area life-cycle from the early 1930s (Moore and Rhodes 1975), but her geographical layout, particularly the constraints imposed by relief, and her disposition of resources conditioned a distinctive degree of response. The extent of concentration in mining areas like the Rhondda was unparalleled and subsequent readjustment the more agonizing. Iron and steel, and tinplate manufactures grew rapidly in the nineteenth century but during the 1920s and 1930s suffered dramatic changes in location and in technology. 1939–45 brought munitions factories, chemical, aluminium and vehicles plants, helped retrain labour and brought women into the factories, encouraged journeys to work, and led to closer economic ties with England.

Since the 1940s benefits under successive government aid policies have been substantial. Out-migration from Wales was first slowed down and then reversed. Rates of industrial investment were high in the 1950s and early 1960s, partly the

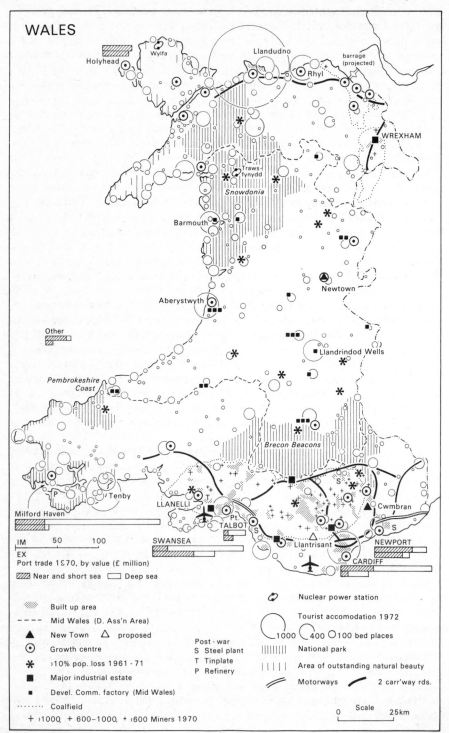

Figure 1.8   Wales

result of major capital-intensive projects in basic industries such as the Llanwern integrated steel-making plant. Diversification had played its part in the growth of new industrial and service jobs, but the limited size of the total labourforce imposed constraints on the tempo of the process. Most of the new employment was located off the S Wales coalfield though nearly half the population continued to live there, amidst industrial dereliction and an outworn social fabric. Between 1958 and 1968, the age of the 'Welsh economic miracle', jobs in manufacturing grew at five times the UK rate, although Wales had a working population only one-tenth that of London. Moreover, new manufacturing jobs replaced 91% of the jobs lost in mining and quarrying (cf 18% in N England, 26% in Scotland) and a useful proportion of the new jobs were provided by overseas companies.

Yet *regional planning* had been disappointing (Hagger and Davies 1961) to the time of the *1967 White Paper* (Sec. State Wales 1967), which defined spatial objectives only secondarily to those for economic and social sectors. Furthermore, the proposals were for three scarcely related economic sub-regions: S Wales, Mid-Wales and N Wales. This strong sub-regional level of strategic thinking has still to be incorporated effectively into a Welsh national context. Yet the basic problems are nation-wide: economic restructuring, especially jobs for men; the inner cities (Welsh Office 1977); improvement of external and internal accessibility, and the need for a coherent geographical overview (Manners 1968).

South Wales The problems of S Wales (Humphrys 1972) tend to overshadow the Welsh scene as did those of the C Lowlands in Scotland. With some two-thirds of the Welsh population living within 56 km of Bridgend, economic restructuring, settlement regrouping and environmental rehabilitation are concentrated in this major industrial and urban area. The *1967 White Paper* proposed to concentrate efforts to attract new industry along improved east-west communications linking up towns at the mouths of the mining valleys where these debouched on to the coastal plain. The valleys would then conserve their communities, journeys to work would develop down the valleys and the environment would be renewed; the Heads of the Valleys road would also attract some industries.

Several growth-points were defined, including importantly the New Towns (Welsh Office 1978) of Llantrisant, designated in 1972, and Cwmbran (1949). Llantrisant, already the site of part of the Royal Mint, was to help reduce out-migration and to attract industry, but in 1974 the Secretary of State ended the project. Cwmbran regroups population from the Monmouthshire valleys whilst other growth centres are at Bridgend, Kenfis (Port Talbot), Landore-Morriston (Swansea) and Fforestfach. As capital of the principality Cardiff is to reinforce its commercial, administrative and educational function.

Developing Severnside as a coherent sub-region would stimulate growth in the Newport sub-region. The M4 motorway powerfully extends economic linkages of S Wales with Greater London, to match those along the M5 to the W Midlands. The tendency to think of the SE coastal tract as a perimeter area of Wales rather than an economic bridge seems endemic in planning circles. On the other hand, current studies on Milford Haven indicate a further and major growth potential. In the early 1980s, however, growth seemed a mirage and the Welsh industrial economy struggled for survival, threatened by massive steel-plant reductions, closure of firms and further rundown of coal-mining.

Mid-Wales The problems here (Welsh Office 1964; Welsh Council 1971A; Development Commn 1972) are almost an exact antithesis to those of the South,

as are those of the Highlands to those of Central Scotland. But, unlike the
Highlands, Mid-Wales lacks a comprehensive development organization, and Welsh
social and economic problems, though smaller in scale, require more sensitive
planning. Depopulation down to threshold levels is the key issue, with political as
well as social and economic undertones (Wenger 1980), but the numbers leaving are
few in total. Unemployment and under-employment are both deepseated, but the
numbers in any one place are often not sufficient to attract an industrialist. The
largest town is Aberystwyth and the New Town of Newtown, Montgomeryshire
(1970) has a very modest population objective. Sceptics feel that the New Town
proposal is rather to serve overspill needs of the English Midlands, but to achieve
its target will necessitate a careful policy of attracting small firms. In any case
repopulation of Mid-Wales is likely to be necessary if the area is to prosper in the
longer term, and this will be singularly difficult to achieve.

The objectives of Welsh rural strategy are to establish a firmer economic base by
restructuring agriculture in commercially viable units, whilst maintaining the family
farm (Welsh Council 1977), building up forestry, using water resources more to the
advantage of Wales, conserving the landscape heritage, developing tourism and
attracting industry to small country towns. Basic to all is the underpinning of
Welsh rural society as a way of life (Houston and Jenkins 1965), threatened
according to some by a proliferation of English-owned second homes (Bollom 1978).
Figure 1.8 shows the sparse and fragmented tourist capacity in hotels in Mid-Wales,
in striking contrast to the north coast. It also indicates the pattern of small rural
growth-points to which small firms are to be attracted. The work of the Industrial
Development Association and the Development Commission has had notable
successes. By these means a self-sustaining economic base may be created, but it
will be a delicate task, and the developing of both internal and external
communications will be a key factor.

North Wales With pockets of SDA status since 1974, N Wales was to have a
concentration of growth at selected centres. Several of these were tourist centres,
with a rising population including those coming for retirement; introduction of
industry to balance seasonal unemployment was proposed. Portmadoc was to serve
as a centre for regrouping population in an area of high unemployment, whilst the
Holyhead—Anglesey area with an aluminium smelter and nuclear power station had
the best growth potential. In NE Wales (Shotton) there is a microcosm of S Wales
problems in coal and steel. The *Dee Estuary Scheme* (MHLG 1967; Sec. State
Environment 1971) showed a crossing to be both feasible and viable, with potential
for water storage, recreation and industrial expansion. Here too in the early 1980s
the accent has had to be on stabilization, not expansion.

N Ireland (fig. 1.9)
More than a decade of political turbulence and armed conflict has troubled Ulster,
and no end is in sight. The province is geographically separated from Britain, with
economic as well as psychological handicaps resulting. Suffering all the economic
and social ills of British AAs, and many of them in a more acute form, N Ireland is
'a client economy within a State in decline'. It is, furthermore, a deeply divided
sectarian community, with a Protestant majority and Catholic minority. Religious
differences are entrenched in the way of life, with privilege and facilities denied to
the minority in fifty years of autonomous political status (Probert 1978; Bew *et al*
1979; Pringle 1980). With a backward countryside and an outdated manufacturing

structure N Ireland has faced a succession of traumatic readjustments during the past few decades. Her regional economy is as deeply in crisis as ever before (Rowthorn 1981) and her society is riven by inequality, widespread poverty, the pressure of population on scarce resources (Compton 1978) and a traditional need for the young and most able to emigrate in search of betterment (−37,000 1961−6; −24,000 1966−71). Unemployment (Murie 1974; Doherty 1980) has been the beacon indicator of persistent malaise, never falling below the UK average and always leading the regional table of deprivation. Not surprisingly, N Ireland has long been subsidized by the British Exchequer (£589 million in 1979−80, or 32% of total revenues in the province). Her trade is no less dependent on Britain: 70% of Ulster imports and 76% of exports in 1970−5.

The present unfortunate situation has not always been the case. At the time of Partition (1920), N Ireland comprised the Protestant industrial base around Belfast, created by shipbuilding, engineering and the linen industry; to the west of the Bann lay the backward Catholic rural hinterland. Yet by 1939 Britain had to support Ulster by subsidies. The 1930s depression created more unemployment in town and countryside, there was little modernization of industry and little detectable improvement in housing or social facilities. In 1939 unemployment still stood at 20%, compared with 7% in Britain, and per capita incomes were only half the size. After a brief wartime boom the old economic problems resurfaced (N Ireland Econ. Council 1981). The threats of the Protestant working class to desert the Unionist cause led to government stimulus in the economy through investment grants, tax concessions, and other inducements to incoming firms. By 1970 65,000 new industrial jobs had been provided, yet the total in manufacturing was only 180,000 compared with a peak of 185,000 in 1956 (Rowthorn 1981, 4). Expansion in synthetic fibres, mechanical engineering and metal goods offset declines in shipbuilding and the linen industry but industrial linkages remained weak (Steed 1968; Hoare 1978). The structure of agriculture was transformed: consolidation of small family farms and mechanization released a flood of labour to the towns. From 25% of all jobs in 1950 farming employed only 10% by 1970. The public service economy boomed after the 1940s. Between 1954 and 1970, for example, employment in secondary-school teaching rose threefold and doubled in the health services. Yet total employment was scarcely increased: the high birth-rate meant that emigration had to siphon away a labour surplus.

In the 1970s the renewed economic depression hit N Ireland particularly hard. Employment fell, factories closed and investment was low. To the adverse effects of world competition and cheap imports were added the cumulative effects of the Troubles (Rowthorn 1981, 9). Table 1.6 shows the extent of de-industrialization in the 1970s and the growth of the services economy, particularly in the public sector. Services indeed grew at more than double the UK rate to 54% of all jobs in 1980, compared with only 22% in manufacturing. 'The old peasantry and industrial proletariat had been replaced by a vast army of service workers' (Rowthorn 1981, 11). Though women benefitted particularly from such transformation of the labour market, it was often in part-time jobs and in 1979 the female labourforce was the same as it had been in the 1920s. The loss of traditional farm and factory jobs for women and girls had been made up by services employment.

The variations in social well-being or its absence were probably greater within N Ireland than even those between the province and the rest of the UK. A principal components analysis, using 8 diagnostic variables to represent 8 significant

TABLE 1.6

N Ireland, Working Population, 1970–80

	Agric. Fish.	FDT	Mech. Eng	Elec. Eng	Text.	Clothing and shoes	Other Manuf.	Constrn	Tpt	Utilities
1980 (000s)	63.2	21.4	9.2	9.0	25.8	17.2	48.4	44.0	22.4	11.7
1970–80 % change	–10.3	–17.7	–35.2	–26.2	–42.8	–30.6	–15.1	–16.5	–8.4	–3.3

	Distrbn	Bank Financ.	Misc. Serv.	Prof. Sci.	Pub. Admin. Defence	Unemploy.	Total
1980 (000s)	64.9	21.1	62.7	111.4	53.1	73.1	651.6
1970–80 % change	–5.4	+59.8	+39.6	+55.2	+52.6	+130.6	+9.1

Source: Rowthorn (1981), 9; Dept Manpower Services

dimensions (Goodyear and Eastwood 1979, 329), mapped differential social well-
being. The least deprived areas clustered around Belfast with a ring of high levels of
social well-being. These were in towns that had benefitted from government
location policies (see below). Within Belfast itself the inner city blight was
reminiscent of other British cities, most acute in Catholic inner wards but difficult
to relieve since it would have meant moving to Protestant areas in the less-developed
north of the city. With increasing distance from the capital, the index of well-being
fell steadily, but remote rural areas had even lower levels than distance alone would
account for. All three Londonderry wards had very negative values.

The seedbed of civil strife lay in the long-term manifestly unequal treatment of
Catholics and Protestants (Miller 1979; O'Dowd et al 1980). The Catholics were
concentrated in the backward rural areas west of the Bann and in the most deprived
city wards of Belfast and Londonderry. The Catholic community had persistently
suffered discrimination, in housing, education and at the workplace. The electoral
system had been manipulated for fifty years and many had been virtually forced to
emigrate for the lack of a job (Rowthorn 1981, 3). Only 5% of shipyard workers
were Catholic, for example, and they were also grossly under-represented in the
public service (Aunger 1975). During the 1970s there were marginal improvements
under the Fair Employment Agency. Ironically, it was in Protestant industrial
strongholds that depression and unemployment hit hardest in the 1970s,
particularly with the virtual extinction of man-made fibres and the decline of
mechanical engineering (Rowthorn 1981, 20). Yet in 1971–8 unemployment was
still higher in the Catholic areas: in 1978 40% of male heads of household in inner
wards of Catholic W Belfast were unemployed, compared to 18% in the comparable
Protestant wards.

Neither government industrial location policy nor physical planning were entirely
free from political distortions. The problems of economic structure and peripheral
location were highlighted early (Isles and Cuthbert 1957). The Wilson Report

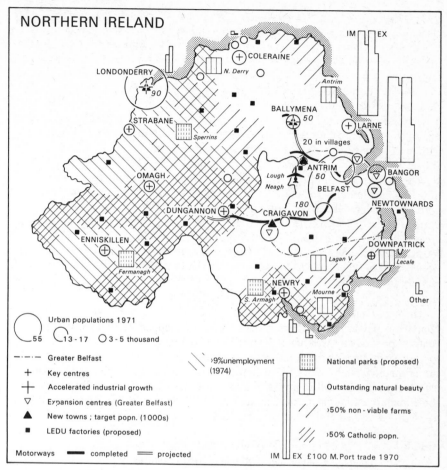

Figure 1.9 Northern Ireland

(Govt N Ireland 1965) advocated orderly planning of physical development, with major spatial redistribution. In the early 1960s the *Belfast Regional Survey and Plan* (Matthew 1963) proposed to limit, even reverse, the growth of Belfast, create a New Town at Craigavon and disperse population to fifteen designated centres. The 1970 Development Programme (Govt N Ireland 1970) confirmed the growth area concept, defining Londonderry and Ballymena for accelerated industrial expansion and eight other key centres. New Towns at Craigavon, Antrim–Ballymena and Londonderry were to be the spearheads of such growth. Though it was intended that such a pattern of growth would diffuse benefits into the rural hinterland, a complementary rural programme was set in train. The Local Enterprise Development Unit scheme (LEDU) (Busteed 1976), was to encourage introduction of small firms into rural areas, by grants, loans, advance factories (300 m²) and nursery workshops (four units, each 59 m²). Fig. 1.9 shows the initial LEDU investment pattern, but since then the level of local initiative has been disappointing and the unstable political situation has further impeded the programme.

The *Regional Physical Development Strategy 1975–95* (N Ireland DoE 1977; Quigley 1976) accepted that population growth would be slowed, that mobility was reduced in the Troubles, that few mobile plants were available for 'steering' and that the emphasis should be on improving social well-being. It was recognized that, though the Belfast stopline policy had been successful, little enough had been done to redevelop the deprived inner city and much of the growth disseminated had gone to small towns and villages rather than designated growth centres.

Of six spatial strategies tested, quantitatively and by consultations, the choice fell on a district-town preference for development. The Belfast stopline was to be held, except perhaps in the SW, and New Town expansion was to be encouraged. In fact, during 1973, the New Town Corporations were dissolved and their functions transferred to the district councils. There has thus been a strong spatial element in growth allocation in N Ireland (Hoare 1976). Detached locational rationale vied with political expediency in choice of growth centres as the Catholic voice became more effectively heard. The differential shift in public investment in the Catholic areas began before the dissolution of Stormont (1972). In 1967–71 36% of new jobs created by the Department of Commerce were located west of the Bann, though that area had only 27% of Ulster population. Similarly the vast government subsidy to the De Lorean car company in West Belfast was to provide industrial jobs for many Catholics (Rowthorn 1981, 20) until it failed in 1982.

The economic impact of the Troubles since 1969 has been variously assessed (Davis and McGurnaghan 1975; Darby and Williamson 1978). Official thinking tends to play down the effects of a conflict which reached its high point in the early 1970s. Since 1975 the IRA has concentrated mainly on security forces targets rather than on destruction of property and workplaces. The bombing campaign affected the private will to invest, damaged tourism and yet, ironically, stimulated the growth of employment in the public services sector. Table 1.7 (Rowthorn 1981, 17) shows an evaluation of the effects of the Troubles on employment.

TABLE 1.7

Effect of the Troubles, Employment in N Ireland, 1970–80

	change	% of 1970
Agriculture	nil	nil
Manufacturing	−25,000	−14
Other Industry	−4,000	−4.5
Private services	−10,000	−8
Public services	+15,000	+14
Total	−24,000	−4

Source: Rowthorn (1981), Table 9, p. 17

The political future of N Ireland remains uncertain, but the prospect of further economic and social decay will fuel the internal conflict, intensifying the competition of Catholics and Protestants for jobs, houses and other social facilities (Rowthorn 1981, 26). Among political solutions being canvassed (Gibson 1975), continuing membership of the UK seems the most realistic, even though greater economic dependency and subsidy are inescapable. Independence would be impracticable, and closer association with Eire would be resisted by the Unionist majority, at least in the short term. The Eireann economy has done better during the 1970s recession and, combined with the continuing economic decline in Ulster, this could have political repercussions. The disillusionment of the Protestant working class in the North may lead to closer rapport with the Catholics there and, who knows, more formal links with Eire as a first step to a reunification of a more peaceful united Ireland (Fitzgerald 1972, Rowthorn 1981, 25).

V.3   The Less Favoured Regions

There is some generalization involved in identifying as less favoured regions the whole of Yorkshire, and Humberside, and the NW. The two trans-Pennine economic regions have very substantial populations living in sizeable, well-established towns and cities. Employment is sluggish or falling, though unemployment since the war has rarely been high enough for DA status to be conferred. The only exceptions to this, apart from Merseyside, were the short term scheduling of parts of SE (1946) and NE Lancashire (1953). Regional incomes have been rising slowly, and the industrial structure has been weighted with slow-growth or decline sectors. Out-migration has been a less severe problem than in the DAs, though it has been ever-present. Furthermore, the regions had a major legacy from the Industrial Revolution in their townscapes, and there was a serious problem of dereliction. To meet all these problems, in aggregate at times scarcely less severe than those of the DAs, there was no special locational aid from successive governments. It was only in 1969 that a lesser scale of aid became available and then only for strictly localized areas. The 1972 extension of IA status to virtually all of Yorkshire and Humberside and to the NW region permitted for the first time a coherent view on economic as well as social or physical objectives in their regional development.

Both regions are less than 320 km from London, linked by the direct motorway network and fast HST or electrified rail services. They are thus subjected to greater locational pulls from the Midlands and SE than are the DAs. In return, they may hope to offer less disadvantageous freight hauls to incoming industry, in respect of service to national markets.

Yorks. and Humberside (fig. 1.10)
Fawcett (1919) spoke of Yorkshire as a 'microcosm of England'. The same might be said for the regional development problem posed today by the entire economic region. It lacks homogeneity or coherence, and there have persisted clear differences of emphasis as between alternative strategies for growth and development. The economic restructuring problem is massive (Brown 1970) but, until the late 1970s, had not given rise to the dramatic downturns of the DAs. It is arguably the primary heavy industrial region of the UK, with the nineteenth-century sinews of coal (27% national output 1979), steel (32% national output 1979) and woollen textiles long established and in all cases trending to secular decline. Adjustments to an EEC role also produced problems (Yorks. and H. EPC 1972B).

Within the *Pennines* and their fringe zone west of the A1(M) are concentrated 3½ millions, no less than 75% of the regional population. This is an urban-industrial zone with major cities and smaller, specialized industrial towns, the home of the woollen 'worsted' clothing and engineering industries. It is also a zone with a relatively low population growth and serious environmental difficulties, notably so in the smaller, single-industry woollen towns in the more remote Pennine valleys. In the south, around Sheffield—Rotherham, concentration on the steel industry and its related special product range means too narrow an employment base and poses particular problems of economic vulnerability. This is even more pronounced around the integrated steel plant at Scunthorpe to the east. In the W Riding conurbation the problems are thus those of a massive slow-growth or declining urban and industrial complex, without obvious means of achieving an industrial transformation.

The *central zone* includes the most productive localities of the Yorkshire coalfield, flanking the major north-south arteries of the A1(M) and the main east-coast rail link, set within a rural hinterland. Since the late 1950s there has been a sharp rundown in mining jobs, even in this prosperous coalfield. The exciting prospects for the new Selby coalfield will not radically transform this basic employment problem. The development issue is that of regrouping mining and agricultural populations and finding alternative work within daily travelling distance to absorb those displaced by redundancies. In meeting this the nodal location on the national communications network could prove a major asset.

The problem in the third zone, *Humberside*, is of a different order. The north bank, around Hull, has had a limited port-based industrial structure and has suffered from relative isolation. There are also physical planning problems, particularly those of urban redevelopment and the conservation of high-grade agricultural land. On the south bank industry has grown rapidly since the 1950s, but many plants have been capital-intensive rather than providing many new jobs. There is, however, ample land in the Humberside region to accommodate both population and industry.

The fundamental regional problem for Yorks. and Humberside is to decide on broad spatial allocations and priorities for growth as between the three zones. Strongly-held convictions in cities and Ridings have not made the tasks of formulating and gaining acceptance of a coherent strategy any easier. Nor is the task lightened by the difficulties of forecasting the tempo and nature of economic growth which may be expected. The woollen and worsted industry has been struggling to adapt to foreign competition, diversifying into man-made fibres and concentrating on up-market production lines. Though there has been considerable rationalization and closure of firms, there are still many small-to-medium family-owned concerns. In 1973 the Wool Textile scheme sought to improve the industrial structure and provide much-needed investment. Closures and short-time working became endemic in the clothing industry, too, during the 1970s. Engineering was mainly concentrated in the heavy branches, initially related to textile machinery and transport equipment, but widening to electrical engineering and the lighter branches during the past few decades. Employment held up well but little restructuring had taken place. In steel production serious employment declines took place through the 1970s but jobs in coal-mining fell less than anticipated. Service jobs have grown slightly faster than the national average since 1971, but from a lower base level.

Government scheduling for industrial location aid came late. In 1969 the coalfield and N Humberside became IAs and in 1972 most of the planning region was included. The part of the N Region (Cleveland) transferred in the same year kept its DA status, until downgraded to an IA in 1978. Hull and Grimsby were

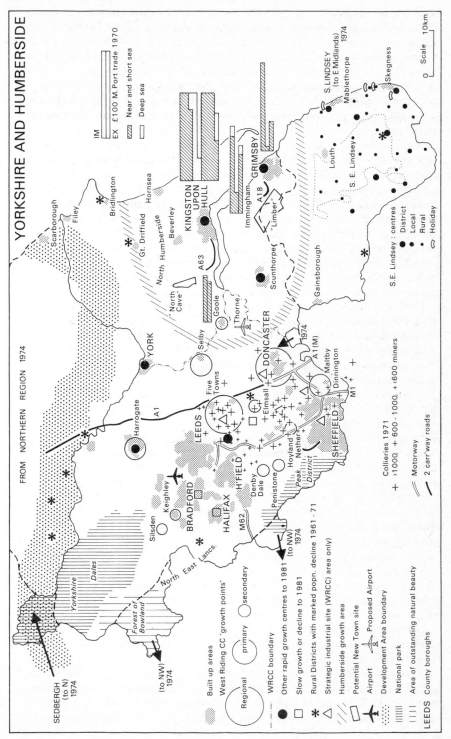

Figure 1.10   Yorkshire and Humberside

scheduled as DAs in 1977, but in 1979 the entire region lost scheduled status.

Regional planning A succession of regional planning reports developed a spatial strategy. The 1966 review (Yorks. and H. EPC 1966) emphasized the complexity and diversity of the region and underlined the varied needs and problems of each sub-region. The 'collective regional action and new sense of coherence' then called for have since been slow to materialize. Basic to the arguments of the review is the proposition that the problems of each sub-region should be mitigated largely *in situ*. There were no proposals for intra-regional transfers of population, or selective investment in areas where economic growth might be more readily induced. The defence may well have been that mobile industry would be difficult to attract without greater government incentives, that indigenous industry had prospects for regeneration and this would have to take place on existing sites. With the prospect of only very modest additions to the labourforce, dramatic intra-regional transfers were neither practicable or desirable. Future development should be concentrated mainly on established centres of population, native industries should power such development, and there should be priority for improving the general urban environment in the Pennines (Yorks. and H. EPC 1976A). Planning emphasized sub-regional analysis (Yorks. and H. EPC 1968, 1969A, B) but lacked an overall framework. For example, in the Halifax and Calder Valley study the recommendation was made for growth at the mouths of the valleys and along the M62, a micro-strategy similar to that for S Wales, but this sub-regional solution was not set within any wider regional context.

In the *Hunt Report* (Sec. State Econ. Affairs 1969) on the Intermediate Areas, a clear difference of opinion arose on prescription for future development. The majority view was that there should be a strategy of selective investment in growth centres. Industrial estates at strategic points, capable of drawing in labour from a wider hinterland, would play the role they had already had in DAs. Concentration on growth centres should not be at the expense of other parts of the region, and, indeed, no inherent conflict of interests was envisaged. A.J. Brown laid stress rather on the scale of the large urban concentrations and the importance of channelling growth there. He further saw the coalfield as the one location in Yorks. and Humberside where a growth centre might be justified. To him the growth-centre concept was appropriate only when the entire pattern of settlement was being changed, as in the regrouping of agricultural or mining populations, or when substantial moves from congested cities were being made through overspill schemes. Growth centres would contribute less to the problems of a massive slow-growth industrial and urban complex.

The division of views on strategy surfaced again in the *Development Plan Review* of the W Riding CC (1969, 1971), which admittedly did not have responsibility for the problems of its included county boroughs. The strategy proposals were firmly based on the designation of growth points and, indeed, an even greater emphasis upon such selective investment, as the future population for the region seemed likely to be lower. The pattern of suggested growth points, at regional, primary and secondary levels is seen on fig. 1.10; the selection of Doncaster confirmed the potential already identified in the EPC sub-regional study. The pattern of growth points was carefully chosen to exploit under-utilized resources of land or labour, capitalize in other cases upon favourable location, and on other occasions lead to environmental improvement. In addition, a series of strategic industrial sites were proposed. Furthermore, no fewer than fifty-one key villages were selected for expansion.

The *Regional Strategy* (Yorks. and H. EPC 1970) confirmed the basic recommendation of the 1966 Review and suggested that in view of the longer time-scale of the WRCC Development Plan (2001 rather than the year 1984), there was no fundamental conflict between the different perspectives. The regional strategy re-emphasized that growth should follow the broad pattern of existing settlement, that the larger towns had the better and more diversified growth prospects, particularly for attraction of service industries, but that growth should also be disseminated throughout the urban system at all levels. For Bradford, Huddersfield and Halifax the current adverse trends were to be stabilized, with some increase at Huddersfield, whilst in the longer term Leeds was recommended as a major growth area. Urgent provision of new jobs for men was prescribed for Greater Doncaster, Barnsley, the Five Towns (fig. 1.10) and Wakefield, with some decline in population in the central coalfield. For Sheffield and Rotherham the economy was to be diversified and the possibility kept open for accommodating regional population growth in the longer term. The strengthening of the economic base and improvement of the environment were priorities for Humberside, whilst conservation or modest development were envisaged for country areas and market towns.

The problem posed by the future development of *Humberside* is longer term and national in the first instance but its regional implications are profound. Had the government accepted the case for rapid estuarine growth on Humberside by the end of the century (CUEP 1969), a safeguard would have been built in to protect the DAs, but no such protection had been vouchsafed for adjacent areas of Yorks. and Humberside. In national and local terms (Lewis and Jones 1970; Craig, Evans and Showler 1970) the long-term case for Humberside development remains strong, potentially dramatic. It was anticipated that major growth would have taken place by spontaneous mass movements from the 1980s onwards, but that in the short term industry and people might be attracted more from the Midlands and the SE, partly by planned overspill. Had they been acceptable to government, the impact of such major developments upon the massive slow-growth industrial and urban complex in the Pennines and the general strategic balance within Yorks. and Humberside would have posed extraordinary problems, even within an enhanced European future.

The *1975 Regional Strategy Review* (Yorks. and H. EPC 1976B), considered the implications of a slow-growth economy at a time of rising national recession. In some respects the region was more favoured than at the time of the 1970 review. Net out-migration had fallen; the communications pattern had improved, with virtual completion of the M62, and a start had been made on the Humber Bridge (completed 1981). UK entry to the EEC bid fair to favour the Humberside ports, even though the government had decided against the MIDAS concept there. The Humber fishing industry, however, languished (Yorks. and H. EPC 1977). At the newly-discovered Selby coalfield there was the prospect of 8 million tonnes of coal per annum by the mid-1980s and 4,000 mining jobs. At Scunthorpe the Anchor scheme had been commissioned by the BSC in 1973, though by the end of the decade it was under threat.

Sectoral priorities in the review stressed the overriding need to develop productive industry, then to complete essential communications and only thereafter to focus upon environmental problems. Among environmental problems pride of place was to be given to housing, followed by water and sewerage, air pollution, health, education, derelict land and river pollution, in that order of importance. It was strongly asserted that regional policies should increasingly be concerned with reducing out-migration, improving the quality of life, and raising average incomes, rather than excessively preoccupied with unemployment levels.

The North West (fig. 1.11)
The problems of the NW (Smith 1969; Nuttall and Batty 1970; Lloyd and Mason 1979; Lloyd and Reeve 1981) arise initially from the very size of the regional population, its concentration between the Ribble and the Mersey (5.9m), a low population growth-rate, and the scale of industrial transformation and rundown which have taken place in cotton, coal and engineering since the war. Though there has been some replacement of jobs by growth industries, especially so in services, the region is still characterized by a low level of autonomous economic growth. In common with Yorks. and Humberside the urban-industrial problem is most serious in the traditional single-industry towns in the Pennines, but in the NW the decline of employment in cotton textiles has been more profound and its sub-regional effects more traumatic.

Furthermore, the presence of major conurbations on Merseyside (1.5m, 1981) and at Greater Manchester (2.6m, 1981) in lowland Lancashire, each until 1974 controlled by independent planning authorities, has weighted the restructuring problem and coloured policies for development and change. Merseyside has been consistently scheduled as a DA since 1949 (SDA since August 1974), to its great advantage (DEA 1965). The only other DA has been Furness, on the borders of the N Region, and transferred to that region in 1974. Manchester, on the other hand, failed to attract the same scale of new industrial investment but has built up service employment. Both conurbations need substantial and continuing overspill schemes to permit redevelopment and decrease congestion, and there is a major problem of priorities as between the sub-regions for the distribution of such population and employment.

Nowhere in Britain is the range of possible regional development options greater: dissemination of growth and sub-regional balance; perimeter additions to one or both conurbations; major developments at the New Towns including the Central Lancashire New Town (CLNT); balance between growth in the Ribble Belt (CLNT and NE Lancashire) and the Mersey Belt, particularly in the sub-region between the conurbations; concentration of growth in areas most attractive to industry or remedial measures in problem sub-regions. Nowhere in Britain has there been such a slow growth momentum, in population or employment, in relation to the scale of problems to be faced, and scarcely anywhere else has the fragmentation of planning authorities made coherent policies so difficult to achieve. On the other hand, the growth of the motorway network and the completion of main-line electrification on the west-coast route offer fresh regional economic potential.

In the 1970s economic recession deeply intensified the regional problems of the NW. Far from fulfilling planning predictions as the 'engine for regional economic growth', Merseyside (Lane 1981) became the most serious problem area within a regional economy itself in sharp decline. Its rather more prosperous traditional service base was in contrast to the longer term decline of port-based industries, but it was the rash of closures and redundancies at the newer industries on suburban industrial estates which precipitated the socially disturbing escalation of

TABLE 1.8

Merseyside SDA, Closures and Redundancies, 1976—81

	Closures	Employees	Redundancies	Employees	Total
Vehicles	2	4,400	8	6,144	10,514
Miscell. manufs	20	6,686	27	3,392	10,078
Elec. engineering	8	4,213	11	2,513	6,726
Food, Drink, Tob.	10	3,547	17	2,290	5,837
Textiles and Clothing	8	4,072	1	60	4,132
Engineering	10	1,427	14	1,220	2,647
Ships and Marine Eng.	5	1,289	7	1,240	2,529
Packaging	3	850	10	988	1,838
Chemicals	4	390	11	1,393	1,783
	70	26,874	105	19,210	46,084

Sources: MSC; Lane (1981); *RSA*

unemployment (table 1.8). Manchester fared better in spite of a vulnerable range of traditional manufactures (Dicken and Lloyd 1978) and attracted the 'giant's share of regional growth in office-based services' (Lloyd and Reeve 1981, 7). De-industrialization hit the NW particularly hard. Between 1971 and 1977 there was a job loss of 34,000 in textiles (22.5%), 29,000 in mechanical engineering (24.4%) and 9,000 in clothing (12.3%). After 1977 there was a spectacular decline in motor-vehicle employment with the closure of British Leyland capacity.

Regional planning The North West Study (DEA 1965A) stressed the twin objectives of better living conditions and the need to stimulate economic growth. The problem of housing obsolescence was placed in the forefront, and has remained a major preoccupation (N West EPC 1970). The forward projections for the regional population were then more sizeable (plus 800,000—930,000 by 1981), even though out-migration was assumed to continue. Overspill schemes for intra-regional redistribution (fig. 1.11) were numerous but for the most part small and separately negotiated by the conurbation local authorities. The New Town designated at Skelmersdale, together with proposals for similar developments at Runcorn, Warrington and Leyland—Chorley were also to accommodate overspill, and it was not anticipated that other overspill schemes would be required, certainly not before the last decade of the century. The problem industrial areas within the Pennines were scarcely touched upon.

A counterpart study for *Merseyside* (DEA 1965B; Lawton and Cunningham 1970) noted the youthful population and a high natural increase rate in spite of a traditional net migration loss. The industrial economy was changing during the same period from narrowly port-based to a greater diversification linked to the hinterland of the NW. Yet industrial transformation had not been sufficient to offset job loss in port-based industries and still meet the needs of an increased labourforce. Unemployment persisted, particularly for young persons, and justified the scheduling of Merseyside as a DA as far back as 1949.

The *1966 Strategy* (NW EPC) optimistically proposed to reduce net out-migration and contemplated a population increase of one million by 1981. Two growth areas were proposed: in N Lancashire and S Cheshire. The green belts around the conurbations were to remain inviolate and there was to be no infilling in

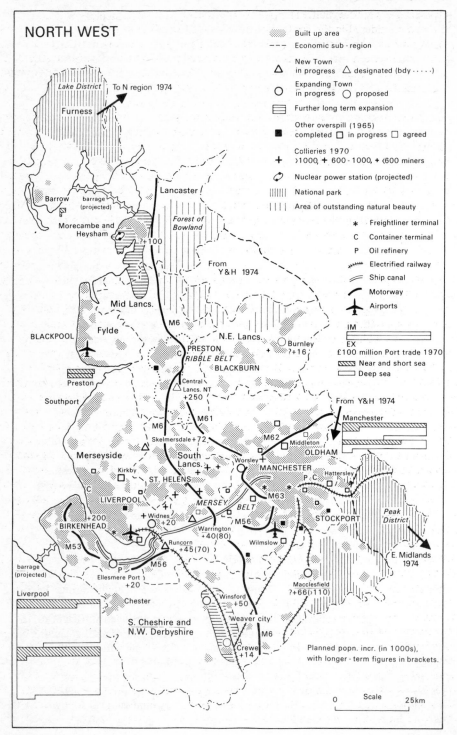

NORTH WEST

	Built up area
---	Economic sub - region

New Town
△ in progress   △ designated (bdy ·····)

Expanding Town
○ in progress   ○ proposed

▱ Further long term expansion

Other overspill (1965)
■ completed ▱ in progress ▱ agreed

Collieries 1970
✛ >1000, + 600 - 1000, + <600 miners

↻ Nuclear power station (projected)

|||||| National park

|||| Area of outstanding natural beauty

✳ Freightliner terminal
C   Container terminal
P   Oil refinery
⊬⊬⊬⊬ Electrified railway
≈ Ship canal
◗ Motorway
✈ Airports

IM
EX
£100 million Port trade 1970
▨ Near and short sea
▭ Deep sea

Lake District
To N region 1974
Furness

Barrow   barrage
(projected)
Morecambe and
Heysham
?+100
Lancaster
*Forest of
Bowland*

From
Y&H 1974

Mid Lancs.

BLACKPOOL
Fylde
N.E. Lancs.   ○ Burnley
M6   + ?+16
C   PRESTON
RIBBLE BELT
BLACKBURN
Preston
Central
Lancs. NT
+250
Southport
From Y&H 1974
M61
M6   Manchester
Skelmersdale +72
M62
Merseyside   △   Middleton OLDHAM
Worsley ○ MANCHESTER
Kirkby   South   P C Hattersley
St. HELENS   Lancs.
C   ✳   M63
LIVERPOOL   *MERSEY* *BELT*   *Peak
+200   District*
BIRKENHEAD • Widnes +20   STOCKPORT
M53   △ Warrington M56
Runcorn +40(80)   Wilmslow   E. Midlands
barrage   +45(70)   1974
(projected) P M56
Ellesmere Port
+20   Macclesfield
Liverpool   ?+66(>110)
Chester   Winsford
+50
S. Cheshire and   'Weaver city'
N.W. Derbyshire   M6
Crewe
+14
Planned popn. incr. (in 1000s),
with longer - term figures in brackets.

Scale
0   25km

Figure 1.11   The North West

the intervening Mersey Belt. The industrial problem areas of Rossendale and the NW were considered in the context of the effects of the *Cotton Industry Act* (1959) which had achieved massive rationalization and reduction of both capacity and employment in that industry. Yet NE Lancashire had been descheduled under the 1960 *Local Employment Act* and the prospects of attracting sufficient new industrial growth correspondingly reduced.

The *Strategy II* (NW EPC 1968) had less regard for allocations of the lesser expected population growth but much greater emphasis upon the need for industrial location efficiency, buttressed by effective action on transport, housing and schools. The environment was to be improved by urban renewal and an attack on the problems of derelict land (N West EPC 1971) and pollution. Peripheral growth of the conurbations by inroads into green-belt land was rejected in favour of continued growth at the New Towns and by town-expansion schemes. Increased journeys to work were anticipated, both to these new developments and to industrial sites within the marginal problem localities in Rossendale, the NE and the Pennine fringe. The early development of the CLNT was firmly supported and the urgency of local government reform seen as necessary if a coordinated strategy was to be achieved.

In its proposal, not accepted by the government, to deschedule Merseyside as a DA, the *Hunt Report* (Sec. State Economic Affairs 1969, 159) brought into the open one of the principal strategic issues, the role of the conurbations in regional economic growth, and particularly the extent of distortions which DA scheduling may have introduced. Attracting industrial moves from neighbouring areas, mostly from Manchester, Merseyside then represented the major North West growth complex. Its assets included perimeter industrial estates with major housing developments, the green-field industrial sites capable of taking motor-vehicle plants, the nearby New Towns of Skelmersdale and Runcorn and the overspill town of Winsford. Descheduling was opposed by Brown (Sec. State Economic Affairs 1969, 159), arguing that the high natural increase and immigration required continued government support policies for creating new employment. If the area was to be descheduled it did not follow that the same industrial growth would be available for other sites in the North West. In the event DA status was retained and in August 1974 SDA status was conferred. NE Lancashire was designated an IA in 1970, a status extended to the entire North West in 1972.

The now-abortive Central Lancashire New Town (MHLG 1967), speculatively intended to build up to a population of no less than 430,000 by 1991 from the 250,000 in the initially designated area, clearly had the potential to act as a counter-magnet to the two principal conurbations. It was also, prospectively, a major growth centre to underpin the industrial economy and help stabilize the population of the entire Ribble belt. Indeed, it was intended deliberately to relieve growth pressures in the Merseyside—Manchester axis, to act as a base for concentrating large immigrant growth industries, and to provide an attractive environment and modern living conditions. There is extreme uncertainty about the prospects of attracting sufficient mobile large-scale industry and some doubt about the potential adverse effects upon NE Lancashire. Some regretted that the designated area did not extend further south, to help relieve unemployment problems in the area north of Wigan. To clarify the possible effects upon NE Lancashire an Impact Study (Matthew *et al* 1968) was commissioned, followed by a project study for a fast road link to the NE. It was felt that the effects of CLNT on the sub-region would on balance be favourable.

The *Strategic Plan for the North West* (DoE 1974) was formulated before economic recession became pronounced; by the early 1980s its thinking seemed wildly optimistic. Its attitude to growth was more catholic and there was a proper regard for quality of life in its proposals (Powell 1974). The plan aimed to optimize job distribution rather than maximize growth and its proposed patterning of change was not limited to the most likely growth areas. The method of evaluating options (Activity Allocation Model) seems to have involved a blend of measurement with judgement. The first cycle of evaluation established weighted objectives within a goals achievement matrix. The second moved from preferred emphases of policy to preferred spatial patterns of employment, degree of population displacement and assessment of land release required for new development. The third cycle produced the recommended physical pattern to 1991.

The spatial patterns tested varied from concentration to dispersal (Mersey belt; CLNT-Ribble belt; Weaver city; peripheral growth around conurbations; Lancaster–Morecambe; Deeside). Concentration was favoured: greater job choice; access to urban facilities; level and costs of provision; benefits of public transport; better treatment of the underprivileged. Disadvantages were seen as more a matter of urban form and structure rather than those of sheer weight of numbers. It was determined that the best prospects for regional employment growth lay in existing centres of industry and commerce. This favoured the Mersey belt, already showing signs of serious economic decline within which also the greatest environmental problems were to be found.

The recommendation was that job growth should thus be greatest in S Lancashire, especially around the three New Towns and to the north and east of the Merseyside and SELNEC conurbations, in each of which there should be maximum job retention. Corridor growth in the directions of Bolton, Bury and Tyldesley–Westhoughton would focus this outward growth, and southwards only the Macclesfield corridor should be developed. There should be careful management of the rates of job creation, fast in S Lancashire, much slower in S Cheshire. Overall, the displacement of population should be moderate rather than high.

The price of such a priority for the Mersey belt necessarily implied slower rates of growth elsewhere. The CLNT grew slowly in the short term, but could have made a major contribution to growth later in the century. Priority for CLNT was discontinued in the early 1980s and it is now unlikely ever to fulfil earlier ambitions. For NE Lancashire, the Fylde and Furness, existing policy restraints were to continue. At first sight this implied a harsh policy towards marginal areas of all types and many former single-industry textile towns faced difficult problems of readjustment. The degree of mismatch between population growth locations and economic potential indicated that mobility needed to be high at a time of mounting recession and retrenchment.

The SPNW was vigorously attacked by the *Lancashire County Co.* (1974), for its degree of pessimism, its alleged unjustified and untested change of direction in major planning policy, and for its preferred strategy of concentration on the Mersey belt. It was argued that such a concentration policy would add seriously to environmental problems, that it was incompatible with an objective of improving the quality of life and that in any event the policy had not been costed. Furthermore, the creation of growth corridors would consume valuable open land and there would be peripheral accretion around the conurbations as a result.

In the view of Lancashire CC economic growth should be promoted where it had the greatest possibility of success, but the search for quality of life should always be an important qualification on purely economic strategies. The CLNT was seen as the best prospect for growth upon land already allocated, and the SPNW report was accused of overestimating the growth intended there. A further condemnation of the SPNW was that it did not provide a realistic, flexible and balanced view of the future.

V.4   Regions of Mixed Trends

The SW and E Anglia economic regions do not fall into any clear category, though they share certain common features. Neither has coherence, least of all the SW, and indeed each has four distinctive sub-regions. As a result, there are built-in conflicting economic and social trends, and a marked territoriality between urban and rural interests. Both are identified by the lowest population densities among UK economic regions, but nevertheless there are strong pressures for growth and development in parts of both the SW (Severnside, Swindon) and E Anglia (New Town and town expansion schemes). In both regions the influence of the metropolis is increasingly felt and is spreading. This adds to the problems of developing a regional sense of purpose.

The South West

The *Draft Strategy for the South West* (SW EPC 1967) accepted from the outset that very different treatment would be required for each of its four component sub-regions: Bristol and Severnside; the Central area; Devon; Cornwall. Indeed, in view of the distinctive economic and social problems of each, the strength of county-based loyalties, the lack of a clear capital for the region and the extent of outside, particularly metropolitan influences, it is not surprising that a coherent and universally agreed strategy did not emerge. Nine sub-regions were identified in 1967 and twenty economic planning areas in 1974 (SW EPC 1974).

Bristol and Severnside   The strategic issues facing this sub-region arise from strong population and economic growth pressures. There is a need to define priorities for proper physical planning of growth, to avoid congestion and loss of amenity; furthermore, expansion of manufacturing ought to be balanced by the growth of services. The verdict of the now-abortive Severnside study (CUEP 1971) was that the potential for population growth by the end of the century was double even that by projection of the buoyant economic trends of the 1960s. The industrial mix is diverse with many powerful growth elements (Walker 1965; Britton 1967): aircraft and aerospace, engineering, paper and printing at Bristol; mechanical and instrument engineering in N Gloucestershire; and the iron and steel industry in Monmouthshire. The effects of the 1970s recession were minimal and the loss of only 4.8% of manufacturing jobs 1971–80 was easily the most favourable among British regions. Nevertheless, the Concorde project is threatened, which could bring distress to many SW towns. Port development may be an income generator, but is unlikely to provide many new jobs. Tertiary employment, particularly in offices, is a better prospect, with Bristol already the fourth office centre outside London though only eighth in urban size.

The nodal communications location is the surest guarantor of the future for Severnside. The building of the Severn bridge, the M4 and M5 motorways and the

introduction of the HST rail service have strengthened the infrastructure of a
coherent Severnside sub-region. They have also linked Severnside effectively with
the South East and the W Midlands.

The *central sub-region* is a largely agricultural and rural belt, with limited
growth potential in its market towns and at selected S Coast resorts. It is subjected
to strong growth influences from Bristol—Severnside to the north and, to a lesser
extent, from the metropolis. Conservation of the environment and the special
character of the smaller towns, underpinning of community life in the rural areas,
and accommodation of growing retirement populations in the coastal resorts were
elements of regional planning policy (SW EPC 1975).

Devon and Cornwall The problems of the outer sub-regions of the SW could
scarcely be more different: to promote rather than restrain growth, and to do so
from a narrow agriculture-tourism base; to create better accessibility rather than
channel growth arising from a modern spinal communications net; to attract
industry and reduce unemployment rather than avoid 'over-heating' arising from
rapid economic growth; to create many small centres of growth rather than major
growth concentrations.

The *1966 Strategy* (SW EPC 1967) stressed the importance of strengthening
agriculture and horticulture, whilst accepting that employment in these sectors
would continue to fall, by amalgamation of holdings, increase in gross output per
holding and more effective marketing. Tourism was seen as a major but vulnerable
growth industry (SW EPC 1976), which might be inter-related with other elements
of the rural or coastal economy, but one whose prospects could not alone carry
Devon and Cornwall to prosperity (MHLG 1970). Farming and tourism would
provide the base from which self-sustaining economic growth might be promoted
by the introduction of manufacturing and its location at selected regional or local
growth centres. Plymouth was recommended as a major centre for growth, with
further potential at the two growth triangles, Exeter—Honiton—Taunton and
Truro—Camborne—Falmouth. Prospects for self-supporting growth would be
enhanced by planned overspill from Greater London.

Population growth came disproportionately from the influx of retired persons,
whilst younger people continued to leave Devon and Cornwall in search of work.
The multiplier effect of retired people on the local economy might be as much as
the equivalent of one service job equivalent per retired household. Manufacturing
jobs were likely to be a more stable long-term investment.

During the period 1966—70 Devon CC carried out feasibility studies for several
growth centres, the Cornwall Council investigated the proposals for West Cornwall
(Cornwall CC 1970) and the EPC published the Plymouth area study (SW EPC
1969). Neither county council accepted that the growth triangles should have
precedence for investment, or indeed that population or employment should be
channelled into such areas. Furthermore, the proposal that Greater London
overspill should contribute to the build-up was strongly resented locally. In Devon
and Cornwall the strategy is rather for smaller-scale and inter-related growth points,
with redistribution of population from larger towns like Exeter or Plymouth into
an immediate hinterland. As in Wales there is a strong sentiment for promoting
development from indigenous resources and population.

Studies in industrial development at Plymouth and in Devon and Cornwall
(Braithwaite 1968; Spooner 1972, 1974) showed the difficulties of generating and
maintaining sufficient momentum without government aid and, even with it, the

problems of attracting new developments on the necessary scale and with adequate growth prospects. There is some expectation that EEC membership will continue to help rather than damage the SW. A roll-on/roll-off Plymouth—Roscoff (Brittany) ferry service, a possible container outport at Falmouth and a potential increase in tourism from Europe are all positive features.

The *1974 Strategic Settlement Pattern* (SW EPC 1974) reformulated the principle of securing economic growth to match population growth, consistent with consideration for the environment. Interestingly, the process of hypothesizing and testing alternative spatial strategies was held to be inapplicable for the SW, in view of the limited economic interaction between the sub-regions. Regional-scale options for influencing population flows were thus regarded as very limited and the principle of redeploying or inter-relating growth was firmly rejected. The population proposed for most of the twenty economic planning areas, each broadly homogeneous in economy and environment, was that likely to occur by extrapolation of existing trends. Capacity to move against the trends was thought to be very limited, even though half the anticipated population growth was to be by net in-migration. The most interesting features distinguishing this 1974 document were: the long time-scale (to 2001), the stress upon marginal influencing of population location without a thoroughgoing analysis of employment potential, and the extreme compartmentalization of what was proposed.

East Anglia

Difficult to establish in the first place, the identity of this region risks being increasingly submerged by metropolitan influences expressed through the communications network and the pattern of New and overspill towns. The Outer Metropolitan Area (OMA) bounds the region on the south and London lies only 193 km from the furthest point of the Norfolk coast. The location of E Anglia has traditionally been interpreted as oblique to the main axis of national economic life. Its identity has been built up as one of the foremost agricultural regions in the UK, somewhat isolated by poor communications, but with a degree of coherence from the interlinking of sub-regions based on Norwich, Peterborough, Cambridge and Ipswich. The EPC came into being later than others (1966), for in official circles E Anglia had hitherto been a statistical abstraction.

The *East Anglia Study* (E Anglia EPC 1968) recognized the problem of consolidating an identity for a region lacking homogeneity and subject to strong external influences from the south. The regional development problem is compounded of conflicting trends. On the one hand, the population mass is small, the overall density is low, whilst the traditional economic structure has been built from an agrarian base. Manufacturing is poorly developed, with many small firms in food- or fish-processing and light engineering (Sant and Moseley 1977). Labour has a restricted range of skills and average incomes are low. Furthermore, there have been persistent but highly localized unemployment 'black spots' in coastal and rural Norfolk. Not only is the internal road system inadequate but rural transport, both road and rail, has declined markedly. Housing, education and health standards have been lower than those of the nation. Not surprisingly, rural depopulation has proved to be a characteristic feature, though tourism has underpinned the coastal economy (E Anglia EPC 1978A).

On the other hand, the total population of E Anglia has shown the fastest regional growth rate since 1951 and this is likely to be sustained (E Anglia EPC

1978B). Growth came from the SE with the influx of sizeable London overspill
population. From 1966 to 1981 about 100,000 additional males sought jobs,
three-quarters of them at the New Town of Peterborough or in overspill areas. The
distribution of overspill schemes is seen on fig. 2.20. Under the *Town Development
Act* (1952) ten local authorities made overspill arrangements with what is now the
GLC and a total capacity, 1966–81, for about 250,000 people was made available
in E Anglia.

The strategy problem facing the E Anglian Council was to draw up a plan which
would strengthen the regional economy and benefit from the London-inspired
growth momentum, without at the same time becoming no more than a peripheral
extension of the SE. Indigenous growth was likely to be small and hard to realize,
since the region had never had DA status and only intermittently and in piecemeal
fashion aid under the 1960 and 1963 *Local Employment Acts*. Additionally, office
development had been restricted, and firms could not be attracted, under overspill
arrangements, from the adjacent OMA.

A strategy for concentration of development along radial growth corridors from
the SE to Peterborough (A1(M)), or to Ipswich (A12) and thence to Norwich, was
rejected as damaging to the coherence of E Anglia. Transverse growth corridors
seemed unlikely to be realized, although a Haven Ports–Cambridge–Northampton
axis developed in the 1960s, with some loss of sub-regional balance. Nor did a
major New Town growth in Breckland seem in the interests of the region and the
proposed scale of such a development, at Thetford, also threatened amenity.

The proposed strategy envisaged the build-up of the *four city regions*, each with
a dispersed hinterland of about 24 km radius. Norwich, Peterborough, Cambridge
and Ipswich were nodally located, though large parts of the hinterland of the first
three lay outside the E Anglian planning region. Second-order urban regions were
to be based on King's Lynn, Great Yarmouth–Lowestoft and Bury St Edmunds,
and it was intended to select smaller-scale rural growth-points. In commenting on
the proposed strategy the government agreed that there was no reason to
concentrate development in any one part of the region, but rejected any notion of
uniform sub-regional growth. Sub-regional studies were undertaken to identify
areas with the greatest growth potential. Office development controls were lifted
and firms from the OMA permitted to move to New or expanding towns. The rural
growth-point strategy was accepted and some IDC relaxation took place.

The *Strategic Choice Report* (DoE 1974) is conceptually in strong contrast to
that for the SW, published in the same year. The exceptional growth pressures
upon E Anglia, accelerating and particularly heavy over the years to 1985, were
seen as a great opportunity to redress imbalances sub-regionally and at different
levels in the urban hierarchy. Manipulation of the immigrant streams under a
selective growth and location policy would be the means, and the merits of diversity
and continuity with the past would be secured by flexible, small-scale units of
provision. The effective solution to the longer-term problems of E Anglia should
not be sacrificed by short-term maximum-growth policies. These might in fact
heighten existing spatial imbalances through the sheer speed of development.

External pressures for growth would be expressed centrifugally from Outer
London in zones of diminishing intensity across the western and southern sub-
regions of E Anglia. Policy should be directed to building up the four sub-regional
centres (Norwich, Cambridge, Peterborough and Ipswich) but there should also be a
deliberate attempt to stimulate greater growth proportionately in the northern and

eastern sub-regions. A small-towns policy (E Anglia Consult. Commn 1973) should
be fostered to diffuse growth and to assist in evening out growth and change. The
economic vigour of the Haven Ports (E Anglia EPC 1977), in trade with Europe, has
stimulated growth along the SE perimeter.

V.5   The 'Growth' Regions

As far back as the *Barlow Report* (1940) the growth potential of the Midlands–SE
axis had been recognized. Indeed in the 1930s it had been the reception area for
the so-called 'drift to the south'. It had and still has the cardinal advantages of
location on the modernized rail and motorway network, access to the major
gateway ports, and has long had the sites preferred for a wide range of twentieth-
century growth industries. The living environment, for the most part, escaped the
worst of the Industrial Revolution heritage. With all these assets, confirmed by
agglomeration, the economies of scale, the creation of an ever-larger market in the
rising population, it was entirely justifiable until the early 1970s to speak of
'growth regions'. Yet the term is not applicable in all parts of the regions and
already in the late 1960s there emerged ominous signs of rising unemployment even
in such hitherto prosperous cities as Coventry and Birmingham. During the 1970s
the employment situation in the W Midlands so worsened that there is a case for
excluding it from the category of 'growth' regions altogether. This would assume
that its problems are secular rather than cyclical, a judgement which might for the
moment be premature.

The East Midlands
The region lies in the heartland of England, nodally located astride four major
national communication arteries: the M1 and A1(M), and the east-coast HST route
and the electrified Euston–Manchester–Glasgow rail links. It also has the most
striking regional concentration of thermal electric-power generation. Though not
without its weaknesses (steel, shoes, man-made fibres), the industrial structure has
useful representation of growth industries, in engineering and electrical products.
During the 1970s recession the E Midlands fared better than most. Between 1971
and 1981 employment in manufacturing fell by only 8% and service jobs rose by
30%. Its industrial cities are sufficiently close-knit to permit linkages and
economies of scale to develop. The population growth trend is a stimulus to
economic development, and regional unemployment levels have consistently been
below the national average. Unlike the W Midlands or the SE, the E Midlands has
no single massive and congested conurbation to dominate its development strategy.
Not least among its many assets are reserves of space for industrial and urban
development, or redeployment of people and work. It includes, furthermore, one
of the most prosperous agricultural areas of Europe.

On the other hand, the region is lacking in coherence, not only by virtue of its
internal diversity, but also because there are powerful and independent economic
influences just beyond its borders. The metropolitan influence is strongly felt in the
Northampton sub-region, only 96 km from London, and its growth potential has
also to be measured against that of nearby Milton Keynes or Peterborough. The
influence of Sheffield penetrates southwards to Chesterfield, whilst Greater
Birmingham is a powerful magnet to the south-west of the region. Until the transfer
of S Lindsey to the E Midlands in 1974, Lincoln remained very much a border

town, but with the opening of the Humber bridge it has been more closely linked with Humberside. In the face of these many conflicting pulls around the perimeter, the E Midlands has sought a corporate identity with the creation of many regional bodies and the strengthening of others. Nevertheless, city-based loyalties remain strong and on occasion have proved competitively disruptive.

Diversity in the regional economy has been a force for stability and cushioning recession, but because of their specialization not all parts of the region are prosperous or have equal prospects. Since the mid-1950s the emphasis on jobs in hosiery, knitwear, footwear, coal and leather products has diminished, though these groups are twice as strong as in the rest of the country. Newer industries such as chemicals, electronic engineering or vehicle components have been growing strongly. Aero-engine production has passed through a shadow, and the recession in footwear, knitting and textiles has been locally severe in virtual single-industry towns, under increased competition from developing countries. Growth in service jobs during the 1970s has been at almost double the national rate, but from a traditionally low baseline.

Though agriculture is perhaps the most productive and efficient in Britain, growing 20% UK wheat and sugar beet, 12% of barley and 16% of potatoes on only 7% of the national agricultural area, there has been a heavy loss of agricultural jobs. Coal-mining, too, has reduced its labourforce, but the newer pits, eastward down the dip-slope, are among the most productive in the UK. In older, worked-out mining districts of the Erewash valley and parts of Leicestershire there have been restructuring problems, but the accent elsewhere is upon high-technology invest-ment in the mines. Planning application for three mines in the Vale of Belvoir, to tap up to 500m tonnes of reserves, has been refused on environmental grounds (1981), even though vigorously supported by the mineworkers and local authorities (Spooner 1981, 50).

The growth allocation problem in the E Midlands is a matter, on the one hand, of diffusing some employment from the major cities to less prosperous parts of the hinterland; on the other of matching new job provision with the decline of employment in single-industry towns or parts of the coalfield. The continuing polarization of growth onto Leicester and the technological centre of Loughborough will take care of itself. Some mobility of industry will be necessary to facilitate better matching of growth and decline at sub-regional level. In the straightened economic circumstances of the 1980s a 'best-first' policy of investment at a time of scarce mobile industry is likely to aggravate further the already disturbing sub-regional inequalities.

Assisted Area status has been tardy, partial and fragmentary (Smith 1979). High unemployment localities gained IA status in 1969, extended in 1972 (N Lincolnshire, High Peak) and 1974 (Chesterfield). The ending of steel-making at Corby (1979) caused 5,800 jobs to be lost, though the tube-works continued to be prosperous and will use an alternative steel supply. The town was granted SDA status, became a Steel Closure Area (higher training costs assistance; aid from BSC Consultancy Ltd; ECSC loans of up to 50%) and was awarded an Enterprise Zone (1980). At the same time the town lost its New Town status and embarked not without success on a vigorous programme of self-help. The tourist resorts of Mablethorpe and Skegness were other unemployment 'black-spots' of the early 1980s.

The prospects for the sub-regions may be summarized. The Northampton area might have the most substantial growth, but it would be in population overspill from the SE and W Midlands. Such overspill may in fact wither in the current adverse economic climate and, in any case, there would be an almost insuperable problem of attracting sufficient mobile industry or building up the services to match households with jobs. The restructuring problems of the footwear industry and replacement of the Corby steel industry are likely to pre-empt industrial investment. When Mr Heath referred to Leicester in the early 1970s as 'Britain's most successful city' he was no doubt thinking of a population set to reach one million by end of the century. The growth of light engineering, electronics, food-processing and warehousing underpinned the labour market. The growth ethic permeated the sub-regional plan (Leicester City and County 1969), with a fashionable alternative spatial strategy for allocating a growth which will now be less and longer in coming.

Nottingham and Derby are the complementary industrial poles of their sub-region (Notts. and Derby. Sub-Reg. Study 1969), which includes half the population and the more serious economic problems of the E Midlands. Large indigenous companies dominate the industrial landscape: Boots, TI-Raleigh (Nottingham); Rolls-Royce (Derby, Leicester, Hucknall). Nottingham has the more diverse economy, including a wider range of consumer goods, such as textiles and tobacco. Derby is a more concentrated capital-goods centre, with half its industrial jobs in vehicles, only 8% in textiles and 7% in engineering. To the north, along the Erewash and Rother valleys, coal-mining decline and industrial decay have been endemic, with difficult problems of landscape rehabilitation and settlement renewal.

The E Lowlands (Fennell 1971) is an agricultural zone, with sparse population, low density of small or dispersed settlements, low rateable values and small-scale local finances. Somewhat neglected at the regional strategic level, depopulation has continued. Holland CC (1970) worked out an ingenious and inter-related pattern of rural growth points to stabilize the local economy. The 'development shadow' effect of more profitable investment in larger centres on the western and northern fringes of the C Lowlands may imperil such a sensitive plan mechanism.

The West Midlands

Though there are differences in scale, economic structure and national location, the regional development problems of the W Midlands have certain features in common with the SE. Until the 1970s both had been areas of faster economic and demographic growth, with low unemployment rates and a persistent attraction for migrants from elsewhere in the UK or from overseas. Each region has at its heart a major conurbation, Birmingham—Black Country (W Midlands Metro County) and Greater London. Though the W Midlands has less than one-third the numbers of the SE, the Metro counties in both contain a significant part of the regional population: Birmingham—Black Country 51%; Gtr London 40%. The problems of these great city clusters thus dominate those of the region and have inevitably had pride of place in regional strategies. Furthermore, the W Midlands has shared with the SE a nodal location on the main axes of economic growth in the UK since the early 1930s. This was later confirmed by the continuing polarization of national life through the radial motorway network and the electrified Euston—Glasgow rail route. For some decades, until the 1970s, the growth momentum in the W Midlands and SE has been productive of mobile industries to be steered to the AAs.

The dramatic economic downturn of the 1970s has enforced a concentration upon their own difficult internal problems, of locating and accommodating a growing number of people when there has been a declining volume of work, and no government locational aid (Tyler 1980).

The economic prosperity of the W Midlands rests upon five manufacturing sectors: vehicles, mechanical and electrical engineering, metal manufacture and metal goods. These account for 68% of industrial output and 70% of industrial employment; the corresponding national figures are 45 and 47%. In the ten years 1966–76 the five sectors had a net loss of 175,000 jobs in the W Midlands. New technology has reduced manpower needs, foreign competition has squeezed markets; manufacture of motor cycles, for example, has disappeared. The resulting large-scale unemployment is foreign to the history of the W Midlands, a situation not likely to improve since the population growth momentum of past decades is swelling the prospective labourforce annually. Between 1975 and 1991 some 15,000 new jobs will be required each year to accommodate the entrants to work, without taking account of the unemployed. From 1971–8 only 850 jobs per year became available but some 8,500 were lost every twelve months.

Declining employment in the car industry has had widespread negative multiplier effects, the more serious since the region has long been distinctive for its pattern of close and proliferating industrial linkages. Manufacturers have been reluctant to develop new capacity outside the region or, indeed, in many cases even outside the conurbation. The extent of sub-regional specialization by industry is well known and introduces further rigidities: the conurbation with metal manufacture, metal-using industries, car assembly, electrical engineering and small-scale metal fabrication; the Coventry belt with car assembly, electrical and mechanical engineering and aerospace industries; N Staffs with pottery manufacture, engineering and electrical goods. Immobility of firms is underpinned by localization of skilled labour, constraining mobile solutions in regional planning.

Regional planning There are two central issues in the spatial allocation of growth, or the sharing of readjustment and decline. First, the balance and equilibrium between the conurbation and its hinterland, and, secondly, the differential growth pressures along communication axes passing through the region. A third issue is the vexed question whether the W Midlands can or should have a continuing role in providing industry for the needs of the AAs as the national economy revives in due course. Of the three issues, that of the allocation between conurbation and hinterland has proved the most controversial, even politically vexatious. During the 1970s indeed the spatial strategy was virtually reversed (Mawson and Skelcher 1980, 158). From a decentralizing policy for both people, by planned overspill, and industrial firms, there is now an emphasis on stimulating firms within the conurbation and redeveloping the urban fabric to hold more population.

As for Gtr London, a conurbation containment policy had been followed for some decades (Wise 1972; DEA 1965; W Midlands EPC 1967; Coventry CC *et al* 1971; Joyce 1977). Definition of an overspill population and its relocation by bilateral local authority agreements is a well-known British policy. In the W Midlands it took off very slowly and only 25,000 were relocated between 1945 and 1965. At the most optimistic phase, when jobs could be taken for granted and resources were more readily available, no fewer than 867,000 were to be relocated within 30 to 40 years. The sheer scale of such redistribution is staggering; the fine-tuning to match redistribution of work, of the right variety, to the right places at the right time, was no less problematical. Though the volume of movement never took place the immobility of workplaces in comparison to suburban extensions by decentralization of residence was responsible for a dramatic congestion along all commuter routes into the conurbation.

The 1971 *Strategy* (WM EPC 1971; WM Reg. Study 1971) was in two parts: an economic appraisal from the EPC and a more general strategy from the local authorities. The EPC study made a strong case for greater regional powers to promote economic growth and greater autonomy for local industrialists to choose their locations. It also emphasized the economic health of the conurbation as the most vital regional issue and that this should have at least parity in shared economic growth with other sub-regions, New Towns or expanded towns, for the remainder of this century. The argument was that the advantages of agglomeration, the linkages and the growth prospects were greater in the conurbation and that industry could not be made more mobile without unacceptable economic loss.

This thinking contrasts with that for Gtr London or, indeed, even with that of the 1970 *Strategic Plan for the SE*, where decentralization and the development of powerful counter-magnets on the perimeter of the region were major spatial proposals. Limited decentralization from Birmingham and the Black Country has been a continuing theme in W Midlands regional planning since the 1940s. Certainly the rezoning of industry in the five 'comprehensive redevelopment areas' of central Birmingham or the clearance of dereliction in the Black Country are both impressive achievements, and the preservation of a green belt around the conurbation is no less so. On the other hand, the limited success in building up the New Towns at Telford (1968 in its present form) and Redditch (1964) and the small scale of overspill redistribution thus far make the 1971 plan seem remarkably over-ambitious.

The local authorities' planning strategy was thus very conurbation-oriented, identifying there the nodal points for longer-term economic growth, even admitting the shorter-term and continuing problem of renewal, restructuring and elimination of pockets of serious deprivation. Around the central city activities there were to be new industrial zones on the conurbation rim, flanked by service-industry growth corridors from Solihull to Redditch on the south and Sutton Coldfield to Lichfield on the north. Critique of the 1971 strategy pointed out the absence of policies for the N Staffs sub-region or for the rural economies of the western and southern areas. The impression is that what is good for the conurbation must be good for the W Midlands, just as what is good for the W Midlands must surely be in the national interest.

In 1979 the *W Midlands Strategy* was updated and rolled forward to 1991 (Jt Monitoring Steering Gp 1979; WM EPC and WM PAC 1979). Though the 1971 *Strategy* had been approved by the Minister in 1974, the W Midlands was the first to evolve a monitoring system and only the second, after the SE, to produce a major Strategy Review. Unfortunately, the Planning Board (civil servants) dissociated itself from the regional strategy, since it recommended government economic policy changes at national level. Though logical in the light of the past experience of the W Midlands as an exporter of mobile industry, a role it could no longer fulfil, the call for new regional policies transgressed central government prerogatives. During the 1980s, indeed, regional planning was destined to become local physical planning, whilst economic planning reverted to a national level.

For the 1980s, the strategic issues are almost the reverse of those throughout the past few decades. From actively promoting the overspill of people and jobs to outer locations, beyond the green belt, policy today focusses on the inner urban areas. The revitalization of the urban areas, and containment of decentralization beyond, highlights the tension between economic and social policy, between centrifugal market forces and social concern for the deprived dwellers in the decaying inner city (Paris and Blackaby 1979). Nevertheless, the city region was seen as the appropriate level for a growth allocation strategy: the conurbation, enclosed by a Middle Ring, one shire county in width (containing much of the statutory green belt), with an Outer Ring beyond. The N Staffs industrial area and the Rural West were the outermost zonal extremities. Disagreement on the definition of the critical Middle Ring led to alternative boundaries for analysis or for policy purposes.

Three versions of the strategy were considered: version A continued the 1974 policy of physical containment of the conurbation and relocation of excess population and housing growth in the shire counties beyond the green belt; strategy B concentrated on regenerating the existing build-up area, with tighter control over dispersal, and in fact an inward shift of resources; strategy C, the preferred option, was to revitalize the regional economy and regenerate the urban areas. This preferred option relied more on market forces, assumed a realistic view on public resources available, and interpreted physical planning possibilities only within these constraints. Physical and economic policies should be complementary and the Metro County and Middle Ring planned as interdependent parts of a city-region. Additional service jobs, urban regeneration and derelict-land clearance were priorities for N Staffs.

The three strategy options were only qualitatively tested and the preferred version had all the hallmarks of political compromise. The extent of the concentration-dispersal balance for people and jobs was left vague. In his response the minister stressed the importance of freedom for industry and commerce to locate where the best prospects were deemed to be. Comprehensive urban regeneration should be undertaken and sites on the periphery of the conurbation would be needed. The focus on land-use issues and the ignoring of economic policy set the stage for the demise of strategic regional planning in the 1980s (Focus GP 1979).

The South East (fig. 1.12)
With almost one-third of the UK population, the greatest concentration of fast-growth services and manufacturing and the most favoured nodal location at the hub of the radial communications network within the UK, facing Europe and overseas, the SE has been uniquely important in British regional planning. Until the 1970s the basic issue had been the extent to which Gtr London was to be permitted to make its distinctive and vital contribution to the national economy, with least detriment and indeed maximum stimulus to policies of regional balance or social justice for other parts of the UK. Allied with this has been the question of how, if at all, the growth pressures throughout the South East might or should be restrained, not only in the interests of its citizens, but also those of the region and the nation. By the 1980s, however, the dramatic downturn in London's fortunes had totally changed the situation. Population was declining by almost 50,000 a year and unemployment, particularly in manufacturing, at an even faster rate. Decay of the

inner city fabric reflected the social malaise of the deprived residents. The attraction of London for people and firms must be the overriding priority (Standing Conf. 1981, 3).

As far back as 1940 the *Barlow Report* spoke of the continued drift of the industrial population to London and the Home Counties as 'a social, economic and strategic problem demanding attention'. In 1921–51 there had been a 30% rise in employment in Gtr London compared with only 19% nationally. The role of London had grown steadily, nationally and internationally, in a wide range of manufacturing and services. The arguments against longer-term growth concerned: physical and mental health, yet on both counts London came out well; overcrowding and poor housing, but slum clearance and urban renewal had greatly decreased this problem; air pollution and environmental hazards; the social costs of congestion, traffic and journey to work; strategic aspects of the vulnerability of large population concentrations; and wider issues, such as the promotion of regional balance in the UK or the rising strength of provincial regionalism (Hall 1963). Many of these issues were town planning problems, though indissolubly interlinked with wider regional questions.

The *Greater London Plan* (Abercrombie 1945) set London within its regional context and ambitiously sought, first, to plan for a stabilized population of 10 millions in the plan area; secondly, to reduce urban sprawl by establishing a green belt; and thirdly, to reduce net residential density in London by a massive overspill programme to relocate some 750,000 from the LCC area and a further 500,000 from areas outside, to a ring of New Towns and expanded towns beyond the green belt. The plan was approved in 1947, with raised population targets, but several basic assumptions proved to be false. Employment was not effectively controlled by restrictions on new industries in the London area. Indeed, no less than 52% of all new employment growth in the UK, 1952–8, took place in the SE and 32% in London. Much of the manufacturing growth was in the outer urban ring whilst the inner ring lost jobs heavily. C London attracted much of the growth in services, and there was a massive increase in commuting, especially to office employment. Secondly, the overspill movement fell short of expectations: in 1946–61 the New Towns took 235,000 but not all came from London and many who did so commuted back to work; the expanded towns took only 28,000 through overspill schemes in the same period. Thus the interdiction policy on growth in London and the SE largely failed. The government did not press restrictions for fear of damaging national economic growth or the export trade. Many central services could not effectively be decentralized and, overall, the growth pressures had been much greater than anticipated. In particular, there had been an unexpected surge in the national birth-rate in the mid-1950s and a sharp influx of immigrants from overseas.

In the early 1960s a more rigorous restriction policy came in through the *Local Employment Acts*, but the growth in service jobs continued largely unchecked, since only *new* office space was controlled. Growth was especially fast in technological services, research and development, and in new manufactures, such as light engineering, vehicles or electronics. Economic growth generally was more rapid and structural than the plan process could accommodate. Between 1948 and 1959 the LCC licensed no less than 5.3 million m^2 of new office space. There had been some movement out by manufacturing firms, but these jobs were more than replaced by the growth in construction and services in the same period. The Outer

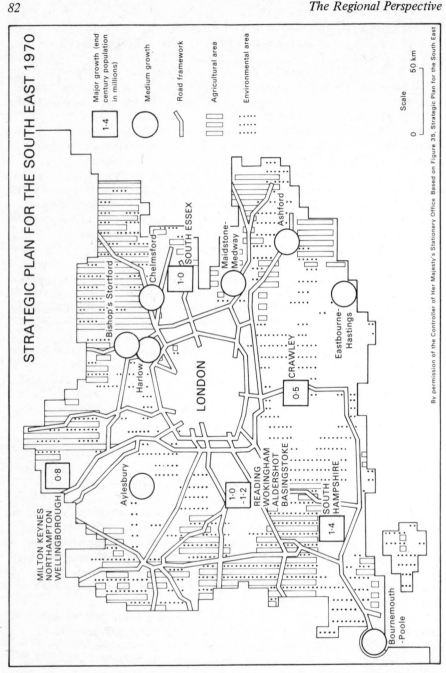

Figure 1.12   The South East: Strategic Plan 1970

Metropolitan Area (OMA), beyond the GLC boundaries but within 64 km of London, increased in population by 40% 1951—66, the product of the first generation of New Towns, the strong immigration from other parts of the UK and its own youthful age structure. The Outer South East (OSE) began to grow more rapidly during the 1960s and regional planning became increasingly concerned with allocations of growth, in population and employment, between the concentric zones around Gtr London.

The *South East Study* (MHLG 1964) proposed a second generation of New Towns and major town expansion in the region, proposals which envisaged some very large concentrations of people and work between 80 and 160 km out from C London. Such major growth might create cities in their own right to act as a series of counter-magnets to the continuing attractions of agglomeration around Gtr London. From 1965, office development throughout the metropolitan region was brought under permit control (ODPs), whilst in the following year creation of the SE EPC strengthened the regional voice against that of the GLC.

The *South East Strategy* (SE EPC 1967) had similar policies, but added new priorities: the urban renewal of London; redesign of the transport system, with corridors and orbital roads; stimulus to the large new city regions, to act as counter-magnets to the metropolis; and protection of the countryside. If London was to be more efficient its growth should be restricted to not more than 8 millions, whilst the remainder of the SE region should be able to absorb into employment not only its own natural increase, but also most of London's continuing overspill and, additionally, a much reduced immigration from other parts of the UK. For the first time overspill was programmed outside the regional boundaries.

A more coherent spatial strategy was postulated by proposals for radial growth along corridors linking Gtr London with the counter-magnet cities. Within the corridors urban growth was to be concentrated in a few localities, and each corridor had parallel major and minor axes. Industrial investment was to be concentrated into medium- and large-scale firms and commuting to London reduced. Rural land was to be conserved, extending the concept underlying the green belt to all parts of the SE.

The 1967 Strategy thus sought to solve the problems inherent in prospective population growth of four millions by the end of the century, through spatial allocation within the economic orbit, but not altogether within the boundaries of the SE. Such redeployment of growth was to improve the efficiency of the region, both nationally and internationally, but the effects upon the prospects for less-favoured regions were left uncertain. In short, the strategy of 1967 recognized that growth pressures in the SE were, at that time, too great to be effectively countermanded. Economic growth had displaced welfare as the fundament of regional policy.

The *Strategic Plan for the South East* (SE Jt Planning Team 1970), was the first definitive tripartite regional planning study, the product of central government, regional planning council and board, and local authorities. The strategy (fig. 1.12) was primarily concerned with the years 1981—2000. A main feature was confirmation of development at a limited number of major growth areas at varying distances from London, using existing or planned urban settlements as bases for growth. The far-sighted corridor concept was abandoned in favour of a more flexible strategy, to allocate growth both within and outside the London metropolitan region, according to changing needs. With slow growth, the three

designated areas — Reading–Wokingham–Aldershot–Basingstoke, South Essex and
the Crawley area — were likely to absorb a higher proportion. If faster growth, then
the South Hampshire (Buchanan 1966) or Milton Keynes–Northampton–
Wellingborough schemes might be accelerated, so that these self-contained counter-
magnet cities might play their role earlier and more substantially.

Additional flexibility in the plan was to come from the expansion of a number
of medium-sized employment centres, which might be used to relieve unacceptable
pressures in the major growth areas or compensate for failure to achieve desired
rates of growth. Such smaller centres would also assist in the restructuring of the
metropolitan region. Gtr London was to 'accommodate the maximum number of
residents consistent with the achievement of improved housing conditions and
improved environmental standards at reasonable cost'. Commuting should not
increase, which meant phasing the outward movement of jobs with that of population. Hitherto there had been optimism on this point, in contrast to the views for
Birmingham and the Black Country. The consultants' advice was that all parts of
the SE were acceptable to industrialists, provided labour was available and the
environment reasonable. The strategy would succeed or fail on the ability to adjust
job relocation with population redistribution. Its novelty lay in the flexible
approach, even if the preferred development pattern was less imaginative and more
permissive than the 1967 Strategy.

Greater London Published about the same time as the SPSE, the *Greater
London Development Plan* (GLC 1969) was the prototype structure plan for what
is certainly the most complex and large-scale planning unit in the UK. Its
recommendations were subjected to a most searching critique in the *Panel of
Inquiry* (*Layfield Report*, DoE 1973). The problem of planning a major
conurbation within the context of its economic region is one common to five other
regions of the UK. The case of Gtr London within the SE is exceptional, however,
both in scale and in the multifarious national and international roles played by the
capital city. To safeguard these vital roles by planning for a suitable level of
growth, and its allocation either within the conurbation or as between Gtr London
and the rest of the SE, is a difficult conceptual and management problem. This is
greatly aggravated by the lack of economic planning powers at GLC level, by the
strength of market forces generally in relation to limited powers of planning
control on allocations, and, thirdly, by the escalating social and economic problems
within the GLC.

The social problems of Gtr London concern housing (quantity, quality and cost),
imbalance both structurally and spatially between labour supply and demand,
persistent localized pockets of severe unemployment and social deprivation, traffic
congestion, and the deteriorating general urban environment. Both the adverse
structural changes in employment and the net demographic changes (table 1.9) in
the GLC area have been dramatic in recent times.

The GLC Strategy was to provide for a more equal geographical spread of
employment opportunity, with a balanced structure of industry, commerce and
services to match the skills available in each area. Secondly, a determined attack
was made on the social polarization developing within Gtr London, through housing
policies as well as job provision. This task became more difficult as jobs in
manufacturing declined and there was a steady net outflow of lower-middle-class
and skilled workers from both Inner (LEA) and Outer London. The prospective
danger is that further social polarization will create an even larger elite in the central

TABLE 1.9

SE Region: Population Change, 1951–79, by Economic Sub-region (av. ann. change in 000s)

	Natural change 1951–61	1961–71	1974–9	Migration 1951–61	1961–71	1974–9
Gtr London	+33.3	+44.9	+2.7	−61.0	−98.2	−63.6
OMA	+24.2	+41.4		+77.5	+43.8	
OSE	+8.9	+13.5		+27.3	+50.6	
South East	+66.4	+99.6	+10.9	+43.8	−3.7	−24.6

Source: Reg. Stats; Reg. Trends

area, a greater commuting flow of office workers and professional people from the GLC periphery and beyond, with a marked concentration of low-paid unskilled workers and socially-deprived households in an expanding, intervening belt. The GLC might then be unable to solve its mounting welfare problem and would wish to see a larger resident population retained. Tertiary growth was to be stimulated at twenty-two (shopping) centres plus six *major* strategic centres, together with Brent Cross (fig. 6.6b). There is a paradox in that to create more congenial living conditions in Gtr London fewer people should live there, but on the other hand without an enhanced employment base and a greater representation of medium- and higher-income groups the welfare problem will not be solved and community life will not improve. If the overspill areas had accepted a balanced proportion of the aged, the poor and the unfortunate, the problem might have been reduced. If only the more able, the more skilled and the better paid continued to be attracted away, the problem would become steadily worse. In 1976 the GLC ended its policy of dispersing population and jobs to areas outside the capital, declined to enter into any further 'overspill' agreements (ch. 2.IV.6) and sought to renegotiate a reduction in those already in force.

The Panel of Inquiry (Layfield Report, DoE 1973) did not accept that the rate of decline in the GLC population should be slowed down, and surprisingly, argued that the imbalances in labour supply and demand were only transitional in their implications. The ODP system was thought to be inappropriate and it was recommended that IDCs should be more freely available to firms which wished to move within London. The GLC policy for strategic growth centres was endorsed, but refined by the designation of four of the six major strategic centres as deliberate employment, and not simply tertiary, growth points; the others were to become more local shopping and service centres. The need for an integrated GLC transport strategy was strongly underlined.

The Conservative government view in the early 1970s was that Gtr London's population should be allowed to decline further, and that the rate of continuing decrease in employment as well as in population was of benefit both to those who leave and those who stay. The concentration policy for industries and offices was endorsed, but the recommendation to relax the IDC system was not acceptable, nor were powers over ODPs to be transferred to the GLC.

Crucial to the effective spatial redeployment of population in the SE are the volume of mobile jobs, and the nature and strength of public industrial location policies. It has been estimated (Stewart 1971) that 30–40,000 mobile jobs per annum will be needed for the SE, 1981–91, but that only 20,000 are likely to be available. The SPSE Team (1970) emphasized the need for maximum short- and medium-distance moves, since flows of more than 80 km would potentially conflict with AAs policy; yet longer-distance moves, e.g. to S Hampshire or S Essex, would also be needed. The SE EPC preferred more development at greater distances from London but, on balance, the *Strategic Plan* (SE Jt Planning Team 1970) saw inter-regional (AAs) and intra-regional (South East) policies on industrial employment as complementary. The spatial restructuring of the SE and the GLC area in particular were important and difficult objectives in their own right.

The SE in transition The government statement (DoE 1978) on the 1976 *Review* underlined the major subsequent legislative changes: the *Inner Urban Areas Act* 1978; the *Transport Act* 1978; changes in New Towns policy, on office location, housing and airports. Priority was accorded to the regeneration of inner London, the restraints on growth within the green belt were to be maintained (though the zone beyond 12 to 15 miles might be more flexibly treated), and growth should continue to be channelled to the SPSE major growth areas; medium-growth centres were to be determined in structure plans. Within the GLC area the revival of the London Docklands was vested in a Development Corporation (LDDC) in 1981, following approval of the *London Docklands Strategic Plan* (1976). Special Partnership areas with local government were created for the Docklands and Lambeth, Islington and Hackney (1977). In the same year the target population of New Towns competing for London overspill were reduced: Milton Keynes – 50–70,000, Northampton – 50,000, Peterborough – 20,000. Under the national, *Industrial Strategy* firms were to be encouraged to move first to the AAs, but thereafter the London Docklands and the Partnership areas should have precedence over New Towns or expanded towns. Offices of less than 2,800 m^2 (with about 250 jobs) were to be exempted from ODPs in Gtr London, whilst the Location of Offices Bureau (LOB) was to concentrate on attracting international concerns and 'steering' offices towards London inner city locations.

The reduced economic expectations of the 1980s have thus virtually reversed the longer term trends of spatial planning in the SE. The role of the SE in providing industrial and office development for dispersal to other regions has been significantly cut back. Within the SE, the policy of London decentralization has been transformed into one of improving London's relative attractions, to bring to an end the increasingly unsatisfactory economic and social trends in the nation's capital (Standing Conf. 1981, 6).

The 1976 Review of the SPSE (SE Jt Planning Team) took account of the revised static population forecast for 1991, increasing migration of people and businesses out of London, and the general effect of economic recession. The problems of London were the centrepiece of the Review: bad housing; a significant proportion of the homeless; extensive areas of dereliction; pockets of high unemployment and low income; congested roads and inadequate public transport services; and high costs for land, housing, rents, rates and labour. The principle of five major- and six medium-growth areas outside Gtr London was confirmed, but the rates of growth in such urban clusters would need to be contingent upon what happened in London. For the first time since the *Abercrombie Plan* (1944) the need to restrain rather than promote the flow of people and industry out of London became a prime objective for the regional planners.

V.6   A Final Note

The abolition of the EPCs in 1969 brought to an end the formal process of regional economic planning. In future, the accent will be on economic planning at national level with physical planning the responsibility of local government, through the strategic structure plan system. Structure plans continue to require ministerial approval, but the valuable regional consultative dimension has disappeared. It is illusory to believe that an informal group of departmental civil servants at regional level is an adequate replacement. The range of strategies produced had their shortcomings, but collectively they highlighted regional problems and proposed structural and spatial improvements. In their last phase, the strategies for N Region and the W Midlands challenged national economic policies and, in the case of N Region, costed the public expenditure required for regional betterment. In the early 1980s, however, the political climate was firmly set against a regional dimension in planning. Furthermore, there were not lacking those who contended that it was the urban network that needed planning and the region was a less relevant abstraction. It remains to be tested how far a regional voice can be effectively neutered in a reforming democratic society.

REFERENCES

Section I   The UK at the Crossroads

BECKERMAN, W (ed.) (1979) *Slow Growth in Britain,* Oxford

BEST, R H (1959) *The Major Land Uses in Britain,* Wye College, Ashford

BEST, R H and COPPOCK, J T (1962) *The Changing Uses of Land in Britain,* London

BLACKABY, F (ed.) (1979) 'De-industrialization', *NIESR,* London, *Econ. Pol. Pap., 2*

BUTLER, D and SLOMAN, A (1980) *British Political Facts,* 5th edn, London

CEBULA, R J (1980) 'Geographic Mobility and the Cost of Living: An Exploratory Note', *Urb. Stud., 17,* 353–5

CHAMPION, A G (1974) 'An Estimate of the Changing Extent and Distribution of Urban Land in England and Wales, 1959–70', *Centre for Environ. Stud. Res. Pap., 10*

CHISHOLM, M D I and MANNERS, G (eds) (1971) *Spatial Policy Problems of the British Economy,* Cambridge

DURY, G H (1968) *The British Isles: a Systematic and Regional Geography,* London

ELSON, M (1981) 'Farmland Loss and the Erosion of Planning', *Town and Country Plann., 50,* 1, 20–1

FORDHAM, R C (1974) 'Measurement of Urban Land Use', *Univ. Cambridge, Dept Land Econ., Occ. Pap., 1*

HANNAH, S P (1981) 'The Level and Structure of Unemployment', *Univ. Keele, Discuss. Pap., 32*

HARRIS, D and TAYLOR, J (1978) 'The Service Sector: its Changing Role as a Source of Employment', *Centre for Environ. Stud. Res. Pap., 25*

HOUSE, J W (1973) 'Geographers, Decision-takers, and Policy Makers', in CHISHOLM, M and RODGERS, B (eds) *Essays in Human Geography,* London, 272–305

KEEBLE, D (1981) 'Deindustrialization', *Geogrl Mag., LIII,* 7, 458–64

KILPATRICK, A and LAWSON, T (1980) 'On the Nature of Industrial Decline in
   the UK', *Cambridge J. Econ., 4,* 85–102
LAYARD, R (1981) 'Unemployment in Britain: Causes and Cures', *London School
   of Economics Discuss. Pap., 87*
LEWIS, T M and McNICOLL, I H (1978) *North Sea Oil and Scotland's Economic
   Prospects,* London
MANNERS, G *et al* (1980) *Regional Development in Britain,* Chichester
MASON, C M (ed.) (1979) *The Effective Management of Resources: the
   International Politics of the North Sea,* London
MOORE, B and RHODES J (1976) 'The Relative Decline of the UK Manufacturing
   Sector', *Cambridge Econ. Pol. Rev., 2,* 36–41
MUNTON, R (1981) 'Agricultural Land Use in the London Green Belt', *Town and
   Country Plann., 50,* 1, 17–9
NELLIS, J G and LONGBOTTOM, J A (1981) 'An Empirical Analysis of the
   Determination of House Prices in the United Kingdom', *Urb. Stud., 18,* 9–21
QUINLAN, M (1981) 'The Need for New Oil', *Pet. Econ., XLVIII,* 6, 247–50
SHERIFF, T (1979) 'A Deindustrialized Britain', *Fabian Res. Ser., 341*
SMITH, W (1949) *An Economic Geography of GB,* London
STAMP, L D (1962) *The Land of Britain: its Use and Misuse,* London
STAMP, L D and BEAVER, S H (1971) *The British Isles: a Geographic and
   Economic Survey,* London
STOUT, D K (1979) 'De-industrialization and Industrial Policy', in BLACKABY, F
   (ed.) 'De-industrialization', *NIESR, Econ. Pol. Pap., 2,* 171–201
TOLAND, S (1980) 'Changes in Living Standards Since the 1950s', *Soc. Trends,*
   HMSO, 13–38
WATSON, J W and SISSONS, J B (eds) (1964) *The British Isles: a Systematic
   Geography,* Edinburgh
WIBBERLEY, G (1981) 'Permanent Change in Land Use and Agricultural Realities',
   Town and Country Plann., 50, 1, 13–6

Section II   Regions: Identity, Significance and Functions

ARCHIBALD, G C (1967) 'Regional Multiplier Effects in the UK', *Oxford Econ.
   Pap., 19,* 1, 22–45
BROOK, C and HAY, A (1974) 'Export Base Theory and the Growth and Decline
   of Regions', unit 4 in *Reg. Analysis and Devel., 2,* Open Univ.
BROWN, A J (1972) *The Framework of Regional Economics in the UK,* Cambridge
CARRUTHERS, W I (1957) 'A Classification of Service Centres in England and
   Wales', *Geogrl J., 123,* 371–85
                    (1962) 'Service Centres in Greater London', *Tn Plann. Rev.,
   22,* 4, 345–56
CHISHOLM, M D I (1971) 'Freight Costs, Industrial Location and Regional
   Development', ch. 8 in CHISHOLM, M and MANNERS, G (eds) *Spatial Policy
   Problems of the British Economy,* Cambridge, 213–44
COATES, B E and RAWSTRON, E M (1971) *Regional Variations in Britain,*
   London
COVENTRY CY COUN. *et al* (1971) *Coventry–Solihull–Warwickshire. A Strategy
   for the Sub-region,* Coventry
DENNIS, R and CLOUT, H (1980) *A Social Geography of England and Wales,*
   Oxford
DoE (1974) *Strategic Plan for the NW,* HMSO
E ANGLIA REG. STRATEGY TEAM (1974) *Strategic Choice for E. Anglia,* HMSO
EVERSLEY, D E C (1973) 'Problems of Social Planning in Inner London', in
   DONNISON, D V and EVERSLEY, D E C (eds) *London, Urban Patterns*

Problems and Policies, London
FAWCETT, C B (1919) *Provinces of England and Wales,* revised by East, W G and Wooldridge, S E (1961), London
GILBERT, E W (1939) 'Practical Regionalism in England and Wales', *Geogrl J., 94,* 29–44
GREEN, F H W (1950) 'Urban Hinterlands in England and Wales. An Analysis of Bus Services', *Geogrl J., 116,* 64–88
　　　　(1952) 'Bus Services as an Index to Changing Urban Hinterlands', *Tn Plann. Rev., 22,* 4, 345–56
GRIEVE, R and ROBERTSON, D J (1964) 'The City and the Region', *Univ. Glasgow, Soc. and Econ. Stud., Occ. Pap., 2*
GROVE, D M and ROBERTS, C A (1980) 'Principal Component and Cluster Analysis of 185 Large Towns in England and Wales', *Urb. Stud., 17,* 1, 77–82
HALL, P G (1971) 'Spatial Structures of Metropolitan England and Wales', ch. 5 in CHISHOLM, M and MANNERS, G (eds) *Spatial Policy Problems of the British Economy,* Cambridge, 96–125
HALL, P G, GRACEY, H, DREWETT, R and THOMAS, R (1973) *The Containment of Urban England,* London, 2 vols
HIRSCHMAN, A O (1958) *The Strategy of Economic Development,* New Haven
HOBSON, A C (1951) 'The Great Industrial Belt', *Econ. J., 51,* 562–76
HOUSE, J W (1966) 'Margins in Regional Geography: an Illustration from Northern England', in HOUSE, J W (ed.) *Northern Geographical Essays,* Newcastle upon Tyne, 139–56
　　　　(1969) 'Future Trends of Regionalism in Britain', *Br. J. Marketing, 3,* 176–82
HOUSE, J W (1976) 'UK Marginal regions in the context of EEC Policies', ch. 11, in LEE, R and OGDEN, P E (eds) *Economy and Society in the EEC: Spatial perspectives,* Farnborough, 194–216
KEMP-SMITH, D and HARTLEY, E (1976) 'UK Regional Accounts', *Econ. Trends, 277,* 78–90
KNOX, P L (1974) 'Spatial Variations in Level of Living in England and Wales in 1961', *Trans. Inst. Br. Geogr., 62,* 1–24
　　　　(1975) 'Social Well-being: a Spatial Perspective', *Theory and Practice in Geography,* Oxford
LEICESTER CY COUN. AND CC (1969) *Leicester and Leicestershire Sub-regional Study,* Greenfield
McCRONE, R G L (1969) *Regional Policy in Britain,* London
MOSER, C A and SCOTT, W (1961) *British Towns: a Statistical Study of their Social and Economic Differences,* Edinburgh
MYRDAL, G (1957) *Economic Theory and Underdeveloped Regions,* London
NEVIN, E T, ROE, A R and ROUND, J I (1966) 'The Structure of the Welsh Economy', *Welsh Econ. Stud., 4,* Univ. Wales
NOTTS.–DERBYS. SUBREG. PLANN. UNIT (1969) *Notts. and Derbyshire Sub-regional Study,* Alfreton
RENTON, G A (1974) *Modelling the Economy,* London
ROBERTSON, D J (1965) 'A Nation of Regions?', *Urb. Stud., 2,* 121–36
ROY. COMMN LOCAL GOVT IN ENGLAND 1966–9 (1969) (Redcliffe-Maud) *Report,* Cmnd 4040, HMSO, 3 vols
SAIGAL, J C (1965) *The Choice of Sectors and Regions,* Rotterdam
SELF, P (1965) 'North versus South', *Tn Ctry Plann., 33,* 330–6
SENIOR, D (ed.) (1966) *The Regional City,* London
SHORT, J (1978) 'The Regional Distribution of Public Expenditure in Great Britain 1968/70–1973/4', *Reg. Stud., 12,* 5, 499–510
　　　　(1981) *Public Expenditure and Taxation in the UK Regions,* Aldershot

SMAILES, A E (1947) 'The Analysis and Delimitation of Urban Fields', *Geogr., 32,* 151–61
SMITH, R D P (1968) 'The Changing Urban Hierarchy', *Reg. Stud., 2,* 1–19
SE JOINT PLANN. TEAM (1970) *A Strategy for the SE,* HMSO
WIBBERLEY, G P (1954) 'Some Aspects of Problem Areas in Britain', *Geogrl J., 120,* 43–61
WILSON, A G (1974) *Urban and Regional Models in Geography and Planning,* London
WILSON, T (1968) 'The Regional Multiplier: a Critique', *Oxford Econ. Pap., 20,* 374–93
WISE, M J (1966) 'The City Region', *Advmt Sci., 22,* 104, 571–88
WOODWARD, V H and BOWERS, J (1970) 'Regional Social Accounts for the United Kingdom', *NIESR, Reg. Rep., I,* Cambridge

Section III   Public Policies on the Regions

ASHCROFT, B (1978) 'The Evaluation of Regional Economic Policy: the Case of the UK', *Univ. Strathclyde, Centre for the Study of Public Policy*
ASHCROFT, B, STEPHEN, F and SWALES, J K (1979) *Report to Civil Service National Whitley Council on the Consequences of Government Office Dispersal,* Dept Econ., Univ. Strathclyde
BROWN, A J (1972) *The Framework of Regional Economics in the UK,* Cambridge
BROWNRIGG, M and GREIG, M A (1980) 'UK Regional Policy: its Development over the 1970s', *Economics, XVI,* 69
BUCK, T W and ATKINS, M H (1976) 'The Impact of British Regional Policies on Employment Growth', *Oxford Econ. Pap., 28,* 118–32
CAMERON, G C (1974) 'Regional Economic Policy in the UK', in SANT, M (ed.) *Regional Policy and Planning for Europe,* Farnborough, 1–41
             (1979) 'The National Industrial Strategy and Regional Policy', ch. 14 in MACLENNAN, D and PARR, J B (eds) *Regional Policy: Past Experience and New Directions,* Oxford, 297–322
CHISHOLM, M D I (1974) 'Regional Policies for the 1970s', *Geogrl J., 140,* 2, 215–44
             (1976) 'Regional Growth Policies in an Era of Slow Population Growth and Higher Unemployment', *Reg. Stud., 10,* 201–13
CIVIL SERVICE DEPT (1973) *Dispersal of Government Work from London* (Hardman Report), Cmnd 5322, HMSO
COMMN EUROPEAN COMMUNITIES (1975) *General Regional Aid Systems,* COM (75) 77, Brussels
DTI (Dept Trade and Industry) (1972) *Industrial and Regional Development,* Cmnd 4942, HMSO
DEPT INDUSTRY (1975) *An Approach to Industrial Strategy,* Cmnd 6315, HMSO
DIAMOND, D R (1974) 'The Long-Term Aim of Regional Policy' in SANT, M (ed.) *Regional Policy and Planning for Europe,* Farnborough, 217–23
DUNFORD, M, GEDDES, M and PERRONS, D (1981) 'Regional policy and the crisis in the UK', *International J. Urb. and Reg. Res., 5,* 3, 377–410
EVERSLEY, D E C (1973) 'Problems of social planning in Inner London', in DONNISON, D V and EVERSLEY, D E C (eds) *London, Urban Patterns, Problems and Policies,* London
FOTHERGILL, S and GUDGIN, G (1978) 'Regional employment statistics on a comparable basis 1952–75', *Centre for Environ. Stud., Occ. Pap., 5*
GODDARD, J B (1981) 'Prospects for Regional Economic Development: Implications for Planning', *Reg. Stud. Assocn, Discuss. Pap., 13,* 43–54

HOLLAND, S (1976) *Capital versus the Regions,* London
        (1976) *The Regional Problem,* London
HOUSE OF COMMONS (1979) *Hansard,* Regional Policy, 1146, 20—25 July
        (1981A) *Industry Act 1972. Annual Rept year ending
31 March 1981, 460,* HMSO
        (1981B) 'Measuring the Effectiveness of Regional
Industrial Policy', *H of C Pap. 206,* 30 April
HOUSE, J W (1976) 'UK Marginal Regions in the Context of EEC Policies', ch. 11
in LEE, R and OGDEN, P E (eds) *Economy and Society in the EEC: Spatial
Perspectives,* Farnborough, 194—216
HUGHES, J T (1979) 'An Urban Approach to Regional Problems', ch. 8 in
MACLENNAN, D and PARR, J B *Regional Policy: Past Experience and New
Directions,* Oxford, 173—90
KEEBLE, D (1976) *Industrial Location and Planning in the UK,* London
        (1977) 'Spatial Policy in Britain: Regional or Urban?', *Area, 9,* 1, 3—8
        (1980) 'Manufacturing Dispersion and Government Policy in a
Declining Industrial System: the UK Case, 1971—6', *Environ. and Plann. A.*
LAW, C M (1980) *British Regional Development Since World War I,* Newton
Abbot
LOCATION OF OFFICES BUREAU (1972) *Annual Rept 1971—2,* London
McCALLUM, J D (1979) 'The Development of British Regional Policy', in
MACLENNAN, D and PARR, J B (eds) *Regional Policy: Past Experience and
New Directions,* Oxford, 43—64
McCRONE, R G L (1969) *Regional Policy in Britain,* London
        (1972) 'The Location of Economic Activity in the UK', *Urb.
Stud., 9,* 369—75
MACKAY, R R (1976) 'The Impact of the Regional Employment Premium', in
WHITING, A (ed.) *The Economics of Industrial Subsidies,* London, HMSO
        (1979) 'The Death of Regional Policy — or Resurrection Squared?',
Reg. Stud., 13, 3, 281—95
MACLENNAN, D and PARR, J B (eds) (1979) *Regional Policy: Past Experience
and New Directions,* Oxford
MACLENNAN, M C (1979) 'Regional Policy in a European Framework', ch. 12 in
MACLENNAN, D and PARR, J B (eds) *Regional Policy: Past Experience and
New Directions,* Oxford, 245—71
MARQUAND, J (1978) 'The Role of the Tertiary Sector in Regional Policy', *Rept
to EEC Commission, Reg. Pol. Directorate*
        (1980) 'Measuring the Effects and Costs of Regional Incentives',
Government Economic Service Wkng Pap. 32
MASSEY, D (1979) 'In What Sense A Regional Problem?', *Reg. Stud., 13,* 2,
233—43
MASSEY, D and MEEGAN, R A (1978) 'Industrial Restructuring versus the Cities',
Urb. Stud., 15, 273—88
MINIST. OF TRANSPORT (1963) *The Reshaping of British Railways* (Beeching
Report), HMSO
MOORE, B C and RHODES, J (1973) 'Evaluating the Effects of British Regional
Economic Policy , *Econ. J., 83,* 329, 87—110
        (1974) 'Regional Policy and the Scottish Economy',
Scott. J. Pol. Econ., XXI, 3, 215—35
        (1976) 'Regional Economic Policy and the
Movement of Manufacturing Firms to the Development Areas', *Economica, 43,*
17—31
MOORE, B C, RHODES, J and TYLER, P (1977) 'The Impact of Regional Policy in
the 1970s', *Centre for Environ. Stud. Rev., 1,* 67—77

(1980) 'New Developments in the
Evaluation of Regional Policy', *SSRC Urban and Regional Economic Conf.,*
Birmingham
NEVIN, E T (1972) 'Europe and the Regions', *Three Banks Rev., 94,* 54—78
PITFIELD, D E (1978) 'The Quest for an Effective Regional Policy 1934—1937',
Reg. Stud., 12, 429—43
RHODES, J and KHAN, A (1971) 'Office Dispersal and Regional Policy', *Univ.
Cambridge, Dept Applied Econ., Occ. Pap., 30*
ROBERTSON, D J (1965) 'A Nation of Regions', *Urb. Stud., 2,* 121—36
SANT, M (1975) 'Industrial Movement and Regional Development: the British
Case', *Urb. and Reg. Plann. Ser., 11,* Oxford
SCHOFIELD, J A (1979) 'Macro Evaluations of the Impact of Regional Policy in
Britain: a Review of Recent Research', *Urb. Stud., 16,* 3, 251—71
SEC. STATE ECONOMIC AFFAIRS (1969) *The Intermediate Areas* (Hunt Report),
Cmnd 3998, HMSO
SEC. STATE TRADE, INDUSTRY AND REG. DEVEL. (1963) *The North East: a
Programme for Regional Development and Growth,* Cmnd 2206, HMSO
SEC. STATE TRADE AND INDUSTRY (1972) *Industrial and Regional
Development,* Cmnd 4942, HMSO
SCOTT. DEV. DEPT (1963) *Central Scotland: a Programme for Development and
Growth,* Cmnd 2188, Edinburgh HMSO
SEGAL, N S (1979) 'The Limits and Means of Self Reliant Regional Economic
Growth', ch. 10 in MACLENNAN, D and PARR, J B (eds) *Regional Policy: Past
Experience and New Directions,* Oxford, 211—24
SWALES, J K (1979) 'Entrepreneurship and Regional Development: Implications
for Regional Policy', ch. 11 in MACLENNAN, D and PARR, J B (eds) *Regional
Policy: Past Experience and New Directions,* Oxford, 225—42
THWAITES, A T (1978) 'Technological Change and Regional Development', *Centre
for Urb. and Reg. Devel. Stud., Univ. Newcastle upon Tyne, Discuss. Pap., 9*
TOWNSEND, A R (1980) 'Unemployment Geography and the New Government's
"Regional" Aid', *Area, 12,* 1, 9—18
TURNBULL, P (1967) 'Regional Economic Councils and Boards', *J. Tn Plann. Inst.,
London, 53,* 41—9
WILSON, T (1979) 'Regional Policy and the National Interest', ch. 4 in
MACLENNAN, D and PARR, J B (eds) *Regional Policy: Past Experience and
New Directions,* Oxford, 81—107

Section IV   New Patterns for Democracy

ARTHUR, P (1977) 'Devolution as Administrative Convenience: A Case Study of
Northern Ireland', *Parliamentary Aff., 30,* 97—106
BALSOM, D (1979) 'The Nature and Distribution of Support for Plaid Cymru',
Glasgow, Univ. Strathclyde, Centre for the Stud. of Pub. Pol.
BALSOM, D and McALLISTER, I (1979) 'The Scottish and Welsh Devolution
Referenda of 1979: Constitutional Change and Popular Choice', *Parliamentary
Aff., 32,* 4, 394—409
BARRAS, R (ed.) (1978) 'Current Issues in Structure Planning', *Centre for Environ.
Stud. Pol. Ser., 4*
BOGDANOR, V (1979) *Devolution,* Oxford
BUSTEED, M R (1975) 'Geography and Voting Behaviour', *Theory and Practice in
Geography,* Oxford
CAIRNCROSS, A K (ed.) (1954) *The Scottish Economy,* Cambridge
DEARLOVE, N (1979) *The Reorganization of British Local Government: Old
Orthodoxies and a Political Perspective,* Cambridge

FIRN, J R and MACLENNAN, D (1979) 'Devolution: The Changing Political Economy of Regional Policy', ch. 13 in MACLENNAN, D and PARR, J B (eds) *Regional Policy: Past Experience and New Directions,* Oxford, 273–95

FREEMAN, T W (1968) *Geography and Regional Administration,* London

GILBERT, E W (1939) 'Practical Regionalism in England and Wales', *Geogrl J., 94,* 29–44

      (1948) 'Boundaries of Local Government Areas', *Geogrl J., 111,* 172–206

GOVT N IRELAND (1967) *The Reshaping of Local Government: Statement of Aims,* Cmnd 517, Belfast HMSO

      (1969) *The Reshaping of Local Government: Further Proposals,* Cmnd 530, Belfast HMSO

GRONNENBERG, R (ed.) (1978) *Island Futures: Scottish Devolution and Shetland's Constitutional Alternatives,* Shetland

GUDGIN, G and TAYLOR, P J (1979) *Seats, Votes, and the Spatial Organization of Elections,* London

HOUSE OF COMMONS (1974) *Democracy and Devolution – Proposals for Scotland and Wales,* Cmnd 5732, HMSO

      (1975) *Our Changing Democracy: Devolution to Scotland and Wales,* Cmnd 6348, HMSO. Supplementary Statement, Cmnd 6585

JAMES, J R, HOUSE, J W and HALL, P G (1970) 'Local Government Reform in England', *Geogrl J., 136,* 1, 1–23

JOHNSON, J H (1970) 'Reorganization of Local Government in N. Ireland', *Area,* 4, 17–21

LOCAL GOVT BOUNDARY COMMN FOR ENGLAND – DESIGNATE (1972) *Memorandum on Draft Proposals for New Districts in the English Non-Metropolitan Counties proposed in the Local Government Bill,* HMSO

LORD PRESIDENT OF THE COUNCIL (1975) *Our Changing Democracy. Devolution to Scotland and Wales,* Cmnd 6348, HMSO

      (1976) *Devolution: the English Dimension,* HMSO

      (1977) *Devolution: Financing the Devolved Services,* Cmnd 6890, HMSO

McCRONE, G (1969) *Scotland's Future: the Economics of Nationalism,* Oxford

McDONALD, J F (1979) 'The Lack of Political Identity in English Regions: Evidence from MPs', *Glasgow, Univ. Strathclyde, Centre for the Stud. of Pub. Pol.*

MACKAY, D I and MACKAY, G A (1974) *Scotland: A Growth Economy,* Edinburgh

MACKINTOSH, J P (1968) *The Devolution of Power,* Harmondsworth

OSMOND, J (1978) *Creative Conflict: The Politics of Welsh Devolution,* Llandysul

PAGE, E (1978) 'Why should Central-Local Relations in Scotland be any Different from those in England?', *Glasgow, Univ. Strathclyde, Centre for the Stud. of Pub. Pol.*

PEACOCK, A (1977) 'The Political Economy of Devolution: The British Case', *Univ. York Reprints, 236*

PHILIP, A B (1975) *The Welsh Question,* Univ. Wales

PUBL. GEN. ACTS, see list on pp. 505–7

REV. BODY ON LOCAL GOVT IN N IRELAND (1970) *Report,* Cmnd 546, Belfast HMSO

ROY. COMMN CONSTITUTION 1969–73 (1973) (Kilbrandon) *Report,* Cmnd 5460, HMSO

ROY. COMMN LOCAL GOVT IN ENGLAND 1966–9 (1969) (Redcliffe-Maud) *Report,* Cmnd 4040, HMSO, 3 vols

ROY. COMMN LOCAL GOVT IN GREATER LONDON 1957–60 (1960) *Report*,
    Cmnd 1164, HMSO
ROY. COMMN LOCAL GOVT IN SCOTLAND (1969) (Wheatley Commn), *Report*,
    Cmnd 4150, Edinburgh HMSO, 2 vols
SCOTT. COUN. RES. INST. (1974) *Economic Development and Devolution*,
    Edinburgh
SCOTT. OFF. (1971) *Reform of Local Government in Scotland*, Cmnd 4583,
    Edinburgh HMSO
SEC. STATE ENVIRONMENT (1971) *Local Government in England. Government
    Proposals for Reorganization*, Cmnd 4584, HMSO
SEC. STATE LOCAL GOVT AND REGIONAL PLANN. (1970) *Reform of Local
    Government in England*, Cmnd 4276, HMSO
SEC. STATE N IRELAND (1973) *N Ireland Constitutional Proposals*, Cmnd 5259,
    HMSO
SEC. STATE SCOTLAND (1971) *Reform of Local Government in Scotland*,
    Cmnd 4583, Edinburgh HMSO
SEWELL, W R D and COPPOCK, J T (eds) (1977) *Public Participation in Planning*,
    Chichester
SMITH, B C (1964–5) *Regionalism in England*, London, 3 vols
TAYLOR, P J and GUDGIN, G (1976) 'The Myth of Non-Partisan Cartography:
    A Study of Electoral Biases in the English Boundary Commissioners
    Redistribution for 1955–1970', *Urb. Stud*, *13*, 13–25
THOMAS, D *et al* (1969) 'The Redcliffe-Maud Report: Royal Commission on Local
    Government in England, 1966–9', *Area*, *4*, 1–20
THOMAS, J G (1952) 'Local Government Areas in Wales', *Geogr.*, *37*, 9–18
WELSH OFFICE (1970) *The Reform of Local Government in Wales, Consultative
    Document*, Cardiff HMSO

Section V   Economic Regions and Nations

BARRAS, R (ed.) (1978) 'Current issues in structure planning', *Centre Environ.
    Stud., Policy Ser.*, *4*
BROWN, A J (1972) *The Framework of Regional Economics in the UK*, Cambridge
GODLEY, W (ed.) (1980) 'Urban and Regional Policy with Provisional Regional
    Accounts', *Cambridge Econ. Pol. Rev.*, *6*, 2

Northern Region

BOWDEN, P J (1965) 'Regional Problems and Policies in the North East of
    England', in WILSON, T (ed.) *Papers on Reg. Devel.*, Oxford, 20–39
CARTER, K R *et al* (1978) *Regional Planning and Policy Change: The Formulation
    of Policy Guidelines in Regional Strategies*, DoE, HMSO
COMMN PUBLIC PARTICIPATION IN PLANNING (1969) *People and Planning*
    (Skeffington Report), HMSO
FULLERTON, B (1960) 'The Pattern of Service Industries in North-East England',
    Univ. Newcastle upon Tyne, Dept Geogr., Res. Ser. 3
            (1966) 'Geographical Inertia in the Service Industries: an example
    from N England', in HOUSE, J W (ed.) *Northern Geographical Essays*, Newcastle
    upon Tyne, 157–77
GODDARD, J B (1981) 'British Cities in Transition', *Geogr. Mag*, *LII*, 8, 523–30
HOUSE, J W (ed.) (1964–72) *Papers on Migration and Mobility in Northern
    England*, *1–11*, Univ. Newcastle upon Tyne, Dept Geogr.
HOUSE, J W (1969) *Industrial Britain: the North East*, Newton Abbot
HOUSE, J W *et al* (1978) 'Strategic Plan for the Northern Region: A Review
    Symposium', *Tn Plann. Rev.*, *49*, 1, 14–28

JAMES, V Z (1978) 'Office Employment in the N Region. Its National, Regional and Organizational Context', *Univ. Newcastle, Centre for Urb. and Reg. Devel. Stud., Disc. Pap., 12*

JOHNSON, P S (1978) 'New Firms and Regional Development: Some Issues and Evidence', *Univ. Newcastle, Centre for Urb. and Reg. Devel. Stud., Disc. Pap., 11*

NORTHERN EPC (1966) *Challenge of the Changing North,* HMSO
    (1969) *An Outline Strategy for the North,* Newcastle upon Tyne
    (1969) *Regional Ports Survey,* Newcastle upon Tyne
    (1970) *Report on Education,* Part 1, Newcastle upon Tyne
    (1971) *Report on Housing Needs for the N Region,* Newcastle upon Tyne
    (1972) *The N Region and the Common Market,* Newcastle upon Tyne

N REGION STRATEGY TEAM (1975) 'Evaluating the Impact of Regional Policy on Manufacturing Industry in the N Region', *Tech. Rept, 2,* Newcastle
    (1976A) 'Linkages in the N Region', *Work. Pap., 6,* Newcastle
    (1976B) 'Spatial Patterns and the Development of Service Industries', *Work. Pap., 9*
    (1976C) 'Office Activity in the N Region', *Tech. Rept, 8,* Newcastle
    (1976D) 'Rural Development in the N Region', *Tech. Rept, 16*
    (1977A) 'Urban Environment in the N Region', *Work. Pap., 16*
    (1977B) 'New Towns in the N Region', *Work. Pap., 7*
    (1977C) *Strategic Plan for the N Region,* Newcastle, 5 vols

NUNN, S (1980) 'The Opening and Closure of Manufacturing Units in the UK', *Dept Industry, Govt Econ. Service Work. Pap., 36,* London

SEC. STATE TRADE, INDUSTRY and REGIONAL DEVELOPMENT (1963) *The North East: a Programme for Regional Development and Growth,* Cmnd 2206, HMSO

SMITH, I J (1979) 'The Effect of External Takeovers on Manufacturing Employment Change in the N Region between 1963 and 1973', *Reg. Stud., 13,* 5, 421–37

THWAITES, A T (1978) 'The Future Development of R and D Activity in the N Region: a Comment', *Univ. Newcastle, Centre for Urb. and Reg. Devel. Stud., Disc. Pap., 12*

Scotland

ABERCROMBIE, P and MATTHEWS, R H (1946) *Clyde Valley Regional Plan,* HMSO

CAIRNCROSS, A K (1952) *Local Development in Scotland,* Edinburgh

CAIRNCROSS, A K (ed.) (1954) *The Scottish Economy,* Cambridge

CAMERON, G C and REID, G L (1966) 'Scottish Economic Planning and the Attraction of Industry', *Univ. Glasgow. Soc. and Econ. Stud., Occ. Pap., 6*

CAMPBELL, A D and LYDDON, W D C (1970) *Tayside: Potential for Development,* Edinburgh HMSO

FIRN, J R (1974) 'Indigenous Growth and Regional Development; the Experience and Prospects for W Central Scotland', *Univ. Glasgow, Urb. and Reg. Stud., Disc. Pap., 10*

(1975) 'External Control and Regional Development: the Case of
Scotland', *Environ. and Plann. A., 7*, 393–414

GASKIN, M (1968) *Survey of the Economy and Development Potential of NE
Scotland,* Edinburgh HMSO

GASKIN, M and MACKAY, D I (1978) *The Economic Impact of North Sea Oil on
Scotland: Final Rept to the Scottish Economic Planning Dept,* Edinburgh
HMSO

HENDERSON, R A (1973) 'Industrial Overspill from Glasgow: 1958–68', *Univ.
Glasgow, Urb. and Reg. Stud., Disc. Pap., 9*

HIGHLANDS and ISLANDS DEV. BD (1968) *The Moray Firth. A Plan for Growth
in a Sub-region of the Scottish Highlands* (Jack Holmes Planning Group),
Glasgow

KNOX, P and COTTAM, B (1981) 'Rural Deprivation in Scotland: A Preliminary
Assessment', *Tijd. Econ. Soc. Geogr., 72*, 3, 162–75

McCRONE, G (1969) *Scotland's Future: the Economics of Nationalism,* Oxford

McDONALD, S T (1977) 'The Regional Report in Scotland: a Study of Change in
the Planning Process', *Scott. Geogr. Mag., 93*, 2, 109–20

McGUINESS, J H (1968) 'Regional Economic Development, Progress in Scotland',
J. Tn Plann. Inst., London, 54, 103–11

MACKAY, D I (ed.) (1979) *Scotland: the Framework for Change,* Edinburgh

MACKAY, D I and BUXTON, N K (1965) 'The North of Scotland Economy:
a Case for Redevelopment', *Scott. J. Pol. Econ., 13*, 23–49

MACKAY, D I and MACKAY, G A (1974) *Scotland: a Growth Economy,*
Edinburgh

MINAY, C L W (1965) 'Town Development and Regional Planning in Scotland',
J. Tn Plann. Inst., London, 51, 13–9

MOORE, B and RHODES, J (1974) 'Regional Policy and the Scottish Economy',
Scott. J. Pol. Econ., 21, 215–35

NICOLL, R E (1966) 'The Physical Implications of the White Paper on the Scottish
Economy, 1965–70', *J. Tn Plann. Inst., London, 52*, 314–8

                    (chairman) (1973) *A Future for Scotland,* Scottish Council,
Edinburgh

PARSLER, R and SHAPIRO, D (1980) *The Social Impact of Oil in Scotland,*
Farnborough

ROBERTSON, D J, JOHNSON-MARSHALL, P E A and MATTHEW, Sir R H
(1966) *Lothians: Regional Survey and Plan,* Edinburgh HMSO, 2 vols
(1968) *Grangemouth/Falkirk Regional Survey and Plan,* Edinburgh HMSO,
2 vols

ROBERTSON, I M L (1975) 'Scottish Population Distribution: Implications for
Locational Decisions', *Trans. Inst. Br. Geogr., 63*, 111–24

SCOTT. COUN. (1968) *Lochaber Study,* Edinburgh
            (1970) *Oceanspan I: a Maritime-based Development Strategy for a
European Scotland, 1970–2000,* Edinburgh

SCOTT. COUN. RES. INST. (1974) *Economic Development and Devolution,*
Edinburgh

SCOTT. DEV. DEPT (1963) *Central Scotland: a Programme for Development and
Growth,* Cmnd 2188, Edinburgh HMSO
            (1968) *The Central Borders: a Plan for Expansion,* Edinburgh
HMSO, 2 vols
            (1970) *A Strategy for SW Scotland,* Edinburgh HMSO
            (1978) *The New Towns,* London

SCOTT. ECON. PLANN. DEPT (1978) *The Economic Impact of North Sea Oil in
Scotland,* HMSO

SCOTT. OFF. (1966) *The Scottish Economy, 1965 to 1970: a Plan for Expansion,* Cmnd 2864, Edinburgh HMSO
SCOTT. TOURIST BD (1968) *Galloway Project,* Strathclyde Univ.
SELF, P *et al* (1967) 'Scotland: Planning and Economic Development', *Town and Country Plann., 35,* 265–325
THOMSON, D C and GRIMBLE, I (1968) *The Future of the Highlands,* London
TOOTHILL, J N (1961) *Inquiry into the Scottish Economy,* Scottish Council (Dev. and Ind.), Edinburgh
TURNOCK, D (1970) *Patterns of Highland Development,* London
             (1979) *Industrial Britain: The New Scotland,* Newton Abbot
WEST CENTRAL SCOTLAND PLAN (1974) *West Central Scotland – A Programme of Action,* Glasgow

Wales
BOLLOM, C (1978) *Attitudes and Second Homes in Rural Wales,* Cardiff
BOWEN, E G (ed.) (1957) *Wales: a Physical, Historical and Regional Geography,* London
DAVIES, G and THOMAS, I (1976) *Overseas Investment in Wales – The Welcome Invasion,* Swansea
DEV. COMMN (1972) *Mid Wales: An Assessment of the Impact of The Development Commission Factory Programme,* HMSO
HAGGER, D F and DAVIES, H W E (1961) 'Regional Planning in S Wales', *Advmt Sci., 18,* 65–73
HOUSTON, E and JENKINS, R (1965) *The Heartland: A Plan for Mid Wales,* London
HUMPHRYS, G (1972) *Industrial Britain: S Wales,* Newton Abbot
LLOYD, M G and THOMASON, G F (1963) *Welsh Society in Transition,* Coun. Soc. Serv. Wales and Mon.
MANNERS, G (1968) 'Wales: The Way Ahead', *J. Tn Plann. Inst., London, 54,* 67–9
MIN. HOUSING and LOCAL GOVT (1967) *Dee Crossing Study, Phase I,* HMSO
MOORE, B and RHODES, J (1975) *Regional Policy and the Economy of Wales,* Welsh Office, Cardiff
NEVIN, E T, ROSE, A R and ROUND, J I (1966) 'The Structure of the Welsh Economy', *Welsh Econ. Stud., 4,* Univ. Wales
ROY. COMMN CONSTITUTION (1973) 'Survey of the Welsh Economy', *Res. Pap., 8,* HMSO
SEC. STATE ENVIRONMENT, WALES *et al* (1971) *Dee Estuary Scheme, Phase 2,* HMSO, 2 vols
SEC. STATE WALES (1967) *Wales: The Way Ahead,* Cmnd 3334, Cardiff HMSO
THOMAS, B (1962) *The Welsh Economy in Transition,* Cardiff
THOMAS, D (1977) *Wales: A New Study,* Newton Abbot
TOMKINS, C R (1971) *Income and Expenditure Accounts for Wales, 1965–8,* Welsh Council
WELSH COUNCIL (1971A) *A Strategy for Rural Wales,* HMSO, Cardiff
               (1971B) *Wales and the Common Market,* Cardiff
               (1977) *Agriculture in the Welsh Economy,* Cardiff
WELSH OFF. (1964) *Depopulation in Mid Wales,* HMSO
            (1977) *Policy for the Inner Cities,* London
            (1978) *The New Towns,* London
WENGER, G C (1980) *Mid-Wales: Deprivation or Development. Study of Patterns of Employment in Selected Communities,* Aberystwyth

N Ireland

AUNGER, E A (1975) 'Religion and Occupational Class in N Ireland', *Econ. and Soc. Rev., 7,* 1, 1—18

BEW, P, GIBBON, P and PATTERSON, H (1979) *The State in N Ireland,* Manchester

BUSTEED, M (1976) 'Small-scale Economic Development in N Ireland', *Scott. Geogr. Mag., 92,* 3, 172—81

COMPTON, P A (1978) *N Ireland: a Census Atlas,* Dublin

DARBY, J and WILLIAMSON, A (eds) (1978) *Violence and the Social Services in N Ireland,* London

DAVIS, R and McGURNAGHAN, M A (1975) 'The Economics of Adversity', *Nat. West. Rev.,* May

DOHERTY, P (1980) 'Patterns of Unemployment in Belfast', *Irish Geogr., 13,* 65—76

FITZGERALD, G (1972) *Towards a New Ireland,* Dublin

GIBSON, N (1975) 'Some Economic Implications of the Various Solutions to the N Ireland Problem', in VAIZEY, J (ed.) *Economic Sovereignty and Regional Policy,* Dublin, 200—18

GOODYEAR, P M and EASTWOOD, D A (1979) 'Regional Development and Spatial Inequality in N Ireland', *Econ. and Soc. Rev., 10,* 4, 321—40

GOVT N IRELAND (1965) *Economic Development in N Ireland* (Wilson Report), Cmnd 479, Belfast HMSO

———————— (1970) *N Ireland Development Programme 1970—5,* Belfast HMSO

———————— (1970) *N Ireland Development Programme 1970—5, Government Statement,* Cmnd 547, Belfast HMSO

HOARE, A G (1976) 'Spheres of Influence and Regional Policy: the Case of N Ireland', *Irish Geogr., 9,* 89—99

———————— (1978) 'Industrial Linkages and the Dual Economy: the Case of N Ireland', *Reg. Stud., 12,* 167—80

ISLES, K S and CUTHBERT, N (1957) *An Economic Survey of N Ireland,* Belfast HMSO

MATTHEW, R H (1963) *Belfast Regional Survey and Plan,* Cmnd 451, Belfast HMSO, 2 vols

MILLER, R L (1979) *Occupational Mobility of Protestants and Roman Catholics in N Ireland,* Belfast

MURIE, A (1974) 'Spatial Aspects of Unemployment and Economic Stress in N Ireland', *Irish Geogr., 7,* 53—67

N IRELAND, DEPT ENVIRONMENT (1977) *Regional Physical Development Strategy, 1975—95,* Belfast HMSO

N IRELAND ECON. COUNCIL (1981) *Employment Patterns in N Ireland 1950—80,* Belfast

O'DOWN, L, ROLSTON, B and TOMLINSON, M (1980) *N Ireland: Between Civil Rights and Civil Strife,* London

PRINGLE, D G (1980) 'Electoral Systems and Political Manipulation: A Case Study of N Ireland in the 1920s', *Econ. and Soc. Rev., 11,* 3, 187—206

PROBERT, R (1978) *Beyond Orange and Green: the Political Economy of the N Ireland Crisis,* London

QUIGLEY REPT (1976) *Economic and Industrial Strategy for N Ireland: Rept of a Review Team,* Belfast

ROWTHORN, R (1981) 'N Ireland: an Economy in Crisis', *Cambridge J. Econ., 5,* 1—32

STEED, G P F (1968) 'Commodity Flows and Inter-Industry Linkages in N

Ireland's Manufacturing Industry', *Tijd. Econ. Soc. Geogr.*, *59*, 245–59

Yorks. and Humberside
ATKINS, W S and PARTNERS (1969) *The Strategic Future of the Wool Textile Industry*, Econ. Dev. Comm. Wool Ind., HMSO
BROWN, M B (1970) 'The Concept of Employment Opportunity with Special Reference to Yorks. and Humberside', *Yorks. Bull. Econ. and Soc. Res.*, *22*, 2, 65–100
CENT. UNIT ENVIRONMENTAL PLANN. (1969) *Humberside: a Feasibility Study*, HMSO
CTY COUN. W RIDING YORKS (1969) *The County Strategy*, Wakefield
(1971) *The County Strategy for Development*, Wakefield
CRAIG, J, EVANS, E W and SHOWLER, B (1970) 'Humberside: Employment and Migration', *Yorks. Bull. Econ. and Soc. Res.*, *22*, 2, 123–42
LEWIS, P and JONES, P N (1970) *Industrial Britain: The Humberside Region*, Newton Abbot
SEC. STATE ECON. AFFAIRS (1969) *The Intermediate Areas* (Hunt Report), Cmnd 3998, HMSO
YORKS. AND HUMBERSIDE EPC (1966) *A Review of Yorkshire and Humberside*, HMSO
(1968) *Halifax and Calder Valley*, HMSO
(1969A) *Doncaster: An Area Study*, HMSO
(1969B) *Huddersfield and Colne Valley*, HMSO
(1970) *Yorkshire and Humberside Regional Strategy*, HMSO
(1972A) *Growth Industries in the Region*, Leeds
(1972B) *Implications of UK Entry into the Common Market for the Yorkshire and Humberside Region*, Leeds
(1976A) *The Pennine Uplands, Socio-economic Interactions and Opportunities in the Yorkshire Pennines*, HMSO
(1976B) *Regional Strategy Review 1975. The Next Ten Years*, Leeds
(1977) *Fishing Industry: its Economic Significance in the Yorkshire and Humberside Ports*, Leeds

The North West
DEPT ECON. AFFAIRS (1965A) *The NW: a Regional Study*, HMSO
(1965B) *The Problems of Merseyside*, HMSO
DoE (1974) *Strategic Plan for the NW*, HMSO
DICKEN, P and LLOYD, P E (1978) 'Inner Metropolitan Industrial Change, Enterprise Structures and Policy Issues', *Reg. Stud.*, *12*, 2, 181–98
LANCS. CC (1974) *Observations on the Strategic Plan for the NW*, Preston
LANE, T (1981) 'What Future for Merseyside?', *Reg. Stud. Assocn*, Manchester Conf
LAWTON, R and CUNNINGHAM, C M (eds) (1970) *Merseyside: Social and Economic Studies*, London
LLOYD, P E and MASON, C M (1979) 'Industrial Movement in NW England', *Environ. and Plann. A.*, *11*, 1367–85
LLOYD, P E and REEVE, D E (1981) 'NW England 1971–1977. A Study in Industrial Decline and Economic Restructuring', *Reg. Stud. Assocn*, Manchester Conf

MATTHEW, R H *et al* (1968) *C Lancashire New Town Proposal. Impact on NE Lancashire,* HMSO
MINIST. HOUSING and LOCAL GOVT (1967) *C Lancashire. Study for a City,* HMSO
NORTH WEST EPC (1966) *An Economic Planning Strategy for the NW Region,* Strategy I, HMSO
      (1968) *The NW in the Seventies,* Strategy II, Manchester
      (1970) *Housing in the NW Region,* Manchester
      (1971) *Derelict Land in the NW,* Manchester
NUTTALL, T and BATTY, M F (1970) 'The NW – Problem Area for Regional Planning', *Tn Plann. Rev., 41,* 372–82
POWELL, A G (1974) 'Regional Policy and Sub-regional Planning in the NW', in SANT, M E (ed.) *Regional Policy and Planning for Europe,* Farnborough, 157–70
SEC. STATE ECON. AFFAIRS (1969) *The Intermediate Areas* (Hunt Report), Cmnd 3998, HMSO
SMITH, D M (1969) *Industrial Britain: The North West,* Newton Abbot

The South West
BRAITHWAITE, J L (1968) 'The Post-War Industrial Development of Plymouth: an Example of National Industrial Location Policy', *Trans. Inst. Br. Geogr., 45,* 34–50
BRITTON, J N H (1967) *Regional Analysis and Economic Geography. A Case Study of Manufacturing in the Bristol Region,* London
CENT. UNIT ENVIRONMENTAL PLANN. (1971) *Severnside: A Feasibility Study,* HMSO
CORNWALL CC (1970) *West Cornwall Study,* Truro
DEVON CC (1966–70) *Feasibility Studies,* Barnstaple, Exeter and District, Honiton, South Brent and Ivybridge, Tiverton–Sampford Peverell
MINIST. HOUSING AND LOCAL GOVT (1970) *The Holiday Industry of Devon and Cornwall,* HMSO
SOUTH WEST EPC (1967) *A Region with a Future: A Draft Strategy for the South West,* HMSO
      (1969) *Plymouth Area Study,* Bristol
      (1974) *A Strategic Settlement Pattern for the South West,* HMSO
      (1975) *Retirement to the South West,* HMSO
      (1976) *Economic Survey of the Tourist Industry in the South West,* London
SPOONER, D J (1972) 'Industrial Movement and Rural Periphery: the Case of Devon and Cornwall', *Reg. Stud., 6, 2,* 197–215
      (1974) 'Some Qualitative Aspects of Industrial Movement in a Problem Region of the UK', *Tn Plann. Rev., 45,* 63–83
WALKER, F (1965) 'Economic Growth on Severnside', *Trans. Inst. Br. Geogr., 37,* 1–13

E Anglia
DoE (1974) *A Study of the Cambridge Sub-region,* Parts I and II, HMSO
E ANGLIA CONSULTATIVE COMM. (1969) *E Anglia: A Regional Appraisal,* Bury St Edmunds
      (1973) *Small Towns Study,* Cambridge
E ANGLIA EPC (1968) *E Anglia. A Study,* HMSO
      (1977) *Seaports in E Anglia,* London

(1978A) *Tourism in the Coastal Strip of E Anglia,* London
(1978B) *Future Population of E Anglia,* Norwich
E ANGLIA REG. STRATEGY TEAM (1974) *Strategic Choice for E Anglia,* HMSO
MINIST. HOUSING and LOCAL GOVT (1966) *Expansion of Peterborough,* HMSO
SANT, M E C and MOSELEY, M J (1976) *Industrial Britain: E Anglia,* Newton
Abbot
(1977) *The Industrial Development of E Anglia,*
Norwich

E Midlands

BURROWS, M and TOWN, S (1971) *Office Services in the E Midlands: An
Economic and Sociological Study,* Nottingham, 2 vols
E MIDLANDS EPC (1966) *The E Midlands Study,* HMSO
(1969) *Opportunity in the E Midlands,* HMSO
(1976) *A Forward Economic Look,* Nottingham
FENNELL, K R (1971) *The Eastern Lowlands Sub-regional Study,* Kesteven Cty
Plann. Dept
GIBSON, M and PULLEN, M (1971) *Retail Patterns in the E Midlands, 1961−81,*
Leicester
HOLLAND CC (1970) *Rural Policy Structure,* Boston
LEICS. CY COUN. and LEICS. CC (1969) *Leicester and Leicestershire Sub-regional
Planning Study,* Glenfield
MINIST. HOUSING and LOCAL GOVT (1966A) *Expansion of Northampton,*
HMSO
(1966B) *Northampton, Bedford, North
Bucks Study,* HMSO
NOTTS.−DERBYS. SUBREG. PLANN. UNIT (1969) *Notts. and Derbyshire Sub-
regional Study,* Alfreton
SMITH, D J (1979) 'The Assisted Areas of the E Midlands', *E Midland Geogr.,* 7, 3,
113−22
SPOONER, D (1981) 'Mining and Regional Development', *Theory and Practice in
Geogr.,* Oxford

W Midlands

COVENTRY CY COUN. *et al* (1971) *Coventry−Solihull−Warwickshire: A Strategy
for the Sub-region*
DEPT ECON. AFFAIRS (1965) *The W Midlands: A Regional Study,* HMSO
FOCUS GROUP (1979) *W Midlands Regional Issues: a Commentary on the W
Midlands Regional Strategy 1979,* Birmingham
JT MONITORING STEERING GROUP (1975) *A Developing Strategy for the W
Midlands,* DoE, Birmingham
(1979) *A Developing Strategy for the W
Midlands,* DoE, Birmingham
JOYCE, F (ed.) (1977) *Metropolitan Development and Change. The W Midlands:
a Policy Review,* Birmingham
MAWSON, J and SKELCHER, C (1980) 'Updating the W Midlands Regional
Strategy: a Review of Inter-authority Relationships', *Tn Plann. Rev.,* 51, 2,
152−70
PARIS, C and BLACKABY, B (1979) *Not Much Improvement: Urban Renewal
Policy in Birmingham,* London
TYLER, P (1980) 'The Impact of Regional Policy on a Prosperous Region: the
Experience of the W Midlands', *Oxford Econ. Pap.,* 32, 1, 151−62
W MIDLANDS EPC (1967) *The W Midlands: Patterns of Growth,* HMSO

(1971) *The W Midlands: An Economic Appraisal*, HMSO
W MIDLANDS EPC and W MIDLANDS PLANN. AUTHOR. CONF. (1979)
   *A Developing Strategy for the W Midlands. The Regional Economy. Problems
   and Proposals*, Birmingham
W MIDLANDS REG. STUDY (1971) *A Developing Strategy for the W Midlands*,
   WMRS
WISE, M J (1972) 'The Birmingham—Black Country Conurbation in its Regional
   Setting', *Geogr.*, *57*, 89—104
WOOD, P (1976) *Industrial Britain: The W Midlands*, Newton Abbot

South East
ABERCROMBIE, P (1945) *Greater London Plan 1944*, HMSO
BUCHANAN, C and PARTNERS (1966) *South Hampshire Study*, HMSO, 3 vols
DoE (1971) SE Joint Planning Studies, vol. I: *Population and Employment;*
   vol. II: *Social and Economic Aspects;* vol. V: *Report of Economic Consultants
   Ltd*, HMSO
       (1973) *Greater London Development Plan. Report of the Panel of Inquiry*
   (Layfield Report), HMSO, 2 vols
       (1978) *Strategic Plan for the SE: 1978 Review*, Government Statement, HMSO
EVERSLEY, D E C (1973) 'Problems of Social Planning in Inner London', in
   DONNISON, D V and EVERSLEY, D E C (eds) *London: Urban Patterns,
   Problems and Policies*, London
GLC (1969) *Greater London Development Plan*, London
HALL, P G (1963) *London 2000*, London
MILTON KEYNES DEV. CORPN (1970) *The Plan for Milton Keynes*, Bletchley,
   2 vols
MIN. HOUSING and LOCAL GOVT (1964) *The SE Study, 1961—81*, HMSO
SOUTH EAST EPC (1967) *A Strategy for the SE*, HMSO
                     (1971) *Views on the Strategic Plan for the SE*, London
SE JOINT PLANN. TEAM (1970) *Strategic Plan for the SE*, HMSO
                     (1976) *Strategy for the SE: 1976 Review*, DoE
                     (1978) *Strategy for the SE: 1978 Review*, DoE
STANDING CONF., LONDON AND SE REG. PLANN. (1981) *SE Regional
   Planning in the 1980s*, London
STEWART, J M W (1971) 'Planning and SE England', *Area*, *3*, 267—70

2

People and Work

I INTRODUCTION

I.1 General Context

In a mature industrial society and long-settled land such as the UK, the population
map mirrors environmental, economic and social contrasts and changes in these over
both time and space. The population distribution map (fig. 2.1) therefore reveals
much of earlier origin as well as more recent trends and forces. Many consequences
are still with us from nineteenth-century industrial and urban growth, when
population was concentrated by a coal-based, steam-powered and railway-linked
economy, and from eighteenth- and nineteenth-century agrarian reform, which
resulted in much increased output per unit of land and of manpower, and led to a
declining agricultural labourforce. Thus, powerful and long-established economic
and social forces underlie long-standing population trends: losses from many parts
of the countryside; a continuing move from older industrial and urban areas; a
focusing on the metropolitan region of London and the major provincial cities.
These pose continuing problems in population and regional planning for the present
and the immediate future.

To these long-established forces have been added variants of specifically
twentieth-century origin. More mobile, technologically-based and assembly-line
industries which demand access to labour and markets rather than to power or raw
materials have broken the dominance of the peripheral industrial regions and drawn
population to the core area of Southern England. The growing significance of
services and commercial activities in the economy have focused a large and
increasing section of employment on the conurbations. Mass transit systems and
greatly augmented car ownership have markedly increased mobility, permitting
increasing separation of home and workplace and accentuating the growth of city
regions, within which dispersal of housing areas and concentration of jobs are
pulling in different directions. Thus, while in purely agricultural areas until very
recently population has continued to decline, in a growing rural—urban fringe
around *all* large cities population increased rapidly, both through private house-
building and, especially after the Second World War, on local authority estates and
by overspill agreements with adjacent towns. Moreover in the 1970s these
influences seem to be extending into remoter rural hinterlands (Champion 1981).

Such trends reflect not only the process of urbanization (ch. 6), which has been
such a prominent feature of the UK since early Victorian times, but also the recent
and present inter- and intra-regional mobility which is reshaping its real social
regions. Population change, in turn, is basic to many aspects of present and future
economic, social, political and administrative organization.

A population of some 56m living on only 24.4m ha, much of which is unsuitable
for cultivation or settlement, especially in highland Britain, creates densities of

population second in Europe only to the Netherlands and among the highest in the world. At the beginning of this century only 5% of England and Wales was in urban land use but interwar sprawl of towns reduced farmland by over 25,000ha per year (Best 1972). Better planning controls since the war have seen this loss reduced to an average 15,800ha per year up to 1970. Even so, the built-up area of England and Wales had increased from 5% of the total area in 1900 to 10% in 1950 (UK, 1950: 7.3%) and, despite the reduced rate of consumption of land, to over 11% at present (UK, 1965: 8.5%). Slowing down of population growth and house-building have reduced the pressure but urban land in England and Wales could form some 15% by the end of the century, though for the UK as a whole (11.3% in 2000 AD) the long-term prospect is somewhat less daunting (table 1.2) (DoE 1971).

Improvements in housing and urban amenities have also contributed considerably to urban demands for land. Pressure on land for communications, water supplies and recreation will increase. Thus, in the early 1970s it was urged that we should not add to the pressures arising from existing population by further population increases, even if in many parts of the UK there is room for more population.

The economic value of a numerous and growing population depends on its ability to release greater productive power than its demands on resources generate. During the postwar years there was a relative decline of population in the productive age-groups – a product of the low interwar fertility rates – and shortage of labour led to acute pressure of demand for both skilled and unskilled workers. This contributed to the considerable influx of immigrants in the late 1950s and early 1960s (ch. 2.II.6) and to the general feeling that population growth was no bad thing. The combined effects in the 1970s of severe economic problems and the growth of the potential workforce has led to a belief that the UK cannot provide for a larger population, a fact reflected in the recent rapid decline in births. Moreover, the present inability of the economy to absorb the large 1960s birth cohorts into the labourforce is a major factor in unemployment.

I.2   Demographic Trends: Some Basic Factors

Following upon the toll of the First World War on the young men of Britain and its consequent effect on marriage-rates, the economic depression of the early 1930s contributed to the continuing fall in fertility. The crude birth-rate in the UK, which had reached a peak of 35 per 1,000 in the early 1870s, declined gradually to 1914 and fell rapidly in the interwar years. The idea of the smaller family spread through all sections of society and fertility fell below replacement level in the 1930s. Although population continued to increase slowly, supported by a net gain by migration, the long-term prospects for population growth were poor. A continuing decline in death-rate contributed to a slowly growing, but ageing, population (table 2.1). Hence, the population predictions of the 1930s, almost without exception, were of future decline. The most optimistic forecast of the Report of the Royal Commission on Population (1949) for GB was of a population of 52m by the end of the century; the least optimistic assumption placed it as low as 41m.

Three sets of forces have produced wide fluctuations in population trends since 1945. First, birth-rates increased markedly in the baby boom of the immediate postwar years when crude birth-rates reached an average of 18 per 1000 in 1946–50. Despite considerable fluctuations in birth-rate, involving a fall in the early 1950s, birth-rates generally remained above those of the interwar years until

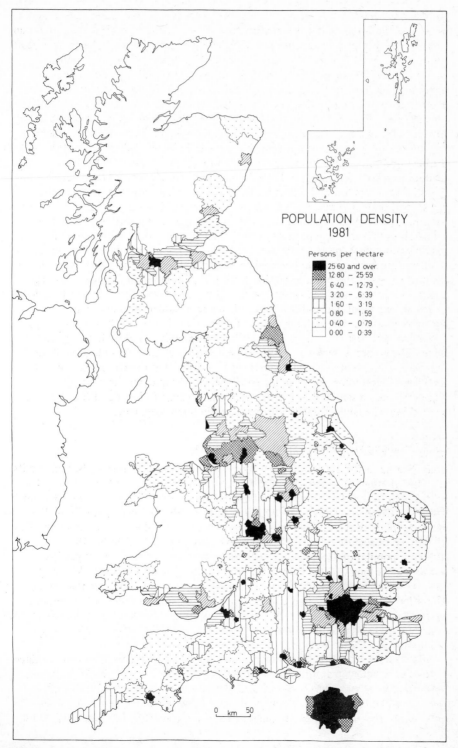

POPULATION DENSITY
1981

Persons per hectare

■	25·60 and over
	12·80 — 25·59
	6·40 — 12·79
	3·20 — 6·39
	1·60 — 3·19
	0·80 — 1·59
	0·40 — 0·79
	0·00 — 0·39

0   km   50

Figure 2.1   Population density, UK, 1981

TABLE 2.1

Birth, Death and Marriage Rates UK, 1901–80

	1911	1931	1951	1961	1966	1971	1977	1980
Births per 1,000	24.6	16.3	15.8	17.8	17.9	16.2	11.8	13.5
Fertility rates per 1,000 women 15–44	99.1	66.5	73.0	90.1	91.1	84.4	62.0	65.0
Percentage illegitimate births	4.7	4.8	4.9	5.8	7.7	8.2	10.0	11.5
Deaths per 1,000	14.1	12.2	12.6	12.0	11.8	11.6	11.7	11.8
Male deaths/1,000	15	13	13	12.6	12.5	12.2	12.1	12.5
Female deaths/1,000	13	12	12	11.4	11.2	11.1	11.3	11.7
Av. age of first marriage								
male	27.3	27.4	26.8	25.6	24.9	24.6	25.1	25.2
female	25.6	25.5	24.6	23.3	22.7	22.6	22.8	23.0
Percentage women ever								
married: 20–24	24.0	25.5	47.3	57.4	58.2	59.0		
25–29	55.8	58.4	77.5	84.3	85.5	85.8	NA	NA
40–44	81.6	81.4	85.3	90.1	91.3	91.9		

Source: Social Trends; Popul. Trends; Registrar General's Quarterly Returns
NA = not available

1972, but in 1977 fell to their lowest level since civil records started in 1837 (fig. 2.2, table 2.1). General fertility also increased due to earlier and more universal marriage. In GB the average age of first marriage for women, at 25.5 years in the 1920s and 1930s, fell to less than 25.0 after 1945, and continued to fall in the 1960s to 22.6 in 1971 before rising to its present level of 23.0 years. Moreover, the proportion of women aged 15–49 with experience of marriage increased in England and Wales from 529 per 1000 in 1931 to 700 in 1961 and 698 in 1970, with equivalent figures for Scotland of 483, 677 and 697.

All these factors are reflected in the growth of the average number of children per marriage in Britain from the low level of 2.05 for marriages in 1936, to 2.23 for 1951, to an estimated 2.50 for 1961, but to some 2.20 for those of the mid-1970s. These changes were enough to create growth and projected future growth up to the early 1970s but the fall in births has produced a 1979-based forecast for 2000 of 58.4m, 5–6m less than the 1969 estimate, whilst a reduction in births of one child in three families would eventually stabilize population numbers. Birth-rate fell from a second postwar peak of 18.6 in 1964 to 11.8 per thousand in 1977, well below the level even of the mid-1930s. If the families born to the generation of the 1960s baby boom fall to below 2.00, as suggested by recent birth trends, this could lead to a further downward revision of future population totals. Indeed, if the 1974 net reproduction rate of 0.89 were to continue, it would lead to future population decline (Pearce 1975).

While increased births in the 1960s have increased the numbers and proportion of young dependants, continuing improvements in health and standards of living have been reflected in a slow lowering of mortality. Although due in part to an ageing population structure, crude death-rates have fallen, but slowly, from 12.7 per 1000 in 1921, to between 11.6 and 12.2 since the 1960s (fig. 2.2). Expectation

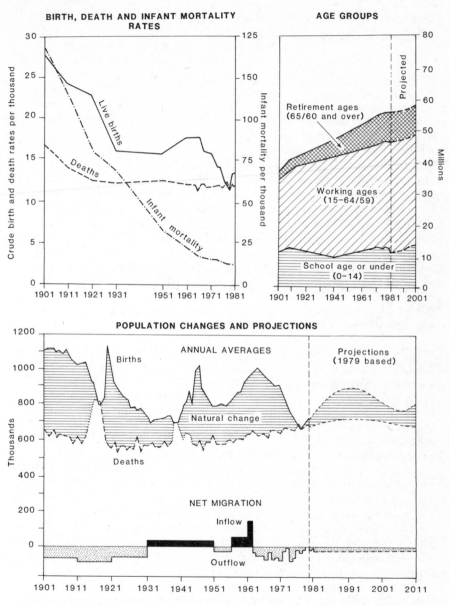

Figure 2.2   UK vital trends, components of population growth, 1901–81; Age structure,
1901–2001; Population changes and projections, 1901–2001

of life has increased steadily, especially for women, and is reflected in the increased
proportion of retired people in the population (table 2.6), one reason for the
increased dependency ratios which have been a feature of the postwar years.

A third factor in population growth since the 1930s has been the fluctuating
pattern of overseas migration. In contrast to the losses from migration sustained

during the nineteenth and early twentieth centuries, during the 1930s and 1940s a
slowing down of emigration and increased immigration, much of it of refugees from
Europe, combined to reverse the UK's long-standing net loss from migration.
Moreover, in the mid-1950s to the early-1960s immigration from the New
Commonwealth countries contributed to a considerable continuing inward
movement, which produced a net gain due to migration of 20,000 in the civilian
population 1951–61 and of 113,000 in 1961–6 (table 2.2). This was slowed down
by the 1962 *Commonwealth Immigrants Act* and nearly arrested by the 1968 Act.
Though the influx of dependants of previous migrants has continued to generate
considerable immigration, economic conditions and the 1981 *Nationality Bill*,
which restricts British citizenship, will reduce this flow. Increasing control of
immigration and deteriorating economic conditions, especially in terms of labour
surpluses, have resulted in a considerable recent loss by migration (see table 2.2).
In a sample of the migrants passing through major sea and air ports, 1964–74, a net
migration loss of 452,000 was recorded in the UK (Davis and Walker 1975).
However, gains of foreign and Commonwealth migrants, especially from the New
Commonwealth, and losses of UK nationals have led to continuing diversification of
the UK population. The effects of this distinctive, if short-lived, process on the
composition of the population have been considerable and will have longer-term

TABLE 2.2

Components of Population Change, UK, 1921–81

(1,000s)	1921–31		1931–51	
Population at start of period	44,027		46,038	
Average ann. change	Total	%	Total	%
Births	824	1.87	785	1.71
Deaths	555	1.26	598	1.30
Net natural change	268	0.61	188	0.41
Net migration	–67	–0.15	+22	+0.05
Total av. ann. change	201	0.46	213	0.47

1951–61		1961–71		1971–81	
50,290		52,816		55,610	
Total	%	Total	%	Total	%
839	1.64	963	1.76	736	1.32
593	1.16	639	1.17	670	1.20
246	0.48	324	0.59	67	0.12
+9	+0.02	–3	–0.01	–29	–0.05
253	0.50	322	0.59	37	0.07

Source: Soc. Trends; Popul. Trends

effects upon population trends (ch. 2.II.6). Moreover, in certain areas overseas immigrants have become dominant in social and demographic structures.

I.3 General Population Trends, Rural and Urban

The dominant trends of the last 60 years have been the drift from the older industrial regions; movement from rural to urban areas; the counterflow from city centre to suburb (fig. 2.3). Since 1961, however, significant variations on these themes have become apparent (fig. 2.4). The large cities and conurbations have all experienced marked losses to adjacent areas (tables 2.3 and 2.4). In the rural areas of the UK, characterized by population losses throughout the Victorian period, out-migration and decline continued during the interwar years, especially from marginal areas. Since the Second World War losses from the rural areas have progressively diminished, though depopulation of the remoter rural areas continued into the 1960s. Rural districts increased their population by overspill from adjacent towns, chiefly in response to suburban dispersal and the increase of commuting, and of movement by people on retirement (table 2.3). In the 1970s there have been widespread gains in rural areas in many parts of the UK. Actual numbers are often

TABLE 2.3

Population Change in Urban and Rural Areas, UK, 1951–71

	Total 1961	% change 1951–61	Total 1971	% change 1961–71
England and Wales	46,104.5	5.2	48,593.7	5.3
Conurbations	16,741.9	–3.4	15,928.0	–4.8
Urban areas				
over 100,000	6,640.4	5.8	6,754.1	1.7
50–100,000	5,008.7	13.2	5,392.2	7.5
under 50,000	8,759.7	8.5	9,961.2	13.7
Rural districts	8,953.9	9.3	10,568.3	18.0
Scotland	5,179.3	1.6	5,227.7	0.9
Conurbation	1,807.8	2.7	1,731.0	–4.2
Other cities and				
large burghs	1,441.9	9.6	1,491.8	3.5
Small burghs	866.6	9.2	994.8	14.8
Districts of County	1,065.4	–11.9	1,018.4	–4.4
N Ireland	1,425.0	3.9	1,527.6	6.8
County boroughs	469.6	–4.9	412.0	–12.3
Other urban areas	300.4	17.2	429.9	43.2
Rural districts	655.0	5.5	685.7	4.7
UK	52,708.9	4.9	55,346.6	5.0
Conurbations	18,549.7	–0.5	17,659.0	–4.8
Large urban areas	8,551.9	5.7	8,657.9	1.4
Other urban areas	14,935.4	10.3	16,768.1	12.3
Rural districts	10,674.3	6.3	12,272.4	15.0

Source: Census of 1961 and 1971
Because of the different basis of classification in Scotland, figures for urban and rural areas have had to be adjusted and do not exactly equal the total.

TABLE 2.4

Population Change by Categories of District, England and Wales, 1971–81

Category of district	No. of districts	% change 1961–71	Population change 1971–81 000s	%	Population 1981
Gtr London Boroughs	33	–6.8	–756	–10.1	6,69ε
Metropol. Districts	36	0.5	–546	–4.6	11,235
Non-Metropol. Districts					
Cities	27	–0.2	–204	–4.6	4,450
Northern and Welsh					
Industrial	39	3.7	42	1.3	3,348
Southern Industrial	34	12.1	158	5.0	3,320
New Towns	21	21.8	283	15.1	2,165
Resort and retirement	36	12.2	156	4.9	3,335
Other urban and					
accessible rural	99	22.0	661	7.0	9,449
Remoter rural	78	9.7	468	10.3	5,013
England and Wales	403	5.7	262	0.5	49,011

Source: Census 1981, Preliminary Report, England and Wales

small and are mostly due to net in-movement, so it would be premature to see this as 'counter-urbanization', rather perhaps as an extension of residential migration into small towns and accessible country areas.

Since 1945 large cities and conurbations have experienced marked and increasing losses of population. In the 1950s and sixties in closely settled areas of the UK most large urban authorities lost population to adjacent suburban areas, often in rural districts. Accompanied by loss of rateable value and, often, by increasing social segregation of centre and periphery in essentially interdependent urban regions, this process has been reflected in the growth of population in the smaller urban areas, many of which, since the 1972 Local Government Act, are concealed within large Districts – many in remoter areas – in which the greatest percentage increases have been recorded for 1971–81 (fig. 2.4).

The result has been to shift the balance of regional growth within the UK. During the nineteenth century the most rapidly growing regions included N England and the industrial areas of C Scotland and S Wales. But since the First World War, the Northern, Yorks. and Humberside, and NW regions of England, together with Wales and Scotland, have suffered a relative fall in population, while the Midlands and South East increased their relative share of population up to 1971. That share fell in the 1970s, but the E Midlands, E Anglia and the South West – like the Outer South East – continue to attract migrants both from other regions and by residential movement from Greater London (table 2.5).

I.4 Effects on Population Structure

These changing distributions reflect changing economic forces, but the demographic results of changes in natural and migrational components of population trends also carry considerable economic and social implications at both national and regional levels. The declining birth-rate and falling mortality of the early twentieth century

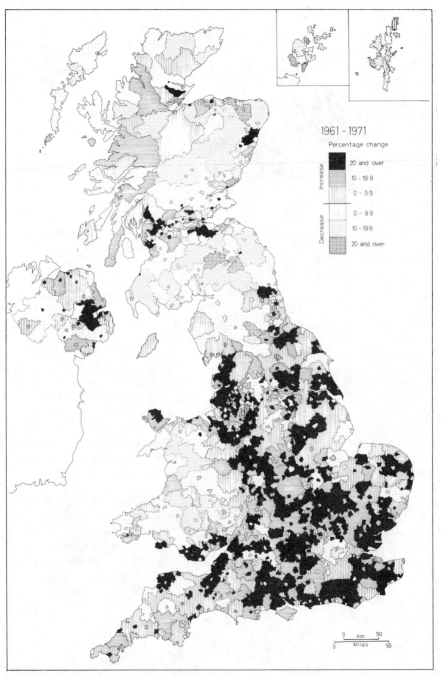

Figure 2.3   Population change, UK, 1961–71

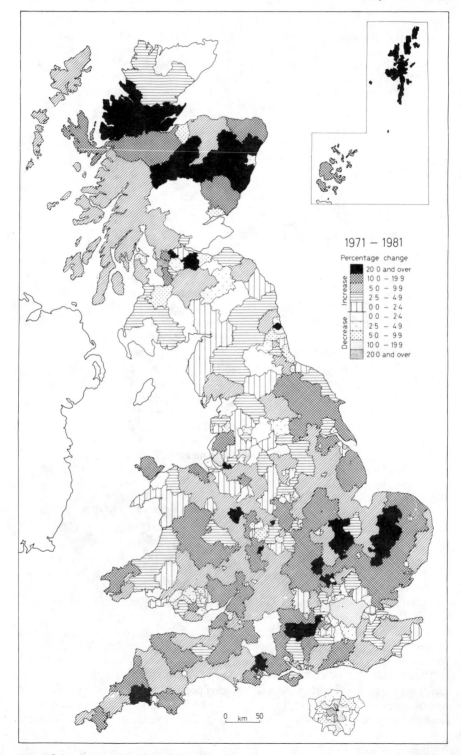

Figure 2.4   Population change, UK, 1971–81

TABLE 2.5

Components of Population Change, UK Regions, 1951–81 (000s)

Region	1951	1951–61 Average annual change Natural	Migration	1961	1961–71 Average annual change Natural	Migration	1971	1971–81 Average annual change Natural	Migration	1981
Northern	3,127	19.3	−8.0	3,246	17.4	−8.1	3,293	2.0	−6.5	3,097
Yorks. and H.	4,509	19.5	−9.6	4,631	26.6	−6.5	4,811	3.5	−3.8	4,854
North West	6,417	23.5	−12.4	6,545	34.0	−9.4	6,747	2.2	−21.1	6,406
E Midlands	2,896	15.8	+3.9	3,108	22.2	+7.4	3,380	7.0	+10.4	3,807
W Midlands	4,426	27.6	+4.7	4,761	39.6	+3.5	5,121	13.0	−10.3	5,136
South East	15,216	66.4	+43.8	16,346	99.6	−3.6	17,289	27.4	−47.5	16,729
Gtr London	8,206	33.3	−61.1	7,977	44.7	−97.4	7,441	7.7	−83.4	6,696
OMA	3,509	24.2	+77.5	4,521	41.3	+44.4	5,345 }	19.6	+35.9	10,033
OSE	3,502	8.9	+27.3	3,848	13.3	+49.9	4,502 }			
E Anglia	1,388	6.5	+2.7	1,489	8.4	+13.5	1,686	3.7	+15.9	1,865
South West	3,247	10.5	+9.9	3,436	15.0	+22.4	3,792	−3.5	+28.1	4,326
Wales	2,589	8.4	−4.9	2,635	9.8	+0.5	2,723	0.2	+5.7	2,791
Scotland	5,103	33.9	−28.2	5,184	35.4	−36.4	5,230	1.8	−13.0	5,117
N Ireland	1,373	14.6	−8.9	1,427	17.2	−6.5	1,534	10.2	−10.5	1,547
UK	50,291	246.0	+7.0	52,807	326.3	−23.7	55,610	66.7	−31.2	55,921

Figures are derived from *Registrar General's Mid-year Estimates of Home Populations*.
See also: Eversley (1971); *Abstract of Regional Statistics* (1971); *Long-term Population Distribution in GB: A Study* (1971); *Registrar General's Revised Estimates . . . Regions* (1975); Champion (1976).

caused a considerable increase in the elderly (over 60 years), both numerically and as a proportion of the total population (table 2.6). In 1911 the 60+ age-group formed 9.2% of the total population, but by 1941 it was estimated at 13.9 and, in 1971, 18.6%. The increase in older dependants was offset between the wars by falling birth-rates; the proportion of those under 15 years fell from 30.8% in 1911 to 21% in 1941. Hence, the dependency ratio (conventionally measured by the proportion of those aged 0–14 years and of retirement age, here reckoned as 60 years and above, as related to the 15–59 age group) which was 61.5 in 1911 had dropped to 53.9 in 1941. By 1971, because of generally higher birth-rates since 1945 and increased expectation of life among older people, the dependency ratio was 70.8. While from 1941 to 1971 the under-15s increased by 34% and the over-60s by 53%, the main workforce increased by a meagre 2%. Hence, in the 1950s and 1960s we experienced a relative decline in the workforce, though the actual numbers of the population of working age increased slightly. During the 1970s the dependency ratio fell to 67.0 in 1975, and to 63.0 in 1981. Though raising of the school-leaving age to sixteen in 1973 offset the rise in numbers of the workforce (Davis 1976), they rose by 1.3m in 1971–81 and it is estimated will increase by a further 1.0m in the 1980s before their rate of increase slows, with the addition of 0.4m in the 1990s. This sharp increase in the number of those of working age (2.7m between 1971–2001) is in marked contrast to the stagnation in the potential workforce in the 1950s and 1960s. This was partly offset by drawing more women into gainful employment, a trend accelerated by two world wars and by changing attitudes to the role of women in society and their potential role in professional, commercial and industrial life. These changes have been reflected in the increase in the proportion of women in employment, especially during and since the Second World War, though there are considerable regional variations in female activity rates.

Thus, one of the factors in 'full employment' since 1945 has been the coincidence of labour shortage, due to changing population structure, with a generally expanding economy. These were also basic factors attracting immigrant labour to the UK in the 1950s and early 1960s. The recession of the 1970s, coupled

TABLE 2.6

Age Distribution, UK, 1911–2001

Age group	Total popn (millions) Census enumeration			Projections*		Per cent of total popn Census			Projections		Percentage changes			
	1911	1941	1971	1981	2001	1911	1941	1971	1981	2001	1911–41	1941–71	1971–81	1981–2001
0–14	13.0	10.1	13.5	(11.6)	(12.8)	30.8	21.0	24.1	(20.8)	(22.1)	−22.3	+33.7	−14.1	+10.3
15–59	25.7	31.4	32.1	33.1	(34.4)	61.1	65.1	57.2	59.4	(59.3)	+22.2	+2.2	+3.1	+3.9
60 and over	3.4	6.8	10.4	11.2	10.8	8.2	13.9	18.6	20.0	18.6	+100.0	+53.0	+7.7	−3.6
All ages	42.1	48.3	55.5	55.7	58.0	100.1	100.0	99.9	100.0	100.0	+14.8	+15.9	+0.4	+0.5

*The projections are those of 1978, bracketed figures are estimates including those as yet unborn.

Source: Soc. Trends, 1 (1970) and *3* (1972); Registrar General, *Popn Projections, 1978–2018* (HMSO, 1980)

with increasing economy in the use of labour in the face of rapidly rising labour costs, has now changed this situation in a period of sharply rising numbers of people of working age. It is reflected in increases in unemployment, a fall in activity rates and a decline in the immigration of workers though not yet of dependants. The problem is now one of an expanding workforce in a stagnant economy.

Sex structure From the 1920s to the 1940s the catastrophic casualties of the First World War, reflected in the relatively high ratios of women to men (table 2.8), were a factor contributing to reduced fertility between the wars. Since the Second World War much improved ante- and post-natal care has resulted in a marked increase in the surplus of male births. Despite higher male mortality, especially in later life, the imbalances of the sexes in the interwar years in the UK is now much reduced. Current estimates show that men outnumber women in all age-groups up to 44 years in England and Wales, to 40 years in Scotland and 34 in N Ireland where the lower age of male deficits is due largely to differential migration.

TABLE 2.7

Older Age-groups, UK, 1941–2001, as a ratio of 1969 (= 100)

		Actual (1)				Estimated (2)		
		1941	1951	1961	1969	1981	1991	2001
All retirement ages	Total	63	76	86	100	109	110	105
	M	67	80	85	100	115	119	115
	F	61	74	86	100	106	106	101
85 and over	Total	36	47	72	100	119	157	180
	M	42	56	83	100	106	146	173
	F	34	44	68	100	123	161	183

Source: (1) *Soc. Trends, 1,* (1970), Table VIII, p. 29;
(2) OPCS, *Population Projections,* 1978–2018 (1980)

One very notable feature of changing age and sex structure is the increasing dominance of women in later age-groups. Among the over-60s the ratio of men to women is about 1:1.44 but among the over-70s it is 1:1.79 and 1:2.65 for the over-80s; the increasing number of very elderly people is due mainly to an increasing proportion of elderly women (Thompson 1970).

I.5 Population Composition and the Workforce

In a Select Committee report for 1970–1 (House of Commons 1971) it was noted that, after a postwar phase of increased dependency rates perpetuated by the proposal to raise the school-leaving age to 16 in 1973, the working population would increase from 1974. Compared with the period 1941–69, when the population of working age increased by a mere 4%, and with a decrease of some 1% 1969–73 there has been an increase of 3.6% in the population of working age by 1981, with a projected increase of 13.6% between 1981–2001.

This is a major challenge. Though an increased labourforce may contribute to increased output, it may also present problems in a contracting labour market. Thus the changing demographic structure is of considerable economic significance.

The changing employment situation in the 1950s and 1960s was partly related to a changing manpower situation. The present labour surpluses are a product of increased supply, especially in the younger age-groups, at a time of economic recession and increasing economy in the use of manpower in a high-wage economy. There will be an excess rather than shortage of labour in the 1980s unlike that which hampered the economy in the 1950s and 1960s and generated a demand for immigrants to fill the gap in home labour supplies. Nevertheless varying regional demands for labour and changing skills will no doubt involve continuing labour mobility involving both population migration and structural changes in the labourforce.

I.6   Population Trends and Social Provision

If the increased manpower can be put to work, some of the burden of dependency which has fallen upon a relatively static working-age population until recent times may be eased. Postwar increases in both children and old people have placed heavy pressures upon the whole range of social services — education, health, social and family benefits — and also upon housing. For example, the boom in births of 1945—7 led to a 30% increase in school intake in 1950—2 which reached the universities and colleges in the Robbins boom period of 1963—5. Similarly the upward trend of births of the period 1955—64, which produced a second postwar increase of 29% in school entries, has exerted a more gradual, but increasing, pressure on educational facilities, youth services, etc., which has yet fully to work its way through. However, the fall in births of the 1970s is reflected in the sharp fall in the number of teachers needed in the late 1970s and 1980s and the anticipated fall in university places in the 1980s.

Meanwhile, increased longevity is requiring the provision of more special services for the elderly. These fall unequally on the community both in regional terms (fig. 2.10), as between urban and rural areas, or between older-established and more recently formed communities. The general tendency to an ageing population since the First World War has not been offset by increased births since 1945. Taking 1969 as base year, the index of rates of change in the older age-groups has shown a marked upward trend which is expected to continue, especially among the aged, calling for much greater provision of special homes, hospitals and other services than is yet available (table 2.7).

II   POPULATION DISTRIBUTION AND TRENDS

II.1   Intra-regional Contrasts

With an average of 2.27 persons per ha, the UK is one of the most densely populated areas of the world. Moreover there are very wide variations, ranging from the extremely crowded inner-residential areas of the large towns, with densities of over 25 per ha rising to 120 per ha, to thinly populated rural areas of under 0.40 per ha and extensive, uninhabited moorlands which cover much of upland Britain (fig. 2.1). The key to the intensity of occupation lies in an unusually high degree of urbanization (ch. 6). In 1911, after over a century of rapid urban growth, 78% of the population of England and Wales lived in urban districts and perhaps as many as nine-tenths were 'urbanized'. Similarly in Scotland population numbers were dominated by the large towns and industrial districts of C Scotland. Even in N Ireland, where Belfast is the only large industrial city, about one-half of the population were urban-dwellers.

The proportion of *urban-dwellers*, narrowly defined as those who live under urban administrations, was still at about the level of fifty years ago according to the 1971 census: 77.7% in the UK; 78.3% in England and Wales; 81.5% in Scotland; and 55.1% in N Ireland. Many large towns, Greater London included, reached their peak population before the First World War, however, and have since maintained growth by outward movement. Even where land has been available within the city boundaries for new housing, slum clearance and lower-density house-building have led to large net losses of population by migration and, since the Second World War, a fall in total numbers of people in large cities which had become general by the 1970s.

In 1971 32.7% of the population of England and Wales lived in the 6 conurbations officially designated in the 1951 Census (Greater London, Merseyside, SE Lancashire (SELNEC), Tyneside, W Yorkshire and the W Midlands), a decline from the 38% of 1951 due largely to a fall of 725,000 in the conurbation population, 1961–71. A similar reduction from 35 to 33% in the population of Scotland who lived in the central Clydeside conurbation was due to a fall in the total since 1961.

This relative loss of population from the conurbations was paralleled in most large towns over 100,000 inhabitants; in 1961–71 these grew more slowly than small towns, both relatively and absolutely (table 2.3). In England and Wales during that period their growth was only one-third of the national average (Champion 1976, 412–3). Direct comparison of the former urban local government areas with the 1974 Districts is difficult, but there has been a fall in the population of *all* larger towns (table 2.4). Yet in many cases urban losses are illusory. Reduced densities in the inner areas are the result of clearance either for commercial and other redevelopment, or for housing renewal at much lower densities, even where high-rise apartments have been built. However, compared with the very high intensity of occupation in nineteenth-century housing areas, and due to enhanced standards of space for amenities such as schools and open spaces, even such intensive redevelopment does not usually absorb more than half the pre-existing population. The people displaced do not usually 'leave' the city but are rehoused on the periphery, often in adjacent local authority areas, many of which were formerly designated as 'rural districts'. Thus the moderately high density areas have progressively extended their bounds around large towns with some evening-out of the population gradient between cities and peripheral areas. While less marked than in the interwar years, the physical expansion of towns continues (ch. 6.I.3). Hall *et al* (1973) identified 100 labour centres which form the core of labour areas, jointly making up Standard Metropolitan Labour Areas (SMLAs). In these there was general and progressive decentralization of population 1951–66, a tendency which Champion (1976) has shown is continuing and extending to outer city areas beyond the SMLAs.

Fears have been expressed of 'megalopolitan' tendencies in the corridor from Greater London to NW England and W Yorkshire, which contains about 51% of the population of England and Wales, though Best (1972) suggests that this danger is not immediate and Hall (1973) has argued that urban England has been 'contained'.

Moreover this is only one aspect of a general problem of concentration. Certainly in 1961 only two million, less than 5% of the population of England and Wales, lived over 16 km from a major city (Smailes 1961). The activities of a large part of the workforce focus upon the major urbanized areas (ch. 2.IV.5) and with the widening of commuter hinterlands people are living progressively further from their jobs.

TABLE 2.8

Female/Male Ratios, UK, 1911–2001

Census of population

Total in millions	1911 Total M	F	F per 100M	1921 Total M	F	F per 100M
England and Wales	17.45	18.62	106.8	18.01	19.81	109.6
Scotland	2.31	2.45	106.2	2.35	2.53	108.0
N Ireland	0.60	0.65	105.9	0.61	0.65	106.2
UK	20.36	21.72	106.7	20.97	22.99	109.5

Source: Censuses; Registrar General's Estimates (1973 base)

Up to the 1960s population densities within purely *rural areas* continued to decline, following nearly a century and a half of outward migration from the countryside. Within the remoter areas of highland Britain, a mere 1% of the country's population lives on over one-third of its land area. Up to the 1970s such thinly peopled areas, with a progressively ageing structure, experienced excess of deaths over births, and, slowly but surely, were dying in demographic as well as in economic and social terms. Declining amenities, including transport, difficulty of access to schools and other services, suggested that in much of central Wales and the Scottish Highlands and Islands further depopulation was likely except in more accessible recreational areas. Even where farming prospered and supported a range of active professional and service functions in local market towns, population decline or stagnation often continued. Increased food output has been achieved by greater productivity, much of it by increased mechanization. The farm labourforce has declined to less than half its 1945 total, while amalgamations continue to reduce the number of farms. Indeed, the UK now has only 3% of its working population engaged in agriculture, though the area of tillage and stock numbers alike are considerably above interwar levels (Coppock 1972, 36).

In the 1970s the fall in aggregate rural population has been reversed in many parts of England and Wales, in central and eastern Scotland and the Highlands and Islands, and in N Ireland. Such trends may be illusory, for increasing population and higher densities in the rural areas of the UK are mostly the result of dispersal of town-dwellers beyond urban administrative limits or, in certain favoured seaside and country districts, are due to the inward movement of population to live in retirement, though some areas of considerable rural increase are remote from major urban areas. Residential dispersal into adjacent rural areas has not been confined to the private housing sector. Increasingly since the 1950s, local authority housing estates and overspill agreements have moved outside urban boundaries into rural districts, enlarging commuter hinterlands and extending the real city regions. Thus highly urbanized areas in England and Wales and central Scotland have tended to coalesce (fig. 2.1) (ch. 6.III).

II.2 Regional Components of Population Change

Within the basic pattern of population distribution and change, there are considerable contrasts in regional trends. Moreover, despite the persistence of

Table 2.8 (cont.)

1951			1971			1981			2001 (est.)		
Total		F per 100M	Total		F per 100M	Total		F per 100M			F per 100M
M	F		M	F		M	F		M	F	
21.02	22.74	108.2	23.62	24.98	105.8	24.83	25.19	105.7	25.15	26.12	103.9
2.43	2.66	109.2	2.52	2.71	107.5	2.46	2.66	107.9	2.52	2.63	103.8
0.67	0.70	105.3	0.75	0.78	103.8	0.76	0.78	102.6	0.80	0.82	102.2
24.12	26.10	108.3	26.89	28.47	105.9	27.05	28.63	105.8	28.48	29.57	103.8

trends characteristic of the years 1921−71 − rural decline, urban overspill and the drift south-east − there have been recent shifts in the scale and intensity of population movements which presage future change. During the first half of the twentieth century the major population growth was concentrated into three standard Regions (as at present defined): the South East, and the W and E Midlands. The redistribution of the late eighteenth and nineteenth centuries had been partially reversed. The SE Region increased its share rapidly and the Midlands Regions more gradually. In the older industrial areas higher birth-rates were offset by massive out-migration. During the depression years of the 1930s unemployment rates in the Midlands and SE were often only half the national average while in the depressed industrial areas of S Wales, Scotland and Northern England they were well above average (ch. 1.III.2). Between 1921−51 the SE Region gained nearly 1.2m people by migration, the Midlands Region over 300,000 between 1931−51 and the SW Region rather fewer over the same period. In contrast, between 1921−51, the net migration losses of Northern England were 912,000, Wales 434,000 and Scotland 675,000. N Ireland's losses, a continuance of nineteenth-century rural-urban movement to Britain, were somewhat abated in the stagnant UK industrial economy of the interwar period; against an increase of 23,000 in population from 1926−37 must be offset an estimated net migration loss of 70,000 during the same period.

One of the aims of postwar planning has been to diminish the continuing drain of population from the so-called depressed areas of the interwar period. The extent to which planning policy has succeeded in this may be judged, in part, from population trends, not least rates of net migration. Between 1951 and 1961 the South East's population increased by 1.13 million with a net migration gain of 438,000, the adjoining Regions, E Anglia and the South West, which received overspill from and growth associated with the SE, had increases of 111,000 and 189,000 respectively (table 2.5). The other regions of population growth, the W

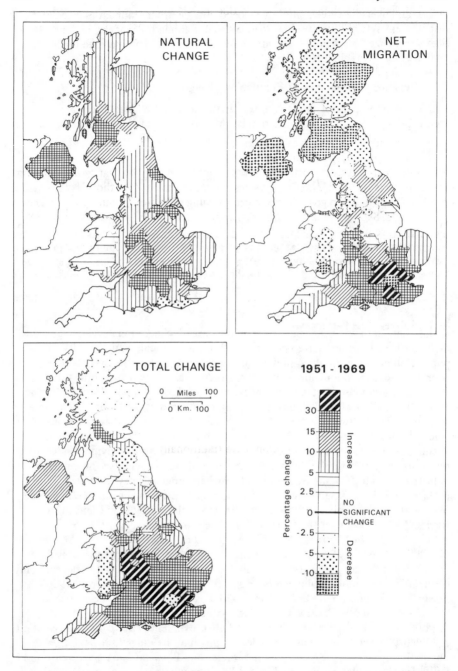

Figure 2.5   Natural, migration and total population change, economic planning sub-regions,
1951–69

and E Midlands, which increased by 335,000 and 212,000 respectively, also had considerable migration gains. All other areas of the UK experienced losses by migration between 1951 and 1961, which were substantial in some cases, as, for example, from Scotland and the North West.

Despite vigorous attempts in the 1960s to attract industry to the development areas and to control the supply of new jobs in the growth regions (chs 1 and 4) these population trends have persisted. Although from 1966, the SE Region has lost population by migration, essentially due to massive losses from Greater London, whose population decreased by 540,000 from 1961–71, these mainly went to the adjacent regions of E Anglia and the SW. In the Midlands, however, there has recently been a significant slowing down in the growth rate of the W Midlands. This last case apart, however, the ratio of regional to national population trends reflects the same essential features as those of the 1950s, though relative recovery of population growth, and corresponding reduction of outward movement, in N Ireland, Scotland, Wales and Yorks. and Humberside is interesting. On balance, we must agree with the verdict of Eversley (1971) that, although regional policies have not succeeded in arresting population losses from areas of long-standing decline, 'Without government policies the situation would be far worse' and it may well be that some levelling-out of regional rates of change may be expected in the future.

II.3 Sub-regional Patterns of Change

(i) 1951–71

While regional trends pick out the main features of population change since the war, they are on too broad a scale to permit accurate assessment of the relationship between components of population change involving considerable intra-regional contrasts, such as between urban and rural areas or between urban core and periphery; furthermore, both natural and migrational components must be considered. Areas of high natural growth, such as the coalfields of NE England and S Wales, or the Merseyside sub-region, have traditionally exported surpluses arising from high birth-rates. Many rural areas still have a higher natural growth than they can support. Thus a certain level of migration must always be expected at both regional and sub-regional level as a regulator of population growth; but when such migration seriously affects population and social structure, especially by continuously draining away the younger and more talented sections of the population, it may create serious problems.

From the Registrar General's mid-year population estimates and census tabulations for sixty-three planning sub-regions in England and Wales and twenty-two in Scotland it is possible to analyse components of population change in fair detail up to 1971 (SDD 1972, DoE 1971) (fig. 2.5). While a full analysis for 1971–81 must await full publication of the 1981 Census, the preliminary results, together with the Registrars' General mid-year estimates permit some calculation of regional trends (fig. 2.6).

Total change The pattern of total population change at sub-regional level between 1951–69 (fig. 2.5) underlines those features already analysed, drawing particular attention to the contrasts between decrease in the remote rural areas, the stagnation or decline in such old industrial regions as the S Wales coalfield, and the W

Yorkshire and E Lancashire textile districts. The fall in Greater London's total population is typical of the inner areas of conurbations and has also occurred in all other conurban sub-regions during the 1960s and 1970s. Indeed the combined population decline of Greater London and the central County Boroughs (CBs) of the five other English conurbations, 1961–71, was 952,024, while in the more extensive conurbations themselves the population fell by 724,557.

Natural change Some of the features of total change are quite closely related to natural change, i.e. the balance between births and deaths. High-growth areas in SE England and the Midlands are marked by above-average natural increase, except in inner urban areas. But many areas of slow overall growth or even of decline have relatively high rates of natural increase: such are the Glasgow region and industrial NE England, while in N Ireland the moderate total increase since 1951 is considerably below the rate of natural growth. Much of rural Scotland has a moderate level of natural increase, but overall population stagnation or decline. In contrast, the south coast of England, an area of generally high total increase of population, has little or no natural increase or may actually show a natural decrease, as in the Sussex coast sub-region. While certain of these contrasts are due to differences in age structure, they also imply considerable variations in migration.

Net migration Even at sub-regional level net migration conceals a good deal of inter- and intra-regional mobility which can only be fully analysed from information on changes of residence first collected in the 1961 census. Net migration figures reflect the resultants of more complex patterns of inward and outward movements and are often regarded as a good indicator of the relative power of 'push. and 'pull' forces acting upon population at a regional level. The pattern in fig. 2.5 is a remarkably concise commentary on the continuing pull of population to the more prosperous economy and attractive social image of the south-eastern quadrant of Britain. Apart from migration losses from the Greater London and W Midlands conurbation sub-regions, much of which has been due to outward movement to adjacent areas in a process of intra-regional overspill of housing and population, with corresponding increases in commuting, this quadrant was one wholly of migration gain. This growth now extends into the SW and Bristol–Severn areas, and into E Anglia, both of which have had higher migration gains in the 1960s than the inner metropolitan sub-regions (table 2.5). In part such increases have been due to retirement migration to rural or seaside areas, especially in the South West and along the south coast.

Components of population change In summary, in the 1950s and 1960s, population increased in most sub-regions. In a very few cases, confined to the retirement areas of the Fylde, Morecambe–Lancaster, the Sussex and N Wales coasts, natural losses were more than compensated for by net migration gain, leading to population increase. In contrast, natural increase exceeded migration loss in most conurbations and older industrial areas, and in the less remote rural areas of S Wales, N England and S Scotland which, either by retaining sufficient of their natural increase or by attracting migrants from adjacent areas, have increased in population over the postwar period.

Fastest growth occurred in areas of both natural and migrational increase. Natural increase predominated over migrational gain in much of the E Midlands,

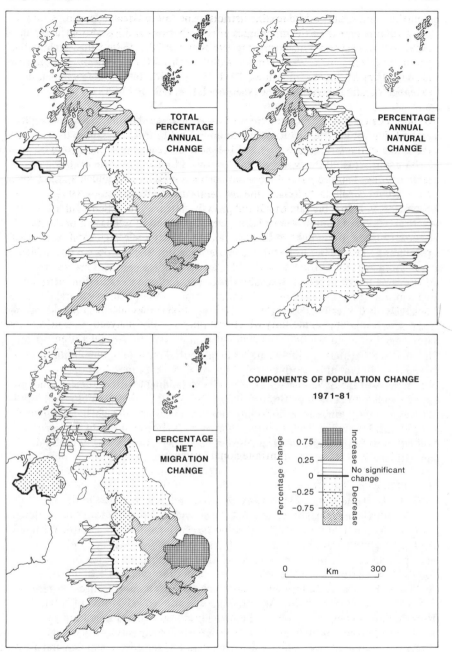

Figure 2.6   Components of population change, 1971–81

peripheral areas of the W Midlands and the north-western parts of the Outer
Metropolitan Area. Apart from the growth area of Bristol, the Severn estuary and
parts of the Welsh border influenced by overspill from the W Midlands, such growth
patterns were virtually absent from the rest of the UK. However, rural N Yorkshire
and the Falkirk—Stirling area were affected by outward movement from adjacent
urban regions, the latter especially by overspill from the central Clydeside
conurbation and east-central Scotland.

The major areas of attraction for population retained their natural increase plus a
larger element of growth due to net migration. This type of growth accounted for
large increases in population in most of the inner and outer metropolitan areas.
Much of southern and the whole of south-western England now shares these
characteristics, due to considerable recent gains by migration, as does much of E
Anglia, where considerable recent in-movement has resulted from overspill
agreements with Greater London (fig. 2.20). Similar features have occurred in the
outer sub-regions of the W Midlands but, apart from the suburban commuter belts
of north Cheshire (with links to Manchester and Merseyside) and of mid-Yorkshire
(with links to Leeds—Bradford and Hull), this 'healthy' type of population trend is
absent from the rest of the UK.

In this period there were two categories of population loss. In NE Lancashire, a
long-continuing net outward migration was combined with a slight natural decrease,
due largely to the region's ageing population structure, the only example of natural
losses outside the 'retirement' areas. Areas where net out-migration exceeded
natural gain to produce a fall in total population were of two distinct types. The
first included Greater London where, as in all central city areas, population has
moved out. In two nineteenth-century industrial areas, Furness and the north-
eastern parts of the S Wales coalfield, both long-standing industrial decline and an
ageing population contributed to population loss. The second type of population
loss was in remote rural areas, including most of southern and highland Scotland,
and Mid and North Wales, where long-standing out-movement created an aged
population with a low rate of natural growth and stagnating or slowly declining
populations.

(ii)   1971–81

While the larger area and more mixed character of most of the 1974 Local
Government Districts makes direct comparison with the pre-1974 map difficult, the
1981 population density (fig. 2.1) reflects a northwest-southeast gradient from low
densities in peripheral rural areas of the British Isles to the close network of
metropolitan centres and large cities which dominate the core region of Greater
London—Midlands—Lancashire—Yorkshire and outliers such as Central Scotland,
North East England and South Wales. Though the new administrative areas hide
some of the detail, as compared with the maps in the second edition of this book
(House 1977), extensive clearing and rehousing in inner cities has reduced some of
the highest densities, producing a core of relatively low density surrounded by
closely occupied late nineteenth- and early twentieth-century terrace housing.
Despite rehousing in high-rise dwellings in the inner areas, particularly in the 1960s,
most people from cleared areas have been dispersed to local authority estates
around the periphery of large towns and farther afield in overspill and New Town
schemes (see section IV.6).

In the Standard Metropolitan Labour Areas (SMLAs) designated by Hall (1973), the outer rings have grown faster in the 1970s (Kennett and Spence 1979) and journeys to work in city centres have lengthened though, as industry and warehousing and distribution have dispersed, commuting around the periphery of large urban areas has increased.

These features and the halting of the decline in rural population densities are more clearly shown in population changes in the 1970s (fig. 2.4), especially as compared with those in the 1960s (fig. 2.3). There has been a change in dominant postwar trends, with a decline in metropolitan counties and all larger cities due largely to increased net out-migration from their older residential areas, including older suburbs. This has been combined with increases in nearly all rural areas especially those of the 'remoter' areas of the British Isles. These have been caused primarily by net in-migration, due both to residential movements from cities and by retirement migration and by attraction of some new industries to small towns and, in Scotland, to oil-boom areas. The precise reasons for this turnround in rural population trends must await data on the structure of such urban–rural movements.

Between 1971 and 1981 the natural growth rate slowed to a mere 0.1% per annum as compared with 0.5% between 1945 and 1971. In contrast to the fall in the population of all metropolitan counties, many non-metropolitan counties and districts recorded increases, some around the major conurbations, especially in the Outer South East, but the largest in more rural areas such as South West England, East Anglia, mid-Wales and the border, and eastern and northern Scotland. 319 of the 403 districts in England and Wales grew less rapidly (or declined faster) than in 1961–71, mainly in and around city and industrial areas. The 84 which had higher growth rates in the 1970s were virtually all in remoter areas. Parallel trends were recorded in Scotland where the biggest decreases still occur in Greater Glasgow and C Scotland. There was modest growth in most rural areas, with the biggest increases in Grampian and the Highlands and Islands, especially in areas such as Shetland most affected by the oil boom.

The actual numbers involved in these rural increases are relatively small as compared both with those who live in or who have recently moved from large towns. Nevertheless, there ha. clearly been a reversal of rural population decline in the late 1960s and 1970s. Whether this is due to wider dispersal from city regions or a genuine pull towards greater job opportunities in small towns and villages is as yet uncertain. Champion (1981) has stressed the changing role of differential migration in these shifts in population. The 78 Districts of rural England in which an increase of over 10% was recorded for 1971–81 were also areas of net in-migration according to OPCS population estimates. In contrast, very high and persistent migrational losses occurred in Greater London and all Metropolitan Counties, and there is growing out-migration from other major towns and industrial areas. Moreover, a decline in the level of movement to the 'suburban counties' of the axial belt and C Scotland is reflected in a deceleration in population growth between the 1960s and 1970s with a marked fall in net in-migration.

Movements to rural areas appear to have been most marked from the late 1960s to the mid-1970s, but are still at a relatively high level as compared with the 1960s in remoter areas. The extent to which these focus on a few 'growth' points within quite large rural districts with relatively small populations, and are part of a general movement to smaller towns, is not yet established. Similarly, the extent to which in some areas movement is mainly for retirement or is related to long-distance commuting, awaits the evidence of the workplace and occupational tables of the

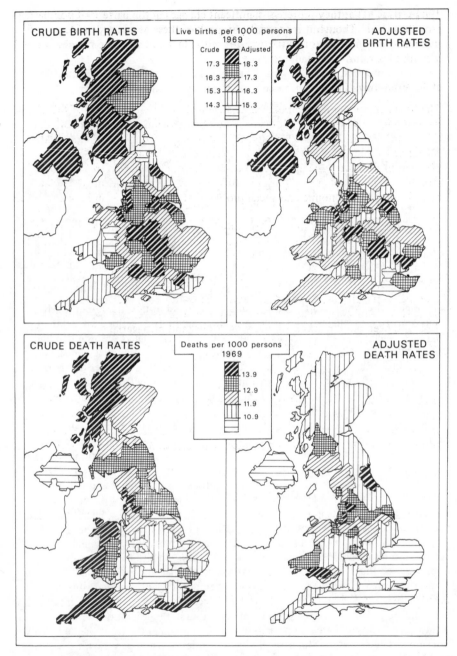

Figure 2.7   Birth- and death-rates, UK economic planning sub-regions, 1969

1981 census. That they represent significant changes in the pattern of population growth is clear. Though it is too early to speak of these as evidence of 'counter-urbanization', they point to a partial shift in the location of economic activity and a continuing return to the countryside.

II.4 Vital Trends

The broad components of population change reviewed in section II.3 of this chapter are resultants of three basic factors in population dynamics: births, deaths and migration. Variations in the fertility, mortality and morbidity of the population reflect economic and social conditions; they are also the outcome of present population structures and are determinants of future population trends and structure. Thus, vital and migrational differences are basic elements in explaining and planning for economic and social problems at both national and regional levels.

Birth-rates The rapid decline of birth-rate in all social classes and all regions of the UK was one of the most remarkable demographic features of the early twentieth century and the interwar years. While the reduction in family size was general, significant variations in fertility and family size remain between social classes and are found between the various parts of the UK. Glass and Grebenik (1954) showed that higher fertility persisted among wives of manual workers, despite the general decrease in family size. The tendency to a somewhat larger average family since 1945 has been more marked among professional and managerial classes, changing the progression of high social class/small family to low social class/large family which was characteristic up to the Second World War.

The 1961 census revealed that between couples of equivalent age of marriage, e.g. those married between ages 20–24, the average size for *all* durations of marriage among manual workers was higher than among non-manual workers. But the 1971 census showed that for couples marrying in the 1950s the range had narrowed (table 2.9), the number of children per marriage had fallen and the differential fertility between social classes had narrowed. Earlier, according to

TABLE 2.9

Variations in Family Size, Great Britain, 1971

Children per marriage by social class of husband

Duration of marriage in 1971	manual workers			non-manual workers			
	V unskilled	IV semi-skilled	III M skilled	I professional	II employers and managers	III N intermediate	ALL
15–19 years (married approx. 1951–5)	2.74	2.40	2.37	2.26	2.18	2.02	2.33
10–14 years (m. approx. 1956–60)	2.62	2.32	2.31	2.23	2.13	2.00	2.26

Source: Census (1971)

Glass and Grebenik (1954), 'The ratio of fertility of manual to non-manual groups, which has been around 1.4:1.0 for the marriages of the 1920s and early 1930s, fell to less than 1.2:1.0 for the marriages of the 1940s'.

While fertility among semi-skilled and unskilled workers has tended to stabilize at relatively low levels, that for employers and professional workers had, until recently, tended to rise since 1945. The *Population Investigation Committee*'s national survey of Britain (1967–8) observed little difference between social classes in the proportion of recently married couples adopting birth-control methods and noted that the gap between manual and non-manual groups had narrowed considerably over the previous twenty years (House of Commons 1971, 189).

This is reflected in a faster decline in births in the 1970s in manual than in non-manual classes. Moreover, in *all* social classes women who married from the mid-1960s have tended to delay child-bearing, though this is more marked in non-manual groups (Pearce and Britton, 1977). Secondly, the intervals between births of children has tended to become larger: the median for first birth was 20 months after marriage in 1971 but 30 months in 1977. Though this was higher in non-manual than manual groups the ratio of birth intervals, 1971–7, was very similar in all social classes. With a similar, though smaller, increase between first and second and third births, this trend will tend to reduce the size of completed family for women marrying in the late 1960s and 1970s (Britton 1980).

Geographical patterns of birth-rates substantiate the social differences in fertility within all cities. For example, on Merseyside, traditionally an area of high fertility, in the 1960s birth-rates were clearly zoned from high rates, 75% above national rates, in the central and inner residential areas of Liverpool and Bootle CBs, through moderate levels 50–75% above national average in intermediate areas, including both interwar corporation and private residential areas, to low values 20–25% above national average in outer areas of recent corporation and private housing estates (Pickett 1970A, 92–7). But there has been a general evening-out of birth-rates during the 1960s and seventies. Crude regional birth-rates ranged from 12.1 to 23.6 per thousand in 1969 (fig. 2.7), as compared with 16.3 per 1000 for England and Wales, 17.4 for Scotland and 21.4 for N Ireland. High crude birth-rates remain in the rural areas of N Ireland and Scotland which, despite heavy and long-continued out-movement of young adults and quite high proportions of older people, have relatively high levels of fertility. As Compton (1976) has shown, there are considerable disparities in birth-rate between Protestant and Roman Catholic communities in N Ireland, the Catholic birth-rate being over one-third higher, a fact reflected in regional patterns of fertility and natural change. Similarly, in industrial regions in C Scotland and the axial belt from London to S Lancashire and W Yorkshire manual-worker groups and younger population structures both seem to lead to rather higher birth-rates. In contrast, lower crude birth-rates are associated with the rural regions of Wales and N and S England, and, not surprisingly, with many of the retirement areas of N Wales, Southern and SW England. Thus, while in the past higher birth-rates prevailed in the north and west of Britain (especially Scotland and N Ireland), by the mid-1960s this differential had to some extent been ironed out. Indeed, the fall in birth-rate since 1969 to 11.6 per 1,000 for England and Wales, 12.0 for Scotland, and 16.5 for N Ireland in 1977 (UK 11.8) seems to have affected the North relatively more than the Midlands and South.

However, crude birth-rates are affected by the age structure of the population and the Registrar General's adjusted rates allowing for this show the regional position more clearly. High rates still characterize N Ireland and the Highlands and Islands of Scotland. The highest adjusted birth-rates in England and Wales and S Scotland tend to occur in the suburban and peripheral areas of the large cities and industrial areas, a feature of growing significance in the 1970s. Adjusted rates narrow the overall range of birth-rates and certain rural areas, for example in N Wales, SW England and N Yorkshire, achieve moderate or above-average birth-rates when age structure and the small number of total births are taken into account.

Death-rates The patterns of mortality in the UK, though offering many parallels, are in certain respects more clear-cut than those of fertility. General mortality-rates and those from many specific diseases are above average in many urban areas and below average in rural districts. There is also a general regional gradient from relatively high death-rates in NW Britain to relatively low rates in SE Britain in areas of equivalent character, whether urban or rural.

Some of the highest death-rates in the UK are found in association with poor environments and higher-than-average incidence of social and economic problems. Many such conditions occur in the large nineteenth-century industrial towns and, in turn, within all urban areas there is still a marked gradient between unhealthy inner areas and the suburbs, partly due to environmental conditions, partly to social and demographic characteristics. The average risk of death in Salford, one of the highest mortality areas, was 33% higher than in Bournemouth, one of the lowest, in 1969. Similar contrasts occur between inner urban areas and the outer suburbs, in which there are also substantial differences between local authority overspill areas, with higher rates, and lower mortality in private residential areas. The larger 1974 Districts conceal many such variations. Yet, even though the range has narrowed to 8.9–16.9 per thousand (or 10.5–14.2, adjusted) at county level and from 6.6 to 18.6 (6.4–16.4 adjusted) at District level and the precise distribution of high and low values has changed, the higher rates are still found in industrial cities (Salford at the top) and the lowest in the residential South.

TABLE 2.10

Male Standardized Mortality Rates by Socio-economic Class, England and Wales, 1921–72 (England and Wales = 100)

Class	1921–3 (age 20–64)	1930–2	1949–53	1959–63 (age 15–64)	1970–2
I	82	90	86	76	77
II	94	94	92	81	81
III	95	97	101	100	104
IV	101	102	104	103	113
V	125	111	118	143	137

Class I = professional
II = employers and managers
III = intermediate and junior non-manual (N); skilled manual (M)
IV = semi-skilled manual
V = unskilled manual
Source: Social Trends 6 (1975), Table 7.1, 26

Many contrasts are, however, generic rather than regional in character. Clearly, different social classes have very different mortality experience (table 2.10). Despite the reduction of mortality differentials in all social classes, due doubtless to the progressively better health, dietary and housing conditions of the lower classes, a considerable range remains, involving many factors, social, environmental and, perhaps, genetic. Among indices of class differentials in mortality experience, infant mortality, regarded as a sensitive measure, was 2 to 2.5 times higher among children of socio-economic class V parents than of class I (table 2.11). In 1973, on the basis of data for Scotland, it was twice as great among social class V as in class I in the 1960s (stillbirths 16.2 and 7.4 per 1,000 respectively). In Great Britain infant mortality in social classes IV and V exceeded that in classes I and II by 73% in 1970–2 (OPCS 1978). Factors quoted include the higher incidence of premature births, linked to the earlier age of child-bearing among working-class mothers, more closely-spaced pregnancies, poorer ante- and post-natal care, and greater risk and poorer treatment of infection in children such as bronchitis and gastro-enteritis, all of which are often coupled with poor and overcrowded housing conditions.

TABLE 2.11

Infant Mortality, England and Wales, 1964–5

	Socio-economic classes		
Infant deaths per 1,000 live births	I and II	III	IV and V
Neonatal	9.2	11.8	13.2
Post-natal	3.5	5.4	7.6

Source: Kelsall (1967), 49

The pattern of crude death-rates by planning sub-regions (fig. 2.7) partly reflects areas with a high proportion of old people, for example in NW Scotland, N and SW Wales, SW and Southern England; when adjusted for age-structure, these relatively high rates are modified in most cases.

Above-average adjusted death-rates pick out C Scotland, especially the Glasgow region, the industrial NE of England, a belt from S Lancashire through W Yorkshire to Humberside, and the S Wales coalfield. The W Midlands have generally modest rates, though mortality is higher in the Potteries and the W Midlands conurbation. In general, the rural Midlands and the Welsh border, E Anglia, SE and SW England have low or moderate rates, though the higher figures for Greater London underline the less healthy and poorer social conditions of inner urban areas.

The regional patterns of general mortality and of morbidity of particular diseases have been fully mapped and analysed by Howe (1970), whose maps, using standardized mortality-rates, support the more general picture given in fig. 2.7. He observes that in the 320 administrative units mapped, 53 areas had very high male mortality ratios of which only 4 were in the London area, the rest being in N and W Britain, with the Glasgow and S Lancashire areas having the greatest concentration of high rates. While the pattern of female mortality differs in detail it is similar to that for men, though there is a rather less marked concentration of high rates in Greater London, NE England, S Lancashire and S Wales.

A recent analysis has shown that such regional differences in mortality persist (Chilvers 1978). Mortality from all causes is higher than the national rate in conurbations and large towns (over 100,000). In general and for many individual diseases — especially heart and chest — levels of mortality are lower in rural areas and small towns. Secondly, there is a marked regional gradient from north to south in Britain, with the rural Midland, E Anglia, the SE and SW below the national level of general mortality, but other regions above it.

Infant mortality One of the most telling demographic indicators of social and environmental conditions and, indeed, of overall living standards, is the rate of infant mortality. Not only are there marked class differences in its national incidence (table 2.11), but there are pronounced regional differences (Coates and Rawstron 1971, 227–35). Despite the fall in infant mortality in the UK since 1945, in continuance of a marked downward trend since the mid-Victorian period (fig. 2.2), which has reduced rates from around 31 per 1,000 in 1917 to about 13.2 per 1,000 in 1979 in England and Wales (12.4 in Scotland and 14.8 in N Ireland), significant regional variations persist. For example, whereas the infant mortality rates in the central Clydeside conurbation in 1969 were 24.2 per 1,000, they ranged from 19.8 to 14.0 in the Scottish New Towns. Similarly, there was considerable variation at sub-regional level in England and Wales, the highs (24 per 1,000) being experienced in the SE Lancashire and NE Cheshire (SELNEC) and Merseyside conurbations and in the central and eastern S Wales valleys, while in the Essex sub-region the rate was only 13 per 1,000. In 1978, in England and Wales, most health authority regions in the north, the W Midlands and Wales were at or above average. But in the smaller area health authorities the position is more complex: while most urban and industrial areas have above-average infant mortality, the record of many large provincial cities — Newcastle, Leeds, Sheffield and Liverpool, for example — is good. In contrast many inner areas of London have relatively high rates, pushing the regional figures for NE Thames above average.

Ironically, those areas with the poorest mortality and health records are still frequently those with the poorest medical and health services (Smith 1979). Despite the overall improvement in provision under the *National Health Acts* of 1946–8, the National Health and Social Services have not yet succeeded in levelling out substantial regional inequalities. Thus the average number of patients on general practitioners' lists tend to be higher in industrial towns in the North than in towns of the Midlands and South, and the list is bigger in poor inner-city residential areas than in the middle-class suburbs (Coates and Rawstron 1971, 188). There is a strong case for positive discrimination in favour of such areas in the provision of social services.

Life-expectancy These mortality differentials are summed up in the considerable variations in life-expectancy between regional health authorities (RHAs). Using standardized mortality rates in a life table Gardner and Donnan (1977) have shown that in the mid-1970s all southern RHAs had above-average life-expectancy for both males (69.9–71.3 years) and females (76.3–76.9), whereas those of the Midlands, Wales and all more northern areas were below average, 67.9–69.4 for men and 74.3–75.4 for women. Male and female averages for England and Wales were 69.5 and 75.7 years, respectively.

II.5 Migration

After a flurry of movement in the early war years involving 19% of the population
of England in non-local moves in 1940 (7.5 million) this mobility had dropped to
7.4% by 1950 (3.2 million moves). According to the figures of residential mobility,
gathered by the sample census of 1966, the percentage of movers respectively over
one and five years had fallen to 4.7 and 4.8; moreover, only 29% of the non-local
moves involved distances of over 64 km. Thus, though the total volume of
migration increased, there was much greater growth of short-distance movement,
strengthening the ties between cities and their hinterlands and leading to a much
greater volume of daily journeys to work, to school, to shop and to share in all city
services.

TABLE 2.12

Regional Mobility, GB, 1970–1 and 1966–71

Regions	Migrants 1970–1 (000s)			Migrants 1966–71 (000s)		
	(1) Total region	(2) from local	$\frac{2}{1}\%$	(4) Total region	(5) from local	$\frac{5}{4}\%$
Northern	349.5	299.2	86(84)	1,112.7	947.4	85(85)
Yorks. and Humberside	505.3	422.5	86(86)	1,577.8	1,363.0	86(86)
North West	697.5	607.3	87(88)	2,135.6	1,865.1	87(89)
E Midlands	339.8	271.3	80(81)	1,015.8	821.7	81(83)
W Midlands	536.5	454.2	85(85)	1,650.3	1,400.5	85(86)
E Anglia	170.4	131.7	77(76)	479.7	374.2	78(80)
South East	2,004.7	1,773.7	89(89)	5,698.6	5,029.7	89(90)
South West	413.5	326.2	79(81)	1,167.6	931.2	80(82)
Wales	245.4	204.4	83(84)	765.7	642.5	85(85)
Scotland	606.1	546.1	90(NA)	1,810.3	1,643.8	91(NA)

The tabulations are on a 10% sample base. Comparative figures for 1966 are given in brackets
in columns 3 and 6: 'local' refers to the number of migrants not moving outside the region in
which they were enumerated.

The figures for Scotland are not comparable with those for the less extensive English regions.

Source: Census 1971, Great Britain Migration Tables, Part I

Inter-regional migration Though of considerable importance to regional variations
in population growth, net migration conceals both the volume and patterns of
movement which are difficult to study from British census sources before 1961,
when information concerning changes in residence was first collected. Unlike many
European countries the UK has no system of continuous registration of personal or
residential mobility, though for wartime and early postwar years the National
Register could be used for this purpose (Newton and Jeffrey 1951). Contrasts in
migration between town and country or between inner and outer zones or urban
regions are part of a mobility continuum which involves not only inter- and intra-
regional residential migration but also considerable personal mobility in all sections
of the community. Up to 1961 the only census source of information on migration
flows was derived from birth-place statistics which do not permit direct study of
movement over specific time periods. In its 10% sample the 1961 census enquired

about change of address over the year prior to the enumeration. The 1966 and 1971 censuses extended the question to include change of residence over a five-year, as well as a one-year, period prior to the census (table 2.12). These data permit analysis of in-, out- and gross migration in varying regional detail down to local authority areas and may be cross-tabulated by age, sex, occupational group, etc.

Net inter-regional mobility The relatively small net balance of migration in all regions in both 1960–1 and 1965–6 concealed considerable in- and out-movements; indeed gross migration usually exceeded net by over 10 to 1 and for many regions was a good deal higher (table 2.13). It is not easy to summarize inter-regional movements, even at the very general level of the UK economic planning regions, since it is difficult to link these various components to the population at risk. The scale, direction and balance of the migration streams are much what one would expect from general population trends. Net balances are small, mostly under 5 per 1,000 of the resident population, but gross migration indices for population aged one year and over exceed 40 per 1,000 in some areas (table 2.13). The greatest mobility rates in 1960–1 occurred in E Anglia and the SW region, followed by the E and W Midlands. Though by far the greatest numbers moved into and from the SE region, its gross migration rates were relatively small, especially in Greater London. Many regions had very similar degrees of movement and very small differences between inward and outward rates of migration as shown by modest net balances. Such features well exemplify the dictum that every migration flow produces a counter-flow. Hence, the differentials in migration rates between such regions as the NW, Yorks. and Humberside, and Wales differ little from the then 'healthy' growth areas of the W Midlands or even the SE.

In 1965–6 migration rates confirmed the attraction of E Anglia, the SW and the E Midlands. The most sluggish were those for the NW and Scotland and, in terms of migration rates, Greater London, despite the latter's large volume of both in- and out-movement. The migration rates to the development areas were generally higher than in 1960–1; in particular, the inward balance of movement to Wales suggests that development area policies in the 1960s were beginning to make an impact on population trends. Scotland's very low rate of inward migration and considerable net loss remained, however.

It is not possible to show the complexity of inter-regional movements on a single map, but the balance of migration of population for the period 1966–71 gives a graphic picture of both the essential mechanism and the resultants of such movements (fig. 2.8). The inset map of net migration rates and the actual net flows are a clear commentary upon the continuing decline of the northern and older industrial regions of Britain. Inter-regional migration may be seen to be not so much a direct transfer from areas of loss to areas of gain but rather a 'shunting' movement culminating in the transfer of considerable numbers of people to only four major regions: E Anglia, the E Midlands, the SE and the SW. Within the South East, migration has increased rapidly since the war by movement from inner London. By the 1960s, this involved Greater London, the Outer Metropolitan Area (OMA) and the Outer South East (OSE) in rehousing, in private residential schemes and in a second generation of New Towns and overspill schemes mainly located in the three adjacent planning regions.

Those regions which gained population by residential migration in the 1960s all reflect the same basic features. The SW gained from all other regions, not only

TABLE 2.13

Inter-regional migration, GB, 1960–1 and 1965–6

Planning region	All ages above one year (000s)						Net balance of working age 15–59			Migration rates of resident population (per 1,000)							
	1960–1			1965–6			1965–6			1960–1				1965–6			
	in	out	net	in	out	net	male	female	total	in	out	gross	net	in	out	gross	net
Northern	35.9	45.6	−9.7	45.3	48.1	−2.8	−0.8	−1.2	−2.0	11.0	14.0	25.0	−3.0	13.6	14.5	28.1	−0.9
Yorks. and Humberside	53.4	60.8	−7.4	66.4	66.0	+0.4	+1.0	−0.8	+0.2	11.5	13.1	24.6	−1.6	13.9	13.8	27.7	+0.1
North West	61.9	68.9	−7.0	70.5	72.9	−2.4	−0.4	−2.2	−2.6	9.4	10.5	19.9	−1.1	10.5	10.9	21.4	−0.4
E Midlands	55.9	48.6	+7.3	67.4	55.6	+11.7	+4.3	+3.3	+7.6	18.0	15.7	33.7	+2.4	20.6	17.0	37.7	+3.6
W Midlands	63.5	61.4	+2.0	66.0	70.5	−4.5	−0.3	−3.0	−3.3	13.4	12.9	26.3	+0.4	13.2	14.1	27.3	−0.9
South East	173.3	153.2	+20.2	174.6	194.8	−20.1	−3.8	−0.7	−4.5	10.7	9.4	20.1	+1.2	10.3	11.4	21.7	−1.2
Greater London	61.7	59.7	+2.1	60.7	78.7	−18.0	−3.1	−1.9	−5.0	7.6	9.9	17.5	−2.3	7.8	10.1	17.9	−2.3
OMA	111.6	93.5	+18.1	52.0	60.1	−8.1	−1.9	−1.8	−3.7	11.5	13.3	24.8	−1.8	10.4	12.0	22.4	−1.6
Rest				61.9	55.9	+5.9	+1.2	+3.1	+4.3	16.1	14.5	30.6	+1.5	14.9	13.4	28.3	+1.5
E Anglia	35.0	30.8	+4.2	48.1	36.1	+12.0	+3.0	+3.9	+6.9	23.8	20.9	44.7	+2.9	30.4	22.8	53.3	+7.6
South West	87.0	67.7	+19.3	93.2	72.6	+20.7	+4.1	+6.3	+10.3	25.5	19.8	45.4	+5.7	25.6	20.0	45.6	+5.7
Wales	33.9	38.7	−4.8	36.7	36.0	+0.7	−0.5	−0.3	−0.8	12.8	14.6	27.5	−1.8	13.6	13.3	26.9	+0.3
Scotland	27.4	51.6	−24.2	37.0	52.7	−15.7	−6.6	−5.3	−11.9	5.3	10.0	15.3	−4.7	7.1	10.1	17.2	−3.0
GB	627.1	627.1	–	705.2	705.2	–	–	–	–	–	–	–	–	–	–	–	–

Source: Long Term Population Distribution, GB: A Study (HMSO, 1971), Appendix 2, Tables 1a and 1e

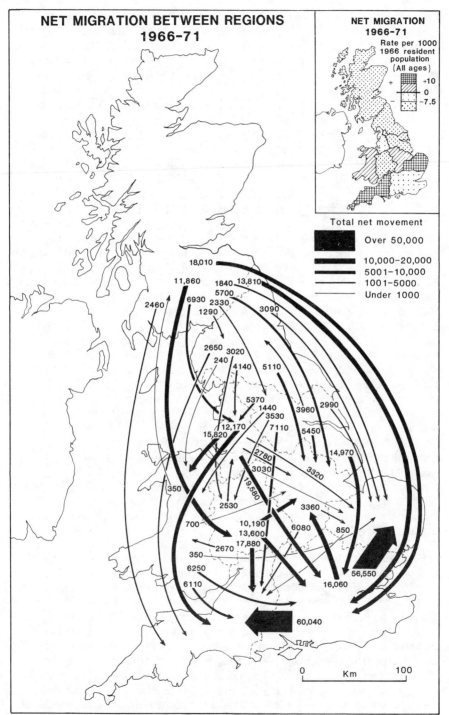

Figure 2.8   Net inter-regional migration, UK, 1966–71

from gains by outward movement from the metropolitan area but due also to its
own attractions in the Bristol—Severnside growth area and in the rural and coastal
retirement areas of Devon and Cornwall (Law and Warnes 1976), a fact reflected in
the age structure of the migration (table 2.15). However, in 1966—71 over 90% of
the region's gains were from the SE, W Midlands and NW. E Anglia gained from all
other regions except the SW. The E Midlands similarly gained from all regions,
except E Anglia and the SW, to both of which there were small net losses. The SE
epitomizes many of the features of both intra- and inter-regional movement. While
there were large net losses from the Greater London sub-region to the OSE and
adjacent regions, it attracted large numbers in the 15—24 age-group, a feature also
found in the OMA. London's labour market lost 400,000 people in 1966—71, of
which 325,000 went to the rest of the South East (Kennett 1978). Residential
dispersal from the centre to the periphery is seen in the gain in all age-groups of the
OSE sub-region which is comparable in this respect to E Anglia and the SW.

All other regions suffered a net loss of population by migration, though this did
not occur in every age-group. The W Midlands' losses were previously mainly to
adjacent regions, the NW and E Midlands, and to the 'gain' areas of E Anglia and the
SW, but by 1966—71 it gained only from Scotland, N England and Yorkshire and
Humberside. The NW gained from other regions of N England, from Scotland and
the W Midlands, but lost to all other regions; while Wales gained from the NW, W
Midlands, the North, Scotland and E Anglia. Those with the weakest attraction in
this phase were Yorks. and Humberside, which lost to all regions except Scotland;
the North, which lost to all save Scotland and Yorks. and Humberside; and
Scotland, which lost population to every other region and in every age-group. As
Champion (1976) showed, these tendencies persisted in the last decade. Scotland,
the three regions of northern England, the W Midlands and SE have all continued to
lose population by migration. The only regions of consistent gain are the E
Midlands, E Anglia and the SW, though Wales — having staunched the outflow
which has characterized it for much of the century — actually had a small gain by
migration in 1966—71, a gain due in part to retirement migration to N Wales.
Within all regions, however, a factor of increasing importance in population
redistribution is the movement of people out of the inner areas of large cities, a
factor which is now giving cause for considerable concern in relation to age structure
(section III.2), housing and social structure (sections III.3 and III.4). Moreover,
employment is being decentralized, with 85% of SMLAs affected, markedly so in
the larger cities (Kennett 1978).

Age-selective migration Population migration is highly age-selective. All recent
studies of migration in the UK confirm the tendency of young Britons to be more
migratory than the population as a whole. There is a strong movement of school-
leavers and people in their late teens and early twenties from both rural areas and
stagnating industrial regions of limited employment opportunities. In areas of
residential development accessible to large towns, rural out-migration is offset by
in-migration of young families. But the inner residential areas of the cities (the
'cores'), especially London, are generally a zone of population loss mainly of the
15—44 age-groups, partly offset by an influx of overseas immigrants and of single
young people, including students. Cumulatively, such differences contribute to
striking contrasts between the age structure of migrants and that of the population
as a whole (table 2.14). The 15—24 age-group is by far the most mobile with

TABLE 2.14

Age Structure of Inter-regional Migrants and Total Population, GB, 1961 and 1971

	Per cent of age-group				All ages
	1–14	15–24	25–44	45+	1+
Population 1961	22	13	27	38	100
Migrants 1960–1	23	23	35	19	100
Population 1971	22	15	24	39	100
Migrants 1970–1	24	27	30	19	100

Source: Census 1961; Census 1971

migration-rates in 1970–1 35% above that of the next most mobile 10-year group, 25–34 years. On the limited evidence of the 1960–1 and 1970–1 data, migration rates seem to be rising more quickly in the 15–24 age-group than in any other. Inasmuch as there has been a considerable increase in the number of people in full-time higher education, a proportion of this may be ascribed to temporary migration but there is much evidence to support the belief that such migration leads to permanent movement away from home, especially in the case of those moving from rural areas or depressed industrial regions.

Such age-selective migration is reflected both in the structure of the migration itself and in the age structure of both sender and receiver areas. The clear-cut losses of 1960–1 in virtually all age-groups from the three northern regions of England and from Scotland and Wales had been ameliorated by 1965–6 (fig. 2.9). By 1970–1 the trend to loss was reasserting itself in the NW and in Yorks. and Humberside. Scotland alone showed a net migration loss in every age-group throughout the period and this was quite severe for the young and mature age-groups of 15–44 years, representing a substantial draining of vigorous, working-age population of both sexes from the region. This loss of the active, youthful population persisted in the NW and for Wales, despite a general slowing down of the migration flow in the mid-1960s. Indeed in the NW there was an increase of one-third in the net loss from the 15–24 group between 1960–1 and 1965–6, and from 1966–71 the losses from this region were double what they had been in 1961–6. The population situation of Yorks. and Humberside, encouraging in the mid-1960s in that loss in all three younger age-groups (0–44 years) was arrested, reverted to the former pattern of high losses in the younger age-groups by 1970–1. But in the W Midlands there was a reversal of the modest gains in the younger age-groups by the mid-1960s, though the losses in the 15–24 groups were mainly female. The 1971 census confirmed the change in this region's fortunes by showing an increased net loss of population in all age-groups, 1970–1 (fig. 2.9), a trend confirmed by table 2.15.

In contrast, the regions of gain not only added considerable numbers of population but, apart from the SW, had their greatest gains among the under-45s. It is clear that E Anglia and the SW in particular, and the E Midlands to an extent, were closely linked with the SE in an age-selective redistribution of population. In the SW the growing dominance of migration by the age-groups over 45 is reflected in the fact that by 1965–6 over one-third of the net migration gain was in the

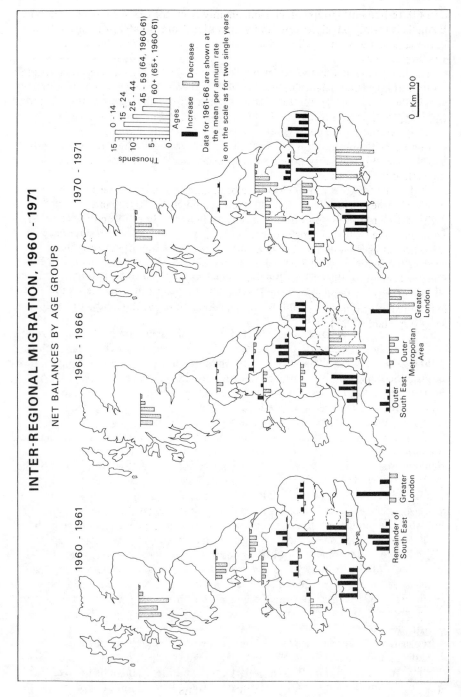

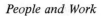

Figure 2.9   Inter-regional migration by age-groups, GB economic planning regions, 1960–71

over-60 'retirement' groups which came mainly from the SE, W Midlands and NW.
E Anglia is mainly a recipient of family migration from Greater London, reflected
in the large net gains in the 25–44 and 0–14 groups and the smaller gains of
15–24-year-olds.

The key to much selective redistribution lies in the SE region. Despite a striking
reversal of migration balance between 1961 and 1966, there was still a considerable
gain in the 15–24 age-group, the migrants coming from all regions of the UK and
from overseas. However, by 1965–6 major out-movement had developed in all
other age-groups with a considerable overspill movement of young families to
E Anglia (the 0–44 year group). That to the SW was dominated by the over-45s,
and the over-60s were very important, especially women. These trends had
intensified by 1970–1.

Within the SE gross movements have been almost as large as the gross movements
within all other regions (e.g. 304,000 as compared with 370,000 in 1965–6). This
massive dispersal of families from the centre of Greater London and the OMA to the
periphery (the OSE) involves two distinct types of mover: first, a residential
migration of ages 1–14 and 25+; secondly, retirement migration of the over-60s to
the south coast in particular, reflected in the fact that one-third of the flow from
Greater London to the OSE in 1965–6 was of those over 60 years.

The effects on population structure may be derived from the relationship
between the regional net migration balance and the gross movements in each
age-group (table 2.15).

TABLE 2.15

Regional Migration Gain or Loss 1961–71, by Major Age-groups, GB (net balances by age-group in 000s)

Region	5–14	15–24	25–44	45–59	60+	All ages 5+
A. 1961–6						
Northern	−12.1	−14.5	−20.3	−6.0	+1.7	−51.2
Yorks. and Humberside	−1.8	−6.3	−8.2	−4.2	−4.8	−25.2
North West	−1.4	−9.5	−7.2	−4.6	−5.8	−28.5
E Midlands	+6.8	+2.8	+16.8	+3.4	+1.8	+31.6
W Midlands	−0.2	−6.1	−1.9	−8.1	−8.3	−24.6
E Anglia	+8.4	+3.7	+14.8	+8.3	+12.5	+47.7
South East	−14.8	+34.0	−18.0	−13.0	−32.8	−44.6
South West	+13.6	+6.1	+25.2	+21.5	+29.7	+96.1
Wales	+1.5	−10.3	−1.2	+2.7	+6.0	−1.2
B. 1966–71						
Northern	−5.2	−15.3	−8.1	−0.7	+2.3	−27.0
Yorks. and Humberside	−5.0	−17.7	−15.9	−3.8	−2.3	−44.7
North West	−1.9	−20.5	−5.3	−5.9	−8.9	−42.4
E Midlands	+6.7	+3.0	+16.9	+2.0	+0.7	+29.3
W Midlands	−5.0	−7.3	−10.1	−9.3	−11.2	−43.0
E Anglia	+12.4	+9.5	+22.7	+10.9	+16.4	+71.8
South East	−15.8	+47.3	−24.9	−23.6	−47.6	−64.6
South West	+12.5	+11.4	+23.1	+24.5	+42.3	+113.9
Wales	+1.3	−10.3	+1.6	+6.0	+8.3	+6.8

Source: Champion (1976), table IV

Two aspects of migration have shaped trends in the distribution and structure of population since 1945. First, fluctuations in *net overseas migration* have had considerable impact at both national and local level. Secondly, *differential inter-regional movement*, the net resultants of which explain much of the regional variations in population growth, is of considerable importance in its effects on regional structure and future population trends. Though in demographic terms both have much in common, their social impact is very different: thus each will be discussed in turn.

II.6 Immigration from Overseas

General review Despite its importance, precise information on the scale and regional impact of immigration is limited. Immigration statistics leave many gaps, while census data on immigration are defective in a number of ways. British census tables of birthplace before 1971 show nothing of the date of movement and give nationality but not ethnic origins. Moreover, the census probably under-enumerated the overseas-born in both 1961 and, especially, in the 10% sample census of 1966. Furthermore, it was difficult to distinguish persons born overseas of British parents. The questions in the 1971 census concerning place of birth, nationality and place of birth of parents and year of first entry into Britain of overseas-born have provided the basis for a fuller and more accurate picture of immigration from census sources.

There have been three phases in postwar immigration to the UK. Between 1945–55 renewed emigration to the Dominions led to slight net migration losses, despite a considerable gain of European refugees, especially those of Polish origin. Nevertheless, during this period England and Wales gained by migration, not least because of continuing immigration from Eire (fig. 2.2). After 1955, immigration from the New Commonwealth increased considerably, leading to a relatively large net inward movement of 479,000 in 1958–62. Rising labour demands, especially in the early 1960s, had much to do with this influx which produced net gains of 45,000 in 1958. This rose to 172,000 in the peak year of 1961, leading to restriction of movement under the *Commonwealth Immigrants Act* (1962). This Act created a graded system of employment vouchers which immigrants were required to hold to obtain entry: 'A' vouchers were issued to those who had jobs to come to, 'B' vouchers were for those with particular needed skills or qualifications (such as nurses or doctors), and 'C' vouchers were issued to unskilled workers. Preference was given from the outset to A and B categories. C vouchers were officially discontinued from 1965, and the policy of selective recruitment of highly-qualified persons was confirmed by new regulations in 1968.

The 1962 Act allowed dependants of immigrants already in the country freedom of entry, though this was tightened up under the 1968 *Commonwealth Immigrants Act*. Since 1962, therefore, the emphasis has shifted from the immigration of workers to their families and dependants: thus, in 1969 of 36,557 Commonwealth immigrants 29,459 were dependants. In 1968 250,000 dependants were estimated to be eligible for entry into the UK, mostly from India and Pakistan (Eversley and Sukedo 1969). A further group of coloured Commonwealth immigrants are the holders of British passports, mainly East Africans of Asian origin, the estimates of whom vary considerably: for example, estimates of the potential numbers involved in expulsions from Uganda varied from 23,000 to over

50,000, against the 26,000 who had arrived in Britain around the expiry of the expulsion deadline in November 1972. The 1971 *Immigration Act* restricted acceptance to those with UK passports or families of those already in the UK, while the 1982 *British Nationality Act* has further tightened up on entry.

In relation to the total population of the UK, the increase of immigrants, more particularly of coloured Commonwealth immigrants, is not large (table 2.16); but it has led to considerable changes in the characteristics of the overseas-born population of the UK since 1945 and, in some localities, has had very marked social and demographic consequences. As compared with about 1% overseas born in 1931 (perhaps 1.5% allowing for those whose birthplace was not stated), the increase in GB to 1,053,200 (2.1%) in 1951, 1,507,600 (2.9%) by 1961, to 1,876,300 (3.5%) by 1966 and to 3,100,000 (5.8%) by 1971 represents a considerable change. In 1966 less than half the 1.88m people of overseas birth in Britain were coloured (852,750), a figure which was estimated to be 1,030,000 by 1971; it is around these figures that most of the debate on immigration has focused. It is difficult to estimate precisely the numbers of coloured population, since this also involves children born to immigrants in the UK. It has been suggested that by 1981 822,000–839,000 children be added to the 943,000 people from the New Commonwealth recorded in the 1971 census. Such figures indicate a total of about 1.49 million of New Commonwealth and Pakistan birth in GB in 1971 (2.7% of total population), about 1.64m in mid-1976 (3.5% of the total) (Rose *et al* 1969, Runnymede Trust 1980) and 1.96–2.03m by 1981 (*Social Trends* 1981, *Population Trends* 16 1979).

Distribution
The problem is not primarily one of overall numbers of immigrants, but rather of their proportionate distribution. Like most immigrant communities, past and present, coloured immigrants tend to concentrate in relatively few areas. In 1951 the greater part of the overseas-born population of the UK lived in London and SE England, though at that time these were chiefly European-born. Since that time the overseas-born have increased much more rapidly than the population as a whole and have become even more concentrated in distribution. While the SE planning region (including Greater London) was by far the main focus of coloured immigrants, considerable increases had taken place in the W Midlands and, especially of Indians and Pakistanis, in the NW, Yorks. and Humberside, and the E Midlands (table 2.17). By 1971 these proportions remained much the same. While the percentage of New Commonwealth immigrants in the conurbations had fallen slightly, it had done so at about the same rate as the total population.

By far the greater proportion and the highest densities of coloured immigrants are to be found in the inner areas of the major cities, particularly metropolitan boroughs and the W Midlands conurbation. Every local authority with over 5% coloured population in 1966 was in Greater London (Coates and Rawstron 1971, 122–73). In 1971 eight areas of Greater London had over 20,000 New Commonwealth-born residents (with a total in London of 476,000 or 6.4% of its population), but only 4 other provincial cities did, forming between 4.9 and 8.2% of their populations. The highest rates of increase in the 1960s were in a few areas of Greater London and other major cities, so that the degree of concentration is becoming even more marked at the local level. In 1966, 16,770 (5.6%) of the population of Ealing was from New Commonwealth countries, but in Northcote

TABLE 2.16

Estimated Population of Major Immigrant Groups, England and Wales, 1966–86 (in 000s)

Area of origin	1966 Born overseas	Born in UK	Total	1971	1981	1986 Low fertility estimate	High fertility estimate
India	180.4	43.2	223.6	377	579	768	890
Pakistan	109.6	10.1	119.7	211	306	408	485
Ceylon	12.9	3.2	16.1	NA	NA	NA	NA
Jamaica	188.1	85.7	273.8	343	411	474	529
Other Caribbean	129.8	50.5	180.3	229	293	341	375
W Africa (former Br.)	43.1	7.6	50.7	68	80	83	94
Far East	47.0	13.0	60.0	NA	NA	NA	NA
Total	710.9	213.3	924.2	1,228	1,669	2,074	2,373

NA = Not available
The estimates exclude Indians and Pakistanis of British origin.
For 1971 and 1981 the estimates are based on low fertility assumptions.
Source: Rose *et al* (1969), tables 10.2 and 30.1

Ward 31% of the population was coloured (Deakin *et al* 1970). Even with such a high proportion of immigrants and the widespread belief that this was a predominantly Indian area, half the households surveyed were European. While Glass (1960, 41) argued that these concentrations did not then constitute ghettos, the continuing inflow and considerable concentration of coloured immigrants into such areas *is* of concern. While Ealing's New Commonwealth population increased to 33,000 in 1971 (11.1%), the Southall district, with a population of about 70,000 in 1976, has an immigrant population of 20–30,000, most of whom belong to Sikh families from the N Punjab, as compared with only 2,000 Commonwealth immigrants in 1961, 1,600 of whom were Indian-born. It has been suggested that other parts of the Borough of Ealing are developing marked concentrations of immigrants, for example Acton Town, but some parts of the Borough have scarcely any immigrants (Dalton and Seaman 1973); such sharp spatial contrast within a town is typical of this problem. Studies of mainly West Indian working-class areas of Birmingham show that over half the enumeration districts of the CB had no West Indians, while 30% of this group was concentrated into wards in which they formed over 15% of the total population (Jones 1967). At such a stage of assimilation this is, perhaps, to be expected; historical parallels may be seen in the segregation of Irish immigrants in the mid-nineteenth century and of Jewish immigrants from Eastern Europe in the late nineteenth century. But difficulties arising from colour and custom, aggravated by unemployment, housing shortages and problems of education, hinder rapid acceptance by or assimilation into the community at large.

Structure and trends in immigrant populations Immigration is highly age-selective, particularly in the early stages when it is dominated by young persons, especially men. Dependants usually follow to give a more normal age and sex structure to the immigrant community. In the case of the Commonwealth immigration of the late

1950s and 1960s this process is still in train, with consequent effects on the
demographic and social structure and on fertility patterns.

A large-scale survey of Irish, and Old and New Commonwealth immigrants in
1961 showed that 75% were men, 62% were between 18 and 34, and 83% under 45,
as compared with 62% in the population at large; only half the men were married as
compared with 73% of the population over 19 years in England and Wales (Krausz
1971, 45, 146). These characteristics were still apparent in the remarkably low
proportions of over-45s and the predominance of mature adults of 25–44 in the
early 1960s. The effects of immigrant births and the arrival of dependants in the
mid- and late 1960s are apparent in the changes between 1966 and 1971 (table
2.18). While the female/male ratios are low, especially among Pakistani (39:100 in
1971) and, to a lesser extent, Indian and W African groups, a trend towards
normality may be seen in lower sex ratios among the 1961–6 arrivals and especially
among those coming between 1966 and 1971. The considerable number of
dependants is leading to a further balancing of the population structure. The large
number of women among West Indian immigrants to London in the 1960s was
reflected in very low male/female ratios.

The 1971 Census revealed a very youthful structure in New Commonwealth
populations, with 41% aged under 15 and 49% aged 15–44, as compared with 24
and 39% respectively in Great Britain. This helped to promote a high rate of
natural increase. It is difficult to compare the fertility of immigrants with British
rates, since most immigrant families are still in the process of formation. 1961
census data suggested that for marriages of comparable duration, immigrant fertility
was generally higher than among native-born English; but the highest rates were
among Irish women (40% above the English rates) while those for coloured
immigrant women were 20% above native-born (Thompson 1969). There is some
evidence that the differential is lower among completed immigrant families and not
significantly different from British-born people of comparable social class. Much
has been made of a survey 1969–73 by the Ministry of Health and Social Security
showing that 11.5% of all births in England and Wales were to foreign-born mothers
but, of the 11.5%, 2.9% were to Irish mothers and 2.9% to other white immigrants,
leaving 5.7% of births to coloured immigrants. True, in areas of high concentration
of immigrants much higher figures obtained; e.g. in Lambeth and Brent (1969),
1 in 3 births were to mothers from the New Commonwealth; in some parts of the
Midlands similarly high proportions were found, e.g. 1 in 4.5 in Wolverhampton and
1 in 6 in Birmingham and Leicester, while in Huddersfield the figure was 1 in 5.
How long these proportions will persist depends partly on age structure. In 1971,
however, as compared with the 5.6% of the British population who are of New
Commonwealth origin (1.49 millions) 3.7% were aged 15–19, 4.0% 10–14, 4.7%
5–9 and 6.6% under 5.

With many immigrant women in the younger, child-bearing ages, such crude
statistics can be very misleading. Limited calculations of fertility rates among
immigrant families suggest that they 'are larger by about one-third than those of the
English population' (Krausz 1971, 49; Moser 1972, 20–30). Studies by the OPCS,
based on data showing the country of birth of parents of new babies, data collected
since 1969, indicate that in 1974 6.2% of all births in GB were to parents one or
both of whom were of New Commonwealth origin, as compared with an estimated
4.5% in 1966 and 5.9 in 1971. With a youthful population, death-rates among the
New Commonwealth population in GB are low and the natural increase considerably

TABLE 2.17

Main New Commonwealth Immigrant Groups, England and Wales, 1966 and 1971

	(1) India 1966*	1971	(2) Pakistan 1966	1971	(3) West Indies 1966	1971	Total of 1–3 1966	1971	Total population 1966	1971
Total (000s) in England and Wales	163.8	313.4	73.1	135.7	267.9	301.4	504.9	750.5	47,135.5	48,602.9
Percentage in Conurbations										
Tyneside	0.9	0.6	0.8	0.6	0.1	0.1	0.5	0.4	1.8	1.7
W Yorks.	5.6	5.1	17.3	16.1	3.1	3.4	6.0	6.4	3.6	3.6
SELNEC	3.7	4.0	7.0	9.1	4.0	3.5	4.3	4.7	5.1	4.9
Merseyside	0.9	0.7	0.6	0.3	0.6	0.5	0.7	0.5	2.8	2.6
W Midlands	14.9	14.3	19.3	17.0	13.4	13.1	14.7	14.3	5.0	4.9
Greater London	33.9	34.2	22.0	22.1	56.7	55.4	44.3	40.5	16.3	15.2
Total	60.0	58.9	67.0	65.2	77.9	76.0	70.5	66.8	34.6	32.9
Rest of England and Wales	40.0	41.1	32.9	34.8	22.1	24.0	29.5	33.2	65.4	67.1
Scotland		9.2		3.8		1.6		14.6		

*excluding White Indians
Source: *Sample Census 1966* and *Census 1971*

higher than that for the population of UK origin. Natural increase rates for immigrants have thus been high over the past decade, compared with the rest of the GB population: 4.1% in 1966–7 as compared with 0.7, but falling to 3.4 as against 0.5 in 1970–1 and 2.4 as against 0.12 in 1973–4 (OPCS, 1975). As with the total UK births, births to West Indian immigrants fell sharply from 14,100 in 1971 to 6,900 in 1977. But those to mothers from the Indian subcontinent remained fairly steady at 20–23,000 per year (Runnymede Trust 1980). This overall decline in fertility suggests the early stages of a convergence towards average national fertility rates. If recent estimates of completed families of 3.9 (1971) falling to 3.5 (1976) among New Commonwealth immigrants are correct and assuming rather smaller families among UK-born coloured women, the average annual increase of population of New Commonwealth and Pakistan origin is likely to fall from the estimated 5.1% per annum level of 1971–6 to 2.2% p.a. in 1986–91 at a lower estimate, or 3.5% at a higher.

On the basis of such evidence, while admitting that the proportion will increase, it is difficult to justify some of the wild forecasts of future coloured population. Using 'high fertility' assumptions, Rose *et al* (1969) suggested that the numbers in England and Wales are unlikely to exceed 2.37 million by 1986 (4.5% of the estimated total population), perhaps 3.5m (6%) by the end of the century, far below the 4.5–7.0m quoted in some quarters. A recent estimate for population of wholly New Commonwealth origin suggests 2.5–3m in Britain by 1991 and 3–4m by the end of the century (5–7% of the total estimated population). The decline in fertility with the length of stay in Britain of coloured immigrants supports this view (OPCS 1979).

II.7 Differential Inter-regional Movement

Two further aspects of population migration in the UK deserve special mention: rural-urban movements and differential migration according to socio-economic groups. Though the massive flood-tide of rural migration of the nineteenth century has since abated, there are still considerable losses from many rural areas. Since 1951 aggregate population of rural districts increased (table 2.3) due to urban overspill, whilst areas within commuting distance of town jobs retained natural increase. A second factor in growing rural populations, notably in coastal areas, is retirement migration, an important aspect of growth in N Wales, the OSE, the SW, and in parts of E Anglia, N Lancashire, Yorkshire and the Lake District (Law and Warnes 1976). In contrast to these more accessible areas, the remoter country districts, especially the hard core areas of depopulation in upland Britain (Wibberley 1954), continued to lose population up to the late 1960s.

Rural population loss is markedly greater among youthful than among mature age-groups (DoE 1971, 89–131). Limited opportunities for jobs and higher education in rural areas force young people to leave home. Though facilities for primary and secondary education are generally good in the countryside, in some remote areas of Wales and especially of Scotland closure of schools has been one factor in continuing family migration. Higher education or instruction for the professions or skilled trades requires a move to town. Hence, country districts tend to be 'denuded of people of superior abilities' (Musgrove 1963, 3). Once gone, they seldom return. Jones (1965) showed that in C Wales 'over half the distant migrants were taking their first job after leaving school or college', many of them in large

TABLE 2.18

Age and Sex Structure (percentage) among Selected Groups of Commonwealth Immigrants, GB, 1966 and 1965–71

Age	India (1) 1966	(2) 1965–71	Pakistan 1966	1965–71	Jamaica 1966	1965–71	Rest of Caribbean 1966	1965–71	Former British W Africa 1966	1965–71	Cyprus 1966	1965–71	Total Popn 1966–7	1971
0–14	33	21	24	32	40	36	39	40	23	37	35	42	23	24
15–24	16	28	15	38	11	39	12	40	16	37	18	33	14	14
25–44	40	38	51	26	41	22	41	16	59	25	34	18	25	24
45+	11	14	10	3	8	4	8	4	2	2	13	7	38	38
Males per 1,000 1966	1,479		4,231		1,066		1,026		1,614		1,191		940	
Females 1971	1,193		1,568			1,004*				1,205†	1,165		944	
M:F 1961–6 arrivals (1) 1965–71		1,373	3,541		733		809		1,452		1,016			
arrivals (2)		891	1,465		679		715		1,095		922			

OPCS (1975), table 2, gives similar estimates
*West Indies as a whole
† Africa as a whole
Source: (1) Rose *et al* (1969) and (2) *Census 1971*

cities such as Liverpool or Birmingham, with the main flow to London and the South East. An official enquiry (MHLG 1964) noted that such selective out-migration '. . . must influence adversely the quality of the community'.

A similar drain of population from rural Scotland was the cause of actual or threatened depopulation (Turnock 1969; Caird 1972). It was observed that the extent of such migration from Scotland 'increases with education attainment': the rate of migration of highly qualified persons is some two and a half times that of the population of Scotland in the same age-group (MacKay 1969, 209).

Detailed studies of Northern England have indicated that while all young people in rural areas are mobile, school-leavers were especially so (House, Thomas, and Willis 1968). Though they went mainly to adjacent towns, the next most important flow was a long-distance movement to London and the SE. In some cases family migration resulted from the wish to give children a better chance of a career without them having to leave home.

These examples may be multiplied from other parts of the UK. As population in remoter rural areas contracts, educational opportunities there tend to narrow and the gap in opportunity between urban and rural areas is likely to continue to widen, thereby increasing the flow of able young people from the countryside. The less skilled remain, though the girls tend to be more mobile. Farm families also tend to be less migratory, in contrast to the nineteenth-century situation when many farm labourers left the countryside. It remains to be seen to what extent the arrest in the decline of rural population in the 1970s has halted such trends.

Varying social and economic opportunities are also key factors in the pattern and scale of both inter-regional and intra-urban migration. The growing concentration of higher services upon a relatively few major cities has increased socio-economic differentials between regions in the postwar period, increasing the differential mobility of highly qualified manpower. Few investigations have been made of this aspect of migration, though a general relationship between levels of education and inter-regional movement has been observed in the context of manpower and employment (Roberts and Smith 1960). Friedlander and Roshier (1966, 57) have observed that '. . . in general, the higher occupational (and education) groups were found to be more mobile and this differential increased with distance moved'. A detailed study of professional and managerial manpower in the 1960s showed that the greater opportunities for upward social mobility led to a pronounced movement of these groups to the major cities, especially to Greater London (Waugh 1969). Conversely, the progressive decrease in the proportion of high-status jobs in both rural and declining industrial regions highlights the contrasts in this type of inter-regional migration. The migratory elite, as they have been described, are more mobile both in terms of distance moved and as a proportion of their age-group. Whereas 70% of manual household heads had *not* moved house in the five years previous to the *General Household Survey* of 1972, 50% of professional and non-manual heads had done so. Moreover, the latter group made more frequent moves.

Much present-day migration in the UK is local or intra-regional. In the 1960s short-distance movements, often primarily changes of residence mainly for social reasons, accounted for 80% of the moves, nine-tenths of which are under 16 km (Harris 1966). Such movements are mainly within urban regions and take two forms: first, the displacement of working-class families from rented accommodation in the residential areas affected by slum clearance, who move to peripheral local authority housing or, more recently, farther afield to New Towns or overspill areas; secondly, a large outward migration to private residential areas, often in adjacent rural districts, of managerial and professional classes and certain types of skilled workers. Such people rise professionally and socially through a series of higher positions, moving residence within the community in which they live. This 'spiralist society', as it has been called thus produces 'a characteristic combination of social and spatial mobility' (Watson 1964).

Peripheral migration from the inner areas of large cities is exemplified by migration on Merseyside (Lawton and Cunningham 1970, ch. 5). Internal migration between and within local authorities on Merseyside has increased with the rapid sprawl of the conurbation in the twentieth century. Movement within the region has increased considerably since 1950, a fact underlined in the 1960s by overspill agreements and the development of the New Towns of Skelmersdale and Runcorn. Between 1961 and 1971 the population of Liverpool CB fell by 138,916, a decrease of 19.9%, almost the same percentage loss as experienced by Manchester and paralleled by some of the inner London boroughs, and a further fall of 100,000 (16.4%) was experienced in 1971–81 (Lawton 1982). Movement to outer Merseyside extended into adjacent areas of south-central Lancashire and N Wales, symptomatic of a national trend towards residential decentralization from cities (Champion 1976). One aspect is the decline in both the inner core of the city and, more recently, in the outer city ring, both of which have lost population to the outer city region; another aspect is the problem of the adjustment of all classes of society to changing residential patterns through more complex commuting links (Hall 1971; Johnson, Salt and Wood 1974).

Most residential migration to the periphery in the 1960s was of professional and managerial households. In the rapidly growing Merseyside suburb of Formby, from a 12% increase in 1951–6, population growth was a staggering 100% in 1961–71. The population structure was mainly young in 1966: 31% were between 25–44 years as compared with Liverpool's 24%, and 28% under 15 years (Liverpool 25%). Formby is a predominantly middle-class area with 39% in the social classes 1 and 2 (Liverpool 10%). One-quarter of the population had changed address in 1965–6 and of a sample social survey conducted in 1968 (Pickett 1970, 133) nearly one-half of the movers had come from the Merseyside conurbation, over one-quarter from Liverpool itself. This is endorsed by the survey finding that 49.5% of the whole sample but 58.9% of the migrant heads of households travelled to work in the inner areas of the conurbation. These findings are supported in a wider context by a research study on migration between major centres and their surrounding areas carried out by the *Redcliffe-Maud Commission* (R. Commn 1969, III, 39–56), which showed a strong positive correlation between migration loss from county boroughs and low indices of men over 15 in professional and managerial classes and of males 25–44 as a proportion of all males of 15 and over. Taking England outside Greater London as = 100, the indices were as shown in table 2.19.

In a more detailed study of fourteen towns it was shown that the migration loss of men aged 25–44 in the professional and managerial classes was roughly twice that of losses among all males over 15 years (Royal Commn 1969, III, 43–5).

While there is some compensatory in-migration to city centres, as observed in Greater London, this does little if anything to offset the loss of the more prosperous and vigorous sections of the population. Indeed many of the vacated residences are occupied by poor people including, in many areas, a large proportion

TABLE 2.19

Mobility of Professional and Managerial Workers, England, 1961–6

	% net migration	Proportion managerial and professional		Proportion of males 25–44 to males 15+	
	1961–6	1961	1966	1961	1966
All CBs	−3.19	79	78	100	97
CBs with migration losses (61 out of 78)	−4.10	74	73	101	98

Source: Royal Commission on Local Government in England (1969), vol. III, appendix 3, table 1, 48–9

of overseas immigrants. In 1961 the four county boroughs of inner Merseyside included 23,820 (2.3%) Irish-born and 14,330 (1.3%) from overseas, while in Liverpool most of the New Commonwealth immigrants were concentrated into a few inner city wards which also have high indices of most aspects of social stress. The 1981 census supplement for the Liverpool Special Area shows that in the city's inner area 2.1% of household heads are from Pakistan and New Commonwealth countries, twice the proportion in Merseyside in general, while Granby Ward, the main focus of immigrants, has 11.2%.

III POPULATION STRUCTURE

Contrasts and changes in natural and migrational trends result from and influence population structure. In the UK differential migration as between different age-groups and between men and women is an important factor in regional differences in population structure and future population trends alike.

III.1 Sex Ratios

Due to the better survival rates of male children and the diminishing importance of the 'lost generation' of men killed during the First World War, the pronounced imbalance between the sexes of the 1921–51 period has been progressively modified since the war (table 2.8). There are, however, considerable regional deviations from the 1971 UK figure of 105.5 females per 100 males. In broad regional terms (fig. 2.10) this average is exceeded only in rural Wales, southern and much of eastern Scotland, SW England, Greater London and the OMA and NW England. At the higher level of definition of administrative county and county borough (fig. 2.11), the main factors involved in these differences become more apparent.

The majority of rural areas have a below-average ratio of women to men, largely because of the long-standing tendency for women to be more migratory than men and the more restricted job opportunities for women in rural areas. In 1971 the lowest female:male ratios were in parts of N Ireland and the Scottish Highlands, but most of the rural areas from the Welsh border to the Fenland counties had relatively low ratios. Women dominate the population structure of retirement areas, in which resorts and spas have notably high ratios; due to their greater longevity, there are very large proportions of elderly women in such areas. This accounts for such ratios as 122 in Peebles and Pitlochry, 126 in Torbay, 128 in Bournemouth, 133 in Eastbourne and 123 in Southport.

In addition, above-average female:male ratios are found first in Greater London and, secondly, in textile districts such as the NW and the Scottish Border country. A detailed study of the Scottish Border counties (Soulsby 1972) showed that differential migration and occupational structure account for considerable variations in sex ratios at local as well as at regional level, in which a sharp upswing in the proportion of women in the population in the later nineteenth century was due to female employment in the textile industry. Though much less pronounced than in the past, due to the absolute and relative decline of jobs in the cotton mills, some E Lancashire textile towns, for example Blackburn and Burnley (108), have above-average ratios, though the Lowry-like image of shawled and beclogged women clattering over cobblestones to work in the spinning mills is now a picture from the past, as below-average sex ratios and large numbers of immigrants in many SE Lancashire mill-towns show. In a very different context, the majority of Greater London boroughs have high proportions of women, though the highest ratios tend to be found in west London. This tendency for higher proportions of women is indeed typical of the inner residential areas of many large towns.

Apart from the male-dominant rural areas, districts with below-average sex ratios, and hence relatively more men than average, tend to be associated with heavy industrial areas. Some of the lower ratios are found in coalfield areas of south-east Wales (e.g. 104.8 in Glamorgan AC) and NE England (e.g. Durham AC, 102.6). The lowest tend to be in the heavy industrial districts such as the W Midlands, where Wolverhampton, Walsall and West Bromwich all have ratios of around 101, or S Yorkshire, where the Barnsley and Rotherham ratios are 102.

III.2 Age Structure

The general increase in numbers in both young and older age-groups since 1945 has already been shown to underlie continuing population growth in the UK (table 2.6). The increased birth-rate of the early 1960s brought the proportion of under-15s to 24.1% in 1971, the same as in 1931, but the sharp fall in births in the 1970s has reduced this figure to 20.8%. Meanwhile population of retirement age has greatly increased, from 16.0 (1971) to 20.0% in 1981 as compared with 9.6% in 1931. However, considerable spatial variations in age-structure persist. These have been analysed for local authority areas by Dewdney (1968). In his study of four age-groups 0–14, 15–44, 45–64 and 65+, Dewdney stressed two aspects: first, the distribution of different age-groups; secondly, the age-structure within the various local authorities or regions in which, he observes, the various age-groups are complementary, so that 'Quite different mechanisms of population growth and movement may give rise to similar results as far as the age composition of a particular area is concerned' (Dewdney 1968, 9).

The essential features of Dewdney's detailed analysis are reflected at the level of UK economic planning sub-regions for 1971 (fig. 2.10). Above-average proportions of young people (0–14 years) result from a variety of causes. Relatively high birth-rates explain the larger proportion of young people in much of rural Scotland and

N Ireland, despite long-standing out-migration and a continuing migrational loss of young adults. Up to the early 1970s, relatively high birth-rates also explained the high proportions of under-15s in certain industrial regions, including C Scotland, NE and NW England, and Yorks. and Humberside. A growing tendency to outward migration of young families from inner residential areas to the periphery of the large towns has progressively increased the proportion of children in the population of many parts of the major city regions, notably in the outer metropolitan areas.

The 15–59 group is a rather large one which tends to conceal differences between the more mobile 15–44 and more stable 45–59 age-groups. Dewdney's analysis showed that relatively high proportions of the younger adult population were found in areas of economic growth and in-migration, and tended to be prominent in the conurbations and large industrial areas, though residential overspill has reduced the proportion of this group in the inner metropolitan areas, as may be seen in the 1971 map (fig. 2.10). In contrast, the 45–59 group has many different tendencies. The inner areas of large cities have considerable numbers of small households made up of parents over 45 whose families are grown up and have left home. Elsewhere, in declining industrial areas of long-standing out-migration, the older mature population has above-average representation, but the broad 15–59 age-group conceals the deficiency of younger adults in the population.

In rural areas of Wales, Scotland and E England, along the south coast of England and in the SW, there are considerable numbers of over-60s, arising from two inter-related factors. Prolonged out-migration of young adults often leads eventually to a deficiency of births, thus creating a predominantly elderly population, as in much of rural Wales and the Scottish Highlands. Indeed this situation is sometimes found in industrial areas, notably in the small industrial towns of NE Lancashire. In the resort areas, of the south coast of England and N Wales for example, the reasons for very large proportions of over-60s are more positive and, as has been shown previously, involve a considerable in-migration of people of retirement age.

Without a very carefully integrated analysis of age–sex structure, area by area, it is difficult to summarize the changing regional inter-relationships of these various age-group patterns.

The sharp decline in fertility and changes in the pattern of population growth (section II.3) in the 1970s have been reflected in a changing balance of population. In particular, the ageing of the populations of conurbations and large cities has continued, while the move to the periphery of most SMLAs is reflected in younger households, with more people in the young-adult and middle-age groups. Meanwhile the continuing movement of retired people to areas such as the South West, the south coast, mid- and North Wales and parts of rural N England and Scotland is partly responsible for increases in their population in the 1970s, as reflected in their age structure.

However, certain broad trends persist. In N Ireland, high birth-rates are reflected in the large proportion of under-15s but the deficiencies in the other age-groups reflect long-standing out-migration. Parts of rural Scotland have relatively high proportions of children but in areas of past depopulation in the Highlands and Southern Scotland this is associated with large proportions in the over-60 group and a deficiency in the 15–59s, especially due to large out-migration of younger adults. The Central Valley of Scotland, in contrast, like many English industrial regions has a high proportion of both children and young adults; above-average proportions of over-60s in the Scottish industrial sub-regions are found only in the Fife coalfield.

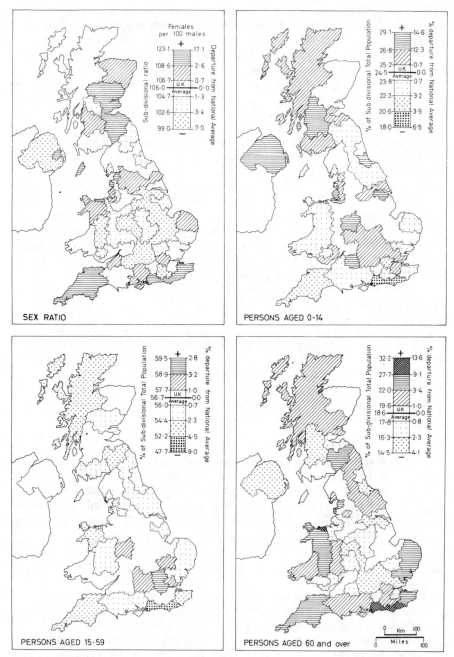

Figure 2.10   Age and sex structure, UK regions, 1971

In England and Wales there is a generally clear distinction between the rural areas, with below-average under-15 and 15—44 age-groups and above-average shares of the elderly which become very pronounced in retirement areas, and the urban and industrial areas. The urban regions are more complex with many contrasting structural features which are not apparent at sub-regional level. Intra-regional migration has produced a series of zones within the city region. The city centres have relatively few young and old, and are often dominated locally by young adults, as in parts of central London. The older residential areas of the inner city are increasingly dominated by mature adults and elderly people, with younger families still actively moving to the suburbs. The peripheral areas complement the inner city and are dominated by families at an active stage of formation, with above-average proportions of children and young adults, though in the outer areas the 45—59 age-groups are dominant, as for example in the outer metropolitan region.

All these situations are dynamic, and age structures reflect economic and social change, especially in the progressive extension of urban-based population into rural areas. The implications of recent and projected changes in age structures, which are of considerable significance to both physical and social planning on a regional basis and national basis (section I.4), will receive close scrutiny when the full 1981 Census tables of population structure are available.

III.3 Social Structure

Experience of fertility, mortality and migration varies regionally to produce differences in age and sex structure. Many of these demographic contrasts are due, in part, to differing social structure. Hence, an analysis of population trends must take account of differing social structures at both regional and local level (Knox 1974). Moreover, social contrasts are themselves often a resultant of aspects of population dynamics; thus selective migration varies not only with age and sex but also with education, skills and job mobility.

Socio-economic indices The analysis of social structure is hampered by the lack of any one generally agreed or readily measured criterion. British population censuses have collected information on occupations in some detail since 1841. In association with the fertility analysis of the 1911 census, the Registrar General adopted a system of social groups and classes based on occupation which has led to the present socio-economic classification (Booth 1886; Marsh 1965); a discussion of social-class composition and contrasts in family, household, demographic, social and economic characteristics between classes is in *Social Trends* (CSO 1975, 10—32). Such classifications are very valuable, especially in cross-tabulations with other population data, but they raise a number of problems of comparison, especially as between 'middle-ranking' manual and non-manual occupations.

Hence they are often used in association with other socio-economic information. Since housing is one of the biggest investments made by a family, it may be expected that the quality and spaciousness of dwellings will reflect household income and may, therefore, be a useful surrogate of living standards and social class. A number of housing variables concerning type of tenure, intensity of occupation and amenities have been used with considerable effectiveness by social geographers and sociologists in defining the social areas of towns (Moser and Scott 1961; Robson 1969). The availability and characteristics of housing in cities and the

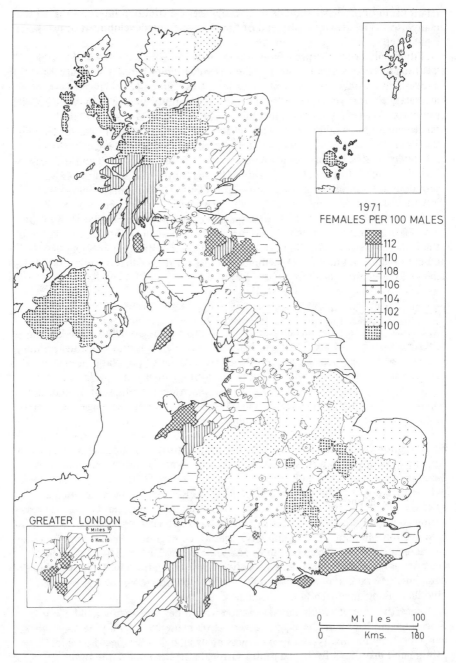

Figure 2.11   Sex ratios, UK, 1971

relationship of residential trends to employment are of direct interest in relation to many aspects of daily mobility and of the structure and development of urban regions (ch. 6.II).

Educational qualifications have become increasingly important in the modern UK for professional, business and technical skills; hence educational achievement is increasingly valuable as a measure of social class. From 1951 there has been increasing information on educational achievement in British censuses which now provide data on the terminal age of education, scientific and technological qualifications (1961 census), higher educational qualifications (1966 census) and, in the 1971 census, school-leaving qualifications. In addition the Department of Education and Science issues annually the six-volume *Statistics of Education* which includes much information on the educational provision by local authorities, the proportions of various age-groups in full-time education, qualifications of school-leavers and the like.

Personal income is one of the best indices of social class but is not available in any detail for the UK. Some aggregate data on personal incomes are published by the Inland Revenue, tabulated for counties. Since 1965 these have been used as the basis of figures published in the annual *Regional Abstract of Statistics*. From these data it is possible to analyse, in broad terms, the distribution and trends in personal incomes (Coates and Rawstron 1971, ch. 2).

While each individually is of value in social analysis, such criteria may be combined with demographic variables through the use of multivariate statistical techniques, such as principal components analysis, to delineate spatial variations in social structure more fully. Work of this kind has been pioneered for British towns by Moser and Scott (1961) and Armen (1971). Such studies are of particular value in distinguishing the differing character of social areas within cities, in which demographic, social and economic conditions are often closely inter-related and in which an understanding of population distribution and trends is inseparable from social geography. Moreover, the growth of studies of 'welfare geography' – which stresses the spatial variations in availability of resources and services and their implications for different sections of the community – has emphasized the significance of this link (Smith 1979).

III.4 Housing and Households

Of the UK's 21.4 million dwellings (1980), 48% have been built since 1945 but 30% are pre-1919 in date. 55% of dwellings are owner-occupied, 31% rented from local authorities or public corporations and the rest mainly rented from private landlords (table 2.20). Although the number of dwellings now exceeds the number of house-holds there are still housing shortages in the conurbations and industrial areas, especially in inner city areas.

The large interwar building and slum clearance programme added nearly four million dwellings to the housing stock of England and Wales, about 30% of which were built by local authorities. Yet this very large increase only slightly exceeded the rate of growth of households; indeed 1901–39 the number of dwellings built lagged slightly behind the increase in families. Hence, if essential slum clearance is taken into account, there was an estimated deficit of housing in 1939 of over half a million homes in England and Wales alone (Cullingworth 1960).

Moreover, at that time conditions of *overcrowding* were still widespread, though the yardstick of 1½ persons per room was generous by nineteenth-century standards. Both the virtual cessation of building during the Second World War and the damage to and loss of property by bombing, which affected one in three of all dwellings in England and Wales, contributed to a general postwar housing shortage in the UK, which was particularly acute in the large cities. Despite the building of nearly three-quarters of a million homes in Britain between 1946 and 1950 (Holmans 1970), there was a shortage of over one million dwellings at the time of the 1951 census, when the ratio of households to dwellings was 1.056 for GB.

Since 1951, the situation has improved considerably, though the continuing high rate of formation of new households, due to high marriage rates and a falling average age of marriage, together with immigration and inter-regional migration to certain areas of rapid population growth, has caused regional shortages of housing to persist. Estimates of formation of new households due to marriage *less* losses due to deaths, together with a falling demand from immigrant households suggested that there was some reduction of demand for new homes from about 145,000 per year in 1970 to some 120,000 per year in the mid-1970s, rising to 130,000 per year around 1981.

A further considerable postwar demand for additional housing has come from slum clearance. Some 992,000 houses were 'demolished or closed' in England and Wales and 250,000 in Scotland from 1955–71 and 2.25m people were rehoused, but 2.1m unfit dwellings remained (DoE 1971, 48). In addition to clearance, an average of 80,000 houses per year were improved in England and Wales, 1965–71, under various sections of the *Housing Acts* (of 1957, 1961, and 1969) and the *Public Health Acts*. In an attempt to upgrade the 4.5m dwellings in England and Wales and 200,000 in Scotland which lacked amenities or were in poor repair though structurally sound (MHLG 1966; SDD 1968), an average of 307,000 improvement grants per year were made in Great Britain in 1970–4 (DoE 1974, 38). While this fell to a total of 356,800 in the years 1978 and 1979, over one-third of these were private, 11% to housing associations, but the majority (54%) to local authorities to update their extensive prewar housing stock, though this has not saved a good many high-rise apartments from demolition.

Although the number of slums in England and Wales was reduced from the estimated 1.8m dwellings of 1967 to around 1.35m by 1970 (Holmans 1970, 38), a considerable number of pre-1919 houses remain (table 2.20). The estimated net increase in households of 120–130,000 per year for the 1970s had not been realized, but the rate of slum clearance of around 100,000 per year fell to 79,000 p.a. 1970–4 and to a mere 38,500 in 1979, so that there is still an annual need for many more new homes than the 152,000 dwellings begun in 1980. With an estimated 547,000 unfit houses in England alone, together with 850,000 overcrowded homes and some 50,000 homeless, there is need for a building programme of around 320,000 dwellings per year in the UK to provide for present needs and for impending obsolescence of some 3m houses. Yet the likely level of provision in the immediate future is only 200,000 per year as compared with 306,000 completions in the UK in 1971–6, which was well below the peak of 426,000 reached in 1968. Although the total stock of 21.5m dwellings in 1981 as compared with an estimated 20.4m households is healthier than in 1974 (table 2.20), there is likely to be continuing pressure on housing in certain regions and, particularly in many inner city areas, in the public housing sector. Above all, there is likely to be deterioration in the quality of much of the existing private housing stock, despite the large numbers of improvement grants made in the 1970s.

Inter-regional housing contrasts There are considerable regional differences in the relative supply of housing in relation to households and population, in the degree of overcrowding, in the characteristics of housing tenure and in the amenity of housing. These partly reflect population trends over a considerable period, partly relate to pressures of recent population movements, and partly reflect broad social and economic contrasts between regions. Most of these features also reflect two distinctive and sometimes pronounced intra-regional contrasts between rural and urban areas and, secondly, more marked contrasts between inner and outer residential areas of large cities.

Tenure One of the characteristics of housing in the UK since 1920 has been the increasing importance of local-authority housing (table 2.20). Interwar corporation housing estates became a distinctive element in the British townscape and gave birth to almost exclusively working-class residential suburbs which were marked by many problems of social adjustment to the new environment. During the 1920s and

TABLE 2.20

Dwelling Stock, UK, 1980

	Number of dwellings (millions)	Tenure of dwellings (percentages)			Age of dwellings (percentages)				
		Owner-occupied	Rented from Local authority[1]	Private owner[2]	Pre-1918	1891 to 1918	1919 to 1944	1945 to 1970	Post-1970
Standard regions									
Northern	1.14	46	41	13	13	16	21	37	13
Yorks. and H.	1.87	55	33	12	15	16	23	34	12
E Midlands	1.45	57	30	13	15	13	21	36	15
E Anglia	0.73	58	27	15	22	9	15	36	18
South East:	6.55	56	27	17	16	14	24	34	12
Gtr London	2.76	46	29	24	–	–	–	–	–
Rest of region	3.79	61	25	15	–	–	–	–	–
South West	1.68	63	22	15	22	11	18	35	14
W Midlands	1.92	56	34	10	13	12	24	39	12
North West	2.46	59	31	10	17	15	23	33	12
England	17.85	57	30	13	16	14	22	35	13
Wales	1.07	59	29	12	23	19	14	32	12
Scotland	1.99	35	54	11	13	16	18	39	14
N Ireland	0.50	49	40	11	11[3]	18[4]	15	38	18
U Kingdom	21.41	55	32	13	30		22	35	13

[1] or New Town
[2] including 'other tenures'
[3] pre-1870
[4] 1870–1919
Source: Regional Trends, 1981

1930s much early Victorian housing, mainly privately rented, was being cleared from city centre slums. While most of the surplus population from these grossly overcrowded areas was decanted to the new local authority estates, a considerable amount of housing renewal, mostly through blocks of flats, was also leading to social and visual changes in the inner city.

Since 1945 these trends towards replacement of slums by local authority housing have continued, leading to a shortage of rented property in the private sector, in great contrast to the nineteenth century or even the interwar situation. From 1950 to 1970 the total housing stock increased at an average annual rate of 1.57%. New building in the private sector (mainly for purchase) increased by 1.2% per year and in the public sector at 1.0% per year. While owner-occupied dwellings grew at the rate of 1.8% per year and local authority and New Town property at 1.1% per year,

TABLE 2.21

Permanent Dwellings Completed, UK, 1945−79

| | Average annual completion of permanent dwellings (000s) | | | | | |
	England	Wales	Scotland	N Ireland	GB	UK
1945−50	115	7	15	3.6	137	141
1951−5	237	13	33	7.3	284	291
1956−60	248	12	30	6.0	290	297
1961−5	284	16	31	8.5	331	340
1966−70	325	18	41	11.4	384	395
1971−5	261	16	33	11.0	310	320
1976−9	242	13	28	9.1	283	292
Total 1945−79	8,435	469	1,049	279.0		
Annual av. 1945−79	241	13.4	30.0	8.0	284	292

Source: Housing Statistics GB, 26 (1974); *Regional Trends,* 1981

the privately rented housing stock *decreased* continuously at an average of 1.2% per year. Thus, the proportion of owner-occupied dwellings has increased from 20% in 1950 to 42% in 1960 and 55% in 1980; renting from local authorities and New Town corporations has grown over the same period from 18% to 27% and now to 32%; privately-owned property has fallen from 45 to 26 and now to 13% (table 2.20). This betokens a social revolution of considerable proportions.

While the proportions of housing in different tenures varies regionally, owner-occupied houses provide the majority of the stock in all regions except Scotland and to a lesser extent in Greater London and some other conurbations. A high level of owner-occupation is the hallmark of rural and many suburban areas, though the further extension of peripheral local authority housing estates is changing this situation. Many areas of the inner city and of the older industrial regions have lower proportions of owner-occupied and privately rented property than in the past. Regionally this situation is reflected in the above-average proportion of owner-occupied property in the south-eastern quadrant of Britain from the Midlands to the south and east coasts (Greater London excepted) and in Wales, and in the below-average proportion in the industrial north and in C Scotland. In detail, as Storrie (1968) has shown, there are contrasts; for example the high percentage of owner-occupied houses in the textile towns of E Lancashire.

Privately rented dwellings dominated the housing stock up to the mid-1950s, especially in the large cities and industrial towns. Slum clearance and the gradual decline of the small-scale property owner (Cullingworth 1963), who was most affected by rent control, led to a rapid reduction in this sector of the housing market; between the *Rent Acts* of 1957 and 1965 there was a fall of one million in such properties (one-quarter of their total). Rural areas have been less affected by this, so that the proportion of privately rented dwellings is above average in many rural areas, especially of N and SW England, of Wales and of N Ireland.

As privately rented property has declined, so local authority rentings have increased, especially in the urban areas. The proportion of such property is most marked in those regions of greatest housing need, especially in those areas where local administrations, often Labour-controlled councils, have invested heavily in housing as one of the most vital social services. Hence, C Scotland, industrial NE England, S Yorkshire, the Black Country and much of the S Wales coalfield stand out on a detailed map of local authority tenure (Storrie 1968, fig. 10). More recently, local authority overspill to peripheral areas such as New Towns and overspill areas (figs. 2.19 and 2.20) have led to rapid increases in such tenures around all city regions. Thus, the major contrasts are intra- rather than inter-regional, apart from the considerably above-average values for Scotland, N England and the W Midlands. The highest proportions of local authority rented property are in Scotland, N Ireland and the industrial and metropolitan counties of England and Wales. Owner-occupiers dominate the Outer South East, the SW, E Anglia, rural Wales and the NW. As may be expected in predominantly owner-occupied areas, such as the OSE, SW England and E Anglia, the proportion of local authority houses is relatively low.

Amenities Housing quality provides a useful measure of the general social characteristics of the population. Amenity is a complex notion involving a wide range of factors influencing property valuations, such as: state of repair; freedom from damp; adequate lighting, heating and ventilation; water supplies; cooking facilities; sanitary arrangements; and food storage. The most easily comparable data are those collected in censuses concerning water supply, bathroom and sanitary facilities. In the 1966 and 1971 censuses the exclusive use of a hot-water supply and fixed bath and WC were regarded as evidence of adequate amenities from this viewpoint. The lack of sewerage in rural areas tends to dramatize relatively poor levels of amenity in the countryside. At the regional level there is a perceptible gradient between the low level of amenities in most inner city areas rising to very high levels in all suburbs (private and local authority), and falling to lower levels in the rural hinterlands (Humphrys 1968). Growing affluence, slum clearance and increasing standards in all housing sectors are rapidly ironing out regional differences in housing quality as judged by such limited criteria, though relatively high proportions of housing without those basic amenities, especially that of a fixed bath, persist in Greater London, the conurbations and older industrial regions of Scotland, Wales and N England; many rural areas also have relatively low levels of amenity (table 2.22).

Overcrowding Many studies of conditions in cities have shown that one of the more useful criteria of social structure is some measure of overcrowding. Though appropriate standards vary over time and between social classes, the number of persons per room is generally regarded as an acceptable measure of overcrowding (Clarke 1960). The currently accepted index of overcrowding in the UK is the proportion of households at an occupancy rate of over 1.5 persons per room, though in the Britain of the 1970s 1 per room might be a better yardstick. The highest proportions of overcrowding are in N Ireland and Scotland, where smaller dwellings and the larger average size of household, together with poor economic and social conditions, are responsible. Similar, though less extreme, conditions are reflected in the higher rates of overcrowding in parts of the industrial North and Midlands, especially in the conurbations, and in Greater London. The proportion of households at over 1½ persons per room is now low, and the major contrasts are intra-regional, with a general emphasis on greater overcrowding in rural areas, especially of western and northern Britain and N Ireland, and in the inner-city areas. City slums still have considerable levels of overcrowding, especially among immigrant communities, where subdivision of housing and 'Rachmanite' exploitation of tenants by private landlords have been a reproach to both national and local administrations in postwar Britain.

TABLE 2.22

Regional Indices of Housing and Households, GB, 1971

Regions and conurbations	TOTAL (1,000s)			PERCENTAGE HOUSEHOLDS	
	Persons	House-holds (Hh)	Occupied dwellings (Dw)	At > 1½ persons per room	Without all three amenities
NORTHERN	3,296	1,100	1,115	1.6	18.3
Tyneside con.	805	277	280	2.3	19.5
Rest	2,491	823	835	1.3	17.9
YORKS. AND HUMBERSIDE	4,799	1,650	1,664	1.2	17.7
West Yorks. con.	1,728	605	609	1.7	15.8
Rest	3,071	1,045	1,055	0.9	18.7
NORTH WEST	6,743	2,273	2,279	1.3	20.0
SELNEC con.	2,393	827	829	1.5	21.8
Merseyside con.	1,267	405	403	1.9	21.3
Rest	3,083	1,040	1,047	0.9	18.0
E MIDLANDS	3,390	1,145	1,151	0.9	19.6
W MIDLANDS	5,110	1,677	1,680	1.6	16.4
W Mids con.	2,372	781	778	2.2	17.6
Rest	2,738	896	903	1.0	15.4
E ANGLIA	1,669	569	578	0.5	17.8
SOUTH EAST	17,230	5,915	5,790	1.8	17.3
Greater London	7,452	2,652	2,501	2.9	24.3
OMA	5,307	1,717	1,726	0.8	10.1
OSE	4,471	1,546	1,563	0.8	13.3
SOUTH WEST	3,781	1,280	1,286	0.7	14.2
WALES	2,731	901	912	0.8	22.5
SCOTLAND	5,229	1,686	1,717	6.5	13.7
C. Clyde con.	1,728	547	553	10.7	16.8
Rest	3,501	1,139	1,164	4.4	12.2

Source: Census 1971, Household Tables

Studies of immigrants' housing in the Greater London and W Midlands conurbations have shown very high densities of occupation, high proportions of sharing of dwellings, very low proportions of local authority housing and very high proportions of rented furnished accommodation among all immigrant groups (table 2.23). Moreover, there has been little overall improvement in the situation since the early 1960s, though more enlightened policy concerning local authority accommodation in some areas is beginning to make an impact. Nevertheless the view that 1961–6 '. . . has been one of improvement for English residents of these boroughs' (of inner London) while '. . . the coloured immigrants were being left even further behind as the general level of housing amenity has risen' (Deakin 1970, 72) is unfortunately still largely true today.

A 1975 sample survey of Greater London Council tenants showed that over 90% of non-whites were allocated homes in inner London (as against 62.5% of whites), mostly in pre-1945 flatted accommodation (51.4% of non-whites as against 24.6% of whites) (Runnymede Trust 1980). Islington Borough reported that 64% of British and Irish applicants were given new accommodation but only 30% of coloured people were. These policies not surprisingly contribute to increasing

Table 2.22 (cont.)

Regions and conurbations	TENURE (% HOUSEHOLDS)			PERCENTAGE HOUSEHOLDS		
	Owner-occupied	Rented from LA or New Town	Privately rented	1- or 2-person hhds with person(s) of pensionable age	Car owning	
					1 car	2+ cars
NORTHERN	41.0	38.6	20.4	26.5	36.8	5.8
Tyneside con.	31.7	43.6	24.7	27.6	30.3	3.8
Rest	44.0	36.9	19.1	26.0	38.9	6.5
YORKS. AND						
HUMBERSIDE	48.6	32.1	19.3	27.7	37.5	6.3
West Yorks. con.	52.6	30.8	16.6	29.1	34.6	5.5
Rest	46.3	32.9	20.8	26.9	39.2	6.8
NORTH WEST	53.8	27.9	18.3	27.4	38.5	7.0
SELNEC con.	51.4	29.7	18.7	27.5	35.8	6.3
Merseyside	40.5	33.5	26.0	25.9	34.8	6.0
Rest	61.0	24.3	14.7	28.0	42.2	7.9
E MIDLANDS	51.1	28.9	20.0	26.0	44.1	8.7
W MIDLANDS	50.7	33.5	15.8	23.7	44.2	9.8
W Mids con.	46.3	39.7	14.0	24.1	40.5	8.2
Rest	55.0	28.1	16.9	23.3	47.6	11.0
E ANGLIA	51.1	27.0	21.9	28.3	49.4	11.2
SOUTH EAST	50.9	24.3	24.8	26.5	44.2	10.2
Greater London	43.4	25.0	31.6	25.8	38.5	7.8
OMA	57.0	26.6	16.4	22.7	51.1	14.5
OSE	57.1	20.6	22.3	31.9	46.4	10.2
SOUTH WEST	56.8	23.4	19.8	29.5	49.2	11.1
WALES	54.0	28.9	17.1	26.7	44.1	8.5
SCOTLAND	29.3	53.5	17.2	25.9	36.5	5.9
C Clyds. con.	24.9	59.2	15.9	24.0	28.9	4.1
Rest	31.1	50.6	18.3	26.7	40.1	6.7

residential segregation, especially of West Indians and Pakistanis, in London as in a number of British cities.

In general, better control of rented housing, slum clearance and local authority building led to the reduction in the proportion of homeless and overcrowded families in the 1960s, though many black spots exist and the UK is still some way from solving its shortage of housing. 30% of Britain's housing stock is pre-1919 in age, a situation which is general in most regions (table 2.20): we are clearly far from satisfactory housing standards for all. Thus, despite half a million demolitions 1955–65, the remaining number of houses classed as unfit was almost unchanged. In the less fortunate areas the proportion of sub-standard property was very much higher: as compared with 12% unfit houses in England and Wales in 1967, the SE's proportion was only 6%, while the North, Yorks. and Humberside and NW regions had 15% (Sec. State Econ. Affairs 1969, 29). Such regional inequalities point to fundamental contrasts in the social geography of modern Britain, and it is in such deprived areas where environmental and social needs are greatest that the house improvement schemes of the late 1960s made the greatest impact. Of the 1.27m improvement grants approved in GB, 1971–4, 0.83m were in the development areas. There remain, however, massive problems of social deprivation in the inner areas of all large towns, the solution to which lies in a much more widely based and more integrated programme of redevelopment than can be achieved through housing policy alone (ch. 2.III.5).

Households During the twentieth century separate households have tended to increase at a faster rate than population in the UK. In part due to decreasing family size, in part to increased mobility of population leading to break-up of two-generation adult households, it also reflects a considerable social revolution, that of a separate home for each individual family unit of parents and children. In England and Wales, for example, the rate of household formation in the interwar period was three times that of the increase in population (Lawton 1963A). Postwar increases in marriage-rates and the reduction in the average age of marriage, together with increasing expectation of life, have accentuated these tendencies since we must now cater for separate homes for three generations: elderly people; mature married couples with children; and young married couples or single persons. Each requires a home of a different type and location, a fact underlying the considerable level of

TABLE 2.23

Housing Tenure of Coloured Immigrants and English in Greater London and W Midlands Conurbations, 1966

Area	Owner-occupiers		From LA		Renting Pri. unfurnished		Pri. furnished	
	Coloured immigrts	English	Coloured immigrts	English	Coloured immigrts	English	Coloured immigrts	English
Gtr London	32.6	38.9	4.2	22.3	18.1	29.0	43.6	7.3
W Midlands conurb.	59.4	41.1	7.7	39.1	9.4	14.6	21.2	2.6

Source: Rose *et al*, p. 133

TABLE 2.24

Population, Dwellings and Households, UK, 1951–71 (in 000s)

	Total population	% change	Total house-holds	% change	Total dwellings	% change	Persons per household	Households per dwelling	% > 1½ persons per room
England and Wales									
1951	43,758		13,118		12,389		3.53	1.056	8.8
1961	46,005	5.3	14,890	13.5	14,646	18.2	3.09	1.017	5.3
1971	48,750	6.0	16,509	10.9	16,455	12.4	2.96	1.003	2.9
Scotland									
1951	5,096		1,436		1,424		3.54	1.008	35.2
1961	5,179	4.8	1,609	12.0	1,627	14.2	3.22	0.989	22.4
1971	5,229	1.0	1,686	4.8	1,717	5.5	3.13	0.982	12.6
N Ireland									
1951	1,371		338		343		4.05	0.985	
1961	1,425	3.9	373	10.3	387	12.8	3.82	0.964	25.5
1971	1,528	7.2	415	11.3	413	6.7	3.08	1.005	5.6

The totals are for all households (present or not) and all dwellings (occupied and vacant)
Source: Censuses of England and Wales, of Scotland (1951, 1961, 1971) and of N Ireland (1951, 1961, 1971)

intra-regional residential migration which reflects changing needs during the family cycle. Thus since 1951 households have continued to grow at over twice the rate of the growth of population throughout the UK (table 2.24).

The regional structure of household size reflects both demographic and social trends. Intra-regional contrasts are often of greater significance than inter-regional differences. The average household remains much larger in N Ireland than elsewhere in the UK, due to higher fertility, and is somewhat higher in Scotland than in England and Wales (table 2.24). The lowest figures of average size of household are generally found in areas where there are high proportions of young adults (especially in single-person households) or of elderly people. Thus central residential areas of cities frequently have small households, as for example in Greater London, mainly because of the large numbers of young people living in flats. At the other end of the scale retirement areas, such as the South West, or areas of long-standing out-migration, both rural (e.g. rural Wales) and industrial (e.g. W Yorkshire and much of E Lancashire), have above-average numbers of one- or two-person households of pensionable age, as do many older, inner residential areas of our large cities.

III.5 Educational Achievement and Personal Incomes

Indices of housing and the like are closely related to other social criteria, such as those based on educational achievement and income, which are often more directly indicative of social status and of social and economic health or deprivation. The better-educated and qualified part of the population are more mobile, both geographically and socially, and the patterns of their mobility reflect regional and intra-regional opportunities.

Public expenditure on **education** increased from 2.2% of GNP after the Second World War to 8.2% in 1979; meanwhile the size of the school-age groups has greatly increased, from 7.0m in 1951 to 10.2m in 1971 and to 11.3m in 1976. The numbers in full-time higher education leapt from only 100,000 in 1951–2 to 432,400 in 1970, then rose more slowly to 460,700 in 1979. Of the estimated 9.3m of school age in the mid-1980s, a higher proportion may stay on into the sixth form, though fewer than were expected in the late 1960s are likely to go on to higher education, not least because of government cuts in provision.

However, there has been no general levelling-up of opportunities in education, even in the public sector. The varying investment in education by local authorities as well as by individual families, points to the diversity in regional opportunities, which in turn reflect levels of prosperity as well as differing choices in the allocation of resources. One important criterion of educational opportunity is the proportion of those who stay on to 16 (the O-level group) or to 18 years (the A-level group). The proportions of pupils staying on after the compulsory age are highest in the SE, Wales and N Ireland (table 2.25). 18+ leavers show less striking variations, but the Welsh tradition of higher education stands out, while the SE and Yorks. and Humberside are also above average. Some of the industrial regions, for example the N Region and the W Midlands, are below average. Whilst many rural districts have below-average numbers of 18+ leavers, E Anglia is the only region among the mainly rural areas which is below average. However, postwar censuses show that while the proportion of both girls and boys in full-time education up to the age of 17 was above average in rural areas, it fell sharply for boys in the 18+ group and was well below average for the 20—24 year group, though the proportion of girls in those age-groups in full-time education was above average.

The general implications of such inequalities were a major concern of the *Report of the Committee on Higher Education* (Min. of Education 1963), the Robbins Report, which underlined the varying opportunities for high-school education, especially as between different social groups. At that time, in areas of generous provision and high social status 14.5% of 17-year-olds were in school in 1960, whereas in low status, low-provision areas, only 6.4% had full-time schooling at that age.

Age of completed school education reflects both affluence and social-class differentials but also the varied emphasis given to education by local authorities. In detail there are many puzzling differences in local authority provision for education, especially as between the former county boroughs. Coates and Rawstron (1971, ch. 10) have shown that not only does provision of private schooling directly reflect regional character and extent of affluence, but many similarities appear in the provision of sixth-form education. Private school places are well above average in all the counties of England south of a line from Suffolk to Gloucester, except Essex, Wiltshire, Somerset and Cornwall, and are important around Edinburgh, while there is above-average sixth-form provision for Greater London, the South East and in Wales. Whilst there has been some levelling-up in opportunities during the 1960s and 1970s, there is still poorer provision in the former county boroughs than in the administrative counties of England; the level of provision of sixth-form places is relatively low, especially for girls, in such industrial areas as Durham, parts of the W and E Midlands and in some of the more rural areas, notably in E Anglia.

The situation is particularly worrying in the inner cities where schools have both declined in enrolment and become socially unbalanced. Despite priority provision for primary schools under the *Plowden Report* (Central Advisory Council for Education 1967), there are still relatively low levels of academic achievement and school-leavers staying on for further study or proceeding to higher and further education. The extent to which this reflects lack of motivation and lack of ability, or is due to lack of opportunity and part of a cycle of deprivation and poverty, is keenly debated. A particularly worrying aspect of the problem in many inner city areas is the inadequate provision for the special educational needs of ethnic groups who now form a significant proportion of the school population in parts of the big cities, for example in inner London, in the W Midlands and in more limited areas of the towns of the E Midlands and N England. With 90% of British-born coloured people under 15 in 1971 and the *proportion* of immigrant births in such areas still high, this will be a continuing challenge in the 1980s.

These features undoubtedly reflect considerable regional disparities in **personal incomes**. Though data available for study of incomes are limited, a number of studies by Coates and Rawstron (1971, ch. 10) have drawn attention to salient features of the distribution of personal incomes in the UK. Their analysis shows that in respect of tax on all types of income — schedule E (basic salaries and wages), schedule D (on fees) or on investment income — the SE quadrant of Britain is a favoured area. Levels of income are highest in Greater London and the SE, shading away west and north through average levels of income over most of the industrial quadrilateral of the Midlands to reach the lowest levels in the Scottish Highlands and Islands and in N Ireland. Moreover, during the 1960s the greatest improvement in incomes was largely within the South East, but outside Greater London; no doubt

TABLE 2.25

School-leavers and Pupils at School beyond the Statutory Age, UK, 1967–79

REGION	Percentage leaving school at				School-leavers Degree courses¹		School-leavers All other full-time education²		Employment		% Pupils* remaining at school beyond school-leaving age (15/16) (State maintained schools only)					
	15	16	18+	18+							1964 at age		1972–3 at age		1978–9	
	1967	1979	1967	1979	1967	1979	1967	1979	1967	1979	16	18	16	18	16	18
North	52	73	11	9	4	7	12	8	84	85	20	4	29	6	39	5
Yorks. and Humberside	49	69	13	11	6	8	14	10	81	82	22	6	30	7	44	6
North West	47	70	13	13	6	8	13	12	81	80	23	5	29	5	41	6
E Midlands	53	68	13	12	5	7	12	14	83	79	21	5	30	6	43	6
W Midlands	49	65	12	13	5	7	13	14	82	79	23	4	32	6	43	6
South East	–	57	–	16	–	9	–	14	–	77	33	6	41	8	–	–
Gtr London	31	–	17	–	7	–	10	–	83	–	–	–	–	–	65	8
Rest	35	–	16	–	7	–	16	–	78	–	–	–	–	–	61	8
E Anglia	47	69	12	13	4	6	16	16	79	78	21	4	29	5	41	5
South West	38	63	16	14	7	8	17	18	76	74	27	5	34	6	45	6
Wales	42	61	17	14	7	9	18	14	75	77	30	9	36	9	48	9
Scotland	30	56	9	4	12	15	5	NA	83	NA	23	3	33	3	54	7
N Ireland	54	51	11	9	NA	NA	NA	NA	NA	NA	14	5	35	12	36	12

* 18-year-old pupils as compared to the 13-year-old group 5 years earlier; N Ireland figures are for all schools
For non-maintained (private) schools, the respective percentages were 71 and 14 in 1964, and 75 and 15 in 1972–3
¹ 1967 figures refer to Universities only
² 1967 figures refer to Polytechnics, Colleges of Education and other advanced Further Education Establishments
Source: *Statistics of Education* (1967, 1973 and 1979); *Regional Trends* (1982)

out-movement of higher-income groups from the centre explains this. The lowest increases and the greatest relative declines in incomes were experienced in Scotland, much of N England and in N Ireland. By the mid-1960s the disparities in personal incomes ranged from an index of 72 in counties Londonderry and Tyrone to 108 in Hertfordshire (UK = 100). Between 1949–65 the best Scottish counties were all in C Scotland, but the highest index of 96 was reached only in West and Mid Lothian; in Ireland the best county, Antrim, had an average index of only 90. Indeed only the SE and the W Midlands had an index of over 100. In 1979–80 as compared with an average weekly household income in the UK of £134, the range was from £113 in N Ireland to £153 in the OSE. Taking the UK as 100 the SE took 115.1 per head of GDP, N Ireland 74.9, Northern Region 92.7 and Scotland 96.0.

It is not unrealistic to speak of continuing *poverty* within the UK, not only in the poorer social classes but in poorer areas. While real wages have increased considerably since 1961, during which time the average weekly earnings of manual workers have increased more than sevenfold, many poorly paid workers still depend on various supplementary payments for support. One of those measured by Coates and Rawstron, free school meals, shows that a similar gradient to that of incomes exists in England and Wales, with low levels of claim in the SE quadrant, increasing westwards and northwards to reach peaks in N England and Mid- and NW Wales. Once more, however, greater contrasts exist within urban areas. While most of the county boroughs of N and NW England, Yorkshire and S Wales have high proportions on free school meals, the proportions are greatest in the inner city. Here they join forces with the various indices of social deprivation which have been discussed in the context of 'levels of living' by Knox (1974) and in terms of housing and social problems within cities by Kirby *et al* (1976). The problems of the inner city with its high incidence of poor housing, poor social provision, high unemployment and various kinds of social malaise have long been recognized (Flynn *et al* 1972; Holtermann 1975) and were the subject of massive Inner Area Studies for Birmingham, Lambeth and Liverpool commissioned by the Department of the Environment in the mid-1970s. Despite a whole battery of inner city programmes and more recent attempts to integrate these via partnership schemes, such areas remain the greatest concentrations of deprivation and social unrest in the UK, as witness the widespread city riots of the summer of 1981. Indeed, the range of most demographic, housing, social and economic measures, including unemployment, is much greater between inner city and outer periphery than between the best-endowed and poorest regions of the UK.

Social segregation in urban residential areas is treated in chapter 6, pp. 442–7.

IV   THE WORKFORCE – DISTRIBUTION AND DAILY MOBILITY

While on a broad regional scale incomes reflect many of the demographic and social contrasts within the UK, they are also closely related to considerable regional contrasts in employment and unemployment.

IV.1   Size and Structure of the UK Workforce

Demographic structure determines the size of the potential workforce now and for the future. The rapid increases in both under-15s and retirement age-groups in the

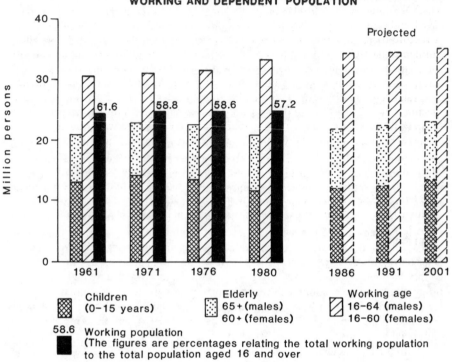

GREAT BRITAIN
WORKING AND DEPENDENT POPULATION

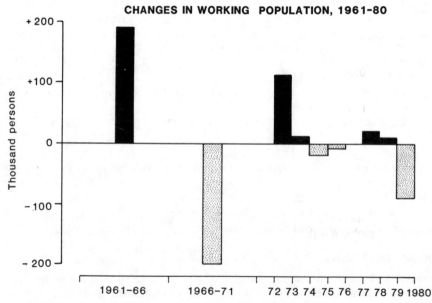

Figure 2.12   Working and dependent population, GB, 1961–80

last thirty years will not be repeated over the next thirty when the greatest increases
will probably occur in the working age-groups, especially in the 15–44 year olds
(table 2.6). Dependency-rates (677 per 1,000 of working age in 1974) fell to 598 in
1981 and estimated as 618 per 1,000 for 2001. It is not easy to relate such age-
structure trends to the available workforce, since this involves knowledge of factors
influencing activity rates in the various sections of the population. The proportion
of married women and elderly people at work varies with labour demand; the
proportion of school-leavers going on to higher education, which rose continuously
and relatively rapidly in the 1960s and 1970s, has now slowed down and will
decline. In 1973 the raising of the school-leaving age to 16 led to a sharp apparent
drop in the workforce for that year. The available workforce was expected to
increase between 1974–85 by an estimated 6.4% (4.7 for men and 9.2% for
women), but recession has negated this. Growing unemployment problems in a
deepening recession have made it impossible to absorb the potential labourforce in
the 1970s, with sharp and progressive increases in unemployment from 849,000 in
1971 to 2.03m in late 1978 and 3.07m in January 1982. A substantial part of this
is due to the big increase in school-leavers from the late 1970s, despite the palliative

TABLE 2.26

Economically Active Population, UK, 1951–79

	Actual 1951	1961	1971	1979
GB				
Economically active (000s)	22,610	23,811	25,103	25,000
male	15,649	16,071	15,917	15,100
female	6,961	7,740	9,186	9,900
married female	2,658	3,886	5,799	NA
Activity rates (%)				
male	87.6	86.0	81.4	78.6
female	34.7	37.4	42.7	46.9
married female	21.7	29.7	42.2	49.0
N IRELAND				
Total working (000s)	466	539	595	
male	295	365	394	
female	171	174	201	
Activity rates (%)				NA
male	62.3	63.2	64.2	
female	35.8	33.6	35.2	

Activity rates: economically active as percentage of total population aged 16 and over (over 15,
1951–71). Data for N Ireland not directly comparable with those for GB.
NA = not available
Source: Social Trends, 5 (1974) and *12* (1982)

offered by various work-experience and job-creation schemes. But a more
fundamental problem is the downturn in the total number of jobs available reflected
in the increase of the level of long term unemployment (i.e. over 6 months) to 45%
of total male unemployment as compared with 40% for men and women. Moreover,
though the proportion of women in the workforce is still increasing, the total of
women employed is no longer rising as quickly as it did up to the mid-1970s, but

this may be due partly to concealed unemployment especially among older married women.

IV.2 Factors Influencing Regional Trends in Employment

The capacity to absorb more potential workers depends on the state of the economy; at regional level this is related to varying trends in employment (ch. 1) and population. Despite attempts to provide additional jobs in the less prosperous regions of high unemployment and slow economic growth, the various measures have had less success than hoped in slowing down population and job losses in the poorer areas. Nevertheless, without such measures things would have been worse. Of 870,000 jobs resulting from movements of manufacturing industry between 1945 and 1961, 427,000 were from Greater London, 98,000 from the rest of the SE and 62,000 from the Midlands, in all 687,000 (79% of the total) from the prosperous regions (Howard 1968). But only 231,000 (34%) of these went to the less prosperous regions, 119,000 between 1945–51, a mere 28,000 from 1952–9 and 84,000 in 1960–5; the rest were redistributed in the better-off areas.

However, for nearly twenty years after the Second World War no attempt was made to influence the distribution of employment in services (ch. 4.IV), the fastest-growing sector of employment and that in which the SE is dominant, especially in administrative and managerial (Standard Industrial Classification – SIC – group 25) and professional and technical (SIC group 26) workers (fig. 1.2). Voluntary movement of offices from London was first encouraged by the Location of Offices Bureau, set up with government assistance in 1963. Initially few firms moved far from Greater London and the main beneficiaries were places like Croydon, whose new office complex led to a remarkable increase in jobs in the borough in the mid-1960s and which by the mid-1970s was itself largely saturated as an office centre, and the New Towns. Some government departments moved to development areas, e.g. the Post Office Savings Bank to Glasgow and the National GIRO to Bootle. Even after the *Control of Offices and Industrial Development Act* of 1965 brought office development under controls similar to those for manufacturing industry and restricted new office building within 65 km of C London, the policy had to be relaxed in the face of shortage of office accommodation in the SE and of reluctance of employees and employers alike to move to a development area. In the period 1963–9 progress was slow even in areas with a surplus of good office accommodation (Manners *et al* 1972, 21) and in the 1970s office devolution, particularly from London, experienced difficulties as the recession slowed down expansion of office jobs. This has resulted in a surplus of office accommodation in most of the six centres around the GLC periphery scheduled for office development under the structure plan as well as in many provincial cities such as Liverpool.

According to the *Hunt Report* (Sec. of State for Economic Affairs 1969, 14–15), the greater part of the 4% growth in employment between 1961 and 1966 was due to a 6% increase in the prosperous regions: in most of the development areas, Merseyside and the South West apart, there were small increases in total employment and a fall in industrial employment. Therefore the less prosperous areas continue to compare unfavourably with national trends. In the 1960s the DAs fared badly in terms of unemployment, changes in employment, female activity rates and average male earnings, and very badly in some of the sub-regions.

TABLE 2.27

Net Inter-Regional Flows of Working-age Migrants (15–59), GB, 1965–6 (hundreds)

Net gain from (+) or loss (−) to		North		Midlands		South		Wales		Scotland		Total	
		M	F	M	F	M	F	M	F	M	F	M	F
North	M			−9.1		−5.0		−9.7		+22.1		−1.7	
	F				−9.5		−38.1		−9.8		+15.6		−41.8
Midlands	M	+9.1				+6.9		+6.3		+17.8		+40.1	
	F		+9.5				−22.9		+1.6		+14.8		+3.0
South	M	+5.0		−6.9				+7.0		+27.1		+32.2	
	F		+38.1		+22.9				+9.9		+24.3		+95.2
Wales	M	+9.7		−6.3		−7.0				−1.0		−4.6	
	F		+9.8		−1.6		−9.9				−1.3		−3.0
Scotland	M	−22.1		−17.8		−27.1		+1.0				−66.0	
	F		−15.6		−14.8		−24.3		+1.3				−53.4

'North' includes the Northern, Yorks. and Humberside and North West planning regions;
'Midlands' includes the East and West Midlands;
'South' includes the South East, East Anglia and the South West.
Source: *Long Term Population Distribution in GB. A Study* (HMSO 1971). Generalized from Appendix 2, Table 6

Not surprisingly, these facts were reflected in the total net migration figures for the regions (table 2.13). Other factors influencing migration are apparent in the high levels of net immigration to the SW, an area of generally low earnings and some pockets of considerable unemployment, but of great environmental attraction, especially to older people. The general 1965–6 pattern of inter-regional mobility of working-age population shows the position very clearly (table 2.27). Considerable losses by Scotland and the North and a small out-movement from Wales were transferred, though not directly, to the Midlands, where the main gains were of male workers, and the South, which had considerable gains of men and, especially, of women. Much of this movement was of highly qualified professional and managerial workers. Waugh (1969) has shown that between 1961 and 1966 the North and West lost both population and 'a disproportionate share of talent and expertise'. This no longer went directly to the SE and W Midlands, and indeed the SW and E Anglia benefited most in the early 1960s. Yet the SE, which had in 1961 the greatest concentration of high-status socio-economic groups (groups 1–4), made the greatest gains in these groups 1961–6, Greater London apart, both in managerial and professional groups. Conversely, most rural counties showed a decline in such groups and in many of the depressed industrial areas, notably the coalfields of NE England and S Wales, the proportions of high-status population were low despite an increase in commuter residents in the 1960s. Thus, regional contrasts in socio-economic status have continued to increase, with upward social mobility reinforcing the already strong position of the more prosperous regions, though the precise details of distribution are being reshaped with intra-regional changes in residence and workplace.

IV.3   Economically Active Population

Two aspects of employment are relevant to the analysis of social and economic health of the regions of the UK: the numbers and proportion of those in employment and of those out of work. Though complementary in many respects, they illustrate different facets of labour demand and supply, and of population structure as related to the actual and potential workforce.

Employed population   The employed population is partly a function of age structure, partly of socio-economic factors, especially the proportions in full-time education beyond the compulsory age, and partly also of demand for labour. For example, opportunities of well-paid jobs for school-leavers may account for relatively low proportions of boys staying on at school in the W Midlands (table 2.25). The relatively high proportions of employed population in E Lancashire result from a long-standing tradition of women mill-workers; the much smaller percentage working population of coal-mining areas is by contrast due to low proportions of women in the workforce, a response to a tradition of women staying in the home in an area of shift workers, as well as of lack of job opportunities for girls. In many areas the reserve of labour among married women not at work offers one of the best ways of expanding the labourforce in the short term, often using part-time labour. Yet when demand for labour falls such women are often the first to be laid off; since they often are not in benefit and do not register as unemployed they may well in times of high unemployment represent a considerable measure of concealed unemployment. Workers of pensionable age, also often employed part-time, perform a similar role in the labourforce.

Activity rates Thus, the proportion of persons in employment, as a percentage of the population over school age (as in table 2.26) is a significant index of the varying intensity of economic activity and labour utilization. A map based on the *1971 Census* (fig. 2.13) shows for administrative counties and county boroughs the higher proportions of the economically active, both men and women, in industrial and urban areas than in rural, though this is more pronounced for the male population. In part this is due to the more elderly population structure of rural areas but it also reflects the narrower range of job opportunities as well as economic activities. Where this is wider, as in the textile areas of the Scottish Border counties, activity rates are much higher.

In 1971 the highest regional proportions of active male population were in Greater London and parts of the inner metropolitan area and in the Midlands (fig. 2.13). There is a general gradient of decreasing activity rates southwards and westwards, though there are exceptions as, for example, in the western parts of the Fenland counties, while the industrial areas of the north and west tend to have higher rates than the regional average (for example, S Wales), though the rates for C Scotland are low.

Female activity rates vary considerably, both at regional level and within regions, or even counties, as between employment exchange areas. But the principal feature is the one-third increase in working women since 1951. In 1969 the proportion of women over fifteen at work in GB was 40%, and regional percentages varied from 22 to 45%. Since then the total number of women working and as a proportion of the workforce has increased, from 9.2m in 1971 to 9.9m in 1979, 37 and 40% respectively of the total workforce. Britton (1975) has shown that a major factor in that increase has been the considerable rise in the proportion of married women, especially older married women, at work. The percentage of the female labourforce who are married increased from 40 to 64 between 1951 and 1971, and the activity rate of married women, aged 45–59, from 22 to 54%. While this partly reflects more universal marriage it is principally due to a shorter period of family formation. 85% of families are now complete within ten years of marriage, with a return to work while children are still young.

In 1971, the highest female activity rates were clearly in the boroughs of the axial belt but, Lancashire apart, were mainly concentrated into Greater London and its surrounding metropolitan area and in the W and E Midlands (fig. 2.13). The highest Scottish rates were mainly in Glasgow, Edinburgh and other major towns and, apart from these, rates were low except in the Border textile districts. Wales, the SW, N and NE England tended to have low or very low female activity rates. This is a pattern which fits closely the differing intensity and patterns of labour demand in the prosperous and less prosperous regions, a pattern which a number of studies have shown to exist also at intra-regional level (Gordon 1970; Coates and Rawstron 1971, ch. 5). Moreover the trends in activity rates fit closely the regional rates of change in employment which between 1966 and 1975 declined more sharply in the less prosperous regions, especially so far as male employment was concerned, and where, apart from the NW, female activity rates are low (Manners *et al* 1972, 40–2; Prest and Coppock 1980, 284).

IV.4 Unemployment

Many local and regional indices of social inequality and of demographic, notably migrational, experience are related to varying regional rates of unemployment.

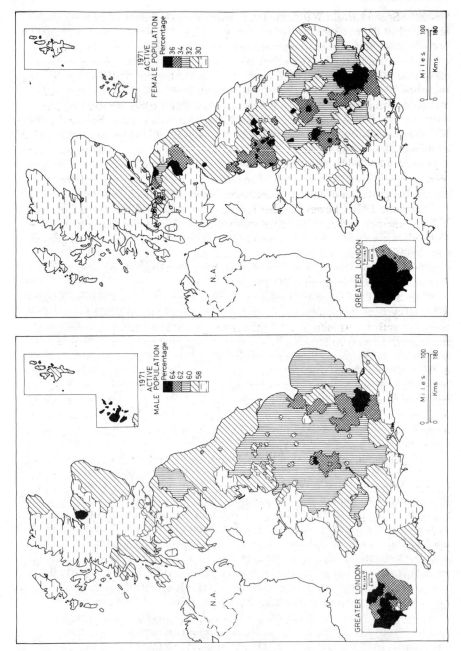

Figure 2.13   Economically active population, GB, 1971

Since the Second World War neither national nor regional rates of unemployment have reached the extremes of the interwar period, but there remains a wide gap between rates in the more prosperous and less prosperous regions. Despite many efforts to diminish the uneven distribution of job opportunities, unemployment rates were above average in the development areas in the period 1961–8, when they had one-fifth of the working population but over one-third of the unemployed and experienced unemployment at up to two and a half times the national rate. Moreover, the North, SW, Wales, N Ireland, together with most of Scotland and the NW, traditionally had higher-than-average proportions of long term unemployed, of unskilled workers and of out-of-work in the 18–44 age-group. Furthermore, these regions have tended to suffer bigger swings in cyclical unemployment. In such areas there is a great need for retraining of labour to attract new types of industry, for the level of provision of industrial retraining is generally much too low.

During the 1970s, however, other regions previously largely immune from high levels of unemployment suffered, relatively and absolutely: for example, in the W Midlands unemployment rates rose considerably, because of cyclical unemployment due to difficult and competitive conditions in the car trade, combined with structural weaknesses in the economy of the region arising from its high level of dependence upon the motor-car industries.

While much of the upsurge in unemployment since 1970 in *all* regions of Britain is due to cyclical unemployment following a prolonged and severe downturn in economic activity, its increased severity as compared with other postwar cyclical fluctuations reflects structural imbalance in the national and in many regional economies. Such structural unemployment is deeper-rooted and likely to be more difficult to deal with, particularly through the existing framework of development area policy. It will demand investment in new industry, retooling of outdated plant and more extensive industrial retraining schemes which go beyond those at present provided even in DAs. Unless and until there is national recovery there will be little prospect of any region, whether in the DAs or the prosperous areas of the postwar period, reaching a better employment level.

One problem in many areas of high unemployment is the extent to which labour mobility may be impeded by housing problems, difficult journeys to work or other factors which tend to inhibit the decanting of surplus labour to jobs, locally or in other regions. Such frictional unemployment could be eased by more flexible housing policies for, as Johnson *et al* (1974) have shown, the migration of labour is considerably influenced by housing availability, and local authority tenants in particular often find it difficult to find accommodation if they should move to a new job. Conversely, people decanted from city centres to overspill estates or New Towns may often have to give up a job if the journey to work becomes difficult and cannot always find secure alternative employment, as the experiences of closures of factories in Skelmersdale, near Liverpool, indicated.

At the core of much unemployment, however, lie imbalances arising from a rapidly changing technology in which new methods of production and of handling and retailing of goods lead to economies in labour in a period of rapidly rising wages and falling market. For example, the drastic reduction in the dock labour-force on Merseyside is due both to the relative decline of the port and the de-casualization of dock labour in 1967 (following the recommendations of the *Devlin Report* on the Port Transport Industry (Min. of Labour 1965) and to a revolution in handling both bulk cargoes (through largely automated loading and unloading) and general cargo, much of which is now containerized and handled and moved by machines rather than, as in the past, by men (Gould and Hodgkiss 1982). Similarly, redundancy in the coal industry since the 1950s is a consequence of a number of factors including alternative fuels and exhaustion of resources but also of greater mechanization.

In such redundancies it is usually the older people who find it most difficult to retrain or to find alternative employment. This is a problem which has spread in the 1970s to the tertiary sector as recession and new technologies (for example, computers and microprocessors) have affected business operations. As Prest (1970, 205–6) has shown, this age factor is a major problem in the re-employment of nearly one-quarter of unemployed men, some 45% of unemployed men being over forty-five. In the case of manual workers in particular, ill-health may add to this problem which is significant in social as much as economic terms. Hence, many of those who become redundant in their late 40s and 50s will form part of the increasing numbers of long term unemployed.

Unemployment rates (excluding school-leavers) in GB have ranged between 1% in the mid-1950s and 11.7% (February 1982). Behind these percentages is the dramatic rise in the unemployed from half a million in the late 1960s to nearly 1m in 1975, 2.2m by the end of 1980 and 3.1m in January 1982. Regional figures have ranged from as little as 0.4% (W Midlands) and 2.2% (Scotland) in 1955, to 8.7% (SE) and over 10.3% (SW) in 1982 in Southern England, while rates in the W Midlands are now much higher (14.3% in February 1982), ranking with those in the NW (14.1%), the North (14.8%), Scotland (13.7%) and Wales (15.0%). Throughout N Ireland's unemployment rate (18.1% in February 1982) has been far above that for the UK as a whole.

Intra-regional unemployment rates have an even wider range. In 1961–6, a period of relatively low unemployment, rates were 10% in parts of the Scottish Highlands and Islands and, according to the *Hunt Report*, most areas of Britain had local pockets of unemployment two to three times the regional rate (Sec. State Econ. Affairs, 1969). Thus while the relative position of unemployment in the regions of the UK has changed little, the gap between the worst and the best figures has widened since 1974. After a sharp increase in unemployment between 1970–2, the national rate fell to 2.7% in 1973–4, increased sharply to around 6.0% in 1977–9 and rose catastrophically to 11.3% at the turn of 1981–2. In the mid-1970s regional unemployment rates were less than 5% except in the N, NW, Scotland, Wales and N Ireland, but the rate was 7.5% in the development areas as a whole and 5.5% in the intermediate areas. In some employment exchange areas, however, unemployment was substantially over 10% and in Strabane (N Ireland) no less than 30.5%. By February 1982 in many of the hardest-hit areas local unemployment rates were around 20% or more, the highest being still in Strabane (37.0%).

As the recession has deepened, the worst-hit areas with the highest numbers of closures of industry have remained in the peripheral areas of Britain, but the relative position of the W Midlands has also worsened considerably as markets in the automobile and other staple industries plummeted. Between 1976 and 1980 only the SE, the E Midlands and E Anglia were consistently below the national unemployment rate, the W Midlands, Yorks. and Humberside, and the SW intermittently so (fig. 2.14). The worsening of the situation was greatest in Scotland, Wales, the North, NW, Yorks. and Humberside and the W Midlands. On

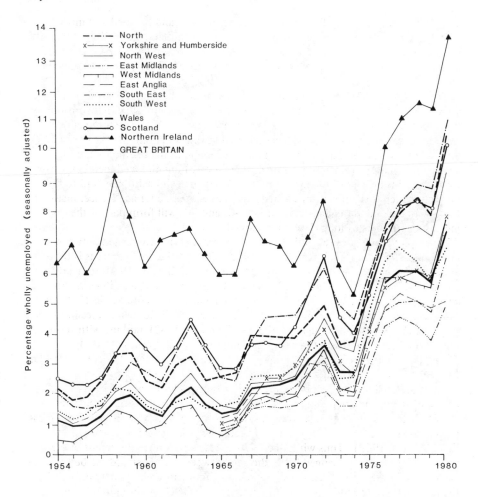

Figure 2.14   Regional unemployment, UK, 1954–80

all counts, N Ireland has been the hardest hit by unemployment, in good times and bad. Yet the pattern is not simply one of uniformly high rates in the deprived areas and good in the core area. In all regions there are employment blackspots. The worst of these are in the large cities. In June 1975, 39% of UK unemployment was in 14 urban markets in each of which there were over 10,000 unemployed (Salt 1976). Moreover, within such areas the unemployment problems of the inner city are much worse than those of their respective regions.

Unemployment statistics alone do not show the full situation, since not all those who are out of work register as unemployed. The data on active population who were recorded in the 1971 census as 'not working' forms a useful basis for analysis of unemployment at county and county borough level (fig. 2.15). Similar regional differences appear, if anything more strongly, with high proportions of both men

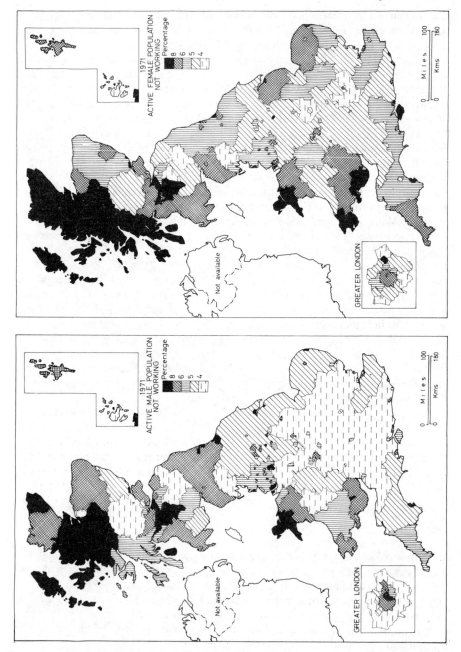

Figure 2.15   Active population not working, GB, 1971

and women not in work in Scotland, N England and Wales and relatively low proportions in the Midlands and SE. The relatively high proportions of women not working in the Midlands, E Anglia and the SE suggest that there may well be much concealed unemployment or under-employment of women, though in certain areas seasonal unemployment may be involved, as for example in the resort areas of the Fylde, the Isle of Wight and SW England. Such seasonal unemployment tends to be dominant in the winter months; mid-year figures (for July) are thus more indicative of deep-seated trends. In rural areas the relatively higher proportions of active females not working suggests a reservoir of labour. Within all regions the 1971 census data suggest higher levels of unemployment in central city areas, especially in Greater London and the conurbations where there are higher proportions of both men and women out of work in the central boroughs than in the surrounding areas. This reflects the higher levels of unemployment among the semi- and unskilled groups among whom New Commonwealth immigrants are particularly adversely affected. Many who came to Britain in the late 1950s and 1960s to make up regional shortages of unskilled labour now find it difficult to get jobs in an economy which finds it increasingly hard to absorb unskilled labour. From 1961 and 1966 census data Davison (1966, 89) showed that even then unemployment among New Commonwealth immigrants was above the 3.2% average for English-born people, especially for Jamaicans (7.4%), other West Indians (6.0%), Pakistanis (5.4%) and, to a lesser extent, Indians (4.4%). These rates are correlated inversely with low proportions in higher socio-economic groups and directly with high proportions in manual and unskilled groups, with higher proportions of New Commonwealth-born out of employment as a percentage of all in this group than are in employment or in the total population (table 2.28). While all the main coloured immigrant groups have higher proportions out of employment than their total numbers would suggest, this is especially so in the case of West Indians.

It has been argued that these people find it hard to break out of this situation and to gain the educational and occupational skills which will permit them to rise in socio-economic status (Krausz 1971, ch. 4, 111–22; Deakin 1970, 72–82). Discrimination in employment and isolation within poor residential areas will only compound the problem. That this *is* now a problem can be seen in the statistics gathered since May 1971 on unemployed minority-group workers. In May 1972 coloured workers formed 2.7% of all unemployed in GB as compared with a total of 2.15% New Commonwealth immigrants living in Britain at the time of the 1971 census, with rates of unemployment particularly high among West Indians and, to a lesser extent, among Pakistanis. Between November 1973 and May 1975, a period of generally rising unemployment, the workless among such groups increased by 156% as against a 65% increase among all unemployed with increases most severe among younger people. An analysis of minority-group unemployment by age (February 1975) showed that 31% of men and 44% of women without jobs were under twenty-five (Dept of Employment 1975).

The position has worsened considerably since the 1970s, primarily due to the rapid rise of unemployment among black youths (Runnymede Trust 1980). Between November 1973 and February 1980, total unemployment doubled but the numbers of black unemployed increased fourfold, the highest levels of increase being among unskilled young people, especially West Indian and Pakistani.

The problem of the immigrants, however, is but a special aspect of the more general problem of high unemployment as an aspect of social deprivation in the inner areas of our cities (Davidson 1976, 108–17). This problem has been exacerbated by the fall in the number of jobs available in such areas following redevelopment of city centres and the movement out of industry under planning policies of the 1960s, a fall which has led to the loss of thousands of jobs and considerable rating revenue. The consequences are twofold: those that remain in the inner areas tend to be the older or less privileged and less well-educated and well-trained sections of the population to whom fewer jobs are open; secondly, housing policies have tended to increase the relative proportion of such groups of people within inner areas which have become increasingly dominated by local authority rented accommodation (often in high-rise flats) and the remaining, often old and poor-quality, private rented housing. There is real need for an urgent drive not only on unemployment but on the associated social and population problems of the inner city. The level of the problem may be judged from the situation on Merseyside. Here, in a region with persistently above-average rates of unemployment, there has been a considerable decline in the population of inner areas since 1951 with Liverpool's population alone falling by 280,000 between 1951 and 1981 accompanied by a decline in jobs. As compared with 750,000 jobs and 15,000 jobless in the area in 1966, there were in 1976 100,000 fewer jobs and over 80,000 unemployed. Moreover, 60,000 jobs have been lost from the inner areas in 1977–81 and as many again may be lost in the next decade. Despite considerable inner area programmes since the mid-1970s, unemployment in the inner city remains a desperate problem on Merseyside as elsewhere. With government policies of reducing public expenditure it is hard to see from where will come the £4,505m needed, according to Merseyside County Council, for inner area programmes.

TABLE 2.28

Commonwealth Immigrants Employed and Out of Employment, UK, 1971

Born in	Population enumerated (1971)		% of total		
	Total (000s)	% of GB	Employed	Out of employment	Student and others inactive
UK	50,514	92.85	92.77	91.34	95.18
Irish Republic	721	1.34	1.87	2.83	0.82
Old Commonwealth	145	0.23	0.29	0.29	0.25
New Commonwealth	1,157	2.15	2.57	3.38	1.72
Foreign and not stated	1,077	2.00	2.28	2.01	1.68
Totals	53,826		23,560	1,355	28,469
India	323	0.60	0.75	0.87	0.46
Pakistan	139	0.26	0.32	0.38	0.20
West Indies	303	0.56	0.81	1.30	0.31
Cyprus	73	0.14	0.15	0.19	0.12
Africa	176	0.33	0.30	0.39	0.34

Source: Census 1971, Advance Analysis

IV.5 Workplace and Residence

General features One of the most distinctive characteristics of population distribution in the modern UK is the increasing separation of workplace and residence. Successive censuses from 1921 have revealed a growing volume and intensity of daily travel to work. By 1961, 36% of the economically active population in England and Wales and 25% in Scotland worked outside the local authority area in which they lived. Between 1921 and 1961 the numbers who travelled to work outside their area of residence in England and Wales increased by 115% from 2.6 to 5.6m as compared with a 29% increase of the working population. The *Redcliffe–Maud Report* (R. Commn 1969, III, App.) estimated that, excluding Greater London, daily travel to work was 70% higher in 1966 than in 1921, and showed that in all regions this increase had been much greater than for the population as a whole. Taking 1921 values as 100, the 1966 index of daily out-movement ranged from 144 in the SE, already a considerable commuter area in 1921, to 250 in E Anglia.

The rapid growth in both numbers and range of commuter journeys has been especially marked since 1945. Two sets of forces are involved: first, concentration of jobs, with an increasing range of labour recruitment from surrounding residential areas; secondly, residential dispersal from the inner city to commuter suburbs (Lawton 1967), a feature of postwar population mobility reflected in intra-urban migration and commuting alike, and permitted by improvements in both public and private transport. The causes have been conceptualized by Warnes (1972) as the result of structural changes in industry and the economy, principally increases in real incomes, decreasing hours of work, increasing size and concentration of manufacturing units and a growth in employment in the tertiary sector; the latter is mainly located in central city areas. These may lead to concentration of employment in fewer units, focused in fewer locations, particularly in the urban areas. Higher incomes, however, leave more money for increased travel costs which, combined with a widening search for land for housing outside the city centres, has led to dispersal of both private and local authority housing. Even where, as in the case of London's New Towns and overspill agreements, the intention is to disperse both homes and jobs, the outcome is usually an increase rather than a decrease of both volume and distance of journey to work.

One of the features of recent changes in population has been a growth of adventitious population resident in rural areas but working in the towns. The growing extent of the dependence upon urban employment is reflected in the considerable increase in the proportion of people commuting from rural districts. Between 1921 and 1966 daily out-movement of resident working population from rural districts in England increased from 22 to 47% as against 21 to 34% in all types of area (excluding Greater London), and rural commuter flow to urban areas increased from 387,000 (14.2% of the occupied resident population) in 1921 to nearly 1.5m (37.4%) in 1966. In over one-third of rural districts in 1966, over 40% of the active population travelled to work in urban areas as against 3.5% at this level in 1921; conversely, in 22% of rural districts of England in 1966 there was less than 20% daily out-movement as compared with 78% of rural districts in 1921 (Roy. Commn 1969, III, App. 2).

TABLE 2.29

Aspects of the Journey to Work, Major British Cities, 1951–71

		TOTAL POPULATION				DAILY MOVEMENT IN			OUT			JOB RATIO		
		Resident active Total 1971	% change 1951–71	Working Total 1971	% change 1951–71	Total 1971	1951–61	1961–71	Total 1971	1951–61	1961–71	1971	Change 1951–61	1961–71
City of London	(CL)	3.55	–1.1	340.46	+0.6	338.50	+15.6	–14.6	1.09	–1.3	+43.4	9,590.4	+1,927	–7,664
Croydon	(Cr)(1)	165.42	(+34.0)	134.79	(+39.1)	50.67	+46.0	(+20.8)	64.49	+7.1	(+15.7)	82.1	+5.6	–1.0
Birmingham	(B)	501.37	–11.1	565.14	–11.8	163.20	+44.7	+15.4	47.21	+36.8	+14.5	112.7	+3.0	–2.3
Bradford	(Bd)	140.15	–6.6	140.14	–13.6	32.95	+26.8	+7.1	18.21	+10.6	+36.5	100.0	+0.5	–8.6
Bristol	(Br)	197.25	–1.0	203.29	+17.8	53.59	+62.4	+38.4	25.83	+12.4	+1.7	103.1	+3.4	–0.6
Cardiff	(Ca)(1)	126.92	(+4.5)	137.62	(+19.6)	35.99	+37.8	(+15.7)	10.28	+34.9	(–11.2)	108.4	+1.2	–8.4
Coventry	(Co)(1)	161.74	(+27.1)	171.32	(+24.3)	41.48	+12.1	(+8.9)	17.26	+49.5	(–25.1)	105.9	–6.1	–5.4
Derby	(De)(1)	100.23	(–13.1)	107.83	(–1.6)	23.72	+25.7	(+1.9)	7.44	+25.9	(+24.7)	107.6	+12.0	(+4.8)
Hull	(H)	130.67	+1.5	127.38	–6.7	25.91	+28.4	+28.0	13.35	+29.1	+26.4	97.5	–3.3	–5.1
Leeds	(Le)	233.62	–7.6	244.78	–9.1	57.78	+25.6	+37.3	22.19	+7.5	+19.7	104.8	+0.0	–1.7
Leicester	(Lr)	140.55	–4.9	171.98	+2.1	57.90	+68.3	+20.9	13.97	+32.4	+36.1	122.3	+8.8	–0.5
Liverpool	(Li)	280.94	–22.8	312.31	–24.3	119.08	+22.3	+6.1	47.49	+4.4	+15.5	111.2	+0.7	–2.9
Manchester	(M)	257.08	–28.3	321.48	–25.9	156.87	+23.4	–7.6	56.98	–0.5	–9.6	125.1	+7.5	–3.0
Newcastle	(Nc)	102.10	–24.3	148.02	–25.9	82.68	+25.1	+1.5	22.09	+10.4	–1.3	145.0	–6.0	+3.0
Nottingham	(No)	141.59	–7.8	168.36	–2.9	66.18	+25.0	+22.7	24.24	+6.4	–1.7	118.9	+2.5	+3.4
Plymouth	(Pl)(1)	103.94	(–1.4)	99.48	(–14.7)	13.24	+14.7	(+6.4)	4.97	+21.7	(+23.9)	95.7	+0.0	–13.9
Portsmouth	(Po)	91.39	–10.1	103.90	–2.3	33.34	+75.7	+43.8	9.61	–10.5	+27.8	113.7	+12.0	–3.0
Sheffield	(Sh)(1)	245.05	(–5.2)	255.95	(+5.9)	48.70	+67.2	(+19.2)	15.79	+16.3	(+2.2)	104.4	+4.0	–5.1
Southampton	(So)	98.45	+27.3	105.99	+29.3	31.95	+48.8	+43.8	13.83	+1.9	+31.2	107.7	+2.8	–1.8
Stoke	(St)	134.27	–6.4	141.98	–10.1	36.50	+26.2	+3.8	17.05	+10.1	+16.0	105.7	+0.3	–4.7
Aberdeen	(A)	82.24	+6.2	80.37	+0.8	12.60	+21.0	+65.9	6.61	+43.7	+14.8	97.7	–4.7	–0.5
Dundee	(D)	87.97	+5.0	85.40	–1.9	10.74	+19.6	+62.0	3.28	–7.5	+35.7	97.1	–4.9	–1.9
Edinburgh	(Ed)	212.63	+1.3	222.54	+1.1	42.10	+50.2	+54.8	11.81	+7.4	+38.5	104.7	–0.5	+0.4
Glasgow	(Gl)	410.96	–16.1	414.02	–19.5	116.89	+20.4	+16.8	55.21	+6.1	–11.7	100.7	–4.1	–0.1

(1) Substantial boundary changes to Croydon, Cardiff, Coventry, Derby, Plymouth and Sheffield preclude comparison of 1971 with earlier figures: calculations for 1951–66 (cols. 2 and 4) and for 1961–66 (cols. 7 and 10) are substituted for 1951–71 and 1961–71 respectively, and are shown in parentheses as is the job ratio change for Derby, 1961–66.

Source: Based on *Workplace Tables*, Censuses of 1951, 1961, 1966 (Sample Census) and 1971.

Working, residential and commuter population, 1951–71 The basic changes in
journey to work may, therefore, be focused on two aspects: first, on relative
changes in the residential and working population of the major cities of the UK;
secondly, on changes in daily movement to and from these major centres. Attention
has been focused here upon twenty-four metropolitan centres with a working
population of about 100,000 or over in 1971, though a number of such centres
have had to be excluded: West Ham (now part of the London Borough of Newham)
and Wolverhampton because major boundary changes preclude comparison; the
London boroughs of Camden and Westminster, and Teesside and Warley because
they are essentially the creation of major local government changes in the 1960s.
Moreover, boundary changes in several towns since 1966 preclude direct comparison
of certain trends to 1971 (table 2.29).

Between 1951–71 the residential population of the majority of such cities fell,
by as much as one-fifth in some cases, though Cardiff, Coventry, Croydon,
Plymouth, Southampton and Dundee had an estimated increase, and in Bradford,
Leicester and Aberdeen there was little change (fig. 2.16). However, the rate of
increase of working population, which up to 1961 had generally exceeded that of
residential population or which had fallen at a lesser rate, declined and, in many
cases, showed an absolute fall in the late 1960s. The fact that residential populations are still smaller than the numbers who work in the large cities reflects postwar
spread of population into the suburbs, a process which continues with relatively
little abatement. On the other hand, there have been significant changes in the
distribution of workplaces. Up to the early 1960s a high proportion of jobs in the
large urban areas were focused on a few areas, especially in metropolitan centres.
The job ratio, an index of working population:resident active population x 100, still
indicated a surplus of jobs in most such towns in 1971 (which mainly had ratios of
over 100) (table 2.29). Up to 1966, however, all the cities studied except Croydon
had a job surplus and in all except the City of London job ratios were higher than in
1951; moreover, with the exception of small downward trends between 1961–6 in
Bradford, Bristol, Southampton and Stoke, job ratios were *increasing* up to 1966.
But by 1971 there was a general fall in job ratios in the major towns reflecting a
greater fall in their working populations, in the late 1960s, than in their residential
populations. This suggests a flight to the suburbs of both homes and places of
employment. Among the more marked reductions of job ratio, 1961–71, the City
of London's trend reflects office dispersal from central London, while Plymouth
has lost jobs in the town with the decline of its naval dockyards and has located
much of its new industry outside the 1971 Borough boundary. In contrast,
Croydon, which, until the 1950s, was predominantly a commuter suburb of Greater
London with a low job ratio, greatly increased its job potential with the injection of
10,000 new office jobs in the mid-1960s, when it acquired 79% of offices and nearly
60% of office jobs decentralized from London between 1963 and 1968 (Daniels
1969). Yet even here, between 1966–71 job ratios fell as from the late 1960s office
dispersal went further afield.

Analysis of trends in daily in- and out-movement (fig. 2.17) shows that in only
one case, the City of London, did in-movement decline in 1951–71. In every other
large city there were considerable increases in daily in-movement (36.0% in
aggregate) and these generally exceeded increases in daily out-movement (21.1% in
aggregate). This was changing, however, in the 1960s as job dispersal from the
centre to the periphery of cities gained momentum, especially with the develop-

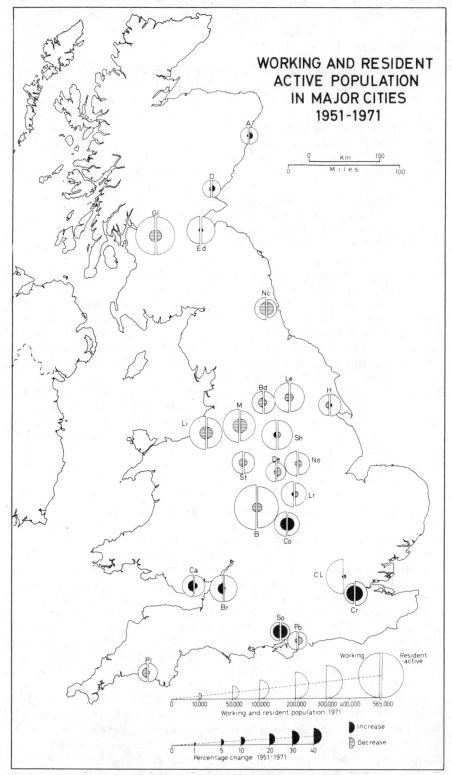

Figure 2.16 Working and resident populations, major cities, GB, 1951–71

*Where the symbol for percentage change is larger than that of total population the latter is superimposed (in white) and percentage change appears as a black border.

Figure 2.17   Daily in- and out-movement, major cities, GB, 1951–71

*Where the symbol for percentage change is larger than that of total population the latter is superimposed (in white) and percentage change appears as a black border.

ment of peripheral industrial estates and dispersal of some office jobs and many distributive industries to sites outside city boundaries. In Greater London, where 51% of the employed population commutes, British Rail suggested that between 1966 and 1973 the number of commuters fell by 8%. However, increases both of in-commuting and out-commuting generally greatly exceeded changes in the resident population between 1951–71 and, collectively, these trends have added to both the volume and complexity of cross-currents of commuting in and around large metropolitan centres.

Two forces are at work in job location, leading to greatly increased daily travel. In the tertiary sector of the economy, the sector of most rapid growth in employment, until recently most jobs were created in the central areas of cities, though some decentralization has taken place since the mid-1960s, mostly in London. On the other hand, many new industrial sites, and a greater proportion of jobs in industry, have moved to the periphery of towns, seeking space, cheaper land and easier transport access and thus leading to a reverse flow of commuting of workers from the city, together with an enlargement of the commuter hinterland into surrounding suburban and rural areas. This peripheral journey to work, as it is often described, is of increasing importance in all advanced industrial economies.

Such trends in journey to work may be epitomized from the example of *Merseyside* (Lawton 1982). The largest concentration of jobs is found in the conurbation centre of Merseyside to which, in 1961, 157,000 workers travelled daily. By 1971 there had been a massive fall in this movement to 93,000, due largely, one suspects, to dispersal of warehousing and industry. Office and service workers are drawn mainly from the suburbs of south Liverpool, Wirral and the commuter areas along the electrified railways to Southport and Ormskirk. Dockside employment in both shipping and industry, though much reduced, still attracts a considerable movement along the waterfront, much of it from the suburbs following widespread slum clearance in the dockside residential areas. Most of the newer labour-intensive industries drawn to Merseyside by development area policy since 1949 have gone to peripheral industrial estates and many 'port industries', such as oil-refining and petro-chemicals, have developed up-estuary and along the Manchester Ship Canal, especially at Ellesmere Port. However, residential dispersal and industrial dispersal are not in harmony. Kirkby, for example, a post-war overspill town for Liverpool, has many new industries on its extensive industrial estates and a job ratio of 131.3 in 1971. But it drew 61.7% of its workers from other parts of Merseyside, while 44.8% of its resident active population travelled to work outside the town, mainly to Liverpool. Similarly, in the early stages of the development of Skelmersdale, Merseyside's first New Town, industry typically lagged behind residential development, as reflected in the 1971 job ratio of 87.0, but 43.6% of residents worked outside the New Town and 39.6% of workers were drawn from outside.

Commuter hinterlands The loss of population from central city areas has not yet been matched by a corresponding redistribution of jobs. Even where employment has been decentralized, it draws labour from wider hinterlands. Over the past fifty years in the NW, according to Warnes (1972, 325), journey-to-work distances have increased by an average of 0.8 km in 1921–51, 1 km in 1951–61 and 1.2 km in 1961–6, resulting in an overall increase of 50% in the mean journey to work from 2.35 to 3.54 kms between 1921 and 1966. These increases were greatest and the commuting range most extensive in the outer suburban areas of the Merseyside and the SELNEC conurbations and in the rural hinterlands of such towns as Lancaster and Barrow-in-Furness.

The journey-to-work tables of the 1971 census show that the number of commuters in England and Wales who travel to work in a local authority area outside their area of residence increased by 309,000 (3.8%) between 1966 and 1971 to 37% of the working population of 22.7m. In Scotland 33% of the working population (3.17m) were involved in such commuting. Despite this there has been a fall in commuting into the centre of most large cities, which is a direct consequence of the decline in employment in inner areas of large cities (ch. 2.IV.4). This decentralization of employment has followed in the wake of postwar decentralizing policies in housing. As Hall (1971 and 1973) has pointed out, this has created a very complex commuting structure, with a number of tiers of journey to work which reflect the hierarchical structure of urban areas, and which contain complex two-way movements between city centre and periphery and considerable and often very complex sets of movements between peripheral centres of employment. Hall *et al* (1973) have described the growing complexity of commuting both between the 'core' and its surrounding 'ring' in one hundred Standard Metropolitan Labour Areas, defined in terms of the size and density of the labourforce, and also with the 'outer city region' within Metropolitan Economic Labour Areas. Their analysis showed that, of 100 SMLAs, 68 were experiencing some decentralization in 1951–61, and 94 were doing so in 1961–6. In a subsequent analysis of 20 of these centres, Champion (1976) has shown that between 1961–71 *all* were showing a decline of population in the 'core' and acceleration in the 'ring'. Warnes (1975) showed that in 1921–66 in Liverpool and Manchester population decentralized faster than employment, with a consequent tendency of commuting to increase, relatively, though the actual volume of movement into the city centre was beginning to decline as compared with the growth of employment around the conurbation fringes. While the strength of movement to the centre is tending to diminish, it is clear that over a lengthy time-period such cities generate forces which are reflected in the organization of employment, population and commuting patterns in the metropolitan region and that these regions have a dominant influence, both directly and indirectly, on population and employment.

Despite the concentration of journeys to work on the major conurbations, rural commuting is also on the increase: in English counties such as N Yorkshire and Westmorland some 20% of the working population are commuters and even in remote and thinly populated counties, such as Radnor, 10% or more of the employed population travel to work outside their area of residence.

The general increase in the extent and complexity of commuter hinterlands is not fully reflected in the volume and pattern of daily movement between towns and their surrounding territories in urbanized and rural areas alike (Lawton 1963B, 61–9; R. Commn, 1969, III, 25–6). The major foci, both in terms of their commuter demand and the range over which daily movement is drawn, are still the large cities. The hinterlands of such cities, together with the City of London, are defined in terms of those local authorities which supplied over one hundred commuters (fig. 2.18). These cover the most populous regions of the UK, and also correspond broadly with the areas from which the greatest proportions of daily out-movement (over 40% of the resident population) are recorded. The extent of these areas of high job-dependence has grown considerably in the last thirty years.

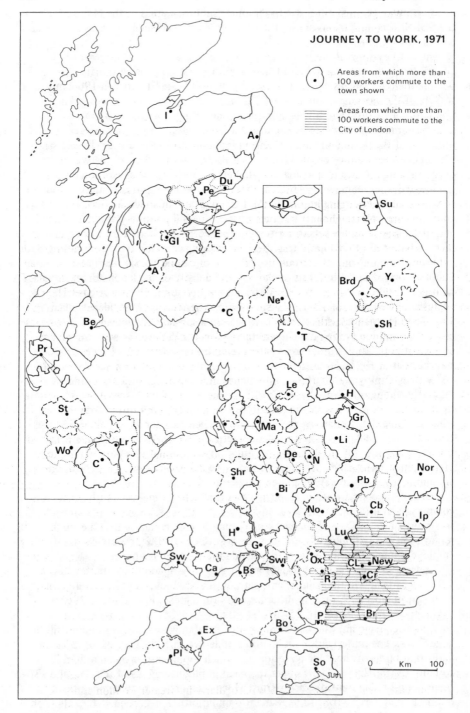

Figure 2.18   Journey-to-work hinterlands, UK, 1971

In the North West, Warnes suggests that by the end of the century the distance travelled to work could increase by as much as 50% on the evidence of recent trends. From a number of recent studies it seems that longer-distance commuting is increasing most rapidly, a process aided by the wider availability of private transport. Major metropolitan areas have increasingly dominated the social and economic life of all regions of the UK and are of fundamental significance to the interdependence of town and country as the various local government studies, including the *Redcliffe-Maud Report* (R. Commn 1969, III, App. 3, 39–47), showed in the 1960s. The Report showed that commuting and intra-regional migration are interdependent. In a detailed study of fourteen towns of varying size and character it was shown that all had lost population in the 15–44 age-group, especially among professional and managerial classes, but that the return daily flow among these groups was stronger than in the journey-to-work pattern as a whole. The towns analysed, ranging in population from 427,800 down to 32,800, were Bristol, Coventry, Nottingham, Leicester, Luton, Northampton, Norwick, York, Exeter, Doncaster, Colchester, Shrewsbury, Taunton and Canterbury. Intra-regional migrants who move to the rural fringes of large towns thus continue to be linked to them through the journey to work as well as for shopping and other services.

Such interdependence is not, however, confined to the hinterlands of large towns or industrial regions but may be found also in rural areas at much lower levels in the urban hierarchy. True, apart from rural Wales, parts of N and SW England, and Southern and Highland Scotland, there are few areas of the UK beyond commuting reach of the employment opportunities in large towns. Yet even in such areas a small town may exert a considerable influence on its region, attracting considerable numbers of workers from an extensive hinterland. For example, Aberystwyth, with important commercial, servicing and cultural functions, in which the University College of Wales plays an important part, had a job ratio of 143.2 in 1971. There are many other similar cases, notably in county towns, though quite small market centres may provide surrounding rural districts with a focus of jobs absorbing 20–40% of their resident occupied population. In most 'rural' counties of England and Wales, therefore, the mean job ratio of municipal boroughs and urban districts is relatively high, while only Merioneth of the rural Welsh counties has a collective urban job ratio of under 100. Somerset's combined urban job ratio in 1971 was 106.4, with very high values in towns like Taunton (136.7) and Yeovil (158.9). Similar examples could be quoted from Hereford, south Lincolnshire, and west Suffolk, to mention only a few counties.

A particularly significant aspect of commuting is that associated with the conurbations. All have job ratios of over 100 and massively large daily movements of population into their industrial and service areas. In the period 1951–71 the numbers travelling to work in the five English provincial conurbations increased by 126.8%. Out-movement also increased substantially, largely due to travel to peripheral industrial estates. Even from a simple analysis of areas contributing over 100 workers per day, the conurbation hinterlands appear very large, extending up to 32 km from the centre in the provincial conurbations and in the case of Greater London forming a vast region containing many complex cross-currents of daily movement of some 80 km in diameter. In all these regions, the level of commuting greatly increased in the 1950s and 1960s particularly in Greater London and the NW conurbations, the greater numbers and longer journeys reflecting the greater dispersal of homes than of jobs. With continuing job losses in city centres in the

TABLE 2.30

Journeys to work, GB, Time and Distance, 1973

Region of residence	% journeys to work taking (minutes)				% journeys to work of distance in miles (km)					
	Under 15	15–30	30–60	Over 60	Under 1 (1.6)	1–2 (1.6–3.2)	2–5 (3.2–8.0)	5–10 (8–16)	10–25 (16–40)	Over 25 (40)
North	35	37	23	5	3	14	42	27	13	1
Yorks. and Humberside	36	39	22	3	7	12	47	23	10	1
E Midlands	42	39	16	3	3	17	56	16	7	1
E Anglia	41	40	16	3	9	16	38	22	13	2
South East										
Greater London	23	26	36	15	3	12	38	25	20	2
Rest of South East	38	34	20	8	6	14	38	19	18	5
South West	55	29	14	2	14	15	42	17	11	1
W Midlands	33	40	24	3	3	15	46	25	10	1
North West	38	35	24	3	5	14	46	24	10	1
Wales	42	38	18	2	7	14	54	13	10	2
Scotland	36	38	22	4	8	17	42	20	12	1
GB	37	35	23	5	6	14	43	22	13	2

Source: Soc. Trends (1974) 5, 106

TABLE 2.31

Journeys to work, GB, Time Taken, 1966–73

	% journeys to work taking (minutes)							
	1966				1973			
	Under 15	15–30	30–60	Over 60	Under 15	15–30	30–60	Over 60
Major urban areas								
London	12	26	42	20	18	29	37	16
Other[1]	14	33	43	10	25	37	33	5
Other urban areas								
Population of:								
250,000–1,000,000	30	46	20	5	23	47	28	3
100,000–250,000	23	42	28	8	37	37	21	5
25,000–100,000	39	34	20	6	35	42	20	3
3,000–25,000	27	34	27	13	35	37	23	6
Non-urban areas	34	31	24	10	33	41	22	4
All areas	25	34	30	11	29	38	26	6

[1] Includes Birmingham, Glasgow, Liverpool and Manchester
Source: *Soc. Trends* (1975) 6

1970s, however, there has been some reduction of journeys to the centre from the outer ring of many SMLAs and a growth in peripheral commuting.

Not surprisingly a considerable part of the working day or, as it may more properly be regarded, of people's leisure time, is taken up by travel to work, since 37% of work journeys are between 3 and 10 miles (4.8 to 16 km), and 16% over 10 miles. The National Travel Survey (Dept of the Environment) has shown that 28% of work journeys in GB take thirty minutes or more and that 37% are of over 8 km. While these figures are highest for Greater London (51% and 47% respectively), even in the SW similar journeys involve 16% of people in half-hour journeys, 29% of which are over 8 km (table 2.30). Rather surprisingly the National Travel Survey suggests that the percentage of journeys taking over thirty minutes fell in London from 62 to 53% between 1966 and 1973, and from 53 to 38% in other major urban areas, though they have increased slightly in large provincial cities (table 2.31). Perhaps the reduction in journey times, not least in the rural areas, reflects the increased use of private cars in work travel. Indeed private transport now accounts for the vast majority of journeys, ranging from 62% of *all* journeys in Greater London to 85.6% in E Anglia. Even so, a small sample taken in Reading in 1973 suggested that men involved in work travel spent on average 2.25 hours per day on it (Bullock *et al* 1974, 57 and 179).

IV.6 New Towns and Overspill

An important aspect of population policy and distribution since 1945, and one of particular significance for the conurbations, has been the attempt to relieve congestion and to provide new homes and jobs through the building of New Towns and the development of overspill arrangements with existing towns (ch. 6.IV.1). Such planned decentralization is not unique, but the first postwar New Towns set up under the 1946 Act were a pioneer venture aimed at providing 'balanced communities of a manageable size, with improved living conditions, employment opportunities of sufficient range to ensure economic stability, besides full social services, including physical and cultural amenities' (Edwards 1964, 279).

The twenty-nine New Towns established in Britain and three in Northern Ireland to date (fig. 2.19), are at very varying stages of development. In 1971 British New Towns already provided 218,000 new dwellings and absorbed a population of 862,000. The *first wave* of New Towns were largely for Greater London, some 40–48 km out, beyond the green belt. Initially mainly concerned with providing housing, they have extended their employment base, though some are still over-dependent on one or two large firms. Collectively, the 'first wave' London New Towns had a population of 493,000 at the end of 1974, of which some 372,000 was overspill, as compared with their planned capacity of 668,500 (table 2.32), but that total had fallen to 486,091 by 1981, reflecting reduction in overspill and also in natural increase due to the falling birth rate. While small in size (the largest, Basildon, was planned to reach 134,000), some have actually seen population fall in the 1970s (e.g. Crawley). The counter-attraction of the conurbation and limited job opportunities within the individual towns have necessitated a considerable degree of commuting, including a sizeable element of travel to work from the New Towns to C London. In 1961 only Bracknell, Stevenage and Welwyn had job ratios of over 100 and the levels of out-commuting ranged from 14 to 40%, while 6.8% of men and 3.7% of women still travelled to work in Greater London. In 1966, 26% of the active population worked outside the eight London New Towns and 29% of their working populations were drawn from outside. Clearly the number and range of jobs was healthier in the 1960s, including more in the service and commercial sector but it would seem that even where the objectives include that of a 'balanced community' a considerable level of commuting is unavoidable in an economy in which more than one member of a household is in work and transport is relatively easy, in terms of cost and accessibility.

Similar problems have been encountered in the New Towns of other regions, though often in a more marked form. The *second wave* of New Towns of the 1960s, in the SE and elsewhere, have generally been focused on existing towns, farther from the major city and often with a considerable initial population of their own (table 2.32 and fig. 2.19). Their original target populations were much larger, presenting a greater opportunity to develop a wider range of jobs and facilities and, since they are farther from the metropolis, giving the chance of becoming more independent than the first wave of New Towns. Such targets were much greater, up to 420,000 in the case of C Lancashire, and an addition of up to 210,000 population at Milton Keynes, perhaps the most ambitious New Town in the UK to date. But in 1977 the government cut these targets. Central Lancashire is no longer needed to house overspill from Merseyside and Greater Manchester, and in other regions target populations have been reduced.

While London has progressed much farther in its programme of New Town building than elsewhere, its case is paralleled in C Scotland where pressing problems of urban renewal, job provision and population overspill, especially from C Clydeside, led to the designation of five New Towns with a present population of 227,400. Glenrothes, the fifth Scottish New Town, was developed in a depressed mining area of Fife and has much in common with Peterlee and Washington in NE England. During 1972 Stonehouse was designated a further Scottish New Town but closed in 1976. The dual motives of overspill housing and job provision are present also in the New Town programme for the W Midlands and the NW, where, in both cases, the later developments are of greater size than the earlier. Wales so far has only one New Town at Cwmbran in south-east Wales, specifically for the problem area of the eastern coalfield. Llantrisant was designated in 1972, but discontinued in 1974 (ch. 1.V.2, Wales). The development at Newtown (Montgomeryshire) is modest and designated to attract some industrial growth to Mid-Wales, perhaps from the W Midlands, rather than to take large-scale overspill. In N Ireland, Belfast and Londonderry, which alike present enormous problems of slums and unemployment, led to the designation of New Towns at Craigavon, Antrim—Ballymena, and Londonderry itself. In 1973, however, the N Ireland New Towns were dissolved and incorporated into the local government structure.

Despite the relative success of GB New Towns in terms of absorbing population **overspill** and attracting new jobs, the scale of development has been inadequate and additional overspill arrangements have been sought by many large cities to relieve pressing problems of housing and population. A variety of arrangements were made in England under the *Town Development Act* (1952) and in Scotland under the *Housing and Town Development Act* (1957). Under these Acts an 'exporting' authority negotiates with a 'receiving' authority for transfer of population, often bearing the cost of housing. Not all such housing is available for overspill, for firms moving to these towns often need accommodation for their labourforce, but the schemes have been of material assistance to large towns in relieving pressure on their housing lists (Scargill 1968).

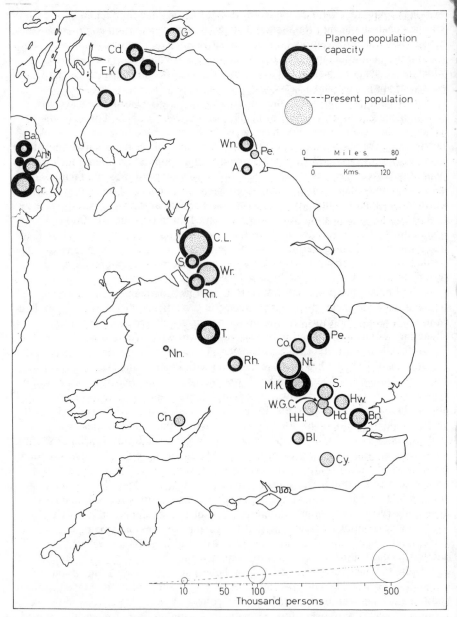

Figure 2.19   New Towns: actual and target populations, UK, 1971

Of the nine British cities which made overspill arrangements under these Acts, by far the biggest scheduled developments were for Greater London (a target of 93,049 dwellings), Glasgow (23,261 dwellings), Birmingham (21,011 dwellings) and Liverpool (18,526 dwellings). No less than sixty-seven schemes involving sixty 'receiver' towns exist in England and Wales. Under separate Scottish legislation

Glasgow has sixty-six schemes scattered throughout virtually the whole of Scotland, ranging from a mere eight houses at Innerleithen to 4,725 in Renfrew county (fig. 2.20). However, the decline in births, reducing the rate of population increase, cuts in public expenditure and the switch in emphasis to rehabilitation of inner city areas are bound to limit such schemes. Thus, in January 1976 the GLC ended its 25-year-old policy of dispersing population and industry to areas outside the capital. The Council resolved not to enter into any more agreements with 'expanding towns' and to negotiate reductions in existing agreements wherever possible.

Altogether fifty schemes were active in the 1960s and 1970s, some of which were of substantial benefit to the towns involved, since they frequently brought new economic activity. As with New Towns, the success of overspill schemes varies with the local and regional economic situation. Thus, Liverpool's overspill agreement with Ellesmere Port made rather slow progress because of the considerable local demand for housing in a rapidly expanding economy. In the Worsley overspill scheme for Salford CB, completed in 1966, the success in providing homes was not matched with success in overspill families obtaining work locally, so that many commuted to work in Salford and Manchester. In 1971 Worsley had a job ratio of 64 and 59% of its active residents worked elsewhere while 48% of its workforce was drawn from outside the town, a situation not dissimilar from that in the earlier stages of the scheme (Rodgers 1959). Another overspill scheme for Liverpool, at Winsford, Cheshire, has been successful both in terms of rehousing Liverpool's population and gaining jobs for the local authority's industrial estate.

✗ There is little doubt that New Towns and overspill schemes have cumulatively made a considerable impact in relieving housing and social problems in many British cities. But progress has been limited and often slow, while many aspects of their economic potential and its relationship to the regional labour market need careful thought (Manners *et al* 1972, 33–4). Over-rapid decentralization of housing and jobs from the inner areas of large cities has been, in the view of many, a factor contributing to an economic and social decline which now presents serious problems. An aspect of this, highlighted in a review of the *Strategic Plan for the South East* (SE Joint Planning Team 1976), is that because of the decline in birthrate in the 1970s and continuing out-migration population will remain around the present 16.73m in the foreseeable future, in contrast to the 3m increase still forecast in 1971. With population moving out of C London at around 100,000 per year in the 1970s and housing policy still geared largely to overspill, population has declined rapidly in the inner areas. Moreover, a considerable loss of both industrial and office jobs, partly through positive policies restricting new developments in inner areas, has limited the provision of the resources and employment opportunities needed for revival of dockland and the inner city. Most parts of inner London have relatively high rates of unemployment by national standards, reaching as much as 10–12% in such areas as Canning Town, and high levels of all indices of deprivation (ch. 2.IV.4). As on Merseyside there are similar massive problems associated with the need to redevelop dockland and the inner industrial areas yet, until recently, there was little active encouragement of industry to locate in the inner areas.

In this situation much of the capital and planning controls devoted to dispersal of industry, houses and population to New Towns and overspill areas will in future be diverted to active programmes of renewal of inner city areas along lines that will

TABLE 2.32

New Towns and Overspill Schemes, UK, 1946–81

REGION (and New Towns) (with date of designation)	NEW TOWNS Population (000s)				OVERSPILL AGREEMENTS			Dwellings (000s)	Overspill population 1968–81 (000s)
	Original	Planned	31 Dec 1974	1981	Towns	No. of schemes	To be built	Completed 31 Dec 73	
LONDON and SOUTH EAST: TOTAL	356.4	1,366.4	800.6	853.2	Greater London	32	93.0	50.9	181
First Wave									
Stevenage (1946); Crawley, Harlow, Hemel Hempstead (1947); Hatfield, Welwyn Garden City (1948); Basildon, Bracknell (1949)	98.4	668.5	493.2	486.1					
Second Wave									
Milton Keynes (1970); Peterborough (1967); Northampton (1968)	258.0	697.6	307.4	367.1					
MIDLANDS and SOUTH WEST: TOTAL	117.7	423.0	196.9	214.9	TOTAL	23	27.8	17.1	
First Wave									
Corby (1950)	15.7	83.0	53.0	47.8	Birmingham	15	21.0	10.3	48
Second Wave									
Redditch (1964); Telford (1968)	102.0	340.0	143.9	167.1	Wolver-hampton	4	4.5	4.5	–
					Bristol	4	2.3	2.3	–
NORTH WEST: TOTAL	413.2	809.0	462.7	484.4	TOTAL	9	31.5	11.9	66
Second Wave									
Skelmersdale (1961); Runcorn (1964); Warrington (1968):	413.2	809.0	462.7	484.4	Liverpool	4	18.5	6.0	41
					Manchester	4	8.5	1.4	25

First Wave									
Aycliffe (1947); Peterlee (1948)	0.3	75.0	51.5	47.5					
Second Wave									
Washington (1964)	20.0	80.0	39.0	47.4	Newcastle	2	2.6	10.5	21
WALES: TOTAL	17.5	68.0	49.7	53.0					
First Wave									
Cwmbran (1949)	12.0	55.0	43.0	44.3					
Second Wave									
Newtown (1967); Llantrisant (1972, discontinued 1974)	5.5	13.0	6.7	8.7					
SCOTLAND: TOTAL	54.2	565.0	222.8	227.4					
First Wave									
East Kilbride (1947); Glenrothes (1948), Cumbernauld (1955)	6.5	275.0	142.5	150.7	Glasgow	66	23.3	9.6	–
Second Wave									
Livingston (1961); Irvine (1966);	40.7	220.0	72.5	71.4					
Stonehouse (1972, discontinued 1976)	7.0	70.0	8.0	5.3					
TOTAL GB	979.3	3,386.4	1,823.2	1,927.8	TOTAL GB	132	186.1	92.1	
NORTHERN IRELAND		320.0	179.8	–					
*Second Wave**									
Craigavon (1965);	–	108.0[1]	61.8	–					
Antrim–Ballymena (1966);	–	120.0	48.0	–	Merged into local govt. units, 1973				
Londonderry (1969)	–	100.0[2]	70.0	–					

Data on overspill population targets are incomplete

* Under *Planning Order (N Ireland) 1973*, Development Commissions were dissolved and Ulster New Towns incorporated into local government structure

[1] by 2001

[2] by 1995

Source: Long Term Population Distribution in GB: A Study (1971), tables 6.2 and 6.3; Manners, *Regional Development in Britain*, tables 5A, B and C; Census 1971 and 1981; Blake (1975), *Town and Country Planning, 43,* 86–97

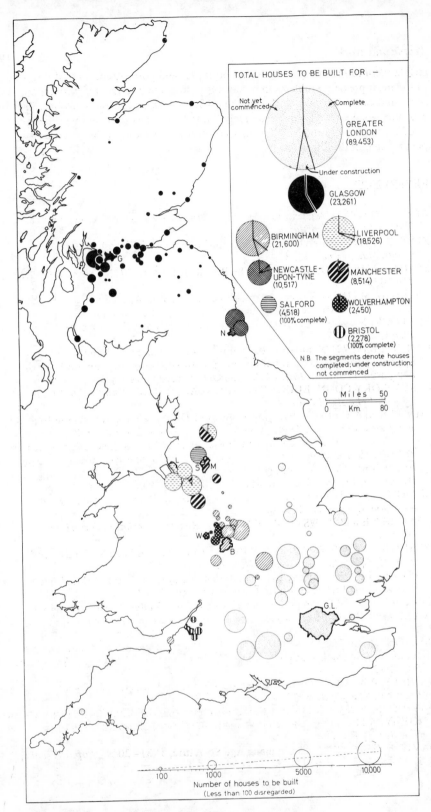

TOTAL HOUSES TO BE BUILT FOR :—

Not yet commenced / Complete

GREATER LONDON (89,453)

Under construction

GLASGOW (23,261)

BIRMINGHAM (21,600)

LIVERPOOL (18,526)

NEWCASTLE-UPON-TYNE (10,517)

MANCHESTER (8,514)

SALFORD (4,518) (100% complete)

WOLVERHAMPTON (2450)

BRISTOL (2,278) (100% complete)

N.B. The segments denote houses completed; under construction; not commenced

Miles 0 50
Km 0 80

Number of houses to be built
(Less than 100 disregarded)
100 1000 5000 10,000

Figure 2.20   Overspill schemes, GB, 1971

enable them to retain and even attract both jobs and population. In so doing, one of the most pressing problems in modern Britain – the interlocking population, social and economic problems of the inner city – may receive more urgent attention at a time when public funds are severely limited. The recent government decision to divert funds from the New Towns to inner area development in the cities is a positive step in this direction.

REFERENCES

ARMEN, G (1972) 'A Classification of Cities and City Regions in England and Wales, 1966', *Reg. Stud.*, *6*, 149–82

BEST, R H (1972) 'March of the Concrete Jungle: Urban Hazards in Britain', *Geogrl Mag.*, *Lond.*, *45*, 1, 47–51

BOOTH, C (1886) 'Occupations of the People of the UK', *Jl R. Statist. Soc.*, *XLIX*, 314–435

BRITTON, M (1975) 'Women at Work', *Popul. Trends, 2*, 22–5
        (1980) 'Recent Trends in Births', *Popul. Trends, 20*, 4–8

BULLOCK, N *et al* (1974) 'Time Budgets and Models of Urban Activity', *Soc. Trends, 5*, 45–63

CAIRD, J B (1972) 'Population Problems of the Islands of Scotland with Special Reference to the Uists', unpubl. paper presented to a symposium on Scottish Population Problems, *Inst. of Br. Geogr.* (Aberdeen meeting)

C. ADVISORY COUN. EDUCATION (ENGLAND) (1967) *Children and their Primary Schools*, HMSO

CHAMPION, A G (1976) 'Evolving Patterns of Population Distribution in England and Wales, 1951–71', *Trans. Inst. Br. Geogr.*, *New Ser. 1*, 401–20
        (1981) 'Counter-urbanisation and Rural Rejuvenation in Britain – an Evaluation of Population Trends since 1971', *Seminar Pap. 38*, Dept Geogr., University of Newcastle upon Tyne

CHILVERS, C (1978) 'Regional Mortality 1969–73', *Popul. Trends, 11*, 16–20

CLARKE, J I (1960) 'Persons per Room: an Index of Population Density', *Tijd. econ. soc. Geogr.*, *51*, 257–60

COATES, B E and RAWSTRON, E M (1971) *Regional Variations in Britain*, London

COMPTON, P A (1976) 'Religious Affiliation and Demographic Variability in N Ireland', *Trans. Inst. Br. Geogr.*, *New Ser. 1*, 433–52

COPPOCK, J T (1972) 'Farming for an Urban Nation', in CHISHOLM, M (ed.) *Resources for Britain's Future*, Harmondsworth, 36–49

CSO (1975) 'Social Commentary: Social Class', *Soc. Trends, 6*, 10–32, HMSO

CULLINGWORTH, J B (1960) *Housing Needs and Planning Policy*, London
        (1963) *Housing in Transition*, London

DALTON, M and SEAMAN, J A (1973) 'The Distribution of New Commonwealth Immigrants in the London Borough of Ealing, 1961–6', *Trans. Inst. Br. Geogr.*, *58*, 21–39

DANIELS, P W (1969) 'Office Decentralization from London – Policy and Practice', *Reg. Stud.*, *3*, 171–8

DAVIDSON, R N (1976) 'Social Deprivation: an Analysis of Intercensal Change', in KIRBY, A M *et al*, 'Houses and People in the City', *Trans. Inst. Br. Geogr.*, *New Ser. 1*, 108–17

DAVIS, N (1976) 'Britain's Changing Age Structure, 1931–2011', *Popul. Trends, 3*, 14–17

DAVIS, N and WALKER, C (1975) 'Migrants Entering and Leaving the United Kingdom 1964–73', *Popul. Trends, 1,* 2–5

DAVISON, R B (1966) *The Black British,* Oxford

DEAKIN, N *et al* (1970) *Colour, Citizenship and British Society,* London

DES *Statistics of Education,* annually, HMSO

DEPT EMPLOYMENT Area Statistics of Unemployment, *Dept Employment Gaz.,* HMSO

(1975) 'Unemployment among Workers from Racial Minority Groups', *Dept Employment Gaz., 9,* 868–71

DoE (1971) *Long Term Population Distribution in GB: a Study,* HMSO

DoE, SCOTT. DEV. DEPT, WELSH OFF. (1964 and 1974) *Housing Statistics GB,* HMSO

DEWDNEY, J C (1968) 'Age Structure Maps of the British Isles', *Trans. Inst. Br. Geogr., 43,* 9–18

EDWARDS, K C (1964) 'The New Towns of Britain', *Geogr., 49,* 279–85

EVERSLEY, D E C (1971) 'Population Changes and Regional Policies since the War', *Reg. Stud., 5,* 221–8

EVERSLEY, D E C and SUKEDO, F (1969) 'The Dependants of the Coloured Commonwealth Population of England and Wales', *Inst. Race Relations, Spec. Ser.,* London

FLYNN, M, FLYNN, P and MELLOR, N (1972) 'Social Malaise Research: a Study in Liverpool', *Soc. Trends, 3,* 42–52

FRIEDLANDER, D and ROSHIER, R J (1966) 'A Study of Internal Migration in England and Wales', *Popul. Stud., 20,* 45–59

GARDNER, M and DONNAN, S (1977) 'Life Expectancy: Variations among Regional Health Authorities', *Popul. Trends, 10,* 10–12

GLASS, D V and GREBENIK, E (1954) *The Trend and Pattern of Fertility in Great Britain,* London

GLASS, R (1960) *Newcomers: West Indians in London,* London

GORDON, I R (1970) 'Activity Rates: Regional and Sub-regional Differentials', *Reg. Stud., 4,* 411–24

GOULD, W T S and HODGKISS, A G (1982) *The Resources of Merseyside,* Liverpool

HALL, P (1971) 'Spatial Structure of Metropolitan England and Wales', in CHISHOLM, M and MANNERS, G (eds) *Spatial Policy Problems of the British Economy,* Cambridge, 96–125

HALL, P *et al* (1973) *The Containment of Urban England,* London

HARRIS, A I (assisted by CLAUSEN, R) (1966) 'Labour Mobility in GB 1953–63', *Soc. Surv. Rep. SS 333,* Minist. Labour and Natn. Serv., HMSO

HOLMANS, A E (1970) 'A Forecast of Effective Demand for Housing in GB in the 1970s', *Soc. Trends, 1,* 33–42

HOLTERMANN, S (1975) 'Areas of Urban Deprivation in GB', *Soc. Trends, 6,* 33–47

HOUSE, J W (ed.) (1977) *The UK Space,* 2nd edn, London

HOUSE, J W, THOMAS, A D and WILLIS, K G (1968) 'Where did the School-leavers go?', *Pap. on Migration and Mobility, 7,* Dept Geogr., Univ. Newcastle upon Tyne

HOUSE OF COMMONS (1971) *Population of the United Kingdom, 1st Rep. Select. Comm. Sci. and Technol.,* HMSO

HOWARD, R S (1968) *The Movement of Manufacturing Industry in the UK,* HMSO

HOWE, G M (1970) *National Atlas of Disease Mortality in the UK,* 2nd edn, London

HUMPHRYS, G (1968) 'Housing Quality' in HUNT, A J (ed.) 'Population Maps of the British Isles 1961', *Trans. Inst. Br. Geogr., 43,* 31–6

INLAND REVENUE *Annual Reports of the Commissioners*, HMSO
JOHNSON, J H, SALT, J and WOOD, P A (1974) *Housing and the Migration of Labour in England and Wales*, Farnborough
JONES, H R (1965) 'Rural Migration in Central Wales', *Trans. Inst. Br. Geogr., 37*, 31–45
JONES, P N (1967) 'The Segregation of Immigrant Communities in the City of Birmingham 1961', *Univ. Hull Occ. Pap. in Geogr., 7*
KELSALL, R K (1967) *The Social Structure of Modern Britain: Population*, London
KENNETT, S (1978) *Differential Migration Between British Labour Markets: Some Policy Considerations*, Dept Geogr., London School of Economics
KENNETT, S and SPENCE, N (1979) 'British Population Trends in the 1970s', *Town and Country Plan., 48*, 221–4
KIRBY, A M *et al* (1976) 'Houses and People in the City', *Trans. Inst. Br. Geogr., New Ser. 1*, 2–122
KNOX, P L (1974) 'Spatial Variations in Level of Living in England and Wales in 1961', *Trans. Inst. Br. Geogr., 62*, 1–24
KRAUSZ, E (1971) *Ethnic Minorities in Britain*, London
LAW, C M and WARNES, A M (1976) 'The Changing Geography of the Elderly in England and Wales', *Trans. Inst. Br. Geogr., New Ser. 1*, 453–71
LAWTON, R (1963A) 'Recent Trends in Population and Housing in England and Wales', *Sociol. Rev., 11*, 303–21
         (1963B) 'The Journey to Work in England and Wales: Forty Years of Change', *Tijd. econ. soc. Geogr., 34*, 61–9
         (1967) 'The Journey to Work in Britain: Some Trends and Problems', *Reg. Stud., 2*, 27–40
         (1982) 'The Distribution and Structure of Population since 1951', ch. 11 of GOULD, W T S and HODGKISS, A G *The Resources of Merseyside*, Liverpool
LAWTON, R and CUNNINGHAM, C M (eds) (1970) *Merseyside: Social and Economic Studies*, London
MACKAY, D I (1969) *Geographical Mobility and the Brain Drain: a Case Study of Aberdeen University Graduates 1860–1960*, London
MANNERS, G *et al* (1972) *Regional Development in Britain*, London
MARSH, D C (1965) *The Changing Social Structure of England and Wales, 1871–1951*, 2nd edn, London
MINIST. EDUCATION (1963) *Report of the Committee on Higher Education* (Robbins Report), Cmnd 2154, HMSO
MINIST. HOUSING and LOCAL GOVT (1964) *Report of the Committee on Depopulation in Mid-Wales*, HMSO
         (1966) *Our Older Homes: A Call for Action*, Report of the Sub-Committee on Standards of Housing Fitness, HMSO
MINIST. LABOUR (1965) *Final Report of the Committee of Inquiry into certain matters concerning the Port Transport Industry* (Devlin Report), Cmnd 2734, HMSO
MOSER, C A (1972) 'Statistics about Immigrants: Objectives, Sources, Methods and Problems', *Soc. Trends, 3*, 20–30
MOSER, C A and SCOTT, W (1961) *British Towns*, London
MUSGROVE, F (1963) *The Migratory Elite*, London
NEWTON, M P and JEFFREY, J R (1951) 'Internal Migration', *Stud. in Medical and Popul. Subjects, 5*, HMSO
OPCS (1972) *Census 1971, England and Wales: Advance Analysis*, HMSO
         (1975) 'Country of Birth and Colour, 1971–4', *Popul. Trends, 2*, 2–8
         (1978) *Demographic Review: A Report on Population in Great Britain*,

series DR No. 1, HMSO
(1979) 'Population of New Commonwealth and Pakistani Ethnic Origin:
New Projections', *Popul. Trends, 16,* 22–7
PEARCE, D (1975) 'Births and Family Formation', *Popul. Trends, 1,* 6–8
PEARCE, D and BRITTON, M (1977) *Popul. Trends, 7,* 9–14
PICKETT, K G (1970A) 'Merseyside's Population and Social Structure', in
LAWTON, R and CUNNINGHAM, C M (eds) *Merseyside: Social and Economic
Studies,* London, 92–7
(1970B) 'Migration in the Merseyside Area', in LAWTON, R and
CUNNINGHAM, C M (eds) *Merseyside: Social and Economic Studies,* London,
108–48
PREST, A R (ed.) (1970) *The UK Economy: A Manual of Applied Economics,*
3rd edn, London
PREST, A R and COPPOCK, D J (1980) *The UK Economy: A Manual of Applied
Economics,* 8th edn, London
PUBL. GEN ACTS, see list on pp. 505–7
ROBERTS, B C and SMITH, J H (eds) (1960) *Manpower Policy and Employment
Trends,* London
ROBSON, B T (1969) *Urban Analysis,* Cambridge
RODGERS, H B (1959) 'Employment and the Journey to Work in an Overspill
Community', *Sociol. Rev., 7,* 213–29
ROSE, E J B *et al* (1969) *Colour and Citizenship,* Inst. Race Relations, London
R. COMMN LOCAL GOVT IN ENGLAND 1966–9 (1969) Vol. III, *Research
Appendices,* Cmnd 4040, HMSO
RUNNYMEDE TRUST (1980) *Britain's Black Population,* The Runnymede Trust
and the Radical Statistics Race Group, London
SALT, J (1976) 'Local Unemployment in the United Kingdom in the 1970s',
Pap. to the Regional Studies Association Annual Conference, July 1976
SCARGILL, D I (1968) 'The Expanded Town in England and Wales', in
BECKINSALE, R P and HOUSTON, J M (eds) *Urbanization and its Problems.
Essays presented to E W Gilbert,* Oxford, 119–42
SCOTT. DEV. DEPT (1968) *The Older Houses in Scotland – A Plan for Action,*
Cmnd 3598, Edinburgh HMSO
(1972) *The Size and Distribution of Scotland's Population:
Projections for Planning Purposes,* Edinburgh HMSO
SEC. STATE ECON. AFFAIRS (1969) *The Intermediate Areas,* Cmnd 3998,
HMSO
SMAILES, A E (1961) 'The Urbanisation of Britain', *Problems of Appl. Geogr.:
Polish Academy Sci. Geogr. Stud.,* Warsaw, *25*
SMITH, D M (1979) *Where the Grass in Greener,* Harmondsworth
SOULSBY, E M (1972) 'Changing Sex Ratios in the Scottish Border Counties',
Scott. Geogr. Mag., 88, 5–18
SE JOINT PLANNING TEAM (1976) *Strategy for the South East: 1976 Review,*
HMSO
STORRIE, M C (1968) 'Household Tenure', in HUNT, A J (ed.) 'Population Maps
of the British Isles 1961', *Trans. Inst. Br. Geogr., 43,* 25–60
TAYLOR, J (1968) 'Hidden Female Labour Reserves', *Reg. Stud., 2,* 221–31
THOMPSON, J (1969) 'Differential Fertility among Immigrants to England and
Wales and some Implications for Population Projections', *Jl of Biosocial Sci.,*
Suppl. 1
(1970) 'The Growth of Population to the End of the Century',
Soc. Trends, 1, 21–32
TURNOCK, D (1969) 'Regional Development in the Crofting Counties', *Trans.
Inst. Br. Geogr., 48,* 189–204

WARNES, A M (1972) 'Estimates of Journey to Work Distances from Census Statistics', *Reg. Stud., 6,* 315—26
         (1975) 'Commuting towards City Centres: a Study of Population and Employment Density Gradients in Liverpool and Manchester', *Trans. Inst. Br. Geogr., 64,* 77—96
WATSON, W (1964) 'Social Mobility and Social Class in Industrial Communities', in GLUCKMAN, M (ed.) *Closed Systems and Open Minds: Limits of Naivety in Social Anthropology,* Edinburgh, London, 129—57
WAUGH, M (1969) 'The Changing Distribution of Professional and Managerial Manpower in England and Wales 1961—6', *Reg. Stud. 3,* 157—69
WIBBERLEY, G P (1954) 'Some Aspects of Problem Rural Areas in Britain', *Geogrl J., 120,* 43—61

3

Environment and Land Use

I LAND USE

I.1 Land-Utilization Surveys

The first land-utilization survey of Britain, directed by Stamp from 1930–47 was designed as a national inventory which could be used as a basis for land-use planning. To achieve national coverage in an acceptable length of time (the field survey was completed between 1931 and 1934), detail was not possible and the classification had to be simple enough to allow accurate mapping by volunteers, many of them school-children. Seven forms of land use, subdivided, were mapped at the six-inch scale and subsequently plotted on one-inch maps. Between 1936 and 1948 one-inch sheets and county reports were published as they were completed. A summary of the work done in the survey and an analysis of the findings was published by Stamp (1947). The Geographical Association of N Ireland became interested in the survey in 1936 and by 1939 had completed a survey of N Ireland, using the same classification. Due to different farming methods and the amount of land of a marginal character in N Ireland, some modifications were adopted; for example, all grassland whether rotation or permanent was grouped in one class. One-inch sheets were published by the Government of N Ireland between 1945 and 1951. A memoir was written for the Belfast sheet (Hill 1947), but a description and analysis for the whole of N Ireland was not published until 1963 (Symons 1963), which allowed the work of the original survey to be extended by considering trends up to 1953.

Stamp's land-utilization survey proved invaluable in postwar planning, but rapid changes in agriculture and urban growth soon rendered it obsolete. A second survey was inaugurated in 1960 (Coleman 1961) and, in it, an attempt to map more detail. Factories were mapped according to industrial group and crops identified. The twelve types of vegetation proved too difficult for volunteer surveyors and this aspect of the mapping was undertaken by the Nature Conservancy to be published on 1:100,000 maps in *A Wildscape Atlas for England and Wales*. This scale will permit mapping communities of at least 2ha in extent. The land-use maps have been produced at the scale of 1:25,000 showing sixty-four categories grouped to give two levels of intensity: first, the old World divisions of the World Land Use Survey, but with transport, open spaces, derelict and unvegetated land added; secondly, subdivisions were made by variations in tone and the overlay of symbols. For example, grassland was indicated in green with symbols and letters to show ley, infestation by rushes, scrub and bracken, etc. By 1968 all England and part of Wales had been completed in manuscript and by 1975 just over 100 sheets had been printed. Many of these are scattered widely, but there is a useful cover in the London area, S Wales, the Vale of York and NE England. The survey of Scotland is incomplete, but some sheets have been published. It is unlikely that any further printing will be undertaken as the cost cannot be justified for a survey of land use as it was in the 1960s.

I.2   Land Classification

On the assumption that land utilization in the years 1931–9 was a consequence of the nature of the land, Stamp produced a classification which was used in many planning reports (Abercrombie 1945; Watson and Abercrombie 1943; Thompson 1945). Although criticized by soil scientists because of its basis in use rather than soil (Stamp 1947, 353), the Soil Survey could not meet the urgent need for a complete mapping cover. With rapidly expanding urban population, good agricultural land needed delimitation if the country were to avoid serious losses of good land. The Land Utilization Survey divided England, Wales and Scotland into 10 categories: 1–4 were of high agricultural value, 7–10 land of low agricultural value, and types 5–6 of intermediate quality (fig. 3.1). First-class arable land was considered to be as valuable as first-class grassland, but would be defined by different physical conditions. In N Ireland land classification began in 1954 but was made difficult because of lack of information apart from the land-use maps and only a few soil survey maps. While the same principles of classification were applied, a scheme emerged which was similar to that of the Dept of Agriculture of Scotland. However, the field-by-field analysis carried out in Scotland could not be attempted in N Ireland because of the smaller fields and the quantity of small farms which produced a greater variation in management. The first-class land in N Ireland was that considered suitable for all crops which the climate permitted and some of this would not have been graded for first-class land in Scotland. All these classifications attempted an assessment of short-term potential assuming reasonable drainage, fertilization, etc. However, it is important to realize that herbicides and fertilizers have since led to greater intensification of use and many of the lands classified as poor or very poor have proved productive under forest.

The *Agricultural Land Service Research Group* (1962) attempted to improve on these classifications by finding a classification which would have relevance at the scale of the individual farm and yet be consistent in its grading throughout Britain. Following the principle adopted by earlier surveys (NEDA 1950), physical characteristics of the land were considered most important, largely because of their permanence and the difficulty in altering them. The difficulty, clearly recognized by the survey, is that it is impossible to evaluate the land without considering the uses to which it might be put. Moreover, it was difficult to be objective in the absence of a comprehensive soil survey and data on local climates. The inter-relations between physical factors and land productivity being imperfectly known made the choice of parameters often purely arbitrary. Five grades were chosen according to the limitations imposed by physical factors and mapped at the 1:63,360 scale (fig. 3.2). At the same time productivity, assuming standard management, was estimated as a check for each area mapped. The great number of holdings within any one physical group makes this a difficult exercise without considering farm structure, equipment and location. Grade I is land with very minor or no physical limitation to agricultural use, which because of climate, soil and slope conditions occurs most readily on the lowlands of S and SE England. Limitations associated with the soil will produce grade II, while more serious limitations of soil such as the poor drainage of the Lias, Oxford and London Clays as well as the glacial drifts, and slope and climate produce grade III classifications.

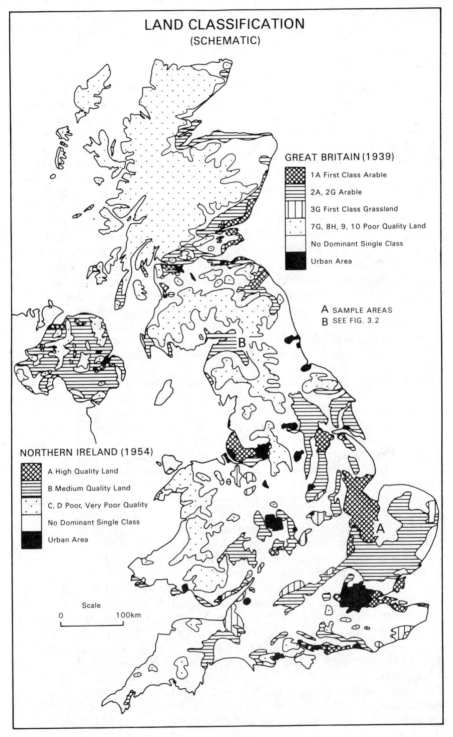

LAND CLASSIFICATION
(SCHEMATIC)

GREAT BRITAIN (1939)

1A First Class Arable

2A, 2G Arable

3G First Class Grassland

7G, 8H, 9, 10 Poor Quality Land

No Dominant Single Class

Urban Area

A SAMPLE AREAS
B SEE FIG. 3.2

NORTHERN IRELAND (1954)

A High Quality Land

B Medium Quality Land

C, D Poor, Very Poor Quality

No Dominant Single Class

Urban Area

Scale
0   100km

Figure 3.1   Schematic land classification, GB 1939, N Ireland 1954

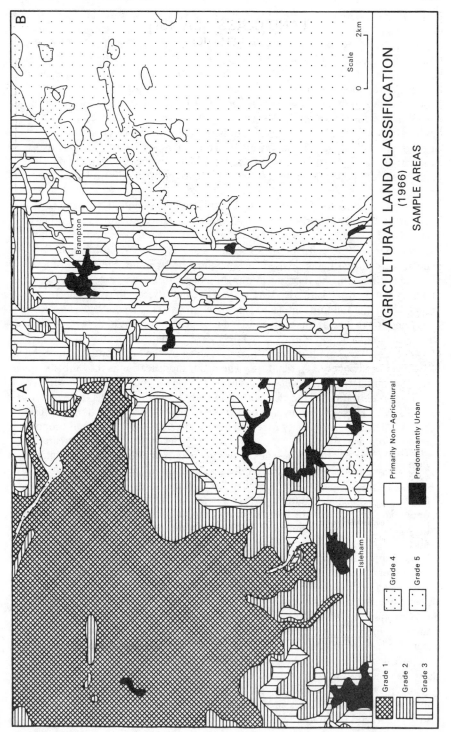

Figure 3.2   Agricultural land classification, sample areas, UK, 1966

Grade IV has severe limitations of soil, either wetness or low water-holding capacity, shallowness or stoniness. The steepness, high rainfall and short growing season of the upland margins also will put these areas into this grade. About 50% of England and Wales is grade V which is of little agricultural value because the limitations of soil, slope and climate are very severe. Thus flood plains of rivers, as well as much of the uplands above 300 metres, are grouped in this class together with areas seriously affected by pollution either from the atmosphere or due to waste disposal. Insufficient information on the range of output per unit area for each of these five grades and the differences in type of farming within any one grade makes interpretation difficult. The survey gives merely an indication of the range of productivity for the dominant type of farming likely to occur within the physical class. It serves no more than to test the accordance between physical and economic gradings.

At the same time the Soil Survey of England and Wales and of Scotland produced a land-use Capability Classification with the aim of assisting planners and other land users. This is a cooperative effort between the Agricultural Development and Advisory Service, the Soil Survey of England and Wales, the Meteorological Office and the Agricultural Land Service. In 1972 these bodies jointly reviewed progress in land classification and its application within agriculture, advisory work, forestry, planning and multiple land use (MAFF 1974). Land-use capability has been described for the soil units in recent soil survey memoirs (Clayden 1971; Scale 1975) and for two areas one-inch and land-use capability maps have been published with the memoirs (Thomasson 1971; Jarvis 1973). The classification (Bibby and Mackney 1969) was modified from that developed by the Soil Conservation Service of the US Department of Agriculture. The major modification is the omission of class 5 which relates to flat wet land. Thus seven classes range from land with minor or no limitations (I) to that with extremely severe limitations that cannot be rectified (V). These are subdivided by the physical limitations which put them in this class. The system is firmly based on purely physical limitations, and economic considerations are completely ignored. It does, however, attempt a more careful evaluation of the physical properties of the soil and draws upon the basic soil maps of this survey. Interpretation of the soil data depends on the more detailed studies of selected soils, which have been termed 'benchmark' soils. These studies cover four years and consider potential yields under normal rotation conditions in commercial farming. One of these studies in the Vale of Belvoir, Nottinghamshire and Leicestershire, was commenced in 1968 and involved six soil series. Soil profile analyses, together with meteorological observations, were related to problems of soil preparation, fertilizer application and crop yields. An attempt was also made to assess susceptibility to disease and physiological limitations at each site. This would have been an impossible task if applied universally, but the aim was to concentrate on key agricultural areas and apply the results to similar soils elsewhere. Information on crop responses exists and is accumulating in results of field experimental studies of crop response to nutrients, effect of crop variety, technique and management on crop yields, together with weed, pest and disease effects, as well as data provided for advisory work and a great body of farming experience. This classification involves both analysis, that is the individual components of the soil system, and synthesis, where the data is interpreted according to the classification. Thus the final classification is an appraisal of soil characteristics, crop yields and management, and it is only the quantitative evaluation of the individual components which reduces its subjectivity. The proposal to use computers for future analysis and mapping will not improve the classification but of course will greatly facilitate its application.

II   ENVIRONMENTAL FACTORS AND AGRICULTURAL LAND USE

II.1   Introduction

Land classifications have been largely concerned with agricultural land use and indeed most had the original aim of preserving the best agricultural land from urban use. The various classifications differ in their relative emphasis on physical characteristics and land use, but they all share the uncertain relationships which exist between land use and environment. Elements in the environment are measurable, though imperfectly, but the real problems lie in identifying those which limit productivity and the weighting given to each in the complex inter-relationships. This section deals with the measurement of these factors in the UK, the parameters derived from them and their relevance to land use and productivity. The opportunities for improving productivity by controlling the environment are also discussed, as well as the consequences of agricultural land use polluting the environment.

II.2   Measurement of the Climatic Environment

Precipitation   Precipitation comes mainly in the form of rain, and an extensive network of about 6,500 rain gauges is in operation (Bleasdale 1965). Since the last century these gauges have been standard, that is 12.7 cm diameter with the rims 0.3m above the ground. The accuracy of the readings varies from site to site. At Wallingford differences of up to 15% in winter months were found between standard and ground level gauges, though this was reduced to less than 5% in June and July. Greatest errors occur with high winds and small raindrop size, when turbulence diverts most of the rain away from the funnel of a standard gauge (Rodda 1970A). It is obvious that rainfall in the wetter areas of the west and upland areas is underestimated. The Institute of Hydrology has developed a grid to be used with ground-level gauges which largely removes the effect of turbulence. Recording rainfall in isolated mountain regions has proved difficult in the past, but automation is likely to overcome this. Experiments by the North of Scotland Electricity Board, using a rotating collecting funnel and thirty-two bottles, have reduced recording to monthly visits. Also at Glen Kingie a radio rain gauge transmits information powered by solar-cell batteries, while at Achnasheen a telephonic gauge allows remote reading in units, tens or hundreds, depending on the frequency of the signals. Less progress has been made in measuring snow, which is a significant proportion of precipitation in highland regions in winter. The interpolation of rainfall is made difficult by the fact that the effect of altitude varies with the synoptic situation and seasonally. In Scotland it has been shown that no satisfactory regression is possible for short periods (Smithson 1969). Point sampling by gauges has limited value when spatial variations in rainfall are required, and even if the rainfall for a crop or forest is required, gauging must be at the site. Radar readings related to gauge recordings may provide clearer patterns for these purposes.

Evaporation   Evaporation, or the transfer of water from the earth's surface, includes the loss from water surfaces, the soil and that transpired by plants; however, loss from a vegetated surface is termed 'evapotranspiration'. The measurement of evaporation by pans or tanks is made difficult by the effects of advection, so that under dry conditions the evaporation rate is much higher than over a large open water surface where advection effects are limited to the edges. Nevertheless at least twenty stations in the UK have tank data, sixteen of these recording data since 1956. This data is from standard evaporation tanks which are sunk in the ground, but the more recent class 'A' pan which is placed above ground level has been installed at many stations as well. The accuracy with which the water level in a tank will indicate evaporation losses depends to a large extent on the gauging of rainfall. Also in winter many pans and tanks cannot be used to record evaporation. It is usual, therefore, to use the summer half-year, April to September, which accounts for about 80% of the annual total, to estimate the twelve-month total and, by assuming a symmetrical curve in evaporation from January to December, redistribute the evaporation between the months to give a 'norm'. Calculations based on this method are published in *British Rainfall*. Using rainfall data and measured runoff, it is possible by subtraction to estimate the amount evaporated or transferred from the surface. This has been calculated by the Meteorological Office for the period 1937–62 for fourteen catchment areas in England and Wales. Both tank data and catchment data indicate evaporation in excess of 51cm in S England and less than 43cm in the North. However it is impossible to construct an accurate map when each site may not be regionally representative as regards exposure.

Estimates of evapotranspiration using lysimeters have only recently been made in this country. By weighing a tank of soil and vegetation, irrigated lysimeters allow a measure of the loss by evaporation. Since irrigation ensures a constant supply of water to the plants, the loss can be considered the potential. The Nature Conservancy has twenty-two stations with lysimeters but with only a short run of recordings (Green 1970A). However, they generally show a ratio of lysimeter potential evapotranspiration (PE) to tank evaporation of between 1 and 1.25.

Calculations by the Penman method (Penman 1948) avoid the error caused by condensation which results in higher tank evaporation readings in winter. However, for summer months, which are most critical for land-use problems, Penman estimates of potential evapotranspiration accord fairly closely with the tank and lysimeter data (Penman 1950). The application of the Penman formula depends on the measurement of meteorological elements, temperature, humidity, radiation, wind and sunshine. The importance of potential evapotranspiration in irrigation, as well as in other problems, prompted the Ministry of Agriculture to publish a detailed description of the Penman method and tables of values for the British Isles (Min. of Agriculture 1967). Averages for the period 1950–64 were calculated or estimated for over one hundred stations. Interpolation beyond these stations depended on distance from the coast, where higher radiation increases the potential evaporation rate, and on altitude.

Height increases wind and relative humidity but decreases temperature and sunshine in a complex relationship. Observations have allowed an empirical correction during summer of 16mm per 100m in England and Wales, and 20mm per 100m in Scotland and N Ireland. In winter these corrections become 12 and 6mm respectively. These corrections have been used to derive values for: the coastal strip 8–16km wide; for each county at the mean height; and at 365m where appropriate. As these values are averages it is important to account for year-by-year deviations of the meteorological controls, of which the dominant in summer is radiation and in winter the saturation deficit. Since the weighting of these factors varies from place to place and month to month they have been published for each station. Thus for a summer month, deviation from average potential transpiration is x times the deviation from the average sunshine. The x factor varies between 0.14 and 0.38, the higher values occurring in June. The factors are generally lower in spring and autumn in the North than in the South but in mid-summer higher factors are needed for northern locations. These tables were prepared for use at any location in the British Isles (Min. of Agriculture 1967), but isoline maps would be unsatisfactory at a small scale although they have been constructed from this data by others. Figure 3.3 shows the pattern of potential evapotranspiration based on average county data. It is useful to reflect that potential evapotranspiration is a theoretical concept and refers to a green crop, completely covering the ground with an adequate supply of soil water at its roots. Variation in plant height and colour of the crop will influence the potential evapotranspiration. Also the supply of water to the roots will depend on the soil type and the rooting habit of the crop. Thus the application of these tables to agriculture, and in particular to irrigation control, requires careful appraisal of the specific problem and location. Errors which exist in the Penman results, notably in summer, are often compensated by under-estimation of rainfall, though it has been suggested that they could still lead to over-irrigation (Edwards 1970). However, since potential evapotranspiration rates change very slowly from place to place and changes from year to year are very small compared with rainfall, most irrigation planning can be based upon the averages for the area as derived from these tables. It is on this assumption that water balances have been calculated for long-term planning of irrigation and these are discussed in the next section.

Temperature Temperature is given particular importance because of its obvious control over growth and in particular the length of the growing season. Maps of temperature have been based upon readings from the standard exposure of a Stevenson screen. Accumulated temperature is an attempt to integrate the excess or deficiency of these temperatures to a fixed datum. $6°C$ is used as a base because of its significance for the commencement and maintenance of growth. Maps of accumulated temperature above $6°C$ by Gregory (1954) were based upon mean monthly temperatures. More detailed calculations were made by Shellard (1959) for forty-nine stations in the UK, and he also calculated accumulated temperature below $21°C$, $15°C$ and $10°C$ because of its importance in heating engineering. More important, however, is his use of the standard deviation of temperature to allow for departures from the means which is a vital consideration when the mean temperature is at or near the base level. An attempt to produce a larger-scale map of more practical use has been made by Birse and Dry (1970) for Scotland. For this map the base was $5.6°C$ but the method was similar to that of Shellard. For each station the accumulated temperature was calculated at intervals of 100m assuming a lapse rate of $0.6°C$ per 100m. Thus contour lines could be used in drawing the isopleths, at intervals of 275 day degrees C, differentiating zones according to length of growing season. Using the same procedure, accumulated deficiency in temperature below $0°C$ provided a measure of frost severity. This work on temperature was combined with calculations of moisture conditions and exposure on two maps at the scale of

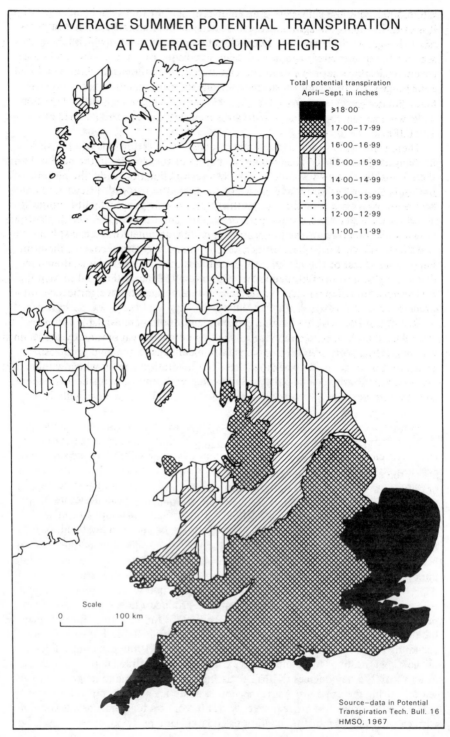

Figure 3.3   Average summer potential transpiration at average county heights, UK, 1967

1:625,000, giving the climate of sites to help in field surveys of soil and vegetation. It is of obvious value in agriculture, particularly in Scotland where relief imposes rapid changes in local climates. Local climates or mesoclimates which take into account the special circumstances of relief, exposure, aspect, soil and vegetation cover are clearly of more value in agroclimatology than the macroclimates (Hogg 1968) suggested by the long-term means from standard meteorological exposures. Mesoclimates can refer to areas less than $25\,km^2$ and can be mapped at 1:25,000 scale, whereas macroclimates refer to areas over $258\,km^2$ and are mapped at 1:250,000 scale.

There is the assumption in all descriptive maps that conditions will remain unchanged. Lamb (1965) has shown the nature of the changes in the past and while there is insufficient evidence to be able to forecast climatic trends, the purpose of the study should determine the choice of the period of records. Elsewhere Lamb has cast doubts on the validity of the thirty-year norm for agroclimatic work. It is also difficult to relate screen temperatures to the conditions under which plants are growing. Soil temperatures have been recorded by agrometeorological stations since the 1920s. The nature of the surface, its colour and vegetation cover is therefore of importance. Most of the readings for depths less than 30cm are taken only once per day and are therefore of limited value. Gloyne (1971) has attempted to map the $8°C$ average annual mean daily earth temperature because of its significance in the processes of soil formation.

Records of hours of bright sunshine and net radiation are available for many stations and both have been used in estimating potential evaporation by the Penman method. The relevance of these to agriculture depends very much on the aspect, exposure and slope of the particular site. The theoretical energy which would result from optimal insolation (Knoch 1963) together with the study of the effects on air temperature or soil temperature (Taylor 1964) is of importance particularly in relation to earliness of crops.

Wind speed is measured at the standard height of 10m in open level country. Friction affects wind speed as high as 305m and land-forms can obstruct or create their own circulations. Gloyne has suggested that wind will follow the surface if windward slopes are less than $40°$ and leeward slopes less than $11°$, which has obvious implications for shelter effects. The effect of wind speed is to reduce temperature extremes but wind speeds in excess of 40kmph can desiccate plants. The map of exposure by Birse and Dry (1970) is the only attempt to consider topography in mapping wind speed. The thirty-four stations in Scotland were inadequate for mapping purposes and were supplemented by an assessment of the visible effect of exposure on broad-leaved trees and on common heather, *Calluna vulgaris*. The map shows five categories of exposure ranging from sheltered, 2.6m per sec wind speed, to extremely exposed, 8.0m per sec. The authors point out that the limits define exposure satisfactorily so long as other factors such as salt spray are not also having an effect on plant life. This shows one of the major problems of equating a single parameter with an effect when relationships are not fully understood.

II.3   Influence of Climate on Agricultural Land Use and Productivity

As in other developed countries, assessment of land potential is important for decisions on the conflicting claims on the land, and displacement of agricultural

enterprises by urban growth has called for reappraisal of other areas to which the
farmers could move with hopes of success. Hogg (1966) quotes a survey of
potential sites for horticulture in England which was prompted by the needs of
displaced growers in the Lea Valley. To some extent the measurement of the
climate described above has been prompted by a practical need so that the
parameters have relevance to land-use problems. However, it is the derived values
such as day degrees or evapotranspiration which are used. The relationships between
climate and the crops which can be grown and their yields are complex. Even if
these relationships are understood it is often impossible to apply these results
beyond the limits of the experimental plots because of lack of data. In general
agricultural surveys the climate can usually be expressed in macroclimatic terms and
uncertainties only exist in marginal areas. Fruit growing has been a rewarding field
of study, for growth of buds, leaf growth, fruit set and maturity can be correlated
with microclimate. Attempts have been made at Long Ashton, Bristol, to relate
fruit-tree microclimates to screen or standard exposures. Practical applications
follow from detailed experimental work only if the knowledge can be applied to
broader areas. The present network of stations is not nearly close enough and the
validity of the principles used to apply the data from them needs verification. The
Met. Office provides a frost-warning service and irrigation advice to farmers. This is
mainly for high-value horticultural enterprises which can afford the cost of
protection. The initial improvement in productivity due to irrigation or frost
protection is undoubtedly large enough to pay for the exercise. It is, however,
difficult to justify further improvements in relation to the cash returns. The
methods used in frost prediction have had some value in planning the expansion of
horticulture, particularly soft fruit-growing. Microclimatic readings over a short
period are related to screen temperatures. The long-term screen records are used to
predict the occurrence of the frost detected in the micro-study. Requests for
irrigation advice based upon generalized water-balance calculations are now largely
met by *The Atlas of Long Term Irrigation Needs for England and Wales* (Hogg
1967B). Practical agrometeorologists are forced to adopt subjective methods
because of the lack of data and knowledge. However, the high-value horticulture is
invariably in more favoured areas and the hazards can be estimated with some
degree of certainty. A more recent area of study of relevance to land use has been
the study of workdays, the climatic requirements depending very much on the type
of work, whether it be sowing, weeding, harvesting, etc. So far most of this work
has been done in grass farming where the distinction between dry days, when work
is possible, and wet days, when it is not, is clear-cut.

Farming activities are not equally sensitive to environmental conditions and in
many cases changes in management can bring about more significant improvements.
Also climate has more influence on crops than on livestock. There is little point in
investigating the actual limits of growth for a particular crop, because economically
it becomes impracticable long before this is reached as this depends on fluctuating
prices as the changing margins of moorland in our uplands indicate. Thus present
land use cannot help in identifying the degree of control imposed by environmental
factors.

Water With the exception of their woody parts, actively growing plants have
75–90% water. Together with the fact that vast amounts of water must pass
through the plant and evaporate from the leaf surface, this accounts for the

importance of water in growth. Alfalfa requires over 431kg of water to produce 0.45 kg dry matter. Drought affects agriculture in the UK to some extent and the degree depends very much on location. A broad view can be obtained from a simple subtraction of average potential transpiration from average rainfall, to give mean potential soil moisture deficit. This relates to crop distribution, the ratio of grass to crops and grass decreases, at a constant rate from a mean potential soil moisture deficit of −150mm to +100mm; above this the proportion of grassland decreases more rapidly (Hogg 1965A). However, this is of limited value to agricultural planning as excess rainfall in winter could cancel out high deficits during the crop-growing season. There is a limit to the amount of water which can be held in storage in the soil and a great deal of the winter excess runs off the land in streams and is lost to plants. Detailed water balances can be made which will take these factors into account. Day-to-day balances will be most accurate, though, for most purposes, five- or ten-day or monthly periods will suffice. The water balance as developed by Thornthwaite (Thornthwaite and Mather 1955) must include some basic assumptions. Apart from the problem of estimating potential evapotranspiration which has been outlined above, the accuracy of the balance depends mainly on the limits of our knowledge of soil−plant−water relationships, and inevitably any agroclimatic model using water-balance data must be simplified for practical application. As a general principle, crop water use is related to atmospheric conditions. A factor is frequently used to reduce Penman E_0 to potential evapotranspiration, in the UK about 0.6 in winter and 0.8 in summer months. For annual crops this factor should increase from a small fraction when the plant emerges, to the maximum when leaf area achieves full ground cover. However, wide spacing can reduce this maximum level. Actual evapotranspiration depends on the presence of water in this root zone. When the soil is fully charged with water it is said to be at field capacity. As the soil begins to dry the tension rises until it reaches permanent wilting point (16 atmospheres) when roots can no longer extract water. The water held between these extremes is termed available soil water (AW). Soil textures can alter the limits; field capacity can range from 4cm per m for sand to 17−21cm per m for clay loam. Permanent wilting point is more difficult to define and is probably a function of plant type as well as soil. Clarke (1971) quotes figures of available water in cm per m according to texture: sand and loamy sands 2−4, sandy loams 8, fine sandy loams 12.5−14.5, loams 16.6, clay loams 25 and clay 29. However rooting depth is probably of more importance than texture. The depth of root penetration depends on the plant, but generally it will be shallow when the water-table is high. Since roots do not extend into unaerated soil, the plant is depending entirely on water from precipitation. If the water-table is kept constant by controlling drainage a significant part of the water used by plants can come from the ground-water; however for most farmland in the UK the water-table rises in wet periods causing roots to die back, and falls in dry weather permitting root extension.

Thornthwaite assumed that potential evapotranspiration (PE) only occurs at field capacity and the rate of actual evapotranspiration becomes a progressively smaller fraction of PE as the soil dries. Another school suggests that water is equally available until permanent wilting point is reached. Denmead and Shaw (1962) have shown that the critical level of soil water above which evapotranspiration occurs at this potential rate depends on atmospheric conditions. For example if the potential evapotranspiration is low ($E_0 = 1$ mm/d), the critical value is near permanent wilting point, so that plants will transpire at the potential rate until all other available water is removed. On the other hand, under high potential evaporation conditions (E_0 = 7mm/d), the rate of evapotranspiration will decrease as soon as soil water falls below field capacity. Penman (1968) has suggested that water is equally available if we consider the root range only. Plants however do extract beyond this and movement of water to the root system would slow down transpiration rates and if potential evapotranspiration is high the actual rate could be a small fraction of this.

The concepts of field capacity and permanent wilting point are an oversimplification of the complex soil hydrological horizons. In the process of drying, water is removed from the surface horizons first and progressively each horizon follows a strict succession of phases, ranging from total saturation to below permanent wilting point of physical desiccation (Rode 1968). The process of soilwetting is usually from above and the water content of each horizon is suddenly increased to the maximum.

Water balances For *The Atlas of Long-term Irrigation Needs for England and Wales* (Hogg 1967B) water balances were calculated for a twenty-year sample, 1930–49, for seventy-nine stations in England and Wales. These balances consider only growth periods between April and September and in calculations assume soil water to be at field capacity at the beginning of each period. Certainly in most areas of the UK the soil has its maximum water content at the end of the winter, but for periods beginning in June, July or August it is unlikely that conditions of field capacity will always occur. A half-monthly balance was considered frequent enough to show the effect of dry spells, though it was probably chosen to correspond with the maximum frequency with which irrigation can be satisfactorily applied. However in SE England heavy rain from summer thunderstorms can balance the total water needs of the fifteen-day period and, in many cases, obscure serious deficits. Since these balances include the application of irrigation water, when required, transpiration was considered to continue at the potential rate. Balances were calculated allowing maximum soil moisture deficit of 25mm, 50mm, 76mm and 127mm at any time. Since water from rainfall or irrigation enters the soil profile from the surface and percolates downwards, each of these calculations refers to soil water deficits within a surface layer whose available water capacity equals this. Thus the total need with a planned 127mm deficit would apply to deeprooting plants; in sandy loams this could be 1.5m and in clay loams 0.6m. Shallowrooting plants where the planned deficit must be smaller, say 25mm, require more frequent irrigation. Crops will undoubtedly respond to a situation where soil moisture deficits are kept at a minimum. However, it has been shown (Winter, Salter and Cox 1970) that the practice of restoring the soil to field capacity by irrigation whenever it reaches a certain deficit may not be economically sound. Because of the costs of irrigation, higher profits per acre can be obtained only by limited irrigation. Watering to achieve only 90% maximum yield would appear to be the most efficient programme for grain crops, but for crops whose vegetative growth is harvested, irrigation for maximum yield would be the most efficient use of water (Fisher and Hagan 1965).

Grass may require irrigation any time between April and September. However, other crops have much shorter growth periods and irrigation may be required only for a short period of the growth cycle. Thus combinations of successive periods of 2, 3, 4, 5 and 6 months have been calculated. For the 2.5cm soil moisture deficit plan (SMD), all lowland England would require irrigation 17 years in 20, but a

12.7cm SMD plan would require irrigation 8 years in 20 in the NE and over 14 in 20 in the SE. Using the 2.5cm SMD plan, the driest year in 20 would require 20cm in the NE and 33cm in the SE. The atlas is a good example of the application of a simplified water-balance calculation to a practical problem. More detailed balances are possible for specific sites where more assumptions can be made appropriate to the crop and soil. For example, a crop of grass can be assumed to transpire at this potential rate as long as water is available in the top layers of soil, the first 5cm AW. The second 5cm AW will be used at one-half of the 'potential and the final 2.5cm AW will be used at one-quarter of the potential. Water balances calculated in this way for growing seasons have agreed with actual field conditions (Min. Agriculture 1967, 17). This method has the advantage that soil moisture conditions are estimated for each horizon in the soil rather than integrated in a single soil moisture deficit for the whole profile.

It has been shown that grass growth is sensitive to the first 7.5cm AW and when this is removed growth practically ceases even though deeper roots may allow continued transpiration (Stiles and Garwood 1964). Nutrition is obviously a complicating factor and as this is concentrated within surface layers of soil, the presence of available water in these horizons is vital for growth. This is further supported by high correlations between hay yields and the actual transpiration during periods when deficits were less than 50mm (Hurst 1964). Hurst calculated daily water balances for fifty stations in East Anglia in 1961 and counted the grass-growing days, that is days when the moisture deficit was 50mm or less. Using empirical relationships with monthly water balances, he mapped grass-growing days in England and Wales, and showed how these rough estimates correlated with milk production.

The use of computers has greatly facilitated the amount of data which can be handled and the number of variables and processes which can be considered. A complete model (MORECS) of the extraction of water from the soil by plants has been devised by the Met. Office, using rainfall and a modified form of the Penman equation. Output is mainly in the form of maps giving average values of soil water deficit for 40 x 40km squares for a variety of soil surfaces and vegetation cover. Broad assumptions have had to be made regarding drainage rates of water in the soil and arbitrary values given to the water-holding capacity of the soil layers. To test the usefulness of the model, a data-bank of soil moisture as measured by neutron probes was set up by the Institute of Hydrology (Gardner 1981). A preliminary comparison indicated that the seasonal form of the measured soil moisture deficits followed that of the estimated values of MORECS but the latter tended to be higher. Changing the arbitrary values of water-holding capacity can improve the estimation of soil moisture, but the data-bank of actual soil moisture measurement for a number of sites in agricultural land, woodland and moorland has value in providing information for drainage and cultivation of similar soils and could be used in models of crop water use and groundwater recharge (Gardner 1981).

Irrigation and growth Most studies of the effects of water on growth have been concerned with the increased production brought about by irrigation. Fisher and Hagan (1965) review research on the effects of water stress on a variety of crops and distinguish them according to their economic yield: vegetative, e.g. in the case of grass; a carbohydrate storage organ, e.g. in sugar beet or potatoes; or a reproductive organ, e.g. grain crops and fruit. Correlations between actual evapotranspiration and yields have been shown for crops of lucerne (Davis and Tyler 1964) in Wales. However, such studies can only be of practical value if they can be used to forecast harvests or, on the basis of accurate seasonal forecasts of water stress, permit an economic assessment of the yield improvement in relation to expenditure on irrigation. Outside the UK investments in weather protection have been assessed using simplified models of operating costs. Certainly where water for irrigation is limited its efficiency becomes important.

In the drier areas of SE England the effects of irrigation are likely to be most important but the availability of water in summer is already a serious constraint to further expansion (Porter 1978). Vegetative production, as in the case of grass, is particularly sensitive to water supply but Goode (1970) showed that the cumulative effect of irrigation on fruit production can also be significant. This is because fruit production depends very much on plant vigour and, in the case of soft fruit, new growth becomes fruit-bearing in the following season. Over a period of 5 years irrigated bushes had 100% more fruit than unwatered bushes. The cumulative effect of irrigation over ten years produced a 50% increase in apple yields. Undoubtedly this is due to the prevention of a growth check when the soil dries out, but as well as this the absence of large soil water deficits reduces the need for an extensive root system, which would deplete the assimilates available for shoot growth and fruit production.

The growing season The studies of grass growth and fruit production in relation to water availability, described above, refer to the summer half-year, April to September, when temperature does not prevent growth. However, the influence of temperature and radiation on the beginning of the growing season and its length is obvious and their variation within the UK considerable. For early production the months January to April are most important. The South West of England has more than 139 day degrees C above 6°C in January and February (fig. 3.4). Radiation and sunshine in these months are noticeably higher in south coastal areas, while the positive temperature anomaly associated with the Atlantic and the SW winds favour the western coasts. In particular, maximum temperatures are raised in coastal areas of the SW, which is important for early growth. The beginning of the growing season has been taken as the average date on which mean screen temperature rises above 6°C (Hogg 1967A). Soil temperatures which will allow germination differ as between crops. Hogg assumed growth will commence when the 10cm soil temperature at 0900 GMT remains above 6°C. However, soil type is a major factor controlling this parameter, as has been demonstrated by the difference in 'earliness' between sand and peat areas in SW Lancashire (Taylor 1964).

The effects of **altitude** on the growing season are most obvious in the highland areas of the West and North. In Scotland there is an average of 1,375 day degrees C on the lowlands of the Moray Firth, Fife and Angus, while the Highlands above 549m have less than 825 day degrees C. However, light is as important as temperature in the growth of hill pastures (Grant 1969). Western areas benefit from the maritime influences, but in day degrees the differences between east and west coasts are not significant and inland from the east coast, higher summer temperatures tend to raise the accumulated temperature figure. In N Ireland equivalent day degree isotherms are believed to occur at generally higher elevations than in GB, although this is based on a very limited number of observations (Symons 1963, 86). The advantages of a westerly position are most apparent in the monthly

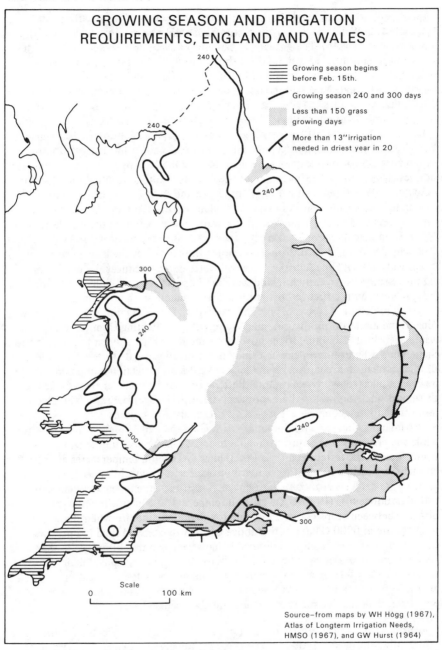

Figure 3.4   Growing season and irrigation requirements, England and Wales

accumulated temperatures of southern England where the effect extends from
January to March; in March, Plymouth has 75 day degrees C above 6°C while
Dungeness has only 46. The growing season decreases by ten days for every 79m of
altitude in the north of England, although such estimates can only be a general
guide. Calculations of accumulated temperature at Chopwell Wood (250m) in
Durham suggest a growing season fifteen days shorter than at Tynemouth (30m,
ASL). Higher altitudes can have the compensating effect of increased moisture but
grass yields can be diminished by 2% per 30m altitude (Hunter and Grant 1971).

The date of the start of the growing season can be greatly influenced by
microclimatic influences, particularly aspect and shelter. Within any region of the
UK, favoured areas may have an advantage in local markets with early crops of
potatoes and vegetables. This is true of the coasts of Co Down in N Ireland and in
Wigtown in SW Scotland. However, mapping of the average date of the start of the
growing season (fig. 3.4) shows the considerable advantage enjoyed by the early-
growing areas of Anglesey, SW Wales, Cornwall, Devon, S Hampshire and the Isle of
Wight. Even here, however, southerly aspect can increase radiation in the short days
of January by as much as 50% on a 10° slope, though the effect is reduced to only
15% in April (Hogg 1967A, 90).

Frost is a hazard to early growing and is an important factor in location. Frost
surveys by the Met. Office in horticultural areas, mainly in the SW, have been
successful in delimiting areas of risk and expressing the probability of satisfactory
crops or the increased production made possible by protecting from frost by
sprinkling. Hogg (1970) describes how the feasibility of installing a frost-prevention
scheme on a Somerset farm can be calculated from an estimate of the probable
duration of night frosts in April. In areas of light soils, irrigation equipment is often
already installed to overcome summer deficits and can be used for frost protection
in spring as well. Soil is usually kept moist when there is a frost risk, estimated by a
grass minimum temperature below −2.2°C. Damage to a crop of early potatoes by
a single night's frost, grass minimum of −3.9°C, at the end of May was averted by
sprinkling. The unretarded crop was able to fetch high prices and the protection
probably saved the farmer about £3,000 (Hogg 1967A, 117). With reliable frost
warning it is possible to plant earlier without undue risk of failure. Frost is very
much a local problem, for cold air drainage at night causes greater frequency of
frost in hollows and valley floors. Differences of 2.7−3.3°C in daily minimum
temperatures have been reported within a few hundred acres in fruit-growing areas
of S England. On the assumption that downflow will cease on slight slopes, i.e. less
than 2°, areas of frost liability in Somerset have been estimated from 1:25,000
topographical maps (Hogg 1965A). Together with air photographs, taken where
shallow radiation fogs occur, this approach could augment the few scattered
meteorological stations to provide maps of local climate with more immediate
application than the macroclimatic maps already discussed.

Exposure Work on the effects of shelter have suggested that yields of crops are
significantly improved if protected even from relatively light winds. Increase of
27% in the yield of lettuces due to lath shelter have been reported (Hogg 1965A).
Sheltered valley sites can have wind speeds 20% below more exposed neighbouring
sites. This has an important effect on crop-growing since the power to damage is
proportional to the cube of the velocity. The frictional effect of trees, hedgerows
or artificial windbreaks are more important in that they can be modified. Artificial

windbreaks have the advantage of being immediately effective, whereas trees are slow to establish themselves and compete with the crops for moisture and nutrition. The shelter given by a windbreak depends on the width/height ratio as well as the degree of permeability. If too wide, the wind on crossing the barrier descends rapidly and the eddy zone to the lee is greatly reduced. If the break has an edge inclined to the windward, the wind is deflected upwards and little penetrates. However for agriculture it is important to prevent stagnation of air which would increase frost risk and for this reason permeability is favoured. Systems of narrow parallel windbreaks can shelter wide areas if the distance between each belt is twenty-six times the height of the windbreak (Caborn 1957). Studies by Hogg suggest that wind and evaporation are more affected by shelter in autumn and winter, while temperature shows its greatest effects in summer. In this connection it is worth mentioning that with increase in field size, hedgerows have been removed and the effect is to increase exposure. The upslope valley winds induced by sun and aspect are not so important in this climate, though near industrial areas they have the damaging effect of carrying pollutants to agricultural areas.

Disease Since disease and pests have strong associations with weather and climate, they have a place in the complex crop-weather interaction. Penman (1962) has thus described them as second-order effects. If the onset of the disease can be anticipated, timely action, e.g. spraying against potato blight, can be done effectively. When the potato plant is receptive to blight, i.e. when carbohydrate reserves are high, it will occur only with suitable local weather conditions. Since the spores will only grow on wet surfaces, attempts have been made to anticipate condensation on leaves. This can be done by moisture meters or estimated from minimum temperature and relative humidity readings (Grainger 1967). Work on black stem rust in wheat (Hogg 1967C) illustrates how the origin of the spores can be traced to countries in Europe. A close connection was found between deposition of spores in SW England and upper air trajectories from the south or south-east during spring and early summer. However, epidemics only developed if humidities were high in June and July, and temperatures high in July and August. Not enough is yet known about most diseases, their vectors and their relationships with the weather to be able to provide effective early warning systems.

The flexibility of land use Green (1970B) discussed this question in relation to the water balance and suggested that the potential land use is rarely achieved because of social and economic considerations. Areas of excess water are less flexible than the deficient areas which can respond to irrigation under conditions of high radiation. Varieties of farm crops and farming systems are used because of their adaptability to the fluctuating seasonal conditions. Reliable long-term forecasts could allow greater flexibility, though the necessary information on the relationships between weather and the performance of different varieties will take some years to accumulate.

II.4   The Amelioration of Climate by Man

Some of the ways in which climate can be improved locally to benefit crop production have been touched upon in the preceding section. Apart from changing the plants' immediate environment by irrigation or shelter, completely artificial climates are created by glasshouses. It has already been suggested that improvements in production are possible if the prevailing conditions can be accurately anticipated, but it is also important to recognize that great improvement is possible by controlling growth to suit sub-optimal conditions.

Drought   Generalized irrigation needs have been discussed in the previous section. A special study of irrigated areas in 1974 (Porter 1978) showed that 65% of irrigated area was in East and SE England. Irrigation is not a complete safeguard, as was proved in the 1976 drought. If all the authorized abstractions in the Great Ouse basin had been taken by farmers, many rivers would have dried up. Water Authorities are able to impose restrictions on irrigation withdrawals under the *Water Resources Act* 1963. The Anglian Water Authority is already heavily over-committed to irrigation and is cautious about further licencing unless farmers provide storage facilities and so reduce their water abstraction in summer (Porter 1978). Irrigation is characteristically on land with good natural or artificial drainage, but there would be problems if drainage were poor or the soil unstable. Suitable water, for example not saline, is not equally available for irrigation. The cost of water and the need to provide storage to take advantage of low winter charges has caused the area in irrigation to shrink, particularly for low-value crops. The irrigated area in 1967 was 104,246 ha (Prickett 1970), 27% more than the 1974 total (table 3.1). Horticulture, particularly small fruit, is becoming a more important water-user. Crops under glass are very heavy users of water, the irrigation needs of a

TABLE 3.1

Areas Irrigated, by Agricultural Regions, 1974 (in ha)

Northern	865
Yorks. and Lancs.	3,246
E Midlands	8,577
W Midlands	9,790
Wales	1,565
South Western	4,658
South Eastern	14,738
Eastern	38,435
Total, England and Wales	81,874

Source: Porter (1978)

glasshouse being equivalent to those of a herd of seventy to a hundred dairy cattle. Crops such as grass and potatoes require sufficient irrigation to maintain water at near field capacity, which ought not to be practised in successive years for it prevents the beneficial effects of cracking during drying out of heavy soils.

Emulsions sprayed on the soil surface can reduce evapotranspiration for up to two months. Soil-water storage is improved if the surface soil is rough, encouraging the retention of water. Yields have been increased by arresting excessive drainage in sandy soils using asphalt barriers below the root zone. These devices, developed largely for arid climates, may have applications in high-value crops and in soils hitherto unproductive.

Soil wetness For most of the UK, wetness is more of a problem than drought. The large-scale drainage schemes in the Fenlands date back to the seventeenth century and illustrate the way in which the water-table in level alluvial areas can be controlled by engineering. They provide over 324,000ha of the richest farmland in GB. Elsewhere drainage can be considered a major soil factor, since moderate drainage can increase yields by as much as 20% (Coppock 1971, 45). It has been suggested that the failure of modern varieties of crops to reach full potential yield is due to defects in soil structure and drainage (Agricultural Advisory Unit 1970). Cereals are particularly susceptible to soil conditions which affect root development. Water-logging excludes air and the anaerobic conditions cause roots to die back, leaving the crop more susceptible to drought later, but it has the effect also of limiting operations with machinery. If a soil is at field capacity or wetter, it usually has insufficient strength to hold machinery or livestock and is too plastic for ploughing or cultivation. Soil texture and structure is important but the smearing effect of ploughing wheels and treading can reduce porosity and cause surface ponding. The early work of Thornthwaite on the water balance was partly concerned with the ability of soil to bear weight. The date of the return to field capacity has been calculated from meteorological records (AAU 1970) for sites throughout England and Wales. These demonstrate the early return to field capacity in the western areas, but also show the advantage of light freely drained soils and the considerable variation between wet and dry years at all sites. However, estimates based upon meteorological data can only be approximate, for no universal relationship exists between soil-water tension and estimated soil-water deficits. It is suggested that a more useful correlation may be found between interpolated soil shear strength and accumulated moisture deficit (Mil. Eng. Experim. Estab. 1969).

Extensive areas of farmland were underdrained prior to 1939, though many systems no longer function effectively and need replacement or improvement. Collapse or silting of old drains is common but more intensive use of this land can lead to puddling of surface soil which prevents water percolating to the underdrains. Removal of the old ditches associated with the small fields of Wales to create the large units of arable farming frequently necessitates new systems of drainage, though cultivation is in any case less flexible than grass in its soil-water requirements. In the wetter areas of the west, higher stocking rates increase the need for more drainage or subsoiling. Since 1966 there has been an annual increase of 10% expenditure on drainage in the SW. Without improved drainage, overstocking can lead to poaching of pastures and this is a feature of the intensive dairying area of Cheshire. Wetter than normal summers extend the dangers of poaching throughout the season, particularly in the low-evaporation areas of the Pennine foothills. For cultivation in the wetter areas, drainage is usually the only way of ensuring enough workdays. Even in the drier areas of the east, heavy soils are manageable only within a very narrow moisture range and only regular subsoiling and mole drainage can keep them in production. Among these difficult soils are the keuper marls, coal measure soils and boulder clays of the E Midlands, Oxford clay, London clay and the clays of the low Weald. However, drainage in many of these areas is not practicable because of their flatness and low elevations. Improvements in arterial drainage can make the drainage of low-lying areas feasible. For example in N Ireland drainage schemes had given flood relief to 26,600ha by 1978 and ultimately drainage of about one-quarter of the province will be affected. The danger of continual ploughing is to create sub-surface pans which seriously restrict the depth of rooting, and yields are greatly reduced. Intensive arable can cause serious structural changes. Continual cultivation of early potatoes in Pembrokeshire has led to clod formation in the soil, which may limit future use.

Drainage of any kind brings improvements and the problem is usually the degree of water control required, which is often decided on the lines of cost. It has been estimated that over 2.8 million ha, or 26% of the total UK farmland, could be improved (AAU 1970, 33). Because of soil and relief and its intensive land use, E England has a very large area (650,000ha) which could be usefully drained. Since 1972 the average annual increase in drained area in the UK has been 3,875ha and by 1978 the total was 138,572ha (DoE 1978A).

Temperature and radiation Modifications of temperature are possible by using windbreaks or spraying to prevent frost, but major changes are possible by using glass and artificial heating. Hogg (1966) quotes heating periods for some horticultural crops which range from approximately four months for chrysanthemums to ten months for cucumbers. Heating requirements in terms of fuel have been estimated using accumulated temperatures below 15°C (Shellard 1959) and Hogg has calculated this for the heating periods of each crop (table 3.2). Assuming 10 degree days require 1 tonne of coal per 4,046m² of glass, he has estimated that 40–45 tons more coal is needed at Cheltenham for one acre of glasshouse tomatoes than at Weymouth, and there is a similar difference between Weymouth and Penzance.

TABLE 3.2

Heating Requirements for Cultivated Plants, Selected UK Stations, 1966

		Average number of day degrees below 15°C		
Crop	Heating period	Penzance	Weymouth	Cheltenham
Tomatoes	4 Nov–28 May	2,470	2,870	3,290
Cucumbers	4 Oct–4 July	2,780	3,180	3,700
Lettuce	11 Nov–27 Apr	2,190	2,585	2,975
Carnations	4 Nov–27 Apr	2,260	2,665	3,080
Chrysanthemums	27 Nov–28 Mar	1,710	2,015	2,325

Source: Hogg (1966)

II.5   Harmful Accidental Effects of Agricultural Activity

Farming activity can lead to damaging effects and this is more likely if there is a change in the type of farming or its intensity. The more obvious are effects on soil-water conditions, but equally serious are the structural changes which can reduce productivity and in many cases lead to soil erosion. Exposed flat lowlands of E England suffer from soil erosion by wind on the sandy soils; those with more than 35% organic matter, such as Fenland soils, are particularly susceptible. High windspeed, in excess of 80kmph is the main cause, and it is also related to soil moisture content. The methods of preparing seed beds for vegetables and the application of herbicides have recently aggravated the situation (Pollard and Miller 1968). Large-scale sugar-beet growing which began in the 1930s is considered an important factor in the peat fens. The removal of hedges is thought to have contributed to the severe blowing of soil in the Vale of York in 1967 (Douglas 1970) but the decrease of hedgerows in areas of stable soils is not having any serious effect. Studies of sediment yields from catchments have not provided any conclusive evidence that there has been any general change in the rate of soil erosion and suggest that it is only serious locally. For control it is necessary to reduce windspeed, stabilize the soil and trap blowing soil. Windbreaks have a limited effect, especially if strong winds come from several directions. Strip-cropping and inter-row cropping can also reduce wind velocity, and soil moisture can be retained better by reducing cultivations, creating rough soil surfaces or mulching. Only high-value cash crops warrant such expensive control measures.

The practice of growing grass leys and green manuring are declining in farming and the soil structure deteriorates due to reduced organic content. Inorganic fertilizers are preferred as the balance of nutrients can be easily controlled. There has been an increase of about 150% in nitrogen application since 1957. However, organic fertilizers are important in the livestock areas of the UK. In 1969 farmyard manure was used on 23% of the arable land of N England and Wales; the percentage was less elsewhere, but 36% of the permanent pasture of Yorkshire and Lancashire was so treated. Inorganic fertilizers do confer benefits in that they encourage better root growth and thus improve soil structure and they give better vegetative growth which can be ploughed into the soil. Nitrogenous fertilizers have the effect of reducing the calcium in soil and thus increase its acidity. Damage to organisms by pesticides is less in soils with a high organic content. The most serious are the organochlorides which harm beneficial insects and persist in food chains, to appear ultimately in milk and meat (R. Comm. Environ. Pollution 1971). The pesticide industry has accepted a good measure of control, so that legislation to restrict the use of more harmful chemicals has been unnecessary. However the need to harmonize the regulations of member countries will probably lead to EEC pesticide legislation (Irvine and Knights 1974). Use of the more persistent organochloride insecticides by agriculture in England and Wales fell from 460 tons in 1963 to 250 tons in 1972 (R. Comm. Environ. Pollution 1974). It has been suggested that these ecological effects are much less than those in lakes and seas. In Scottish fresh-water lochs, agricultural runoff contributed more nitrates than phosphates and as much as 43% of the nitrogen added as fertilizer is washed from the soil. The absence of any extensive algal blooms may be due to the low temperatures (Stewart, Tuckwell and May 1975). In the UK the contribution of agricultural chemicals to pollution of streams and rivers is very small. Mercury from fungicides used in bulb farming in the Fens is deposited in sediments within a few hundred yards of its entry to the streams so that the reason for the recent ten and twenty-fold increase in mercury levels in the rivers and in waters of the Wash is not yet certain. It has been suggested that future surveillance should use molluscs as monitors of mercury pollution (NERC 1976).

A large proportion of the phosphates in rivers come from sewerage but runoff from agricultural land contributes about 9% of the nitrogen in rivers. Phosphate and phosphorus in fertilizers do not present a problem as they are less mobile, but nitrates are soluble and the quantity reaching rivers from farmland is rising (Irvine and Knights 1974); grassland is likely to have more fertilizer in the future. The use of organic fertilizers does not help as they too increase fertility, which leads to fixation of nitrogen naturally and produces more nitrate to be leached from the soil.

III   WATER SUPPLY

III.1 Hydrology of Water Resources

Considering the demands by evaporation, the amount of rainfall and its seasonal distribution appears adequate, but the problem is really one of annual and monthly departures from the mean. For example, one month's runoff can be as low as 10% of the mean for that month. The severe drought of the summer of 1959 emphasized the inadequacy of the existing water supply and prompted the government action which led to the *Water Resources Act* (1963). Three important trends have aggravated the situation: the rise in population, increasing individual requirements due to rising living standards, and growing industrial needs, calling for action to plan water resources for the future.

It is difficult to define hydrological zones in the UK, because of the lack of coincidence between the physiographic and climatic factors which control the hydrology. Slope is important to runoff, but its effectiveness depends on whether the rock is pervious or not. Potential evaporation is only closely related to runoff if the rainfall is always high enough to meet the atmospheric demand. In SE England actual evaporation often falls below the potential during periods of drought in summer. Granite uplands have a similar effect due to rapid drainage, which limits the amount of water which can be held in the soil and made available for evaporation. Because of the dependence of actual evaporation upon water storage, variability of rainfall is usually adopted as a guide to runoff characteristics. In eastern areas the summer months have more than 50% of the annual total, while elsewhere summers are drier and in the SW summers have 38% of annual total rainfall. High mountains have the highest runoff, exceeding 2,000mm pa in the wettest areas, but in SE England the average annual runoff is 125mm and in dry years it can fall to 25mm. The coefficient of variation of rainfall in the SE is more than 16%, so that rainfall would be less than 80% of the average once in ten years. The River Greta in Cumberland reflects the runoff regime from a wet mountain area (fig. 3.5) with a minimum flow in May and June when rainfall is at its lowest. The Great Ouse, on the other hand, represents the drier SE and the minimum in September corresponds to the time of the greatest soil-water deficit. The mountains of the north and west have average rainfalls of over 2,500mm and these are areas of lowest evaporation; south-eastwards rainfall decreases to less than 500mm in SE England and evaporation increases. Thus hydrometric areas can be roughly arranged in order of wetness: the Islands and Western Highlands of Scotland; the rest of Scotland, excepting the E Central area, N Ireland, NW England and Wales; the SW peninsula; E Central Scotland and NE England; Severn and Humber; and SE England, including the Wash. The minimum river flow becomes progressively later in the year as one moves from the wetter areas to the dry SE. The absence of any surplus in the SE has created a water supply problem. However, extensive aquifers, especially in chalk, absorb some winter surplus and help to augment summer flows. Winter storage in the form of snow is significant only in the Cairngorms area. Flooding is a feature of the wet mountains of the north and west, but the area most prone is the SW peninsula where storms have produced daily falls in excess of 150mm on five occasions since 1920 (Rodda 1970B, 49). Since the rainfall in these mountain areas is orographic, the heavy falls tend to be widespread. On the drier lowlands the heavy falls are associated with thunderstorms and the North Sea coast

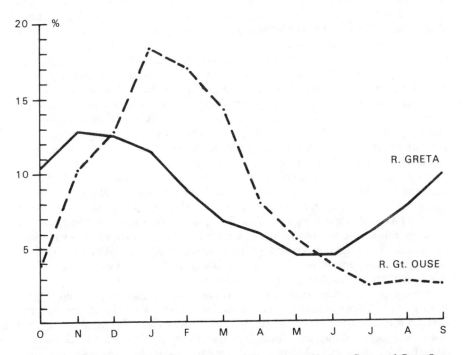

Figure 3.5   Monthly average as percentage annual average runoff, rivers Greta and Great Ouse

is the most prone; however, individual falls rarely exceed 125mm. Land use is as important as rainfall and slope in influencing runoff and flooding. Flooding is not a major problem in the lower parts of UK rivers except on the low-lying east coast, where sinking of the North Sea basin has caused a rise in normal tides of about 77 ± 10cm per century. Deep depressions over the N Atlantic can cause gales in the North Sea and when associated with abnormally high tides can cause serious flooding, as in 1953. Since 155 km^2 of the Thames floodplain are increasingly at flood risk (Horner 1971), a barrage is presently nearing completion.

Water storage   The basic problem is one of storage to provide for times of deficit and to transfer water from areas of plenty to areas where it is scarce. The total requirements exceed the residual rainfall, which is the rainfall less the demands of evaporation and evapotranspiration. At the same time it is necessary to provide for the exceptional drought which may occur only once in a period of a hundred years.

   Upland catchments have been the main suppliers of water for the urban areas of the UK because of their high rainfall and impervious rock, and also because of the short growing season and isolation which have restricted settlement. Until fairly recently there has been little organized resistance to the building of reservoirs (Gregory 1964A). Water supply can be considered as another way in which urban demands for space are threatening agricultural land. The total proposed expansion of water storage for 1981 is 27 km^2 which is small compared with the 202 km^2 lost annually to urban expansion. The benefits of increased water supply and increasing production by irrigation could outweigh the loss of agricultural acreage. The SE has an annual residual rainfall of only 127mm and every acre of urban settlement could demand as much as 700mm (Speight 1968). Sites for storage in the SE would have to be on productive farmland and because of the nature of the topography wide shallow valleys would have to be drowned. The alternative is to impound upper streams and, without affecting existing settlement, four times the present storage could be obtained, only one-third of which would be required this century. The water from these reservoirs could regulate the flow of rivers and ensure a steady supply for abstraction downstream. While management is now possible in short and relatively clean rivers like the Dee, for longer rivers such as the Severn the time-lag of several days for the release from a reservoir to be effective downstream, means that more efficient weather forecasting for the basin would have to be developed. The use of rivers as transporters of water and sources for abstraction has increased the need for better sewerage treatment. The drought of 1976 reduced the flow of rivers, emphasizing the urgency of the problem and it precipitated the Wye Transfer in 1977 (Welsh Water Authority 1979). The quality of water in the Trent makes it unacceptable as a source of supply and doubts have been expressed as to whether the necessary standards could be attained at an acceptable cost. Using the Trent to recharge the Bunter sandstone would be similar in cost to water treatment and furthermore would require a larger area of land.

Storage in *impounded estuaries* or *maritime basins* is another possibility. Estuary storage has been considered for the Dee, Severn, Morecambe Bay, Solway and the Wash, as well as many smaller schemes in Wales and SE England. For most, the cost is a major drawback, especially if the estuary is separated from demand areas by high mountains. The proposed Dee barrage (fig. 3.6) which would yield $1Mm^3$ (million cubic metres) per day, little more than the expected yield of Kielder reservoir $0.95Mm^3$ per day, would cost almost five times as much. Since estuaries are at lower elevations and have larger surface areas than upland reservoirs of similar capacity, higher evaporation losses would make them less efficient. Salt-water intrusion may necessitate desalination, adding further to the cost of estuary schemes, making them less attractive than any other alternative. The Solway barrage was suggested as a source of water for the Tyne, while Morecambe Bay was to serve Lancashire and, by transfer across the Pennines, the W Riding conurbation. The Wash was to serve the water-scarce areas of SE England. Together Solway, Dee, Morecambe and Wash barrages could hold $1,818Mm^3$ and meet all demands this century. Barrage schemes are difficult to evaluate because of the possible effects on silting and fisheries. Because the environmental impact cannot be easily predicted, not more than two estuaries could be developed this century and, in fact, the preferred strategy suggested by the Water Resources Board (1973) included only the Dee estuary for all development up to 2001.

In a complete reappraisal of the needs of the NW Water Authority, it is now considered unlikely that a major resource will be needed by 2000 and so Morecambe Bay has been revived as a serious alternative for future development (North West Water 1979). Although the most expensive of all the alternatives, it avoids the serious land use conflicts of proposed inland storage and it is similar in cost to the Dee scheme without the same water-quality problems. The Morecambe scheme now favours bunded storage of 300M l/d (million litres per day), filled by pumping from the tidal limit of the rivers rather than impounding barrage which would have serious environmental impact on drainage around the bay. It would also require

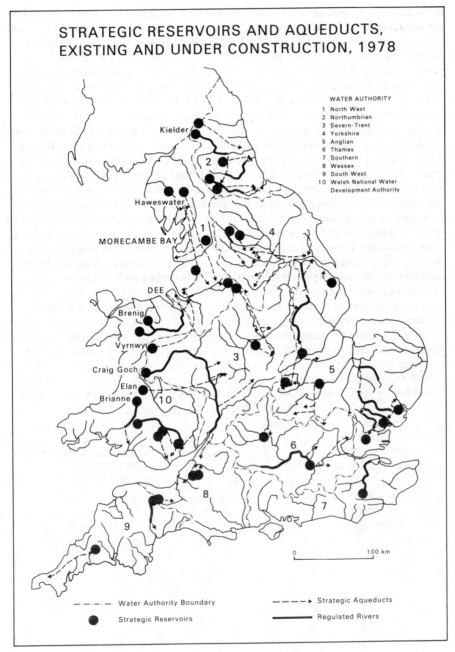

Figure 3.6   Strategic reservoirs and aqueducts, existing and under construction, 1978

treatment of salt and pollution from feeding rivers and affect a large area of the Bay
as well as incurring much higher costs.

In Jersey and Guernsey, where the peak summer demands could not be met by
surface reservoirs, desalination has been developed for public water supply. A
desalination study in connection with the proposed Wash barrage scheme suggested
that it might be competitive by the end of the century in coastal areas of the SE,
but it could not meet all the deficiency in the SE after 1981 as the cost would be
prohibitive (Water Resources Bd 1973, 50). Plans to establish a pilot project at
Ipswich were abandoned by the government in 1972 because the cost of developing
desalination was rising faster than that of conventional sources of water. For inland
areas, where rivers can be regulated, desalination could only be considered if it
proves too difficult and costly to clean up grossly polluted rivers like the Trent.
Apart from the cost of desalination, which includes rapid deterioration due to
corrosion, the Water Resources Board suggested that objections on environmental
grounds to the building of plants at the coast would be as strong as those which
have already faced reservoir proposals.

Another alternative is to use *underground aquifers* for storage. Chalk is the
main aquifer, but like Jurassic limestone the storage in cracks and fissures creates
wide fluctuations in water level. Since they hold water in small pores, the Permian
and Triassic sandstones suffer much smaller variations. In winter, ground-water can
give a high yield in the form of flow from springs but in summer pumping is
necessary. Since the outcrops of these aquifers could receive only a limited amount
of rainfall, artificial recharge would be essential. The Thames Conservancy pilot
scheme for recharging the chalk from 1967 to 1969 proved successful and a

TABLE 3.3

**Potential Potable Water Supplies by Water Authority Areas, England and Wales, Scotland and
N Ireland, 1976–7 (thous. m³ per day)**

	Net total All sources	Surface water	Ground-water
United Kingdom	20,603	13,761	6,854
England and Wales	17,143	10,437	6,718
Water Authority Areas:			
North West	2,848	2,294	626
Northumbrian	788	701	87
Severn–Trent	2,686	1,484	1,230
Yorkshire	1,370	909	412
Anglian	1,818	873	914
Thames	3,570	1,843	1,756
Southern	1,382	310	1,049
Wessex	861	430	431
South West	503	390	113
Welsh Nat. Water Dev. Authority	1,317	1,203	100
Scotland	2,761	2,677	84
N Ireland	699	647	52

Source: Water Data 1977

prototype scheme for artificial recharge has been installed in the Lea valley. If the water used for charging contains effluent then treatment is necessary.

In N Lincolnshire up to 95% of winter percolation could be abstracted in the following summer without causing encroachment of sea water. However, over-development of boreholes in the London Basin has already caused a serious decline in ground-water and any further development must be accompanied by recharging. The chalk and Jurassic limestone of the Thames basin could yield 700,000m^3 per day and the same rocks in the Great Ouse basin 330,000m^3 per day. The other major aquifer is the Bunter sandstone, mainly in the Midlands and on both flanks of the Pennines. The Vale of York sandstone could yield 135,000m^3 per day to regulate the Yorkshire Ouse for abstraction to serve Humberside. The major difficulty with the Triassic rocks is that much of the ground-water is mineralized, which is true also of the coal measures, which have the added problem of pollution from toxic waste dumped in old mine workings. Shropshire has a large potential for ground-water from Triassic rocks, estimated at 225,000m^3 per day, which will be used to augment the Severn. The Severn–Trent Authority has begun drilling for underground storage in the Burton sandstone of the W Midlands, to come into use by 1986. Water from the Severn will be transferred by the Elan Aqueduct and treated before charging the aquifer. The water will then be abstracted by pumping to high-level reservoirs to allow distribution by gravity (Mathews 1981). At present 40% of the water in England and Wales is from ground-water sources, but in Scotland and N Ireland it accounts for less than 10% of the total supply.

III.2 Water Supply and Demand

Rapid urban growth during the industrial revolution led to the development of nearby uplands as sources of water supply, and as demand increased more distant uplands in the North of England and Wales served the industrial belts of the Midlands, Yorkshire and Lancashire. The catchments of the reservoirs were con-trolled to preserve water quality. All major storage works built in the past 120 years were designed for a particular town or city, the main consideration being cost. As potential sites diminished, the larger urban authorities had an advantage (Gregory 1964A, 270). Amalgamation of smaller boards was encouraged in the 1950s: in 1945 there were 1,100 water undertakings in England and Wales, but by 1966 these had been reduced to 286. In addition to statutory undertakings there are water companies operating under individual Acts of Parliament or Orders by the Minister.

In Scotland reorganization stemming from the *Local Government (Scotland) Act* (1973) came into effect in 1975, creating seven river-purification Boards to control pollution of mainland water. Nine regional authorities and three Island authorities control water supply, sewerage and sewage disposal. In N Ireland distribution of water is mainly in the hands of local authorities but grants towards water schemes are made under the *Water Supplies and Sewage Act (NI) 1945*.

Supply The Metropolitan Water Board is the largest water undertaking in the UK, supplying 1.67Mm^3 per day to 6.25 million people. The effects of population concentration were first felt in the industrial areas. Grossly polluted rivers were no problem as long as new sources of water could be found in the uplands, which had been the case up to the Second World War. Subsequent population growth led to water demands which approached the limit of available supplies. Together with an increasing awareness of the recreational value of the uplands, this led to a new concept of water supply. Reservoirs were to be regulators for the rivers, maintaining the volume needed for abstraction in the lower reaches. Extraction of water can reduce the flow of fresh water so that salt-water invasions may increase upstream similar to the effect of the deepening of channels. However, the quality of water, which depends on the volume of river flow and the treatment of effluent, needs to be assured and this is part of the cost of transporting water in this way. The Thames receives $0.81Mm^3$ of sewage effluent per day and $0.18Mm^3$ per day from industry, yet 58% of London's water is abstracted from the river. Manchester and Liverpool have so dominated the water resources development of the Lake District and N Wales, respectively, that any further move for developing river resources is vigorously resisted. Yet Manchester maintains that industry demands high-quality water supplies. The use of rivers as transporters provides the opportunity to economize, but also permits twice the yield obtainable if reservoirs were used for direct piped supply. It also has the advantage of permitting flood control and maintaining dry-weather flow. To be most efficiently used, regulating reservoirs require management on a wider scale than hitherto possible and the *Water Resources Act* (1963) was the first move towards this end; this Act applies only to England and Wales. So far, in Scotland and N Ireland pressures on water resources have not called for this kind of administrative machinery. In N Ireland management of water resources is under review, in anticipation of further industrial development.

Under the Act, twenty-nine River Authorities were created and the government appointed the Water Resources Board as an advisory body to plan and coordinate their efforts, by overseeing their proposals for meeting demand at seven-yearly intervals. Amenity and recreation are considered as well as water supply. The *Water Resources Board* (WRB) undertook three major studies of future demand and formulated strategies for the supply, which they reviewed in their final report (Water Resources Bd 1973). In April 1974 ten regional water authorities were created to take over the function of the river authorities, water undertakings and sewage disposal. The aim was to integrate the activities involved in river management (DoE 1973). The regions are large enough to plan successfully for water needs and pay for any necessary transfers, each having a twenty-year plan and a seven-year programme of investment. The overall national policy is now in the hands of the *National Water Council*, and its review (NWC 1978) provides a framework to consider policy questions arising from the individual plans of the ten water authorities.

It is more economical to meet the needs for several years ahead with one major scheme, rather than by a programme involving a succession of small schemes. By increasing a dam from 18m to 33m in height, the capacity per unit cost is increased three times (Speight 1968). The amount of land flooded would be four and a half times greater, but since land costs are only 2.7% of the total this is not likely to be relevant except for social and amenity considerations. There is a limit to the size, as the larger the storage capacity the longer it takes to refill after a drought. The rate of refill is also dependent on the locality. In NE England an impounded estuary would be drawn down 61cm for six-month periods only twice in thirty-two years, while a pumped storage reservoir in SE England would have a similar draw-down on six occasions, two of which would remain at this level for two years at a time (Rydz 1969).

The average rainfall of the UK is 900mm and this produces an average of 460mm runoff or 190Mm^3/d. The aggregate residual rainfall in the UK (0.068Mm^3 per annum, or 3,864 l per person per day in England and Wales) is much greater than is likely to be required by the community. The maximum possible yield in England and Wales is 185Mm^3 per day (Central Advisory Committee 1959). In England and Wales there has been a decline in abstractions since 1969, when 48Mm^3 per day were abstracted. By 1977 the daily abstractions had fallen to 36Mm^3 (DoE 1978A). The lower populations in Scotland and Northern Ireland demand very much lower abstractions, less than 2Mm^3 in Scotland and 1Mm^3 in Northern Ireland. N Ireland is already fully served by well-distributed uplands and the centrally-placed Lough Neagh, so that any supply problems are local and can be solved by normal development. Scotland is equally well-placed and the problem is one of distribution to the C Lowlands. The Loch Lomond and Loch Bradan Schemes will provide for all industrial and urban growth except in Fife. Apart from the administrative problems, the Southern uplands effectively separate Scotland from England and no water resources of Scotland have been developed for transfer to England.

Demands In England and Wales demands from the public water supply increased from 8.9Mm^3 per day in 1955 to 14.1Mm^3 per day in 1971, but since then demand has levelled off at about 14.5Mm^3/day. Regions differ in their needs. The Severn–Trent Authority estimates demand will rise from 1,921 Ml/d in 1979 to 2,393 by the year 2000, due to population increase, decreased household size, urban redevelopment, the increase in use of water-using appliances and higher losses (Severn–Trent 1981). The Water Resources Board estimated very large deficiencies would occur by the year 2000, especially in SE England (WRB 1973). More recent estimates by the National Water Council (NWC 1978) suggest that demand will be 42% more than the 1975 supply (table 3.4).

Additional supplies will be needed for domestic purposes; industrial processes; and in agriculture, for cleaning as well as irrigation. Apart from these uses, water is

TABLE 3.4

Water Authority Forecasts for Public Water Supply Demands, 1981–2001

Water authority	Actual supply	Forecast demand			Forecast increase
	1975 (Ml/d)	1981 (Ml/d)	1991 (Ml/d)	2001 (Ml/d)	2001 over 1975 (%)
North West	2,450	2,630	3,040	3,280	34
Northumbrian	960	1,200	–	–	–
Severn–Trent	2,180	2,230	2,660	3,020	38
Yorkshire	1,280	1,430	1,700	1,940	52
Anglian	1,450	1,730	2,250	2,670	84
Thames	3,360	3,400	3,640	3,880	15
Southern	1,090	1,220	1,500	1,800	65
Wessex	710	750	850	970	37
South West	380	420	500	590	55
Welsh	1,130	1,300	1,510	1,720	52

Source: NWC (1978); *Water Industry Rev.* (1978)

needed for navigation, mainly in the Trent, Severn and Thames; and amenity and recreation. However, if the rivers are to be used as a source for abstraction, regulating reservoirs will be needed to maintain flow in the upper courses and returned effluent will ensure sufficient volume in the lower reaches. Quality of the water is likely to affect fish before other forms of life. Total abstractions for public supply in 1976 were 15Mm^3/d and if 20Mm^3 will be required by the end of the century then more resources need to be developed, even though the 1976 abstractions were reduced due to the severe drought.

Domestic demand This increases as more new houses are built and older property is modernized. While in 1951 over one-third of houses in the UK had no fixed bath, today the figure is less than 10%. Improvements and urban-renewal schemes will reduce this still further, though the rate of house-building has declined in the 1980s. At the same time, consumption of water is increasing with greater use of washing machines, dish-washers, etc. Although a steady increase in demand was expected to produce per capita use of 450 l per day (WRB 1973, 30), Water Authorities have made more modest estimates in the range 150–170 l/head/day (Severn–Trent 1980). Accurate estimates of population by the end of this century are difficult. Those made in 1965 suggested 66M, but in 1971 this was reduced to 58 million and in 1972 to 55 million. Internal migration due to changing patterns of employment make regional forecasting of water demands even more uncertain.

Industrial demand The most important industrial use of water is for cooling, which at present amounts to 23% of the water abstracted (table 3.5) and the CEGB uses a further 51% for cooling. Assuming that industry will re-use water, industrial demand for water will only be a small part of the future deficiency, since the quantity consumed by industry is small compared with the amount it circulates. About 90% of water abstracted by power stations and about 60% abstracted by industry is returned with no significant change. Since 1973 the decline in industrial output has led to a fall in demand. For example, in Severn–Trent in 1981 there was 4% fall over the previous year (Severn–Trent 1981). Modernization of industrial plants has also led to more efficient use of water. Despite the 2% annual increase in electricity production since 1971, the demand for water has declined, since production has increased in the new coastal stations at the expense of the older stations using river water. The CEGB abstracted 19.4Mm^3/d in 1971 but only 13.3Mm^3 in 1977 (DoE 1978A).

A direct cooling system for power stations uses a great volume of water, but most of this is returned to the source unchanged in quality though at a higher temperature. A 2,000MW station will circulate about 0.27Mm^3/hour. The use of cooling towers needs only 15% of the water for cooling but since it is constantly recycled there are high evaporation losses so that a 2,000MW station will lose 0.06Mm^3 per day. Since there is a trend towards the use of cooling towers, the water consumed by power stations is increasing but little of this is from rivers used for public supplies. The Trent provides 55% of the cooling water used by the CEGB and 45% comes from the Ouse, Mersey and the Severn. The Water Resources Board recommended the siting of new power stations near major water transfers or sewage outfalls (WRB 1966).

The extent to which returned industrial effluent can be re-used depends on the quality requirements. Sewage and saline water can be used for cooling but food industries require high standards. Effluents from food industries are usually of reasonable quality but those from engineering and chemical industries are often

TABLE 3.5

Abstractions of Water in England and Wales, 1971–6 (in Ml/d)

	Public water supplies	Power stations	Other industry	Agriculture
1971	14,400	19,200	7,800	200
1972	14,900	18,200	7,600	200
1973	15,200	17,800	7,400	200
1974	15,200	15,000	7,000	200
1975	15,400	13,700	6,600	300
1976	15,000	13,200	6,600	300

Source: NWC (1978)

highly toxic and may even inhibit the biological processes used by sewage works. Re-use is essential to save substantial construction in meeting the industrial needs of the future.

The *Water Resources Act* (1963) made it obligatory for industry to have a licence and pay a charge for private supply. The maintenance of flow in rivers by regulating reservoirs and the use of sewage effluent will increase the cost of abstraction and this may encourage industry to re-use water internally by the treatment of effluent. Rees (1969) estimated 0.79% increase per annum for the future, but this figure could be altered by a change in the cost of water.

Agricultural demand Although agricultural demand was only 4% of industrial demand in 1976, the peak demand in the growing season is high. Spray irrigation is a high consumer of water as most is evaporated or transpired and lost to the river. The *Water Resources Act* (1963) required licensing of abstractions by the River Authority so that the quantity and rate of withdrawal can be limited.

In 1963 there was enough equipment to irrigate 52,611 ha and this increased to a peak in 1965 of 107,796 ha. There has since been a decline; in 1974 the capacity was 81,874 ha, most of which was in the South and East. The expansion of irrigation was limited by cost and the fact that supply may be restricted or cut off when it is most needed. In fact restrictions were never imposed in the Great Ouse basin, even with the drought of 1976, as abstractions were reduced voluntarily by irrigators to meet the requirements of the Water Authority (Porter 1978). The crops which could significantly benefit from irrigation in E Anglia cover about 340,000 ha, but the 50,000 ha already irrigated fully taxes the resources of the Great Ouse basin. Ignoring costs and availability of water, the area which could benefit from irrigation in the Gt Ouse basin would need 682,000 Ml but actual agricultural demand by the year 2000 may be much lower than this. A survey in 1974 estimated a seasonal demand of 27,000 Ml (Porter 1978).

Spray irrigation is no longer a serious threat to other users of water. Planning has given highest priority to domestic needs, followed by industry and then irrigation. Storage of water in winter to allow for high demands in summer has been considered the responsibility of the farmer but this has made the cost of irrigation much higher than irrigating by direct abstraction. The cost differential in winter is not sufficient to give a financial advantage but it does provide a more secure source of irrigation water. Apart from irrigation, water is also needed for spraying, as a protection against frost, for stock, milk cooling, and cleaning. Only in areas where storage on the farm is not possible, thus requiring additional water, have agricultural needs been considered in the total estimate.

III.3 Strategies

A good deal of integration has been achieved internally in Regional Water Authorities. The links shown in Figure 3.3 were existing or under construction in 1978.

Table 3.6 shows the deficiencies anticipated by the WRB for the end of the century and this greatly influenced the development of strategic resources. The changes in forecast demand and the economic situation greatly changed the programme of development actively carried out by the 10 Regional Water Authorities whose prime concern was for the demands within their regions (table 3.7).

TABLE 3.6

Strategic Water Deficiency in the year 2001

(Mm³ per diem)	Local forecast	Alternative forecast
North	3.45 (±1.5)	3.20
Wales and Midlands	3.20 (±1.3)	2.40
SE and Central	2.85 (±1.2)	2.60
Total, England and Wales	9.50 (±4.0)	8.20

Source: WRB (1973)

Strategies to meet these deficiencies were first outlined by the WRB in its short existence from 1963 to 1974. They have been continued in a national plan considered by the central water planning unit, advising both the government and the new regional water authorities.

The WRB produced three regional reports and a report for England and Wales assessing the probable demand for water up to the end of the century and possible programmes of development to meet these needs. The reports stress the importance of flexibility in long-term planning and the need for regular revision, which since 1974 has become the responsibility of the ten *Regional Water Authorities*. The North, Wales, the Midlands and the SE have special problems which emerge clearly from these detailed regional surveys. All three reports already show that developable resources exist in the UK to meet all foreseeable demands, but the problem is finding the optimal programme of development. The needs are to be met by regulation of rivers, by reservoirs, or ground water, and the combined use of resources. The three regions used to assess the needs and problems of water development are different from the ten regional water authorities set up in 1974; nevertheless they provide a useful framework for a national plan. The Welsh National Water Authority has extra-territorial jurisdiction over the Dee and Wye basins, the Severn—Trent Authority over the entire Severn system including that part within Wales.

In the *South East* the basic problem is lack of internal resources to meet future demands, and development of surface storage would encroach upon valuable farm-

TABLE 3.7

Planned Development of Water Resources, 1978–83 (Ml/d)

Water authority	Reliable yield of existing sources in 1977	Planned development of sources 1978–83
North West	2,839	360
Northumbrian	1,232	834
Severn–Trent	2,450	110
Yorkshire	1,389	340
Anglian	2,000	121
Thames	3,690	65
Southern	1,360	100
Wessex	907	91
South West	428	117
Welsh	1,378	225
Total, England and Wales	17,673	2,363

Source: NWC (1978); *Water Authority Rev.* (1978)

land. The report on the SE (WRB 1966) was most concerned with providing water for the very large deficiency zone within the SE requiring an additional $2.95 \text{Mm}^3/\text{d}$ by the year 2000. A combination of surface and underground storage including schemes like the Chichester barrage, if acceptable, could provide more than the estimated needs at the end of the century. However, it is probably more realistic to assume that long-term schemes must include bulk imports from the west and north. For climatic reasons river regulation can be met only by ground-water. Using ground-water to augment summer flows and artificially recharging the aquifers in winter could yield as much as $0.56 \text{Mm}^3/\text{d}$ in the Ely-Ouse, equal to the internal needs of the Great Ouse area by 2001. The Thames could also be regulated, using ground-water from the chalk to meet all needs this century, provided it is possible to recharge the aquifer which is in places already overpumped and threatened by salt-water intrusions. Many of the rivers in the SE are only indirectly polluted and, if regulated and further deterioration prevented, can continue to be used for abstraction. Re-use of water in the SE is a significant aspect of the water-supply pattern.

The Thames and Lea in 1975 supplied 2Mm^3 per day, which is near the limit of $2.3 \text{Mm}^3/\text{d}$ suggested by WRB. Demand met from other rivers has not been as anticipated, the lower Severn in 1975 providing only 0.2Mm^3 per day (NWC 1978).

The Trent and many of the larger northern rivers are so grossly polluted as to preclude them as sources for public supply. There are of course in Wales and the North many clean rivers, like the Wye, whose obvious amenity and recreational value is likely to safeguard their purity and they will be used increasingly to transport water and for abstraction in the future. Remedial works will further improve the quality of rivers so that abstracting from the Tees will increase from 540m^3 per day at present to $1,250 \text{m}^3$ per day in 2001 and the Dee from 560 to 900m^3 per day. Up to $1,250 \text{m}^3$ per day can be abstracted from the Tyne now regulated by the Kielder reservoir.

Industries sited on the rivers of the *Midlands* and *North* use and re-use the river water. This is particularly so of the Trent which provides 55% of all the river water used by the CEGB. Although the quality prevents its use for public supply it has sufficient dry-weather flow to allow abstraction for industry. Further industrial demand can be partly met by recycling the increased effluent from the industries themsleves. However, the industrial effluents may need treatment and because of the nature of the industries this is a greater problem than in the SE. Industry in the North requires more water than elsewhere in England and Wales and this explains the higher per capita consumption, 278 litres per day compared to 254 litres per day in SE England. However, the North requires less for agriculture since the greater part of the agricultural use is for spray irrigation.

Additional storage needed to regulate rivers for the *Wales* and *Midlands* regions can be found in the Welsh Valleys and Peak district. The Elan reservoir development was approved in 1981 (Welsh WA 1981) but so far no date has been agreed. This has been the cause of some conflict between the Welsh and Severn–Trent Authorities. Severn–Trent objected to the use of Elan to regulate the Wye since it would reduce the security of supply to Birmingham from Elan whose supply will now be augmented by increased pumping from the Severn at higher costs. Carsington reservoir was agreed in 1979 but the first water will not be available before 1985 and restrictions in existing supply will be necessary (Severn–Trent 1980). Public supply in Wales and the Midlands still finds 80% of its water directly from upland reservoirs. Aqueducts carry water from the Elan reservoir on the Wye to Birmingham, from the Vyrnwy, a tributary of the Severn, to Liverpool. Direct supplies from the Derwent, a tributary of the Trent, serve Sheffield, Derby, Nottingham and Leicester. But the Severn, which is regulated by the Clywedog reservoir, is a source for abstractions as far downstream as Gloucester. The dry-weather flow of the Trent is almost entirely effluent so that it cannot be used for direct supply.

In the *North West* the demand in the future is unlikely to need any major developments such as the enlargement of Haweswater envisaged by the Water Resources Board. The NW Water Authority claim that economies could delay the need even beyond the year 2000. Studies in 1979 (North West Water 1979) showed that inland surface development on the Ribble would destroy important agricultural land and the river was so badly polluted, some of which could not be easily rectified, that it would not be a good transporter. Equally the development of tributaries of the Lune including Haweswater would have serious environmental effects in a National Park. Only rather minor increases in Haweswater could be tolerated.

The WRB was concerned with the immediate problem and made proposals for development up to 1981. The urgent need was to be met for the most part by reservoir-enlargement for river regulation. A political argument developed in 1975 over the revenues for water exported from Wales. The Welsh Water Authority seeks to equalize water charges with those of the English neighbours. This is opposed by the Severn–Trent Authority, which is not prepared to pay more for water from Wales than Welsh abstractors would pay. Financial considerations led to the abandonment of the Craig Goch enlargement and the demand in Severn–Trent will now be met by the development of ground water in Shropshire (Severn–Trent 1980). The enlarged Craig Goch with tunnel links to the Severn, allowing transfers from the Severn to the Thames and the Dee, was not flexible enough to allow for changes in demand during construction, a point confirmed by the withdrawal of

Thames Authority from the Severn—Thames transfer proposal.

In the *North* there is no shortage of resources as the region includes the Lake District, with the heaviest rainfall in England and Wales. The problem lies in the siting of storage reservoirs and the systems for transporting the water. The decision to develop the new reservoir at Kielder rather than a stepwise development of several smaller reservoirs serves the immediate future as well as the longer-term demand, though this may have been overestimated. Since it was opened in December 1980, Kielder has regulated the Tyne for abstraction by Newcastle and Gateshead. While the pipeline and tunnels linking it to the Wear and Tees are also complete, demand is not sufficient to justify the cost of transferring water by pumping. The Ouse and its tributaries will be regulated by enlarging the existing reservoirs of Grunthwaite and Gouthwaite. Whilst it is possible to cost the loss of productivity of agricultural or forestry land, it is more difficult to estimate the value of amenity or to judge the demands from the environment of the often conflicting urban and rural users.

The choice by the WRB for development beyond 1981 was between regional self-sufficiency and major inter-regional transfers. Regional self-sufficiency is the least efficient, as it required eighteen additional, and the enlargement of six existing, reservoirs. The cheapest solution lies in continuing to develop inland storage for river regulation, which would require a further seven reservoirs and the enlargement of three existing reservoirs. Two of the new reservoirs would be in national parks and one of the enlargements would destroy a village, so that its effect on the environment would be considerable. While complete dependence on inland reservoirs can be ruled out on environmental grounds, equally the development of estuary storage in the Dee, Morecambe and the Wash is too costly. The preferred strategy involves a combination of estuaries and inland reservoirs. The development of further surface reservoirs is impossible in the SE though the preferred programme includes enlargements of reservoirs in the Wash basin. Thus ground-water development and the transfer of water from the Severn to the Thames was the preferred development for the SE until the end of the century.

Since 1974, planning by the 10 Water Authorities has led to more self-sufficiency (DoE 1976B). Demand for water has been less than anticipated by the WRB and the cost of major schemes has discouraged schemes such as the Severn—Thames transfer. At present, about 90% of the water supply for each of the water authorities is from sources within their region. The drought in the summer of 1976 had greatest impact in areas of high demand and low storage capacity and this revived an interest in the idea of a national grid. However, financial stringency is unlikely to encourage the necessary investment to remove all risk of shortages in the event of another drought similar to 1976. It has already become clear that some Water Authorities cannot meet all possible demands within their regions as this would involve unacceptably high charges (Welsh WA 1979). This further weakens the validity of any national plans.

III.4 Conservation

Water conservation has been defined as the

> 'preservation, control and development of water resources whether by storage,
> including natural ground storage, prevention of pollution, or other means, so as

to ensure that adequate and reliable supplies of water are made available for all purposes in the most suitable and economical way whilst safeguarding legitimate interests'

(WRB 1966, 1970, 1971). In the UK the problem of water conservation lies in the last clause of the official definition, for the reconciliation of conflicting interests becomes more difficult with increasing population pressure. The present water storage provides only 10% of the normal river flow in drought conditions which is insufficient to meet the demands for recreational pursuits. The part of the whole cycle of water use concerning people and recreation is of considerable importance in the management of water.

From 1963 to 1973 water management in England and Wales was controlled by two main categories: the water undertakings who supplied water, and the River Authorities who were concerned with the wider problems of water conservation and management of river basins (MHLG and MAFF 1962). At central government level these two categories were supervised by the Water Resources Board. The *Water Resources Act* (1963) did not, however, overcome the problem of the divided responsibilities for water supply, river management, water conservation, pollution control, sewerage and sewage disposal. The division of responsibility for industrial effluents between the sewerage and River Authorities, in particular, was a major problem. In 1974 the functions of the River Authorities, together with water supply and sewage disposal which were in the hands of some local authorities, were taken over by ten large multi-purpose authorities whose task was to manage rivers on an integrated systems basis (DoE 1973B). Planning at the national level, formerly in the hands of the WRB, became the responsibility of the DoE for water supply, water quality and recreation and the MAFF for land drainage, flood protection and fisheries. The large units could be more self-sufficient than the smaller River Authorities they replaced. In Scotland and N Ireland conservation problems have not yet warranted major reorganization, though *Regional Supply Boards* and a central body are being considered.

Landscaping, ecology and the requirements for leisure activities add a new dimension to the role of water authorities, who will now undertake surveys of potential demand for recreation. The public right of access to reservoirs provided in the 1963 Act has proved satisfactory but without any special provisions for parking or recreation. By the year 2000 a further 16,188ha of reservoir water will be available and in addition the cleaning of many rivers and their regulation for satisfactory abstraction makes them attractive for recreation for a greatly increased number of users. Landscaping and planning for recreational and ecological interests demand a more direct involvement by water authorities in the multiple use of water. Whether these additional uses can be financed by participants or by the country at large has not yet been resolved.

Pressure on the land has led to more opposition to water-storage proposals and the larger Water Authorities claim to be in a better position to consider conflicting demands and especially those of the community directly affected by water development. The changes in policy from direct supply to river regulation will avoid the construction of several new reservoirs. However, practical and less expensive schemes may have to be developed to meet national needs and the larger authorities will be in a better position to choose sites or use landscaping techniques to reduce the impact on the environment and rural communities. Attempts to make better use of present resources by waste prevention, re-use by industry, dual systems for potable and non-potable supplies have come to the fore. In 1979 32% of water in the UK was metered and little information exists on the use of the remaining 13,000 Ml/day. The NWC (1978) estimates losses as high as 25%. Industry frequently uses water of high quality when lower quality would serve as well, but much research needs to be done on the quality of water required by all users as well as that required to maintain aquatic life. Also economies could be encouraged by metering, off-peak tariffs or rationing. Useful as these may be the additional 0.45 Mm^3/d required each year can only be met by surface reservoirs, estuary barrages, aqueduct systems, recirculation and complementary use of ground- and surface-water. The great deficiency in the *Water Resources Act* (1963) was that the River Authorities could not make a comprehensive management plan. The lack of a policy on the quality of river water seriously limited the effectiveness of any of the strategies outlined by the WRB. Now the principal responsibility falls in the 10 autonomous Water Authorities and planning for their regions as far ahead as the end of the century is required by the *Water Act* (1973). These Water Authority plans form the basis for capital expenditure by the government. The National Water Council is responsible for national issues such as environmental pollution and the environmental programme of the European Community. Water supply to industry and to the public must be safeguarded by control over effluent discharges. The building of a new sewage works to raise the quality of river water to permit abstraction may be the alternative to a new reservoir and has the added attraction of improving amenities. The cost of cleaning rivers like the Trent must be considered along with the amount of water made available for abstraction. However, to allow abstraction, the quality must be higher than the Royal Commission standard and the costs can only be met by a levy on all the users.

Cost of water development The greatest influence on costs are the capital works, and the financial constraints of recent years have discouraged the larger reservoir schemes. Authorities have been adopting low-cost schemes or those which can be tackled in steps over a number of years. These considerations have resulted in the abandonment of the Craig Goch reservoir enlargement and the adoption of the very economical ground-water development in Shropshire (Severn–Trent 1980). The NW Water Authority considers that financial constraints will delay any major new developments beyond the end of this century (NW Water 1979).

IV   FORESTS

IV.1   Afforestation

The *Forestry Act* (1919) established the Forestry Commission with the task of replanting areas which had lost timber through decades of uncontrolled exploitation, so replenishing a seriously depleted resource.

Forestry has been an important rural industry employing 15,000 directly in the forests, 8,000 in supporting services and 15,000 in sawmills and associated industries. This employment is particularly important to the more remote areas and expansion would be an important contribution to regional development. Nationally, British forests provide only 8% of our timber needs and the demand

and supply in the UK, the EEC and in the world affects future strategy (CAS 1980). The room for expansion is considerable as the 8% of land in forest is well below the European average of 21%.

The aim in 1943 was to achieve 2 million ha in forest by the end of the century. By 1980 plantations covered 950,000 ha of the UK, 500,000 ha of this in Scotland. The *Countryside Act* (1968) recognized the importance of forests to recreation and extended the powers of the Forestry Commission to plant and manage forests for amenity. In the 1970s, however, a review of forest policy emphasized the need for cost-benefit consideration on all forest management. By the end of the seventies there was an increasing awareness of dwindling natural resources and the need to plant more timber for this purpose, but with the added advantage of providing more rural employment (CAS 1980). The potential area for forest is large, 1,690,500 ha in Scotland, 860,000 ha in England and 480,000 ha in Wales. The impact of various strategies in developing the uplands has been considered by CAS (1980). The fairly modest target of raising our timber production to about 26% of our requirements by the year 2035 would mean 1.96 million ha converted from other users to forest in Britain and 120,000 ha in N Ireland. One of the major effects of forest development in uplands is the water use by increased evapotranspiration. Another effect is on the quality of runoff as well as an increase in the variability in stream flow. The sediment production is only a serious problem in the establishment phase, but nutrients would increase and areas with high-quality water at present may need an extra cost of treatment. Although the area in England and Wales where these effects are a serious threat is large, 748,400 ha, forests rarely cover whole catchments, most are less than 10% under forest, and the highest and wettest areas are usually left bare (CAS 1980). However, forest increase in the Brianne catchment in Wales, already 25% in forest, could lead to a loss of up to 2% in water yield.

The early forestry was on grazing land, and the planting of the lower slopes effectively isolated the high pastures, reducing their value for stock raising. Although present technology allows planting at higher elevations, there is a case for conserving high grazing for red deer, and they too need access to lowland grazing in winter (CAS 1980). Planting of some of the potential forest land would render the remaining farmland usable since rough grazing is essential feed for sheep and cattle. CAS estimates forestry would be possible on only 46% of the potential in Scotland. These considerations show the need for integration in all future planting programmes.

Deciduous hardwoods, mainly in private forests, occur on the more productive soils of the lowlands, but the poorer soil and harsher climate of the uplands is better suited to the introduction of conifers which account for 90% of all Forestry Commission woodland. The conifers have proved that they can be highly productive even on poor site conditions. The average growth rate of Sitka spruce and Douglas fir is more than three times that of oak and twice the growth rate of beech (Grayson 1967). Much of the planting has been in the more favoured parts of the uplands, though recent techniques have allowed the planting of peat bogs. There are still vast areas suitable for forestry so that the difficult areas, such as the exposed west coast of Scotland, may not be developed for extensive forests for some time. The establishment of vast forests of conifers in what seemed to be the less productive uplands has raised one of the most difficult problems of land-use management. Drainage to overcome the serious problem of excessive soil water has been the greatest problem facing reafforestation of the wet uplands (Thompson

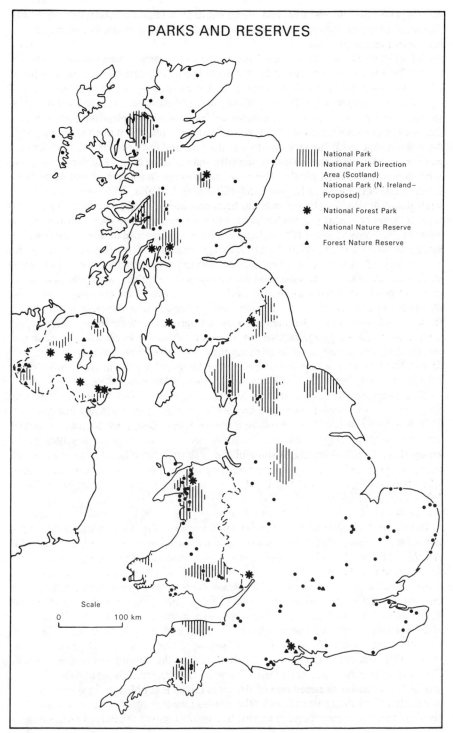

Figure 3.7   Parks and reserves, UK, 1972

1979). The profitability of forests depends to a very large extent on the nature of the site, the soil drainage and exposure in particular. Agriculture and especially sheep or cattle farming would not be so sensitive to environmental qualities and it would be difficult to decide on an optimum land-use pattern based on productivity alone. In any case this would entail a fragmentation of forest blocks which would be uneconomic and may not be compatible, for example, with the practice of the spring burning of grazing areas, which is a hazard to forests. Comparisons of productivity may be meaningless at another time when new techniques of either forest or agricultural management may be developed. A land survey has been carried out jointly by the Departments of Agriculture and Forestry in N Scotland, in which land suitable for forests is identified and, on the basis of its agricultural potential, is either earmarked for purchase by the Forestry Commission or retained for agriculture (McVean and Lockie 1969).

Much afforestation by the Commission in the 1920s was on grazing lands, especially in the Highlands of Scotland. Whilst the presence of forest had the value of providing shelter for stock, the forests were largely planted on the lower slopes and effectively isolated the high grazings from the valley floors, thus reducing their value for stock farming. Technology has made it possible to plant over a wider range of conditions so that this serious conflict need not occur with new plantings.

Forestry Commission planting has been in large units, of which 55% are over 400 ha in extent and the landscape effect is less pleasing than the fragmented pattern of small private woods and farmlands typical of the lowlands. However, attempts to landscape their estates and provide a valuable resource for recreation led the Forestry Commission to establish four large forest parks in Scotland, Snowdonia forest park in Wales, the Forest of Dean and Wye, and the Border forest park in England. Since 1976 the 26 camping and caravan parks have had 1.5 million camper nights annually. The development of Kielder reservoir in the Border forest park and its potential for recreation has led to more specific landscape planning. A 1977 survey showed that 24 million visited Forestry Commission woodlands so that more attention is now paid to that aspect of planning. Forests now have an index of recreation potential to allow planning of facilities (Forestry Comm. 1978).

IV.2 Environmental Factors in the Productivity of Commercial Forests

The large-scale commercial forests established by the Forestry Commission since 1919 have been developed on low-value land, most of which was marginal for agriculture. In the 1950s forests were expanding at the rate of 16,000 ha per annum and most of this was on the rough grazing land of the uplands. From 1966–75 annual planting has averaged 25,000 ha of which 17,000 ha were in Scotland (Forestry Comm. 1975). After 1975 it became increasingly difficult to acquire land and annual planting was reduced to 12,000 ha in 1978–9. Although similar to agriculture in that trees are planted like a crop and harvested at the optimum stage of growth, forestry was forced to develop in areas of difficult conditions of climate and soil. Productivity has been improved through increasing knowledge of the relationships between growth and environment, and the development of technology to take advantage of this knowledge. The scale is also very different from agriculture, which makes the control of temperature and moisture in nurseries a more difficult task. The softwoods have predominated largely because of their rapid growth and their ability to survive in a wide range of conditions. Although

Scots pine is the only native conifer, spruce is preferred for the upland plantations and, in the wetter areas of the west, sitka spruce predominates. Spruce and pine accounted for 80% of postwar planting, lodgepole pine increasing in popularity to become second to sitka spruce (Forestry Comm. 1974).

The sitka spruce, a native of the wet Pacific coast of N America, grows well on the wet western mountains, but under dry conditions the tree becomes susceptible to attack by aphids. For this reason the low rainfall and the dry sandy soils of the Breckland in E Anglia and the Culbin Sands, Morayshire, have suited Scots and Corsican pine rather than spruce. In the Border forests, pine is also grown in the poorest deep peats, while the mid and upper slopes are exclusively in spruce (Pyatt 1966). Larch is usually planted on the areas of better soils, for example the bracken sites of the uplands, and was successfully planted on large private estates in Scotland in the late nineteenth century. For economic reasons, broad-leafed trees, mainly beech and oak, are less important and are confined to the better soils; in 1975 they accounted for less than 1% of total plantings (Forestry Comm. 1975). However a few species in suitable sites have equalled or surpassed the production of conifers and here replacement of conifers is possible in the future. Despite their lower productivity the uplands are now considered for conservation, and landscape benefits account for 3% of plantings.

Despite the generally poor conditions in the forested areas, elevation, topography and position influence the local climate and soil. Growth is dependent on the length of season, temperature and moisture. Since the growth rate in trees depends on the leaf area available, soil-water deficits in winter can retard the new season's growth; girth and volume are increased from April onwards. The conditions for survival in the early years, such as freedom from dried-out surface soil, attacks by rabbits, grouse and deer and late frosts, are not needed once the trees are established, but they do succeed in eliminating forests from many areas unless they can be remedied, as by high fencing in the Highlands of Scotland, to protect seedlings from deer. The effects of environmental conditions on the growth of mature trees can be considerable. The average annual growth increment of $19m^3$ per ha for Corsican pine in E Anglia was reduced by 30% in a dry year (Rouse 1961). However, multi-variate analysis suggests that winter temperature, sunshine, content of clay and stones in the soil, depth of the water table, soil depth, humus type, soil pH and phosphorus content are significant components in the growth of the species (Forestry Comm. 1968, 55). Once trees are established the environmental conditions can change, such as the improved soil-water capacity due to the growth of root systems which can be substantial, even for shallow-rooting trees in peats (O'Hare 1972). Fertilizers can be used most effectively in speeding up the period from establishment to full canopy, when the trees demand less nutrients from the soil as they become more efficient in retaining nutrients from the atmosphere (Miller 1980).

Interception of *precipitation* in forests is appreciable. Together with the direct evaporation from the soil, which may be as much as 10% of the total, it forms an important part of the water balance. Conifers differ from deciduous trees in that they transpire and intercept precipitation throughout the year. In wetter areas the evaporation of intercepted water can be as much as that transpired by the trees. The deep-rooting habits of trees, which under conditions of free drainage are commonly 2m, increase the available water capacity to 300–500mm depending on soil type, which permits a long period of unrestricted evapotranspiration after the onset of drought. For this reason forests transpire more than grassland under the same conditions of potential evapotranspiration and the difference is greatest in SE England. Thinning reduces evapotranspiration; in one case, streamflow from a forest increased by 4.5mm after clearing 10% of the trees. This is only temporary as the branches of the remaining trees rapidly grow to fill up the spaces and the roots extend to occupy all of the soil volume (Rutter 1972; Holmes and Colville 1968).

Temperature is also important to growth, so that altitude and latitude are of significance. In the uplands, records of temperature are sparse and assumptions must be made on crude lapse rates which need not be constant from time to time nor apply without variation over a very wide area. The present tree line in the UK is not entirely determined by nature, but the upper level of potential growth must be based on physical conditions, which in upland areas are complex. In the Cairngorms it is probably about 690m on sheltered slopes, but about 600m on exposed sites (Pears 1972). While the physical limit can be defined broadly as a mean summer temperature of 10°C, the effects of temperature conditions on growth rates are more difficult to isolate. However, the tree line for forests expected to give an acceptable return is about 300m in West and North Scotland.

Studies in Hampshire have shown that Douglas fir starts growth when the mean weekly average rises to 7°C and continues as long as this mean rises, but growth is checked with even a slight fall in this mean (Rouse 1961, 306). However, the mechanism is not understood and in any case is not likely to apply to all species.

Wind effectively excludes trees from the exposed western coasts, where the salt content accentuates its effects, whilst at high altitudes windspeed and temperature are inter-related. However, the dessicating effect of high wind-velocity is more general. Areas in Scotland which have poor tree growth correspond with mean wind-velocities of 4.4–6.2m per sec (16–23 kmph) – though other factors complicate this general relationship in coastal areas and at high altitudes (Birse and Robertson 1970). On sites with mean wind velocities of about 27 kmph, young seedlings of sitka spruce grew better than lodgepole pine but larch failed completely (Forestry Comm. 1968, 38). The effect of strong winds on large plantations is to prevent the emergence of dominant trees and in the Border forests growth is generally restricted by exposure to the south-west and in more exposed sites the result may be rapidly tapering stems which would have limited commercial value (Fraser 1972). Wind is reduced by 10% in a 3–4° hollow, by as much as 40% at the base of a 7–12° lee slope, whilst a reduction of 75% has been noted on a lee slope of 14° (Roberts 1972). Tatter flags are now used to estimate the effects of exposure prior to planting. Experiments in planting at exposed sites began in 1953 at Shetland and Orkney. While trees can grow at altitudes up to 610m in C Wales and Scotland, exposure on the Hebrides and northern islands can limit growth at sea level (Forestry Comm. 1974).

At one time forests were planted with little or no preparation of the *soil* but recent work in Inverness has shown that cultivation before planting can double the height of six-year-old Scots pine and lodgepole pine. Experiments in pruning roots of seedlings to 8 diagonals to increase stability are in progress. The problem is often mechanical and is especially difficult on wet peat and soils with iron pans. Rapid growth on ploughed ridges, thought to be due to increased mineralization of nitrogen under thicker peat, may not be sustained, for the larger trees eventually feel the mineral deficiencies while smaller, less demanding trees will continue to grow. Phosphates have been successful in improving growth on heath and infertile peat soils, and lodgepole pine has proved the best species for these soils (Forestry Comm. 1974).

Pollution, particularly of the air, may present problems, notably on urban and industrial sites which are to be planted in the rehabilitation of derelict land. Sulphur dioxide has caused discoloration of leaves and premature leaf fall in forests near Port Talbot (Jones 1972). Together with dust, which limits photosynthesis, this is thought to contribute to poor growth in sitka spruce, though some genetic variations have a degree of tolerance. Many parts of the Pennines have been dismissed as potential areas for afforestation because of their exposure to sulphur dioxide from Lancashire and the W Riding of Yorkshire (Forestry Comm. 1974).

As knowledge of the nature of environmental problems in forestry grows, it is possible to control the natural hazards and improve soil conditions by nutrients and drainage. Wind throw is a problem in exposed areas. The problem has become increasingly important as trees grow to heights of over 10m, when they become more susceptible. Since 1962 wind throw has become a problem in the Border forests and is essentially due to shallow rooting in poorly aerated soils (Pyatt 1966, 41). Between 1961 and 1967, 970ha suffered wind throw, half of this sitka spruce, mainly 30- to 40-year-old timber which had reached between 9–18m in height. In years of strong winds, as in 1961 and 1962, great damage was done. Damage tends to occur during single severe storms. In January 1968 850,000m³ of timber was lost in C Scotland due to wind throw, during a 75kmph westerly wind which persisted for six hours. Wind is reduced in passing over an extensive forest, and wind speeds in the tree tops of the Border forests are only 10% of the speeds in open country. However, gaps for roads and firebreaks create higher speeds, due to turbulence, and the highest incidence of wind throw is around small clearings. The eddy effect is also obvious near the base of lee slopes. Wind throw can be reduced at forest margins by high pruning which increases permeability but the damage by wind throw in the UK does not justify extensive treatment of all forest margins. Improvements in rooting can be brought about by drainage and cultivation, particularly in compacted heathland and clay soils. It has been estimated that about 90% of the Border area needs improvement, though deep rooting in peaty podsols requires breaking of the iron pan, which can only be done at planting (Wardle 1970). Drainage and cultivation can increase the critical height for winds of 75kmph from 15–20m. While shelter belts can effectively reduce wind speeds by 40% for distances ten times the shelter height, this can only be of use in young forests. Established forests can benefit most from a margin inclined to the wind-ward as this reduces the risk of turbulence (Caborn 1957). Losses due to wind blow are mainly the lost potential growth but the difficulty of recovering the fallen timber incurs additional expenditure. Felling before the timber reaches full height reduces the risk of windfall but the crop has not then realized its full potential. Forest management in the Border forests where the wind blow is a serious hazard has made use of simulated effects to decide on the optimum time for felling (Wardle 1970, 78).

Fire is less of a problem in the UK but its high incidence in spring is related to the dryness of the forest and surrounding vegetation. The risk can be reduced by using herbicides on undergrowth and models of the rate of the spread of fire by physical factors allow the planning of more effective windbreaks (Forestry Comm. 1974). Rouse (1961, 309) has devised an empirically-derived scale of fire risk which depends on the number of days after rain over 6mm in twenty-four hours; temperatures above 15°C; wind speed; and relative humidity. Fire risk can be reduced during these critical periods by forest management. Recent dry summers, notably 1974 and 1976, brought many fires but the area burned was comparatively small.

The most damaging *disease* has been Dutch Elm disease, which killed about 9 million trees between 1960 and 1977. Although mainly confined to the Midlands, South and South East, aggressive strains had reached the North of England and Central Scotland by 1976 (Forestry Comm. 1977). By 1972 so many elms were dead that preservation of trees of high amenity value was the main concern. Control in the areas badly affected has been by injecting fungicide and felling to avoid spreading by roots. The destruction of the source of infection is the best means but only practicable in areas with low incidence (Burdekin and Gibbs 1974). Replanting with other species has been encouraged by grants, but in most cases losses by the disease are still greater than new plantings (Jones 1981).

V   URBAN AND INDUSTRIAL LAND USE

V.1   Introduction

While the location of certain types of industry can be considered the product of economic history, the development of industry in the nineteenth century was to a large extent influenced by the coalfields. With the exception of Belfast, heavy industry is concentrated on or near the coalfields. Twentieth-century growth of light industry has not favoured the northern coalfields, but rather lowland England (ch. 4.II.4). Since the 1950s the growth of urban land has been greatest in an axial zone from Lancashire through the Midlands to London, and the total demand for additional development may be of the order of 700,000ha by the year 2000 (table 1.2). An estimated 1% per annum of land in this area was lost to agricultural use from 1955–60 and the percentage of land in urban use in the SE is likely to reach 36% by the end of the century. The area in urban and industrial use, estimated by Best at no more than 15 to 16% of the land surface of England and Wales, will still be small compared with that in rural use (Best 1968). The effects of industrial activity range from the sprawling New Towns and industrial estates in the SE to the dereliction of the declining heavy industries and old mines in S Wales, the NE, C Scotland and on the flanks of the Pennines. While coalmining and heavy industry have left vast areas of derelict spoil heaps which present major problems of rehabilitation, surface mining and, in particular, gravel extraction have also made increasing demands upon the land. The annual consumption for these latter purposes was above 1,600ha in 1967 (Beaver 1968), and doubled within the next 20 years. Modern power stations make heavy demands on land and because of the need for vast supplies of cooling water are sited on major rivers like the Trent or, in the case of nuclear-powered stations, at the coast (fig. 4.6). Petrochemical industries needing deep-water sites have formed vast complexes on the major estuaries. Through its effects on the atmosphere, the land surface, the rivers and the surrounding seas, industrial and urban land use has influenced the environment far beyond the area of land which it occupies. The most serious effect is that of pollution. The suggested control of pollution by planning buffer zones around major pollution sources would make further demands on land (Royal Comm. Pollution 1976A).

V.2 Pollution

Pollution occurs when man's activity adds substances to the environment which because of their properties or quantity constitute a danger to health and well-being. It is perhaps more useful to broaden the influence to systems in the environment rather than to man alone. It is difficult to define pollution scientifically since many of the substances causing pollution occur naturally. Carbon dioxide, for example, is essential to life, yet in high concentrations it contributes to chronic respiratory disease. Phosphates are also essential to the growth of vegetation yet the great increase in the use of detergents in this country has contributed possibly as much as 50% of the phosphate content of streams and rivers, causing enrichment or eutrophication. Some natural substances, such as lead and mercury, may be more damaging since they can accumulate in organisms and disturb biochemical processes and through food chains present a hazard to man very much greater than if the substances were diluted in the environment. Increasingly, man-made substances such as the chlorinated hydrocarbons used in pesticides have been adding to the pollution problem. As industry increases in sophistication, the emission of effluents whose effects are not yet known will increase.

When an effect of pollution is suspected there are usually moves to control it. The inversion of temperature in London in the winter of 1952–3 had the disastrous effect of unusual accumulations of smoke and carbon dioxide (Bleasdale 1959). The deaths caused by the smog, some 3–4,000 in excess of a normal winter, led to the *Clean Air Acts* (1956 and 1968). In the same year, air pollution in E Lancashire caused lost production estimated at £2,600,000 (R. Comm. Pollution 1974). Toxic pollutants from some individual industries have led to action. For example, fumes from brickworks in the Midlands causing fluoride poisoning in cattle, lead-smelting causing deaths of stock, fluorine in effluent from the aluminium smelters at Fort William contaminating pastures on the leeward side, have all led to the offending industries being required to clean their effluent. The effect of the pollutant depends very much on the toxicity, persistence, mobility and ease of control. These are all-important, for a highly toxic pollutant which breaks down quickly is less serious than a less toxic but more persistent pollutant. For this reason organophosphorous pesticides are preferred to organochlorides though they are equally toxic.

The stability of the environment is important but cannot be seen as a UK problem in isolation. Nicholson (1970) estimates that artificial ecosystems, which constitute most of the UK surface, account for only 10% of the globe, the rest being natural or biologically-exploited natural ecosystems. All our pollutants finally reach the sea, carried by rivers, dumped by man or washed by rain from the air. The sea appears to be able to break down and recycle waste and so far the harmful effects seem to be localized. However, there may be no grounds for complacency in UK waters, as we share the North Sea with other highly populated countries which use it as a sink. Equally, the most enclosed waters of the Irish Sea may be particularly vulnerable in the future. The global atmosphere has shown an increase in carbon dioxide of 0.2% per annum since 1958, largely as a result of fuel combustion. Stratosphere traffic, which must increase in the future, will continue to add water vapour and carbon dioxide. The possible climatic effect of this, together with the impact of sulphur dioxide which finds its way to the stratosphere where its life is prolonged, has not yet been assessed, but in air corridors with dense traffic a 60% increase in water vapour is suspected, leading to more stratospheric cloud (Wilson 1970). Shipping and offshore drilling for oil in the North Sea add to the pollution of the seas. Indeed it has been estimated that approximately two million tons of oil enters the oceans annually.

V.3   Air Pollution

Atmospheric pollution is mainly the result of combustion of fossil fuel, so that the main sources are the built-up areas. The UK climate has required fires in winter and the problem of pollution was recognized centuries ago in Edinburgh and London. The high concentration of pollutants in the cities was largely due to the back-to-back housing, narrow streets and an absence of open spaces which characterized the early growth of industrial cities. While industry was controlled to some extent from 1863 onwards, the emission of household smoke, which constitutes some 85% of total smoke emitted, remained unabated until the *Clean Air Acts* (1956, 1968). Sulphates and carbon monoxide are added to the atmosphere from the sea and the bacterial decomposition of organic debris adds ammonia and hydrogen to the atmosphere. Combustion can occur naturally as forest fires, whilst soil erosion from farmland in eastern England during dry springs adds dust to the air.

There is no question of eliminating all pollution but of finding an acceptable level. The levels of air pollution likely to be harmful are not known but studies showed bronchitis patients had ill-effects when 24-hour mean concentrations of smoke exceeded $250\mu g/m^3$ (microgrammes per cubic metre) and sulphur dioxide $500\mu g/m^3$. However, these cannot be used as safe levels, as other pollutants are always present and more sensitive techniques for monitoring symptoms might have shown ill-effects at lower concentrations (DoI 1976). There is still a need for some guidelines on air quality (R. Comm. Pollution 1976A). Radioactive gaseous effluents from nuclear power stations show a considerable rise since 1976, iodine at Windscale and Calder and tritium oxide from Harwell. However in 1977 the greatest exposure in UK did not exceed 3% of the International Commission on Radiological Protection dose limit for any one radionuclide and in most cases it was less than 1%. However, Iodide 131m, Strontium-90 and Caesium-137 can settle on grass and so reach humans through milk. For this reason milk samples are regularly monitored (DoE 1980).

With exotic pollutants, concentrations must not be allowed to exceed the toxic levels, at threshold limits of seven to eight hours a day. However, less is known about the effects on plants and it is likely that vigour may be adversely affected at lower concentrations than those actually causing damage, and the long-term effects on growth and yield of economic species should be the concern of future studies (Williams and Ricks 1975). It is difficult to measure pollution at low concentrations and therefore most of the evidence is of a crude nature and confined to the most obvious: sulphur, carbon dioxide, carbon monoxide, nitric oxide and particulate matter. The latter includes both larger particles of dust and grit with diameters exceeding $10\mu m$, which quickly settles, and the finer particles which may remain in suspension, forming mist clouds and haze and thus obstructing radiation. The problems of measurement were reviewed by Ball (1971) who suggested the use of laser and low-temperature infra-red spectroscopy for future work, but at present most measurement is of the total deposit or a filtered deposit.

The effect of air pollution on *climate* is measurable. Dust in suspension obstructs solar radiation. Average monthly hours of bright sunshine in the winter months in C London (Kingsway) between 1958 and 1967 showed a 50% increase over the thirty-year normal (Lawrence 1971) when little or no change was recorded in the suburbs. Now the number of hours of winter sunshine in C London is virtually the same as Kew Observatory in Outer London (DoE 1979A). This has been due to a reduction in the smoke and sulphur dioxide. The highest daily concentrations in C London, which exceeded $6,000\mu g/m^3$ for smoke and $3,500\mu g/m^3$ sulphur dioxide in 1952 (DoE 1974B), were reduced to $200\mu g/m^3$ for smoke and $500\mu g/m^3$ for sulphur dioxide in 1979 (DoI 1979). Because of its well-known 'greenhouse' effect of permitting incoming short-wave radiation while obstructing outgoing long-wave radiation, carbon dioxide influences temperature. This is more important on a global scale than within the UK, where the local effects of carbon dioxide concentration are probably counteracted by the reduced insolation caused by smoke and dust. For this reason neither temperature nor radiation change can be reliable indicators. However the global effects of carbon dioxide and damage to the protective ozone layer by fluro-carbons must be the concern of central government and could affect policies of controlling authorities in the UK.

Effects on *life forms* have been explored as possible indicators, and the long term effects on growth and yield of economic species is a matter of priority. The value of indicators depends on whether the effects are known and can be related to other species of resource value. While lichens can be correlated with sulphur dioxide concentrations, it is not possible to extrapolate the effects on crops (Edwards *et al* 1975). Any realistic emission controls must consider not only individual pollutants but interaction between them, for in mixtures the dominant element may differ between species (Williams and Ricks 1975). Research on the damage to lichens by pollution from aluminium smelting and the search for reliable biological indicators of atmospheric pollutants is continuing (NERC 1976). Sulphur dioxide concentrations in Tyneside inhibit the epiphytic flora of ash trees (Gilbert 1971). Fallout on hillsides near Port Talbot is thought to be the reason for the local lichen desert and is considered a contributory factor in the poor growth of sitka spruce in the nearby Margam forest (Jones 1972, 154). The sensitivity of lichens to sulphur dioxide has also been used to map zones of air-pollution levels (Hawkesworth 1971), but a study in Merseyside has suggested the need for care in interpreting the inner limit of species. At lower concentrations of sulphur dioxide other factors influence lichen distributions and it is impossible to use the relationship between lichens and sulphur-dioxide pollution found in the main conurbation to map the sulphur-dioxide pollution in outlying towns (Alexander and Sellars 1980). This suggests that in each locality frequency of species provides a scale for the concentration of sulphur dioxide, but it cannot be universally applied.

Smoke and sulphur dioxide are the most widespread atmospheric pollutants and in the past have done most damage. The National Air Pollution Survey which began in 1961 has 1,200 sites recording sulphur dioxide, smoke dust and grit measured either by filtering of air or rainwater. This survey allows estimates of pollution within 5% accuracy on a national scale and within 10% on a regional scale. In 1975 twenty of these sites began sampling airborne sulphate particles and at another twenty sites 15 substances including heavy metals, oxides of nitrogen, oxidants and hydrocarbons are being sampled.

Sulphur dioxide is produced mainly by the burning of coal. When this was the dominant fuel in the UK sulphur dioxide was a reliable guide to all gaseous pollution. New sources of pollution such as high-temperature furnaces, road-traffic exhaust and jet exhaust at airports are increasing, though the actual level of pollution fell from 1973 to 1976 (DoE 1979A). Pollution at airports is difficult to assess, because of the inadequacy of measuring techniques, but it is assumed to be comparable to that of an industrial estate. In winter Heathrow receives as much pollution from W London as it generates and in summer the difference between the airport and its surrounds is slight (Robinson 1971). Nevertheless it is considered important to monitor nitrogen oxides and hydrocarbons at airports. Road traffic is a more serious problem. Average monthly measurements of carbon-monoxide concentrations in busy streets in England and Wales show that for Manchester and Glasgow a total of sixty hours had more than 10 parts per million (ppm) but levels over 50 ppm averaged less than one minute in a monthly period, except for Cardiff with a total of ten minutes at this level (Reed and Trott 1971). Concentration of 50 ppm is considered the threshold for continuous exposure for eight hours day after day. Industrial furnaces contribute nitric oxide to the atmosphere, though as much as 50% of the total concentration may be due to traffic. Nitric oxide has shown concentrations as high as $29.5\mu g$ per m^3 at Islington (Min. of Technology 1965), but it changes chemically and can be washed from the air by rain. The mean concentration of lead estimated from UK emissions is $0.55\mu g$ per m^3 which is small compared with $71\mu g$ per m^3 mean concentration of smoke in urban areas. However high concentrations of lead are highly localized around smelters and traffic thoroughfares.

As the contribution of lead pollution from factories has been reduced, road-vehicles have contributed a steadily rising proportion of pollutants. Twenty-four per cent of nitrogen oxides, 87% of carbon monoxide and 37% of hydrocarbons are produced by road-vehicles. The damage from lead and the fact that it can accumulate in the body has prompted an EEC directive on the biological screening for lead. In the first lead survey of adults exposed to lead in their work, only Glasgow showed levels above the EEC limit of $35\mu g/100ml$ and this was due to the existence of lead in the water, but children living near motorways in Leeds, the M4 and in Tower Hamlets were below the EEC limits (DoE 1980). The reduction of lead content in petrol from 0.85gm/l in 1972 to 0.40gm/l in 1981 has been a valuable contribution to control. Rural sites have shown a significant fall in lead since 1973.

Measurable levels of photochemically-produced ozone occurred in S England in July 1971 during anticyclonic conditions and at the same time oxidized sulphur dioxide in the form of sulphuric acid and sulphates were much higher than during windy or cloudy weather (Atkins, Cox and Eggleton 1972). This was supported by findings in London in 1972 and it is now possible to predict the weather conditions producing photochemical reactions. Photochemical pollution is not only an urban phenomena as it can be transported up to 1,000km and on occasions emissions from Europe can contribute to photochemical pollution in the UK (Cox 1975). However, because of the topography and climate in the UK the serious photo-chemically-produced fogs in Los Angeles are not likely to occur.

Control is vital because of damage by air pollution to health, living organisms and man-made structures. Control at the point of emissions is in the hands of the

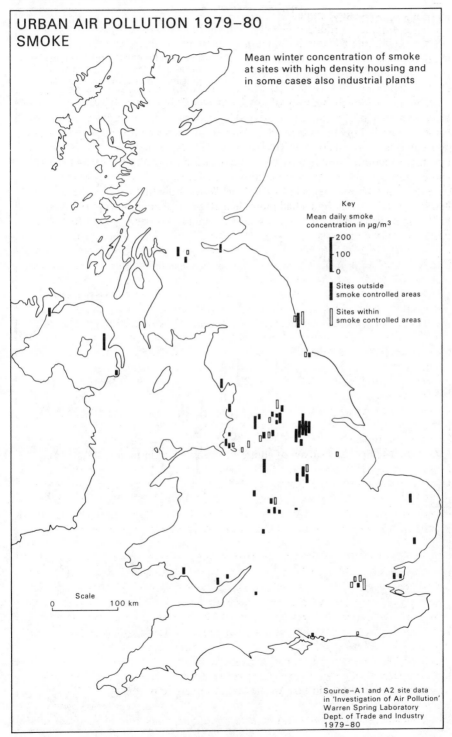

Figure 3.8   Urban air pollution, UK, 1979–80, smoke

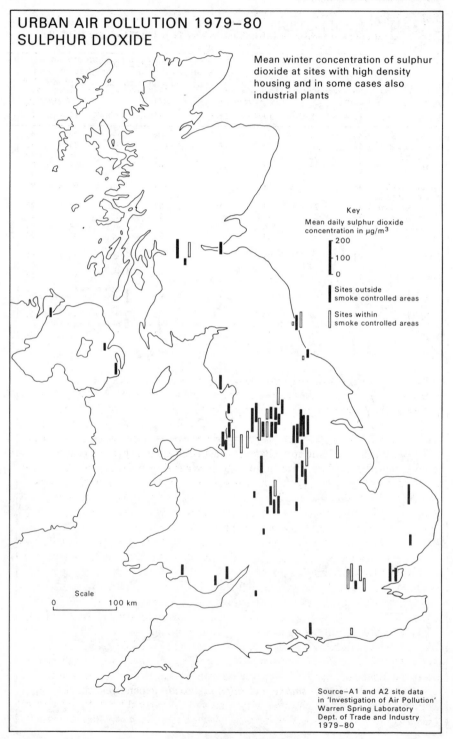

URBAN AIR POLLUTION 1979–80
SULPHUR DIOXIDE

Mean winter concentration of sulphur
dioxide at sites with high density
housing and in some cases also
industrial plants

Key

Mean daily sulphur dioxide
concentration in µg/m³

200
100
0

Sites outside
smoke controlled areas

Sites within
smoke controlled areas

Scale
0   100 km

Source–A1 and A2 site data
in 'Investigation of Air Pollution'
Warren Spring Laboratory
Dept. of Trade and Industry
1979–80

Figure 3.9   Urban air pollution, UK, 1979–80, sulphur dioxide

TABLE 3.8

Daily Concentrations at Individual Urban Sites, Winter Period, 1974–5 and 1978–9

	SMOKE				SULPHUR DIOXIDE			
	Av. concentration $\mu g/m^3$		% of sites with winter mean $>45\mu g/m^3$		Av. concentration $\mu g/m^3$		% of sites with winter mean $>50\mu g/m^3$	
	1974–5	1978–9	1974–5	1978–9	1974–5	1978–9	1974–5	1978–9
North	45	34	44	20	68	57	82	58
Yorks. and H.	58	50	50	42	100	94	95	92
E Midlands	45	42	37	33	73	84	84	92
E Anglia	34	29	18	–	65	62	91	91
Greater London	35	30	18	8	117	100	99	97
South East (excl. Gtr London)	24	23	2	2	62	59	68	72
South West	24	21	–	–	47	49	36	27
W Midlands	45	29	36	30	87	86	84	92
North West	51	38	53	27	96	91	95	95
England	41	36	31	22	86	80	85	84
Wales	27	25	8	5	56	54	63	59
Scotland	39	34	33	19	63	58	57	62
N Ireland	44	50	33	50	60	41	44	35
UK	40	35	30	21	82	76	80	79

Source: DoE (1980)

Alkali Inspectorate (Industrial Pollution Inspectorate, Scotland) and local authorities. This control is most effective for grit and dust. Monitoring of pollutants in the atmosphere is done by sampling, the density of the network depending on whether the control is to be for local or national purposes or to measure spread from a source. While complete control of emissions is the most effective, it is not realistic and a balance must be made between the cost of control and the benefits it brings. The National Survey has shown the progress of control in the former 'black areas' of cities many of which are now cleaner than towns which were considered less polluted and therefore not needing urgent control. Planning authorities can prevent future problems by the siting of houses and industry but would need guidelines on air-quality standards and a knowledge of present patterns of air pollution in developing areas (R. Comm. Pollution 1976A).

Table 3.8 shows the daily concentration at selected urban sites in each of the UK regions in 1974–5 and 1978–9. The North and North West show the greatest improvement in smoke pollution. While 48% of urban sites in these regions in 1974–5 had a winter mean over $45\mu g/m^3$, only 23% were above this level in 1978–9. In the UK as a whole the urban sites with a winter mean over $45\mu g/m^3$ fell from 30 to 21% in the same period. Sulphur-dioxide concentrations showed greatest reduction in the North, with the winter mean at 58% of the urban sites over $50\mu g/m^3$ in 1978–9 compared with 82% in 1974–5. Only 2% of the sites exceeded $100\mu g/m^3$ in 1978–9 compared with 14% in 1974–5 (DoE 1980).

The concentrations of *smoke* and *sulphur dioxide* depend very much on the degree of dispersion, which varies with wind and the vertical temperature gradient. Temperature inversions prevent vertical mixing and lead to the heaviest concentrations. Certain areas may be more prone to inversion because of their topography, for example the valleys on either side of the Pennines (Garnett 1971). Siting of new factories in such areas ought to be avoided, for landscaping can only hope to control shallow radiation fogs by encouraging cold-air drainage. Buffer zones around major polluting industries would improve pollution in residential areas but create economic problems as it would sterilize some high-value land and increase the distance to work (R. Comm. Pollution 1976A). It is difficult to devise generalized models since each pollution source may be affected in a different way by architecture, topography and atmospheric dispersal, but mathematical models which can predict the effects of potential industrial development could be valuable planning tools. Sophisticated models allowing for these variables could only be applied if a much clearer picture of micro and local meteorology becomes possible. The building of high stacks (MHLG 1967) can control ground-level concentration even from large installations to an upper limit of $460\mu g$ per m^3. Ground-level concentrations are inversely proportional to wind speed and the square of the effective height of emission. Low chimneys below 91m have effluents of low buoyancy, while the high stacks which may be over 244m in height send plumes rising to 550m, though even this may not be high enough to penetrate high stratus cloud cover. High stacks relieve the pollution of the immediate surrounds but transport the effluent far beyond the region. Although UK emissions have been held responsible for increasing soil acidity in upland Sweden, it has been argued that they have not the capacity to carry the necessary amount of sulphur and there is no evidence of the same effect in our own uplands. Transfers within the UK have been proved and recent research has shown that more sulphur dioxide may be transported away from the UK than is supposed (Garland 1975). Concentrations of sulphur dioxide on the east coast of UK suggests that easterly winds can bring pollutants from Europe (Barnes 1975). The pollution in country around Leicester can be attributed to more distant urban areas, while in Yorkshire downwind drifting has been shown to carry 50 to 60km from the source (Gooriah 1968). Smoke has been

TABLE 3.9

Atmospheric Pollution at Selected Sites in Open Country*, 1975–80

	Smoke concentrations $\mu g/m^3/day$		
	Mean 1975–80	Highest daily record 1974–5	1979–80
Stornoway, Lewis	3	30	20
Lerwick, Shetland	1	20	11
Eskdalemuir	5	47	27
Pembroke	4	32	39
Amroth, Pembrokeshire	5	37	26
Camborne, Cornwall	5	63	64
Didcot, Berks.	10	39	48
Lytham St Annes	20	166	180
Norton, Runcorn	15	99	164

* These sites are not entirely without sources of pollution. Only Didcot has no sources within ¼ mile.

Source: Warren Spring Laboratory (1971–80)

transported 40km from S Wales and 180km from the W Midlands (Barnes 1975). Light winds favour drifting, for the turbulence and mixing associated with strong winds leads to dispersal. There is a limit to the distance that pollutants can be carried in high concentrations, and coastal sites, for example in Norfolk, record low annual figures. Few records exist for open country and they are usually at sites where a pollution source exists or is suspected. The sites listed in table 3.9 all had some sources of pollution.

Few areas of the UK are completely free from smoke emissions but the control of pollution sources in neighbouring urban areas has greatly reduced the frequency of pollution events and the concentrations at rural sites. Lytham St Annes is on the coast but its proximity to the conurbation of S Lancashire caused two days in 1971–2 to exceed 500μg/m³, but in 1979–80 the two highest days had 122 and 180μg/m³. Areas free from sulphur-dioxide emissions record levels below 10μg/m³ (Barnes 1975), though it has been suggested that a mean of 40μg/m³ is more realistic (Garland 1975). Of the sites in table 3.9, Amroth and Camborne had mean levels of 20μg/m³ since 1975 but those sites near large urban centres had mean levels of 40 to 60μg/m³. The general fall in sulphur-dioxide levels in urban areas has been accompanied by a rise in concentrations in rural areas (R. Comm. Pollution 1976A).

The effect of smoke control under the *Clean Air Act* (1956) is difficult to assess because there has been a change in fuel since its inception, but a general reduction in pollution has occurred and the most dramatic fall has been in urban areas. By 1974 72% of premises in the 'black areas' (MoF 1953) were controlled; after 1974 local authorities became responsible for future control. While in 1952 43% smoke came from domestic sources, industry has since been so successfully controlled that despite a reduction of 80% from domestic sources in 1974 domestic sources contributed as much as 90% of the total smoke emissions (R. Comm. Pollution 1976A).

The overall fall in emissions of smoke since 1960 has been 80% which has caused a fall of about 78% in concentration of smoke. Sulphur dioxide has been more affected by better dispersal through the use of high chimneys so that though emissions have fallen only by 16% since 1960 the ground-level concentrations have been reduced by 50% (DoE 1979B). Smoke control areas have generally lowered pollution levels in all urban areas.

TABLE 3.10

Changes in Atmospheric Pollution, Salford 1970–6[*]

	Smoke (μg/m³)		Sulphur dioxide (μg/m³)	
	mean winter	max. daily	mean winter	max. daily
1970–1	414	1,779	261	898
1971–2	277	872	250	623
1972–3	241	712	203	659
1973–4	142	645	180	807
1974–5	55	338	116	321
1975–6	126	477	90	308

[*] station became smoke controlled in 1972–3 and was closed in 1977

Source: Warren Spring Lab. (1971–7)

The effect of smoke control in 1972 on the mean pollution levels at a site in Salford is shown in table 3.10. Sulphur dioxide depends more on the sulphur content of fuels, and the reduction is partly due to the restrictions on smokeless fuels with a high sulphur content.

Attempts have been made to remove sulphur dioxide from emissions but the processes developed are viable only for large installations like Battersea power station. Even here the expenditure would not relieve SE England of pollution unless similar measures were taken in neighbouring European countries. Much more success has been achieved with smoke control. Fuels have been developed to reduce smoke and their improved efficiency partly compensates for the higher cost; furthermore, grit- and dust-arresting devices are in operation. There are no technical problems in removing pollutants such as oxides of nitrogen and sulphur but the process frequently has noxious effluent and the cost is often prohibitive. Washing of gases lowers their temperature, which reduces their buoyancy. High concentrations of washed gas can be as undesirable as the untreated smoke. Thus despite the cost of approximately £1 million per 200m of chimney, high stacks are still a better way of reducing ground-level pollution.

TABLE 3.11

Changes in Mean Winter Daily Concentrations of Smoke and Sulphur Dioxide, after Smoke Control. Selected UK Sites, 1970–80

	Smoke (μg/m^3)			Sulphur dioxide (μg/m^3)		
	mean winter 1970–2	mean winter 1972–80	% change	mean winter 1970–2	mean winter 1972–80	% change
Colne	88	33	–63	160	93‡	–42
Droylsden	120	55	–54	184	129‡	–30
Leeds	137	44	–68	162	94	–42
Middlesbrough	160	46	–71	163	54	–67
Oldham	133	50	–62	162	132†	–19
Salford	345	141	–59	256	147†	–43
Southampton	58	29	–50	116	86	–26
Tynemouth	173	66	–62	141	73	–48
Wandsworth	80*	42	–48	187	99‡	–47

* data only for 1971–2
† station closed 1976
‡ station closed 1977

Source: Warren Spring Lab.

Table 3.11 shows all available sites in dense residential areas which became controlled after 1971–2. Smoke concentration fell by an average of 58% but sulphur dioxide shows a 40% fall.

Table 3.12 shows the mean concentrations at all available sites with high-density housing in extensive built-up areas. As sites came under smoke control they were excluded from the calculations and new sites were included as recording commenced. From 1963 to 1974 the distinct downward trend in smoke correlates with the increase in smoke-control orders ($r = -0.96$). The annual smoke control reached a peak in 1974 of 70,000ha but thereafter has averaged 30,000ha per annum,

TABLE 3.12

Atmospheric Pollution of High Density Residential Areas (excluding Sites within Smoke Control Areas) Selected years 1963–80

	Smoke concentrations ($\mu g/m^3$)			Sulphur dioxide concentrations ($\mu g/m^3$)		
	mean	std devn	No. of sites	mean	std devn	No. of sites
1962–3	210	87	72	207	89	72
1971–2	71	34	77	112	36	77
1973–4	55	25	44	93	32	44
1975–6	43	22	51	80	22	46
1977–8	35	18	46	70	24	45
1979–80	34	17	48	68	21	48

though a six-month moratorium in 1976–7 reduced the increase. The effect of increasing smoke-control areas by 40,000ha was to reduce the mean daily urban pollution levels by $8.6\mu g/m^3$ for smoke and $6.6\mu g/m^3$ for sulphur dioxide. By 1975, 75% of all urban areas in England and Wales were controlled and some areas like Newcastle upon Tyne had achieved 100% by 1980. Although a downward trend is expected to continue to 1985, the annual mean concentrations of smoke and sulphur dioxide for the years 1976–80 were not significantly lower than the 1975 levels. Only the winter means of smoke and sulphur dioxide in 1977–8 were significantly lower than 1976 (0.1 and 0.8% levels of probability respectively), which is a reflection of the relatively mild period from October to December 1977. However the levels experienced in urban areas are now only twice the rural concentrations. Moreover, the difference between smoke-controlled and other areas is diminishing as the area of control increases. In 1977–8 the mean winter concentrations at 57 sites in high-density residential areas without smoke control was $45\mu g/m^3$, while 61 similar urban sites which had smoke control had a mean smoke concentration of $38\mu g/m^3$.

Monitoring for international control While the policy of using high chimneys to disperse pollution has reduced ground-level concentration in the UK, some is spread beyond the country and this contribution to European and global environmental problems is of interest to international agencies. Six special remote sites in UK, together with a site in W Ireland and one on the east coast of England, monitor the movement of pollutants across the UK, and assess the effects on background pollution in Europe. These stations are also monitoring acidity of rain and total sulphur content. The need for coordination of effort in the UK to provide a framework for control at the national and international level prompted the suggestion of the creation of an Air Management Group (DoE 1974B).

EEC directives on environmental pollution are becoming increasingly important in establishing more formal limits for environmental standards.

V.4 Pollution of the Land Surface

The effects of agriculture on the land have been discussed earlier. Pesticides, herbicides and fertilizers form an important part, though less than in N America, of the total pollution of the land surface. In the UK, industrial and urban activity has

created more tangible effects on the landscape. The effects of early lead and
fluorspar workings have persisted in the carboniferous limestone areas. When soil is
polluted from the air or by surface water it can be controlled by statutory
regulations, but only in 1972, was any attempt made to check the indiscriminate
dumping of toxic materials. Dumping can have an immediate danger to individuals
or can represent a more widespread hazard by contaminating streams or ground
water. Pollution by nuclear waste from industry is much smaller than fallout from
nuclear explosions, but nevertheless important since the danger period before the
complete decay may be thousands of years. For these reasons it is not surprising
that the permissible levels for emissions into the Irish Sea are low, although there is
some uncertainty over standards (R. Comm. Pollution 1976B). However, the
disposal of the residue, which is 99.9% of the total waste produced and is highly
radioactive, presents a major pollution problem. This residue is stored in steel tanks,
encased in 2.4m walls of concrete, with stringent safety precautions, although this
has not prevented leakages of radioactive material. Radiation is more carefully
monitored than any other pollutant.

Increase in nuclear power for the generation of electricity has produced the
problem of disposal of solid waste (R. Comm. Pollution 1976B). The disposal of
solid radioactive waste at Drigg, south of Windscale increased from less than
9,000m^3 in 1971 to 46,000m^3 in 1979. 86% of this was from Windscale and
Calder though the seven CEGB stations built since 1976 have been steadily adding
to the total. Monitoring at the site shows very low levels of airborne radioactivity.
The other approved sites are Dounreay and Clifton Marsh, which together had 10%
of the total volume of radioactive waste in 1979 (DoE 1980). Future needs for
disposal have led to the search for suitable sites. The need to ensure isolation for
very long periods of time has limited the suitable rocks to evaporates, argillaceous,
igneous and metamorphic rocks of sufficient thickness and free from instability.

Pollution by other forms of industrial waste creates problems due more to
volume than to toxicity. About 50% of the volume of raw material used by
industry is waste and its disposal has been treated with much more apathy than if it
were more highly toxic. The increase in the amount of waste will continue and,
with highly sophisticated industrial techniques, more of it will be toxic. In 1978
industrial waste dumped contained 42.4 tonnes of zinc, 217 tonnes lead and 199
tonnes of copper. Both lead and zinc had increased tenfold since 1976. The
problem is to find suitable ways of disposing of this increasing volume of urban and
industrial waste. One alternative, most frequently used up to the present, is the
land surface; another is the sea, with effects described in the next section.

The annual waste has risen from 24 million tonnes in 1974–5 to 25 million
tonnes 1978–9. Of this, 17 million tonnes was household and commercial waste
(DoE 1980). However, many industrial concerns dispose of waste in other ways
and no comprehensive estimate of industrial waste is possible. It is thought that
about 11 million tonnes of toxic waste, including 4 million tonnes of solids, are
produced annually by industry (MHLG, SDD 1970), but over 80% of this toxic
material is relatively inert. Local authorities dispose of 90% of the refuse by direct
tipping on the land, 71% of this being controlled, usually because of a need for
material for reclamation. Large areas have been reclaimed in this way for port
facilities, for example at Southend, Liverpool and Portsmouth. At Belfast mudflats
have been reclaimed for the expansion of aircraft works and runways. Tipping on

the land requires planning permission and the *Coast Protection Act* (1949) controls tipping below the high water mark, though the harbour schemes already completed or in progress have not caused any serious pollution of tidal waters. Tipping is cheaper than the other alternatives, pulverization, incineration or composting. Pulverization has grown in importance since 1960, but in 1973 handled only 3.7% of the refuse and the existing plants can serve only small populations of less than 50,000. Composting is not likely to be encouraged by demand from agriculture, largely because of its low nutrient content and the possibility of toxic elements. Its potential use is probably limited to improving marginal land.

Refuse is increasing in weight annually, though the annual increase rate of 0.7% per person in the ten years 1955–65 has since decreased, largely due to the rapid reduction in consumption of solid fuel.

Household waste is by far the largest component of urban refuse, amounting to 84%. The total household waste per person in 1978–9 was 262 kg compared to 288 kg in 1976–7. Domestic waste in 1979 had about 29% paper and 24% vegetable and putrescible matter. Since 1957 dust and cinder content has fallen by two-thirds, but the rapid increase in paper, plastics, packaging and non-returnable bottles is likely to increase the quantity five times in the next ten years, so that the volume of refuse is increasing, though it is of lower density than in the past.

It has been estimated that less than one-fifth of the excavations made by mineral extractors annually could accommodate all the house refuse produced. Opencast mineral workings are increasing at about 2,023 ha per annum, half of this by sand and gravel excavators. Land made derelict by industry could be improved using refuse as infill and reclamation of tidal mudflats is another possibility. Tipping can create derelict land unless treated. In 1974 there were 100,000 ha of despoiled land in England, one-fifth of this due to the tipping of refuse and waste. Between 1972 and 1978, 2,145 ha of excavations and pits in England were restored, some infilled by urban waste. Large areas of excavations still exist – in 1974 8,717 ha in England and 3,700 ha in Scotland (DoE 1979A).

One of the problems of choosing sites is the pollution hazard to ground-water resources and studies of land-fill sites are in progress. Compacted refuse covered with soil can absorb rainfall and give a low rate of percolation. For the first year percolating water is heavily polluted but it rapidly declines to reach low levels within three years. Sand or gravel can act as a natural filter protecting ground water, but research on the movement of pollutants in the lower greensand and plateau gravels is continuing (NERC 1976). Bacteria will die off within a few feet of the surface, but chlorides and nitrates will persist in solution. Where the underlying rock is fissured, percolation can be very rapid, but sealing with puddled clay can protect ground water if drains are led to filter beds or a sewer. Alternatives are to line the base of the tip with 60–90 mm of aerated gravel or to prevent any percolation by sealing the surface but this causes rapid surface runoff. Tipping directly into water is more of a hazard than dry tipping since de-oxygenation can occur rapidly, allowing bacteria to produce hydrogen sulphide. Wet gravel pits require the added expense of chlorination in hot weather; clay pits on the other hand can be pumped dry before tipping.

Streams emanating from tips can become de-oxygenated or, more commonly, fouled by sewage fungus. River Authorities have been responsible for all discharges but have no powers to control dumping on the land surface. However, because of the risks to water pollution, they have invariably been consulted.

Land-fill is likely to continue as the most common method of waste disposal, accounting for 97% in 1978–9, but in the future as space becomes scarce other methods may be developed, e.g. pyrolysis — where high temperatures are used to reduce all waste including plastics to carbon, oil and gas. Direct incineration has been used increasingly but in 1978–9 was still used for only 8.4% of the total weight of waste in England.

Scrap motorcars increase in numbers annually. After compression and separation of non-ferrous material some can be sold as scrap for steel mills. A few large hammer mills do the separation of ferrous metal magnetically. To use pulverizers economically they must be working continuously, which is only possible in large conurbations. 400,000 vehicles are processed annually at a London plant, 200,000 vehicles at one in Hertfordshire and the same number at a plant in Lancashire. If used to capacity these three could convert 80% of all waste vehicles into separated steel scrap, but the problem is the transporting of vehicles from other areas. Rubber tyres are discarded at the rate of 12 million per annum and, except for Merseyside which has a factory for reclaiming rubber, there is no easy method of disposal. Many London authorities, for example, will not accept them. However, in 1976 2,500 tonnes of car tyres were remoulded and retreaded.

Reclamation of materials by waste-disposal authorities amounted to 41,000 tonnes of paper and 60,000 tonnes of ferrous metal in 1945–6, but since 1975 reclaimed paper has averaged only 12,000 tonnes. Only about 1% of all household waste paper is recycled but industry has a much better record. As much as 70% of the metal used in the ferrous industry, 74% of the lead, 30% of the paper and 25% of the glass comes from waste (DoE 1980).

A recent survey of more than 1,000 firms showed that about 1.8% of all industrial solid and semi-solid waste is toxic. Only 0.8% is dealt with by local authorities, the rest being disposed of by individual contractors. About 75% of this toxic waste is dumped on surface tips, where it creates a serious hazard to ground water. The effect of the toxic material may be to destroy normal biological activity on the surface and if it is soluble no filtering is possible in its percolation through permeable strata. More often the tips are on impermeable strata and so the percolate drains to surface streams. Guidelines on disposal of hazardous waste are being prepared for DoE. There are more cases of river pollution than ground-water pollution. Ground water under a gravel pit used for chemical waste had an oxygen demand of 4,000mg/l and the chemicals inhibited biological oxidation. Tips have been known to pollute ground water for eighty years after all tipping ceased. In 1963 an industrial tip polluted surface water in a neighbouring farm and caused animals to die. These are extreme cases but it is common to have some phenol contamination in water supplies. Large ground-water reserves are less vulnerable because of dilution, and because of their size the authority can exercise more control over surface tipping. The greatest hazard comes from unauthorized tipping which is difficult to solve as tighter restrictions can lead to greater dangers from illegal jettisoning of material. If land sites are to be used for toxic waste, it can be kept dry, compacted and the surface sealed to prevent all percolation; another alternative is dumping at sea. Unused mines are only satisfactory if they are deep and not linked to exploitable aquifers. A large mine in the Midlands is being used in this way but attempts to use old mines elsewhere have been opposed.

V.5 Water Pollution

The great volume of water now abstracted from rivers for public use means that much of the surface of England and Wales is a water catchment and the quality of runoff must be maintained. There is therefore a need to manage river catchments to control the continual low-level pollution from the use of chemicals for industry and agriculture, as well as the accidental spillages which create a high concentration for a short period. At the same time the re-use of treated sewage effluent requires the most stringent standard to avoid health risks.

Runoff carries fertilizer and pesticides from agricultural land and industry discharges effluents which demand oxygen and include chlorine which causes high salinity in estuaries (Volker 1974). Some water pollutants are nutrients, such as nitrates and phosphates, which cause enrichment or eutrophication and the excessive growth of fresh-water plants. These can block dams, whilst some algae produce toxic products and, on dying, oxygen is removed from the water. This has the same effect as excessive organic wastes from sewage which led to a lifeless Thames in the mid-nineteenth century. In England and Wales only 5 to 9% of the nitrogen in rivers comes from agriculture. However, high nitrate levels due to breakdown of organic matter during mild winters and its reduced dilution in periods of low rainfall has caused concern for infant health (R. Comm. Pollution 1974), though in the dry summer of 1976 when nitrate concentration was very high there were no cases of methaemoglobinaemia. However, the possibility that nitrates would react with amines in food and could thus increase the risk of some forms of cancer has caused concern and water authorities are required to report nitrate levels in excess of 50mg/l to the Medical Officer and provide bottled water for infants if levels exceed 100mg/l. Agriculture is the main cause of increased nitrate load carried by rivers, as sewage has been shown to make a small contribution (NWC 1978) (see above, p. 225). The levels are still below the 50mg/l limit set by WHO but the fact that it is increasing has led to pilot plants to remove nitrates (DoE 1979A).

By 1968–9 organochlorate pesticides replaced DDT but despite the persistence of organochlorides less than 0.05mg/l occurred in UK rivers in 1966, well below the 1mg/l threshold for trout. Between 1953 and 1966 the phosphate concentration doubled but this was due to sewage and effluent rather than to fertilizers. Damage to fish population may not be judged by concentrations below a lethal threshold, for lower levels may destroy food and changes in water softness could increase the toxicity of some pollutants. Salmon and trout are the most sensitive to pollution and for this reason often used to indicate levels of toxicity.

Pollution is measured in terms of biochemical oxygen demand (BOD). The *Royal Commission on Sewage Disposal* (1912) produced the standard 30mg/l suspended solids and 20mg/l BOD which are still accepted. However, these levels required dilution by 8 parts of water to 1 of effluent which may not be possible during dry periods in UK rivers. In SE England dilution in summer is often only 2 to 1 so that sewage outfalls have to be far enough apart to allow natural cleansing. Lower dilutions require stricter standards for sewage effluent than those of the Royal Commission.

The Irwell, Tame, Rother, Mersey, Don and Avon (Severn) have as much as half their dry-season flow in the form of treated sewage effluent. Slight pollution is made harmless by dilution; increased pollution and decreased dilution can have the same effect on the concentration of pollutants.

The Royal Commission emphasized that the standards were intended to prevent pollution so that the effect on the watercourse was the most important considera- tion. Control of water pollution has been consistently directed towards the point sources. However, as rivers are being cleaned the pollution from the land surface due to intensive agriculture may be as important in some areas.

TABLE 3.13

Non-tidal Rivers: Survey of Chemical Classification (England and Wales)

Class	1958		1970		1975	
	km	%	km	%	km	%
1 (unpolluted)	23,500	72.9	27,370	76.2	28,037	77.6
2 (doubtful)	4,611	14.3	5,297	14.7	5,458	15.1
3 (poor)	2,058	6.4	1,724	4.8	1,449	4.0
4 (grossly polluted)	2,057	6.4	1,533	4.3	1,178	3.3
	32,226	100.0	35,924	100.0	36,122	100.0

Source: River Pollution Survey of England and Wales (updated 1975), HMSO

In 1958, 73% of the non-tidal rivers of England and Wales were unpolluted, that is with less than 3mg/l BOD, but 6% were grossly polluted with over 12mg/l BOD and so de-oxygenated and without fish. Improvements in the heavily polluted rivers increased unpolluted rivers to 77.6% of the total in 1975 (DoE 1978). Improve- ments have been achieved only on short rivers, such as the Lea, while long stretches of the rivers draining the main industrial regions, the Trent, Mersey and Ouse, remain polluted. Cleaning of these rivers is possible, and a tributary of the Trent, the Derwent, once grossly polluted by the effluents of Derby is now clean enough for fish. Severn–Trent plans to reduce the grossly polluted rivers from 7 to 4% by 1985, but financial constraints may prevent this being realized (Severn–Trent 1980, 1981).

The chemical classification used up to now has been coarse and the NWC (1978) has suggested more explicit criteria to allow uniformity in water-quality standards (table 3.14). Oxygen is the important criteria since other chemicals are related to it. The reorganization of the water industry creating ten multi-purpose regional water authorities has simplified water-pollution control. The increasing need to use rivers as transporters of water has led to sewage improvement schemes. Further industrial development is limited by the availability of water and facilities for discharging effluent. The acceptance of effluent for treatment depends on the sewage-treatment capacity, and discharges directly to the river must be with the consent of the authority.

The EEC now requires information on dangerous substances in rivers and key- points on rivers are monitored for concentration of the principal pollutants including chlorides, nitrates, phosphates and cadmium which give indications of the pollutants reaching estuaries (Commission of the EC 1977).

Industries pay the local authority for treatment either directly or through rates, but some firms may treat effluent, which if sophisticated may require high capital and running costs. The CBI estimates that industries are spending 2–15% of their

TABLE 3.14

Classification of River Quality (suggested criteria)

	Dissolved oxygen (%)	BOD	Ammonia	Drinking water		
1A	80	3mg/l	0.4mg/l	To comply with EEC	} Potable water	
1B	60	5mg/l	0.9mg/l	A2 category		
2	40	9mg/l		To comply with EEC A3	} Potable after treatment	
3	10	17mg/l			} Low-grade industrial water	} Toxic to fish*
4	Inferior to class 3 and probably anaerobic				} Grossly polluted, causing nuisance	
X	10					

Class-limiting criteria (95 per centile)

*European Inland Fisheries Advisory Commission

Source: NWC (1978)

total capital investment on treatment. The expenditure will rise further with demands for higher-quality effluent from River Authorities wishing to abstract public supplies from the river, but could be a serious handicap to many industries competing with European countries where the quality of effluent is less carefully controlled.

Sewage is mainly water and therefore forms a significant part of the flow of many rivers. About 14,000Ml are discharged into sewers, about one half from industry and the other from domestic sources. The GLC sewage works discharges 2,500Ml/d into the Thames and its successful treatment allows the extraction of about one-third of SE England's water needs from the river.

Many sewers built during the last century no longer have the capacity to deal with modern developments. In Coventry, for example, it has been necessary to reconstruct the main sewage system. The problem is aggravated at times of heavy rain since surface runoff can augment the sewers and cause overflow, polluting streams with untreated waste. Storm-water balancing tanks are used to rectify this. Oxygen-demanding water can be readily treated. Sewage works can remove as much as 95% of the oxygen-demanding and sludge-forming constituents by settlement and biological processes. In the past, sewage farms did this by spreading, but the enormous demands that this would make on land today have led to the use of biological filters and a process of activated sludge which accelerates the anaerobic process. At present about four-fifths of the population of the UK is served by such biological plants. Ammonia is oxidized to nitrates, the effluent is clear and can be discharged without seriously affecting the river, and in some cases, as at Luton, the effluent is below 10mg/l solids and 10mg/l BOD and the river Lea can supply London with water. These high standards of treatment must be maintained both by sewage works and industry since in the upper Lea their effluents form as much as 50% of the normal daily flow. However a survey in 1975 showed that 64% of sewage effluents and 52% of industrial effluents were considered satisfactory (DoE 1979B).

TABLE 3.15

Polluting Load Removed at Sewage Treatment Works, 1977
(all estimates in tonnes of BOD per day)

| | Non-tidal waters | | Tidal waters | |
	Carried by sewers to disposal works	Discharged to environment	Carried by sewers to disposal works	Discharged to environment
North West	502	50	214	178
Northumbrian	71	6	128	119
Severn–Trent	616	31	9	7
Yorkshire	401	30	94	77
Anglian	268	30	65	58
Thames	446	16	621	76
Southern	70	4	82	32
Wessex	76	4	65	46
South West	18	1	63	37
Welsh	65	6	135	100
Total	2,533	178	1,476	730
Proportion discharged		7%		49%
Proportion removed		93%		51%
Hence overall removal of polluting load =	77%			

Note: 'disposal works' includes coastal outfalls and it should be noted that a good proportion of the polluting load discharged to tidal waters is through long outfalls which have little effect on the environment.

Source: NWC (1978)

If effluents are to be improved, more extensive treatment must be carried out. For example pathogens are not removed, but would be destroyed naturally by bacteria. Chlorination is undesirable because the effluent contains the toxic by-products of the chemical process and the necessary bacteria would be destroyed. Conventional biological treatment only removes 37–46% of phosphates. These together with nitrates can lead to eutrophication and some UK rivers have shown this effect in years of high sunshine. It is not a problem likely to develop in running water and no large inland water bodies receive enough effluent for the effect to be felt. However, the Irish Sea receives effluent from Lancashire as well as from Dublin and it has been suggested that eutrophic conditions will spread outwards leading to a slow deterioration, similar to what is now happening in the Baltic (O'Sullivan 1971). While 42% of the nitrogen reaching the sea has its origin in agricultural land, as much as 80% of the phosphates comes from domestic and industrial effluents, including 30–50% from detergents. The appearance of synthetic detergents on the market in 1949 created a major treatment problem which led to their replacement by biologically degradable constituents in the 1960s, which eliminated the problem of foam on water-courses. Organochlorides in UK rivers have reached levels in excess of concentrations reported from USA. Most of these come from industry where they are used in mothproofing, etc. Although pesticides have generally low levels in UK water, the danger is through accumulation in algae.

The disposal of the sludge left after treatment is a greater problem as improvements in sewage will generate more sludge. The dry solid in sludge amounts to about 1,250,000 tonnes per annum in England and Wales (Matthews 1981), but wet sludge could be as much as 30 million tonnes (NWC 1978). After a process of anaerobic digestion which largely destroys pathogens, the sludge is dumped on the land, or in the sea, or incinerated. In 1975, the land received 75%, the sea 23% and only 3% was incinerated.

Only the Severn—Trent Water Authority does not use sea-dumping, and of the others Thames and North West together dispose of more than 37% of the sludge at sea and Scotland 58%. This means that the Thames estuary, Liverpool Bay and the Clyde take about three-quarters of the total. Since 1977 increased dumping has occurred in Forth of Firth and off the Northumbrian coast. The effects on the sea are not certain although it has been suggested that sludge disposed of in Liverpool Bay, even if increased six times, would not affect marine life and would not be hazardous to health (DoE 1972A). At present sludge dumped annually in Liverpool Bay contains 2½ tonnes of mercury, one-half of the UK waste mercury. All dumping is controlled by the *Dumping at Sea Act* (1974) which aims to protect the marine environment from damage. There are now recommendations on the safe maximum amounts for 11 metals, and since 1975 there have been considerable reductions in the amount of mercury and cadmium in sludge dumped at sea (Prestidge 1978).

Studies in the Firth of Clyde indicate that sludge-dumping has only a local effect on 20km^2 of the seabed (Thornton 1975). The dilution and purification processes in the sea may not be very effective in disposing of organic material when it is dumped in deep water. Below 1,000m microbial activity is greatly reduced and dilution may put the pollutant beyond microbial attack. Two-fifths of the treated sludge is used as fertilizer, but it will not replace balanced artificial fertilizer as the total output of sludge could supply only 4.5% of the nitrogen and phosphate required and it is very deficient in potash. The presence of toxic metals limits its use and in any case it can only be economically distributed within a 16km radius of sewage works.

It has been assumed that tidal estuaries have unlimited capacity to receive pollution and the practice of discharging untreated sewage and industrial effluent has continued almost unabated. The large volume of water in estuaries dilutes the effluent, and mixing by tidal movements promotes natural purification, but recently the levels of pollution have reached heights which threaten shell fisheries. Moreover tidal scour may not immediately dispose of wastes to the sea so that some potentially dangerous substances like mercury can accumulate in muds (R. Comm. Pollution 1973). It has been suggested that regional geochemical maps based on stream sediment analysis and knowledge of industrial waste disposal can be used to assess the metal status of estuaries (Thornton 1975). Estuaries present a particularly difficult problem as many have become the focus of industry and dense urban concentrations. The unpolluted stretches of estuaries increased from 48.1% in 1970 to 49.6% in 1975. At present the pollution of estuaries can only be estimated, from the population figures of the catchment, but when the relevant provisions of the *Control of Pollution Act* (1974) are implemented all discharges will be controlled and the concentrations of pollutants known (DoE 1979A). At times of reduced flow the Ouse and Trent discharge water with 200 tonnes per day of effective oxygen demand which would use up oxygen from about 22,730Ml of sea-water in the Humber. In these circumstances bacterial pollution extending far out to sea has been reported, as for example up to a distance of 8km beyond the Tyne. The badly polluted estuaries are being cleaned up by sewage improvements, costing on Tyneside, £40 million; Teesside, £20 million; and for the GLC £100 million. In the case of the Tees domestic sewage is only a fraction of the total oxygen demand which is mainly from industry. In 1976 the two major industrial companies, ICI and British Steel, had reduced their polluting discharges to one half of the 1971 amount (R. Comm. Pollution 1974). However, many estuaries like the Solent could become as heavily polluted if they continue to receive untreated effluents. New treatment works at Beckton on the Thames halved the oxygen demand between 1972 and 1975 but there is a limit to such improvements when the cost of abatement exceeds the cost of damage caused by the pollution.

The problem of discharge to the sea is not confined to estuaries, for many sewage authorities dispose of untreated sewage by discharge into the sea. A co-operative research report in 1967, however, came to the conclusion that the coastal waters of the UK showed little pollution and this was localized near outfalls from coastal industries (Woodhead 1971). Yet few existing discharge pipes extend far enough out to sea to prevent beach pollution, though with modern techniques it is now economically feasible to lay pipes 3 to 5km out to sea. Bacterial contamination has its effect on marine life, especially shell fish, but industrial effluents have been known to kill off marine life around the outfall, the most toxic being organo-chlorate pesticides and polychlorinated biphenyls.

Monitoring of discharges and checks on major pollutants and pollution indicators are considered adequate measures (DoE 1979A). Fishery laboratories of England and Scotland have regular sampling programmes for metals and organochlorides. Only recently has the pollution of coastlines been under uniform control through the EEC directive on bathing-water quality. 27 beaches are monitored regularly in summer.

Beyond the 4.8km limit, there is no effective control over dumping at sea, though under the Oslo Convention the UK must record dumping in the NE Atlantic. Disposal of highly toxic materials at sea is usually in very deep water, exceeding 3,650m beyond the continental shelf, where slow diffusion of pollutants from their containers is diluted so much that there is no danger of surface contamination. The total effect is difficult to measure, much of the research being directed towards the influence of heavy metals on ecosystems. More is known about the pollution of the Irish Sea because of the concern over effluents from the Windscale reactors, though it is said that present levels of nuclear waste reaching the sea are unlikely to have any observable effect on the natural environment. The weight of low-level radio-active waste dumped in the NE Atlantic doubled between 1966 and 1979. Since 1974 this has been controlled by the *Dumping at Sea Act* (1974), and has been at 4,000m depth, 950km south-west of Lands End. Liquid radioactive effluent from nuclear sites has been carefully monitored in the Irish Sea but the safety of the permissible levels is by no means certain (R. Comm. Pollution 1976B). Nevertheless the discharges in 1979 have all been less than 40% of that authorized (DoE 1980).

Natural runoff from mineral-rich areas like N Wales or Devon contributes to the presence of metals in coastal waters but high concentrations, for example 47.6µg/l zinc in Liverpool Bay, which is ten times the level in the open sea, and the 4.2µg/l cadmium level in the Bristol Channel, which is thirty to forty times that at sea (Abdullah *et al* 1972), can be attributed to industry. Also the North Sea has shown high cadmium levels offshore from industrial sites, such as NE England. However, these are all localized peaks and concentration falls away rapidly from the coast. The levels have not increased in the past ten years and in fact cadmium has decreased except for the local concentration off Barry in S Wales. However, the detrimental effects of heavy metal concentrations could become serious in the long term if they accumulate in offshore sediments (Bryan 1971). Evidence of biological changes is difficult to interpret. In the 1930s nutrient salts and zooplankton declined in the English Channel seriously, reducing the regular winter herring fishing industry, but recovered again in 1965 probably due to climatic fluctuations which cause north and southward shifts of marine populations (Russell 1971). Marine biological surveillance by NERC has so far linked trends in plankton in the North Sea and the N Atlantic to climatic events. Pollution in near-shore waters and estuaries seems to affect mussels but the variability between animals seems to be due to the inherent characteristics rather than pollution. Because of the difficulty of acquiring, interpreting and applying data, attention has been concentrated on a few of the more toxic pollutants and on oil which is the most significant potential source of pollution (DoE 1979A).

The waste disposal problems of **agriculture** have changed in character in recent years and become more serious with the growth in intensive animal farming. Since 1946 pigs have trebled and poultry doubled. Large units find it difficult to dispose of manure cheaply. Despite the obvious nutrient value for arable farming there are problems of transport and difficulties of application compared with artificial fertilizers. Access to fields is not always possible if soils are heavy and the high water content of slurries could lead to waterlogging if soil water is at or near field capacity. The bacteria present in slurry presents a health hazard especially if used to fertilize grass on dairy farms, and manures from animals fed with chemicals or antibiotics could be harmful to plant growth. Poultry manure which has the highest concentration of NPK (nitrogen, phosphates, potash) of all farm animals has been dried for fertilizer as well as for animal feeding but this disposes of only a small proportion. Some are treated by storage in ditches while oxidation takes place and then discharged to streams. Sewage works have not the capacity to deal with agricultural refuse.

Unlike radioactivity we have no clear idea of the safe level of **oil-pollution**. So far the effects have been limited to the destruction of some marine communities like shellfish and sea birds, though the nuisance of oil on amenity beaches has led to the greatest outcry against oil pollution. Oil persists for fourteen months on beaches, and because of some toxic and persistent constituents may enter food-chains and have far-reaching effects, particularly in sheltered bays and salt marshes. The main disasters so far have been due to accidents to tankers, whose safety is an international problem. The effects of the Torrey Canyon disaster on the coast of SW England in 1967 led the UK government to call a meeting of the IMCO maritime safety committee, which produced stricter regulations on traffic flow. From 1970 to 1975 there were twelve incidents in UK waters, the largest that of the Pacific Glory off the Isle of Wight in 1970 (DoE 1976A).

The development of North Sea oil has increased the hazard of oil pollution. The method of extraction involves injecting sea-water into the sediment which causes a discharge of oil. With normal production this amounts to 325 tonnes annually. The fact that the pollution is from a great number of drilling sites means that it is widely dispersed. Blow-outs present a much greater hazard though of much shorter duration. This hazard has caused concern in the EEC and measures are to be taken on pollution from oil rigs (Comm. EC 1977). A major spill in the North Sea oilfields is not considered a serious long-term threat to plankton (R. Comm. Pollution 1974), but the main aim in treatment of an oil spill is to prevent it reaching shore where ecological damage would be more serious (DoE 1976A).

Thermal pollution of water can occur through the return of water from cooling systems, particularly in power stations and will increase as they reach peak capacity. The Trent has power stations generating 12,000 MW in a distance of 160km (Hawes 1970). Temperatures of discharged water are often $10°C$ above river water temperature, but studies in the USA (Merriman 1970) suggest that this becomes undetectable 3km from the outfall. Tower cooling at power stations also increases the oxygen content of the water. Studies of the effect of discharging sea-water heated $10°C$ above ambient temperature at $91,000m^3$ per hr have been made at Hunterston, Ayrshire. These suggest that the effect on marine life is to prolong the breeding season in the immediate vicinity of the effluent (Barnett 1971), but the overall effect in a temperate climate is very small.

Noise levels have substantially risen in recent years in urban areas largely because of the increase in traffic. Road traffic presents a much greater problem than air traffic. A survey of traffic noise in 1972 showed that 50% of the population of England was exposed to over 35 decibels and 15% had over 65 decibels. In London levels were much higher with 25% of the population exposed to 70 decibels or more (DoE 1979A). Aircraft noise is much more localized and from 1972 to 1974, despite a 10% increase in passenger movements at Heathrow, there was an 8% reduction in the population exposed to high noise levels (DoE 1978B). This is expected to fall still further with the use of larger and quieter aircraft.

VI   CONSERVATION

VI.1 Nature Conservation

The conservation movement in N America was stimulated by the disastrous effects of reckless agricultural exploitation, whilst in the UK the need for conservation has become obvious due to the rapid expansion of urban and industrial life, which has depleted the natural landscapes and through its demands changed the rural agricultural scene. For this reason much of the conservation movement in the UK has been directed towards the preservation of natural habitats (Stamp 1969), but these measures may in many cases only artificially prolong the life of some rare species in danger of extinction. Although man-made, the common lands are open spaces and their preservation desirable on aesthetic grounds. True natural habitats are more difficult to preserve in the UK except in the large areas set aside by the Nature Conservancy in Scotland, the North of England and Wales. The Conservancy, established in 1949, and since 1965 under the wing of the Natural Environment Research Council, is more concerned with management of these reserves by ecological methods than with isolating them, but the present areas protected for their scientific interest may not be enough to maintain variety in wildlife in Britain (NCC 1979). Most of the reserves are in uplands but none can be considered wilderness for their present condition is largely the result of man's activity (Pearsall 1950). The upland moors are largely the result of degeneration. While natural fires occurred before man's occupation, the increased use of uplands for grazing led to the deliberate burning of vegetation to stimulate growth. Burning does not seriously deplete nutrients by removing them in volatile form, but severe burning can destroy the seeds on the ground and thus slow down the rate of recolonization which is in any case a slow process on high exposed sites. Thus many areas of upland Scotland have suffered soil erosion, the degree depending on physical conditions and land use both at the site and in other areas within the same catchment (McVean and Lockie 1969).

In the lowlands, direct *changes in habitats* have been brought about by agricultural developments. Hedges have been removed in the cereal-growing area of SE and E England; in places as much as 70% of the hedges have disappeared. While intensification of grassland has led to similar changes in the pastoral areas the amount of hedgerow removal is much less serious and in any case the small farms of the West, including N Ireland, have a high density of hedges. The removal of some hedges has the effect of reducing species of birds as well as insects, though if the remaining hedges are well cared for the loss could be greatly reduced. The relationship between the wild life and changes in crops is being investigated. Chemicals used on crops or as herbicides on field and road margins can have deleterious effects on wild flowers, with harmful effects to useful insects such as bees which are vital in the pollination of fruit trees. Pesticides used on or near waterways can destroy fish. Intensive rearing units for livestock have the special problem of disposal of waste, but until adequately monitored the degree of pollution can not be assessed. The drainage of the wetter lowlands and marshes, whilst creating new agricultural lands, can have a serious effect on water resources and wild life. Dredging and straightening of rivers greatly reduce the cover for birds and animals as well as fish, apart from the often permanent destruction of water plants.

Semi-natural woodlands of the uplands, including pine and birch forests in Scotland, are most likely to be destroyed by the expansion of forestry, which also threatens upland grassland. These habitats cannot be easily re-created (Ratcliffe 1978). Pure stands of spruce when mature have a very limited fauna except on the margin and along fire-breaks. If the target of 2 million ha forest is reached wildlife might suffer, though the grassed fire-breaks and the existence of young conifer plantings give a rich habitat and commercial timber production need not conflict with nature conservation. Since the *Countryside Act* (1968) the Forestry Commission has been concerned with planning and managing forests in the interests of amenity. The policy of planting a variety of trees, including deciduous species, has improved the habitat though in some cases this has increased the risk of timber loss through windblow. It has been shown in Grisedale Forest that a relatively small area, only one per cent, can be managed for wildlife and give great benefits to amenity and conservation (CAS 1980). In the lowlands, priority is being given to preserving old broad-leafed trees which has become more essential with the ravages of Dutch Elm disease.

VI.2 Land-Use Conflicts

Scarcity of good quality agricultural land in the UK has aggravated land-use conflicts, for although there is a need for space to be used economically, the land is also a natural resource which will be depleted if not used properly. There is a need for effective control of future development, which has proved possible for nature reserves, but where there is economic exploitation principles of ecology are more difficult to apply. There is no overall authority responsible for resource conservation. The uplands can be used productively both for forests and for annual grazing. Planting of coniferous trees is acceptable on the acid soils but the production of acid *mor humus* by these trees can lead to degradation of soils by accelerated leaching, while deciduous trees, particularly birch, can bring nutrient salts to the surface. The application of fertilizers to make up deficiencies has had the effect of accelerating erosion of peats (Parker 1962), and the development of drainage and planting techniques for the wet moorlands has helped to check the accumulation of peat. Grazing is not without its problems, for trampling can destroy soil structure and grazing by sheep has led to the spread of *nardus stricta* previously controlled by cattle. Undesirable effects of sheep grazing can only be remedied by management of the grassland using fertilizers and reseeding. Since returns for these investments depend on soil, areas of the Scottish Highlands, cultivated before the rapid shrinking of arable in the nineteenth century, are being reseeded. Immediate returns must not be the only consideration as soil improvement gives a longer-term return on capital.

The uplands provide facilities for recreation which is almost impossible to evaluate in the same terms as productivity of pasture or forest (Dept Education and Science 1966). Even more than agriculture, forest lends itself to multiple use. The setting-up of forest parks is an example of multiple use and it has been suggested that in future forests should be zoned according to the relative importance they have for timber production, pulp production, or sport and recreation (McVean and Lockie 1969). One of the aims of the water authorities set up in 1974 has been to make maximum use of water for recreation and amenity (DoE 1973B). The Nature Conservancy is attempting to solve the problem of multiple use in the uplands by constructing models to guide future decisions. However, classification of land needs to be further advanced to provide the necessary data.

There are many less obvious ways in which land use affects the environment and, apart from a few areas of National Parks, there is no planning organization to protect the landscape from damage. Market demands and agricultural policy decisions in Europe have recently encouraged farmers in the grazing Broads of Norfolk to cultivate their land for wheat. Drainage schemes using government grants are causing declining water tables which, together with the increase of nitrates and other pollutants, is destroying the ecology of a rapidly expanding area of the Broads. There is a great need for coordination between government policies concerned with economic activity and environment.

VI.3 Industrial and Urban Derelict Land

In the lowlands the most serious problem has been the dereliction left by industry. The disposal of waste, destruction of the surface by extensive opencast working, slag heaps and tips have devastated large areas.

Surveys of derelict land showed 43,273ha in England by 1974 of which 76% justified restoration, 18,500ha in Scotland (1978) and 14,000ha in Wales (1975). In addition, a further 75,000ha in England and 7,000ha in Wales has been classified as despoiled, most of it currently in use as excavations or tips (DoE 1979B).

TABLE 3.16

Derelict Land Reclaimed Annually, 1971–8

	1971	1972	1973–4*	1974–5	1975–6	1976–7	1977–8
Area reclaimed (ha)	1,941	2,168	2,825	1,323	2,460	1,617	2,640

*in 1974 figures calculated from April 1st; 1973–4 figures are for 15-month period January 1973 to March 1974

Source: DoE (1979B)

Reclamation programmes aim to restore all derelict land as quickly as economically possible, and this is undertaken by local authorities in England and by Development Agencies in Scotland and Wales. In England 13,233 ha were reclaimed from 1972 to 1978, and in Scotland 4,500 ha and in Wales 2,000 ha over the same period. In England 30% of the restored land is in the North and 19% in the North West. In the North, E Midlands and Yorks. and Humberside 50% of the restoration was to spoil-heaps, while in SE England 50% of the restoration was to excavations.

Priority has been given to restoration of derelict land in the inner cities. Restoration in the urban area is where possible for housing or industry but most is for public open space, for amenity or recreation. The greatest problem is the restoration of contaminated land but some redevelopment of areas polluted by toxic metals is under way. In rural areas the main aim of restoration is to provide rough grazing and woodland. Unlike the development of the uplands, dereliction, which frequently occurs in areas of urban blight, should present a unique opportunity at least to improve the existing landscape. The question of optimum use need not arise. Although large acreages of conifers have been planted with the help of the Forestry Commission, the nature of the derelict land greatly reduces its potential for timber. Purely rural areas are also affected, such as china-clay tips in Cornwall,

TABLE 3.17

Derelict Land (1974) and Area Restored, England, 1972–8 (ha)

	Spoil heaps		Excavations and pits		Total*	
	Derelict	Restored	Derelict	Restored	Derelict	Restored
North	2,922	1,702	1,690	295	9,411	3,976
Yorks. and H.	1,289	953	1,599	296	5,451	1,683
E Midlands	1,090	714	1,166	264	5,171	1,472
E Anglia	1	–	408	70	1,783	256
South East	53	58	1,136	417	2,360	896
South West	4,307	15	843	80	6,415	261
W Midlands	1,373	828	672	492	4,667	2,129
North West	2,083	852	1,203	131	8,015	2,560
England	13,118	5,122	8,717	2,145	43,273	13,233

*total includes military dereliction, abandoned British Rail land and other forms of dereliction

Source: DoE (1979A)

and within national parks and areas of outstanding natural beauty there are 1,800 ha of derelict land (Oxenham 1966). Reclamation in the urban areas has been largely for housing development or industrial re-zoning and only a small proportion has been developed as open space or for recreation areas.

From a purely physical standpoint the problem of reclamation depends on the type of derelict land. Oxenham usefully differentiates between the mounds and spoilheaps — including those from collieries, quarries, a variety of industries and the opencast workings — and the pits and excavations created in the aftermath of mining. All of these have problems related to their size, shape and the composition of the waste. The number of disciplines involved in the *Swansea Valley Project* (Hilton 1967) demonstrates the extent of the physical problem of attempting to develop a large area devastated by the spoilheaps from heavy iron and steel industries. It has been suggested earlier that instead of creating new tips on fresh pieces of land, the hollows left by the extractive industries could be simultaneously reclaimed. This would not always be possible, but at least some knowledge of the future of the area devastated by tipping could allow effective control over the nature of the tipping. This still does not solve the problem of the great area of existing derelict land. After infilling or levelling, the composition may make landscaping difficult. For example in the Swansea project neither the zinc nor the copper waste tips had much vegetation, though steel slag could support growth and there is little knowledge of the degree of tolerance by plant species. Very often the problem is one of excessive drainage which could lead to wilting during rainless periods, rather than toxicity. Some minerals present in waste, while not preventing grass growth, could accumulate and become a hazard to grazing animals. The surface can be made acceptable by topsoiling, applying fertilizer or organic matter, and pioneer vegetation, most commonly grass, can be established. Many spoilheaps in the W Riding have been successfully planted in grass. Difficult sites have been planted using soil conditioners which create the necessary crumb structure and improve germination. Steep spoilheaps have been rapidly covered, using sets of creeping bent. Derelict land developed for playing fields requires much more careful landscaping and preparation than these efforts to reduce the ugliness of the landscape. Trees have been planted extensively in Co Durham and large schemes in Lancashire have been very successful. Rapid results, though expensive, are obtained by transplanting mature trees, using machinery.

REFERENCES

ABDULLAH, M I *et al* (1972) 'Heavy Metal Concentration in Coastal Waters', *Nature, 235,* 158—60

ABERCROMBIE, P (1945) *Greater London Plan 1944,* HMSO

AGRIC. ADVIS. UNIT (1970) *Modern Farming and the Soil,* HMSO

AGRIC. LAND SERV. (1966) 'Agricultural Land Classification', *Tech. Rep. 11,* MAFF, London

ALEXANDER, R W and HENDERSON-SELLARS, A (1980) *Survey of Lichens and Tarspot Fungus as Indicators of Atmospheric Sulphur Dioxide Pollution in Merseyside,* Dept Geogr., Univ. Liverpool

ATKINS, D H F, COX, R A and EGGLETON, A E J (1972) 'Photochemical Ozone and Sulphuric Acid Aerosol Formation in the Atmosphere over Southern England', *Nature, 235,* 372—6

BALL, D F (1971) 'The Identification and Measurement of Gaseous Pollutants', *Int. J. Environ. Stud.,* *14,* 267–74

BARNES, R A (1975) 'Transport of Smoke and Sulphur Dioxide into Rural Areas of England and Wales' in HEY, R D and DAVIES, T D (eds) *Science Technology and Environmental Management,* Farnborough, 165–79

BARNETT, P R O (1971) 'Some Changes in Intertidal Sand Communities due to Thermal Pollution', *Proc. R. Soc., Ser. B, 177,* 353–64

BARR, J (1969) *Derelict Britain,* London

BEAVER, S H (1968) 'Changes in Industrial Land Use 1930–67', in *Land Use and Resources,* Inst. Br. Geogr., Special Pub. 1, 101–9

BEST, R H (1968) 'Competition for Land Between Urban and Rural Uses', in *Land Use and Resources,* Inst. Br. Geogr., Special Pub. 1, 89–100

BIBBY, J S and MACKNEY, D (1969) 'Land Use Capability Classification', *Soil Surv. Tech. Monogr. 1,* Harpenden and Craigiebuckler

BIRSE, E L and DRY, F T (1970) *Assessment of Climatic Conditions in Scotland,* Macaulay Inst., Aberdeen

BIRSE, E L and ROBERTSON, L (1970) *Assessment of Climatic Conditions in Scotland, 2,* Soil Surv. Scotland, Craigiebuckler

BLEASDALE, J K A (1959) 'The Effects of Air Pollution on Plant Growth', in YAPP, W B (ed.) *The Effects of Air Pollution on Living Material, Symp. Inst. Biol. 8,* London, 111–30

⸻ (1965) 'Improvement of Raingauge Networks', *Met. Mag., Lond., 94,* 137–42

BRYAN, G (1971) 'The Effects of Heavy Metals on Marine and Estuarine Organisms', *Proc. R. Soc., Ser. B, 177,* 389–410

BURDEKIN, D A and GIBBS, J N (1974) 'The Control of Dutch Elm Disease', *Forestry Commn, Leaflet 54,* HMSO

CABORN, J M (1957) 'Shelter Belts and Microclimate', *Bull. For. Commn, Lond., 29,* 3–29

CENTRE FOR AGRICULTURAL STRATEGY (1980) 'Strategy for the UK Forest Industry', *Report, 6*

CENT. ADVIS. WATER COMM. (1959) *First Report of the Sub-committee on the Growing Demand for Water,* HMSO

CHRISTIAN, G (1966) *Tomorrow's Countryside: the Road to the Seventies,* London

CLARKE, G R (1971) *The Study of Soil in the Field,* Cambridge

CLAYDEN, B (1971) 'Soils of the Exeter District', *Mem. Soil Surv. Gt Br.,* Harpenden

COLEMAN, A (1961) 'The Second Land Use Survey', *Geogrl J., 127,* 2, 168–80

COMMISSION OF THE EUROPEAN COMMUNITIES (1977) *State of the Environment,* First Rept, Luxembourg

COPPOCK, J T (1971) *An Agricultural Geography of Great Britain,* London

COX, R A (1975) 'Measurements of Atmospheric Ozone in Rural Locations' in HEY, R D and DAVIES, T D (eds) *Science Technology and Environmental Management,* Farnborough, 181–8

DAVIES, W E and TYLER, B F (1964) 'The Effect of Weather Conditions on the Growth of Lucerne' in TAYLOR, J A (ed.) *Climatic Factors and Agric. Productivity, 6,* Aberystwyth, 12–8

DENMEAD, O T and SHAW, R H (1962) 'Availability of Soil Water to Plants as affected by Soil Moisture Content and Meteorological Conditions', *J. Agron., 45,* 385–90

DES (1966) *Forestry, Agriculture and the Multiple Use of Rural Land,* Rep. of the Land Use Study Group, HMSO

DEPT EMPLOYMENT and PRODUCTIVITY (1968) *Dust and Fumes in Factory Atmospheres,* HMSO
DEPT ENVIRON. (1971) *Refuse Disposal,* HMSO
    (1972A) *Out of Sight, Out of Mind. Rep. of a Working Party on Sludge Disposal in Liverpool Bay,* HMSO, 2 vols
    (1972B) *River Pollution Survey of England and Wales,* updated 1972, HMSO
    (1973A) *The New Water Industry: Management and Structure,* HMSO
    (1973B) *A Background to Water Reorganisation in England and Wales,* HMSO
    (1974A) *The Water Services: Economic and Financial Policies,* HMSO
    (1974B) *The Monitoring of the Environment in the UK,* Rep. by Cent. Unit Environ. Pollution, HMSO
    (1975) 'Controlling Pollution', *Central Unit on Environmental Pollution, Pollution Pap. 4,* HMSO
    (1976A) 'Accidental Oil Pollution of the Sea', *Central Unit on Environmental Pollution, Pollution Pap. 8,* HMSO
    (1976B) *Review of the Water Industry in England and Wales. A Consultative Document,* HMSO
    (1977) *Water Data 1976,* HMSO
    (1978A) *Water Data 1977,* HMSO
    (1978B) *Digest of Environmental Pollution Statistics, 1,* HMSO
    (1979A) 'The United Kingdom Environment, 1979. Progress of Pollution Control', *Central Directorate on Environmental Pollution, Pollution Pap. 16,* HMSO
    (1979B) *Digest of Environmental Pollution Statistics, 2,* HMSO
    (1980) *Digest of Environmental Pollution Statistics, 3,* HMSO
DEPT INDUSTRY (1976) *National Survey of Air Pollution 1961–71 Vol. 4: North Yorkshire and Humberside,* Warren Spring Laboratory, HMSO
    (1979) *The Investigation of Air Pollution. National Survey of Smoke and Sulphur Dioxide, April 1978–March 1979,* Warren Spring Lab., Stevenage
    (1963–80) *The Investigation of Air Pollution. National Survey of Smoke and Sulphur Dioxide,* published annually, Warren Spring Lab., Stevenage
DOUGLAS, I (1970) 'Sediment Yields from Forested and Agricultural Lands' in TAYLOR, J A (ed.) *The Role of Water in Agric., 12,* Aberystwyth, 57–88
EDWARDS, K A (1970) 'Sources of Error in Agricultural Water Budgets' in TAYLOR, J A (ed.) *The Role of Water in Agric., 12,* Aberystwyth, 11–23
EDWARDS, R S, HUGHES, B D and READ, M W (1975) 'Biological Survey in the Detection and Assessment of Pollution' in CHADWICK, M J and GOODMAN, G T (eds) *The Ecology of Resource Degradation and Renewal,* Oxford, 139–56
FISHER, R A and HAGAN, R M (1965) 'Plant Water Relations, Irrigation Management and Crop Yield', *Exp. Agric., 1,* 161–77
FORESTRY COMMN (1968) *Forest Research,* HMSO
    (1974) 'Fifty Years of Forestry Research', *Forestry Commn Bull., 50,* HMSO
    (1975) *55th Ann. Rep. and Accounts of the Forestry Commn for the Year Ended 31 March 1975,* HMSO
    (1977) *Forest Research,* HMSO
    (1980) *60th Annual Report, 1979–80,* HMSO

FRASER, A I (1972) 'The Effect of Climatic Factors on the Development of Plantation Structure' in TAYLOR, J A (ed.) *Res. Pap. Forest Met.*, Aberystwyth, 59–74

GARDNER, C M K (1981) 'The Soil Moisture Data Bank: Moisture Content Data from some British Soils', *Inst. Hydrol., Rept 76*

GARLAND, J A (1975) 'Dry Deposition and the Atmospheric Cycle of Sulphur Dioxide' in HEY, R D and DAVIES, T D (eds) *Science Technology and Environmental Management,* Farnborough, 145–64

GARNETT, A (1971) 'Weather Inversions and Air Pollution', *Clean Air, 1,* 3, 16–21

GILBERT, O L (1971) 'Some Indirect Effects of Air Pollution on Bark Living Invertebrates', *J. Appl. Ecol., 8,* 1, 77–84

GLOYNE, R W (1971) 'A Note on the Average Annual Mean of Daily Earth Temperature in the UK', *Met. Mag., Lond., 100,* 1–6

GOODE, J E (1970) 'The Cumulative Effects of Irrigation on Fruit Crops' in TAYLOR, J A (ed.) *The Role of Water in Agric. 12,* Aberystwyth, 161–70

GOORIAH, B D (1968) *Distribution of Pollution at some Country Sites,* Warren Spring Laboratory

GRAINGER, J (1967) 'Meteorology and Plant Physiology in Potato Blight Forecasting' in TAYLOR, J A (ed.) *Weather and Agriculture,* Aberystwyth, 105–13

GRANT, S A (1969) 'Temperature and Light Factors in the Growth of Hill Pasture Species', *Hill Land Productivity, 4,* 30–4

GRAYSON, A J (1967) 'Forestry in Britain' in ASHTON, J and RODGERS, S J (eds) *Economic Change and Agriculture,* Newcastle upon Tyne, 168–89

GREEN, F H W (1970A) 'Some Isopleth Maps based on Lysimeter Observations in the British Isles in 1965, 1966 and 1967', *J. Hydrol., 10,* 127–40

        (1970B) 'The Flexibility of Land Use in Relation to the Water Balance' in TAYLOR, J A (ed.) *The Role of Water in Agric., 12,* Aberystwyth, 185–94

GREGORY, S (1954) 'Accumulated Temperature Maps of the British Isles', *Trans. Inst. Br. Geogr., 20,* 59–73

        (1964A) 'Some Aspects of Water Resource Development in Relation to Lancashire', *Problems of Appl. Geogr.,* Warsaw

        (1964B) 'Water Resource Exploitation, Policies and Problems', *Geogr., 49,* 310–4

HAWES, F B (1970) 'Thermal Problems "Old Hat" in Britain', *CEGB Newsletter, 83*

HAWKESWORTH, D L (1971) 'Lichens as Litmus for Air Pollution', *Int. J. Environ. Stud., 14,* 281–96

HILL, D A (1947) *The Land of Ulster 1: The Belfast Region,* Belfast HMSO

HILTON, K J (ed.) (1967) *The Lower Swansea Valley Project,* London

HOGG, W H (1965A) 'Climatic Factors and Choice of Site, with Special Reference to Horticulture' in JOHNSTON, C G and SMITH, L P (eds) *The Biological Significance of Climatic Changes in Britain, Symp. Inst. Biol., 14,* London, 141–55

        (1965B) 'Measurements of the Shelter Effects of Landforms and Other Topographical Features', *Scient. Hort., 17,* 20–30

        (1966) 'Climate and Surveys of Agricultural Land Use', *UNESCO Natural Resources Res., 7, Agroclimatological Methods,* Reading

        (1967A) 'Meteorological Factors in Early Crop Production', *Weather, 22,* 3, 84–118

        (1967B) *The Atlas of Long-term Irrigation Needs for England and Wales,* MAFF, London

(1967C) 'The Use of Upper Air Data in Relation to Plant Disease' in TAYLOR, J A (ed.) *Weather and Agriculture*, Aberystwyth, 115—27
(1968) 'The Analysis of Data with Particular Reference to Frost Surveys', *WMO Proc. Reg. Training Semin. in Agromet.*, Wageningen, 343—50
(1970) 'Basic Frost Irrigation and Degree Day Data for Planning Purposes' in TAYLOR, J A (ed.) *Weather Econ.*, *11*, Aberystwyth, 27—43
HOLMES, J W and COLVILLE, J S (1968) 'On the Water Balance of Grassland', *Int. Congr. Soil Sci.*, *9*, Sydney, 39—46
HORNER, R W (1971) 'The Thames Barrier Scheme', *Jl R. Soc. Arts*, *5178*, 119, 369—80
HUNTER, R F and GRANT, S A (1971) 'The Effect of Altitude on Grass Growth in Eastern Scotland', *J. Appl. Ecol.*, *8*, 1, 1—19
HURST, C A (1964) 'Grass Growing Days' in TAYLOR, J A (ed.) *Climatic Factors and Agric. Productivity*, *6*, Aberystwyth, 25—9
IRVINE, D E G and KNIGHTS, B (eds) (1974) *Pollution and the Use of Chemicals in Agriculture*, London
JARVIS, M G (1973) 'Soils of the Wantage and Abingdon District', *Mem. Soil Surv. Gt Br.*, Harpenden
JONES, G E (1972) 'An Investigation into the Possible Causes of Poor Growth in Sitka Spruce' in TAYLOR, J A (ed.) *Res. Pap. in Forest Met.*, Aberystwyth, 147—55
JONES, P (1981) 'The Geography of Dutch Elm Disease', *Inst. Br. Geogr.*, New Ser. *6*, 3, 324—36
KNOCH, K (1963) 'Die Landesklima Aufnahme, Wesen und Methodik', *Ber. dt. Wetterd.*, Offenbach, *85*, 12, 1—64
LAMB, H H (1965) 'Britain's Changing Climate' in JOHNSTON, C C and SMITH, L P (eds) *The Biological Significance of Climatic Changes in Britain*, London, 3—31
LAWRENCE, E N (1971) 'Recent Trends in Solar Radiation, Maximum Black-bulb and Air Temperatures in Britain', *Weather*, *26*, 4, 164—72
McVEAN, D N and LOCKIE, J D (1969) *Ecology and Land Use in Upland Scotland*, Edinburgh
MATTHEWS, P J (1981) 'Sludge Utilization in the EEC', *Water*, *39*, 7—11
MERRIMAN, D (1970) 'The Calefaction of a River', *Scient. Am.*, *222*, 42—52
MILITARY ENGNG EXP. ESTABL. (1969) *The Prediction of Soil Water Tension from Weather Data*, MEXE Rep. 1025, Christchurch
MILLER, H G (1980) 'Nitrites and Forest Soils', *Forest Res.*, Forestry Commn, HMSO
MINIST. AGRIC. (1967) 'Potential Transpiration', *Tech. Bull.*, *16*, HMSO
MAFF (1974) 'Land Capability Classification', *Tech. Bull.*, *30*, HMSO
MINIST. FUEL and POWER (1953) *Committee on Air Pollution*, Interim Rep., Cmnd 9011, HMSO
MINIST. HOUSING and LOCAL GOVT (1967) *Chimney Heights*, 1956 Clean Air Act Memorandum, HMSO
MINIST. HOUSING and LOCAL GOVT and MAFF (1962) *Water Conservation: England and Wales*, Cmnd 1693, HMSO
MINIST. HOUSING and LOCAL GOVT and SCOTT. DEV. DEPT (1970) *Rep. of the Technical Committee on the Disposal of Toxic Solid Wastes*, HMSO
MINIST. TECHNOLOGY (1965) *The Investigation of Atmospheric Pollution 1958—63*, HMSO
NATURE CONSERVANCY COUNCIL (1979) *Nature Conservation and Forestry*, Consultative paper
NE DEV. ASSN (1950) *A Physical Land Classification of Northumberland and*

Durham and Part of the N Riding of Yorks., Newcastle upon Tyne

NERC (1976) *Report for the Council for the period 1 April 1975 to 31 March 1976,* HMSO

NICHOLSON, M (1970) *The Environmental Revolution,* London

NW WATER AUTHORITY (1979) *Report on Regional Water Resource Studies,* Directorate of Resource Plann.

NATIONAL WATER COUNCIL (1976) *Water Prospects for 1977,* London
                        (1978) *Water Industry Review 1978,* London

O'HARE, P J (1972) 'A Comparison of the Effect of Young Forest and Grassland on the Water Table in Blanket Peat' in TAYLOR, J A (ed.) *Res. Pap. Forest Met.,* Aberystwyth, 126–33

O'SULLIVAN, A J (1971) 'Ecological Effects of Sewage Discharge in the Marine Environment', *Proc. R. Soc., Ser. B, 177,* 331–51

OXENHAM, J R (1966) *Reclaiming Derelict Land,* London

PARKER, R E (1962) 'Factors Limiting Tree Growth on Peat Soils', *Ir. For., 19,* 1, 60–81

PEARS, N V (1972) 'Interpretation Problems in the Study of Tree Line Fluctuations' in TAYLOR, J A (ed.) *Res. Pap. Forest Met.,* Aberystwyth, 31–45

PEARSALL, W M (1950) *Mountains and Moorlands,* London

PENMAN, H L (1948) 'Natural Evaporation from Open Water, Bare Soil and Grass', *Proc. R. Soc., Ser. A, 193,* 120–45
            (1950) 'Evaporation over the British Isles', *Q. Jl R. Met. Soc., 76,* 372–83
            (1962) 'Weather and Crops', *Q. Jl R. Met. Soc., 88,* 209–19
            (1968) 'Available and Accessible Water', *Proc. Ninth Int. Congr. Soil Sci.,* Adelaide, 29–37

POLLARD, E and MILLER, A (1968) 'Wind Erosion in the East Anglian Fens', *Weather, 23,* 10, 415–7

PORTER, E (1978) *Water Management in England and Wales,* Cambridge

PRESTIDGE, J B H (1978) *Water,* 12–4

PRICKETT, C N (1970) 'Current Trends in the Use of Water' in TAYLOR, J A (ed.) *The Role of Water in Agric., 12,* Aberystwyth, 101–19

PUBL. GEN. ACTS, see list on pp. 505–7

PYATT, D G (1966) 'Soil Problems in Border Forestry', *Proc. N. England Soils Discussion Group, 2,* 43–5

RATCLIFFE, D A (1978) *A Nature Conservation Review,* Cambridge

REED, L E and TROTT, P E (1971) 'Continuous Measurement of Carbon Monoxide in Streets 1967–9', *Atmos. Envir., 5,* 27–39

REES, J A (1969) 'Industrial Demand for Water: a Study of South East England', *LSE Res. Monogr. 3*

ROBERTS, D G (1972) 'The Modification of Geomorphic Shelter by Shelter Belts', in TAYLOR, J A (ed.) *Res. Pap. Forest Met.,* Aberystwyth, 134–46

ROBINSON, A J (1971) 'Air Pollution', *Jl R. Soc. Arts, 5180,* CXIX, 505–16

RODDA, J C (1970A) 'Definite Rainfall Measurements and their Significance for Agriculture' in TAYLOR, J A (ed.) *The Role of Water in Agric., 12,* Aberystwyth, 1–10
          (1970B) 'Rainfall Excesses in the UK', *Trans. Inst. Br. Geogr., 49,* 49–70

RODE, A A (1968) 'Hydrological Profile', *Proc. Ninth Int. Congr. Soil Sci.,* Adelaide, 165–72

ROUSE, G P (1961) 'Some Effects of Rainfall on Tree Growth and Forest Fires', *Weather, 16,* 9, 304–11

ROY. COMMN (TREATING AND DISPOSAL OF SEWAGE) 1912–3. *Eighth Report*, Cmnd 6464, HMSO
ROY. COMMN ENVIRON. POLLUTION (1971) *First Report*, Cmnd 4585, HMSO
                                    (1972) *Second Report*, Cmnd 4894, HMSO
                                    (1972) *Third Report*, Cmnd 5054, HMSO
                                    (1973) *Pollution in Four Industrial Estuaries*, HMSO
                                    (1974) *Fourth Report*, Cmnd 5780, HMSO
                                    (1975) *Study of Radiological Safety. Evidence by the Dept of Energy*, HMSO
                                    (1976A) *Fifth Report*, Cmnd 6371, HMSO
                                    (1976B) *Sixth Report*, Cmnd 6618, HMSO
RUSSELL, F S *et al* (1971) 'Changes in the Biological Conditions in the English Channel', *Nature, 234,* 468–70
RUTTER, A J (1972) 'Evaporation from Forests' in TAYLOR, J A (ed.) *Res. Pap. Forest Met.,* Aberystwyth, 75–90
RYDZ, B (1969) 'Water Conservation' in *Water Resources Committee, Assocn of River Authorities Year Book,* London, 195–214
SCALE, R S (1975) 'Soils of the Ely District', *Mem. Soil Surv. Gt Br.,* Harpenden
SEVERN–TRENT WATER AUTHORITY (1980) *To 1985 and Onward. The Corporate Plan,* Corporate Plann. Dept
                                    (1981) *To 1986 and Onward. The Corporate Plan,* Corporate Plann. Dept
SHELLARD, H C (1959) *Averages of Accumulated Temperatures and Standard Deviation of Monthly Mean Temperatures over Britain, 1921–50,* HMSO
SMITHSON, P A (1969) 'Effects of Altitude on Rainfall in Scotland', *Weather, 24,* 9, 370–6
SPEIGHT, H (1968) 'Upland Catchment Management: a Water Resources Board View', *Upland Catchment Management Conf.,* Attingham Park Coll., Shrewsbury
STAMP, L D (1947) *The Land of Britain: Use and Misuse,* London
                                    (1969) *Nature Conservation in Britain,* London
STEWART, W D P, TUCKWELL, S B and MAY, E (1975) 'Eutrophication and Algal Growth in Scottish Freshwater Lochs' in CHADWICK, M J and GOODMAN, G T (eds) *The Ecology of Resource Degradation and Renewal,* Oxford, 57–80
STILES, W and GARWOOD, E A (1964) 'Drought, Soil Water and Grass Growth' in TAYLOR, J A (ed.) *Climatic Factors and Agric. Productivity, 6,* Aberystwyth, 19–24
SYMONS, L J (ed.) (1963) *Land Use in N Ireland,* London
TAYLOR, J A (1964) 'Economic and Ecological Productivity under British Conditions' in TAYLOR, J A (ed.) *Climatic Factors and Agric. Productivity, 6,* Aberystwyth, 1–5
THOMASSON, A J (1971) 'Soils of the Melton Mowbray District', *Mem. Soil Surv. Gt Br.,* Harpenden
THOMPSON, D A (1979) 'Forest Drainage Schemes', *Forestry Commn Leaflet 72*
THOMPSON, F L (1945) *Merseyside Plan 1944,* HMSO
THORNTHWAITE, C W and MATHER, J R (1955) 'The Water Balance', *Drexel Inst. Technol., Lab. Clim., 8,* 1, Centerton, New Jersey, 22–67
THORNTON, I (1975) 'Geochemical Parameters in the Assessment of Estuarine

Pollution' in CHADWICK, M J and GOODMAN, G T (eds) *The Ecology of Resource Degradation and Renewal,* Oxford, 157–72

VOLKER, A (1974) 'Management of Water in the Coastal Zone' in FUNNELL, B M and HEY, R D *The Management of Water Resources in England and Wales,* Univ. E Anglia,115–20

WARDLE, P A (1966) 'Land Use Policy: the Claims of Forestry on Resources and its Contributions', *Timber Grower, 19,* 18–25

           (1970) 'Weather and Risk in Forestry' in TAYLOR, J A (ed.) *Weather Econ.,* Aberystwyth, 67–82

WATER RESOURCES BD (1966) *Water Resources of the South East,* HMSO

           (1970) *Water Resources in the North,* HMSO

           (1971) *Water Resources in Wales and the Midlands,* HMSO

           (1973) *Water Resources in England and Wales,* vol 1: Report; vol 4: Appendices, HMSO

WATSON, J P and ABERCROMBIE, P (1943) *A Plan for Plymouth,* Plymouth

WELSH WATER AUTHORITY (1979) *Medium Term Plan 1978–83,* Directorate of Resource Plann.

           (1981) *Policy and Planning, 1981,* Directorate of Resource Plann.

WILLIAMS, R J H and RICKS, G R (1975) 'Effects of Combinations of Atmospheric Pollutants upon Vegetation' in CHADWICK, M J and GOODMAN, G T (eds) *The Ecology of Resource Degradation and Renewal,* Oxford, 127–38

WILSON, C L (1970) *Man's Impact on the Global Environment,* Massachusetts Inst. Technol.

WINTER, E J, SALTER, P J and COX, R F (1970) 'Limited Irrigation in Crop Production' in TAYLOR, J A (ed.) *The Role of Water in Agric., 12,* Aberystwyth, 147–60

WOODHEAD, D S (1971) 'The Biological Effect of Radioactive Waste', *Proc. R. Soc., Ser. B, 177,* 423–37

4

Power and the Industrial Structure

I   THE POWER INDUSTRIES

I.1   Significance and Structure

For most of its long industrial history the UK has been an energy-rich nation, able to supply its own needs from domestic resources and to export a surplus. The spatial distribution of the energy industries exploiting this wealth has always been an important factor in national affairs. In the nineteenth century the development of the coal resources played a major part in moulding the human geography of the UK. The coal-rich regions drew in large numbers of migrants to work both in the coal-mines and in the industries which depended upon coal as a source of power. The Victorian geography of the UK was largely coal-based. In the twentieth century the declining attractions of coal for the new industries which appeared and the decline of the coal industry itself, left large industrial populations stranded. The response by government was to introduce regional development policies. These had considerable influence on the distribution of economic activity in the UK and hence of population, through to the 1970s. In the early 1980s, as the spatial distribution of coal-mining continued to change, important spatial questions arose about whether it was right to develop new coal-mining areas such as the Vale of Belvoir and about the future role of areas of continuing coal-mining decline. The development of the North Sea energy resources raised different geographical questions, about the implications of the non-spatial pricing of natural-gas deliveries and about where the oil being brought ashore should be processed. At the same time the government was faced with increasing difficulties in finding locations which were acceptable to the British people for the planned increase in nuclear power stations. Decisions about these geographical matters will have an effect upon the distribution of development in the UK through to the next century. The aim of this section is to provide a basic knowledge of the geography of the energy industries and in particular about recent spatial changes, the contemporary distribution patterns and the likely future spatial trends, on which judgements about the best future patterns of these industries can be based.

In 1980 energy consumption in the UK amounted to the equivalent of 328 million tonnes of coal or about 6.5 tonnes per person. This high per capita energy consumption reflected the fact that the UK is one of the most highly industrialized and urbanized countries in the world. The way the energy is used bears this out. In 1980 34% was consumed by manufacturing industry, 28% was used for lighting and power in houses, 25% for transport, 6% by public services, another 6% for miscellaneous purposes, leaving only 1% to be used by agriculture.

The demand for energy is met in a variety of ways. In the past there was a simple distinction between the primary energy sources of coal and oil, and the energy provided by converting some of the primary sources into the secondary forms of electricity and manufactured gas. Since 1960 this picture has been complicated by the contribution of nuclear power to electricity generation and the replacement of manufactured gas by the primary energy source of natural gas. By 1980 the major sources of primary energy used in the UK were oil and coal (making almost equal contributions), natural gas and nuclear energy. In addition, water power used to generate electricity made a minor contribution with little potential for expansion (table 4.1).

TABLE 4.1

Energy Consumption, UK, 1980

	Million tonnes of coal equivalent		Used by electricity industry
	Amount	%	
Coal	120.9	36.9	89.7
Petroleum	121.4	37.0	11.2
Natural gas	70.4	21.4	0.6
Nuclear electricity	13.3	4.1	13.3
Hydro-electricity	2.0	0.6	2.0
Total	328.0	100.0	116.8

Source: Digest of Energy Statistics (1981), HMSO

Because coal is relatively inconvenient to use directly, bulky to store, dirty to handle and expensive to transport, wherever convenient it is converted into secondary energy before use. Thus in the UK gas was made from coal and supplied by pipe to houses as early as 1820 and after 1880 coal was used to generate electricity. The use of oil in Britain began in the nineteenth century, but it was not until after 1900 that imports increased significantly as it was used for industrial purposes and in motor-vehicles. However, the total quantities remained small until the 1960s. Then as the cost of coal rose while the cost of oil fell, oil began to replace coal as a fuel. Two other changes hastened the decline of coal consumption after 1960. Nuclear power stations began to supply significant amounts of electricity which otherwise would have been generated in coal-fired power stations and, following the completion of the national gas transmission grid, natural gas replaced gas made from coal. In 1971, for the first time, coal lost its place to oil as the most important contributor to British energy supplies. Demand for oil continued to rise, and reached a peak in 1973. It then fell to a lower level following a sharp rise in oil prices. A further sharp fall in oil consumption occurred after 1979, so that by the end of 1980 the contributions of coal and oil to UK energy consumption were virtually the same. Oil began to be produced from the UK sector of the North Sea in 1975 and by 1981 production equalled national consumption. Once again the UK was essentially self-sufficient in energy supplies.

Within the overall changes in coal consumption, a major change in the use of coal had important implications which are described later. It was *direct* consumption of coal which fell dramatically, while *indirect* consumption increased, as sales to the electricity generating industry rose from 26% of the total in 1960 to 73% in 1980 (table 4.2).

TABLE 4.2

Coal Consumption, UK, 1950–80 (million tonnes)

		1950	1960	1970	1980
Indirect consumption	Electricity power stations	33.5	52.7	77.2	89.6
	Gas works	26.6	23.0	4.2	0.0
	Coke ovens	22.9	29.2	25.3	11.6
	Other fuel conversion	3.0*	2.3	4.1	3.0
Total indirect consumption		86.1	107.2	110.9	104.2
Direct consumption	Agriculture	0.8	0.3	0.2	0.0
	Collieries	10.8	5.1	1.9	0.7
	Industry	45.3	35.4	19.6	7.8
	Rail and water transport	15.6	9.4	0.2	0.1
	Domestic	38.1	36.0	20.2	8.9
	Public services	5.8	4.1	2.9	1.8
Total direct consumption		116.5	92.5	45.8	19.3
GRAND TOTAL		202.6	199.8	156.8	123.5

*estimated

Source: Digest of Energy Statistics, HMSO

The trends in energy use which were apparent by the early 1980s are likely to be maintained until the end of the century. Total energy consumption is expected to remain at around the 1980 level until the end of the decade. Demand is then expected to rise, with supplies of oil and natural gas from the North Sea meeting most of the increased demand. Coal consumption is likely to remain constant at around 100 million tonnes a year or less, and will thus supply a declining share of the market at least until the year 2000 (Robinson and Marshall 1981). Within this picture the consumption of coal by the electricity industry and the siting of coal-fired power stations will play a major role in determining the distribution of coal production. The oil and natural gas industries are likely to make an important contribution to the pattern of industrial development in the UK in the 1990s as they provide important growth points for industrial development (Odell 1979).

I.2   Coal

Coal-mining is the archetype primary industry for the geographer. It suffers from high weight-loss in use since the energy it yields has no significant weight and leaves behind a residue of waste ash. It is tied to fixed locations since it can occur only at the coalfields. It has a high weight-output per employee and needs high-capacity, bulk transport if it is to be carried any distance at an acceptable cost. Its geographical distribution has been considerably influenced by taking advantage of economies of scale and by mechanization. Because of the size of the industry and the national importance of its production, it has suffered from having to balance direct economic return against maximum public good in national and regional economies. Having a much longer history of major development, it has had to deal with a greater inheritance of obsolescence than the other energy industries. Since 1960 it has had the unenviable task of dealing with massive innovational change while experiencing continual contraction of output.

Coal resources The coal resources of the UK occur as layers or seams, in those sedimentary rocks laid down in the Carboniferous geological period which have survived to the present day as coalfields. Structural conditions vary considerably between these coalfields in a generally consistent way which has considerable effect on the geography of the cost of mining. The peripheral coalfields of the north and west suffer most from adverse geological conditions and the central coalfields, extending south from N Yorkshire to the S Midlands, suffer the least. In the peripheral coalfields not only is there much more faulting and folding on a major and minor scale, but variations in coal-seam thickness are much more frequent. In the central coalfields the more uniform conditions allow greater efficiency of mechanized mining and make forward planning and control easier, thus lowering production costs per tonne of coal mined (table 4.3).

TABLE 4.3

NCB Deep-mined Coal Production, by Areas, 1970–80*

	Output (million tonnes saleable coal)		%		Change %	Costs per tonne (£s)	Numbers employed† (000s)	
	1970	1980	1970	1980	1970–80	1980	1970	1980
Scottish	11.4	7.7	8.4	7.0	−32.4	37.2	29.7	20.5
North East	19.2	14.1	14.2	12.9	−26.6	37.0	47.8	32.9
Western	14.7	11.2	10.8	10.2	−23.8	36.5	31.4	22.7
S Wales	11.9	7.7	8.8	7.0	−35.3	51.4	38.6	25.8
N Yorkshire	9.7	8.5	7.2	7.8	−12.4	33.3	17.0	15.4
Doncaster	8.2	7.2	6.1	6.6	−12.2	36.4	17.4	16.7
Barnsley	7.9	8.3	5.8	7.6	+5.1	33.5	18.2	15.6
S Yorkshire	9.6	7.4	7.1	6.7	−22.9	36.0	20.6	16.9
N Derby	9.9	8.3	7.3	7.6	−16.2	28.3	14.7	12.3
N Nottingham	12.3	12.0	9.1	10.9	−2.4	27.9	18.6	18.4
S Nottingham	10.7	8.8	7.9	8.0	−17.8	31.0	16.6	15.8
S Midlands	10.0	8.4	7.4	7.7	−16.0	33.3	16.6	16.8
UK	135.5	109.6	100	100	−18.9	34.9	287.2	229.8

*figures are for the financial years ending March 1971 and March 1981
†wage-earners on books at end of financial year

Source: NCB

The past history of coal-mining also contributes to an understanding of the spatial distribution of the industry. Those areas with coal occurring at or close to the surface, especially near the coast, were the earliest to experience mining on a large scale. Today such areas have the most depleted reserves and also the oldest and generally the smallest collieries. In contrast, where the coal lay deepest or was concealed beneath more recent rocks, mining developed much later. The collieries in these areas have tended to be larger and with more modern layouts. In the first group are the peripheral coalfields of Scotland, Wales and NW and NE England. The newer areas where deep mining has spread are in E Durham and the eastern areas of the Yorks., Derby and S Midlands coalfields.

Estimates of the amount of coal available for mining in the UK vary according to the criteria which are used. What is clear is that at current rates of production of around 120 million tonnes a year, there is sufficient to last for at least two more centuries. How much of this will ever be extracted depends not so much upon the quantity available, as upon the circumstances prevailing in the future when mining decisions are made.

The coal resources and the coal-mining industry of the UK were nationalized in 1947. Since then the National Coal Board (NCB) has controlled all coal production. It operates all but the smallest deep mines, employs contractors to work open-cast mines and licenses small private mines employing no more than 30 men underground to extract coal on payment of fees.

The geography of the deep mining of coal has undergone continual change since nationalization. Closure of collieries to reduce production in line with declining demand caused considerable alteration of the patterns through the 1970s and into the 1980s. Since it exploits a wasting resource, however, even in decline the industry has had to have a continual programme of investment to obtain access to new reserves to replace those being exhausted. By the 1980s therefore, most of the collieries even in the older mining areas had either undergone major reconstruction and redevelopment since 1947 or were new collieries. This dynamic process of renewal has also brought with it significant geographical changes.

At the national level the spatial distribution of coal-mining has undergone a radical shift. Total deep-mined coal output declined by 28% between 1960 and 1970 and by 18% between 1970 and 1980, but the decline was not evenly distributed between regions. As table 4.3 shows, between 1970 and 1980 output from the peripheral coalfields of Scotland, Wales, the NE and the Western Region declined by more than 23.5%, while the central coalfields extending south from Yorkshire to the S Midlands all declined by less than 23.5%. As a result of these changes, the deep mining of coal has become heavily concentrated into the central coalfields. Whereas in 1960 they produced only 46% of deep-mined output, by 1970 this had risen to 58% and by 1980 to 63%. This trend is expected to continue or even accelerate in the rest of the 1980s. A major contribution to this trend will be made by the development of the previously unworked Selby coalfield underlying the predominantly rural area between Selby and York. Production here from the Barnsley seam alone is planned to reach 10 million tonnes a year by 1985 and to continue at that rate well into the next century. Access to the workings will be by five vertical shafts and two inclined drifts, with a total of 50,000 tonnes of coal a day raised via the drifts. The suitable geological conditions will allow the most efficient mining techniques and organization to be used, so that only 4,000 men will be needed compared with the 20,000 required in other coalfields in 1980 to achieve the same rate of output (NCB 1975; North and Spooner 1976). Also extending mining eastwards will be the development of the extensive coal reserves

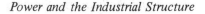

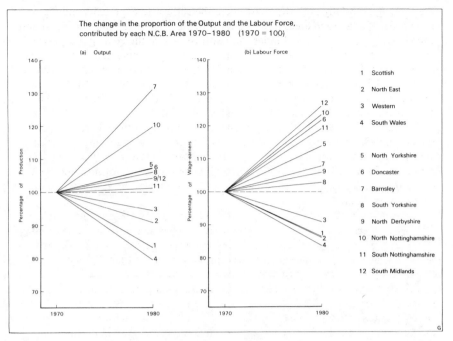

Figure 4.1   The change in the proportion of deep-mined coal output and labourforce
contributed by each NCB Area, 1970–80

discovered beneath the Vale of Belvoir between Nottingham, Grantham and Melton
Mowbray in NE Leicestershire. The reserves of coal here are in excess of 500
million tonnes, in six seams, at depths of between 400 and 500 metres beneath an
area 18 km long and 19 km wide (North and Spooner 1976).

Within individual coalfields there have been two major changes in the distribution
of collieries. In every case there has been a tendency for collieries located on the
long-worked, exposed outcrops to be closed and for production to become
concentrated on the deeper and concealed areas. In NE England for example, most
of the coal is now produced from the concealed coalfield in the east of the area and
mining has largely ceased in the exposed coalfield of the north and west. The other
feature has been the reduction in the number of collieries at a faster rate than the
decline of output. This has occurred because the output per man-shift has
increased, so fewer men and collieries can produce more coal. There has also been
an increase in the average amount of coal each colliery produces. The effect has
been to replace a pattern of a large number of small collieries by one which has a
much smaller number of larger collieries; the distances between collieries has thus
tended to increase (House and Knight 1967). These two changes also mean that
large areas within the geological limits of all the coalfields no longer have any
collieries and are not deep-mining areas.

The rate of geographical change has increased over time. Between nationalization
in 1947 and 1960, demand for coal remained high and there was little change in the
distribution pattern of deep mines, which occurred mainly through closure of
collieries when local coal reserves were exhausted. It was after 1960 and especially

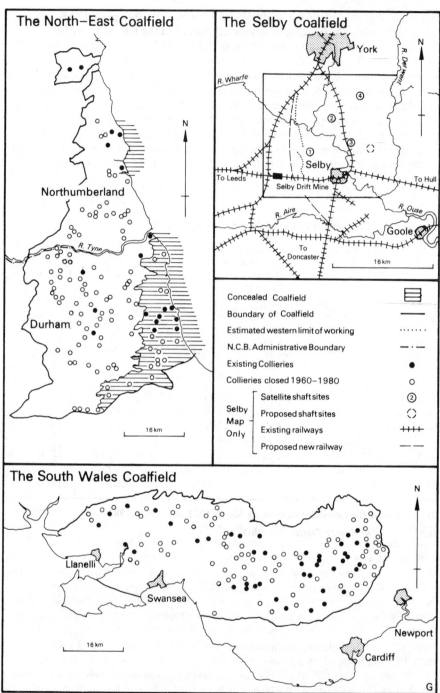

Figure 4.2   The distribution of collieries in the N East and Wales, 1960 and 1980, and of the mines being developed in the Selby Coalfield

after 1965, that the radical transformation of the pattern took place. This was mainly in response to changing economic conditions in the UK. The overall demand for coal fell rapidly in the 1960s as cheaper fuel-oil competed for the energy market. The rise in fuel-oil prices after 1973 reduced this competition. However, by then the availability of cheap natural gas was capturing much of the industrial and domestic consumption which otherwise would have been supplied by coal. These trends were reinforced by the increasingly efficient use of coal by large traditional users such as the steel industry. Other important traditional markets were lost through the dieselization of the railways in the late 1950s, the cessation of the manufacture of town gas when natural gas became available in the late 1960s and the change to more convenient fuels by domestic consumers especially in the 1970s.

TABLE 4.4

Productivity and Number of Collieries, by NCB Area, 1970–80[*]

	Output per manshift overall (tonnes)		No. of collieries in production at end of year	
	1970	1980	1970	1980
Scottish	1.93	1.92	32	15
North East	1.86	2.07	50	24
Western	2.13	2.55	28	21
S Wales	1.51	1.46	51	34
N Yorkshire	2.70	2.68	21	16
Doncaster	2.43	2.18	10	10
Barnsley	2.19	2.62	22	18
S Yorkshire	2.29	2.17	19	18
N Derbyshire	3.09	3.21	14	11
N Nottinghamshire	3.09	3.04	15	14
S Nottinghamshire	2.91	2.68	12	12
S Midlands	2.67	2.36	18	18
UK	2.24	2.32	292	211

[*]figures are for the financial years ending March 1971 and March 1981

Source: Digest of Energy Statistics, HMSO

With such strong competition the NCB reduced total coal output from 184 million tonnes in 1960 to 147m tonnes in 1970 and to 125m tonnes in 1980. These reductions in total output were achieved largely through colliery closures (table 4.4). Output from opencast mine production actually rose from 8m tonnes in 1960 to 15m tonnes in 1980. The geographical distribution of the colliery closures was influenced by other factors. Not all coal is alike. Certain markets require specific types of coal which are concentrated or sometimes found exclusively in the peripheral coalfields. It is also in the peripheral coalfields that production costs are highest so that high quality and high production costs are spatially correlated. The higher prices that can be charged for special quality coals partly compensates for this and as long as the markets remain for these coals output will be continued. Unfortunately, it is the specific markets for these high-cost special coals that have experienced the largest declines. It is colliery closures to cope with this fall in demand that are largely responsible for the contraction of deep mining in the peripheral coalfields. While the markets for special coals contracted, the consumption of coal for electricity generation continued to rise. It increased from 52.7m tonnes in 1960 to 77.9m tonnes in 1970 and 89.6m tonnes in 1980. Electricity generation does not need special coals since boilers can be designed and built to burn any type of coal. What is much more important for this market is not the quality of the coal or even the price per tonne weight, but the price of obtaining one unit of energy from the coal. In the UK the low cost of mining coal in the central coalfields means that although the coal produced there generally has fewer therms per tonne, the cost per therm of using that coal for electricity generation is much less than the cost per therm of using the higher-quality coals of the high-cost peripheral coalfields. It is this which has resulted in the increasing share of national output by the central coalfields.

What is less obvious from this account is why as much as one-third of the UK coal output still came from the high-cost peripheral coalfields in the early 1980s. The existence there of the special high-quality coals is certainly one factor. Transport costs are another. Of all the sources of energy, coal is probably the most expensive to transport. In the UK, transport costs on average add 12% to the cost of production. Distance thus protects the local markets of the high-production-cost coal from competition from coal brought in from other places (Manners 1971, 165). This has certainly been the case in Scotland and parts of Wales which are the remotest areas from the low-cost E Midlands and S Yorkshire coalfields. Similarly, output in NE England has been higher than it would otherwise have been because of the low cost of sending coal by ship to its traditional markets in SE England. It is the use of coal for electricity generation to supply local demand that has especially benefited from this protection in the peripheral coalfields. In Scotland most of the coal produced in 1980 was sent to power stations, in NE England two-thirds of output was used for this purpose and in S Wales about one-third. These figures are of considerable significance for the future of coal-mining in these regions. Total demand for coal for electricity generation is likely to decline from around 90m tonnes a year to no more than 75m tonnes in the year 2000 (Robinson and Marshall 1981). Beginning in the mid-1980s, about ten million tonnes of this coal will come from the new Selby coalfield. In the peripheral coalfields the high cost of coal means that it is uneconomic to transport it to generate electricity elsewhere. Much of the electricity-generating capacity in these regions reaches the end of its most productive life in the period up to 1995. If no new coal-fired power stations are built in these areas, electricity demand now being met from here will be supplied from other sources. This will cause consumption of coal from the peripheral coalfields to undergo further substantial decline.

Political factors have also been important in explaining the maintenance of so much deep-mined coal output in the high-cost areas. The government has always taken account of the fact that coal is an indigenous fuel and that in many parts of the coalfields coal-mining has long been the mainstay of local communities. Reduction of output has regional, social and economic repercussions of considerable significance. With these in mind, successive governments have taken measures to limit the rate of coal-mining decline and to ameliorate the local impact of colliery closures. In 1980 government grants to the coal industry amounted to £250 million of which £12m was for promotion of sales of coal to electricity generating boards.

The government also provided grants to stimulate conversion from oil to coal by industry (NCB 1981). Although this benefited all the coalfields, it is the high-cost areas that have most of the marginal units which would have gone out of production if such support had not been forthcoming.

With the political involvement must be coupled ownership. The geographical effect of planning and operating the industry as a whole since nationalization has been considerable. This allowed production and employment to remain at a much higher level and also ensured the availability of the investment funds which the industry needed to achieve these levels. This would not have been possible had the coal-mines remained as a large number of privately owned companies.

A final geographical feature of the deep-mining coal industry which has undergone significant alteration in a most obvious way, is the landscape of mining. Wherever possible coal is now raised via inclined drifts using conveyor-belts. These have a greater capacity than the vertical shafts with head frames and winding gear favoured previously. At many collieries, too, waste tips are no longer being created and old tips are being grassed over. This is because coal and waste are now raised together and then separated at coal preparation plants. The latter are often at locations separate from the mines and it is at the preparation plants that the waste-tipping thus occurs.

Opencast and private mining The deep mines of the NCB are not the only producers of coal in the UK. Private mines still operate under licence from the Coal Board. Since 1960 their output has not exceeded 2m tonnes a year so that their contribution is insignificant in a national context. Most of the output comes from S Wales, where it helps supplement production of high-quality steam and anthracite coals from pockets too small to make exploitation by the Coal Board worthwhile (Marnell and Humphrys 1965, 328). Opencast mining is much more important: output in 1980 was 15m tonnes. The mines are the responsibility of the Opencast Executive of the NCB who contract the actual extraction out to private firms. Most of the firms involved are well-known national construction companies, such as Wimpey and Derek Crouch, who have the expertise and the equipment available for the heavy earthmoving tasks involved. Opencast sites exploit mainly shallow seams down to about 100 metres, though they do extend to depths of 200 metres or more at times, and are thus normally located on the exposed coalfields, mainly along the outcrops. Any one site is temporary, with an average working life of around five years, seldom more than ten years. The average site covers 120ha and produces 200,000 tonnes of coal annually. Opencast mining has always been very profitable for the NCB and although production has never exceeded 15m tonnes a year, it could easily be increased substantially. With lower costs, opencast production would make coal much more competitive as a fuel than it is at present. One reason for restricted output is the agreement with the unions that opencast coal-mining be limited to that necessary to supplement the deep-mined output where the latter fails to meet the demand. Thus a large proportion of the anthracite consumed in the UK comes from opencast sites in western S Wales. Achievement of profitable deep-mined output there has always been difficult and opencast mining has expanded in supplementation. The present aim is to achieve and maintain opencast output at about 15m tonnes a year, but if controls on opencast mining were to be relaxed there is little doubt that output by this means could expand dramatically and the geography of coal-mining in the UK would undergo a further change.

I.3   Oil and Gas

More of the energy consumed in the UK now comes from the oil and gas fields of
the North Sea than from the coalfields beneath the land. This is a recent
phenomenon. The natural-gas fields of the UK sector of the North Sea were not
discovered until 1964 and the first major oil field was discovered in 1969. Oil and
natural gas together overtook coal as the main supplier of UK energy in 1970. For
much of the next decade, while the natural gas came largely from the North Sea
most of the oil used was still imported. Oil production from the UK sector of the
North Sea began in 1975 and it was not until 1981 that output first began to
exceed UK oil consumption.

Previous to the discovery of natural gas a major manufactured-gas industry had
grown up in the UK, having begun as long ago as 1812. This industry disappeared
in the 1970s and was replaced by the natural-gas industry with a completely
different geography. The changes accompanying the exploitation of North Sea oil
were much less dramatic, but by the early 1980s there were indications of much
more substantial geographical changes likely in the future.

Oil and gas resources

Britain has been an oil producer for a very long time. Oil was extracted from the oil
shales found west of Edinburgh from the early nineteenth century until 1961. For
much of the twentieth century small quantities of oil have been produced from the
oil wells of Dorset and the E Midlands. Recent findings indicate that the Wytch
Farm oil field in Dorset contains between 100m and 200m tonnes and is bigger than
some North Sea fields. Small quantities of natural gas in the form of methane have
also been drained from coal seams at some collieries, providing a lucrative income
for the National Coal Board. These small domestic supplies from the land were
eclipsed by the discovery of major resources in the North Sea beginning in 1964.

By the end of 1981, proven remaining recoverable reserves of oil beneath the
North Sea amounted to 1,125m tonnes and of gas some 739,000 million cubic
metres (Mm^3). Ultimately recoverable reserves, including those in likely future
discoveries, are officially expected to amount to as much as 4,000m tonnes in the
case of oil and to two million Mm^3 in the case of natural gas (Dept Energy 1981).
Odell and Rosing (1974) suggest that the potential recoverable reserves are likely to
be very much more than this. Even accepting the conservative official estimates,
the reserves are likely to meet most UK demands until the early decades of the next
century. In addition, some of the reserves discovered in the Norwegian sector of
the North Sea are being used to supply British needs.

Within the North Sea, the three main areas of discovery of oil and natural-gas
resources are the southern North Sea Basin, the central North Sea Basin and the east
Shetland Basin. The southern North Sea Basin contains the major gas reserves. The
gas there was originally formed in rocks of Carboniferous age, but has migrated
upwards into younger Permian sandstones. There it is trapped from further
upward migration and escape by impermeable layers of salt. The central North Sea
Basin contains major oil reservoirs. These are trapped in deposits varying in age and
type from Permian sandstones and Jurassic sands, to Cretaceous chalk and even
Tertiary sandstones. There the impermeable cap rocks are normally shales. The
richest discoveries of oil have been made in the east Shetland Basin where there are
large oil fields and gas accumulations at various levels. The main source rocks in

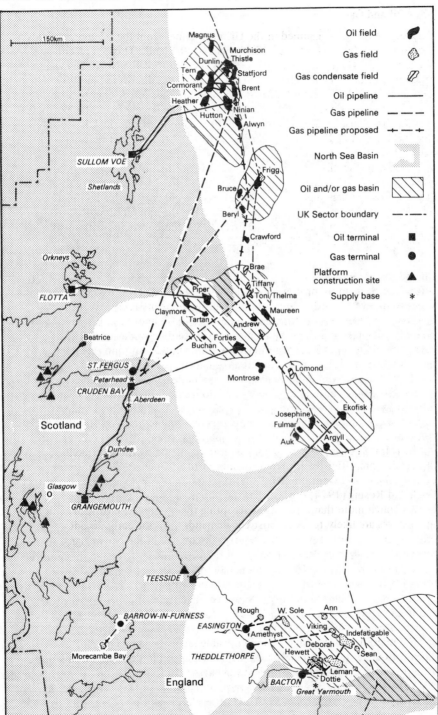

Figure 4.3   Offshore oil and gas fields and pipelines to the UK, 1980

which the oil and gas were formed there were Jurassic sandstones, with the reservoirs found mainly in Jurassic and Tertiary sands, again capped mainly by impermeable shales. The environment of the North Sea makes production of oil and gas very difficult. The oil- and gas-bearing strata lie at depths down to 4,000 metres below the sea bed, which is itself 90—400 metres below sea level. Technical limitations make it uneconomic at present to undertake production from areas where the sea is more than 200 metres deep. Even where the water is shallower, winds of up to 130 knots and 30 metre waves make operations hazardous and costly. Already four drill rigs have been lost through severe weather conditions. In addition, 10—20% may be added to the time taken to drill a well because of bad weather. With operating costs at around £35,000 a day in 1981, this is very expensive.

The British government leases areas in the UK sector of the North Sea to companies for exploration purposes. It also controls the level of taxation on the oil produced and participates in development through the government-owned British National Oil Corporation. The nationalized British Gas Corporation has a monopoly over the marketing of North Sea gas in the UK and negotiates long term contracts with the gas producers for the supply of gas for its needs. How much of the oil and gas will eventually be extracted will depend upon the financial return on the capital investment necessary and upon the relative attractiveness of the financial returns in the British sector compared with those from oil and gas fields elsewhere. The high cost involved in North Sea development, especially in the northern basins, means that, to be exploited, an oil-field must have large reserves to ensure an adequate return on the necessary investment. Already a number of smaller oil-fields discovered have been declared non-commercial because of this.

While most interest and effort has so far been concentrated in the North Sea, oil and gas fields may also exist beneath the seas to the west of the UK, from the Celtic Sea to north of the Hebrides. So far exploration has produced no significant finds, though gas is being produced from small finds in the Irish sector of the Celtic Sea. If finds are made, geological conditions suggest that they will be small in the Celtic Sea, while sea depths and severe winter weather conditions would deter exploitation north and west of the Hebrides.

The main geographical impact of the development of the North Sea oil and gas resources has been on two kinds of places and upon the oil-refining and gas industries. The effect on the industries is dealt with later. Most affected have been the places chosen as the service bases for the exploration and production out to sea. The second centres of activity are where the pipelines arrive onshore. Sometimes the two coincide. At the service centres the main impact has been the modifying and adapting of existing facilities to handle the needs of the new industry. This has included the extension of habours, the building of new jetties and storage facilities and the improvement of airports. New firms have moved in and all this activity has led to the growth of population and extension of settlements. This has often occurred in areas which previously had static or declining populations.

The place which has been most affected by such development and which illustrates the extent of the changes which can occur, is Shetland. The islands occupy a very convenient location as the closest land to the main discoveries in the East Shetland Basin. They also have natural harbours suitable for the building of service bases and terminals. Lerwick Harbour has been the main centre for exploration and servicing work, while at Sullom Voe the biggest oil terminal of its kind in the UK has been developed. Pipelines bring the crude oil here from the Brent and Ninian fields at the rate of about 600,000 tonnes a day (with an energy value approximately equivalent to one million tonnes of coal a day). At the terminal, any gas associated with the oil is removed to stabilize the oil ready for shipment. The terminal has large oil storage tanks, some of which are underground, and pumping facilities. Adjacent to the site are tanker loading jetties. A township houses construction workers and permanent terminal staff with their families. Around the airfield land has been reserved for future industrial development which might include an oil refinery and a gas liquefaction plant.

Two major problems associated with the development are the impact on the local community and the environmental impact. The Zetland County Council has carefully monitored and controlled the development taking place to ensure maximum benefit to the local people living in Sullom Voe. High wages are paid which has attracted people away from the traditional fishing, crofting and woollen industries. The environmental impact is also carefully watched. The construction of underwater pipelines can affect the shell fishing, especially around Yell Sound to the east. There is also the danger of oil spillage occurring. On land, removal of sand from beaches and of rock from quarries for construction purposes, needs to be monitored to minimize the effect on the interests of local residents. Agreement has been reached between the County Council and the oil companies to compensate local people for any disturbance they may suffer.

The benefits of the development include greater wealth for the area, better jobs for local people, job opportunities for young workers and improved air and sea links with other places. However, it must be remembered that unlike the traditional activities of agriculture and fishing which could go on for ever, the oil activities are likely to last for at most two generations. The question must always be asked — what happens when the oil runs out?

Oil Refining

The discovery and production of North Sea oil has had relatively little impact upon the geography of oil refining in the UK. This is mainly because of the nature and extent of oil-refinery development between 1960 and 1975, and partly because of the ownership and control of the refineries and of North Sea oil production.

Until 1975, British oil refineries were almost entirely dependent upon foreign imports of crude oil for their supplies. Before 1960 the oil was imported using small ships of up to 20,000 tonnes deadweight. Oil refineries were sited at convenient coastal sites which were close to industrial areas and large towns which provided large markets. After 1960, as techniques for building and operating large ships were developed, the size of the crude-oil tankers used to import the oil increased dramatically. By 1970 tankers of 250,000 tonnes deadweight were delivering imported oil to deep-water harbours such as Milford Haven. This development was accompanied by a rapid increase in the UK demand for oil. Consumption was confidently expected to continue to rise through the 1970s and 1980s, and large new refineries were built to meet this anticipated demand. Whereas in 1960 the UK consumed 40m tonnes of oil and had 50m tonnes of oil-refining capacity, by 1973 consumption had risen to 97m tonnes and refining capacity to 142m tonnes. After 1973, however, consumption declined and was only 71m tonnes in 1980. Refining capacity peaked at 144m tonnes in 1974 and then fell to only 130m tonnes by the end of 1980 (table 4.5).

TABLE 4.5

Distillation Capacity of Oil Refineries, UK, 1980[*] (million tonnes per annum)

Stanlow	16.8	Llandarcy	5.5
Fawley	14.0	Milford Haven (Gulf)	5.2
Kent[†]	10.4	Teesport	5.2
Coryton	9.5	Milford Haven (Amoco)	5.0
S Killingholme	9.4	North Tees	4.5
Pembroke	9.1	Belfast	1.5
Grangemouth	8.6	Ellesmere Port[†]	1.4
Milford Haven (Esso)	8.5	Eastham	0.5
Shellhaven	8.5	Dundee	0.3
Killingholme	6.0	Ardrossan	0.2
		Total	130.1

[*] at end of year
[†] closed 1981

Source: Digest of Energy Statistics, HMSO

Several factors influenced the way in which the geography of oil refining evolved as these changes took place. A major feature was the increase in the average size of refineries. In 1950 the largest refinery could process only 2.6m tonnes of crude oil a year. By 1975 there were five refineries capable of processing 10m tonnes or more a year and the largest, Stanlow, had a capacity of 18.6m tonnes. Thus as a result of economies of scale in both transporting crude oil and in refining, far fewer refineries were needed than would have been necessary twenty years previously.

Market attraction played a dominant role in the location of much of this refining capacity. It was built to process imported crude oil and so most of it was located at an import point as close as possible to markets. In some cases previously existing refineries were expanded, as at Stanlow and Grangemouth, while elsewhere new refineries were built, as at Fawley and Shellhaven. The largest market for refinery products has always been SE England, with Greater London having the largest single concentration of demand. It is hardly surprising therefore that the Thames Estuary together with Fawley on Southampton Water, had acquired over one-third of UK oil-refinery capacity by 1975. The new refineries built on Humberside to serve Yorkshire and the E Midlands, on Teesside to serve the North East, and at Belfast to serve N Ireland, all indicate the attractions of growing markets in these areas.

Transport economies also played a part in the changes in refinery distribution. The cost of using a 200,000 tonnes deadweight tanker per thousand tonnes delivered oil were only 80% of those of a 90,000dwt tanker and 50% of those of a 25,000dwt tanker. To take advantage of these economies, refineries had to locate at the few suitable deep-water harbours capable of taking the super-tankers, or to be linked with such harbours by pipelines. Both developments occurred. Three terminals capable of taking super-tankers of over 100,000dwt were constructed, at Finnart on Loch Long, western Scotland, Milford Haven in S Wales and the Rhos terminal in Anglesey. The first and last serve long-established refineries at Grangemouth and Stanlow respectively, by pipeline. Milford Haven attracted four refineries with a combined refining capacity of 28m tonnes. An oil terminal there also serves the

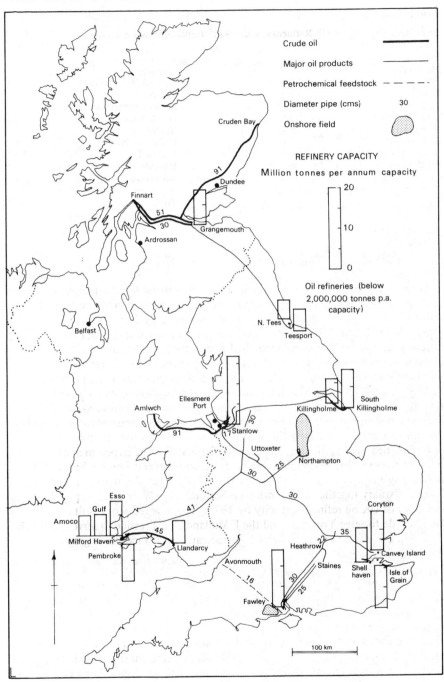

Figure 4.4   Oil-refining capacity and oil pipelines, UK, 1980

5.5m-tonne capacity Llandarcy refinery at Swansea, 130kms to the east by
pipeline. In this way the changes in transport were taken advantage of to bolster
some older refineries in the north and west. It also explains the major refinery
developments at Milford Haven with its deep water and shorter haulages from
extra-European oil-fields, counteracting to some extent the market attraction of the
east of Britain.

While market attractions dominated the oil-refinery distribution pattern,
government policy also played a part. Nearly 70% of the new refinery capacity built
in the UK after 1960 was located in Development Areas. The site attractions in such
areas were reinforced by the grants and tax incentives available, which were very
important because of the very large capital investment needed to construct an oil
refinery. Earlier, strategic considerations were taken into account when Llandarcy
oil refinery in S Wales was sited in 1921 and when Heysham in N Lancashire was
selected as a refinery site during the Second World War.

TABLE 4.6

Fuel Oil Consumption, UK, 1970, 1973 and 1980 (million tonnes)

	1970	1973	1980
Steel industry	5.1	4.4	1.5
Chemical industry, including petrochemicals	2.4	3.6	2.3
Other manufacturing industries	12.1	10.5	6.0
Gas-making	0.2	0.2	–
Electricity generation	11.9	16.6	6.3
Other public utilities	0.1	–	–
Non-manufacturing industries	2.1	1.6	0.8
Non-industrial central heating	4.2	2.7	1.8
Oil refineries	6.5	7.6	6.6
Total	44.6	47.2	25.3

Source: Digest of Energy Statistics (1981), HMSO

The development of the North Sea oil resources had little impact on the
geography of oil refining in Britain in the 1970s. There are several reasons why this
is unlikely to change until the 1990s. The most important is that the beginning of
North Sea oil production coincided with the onset of an economic depression and
with a substantial fall in the demand for oil in the UK. Refinery capacity already
built in anticipation of continuing increases in consumption was not now required.
There was no justification for building new refineries in the east of the UK to take
North Sea oil. In fact, refinery capacity was reduced through reductions at some
refineries and closure of others. The largest reductions took place between 1975
and 1981, at Stanlow from 17.6 to 16.8m tonnes, Shellhaven 9.2 to 8.5m tonnes,
Fawley 17.3 to 14.0m tonnes, and Llandarcy from 7.5 to 5.5m tonnes. Over this
same period refineries were closed at Heysham, in N Lancashire, Isle of Grain in
Kent, and Ellesmere Port near Liverpool. At the time of their closure they had
refining capacities of 0.7, 10.4 and 1.4m tonnes respectively. A second reason for
the limited impact of North Sea oil was the nature of the oil being produced. The
British market uses relatively large amounts of heavy oil products (table 4.6), such
as fuel-oil, and less of the lighter fractions, such as kerosene and gasoline. Thus

heavy crude oil is preferred as feedstock at the refineries since it gives a more suitable yield. The heavy crude oils are imported from the Middle East and the refineries were specifically designed to take them. North Sea oil is generally much lighter, yielding a different and less appropriate mix of products, more suited to the N American market. Since light oil commands a higher price, it is profitable to export the North Sea light oil and import less expensive heavy crude. This again makes new refineries unnecessary. It is for this reason that in 1980, of the 78m tonnes of crude oil produced from the UK/North Sea oil-fields, 39m tonnes were exported and the rest refined domestically (table 4.7). A final factor is likely to be

TABLE 4.7

Disposals of UK Crude Oil, 1980

Destination	Million tonnes		Million tonnes
W Germany	13.2	Denmark	2.5
USA	6.8	Norway	1.5
Netherlands*	6.1	Other countries	2.9
Greece	3.1		
Sweden	2.7	Total exports	38.8
		UK Refineries	39.3

*includes oil for transhipment to other destinations

Source: Digest of Energy Statistics (1981), HMSO

more important in future. Odell (1979) pointed out that because of the surplus of refining capacity and the product mix demand in the UK, new refineries to process North Sea oil will only be built in response to government policy or because of ownership of oil-field production. The governments of most oil-producing countries are anxious to promote domestic refining and the export of products rather than crude oil. This allows the economic benefits of refining, including jobs, value added and taxation, to accrue to the oil-producing nation. The UK is likely to follow suit, especially as the bulk of crude-oil exports are to nearby European countries which could be served with refined products just as easily from the UK. Any new refineries built in response to this will almost certainly be along the east coast of Britain, close to where the oil is landed. Ownership plays a part, in that much of the oil production is in the hands of companies with existing UK refining capacity and they will want the oil to be used in their own suitably modified domestic refineries. Where producing companies do not have UK refineries, then either they will want refineries built to process the crude or they will be encouraged by the government to do this. It is these companies that are likely to be the first to construct new refineries in NE England and E Scotland, causing a change in the distribution of refining capacity. Because of the lead time necessary in building refineries, this new refining capacity is not likely to appear until the late 1980s at the earliest.

Distribution

For distribution, oil products move in increasingly smaller quantities until the final consumers are reached. Because of economies of scale, and especially the large proportion of total costs that are taken up by terminal costs of loading and unloading, the aim is to retain cheaper bulk movement as far as possible. The cheapest means of movement are by water and by pipeline, and both are used in Britain in addition to road and rail. Deliveries are usually made direct to customers located within about 100 km of a refinery. For bulk consumers with rail facilities, these deliveries are made by the trainload. Where justified by large continuous demand, oil pipelines are used. For example, pipelines carry refined products from Stanlow to the Manchester area, from Fawley to Staines and Heathrow airport, and from Llandarcy to the giant Port Talbot steelworks. The oil pipeline network in Britain has grown as individual markets have expanded sufficiently to consume continuous flows of oil products. In 1969 a 394 km pipeline was opened, feeding refined products to N London and the Midlands from refineries and installations on the Thames and Mersey, and another was completed in 1973, from Milford Haven to the Midlands and Manchester. These were in addition to the various specialized pipelines carrying petrochemical feedstock from some refineries to petrochemical complexes. Since 1969 the tonnage of refined petroleum products transferred by pipeline in the UK has exceeded that going by rail. For other consumers delivery is normally by road, but since road transport is the most expensive per tonne-km, bulk oil depots are established to serve customers beyond the refinery supply area. Here physical geography plays a part. The UK has a long coastline compared with area, and all but a very few of the oil refineries are on coastal sites. In addition, few industrial markets in Britain are more than 100 km from navigable water. Depots can thus be sited close to markets, yet be supplied by cheap water transport.

I.4   Gas

Public supply of gas in the UK first began in 1812 and for the next 160 years most of the gas used was manufactured from coal. In 1949 the industry was nationalized, allowing considerable rationalization in production and distribution. In 1964 the first commercial bulk deliveries of natural gas from the Sahara were received and in 1965 the first productive gas-well was discovered in the UK sector of the North Sea. In the next ten years the UK came to depend almost entirely upon natural gas. The inherited industry based on manufactured gas disappeared and the new natural-gas industry took its place. Not only were the gas-making plants scrapped but a new national gas grid was developed. Most of the old pipes used to distribute low-pressure manufactured gas to consumers were replaced by new pipes capable of handling natural gas under high pressure. Gas-burning appliances had to be converted to use the higher-calorific-value natural gas, or were replaced. By 1975 the British public-supply gas industry had become essentially a wholesaler rather than a manufacturer as it was before.

The first pipeline to bring gas ashore from the North Sea was completed to Easington, Humberside in 1967. Since then additional pipelines have been laid to terminals at Bacton, Norfolk; Theddlethorpe, Lincolnshire; and St Fergus, Grampian. Production has been maintained at around 40,000 Mm^3 a year since 1976, at which level production could be maintained into the next century. Until 1977, most of the gas used came from the fields in the southern North Sea. In 1977, gas from the northern fields, including the Frigg Field which is partially in the Norwegian sector, began to be used when a pipeline was completed to St Fergus. A new gas-gathering system is planned to be operating by the late 1980s to bring gas

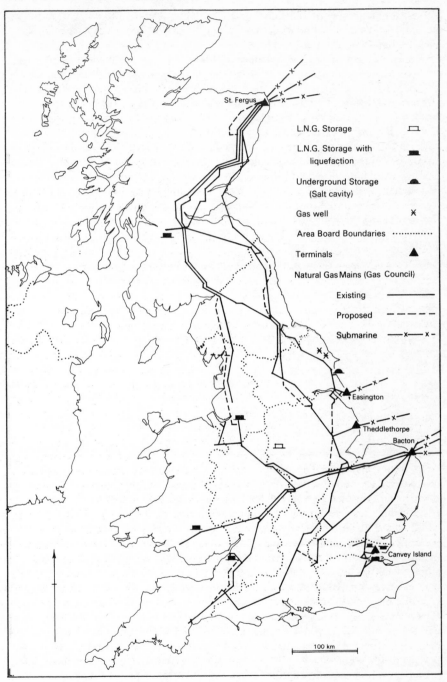

Figure 4.5　The national natural-gas transmission grid, UK, 1980

ashore from a number of additional northern fields, again to a terminal at St Fergus. Before then, a new pipeline will also be piping gas shore from the Morecambe Bay Field to Barrow-in-Furness, Cumbria.

The advantages of gas as a fuel are that it is cleaner to use and can be controlled to a fine degree. Unlike coal or oil, it does not require customer storage facilities. Compared with electricity, however, it has suffered in the domestic market because virtually every home in the UK is already wired for electricity for lighting purposes. Gas has to be provided as a separate service and is essentially competing with other fuels for the space-heating market. Until the 1960s most houses in the UK did not have central-heating and depended upon coal fires for heating. The arrival of cheap natural gas in the late 1960s coincided with the rapid adoption of domestic central-heating and the move away from coal as a general fuel for industry. Gas sales doubled between 1960 and 1970 and more than doubled again by 1980 (table 4.8). By 1980 gas accounted for 53% of domestic fuel consumption and is expected to rise to 60% by 1985 (British Gas Corp. 1981, 25).

TABLE 4.8

Sales of Public Supply Gas, GB, 1970 and 1980* (million therms)

	1970	1980
Domestic	3,653	8,163
Industrial	1,704	6,513
Commercial	702	1,794
National and local government	74	266
Total	6,133	16,736

*years ending March 1971 and March 1981

Source: Digest of Energy Statistics (1981), HMSO

Geographical patterns The changeover from manufactured to natural-gas supplies necessitated the construction of a national natural-gas transmission grid, to replace the local and regional gas grids which had previously been incompletely integrated. In designing the system, the need to operate pipelines at 80% or more capacity continually to be efficient, was important. Unfortunately, gas demand fluctuates seasonally and if pipelines capable of meeting peak demands are laid they would operate well below capacity for much of the time. The obvious solution is to have storage facilities near the markets to meet peak demands (fig. 4.4), with the pipelines capable of meeting base- and middle-load demands. A supplementary technique is to have interruptable supply contracts with large industrial consumers, for which they receive special rates. Both methods are used in Britain. The pattern of the national natural-gas transmission grid is strongly influenced by the geography of demand. Allowing for the sources of supply being off the east coast of Britain, the pattern of the grid coincides closely with other national network patterns of motorways, trunk railways and the electricity supergrid, and for the same reasons. They all conform to the pattern of maximum demand. Over 70% of the gas sales in the UK occur in a belt 60 km wide each side of a straight line through London and Manchester. In 1980 the gas regions with sales in excess of 1,500 million therms in descending order of magnitude were North Western, N Thames, E Midlands and W Midlands.

The development of the North Sea gas resources has so far had little impact on the distribution of industry in the UK. This is mainly because of the non-spatial pricing policy adopted by the National Gas Corporation. Clearly, other things being equal it is cheaper to supply gas to consumers close to the terminals in the north and east of Britain. Yet this is not reflected in differential prices. The costs are largely evened out across the country, so that there is no significant advantage in gas prices from locating in one area compared with another. Unless this is changed gas prices will not influence locational decisions (Odell 1979).

I.5 Electricity

The first public supply of electricity in the UK dates from 1881. From its earliest days the industry has been subject to some degree of public control. In 1926 the government set up the Central Electricity Board to construct and operate a national grid interconnecting individual power stations. In the succeeding twenty years this resulted in generation and transmission being increasingly coordinated. In 1948 all municipal and private undertakings, other than those in N Ireland, were nationalized. The generation of electricity in England and Wales was put in the hands of the Central Electricity Generating Board (CEGB), who were made responsible for transmitting the electricity they produced in bulk to the twelve separate Area Electricity Boards. The Area Boards were made responsible for the distribution and selling of the electricity to consumers in their own areas. In Scotland, the North of Scotland Hydro Electric Board and the South of Scotland Electricity Board both generate and distribute electricity. In N Ireland a joint electricity authority was set up in 1967 to coordinate electricity generation. The electricity is sold in bulk to the Belfast Corporation, the Londonderry Corporation and the Electricity Board for N Ireland, who distribute it to local consumers.

Between 1945 and 1975 the electricity industry experienced three important changes affecting its geography. On nationalization in 1948 the first change was to centralized control and ownership. This had its main impact on the pattern of electricity distribution, since electricity generation has been publicly coordinated since 1926. The second change was in the mix of fuels used for electricity generation (table 4.1).

Coal has always been the most important fuel used to generate electricity in the UK. In 1980 it accounted for 77% of all the fuel used. Between 1955 and 1974 fuel-oil became increasingly important because it was relatively cheap. In the 1970s oil prices rose dramatically, reducing its competitiveness, so that by 1980 it contributed less than 10% of the fuel used compared with 26% in 1974. Natural gas was another competitor for coal in the early 1970s, but rising demands from other users caused use by the electricity industry to fall to less than 0.5% in 1980. The hydro-electric potential of the UK is very limited and is never likely to contribute more than about 2% of needs. Even this is more than the 1.7% share it had in 1980.

Much more important is nuclear power. Britain pioneered the use of nuclear power for commercial electricity generation, when the first large-scale nuclear power station at Calder Hall in Cumbria began to supply electricity to the national grid in 1956. By 1980 11 commercial nuclear-powered stations had been built, contributing 11% of fuel used, and four more stations were nearing completion. These developments have altered the pattern of public-supply generation stations since the locational considerations which apply differ between the different fuels.

The third major change was the continual increase in the demand for electricity in the UK. At nationalization, output capacity was 11.8 thousand megawatts (11,800MW) and sales amounted to 39 thousand million kilowatt hours (39GWh). Subsequent growth is shown in table 4.9, where it can be seen that output capacity and sales more than doubled between 1950 and 1960 and increased by nearly 90% between 1960 and 1970. In the 1970s demand fluctuated, though with a general upward trend. Peak consumption of 240GWh was reached in 1979. The 1980 figure of 230GWh, though lower, was still 16% more than the 1970 figure. Massive investment to meet increases in demand allowed much more rapid modification of the geographical patterns of the industry than would have occurred had demand risen only slowly.

TABLE 4.9

Electricity Supply and Consumption, by Generating Regions, GB, 1950–80

Division	1950 TWh sent out	TWh received	1960 TWh sent out	TWh received	Division	1980* TWh sent out	TWh received
London	9.1	5.2	11.7	8.8			14.8
S Eastern	2.2	2.6	5.4	6.5	SE	22.8	13.9
Eastern	2.6	4.3	6.6	10.1			22.5
S Western	1.9	1.6	4.1	3.9			10.3
Southern	1.5	2.8	5.4	8.5	SW	40.9	19.8
S Wales	2.8	2.8	6.7	6.0			9.8
Midlands	5.8	5.2	9.2	11.0	Midlands	70.6	19.7
E Midlands	3.5	3.9	14.3	8.4			17.7
N Western	8.7	8.3	14.9	15.5	NW	24.0	18.3
N Wales	0.1	0.6	1.2	1.7			13.9
Yorkshire	6.1	5.1	15.0	11.0	NE	53.5	20.0
N Eastern	2.9	3.2	8.6	6.1			13.1
S Scotland	3.4	3.8	6.4	6.4	Scotland	26.0	17.8
N Scotland	1.3	0.7	2.4	2.3			7.8
Britain	51.9	50.1	111.9	106.2		237.8	219.4

TWh = terawatt hours (million million kWh)

*minor boundary changes mean that figures for 1980 are not directly comparable with earlier years

Source: Digest of Energy Statistics, HMSO

There are two ways in which the geography of the public-supply electricity industry has changed since 1960. The first is in the distribution of production facilities and the second is in the development of a national transmission grid for the movement of electricity in bulk. Change did take place earlier following nationalization, as is shown in table 4.9. In 1950, nearly 60% of British electricity production was situated within the axial belt of England stretching from Thameside through to Merseyside. At that time, power stations were located mainly in and around the major urban consuming markets. By 1960, as a result of different rates of growth in installed capacity in the different regions of the UK, this axial belt was providing only 48% of output while the E Midlands and Yorkshire had increased their share to 26%. The biggest changes after 1960 occurred in the period 1965—75. At the regional level there was a shift in the location of production away from markets, with new capacity being developed close to coal supplies and especially near the cheap coal sources of the east-central coalfields.

Despite the doubling of generating capacity between 1950 and 1960 and again between 1960 and 1980, the number of power stations underwent continual decline. This was one indication of the increase in station size. In 1950 the largest were rated at less than 200MW capacity. In 1963 the first 550MW generating unit was commissioned at High Marnam; in 1968 the first 2,000MW stations were brought into operation at West Burton and Ferrybridge; in 1980 there were twelve sites with over 2,000MW capacity and at one of these, Drax in Yorkshire, three generating sets each with a capacity of 660MW were in operation. The rate at which these changes took place was facilitated by the increase in demand, which was rapid until 1973 and which continued more slowly to the early 1980s. This encouraged the building of new stations using the latest technology at a more rapid rate than would otherwise have been possible. It also meant that the distribution of stations was more readily adjusted to the changing situation. Paradoxically, the much slower rate of growth after 1973 also hastened change, through earlier closure of older less efficient stations. Thus, whereas between 1970 and 1975 the number of stations fell from 291 to 261, between 1975 and 1980 it fell from 261 to 216. Closure of older stations and opening of new stations is a regular process because the normal life of any one station is about thirty years. In the first fifteen years of life they are usually relatively high in the efficiency list of stations and are run continuously to meet base-load electricity demand. In the next ten years they fall in the league table as newer more efficient stations are built, so that they are used to supply middle-load demand only. In the final five years they are so inefficient, relatively, that they are maintained on standby to supply peak demand only and at the end of their life may be switched on only two or three times in a year. It is stations in the latter category which were chosen for early closure between 1975 and 1980. The importance of minimizing generating costs through use of the most efficient stations is indicated by the high use of the latter. In 1980 over 75% of all the electricity generated for public supply in England and Wales came from the twenty oil- and coal-fired stations with the highest thermal efficiency in operation, plus the twelve nuclear power stations.

The increase in average size of generating stations and the concentration of production in only a small number of them was dependent upon improvement in the system available for bulk transfers of electricity around Britain. The limited 137kV grid inherited at nationalization was inadequate. By 1960 a new 275kV grid had been built which allowed freer choice in the best location for new power stations. Continuing growth in demand required even greater transmission capacity and in 1965 a new 400kV grid began to be built. By the end of 1980 there were 5,000kms of this 400kV grid available and 2,000kms of 275kV grid. These developments made the UK system the largest integrated power network in the

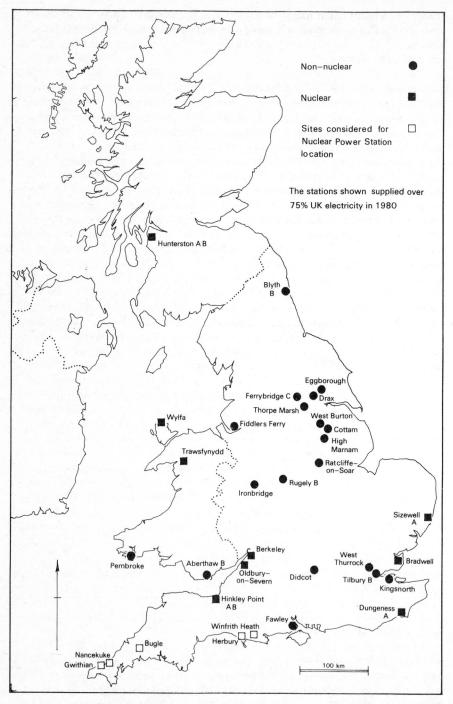

Non-nuclear ●

Nuclear ■

Sites considered for ☐
Nuclear Power Station
location

The stations shown supplied over
75% UK electricity in 1980

Hunterston A B

Blyth
B

Eggborough
Ferrybridge C
Drax
Thorpe Marsh
West Burton
Wylfa
Fiddlers Ferry
Cottam
High
Marnam
Trawsfynydd
Ratcliffe–
on–Soar
Rugely B
Ironbridge
Sizewell
A
Berkeley
Pembroke
West
Thurrock
Bradwell
Aberthaw B
Oldbury–
on–Severn
Didcot
Tilbury B
Kingsnorth
Hinkley Point
A B
Dungeness
A
Winfrith Heath
Fawley
Herbury
Nancekuke
Bugle
Gwithian

100 km

Figure 4.6   Electricity generating stations over 1,000 MW capacity and nuclear power
             stations, UK, 1980

world. As a result, what had been a set of separate regional supply systems was converted into a single system centred on a metropolitan-structured core in the central UK, with links to outlying city-structured systems such as those of the NE England and C Scotland.

Generation Although the explanation of the location of electricity generation is more complex than in the case of the other fuel and power industries, it is possible to recognize the more important factors involved. Transport economies have played a very important part in explaining the changes since 1945. At the time of nationalization, electricity generation was essentially market-oriented. At first sight this is surprising, since transmission of base-load electricity was then competitive with all other forms of land transport of energy over distances of about 80km. It was more efficient therefore to locate base-load power stations at the fuel supply and transmit the electricity to markets, than to put power stations at the market and carry coal supplies to them. In practice this had not occurred before 1948 because generating plant became obsolete so quickly. Technical improvements to make new plant more efficient took effect very rapidly as new plant was continually being built to meet the growth of demand. As a result, any one generator did not contribute to base-load electricity supply for more than a few years. For the rest of its useful life it was used to meet middle- and peak-load demand. But it was not economic to transmit middle- and peak-load electricity over any distance. In this situation even base-load stations were located near to markets, in the certain knowledge that the short-term loss of having them there would be offset by the gains in the longer term when they would be suppliers of middle- and peak-load electricity only (Manners 1971, 161–2). Nationalization changed this. In the late 1940s it was thought unlikely that any further substantial gains would be made in the efficiency of generating plants. To achieve further economies the industry now turned to minimization of transport costs and it was decided to build large new stations to meet base-load demands nearer to the fuel sources, which at this time meant the coalfields. The most attractive for this purpose were those of S Yorkshire and the E Midlands which produced the cheapest coal in Britain and were closest to the south of England and S Lancashire, where electricity demand was growing fast and already exceeded local generating capacity. These inland coalfields also had cooling water for power stations readily available nearby in the valleys of the Aire, Calder and Trent Rivers. It was for this reason that the S Yorkshire and E Midlands areas acquired such a large proportion of the new electricity-generation capacity built in the 1950s. At the same time, however, coal-fired power stations were also being built at some market locations. These were where the market lay close to a coalfield that could supply the fuel, or where coal could be supplied cheaply by water transport. Middle- and peak-load stations using coal were also built close to markets. In those cases it was cheaper to take coal to them than to provide and maintain the extra transmission capacity necessary if they were to be located elsewhere.

These trends in coal-fired power-station location were continued in the 1960s but with the addition of oil- and nuclear-fired stations. Most of the new oil-fired stations were built in areas where transport costs made coal more expensive. Within these areas they were built either near the major oil refineries which supplied the fuel-oil, as at Milford Haven, or on sites easily served by cheap water transport, as at Plymouth. Transport costs are much less important in the location of nuclear stations, which are used almost exclusively to supply base-load electricity; fuel transport costs are a minor element in their operation.

From what has been said already it is clear that market attractions play an important part in the pattern of power-station distribution in Britain. In 1948 the industry was very strongly market-oriented, both at the regional and national levels. Subsequently, although base-load stations were increasingly located closer to their fuel sources, installed capacity also increased at the market. For coal-fired stations this was mainly, though not exclusively, to meet peak-load demand as in the London region. The new oil-fired stations were fortunate in that they could usually obtain their fuel-oil from refineries located close to where the electricity was to be sold. They therefore show much greater market orientation than other forms of generation. For nuclear power, until the late 1960s, the stations were all located in areas deficient in coal, that is that were importing electricity from surplus areas. They were attracted to areas where transport costs made coal-fired electricity generation more expensive. In the late 1960s, however, it was decided to locate a new nuclear station at Hartlepool in the NE. As this was an area with high coal-production costs (table 4.3), this indicated a new trend in nuclear-station location. By the end of 1983 the four latest nuclear stations under construction at Dungeness B, Hartlepool, Heysham and Torness should be in operation. The decisions to build these were made in the late 1960s. Since then questions have been raised about the safety of nuclear power stations and about the cost of the electricity they produce. As a result although several possible sites for new nuclear power stations have been explored no firm decisions on further nuclear power-station construction had been announced by early 1982. Since the time it takes to build such a station is between ten and fifteen years no further nuclear-powered generating capacity can now become available in the UK until the mid-1990s.

Technological development has influenced the patterns in several ways. It was mentioned earlier that in 1947 it was thought the peak of efficiency of stations was very near and this was reflected in a pull to the coalfields. In fact this was not borne out in practice (Manners 1971, 166). Further improvements occurred which tended to reduce the attractions of the coalfield sites in the longer term, as explained earlier. Offsetting this to a certain extent were the economies of scale achieved, from less than 200MW capacity in 1950 to 2,000MW capacity twenty years later. The 2,000MW stations generated base-load electricity and were made possible by the availability of the grid by which their product could be distributed to wherever it was needed, since local demand could not consume all their output. Such developments reflect back on transport economies, since the larger the blocks of energy transmitted the cheaper the transport per unit becomes, and the larger the station the more efficiently it should operate in terms of thermal efficiency. It is technological developments also that have made nuclear power usable for electricity generation. The effect of this has been to locate more capacity nearer to markets than might otherwise have happened if coal and oil had remained the sole fuel sources. Nuclear power has heavy capital costs, making it much more suitable for base-load supplies. This strengthens the attractions of locations away from cheap-coal areas which were originally also base-load oriented. The first nuclear power stations to supply electricity commercially to the supergrid were Bradwell in Essex and Berkeley on the Severn estuary in 1962. The first is located in the heavy electricity-importing areas of the Eastern Region; the second is close, in grid terms, to the heavy demands of the W and SW Midlands. Hinkley Point and Oldbury in the lower Severn estuary reinforced this pattern in the mid-1960s, and Trawsfynydd and Wylfa (1971) on Anglesey helped to supply the NW and Merseyside areas where Heysham (1982) is also located. In Scotland, Hunterston in Ayrshire is suitably placed to supply the Clydeside conurbation which has been a deficit area for electricity since the 1950s (Hauser 1971).

Finally, government involvement has played a role in location throughout the development of the electricity industry. To the control provided in the setting up of the Central Electricity Board in 1926 was added public ownership in 1948. The centralization of ownership gave freedom for the national organization of the industry not fully possible under the mixed ownership which existed previously. From 1948 planning was able to take advantage of national rather than just intra-regional locational advantages. It was this central planning of the industry on a national scale which allowed concentration of production on the cheap coalfields, and of nuclear and oil-fired power stations at the nationally advantageous places. Apart from centralizing ownership, the government also indirectly influenced location through its fuel policy. Sensitive to the social and economic problems associated with the coal industry the government has encouraged the continuing use of domestic coal. In the 1960s a fuel-oil tax was imposed to limit competition from oil. In the 1970s subsidies were given to coal used to generate electricity, and imports of cheaper coal from the USA and Australia were limited. The effect was to encourage dependence on coal, and to attract power-station capacity to where coal was available at an acceptable price. The government also influenced the pattern by financing the basic research necessary to make nuclear electricity generation a commercial possibility. Fierce arguments rage over the true cost of the electricity produced (Posner 1973, 89–105). It can be made to look dearer or cheaper than electricity from coal-fired stations, depending upon whether the government-financed research and development costs are included or excluded in the calculation. Either way it seems unlikely that nuclear power would have been supplying 13% of the electricity used in the UK in 1980 if government sponsorship of the development had not been on such a massive scale. This 13% would have had to come from other sources and stations located differently to the nuclear power stations in 1980.

Distribution The development of the fully integrated distribution grid in the UK reflects all the factors mentioned. Central control was essential for the full develop-ment of a national grid and this was contributed by the nationalization of the industry. Transport economies determined the grid pattern since, as was pointed out earlier, high-voltage lines are justifiable only where bulk movements are to be handled. They became necessary with the central decision to concentrate produc-tion in certain areas, from which large surpluses would have to be transferred. Markets also played their part in the grid pattern. The high-density areas of the grid are to be found within the largest consumption areas in what is now the metropolitan core of Britain, linking it with surplus production centres like the E Midlands. Technology has not really influenced the location pattern of the grid, except in so far as development of higher-voltage lines has minimized the number of transmission lines that would otherwise have been necessary.

II   MANUFACTURING INDUSTRY

II.1   Introduction

Since 1965 the manufacturing geography of the UK has been reshaped. Major
changes accompanied the fall in the total number of manufacturing jobs by nearly
30% from 8.6m in 1965 to 6.1m in 1981. The largest reductions, each of more
than a quarter of a million workers, took place in three industries which had been
prominent since the industrial revolution – metal-making, textile manufacture and
clothing production (fig. 4.7). These in turn had been concentrated in older
industrial regions, largely coalfield-based, where they dominated the local economic
structure. Their decline thus substantially modified regional patterns which had
persisted for so long that they were taken for granted. At the same time locational
trends which had been dominant for decades were overshadowed by new trends or
were simply reversed. Previously, manufacturing in the twentieth century had been
becoming increasingly concentrated in the central regions of the UK economy.
These were in the SE and Midlands, where most manufacturing was already located.
Since 1965 this tendency has been reversed. Manufacturing now shows a preference
for less industrialized areas and has been more spatially dispersed at the sub-regional
level. Even more striking has been the reversal of the drift to the cities. Whereas
before 1965 industry had been concentrating in the major cities and conurbations,
after 1965 it was these urban areas that suffered the largest manufacturing declines.
Instead, industry chose to locate in the suburban periphery of urban areas ranging
in size from the conurbations down to quite small towns. A final feature of the
reshaping was the growth in importance of large industrial enterprises and of foreign
ownership in UK manufacturing. Interplant linkage became more important, as did
spatial segregation of the different functions undertaken by manufacturing
companies. Both have geographical implications of growing significance.

The new patterns and trends began to emerge slowly in the 1960s when UK
employment in manufacturing fluctuated narrowly between a high of 8.6m (1966)
and a low of 8.2m (1968). In 1970 manufacturing employment began a period of
sustained decline. It fell to 7.2m in 1978 and then dropped dramatically to only
6.1m by 1981. The sheer size of the job losses after 1978 reinforced the new
patterns which had by then become obvious.

The main aim of this section is first to describe the main features of the new
patterns and how the changes came about, and then to present an explanation of
why they have appeared.

II.2   New Patterns

There are three important elements which together comprise the contemporary
geography of manufacturing in the UK. The first is the regional distribution of
industry. This includes the industrial structure of the nation as a whole and of the
regions into which it is divided, together with the way in which manufacturing
industry has been redistributed. The second is the systematic industrial geography
of the UK, dealing with the distribution patterns of individual industries. Finally,
there is the internal geography of individual firms, the sum of which is producing
spatial patterns of growing significance. In examining each of these elements in
turn, employment is used as the main measure because of its suitability for most
geographical purposes. The spatial association between changes in the distribution

of economic activity as indicated by employment, and the effects of those changes, is normally very strong. This is because most people in the UK live within about twenty kilometres of where they work. When other measures are used, such as industrial output, productive capacity or investment, the spatial association between changes in these measures and their local effects is much less strong. Employment figures also have the advantage of normally being much more readily available at various spatial scales than other measures. This must be qualified, however, because by 1982, the latest Census of Employment data available dated from 1978. Employment figures quoted for subsequent years are based on official estimates. All the employment figures are classified according to the 1968 Standard Industrial Classification (SIC).

II.3   Industrial Structure

(i)   National

In 1981 the UK had 6.1m employees employed in manufacturing, producing over £60 thousand million worth of goods every year. Moreover, over 77% of the goods and materials exported from the UK are manufactured. This makes Britain one of the most heavily industrialized large countries in the world. It is also one of the most dependent upon manufacturing for earning its living. In the previous sixteen years the numbers employed in manufacturing had undergone a remarkable decline, from 8.6m in 1965 to 7.2m in 1978 and then to 6.1m in 1981. Since the total employment in the UK in all economic activity fell by very much less, manufacturing

TABLE 4.10

Changing Structure of Employment in Manufacturing, UK, 1965–81

	1965		1978		1981*		% change 1965–78
	000s	%	000s	%	000s	%	
Food, Drink and Tobacco	795	9.3	704	9.7	633	10.4	−11.4
Coal and Petroleum Production	44	0.5	40	0.6	} 432	7.1	−9.1
Chemicals and Allied Industries	444	5.2	439	6.1			−1.1
Metal Manufacture	640	7.5	450	6.3	326	5.4	−28.4
Mechanical Engineering	1,075	12.6	932	12.9			−13.3
Instrument Engineering	162	1.9	150	2.1			−7.4
Electrical Engineering	819	9.6	760	10.5	} 2,743	45.3	−7.2
Shipbuilding and Marine Eng.	214	2.5	182	2.5			−15.0
Vehicles	863	10.1	753	10.4			−12.7
Metal goods	601	7.0	542	7.5			−9.8
Textiles	765	8.9	490	6.8			−35.9
Leather goods	56	0.6	38	0.5	} 712	11.8	−32.1
Clothing and Footwear	514	6.0	376	5.2			−26.8
Bricks, Glass, Cement etc.	342	4.0	264	3.6			−22.8
Timber and Furniture	293	3.4	256	3.5	} 1,204	19.9	−12.6
Paper, Printing and Publishing	616	7.2	540	7.4			−12.3
Other Manufacturing	319	3.7	328	4.5			+2.8
Total Manufacturing	8,562	100	7,252	100	6,050	100	−15.3

*provisional

Source: Dept of Employment Gazette

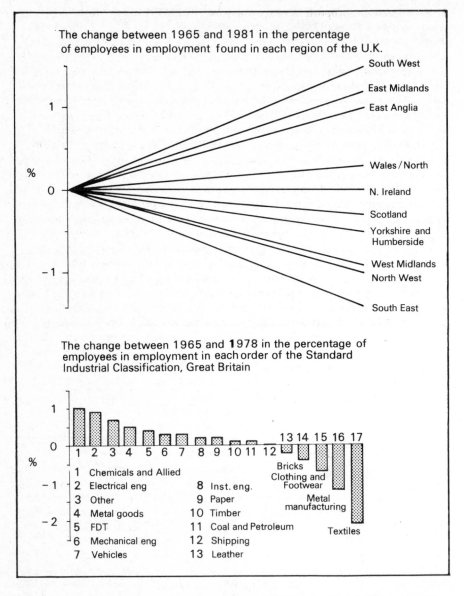

Figure 4.7   Percentage change of employees in manufacturing in (a) each UK region and
              (b) each Order of the Standard Industrial Classification, 1965–81

formed a declining proportion of employment. In 1965 it was as much as 37%, falling to only 32% in 1978 and to 29% in 1981.

Because every industry except Other Manufacturing showed a reduction in employment after 1965, the changing industrial structure of the UK economy tends to be masked. These structural shifts become apparent when the numbers employed in each industry are expressed as percentages of total employment (table 4.10). Of the seventeen industries into which manufacturing is divided by the Standard Industrial Classification, five suffered a relative decline in importance (fig. 4.7). All five had grown to major significance in the nineteenth century and are either concerned with processing or are labour-intensive industries. Processing industries are those which convert raw materials into a more useful form and they provide a declining proportion of employment in most developed countries. Where they are long established, they experience reductions in the numbers employed as capital investment results in marked increases in output per man; unless production expands at the same time, fewer workers become necessary. In the UK, both Metal Manufacture and Textiles provide good examples of this tendency, which also affects the Bricks, Glass and Cement group to a lesser extent. Clothing and Footwear, and Leather are labour-intensive industries. The relatively high cost of labour in the UK makes them vulnerable to competition from low-labour-cost countries. They have also been further adversely affected by increasing mechanization which has reduced the labour input needed per unit output. This has happened in the Footwear industry, for example, where natural leather has been largely replaced by moulded artificial materials which can be more readily handled by machines.

The industries which have increased in importance are, by contrast, largely the newer industries which are concerned with the fabricating and integrating stages of manufacturing (fig. 4.7). Fabricating involves taking processed materials and shaping them into their final form. For example the shaping of car bodies from sheet steel. Integrating is the assembly of shaped components to make a final usable product, as for example in the assembly of car bodies with other components to produce the finished car. Again all developed economies are tending to specialize in such industries and especially in those requiring sophisticated processes and high capital investment and/or skilled labour. The industries with the largest percentage increases in their total share of UK employment in table 4.10 illustrate this trend. They are the Chemicals and Allied products industries, the engineering industries, especially Electrical Engineering, and the Food, Drink and Tobacco Group.

(ii) Regional

It is reasonable to expect that the structural changes at the national level would be reflected in the pattern of regional change in manufacturing employment. Regions where industries suffering the largest declines are strongly represented would be expected to decline most. Regions with a greater proportion of more successful industries would decline least. This in turn would lead to some regions increasing their share of national manufacturing employment at the expense of regions with an adverse industrial structure. These suggestions are borne out to a certain extent by the experience of some British regions (table 4.11). Scotland, Yorkshire and Humberside, and the NW are regions where the textile and clothing industries are strongly represented, with the first two having concentrations of metal-making and mechanical engineering as well. Since Textiles and the Clothing industries together with Metal Manufacture accounted for over one million of the 2.6m jobs lost in the UK between 1965 and 1981, the declining fortunes of these regions is hardly surprising.

TABLE 4.11

Changing Regional Distribution of Manufacturing Employment, UK, 1965−81

Standard region	1965 000s	%	1978 000s	%	1981* 000s	%
South East	2,389	27.9	1,861	25.6	1,605	26.5
W Midlands	1,185	13.9	989	13.6	786	13.0
North West	1,252	14.6	998	13.7	825	13.6
E Anglia	167	2.0	201	2.8	175	2.9
E Midlands	620	7.2	600	8.3	511	8.4
Yorks. and Humber.	860	10.0	708	9.8	573	9.5
South West	422	4.9	427	5.9	383	6.4
Wales	311	3.6	312	4.3	239	4.0
North	459	5.4	419	5.8	341	5.6
Scotland	725	8.5	601	8.3	489	8.1
N Ireland	171	2.0	135	1.9	123	2.0
UK	8,561	100	7,252	100	6,050	100

*estimate

Source: Department of Employment Gazette

One of the effects of these structural changes was that the traditional domination of the older heavy-industry regions by a narrow range of palaeotechnic industries was markedly reduced. In some of these regions, industries which had remained the largest employers of labour since the early industrial revolution lost that claim. This is illustrated in table 4.12 by figures for the NW, Northern region and Wales. In the NW the Textiles industry, historically mainly cotton manufacture, which dominated in 1965 had slipped to third place by 1978 behind Vehicles and Mechanical Engineering and, with 109,000 employees, employed only 3,000 more people than the Food, Drink and Tobacco group. In Northern Region, Metal Making and Shipbuilding and Marine Engineering, which were the two most important industries in 1965, by 1978 employed fewer than the Mechanical Engineering and Chemical industries. In Wales, Metal Manufacture remained the largest employer but with a much reduced share of the total. In other industries the industrial structure of Wales was rapidly approaching that of the UK as a whole. Much of the change occurred as a result of differential decline. Nevertheless, the effect was to make these regions more similar in structure to the UK average. This in turn means that differences in industrial structure are likely to be even less influential in causing regional change in future.

II.4 The Changing Distribution of Industries

Accompanying the structural changes were changes in the regional distribution of the manufacturing industries. Three of the largest which experienced the most percentage decline between 1965 and 1978 were Textiles, Clothing and Footwear

TABLE 4.12

Percentage Employment in Manufacturing by SIC group, in the NW, North, Wales and the UK, 1965 and 1978

SIC Group	N West		North		Wales		UK	
	1965	1978	1965	1978	1965	1978	1965	1978
Food, Drink and Tobacco	9	11	7	7	7	6	9	10
Coal and Petr. Products	1	1	1	1	2	2	1	1
Chemicals and Allied	8	10	12	13	4	6	5	6
Metal Manufacture	3	2	14	10	32	24	8	6
Mechanical Engng	12	12	13	14	7	9	13	13
Instrument Engng	1	1	1	1	1	1	2	2
Electrical Engng	10	10	10	11	9	11	10	11
Shipbuilding and Marine	1	1	13	11	1	0	3	3
Vehicles	9	12	2	3	6	9	10	10
Metal Goods	5	5	3	3	7	7	7	8
Textiles	16	11	5	4	5	4	9	7
Leather Goods	1	1	0	0	1	0	1	1
Clothing and Footwear	7	6	7	7	5	5	6	5
Bricks, Glass, Cement	4	4	4	3	4	3	4	4
Timber and Furniture	3	3	3	2	2	3	3	4
Paper, Printing, Publ.	6	7	3	5	4	4	7	7
Other Manufacturing	4	4	3	4	5	7	4	5
Total Manufacturing	100	100	100	100	100	100	100	100

Source: Department of Employment

and Metal Manufacture (table 4.13). Textiles lost 275,000 jobs. The NW and Yorkshire and Humberside regions which shared almost 50% of the total Textile employment between them in 1965, had only 42% by 1978. During this period the E Midlands increased its share to take over second place from Yorkshire and Humberside and, with 108,300 employees in Textiles, had only 500 fewer than the NW in 1978. The next Census of Employment figures to become available will almost certainly show the E Midlands to have more Textile industry jobs than any other UK region. The Clothing and Footwear industry also experienced marked changes in regional distribution. The SE region recorded the largest decline in its share, with most other regions increasing their proportion. The largest gains were made by the peripheral regions of Scotland, Wales and the North and by Yorks. and Humberside. Metal Making showed only small changes and so these figures are not included in table 4.13. The largest change was in the W Midlands which increased its share from 23.8 to 26.4% of the total metal-making employment in the UK.

At the other end of the scale, Other Manufacturing actually managed to increase employment nationally, while Electrical Engineering and Chemicals and Allied Industries declined the least. In Other Manufacturing the SE and the NW were the major losers, while every other region except Scotland maintained or increased its share. The SW, Yorks. and Humberside and the E Midlands increased their share most. Though changing little in national employment, there were marked changes in the regional distribution of the Chemicals and Allied Industries. Again the SE and the NW experienced declining shares as did the North, though these three regions still accounted for nearly 54% of national employment in 1978. Wales and

TABLE 4.13

Distribution of Selected Industries, by UK region, 1965 and 1978 (%)

	Textiles		Clothing and Footwear		Other Manufs.		Elec. Engng		Chemicals and Allied	
	1965	1978	1965	1978	1965	1978	1965	1978	1965	1978
S East	4.3	4.1	28.0	19.8	36.6	29.3	41.1	39.3	31.6	29.0
E Anglia	0.4	0.6	2.7	2.5	2.5	4.1	2.1	2.4	1.6	2.3
S West	2.0	2.5	5.2	5.3	5.3	7.3	4.4	5.4	3.0	3.8
W Midlands	4.0	4.7	3.9	4.8	14.4	14.4	14.9	13.6	4.5	4.9
E Midlands	16.3	22.1	14.4	15.7	5.6	7.5	4.4	5.1	5.0	5.9
Yorks. and H.	23.1	20.0	9.3	10.7	4.0	5.9	3.3	3.4	7.9	7.9
N West	26.8	22.2	17.3	16.6	17.2	13.5	14.7	12.6	23.4	22.6
North	2.7	3.8	6.2	7.7	3.7	4.5	5.5	5.9	12.6	12.0
Wales	2.0	2.5	2.7	4.1	5.0	6.4	3.4	4.4	2.9	4.0
Scotland	12.1	11.3	5.4	8.5	5.0	4.9	4.9	6.2	7.0	7.4
N Ireland	6.3	6.2	4.9	4.3	0.9	2.1	1.3	1.7	0.5	0.2
UK	100.0	100.0	100.0	100.0	100.0	100.0	100.0	100.0	100.0	100.0

Source: Department of Employment

the SW, and again the E Midlands, all increased their shares the most. These trends illustrate not only the shifts in the regional distribution of different industries which have already occurred, but indicate trends which are expected to continue to the end of the 1980s.

(i)   Sub-regional Change

Prior to 1965 structural changes were used to show how most regional change occurred. Further analysis reveals that this is no longer possible. The influence of industrial structure can be measured by working out for each region the actual changes in employment in each industry, and comparing the figures with the changes which would have occurred if each industry had declined at the same rate as the industry in the nation as a whole. This has been done for the period 1965–78 and the results included in table 4.14. They show that for the W Midlands, Yorks. and Humberside, Scotland, N Ireland and the Northern region, the changes are within 5% of what could have been predicted using national rates of change. Shifts in the internal industrial structure of these regions and in the share they have of total national manufacturing employment, conforms with these structural trends. This cannot be said of the rest of the regions. The SE experienced a disproportionate loss of manufacturing; the E Midlands, E Anglia, Wales and the SW all made substantial gains. For most of the twentieth century the SE was growing and attracting manufacturing to a greater extent than most other regions. This was also true of the W Midlands, where industrial structure has played an important part in recent changes, but which also suffered a reversal of previous trends. The largest proportionate advances were in the SW and E Anglia; both were largely rural regions where manufacturing employment actually increased over the period when there was substantial national decline. The questions raised by these changes are best answered by changing from the regional to the sub-regional scale where other trends are apparent.

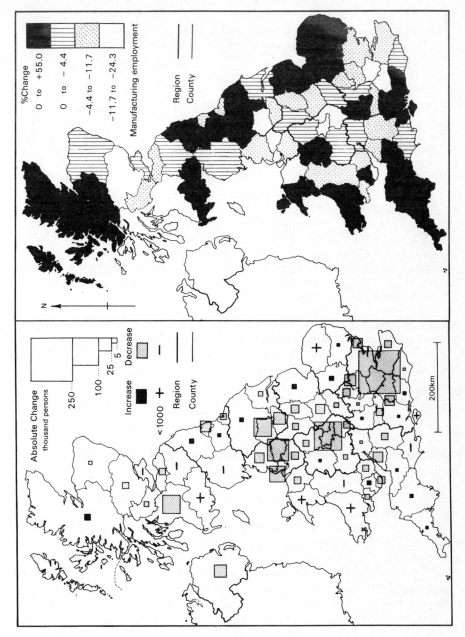

Figure 4.8   Manufacturing employment, UK sub-regions, 1971–6. *Source:* Keeble (1980)

TABLE 4.14

Sum of the Difference for each UK Region between the Actual Change in Employment in each Industry 1965 to 1978 and the Change if the UK Rate of Change for that Industry had Applied (000s)

		% of 1965			% of 1965			% of 1965
S East	−235	9.8	North	+23	5.0	E Midlands	+88	14.2
W Midlands	−27	2.3	Wales	+45	14.5	E Anglia	+58	34.7
N West	−52	2.2	Scotland	−14	1.9	S West	+64	15.2
Yorks. and Humber.	+18	2.1	N Ireland	+4	2.3			

Analysis of sub-regional changes before 1965 showed that even at a time of national manufacturing expansion, some ten sub-regions had begun to experience decline (Keeble 1976). These were Greater London, Glasgow, the sub-regions south of Newcastle and a cluster of sub-regions around Manchester. These losses were masked at the regional level by increases elsewhere in the same region more than offsetting the declines. The largest gains recorded between 1959 and 1965 were in fact in the sub-regions of the Midlands and in the Outer Metropolitan Area of SE England (Keeble 1976). The subsequent period 1966—71 saw the beginning of the decline of UK manufacturing employment, which has continued ever since. All the areas which declined earlier (except the sub-region south of Newcastle) lost even more jobs. More significantly, the previous areas of greatest growth in the Midlands and Outer Metropolitan SE England also began to decline. In contrast and despite the national declines, peripheral sub-regions were actually gaining manufacturing jobs, as were some areas close to the declining major conurbations. These trends continued between 1971 and 1976, as can be seen in figure 4.8. The data on this map is plotted using the post-1974 county boundaries which replaced the pre-1974 sub-regions for statistical purposes (fig. 1.5). A major feature of this map is that with the exception of Mid-Glamorgan, counties recording manufacturing gains after

TABLE 4.15

Manufacturing Employment Change, by type of UK Sub-region, 1959—75

Type of sub-region	Employment 1959 000s	Change 1959—75 000s	%
London	1,549	−586	−37.8
Conurbations	2,728	−434	−15.9
Major free-standing cities	1,827	+62	+3.4
Smaller free-standing cities	362	+64	+17.9
Industrial non-city	1,575	+255	+16.3
Urban non-industrial	110	+42	+38.8
Semi-rural	177	+78	+44.9
Rural	93	+73	+77.2
UK	8,421	−446	−5.3

Source: Derived from Fothergill and Gudgin (1979)

1971 were all traditionally non-industrialized areas. Overall, the map shows a redistribution of manufacturing, with rural or at least previously little industrialized sub-regions increasing their share. The extent of the shifts over the period 1959–75 is well brought out in table 4.15, where the data is classified according to type of sub-region. Later figures are not available in such spatial detail, but the regional trends described earlier and shown in table 4.11 suggest that they persisted at least until the early 1980s.

TABLE 4.16

Inner and Outer City Employments, UK Conurbations, 1952–76 (000s)

	1952	1963	Diff. as % 1952	1968	Diff. as % 1963	1973	Diff. as % 1968	1976	Diff. as % 1973
W Midlands									
Inner city	850	932	+9.6	890	−4.5	796	−10.6	748	−6.0
Outer city	272	360	+32.4	378	+5	443	+17.2	445	+0.5
SE Lancs									
Inner city	492	490	−0.4	441	−10	394	−10.7	378	−4.1
Outer city	308	342	−11.0	339	−0.9	352	+3.8	355	+0.9
Merseyside									
Inner city	477	508	+6.5	494	−2.8	428	−13.4	398	−7.0
Outer city	157	177	+80.6	204	+15.3	193	−5.4	186	−3.6
Tyneside									
Inner city	336	373	+11.0	368	−1.3	346	−6.0	341	−1.4
Outer city	103	110	+6.8	111	+0.9	118	+6.3	123	+4.2
Clydeside									
Inner city	564	568	+0.7	527	+7.8	464	−12.0	447	−3.7
Outer city	281	301	+7.1	305	+1.3	332	+8.9	326	−1.8
London									
Inner city	4,155	4,736	14.0	4,542	−4.1	3,892	−14.3	3,415	−12.3
Outer city	432	594	37.5	620	+4.4	682	+10	685	+0.4

Source: Danson, Lever and Malcolm (1980)

(ii) Urban-Rural Shifts

One final spatial trend which has received increasing attention since the mid-1970s relates not to regional and sub-regional shifts but to the urban decentralization of manufacturing. This has occurred at every urban scale from the conurbations down to small cities and towns. In the major cities and conurbations, the inner cities have been less favoured by manufacturing change than the outer city areas since at least as early as 1945. After 1963, table 4.16 shows that all the inner cities experienced continuing decline, with the outer cities either continuing to grow or declining at a much slower rate. The vast number of manufacturing jobs lost from the inner cities between 1963 and 1976 is striking. Because 60% of the total employment in inner cities is in London and 30% of the total employment in outer cities in the UK is in outer London, this one conurbation tends to dominate the overall picture. Nevertheless, the spatial trends for all the major conurbations included are remarkably uniform. While the changes are dramatic, the pattern must be kept in perspective. By 1976, despite the considerable changes in every case, there was still more employment in the inner cities than in the outer cities. In smaller urban areas similar changes took place. After 1945 new industrial estates and factories became a common feature of the urban fringe but were much less common within the pre-1945 urbanized areas. In the latter, older industry predominates, with increasing losses of industrial sites through redevelopment. Only in the later 1970s did the implications of such changes become translated into action and efforts were made to construct modern industrial buildings to replace those which had been, or were being, removed. Empirical evidence of these urban changes are to be seen in the contemporary landscape of any town or city in the UK.

II.5   The Geography of the Firm

The changes in the distribution of manufacturing already described are not the only spatial changes relevant for understanding the contemporary geography of manufacturing in the UK. The figures used represent the sum total of what is happening at the individual plant level. There has been growing awareness for some time that for a large part of British industry the understanding of geographical change requires also a knowledge of the internal structure and organization of individual firms. The continued growth in the size and importance of large multiplant enterprises in the UK has served to reinforce this point of view. By 1975–6 when there were just over 7m employees in manufacturing employment in the UK, just 12 UK firms employing over 65,000 workers each, had a total labourforce of over 1.3m (Watts 1980). By 1981 just 15 enterprises in this size category employed 1.7m out of a total UK manufacturing labourforce of 6.1m (table 4.17). A further indicator of the significance of large industrial enterprises can be gained from calculating the proportion of output in any one industry accounted for by the five largest firms in that industry. The results for a selection of important UK industries showed that in 1968 over 75% of output was accounted for by the five largest firms in the Vehicles, Food, Drink and Tobacco, Chemicals and Allied, Electrical Engineering and Metal Manufacturing industries. In addition,

TABLE 4.17

Industrial Enterprises Employing over 65,000 Employees, listed on the London Stock Exchange, July 1981[*]

	Employment (000s)		Employment (000s)
General Electric Company	188	Courtaulds	88
BAT Industries	177	Allied Breweries	84
BL	143	Dunlop Holdings	81
ICI	143	Unilever	79
Imperial Group	127	Associated British Foods	72
Thorn-EMI	126	Lucas Industries	68
British Petroleum	118	Bass	66
Guest Keen and Nettlefolds	93		
		TOTAL	1,653

[*] The list excludes certain enterprises for which employment information is not provided, most notably British Steel, Shell, Ford, British Aerospace. Enterprises mainly engaged in the service sector such as banks are also excluded here. Not all employees listed are employed in the UK.

Source: 500 Largest Listed United Kingdom Companies: A Supplement to the Stock Exchange Fact Book

it must be remembered that in many industries there are firms with relatively small numbers employed in the UK and which may not be one of the five major companies in any one industry, but which are owned by large multinational corporations. Examples include the French company L'Oreal (cosmetics), the Australian firm Berlei (clothes), the Japanese firm Sony (television receivers) and the American firm Borg Warner (automatic gears for vehicles). The geographical significance of the organization of all these multiplant firms stems from the implications for individual plant location and for regional socio-economic structure.

For location there are several relevant aspects. It is clear that for most multiplant firms the location of any one of its factories is likely to be strongly influenced by its relationship with the rest of the operations of the firm at other locations. The three main influences can be identified as (externally) the market, and (internally) materials linkages and control linkages. The market influence can be seen in a multiplant firm producing just one product. Each plant thus serves a spatially discrete market so that the whole of the UK is supplied. If it is decided to add another factory, an important factor in deciding its location will be where it can best be fitted in to the existing location pattern of other factories to achieve the maximum benefit (Watts 1978). An interesting example of this is the large brewing firm of Allied Breweries, which has established breweries in each of the standard regions of the UK. Internal materials linkages can be seen to be important in a firm where production is complex, with various components manufactured at different locations and then brought together for assembly. Here the location of any one plant will be strongly influenced by the linkages between the various stages of the operations carried out at different sites. A good example of this is the way the Ford Motor Company has established factories to supply components to the assembly plants it has built around western Europe. Thus the latest large-scale factories it has located are the engine plants at Bridgend in South Wales and in Valencia, Spain. The location of these plants is best understood in terms of the final assembly plants which they serve (Bloomfield 1981). The third element of internal structure which is important, is ease of access and contact between the headquarters from which control is exercised and the production plants. This is usually most important in young companies or where a plant is to produce a newly developed product. Close contact with the decision-makers and with continuing research and development may be necessary in both cases. In all three influences, it can be seen that a vital element is the geography of the multiplant firm rather than the geography of the industry. External factors are features which the geography of the firm is related to in this case, so that the individual plant cannot be studied in isolation from the other plants of the firm to which it belongs.

The significance of multiplant firms for regional differentiation stems from the greater likelihood of different functions of a firm being spatially separated in a large industrial enterprise. Norcliffe (quoted in Watts 1980) has suggested that five functions can be identified — administration, research, processing, fabrication and integration. Within these there is a hierarchy, with the first two forming control functions, monitoring and operating control over the other three which are production functions. The control functions normally require a higher proportion of those in professional occupations and of technically and/or scientifically skilled personnel. These are normally salaried, highly paid, white-collar workers. The production functions by contrast require a large proportion of less skilled and unskilled workers, wage-earning and relatively lowly paid, blue-collar operatives

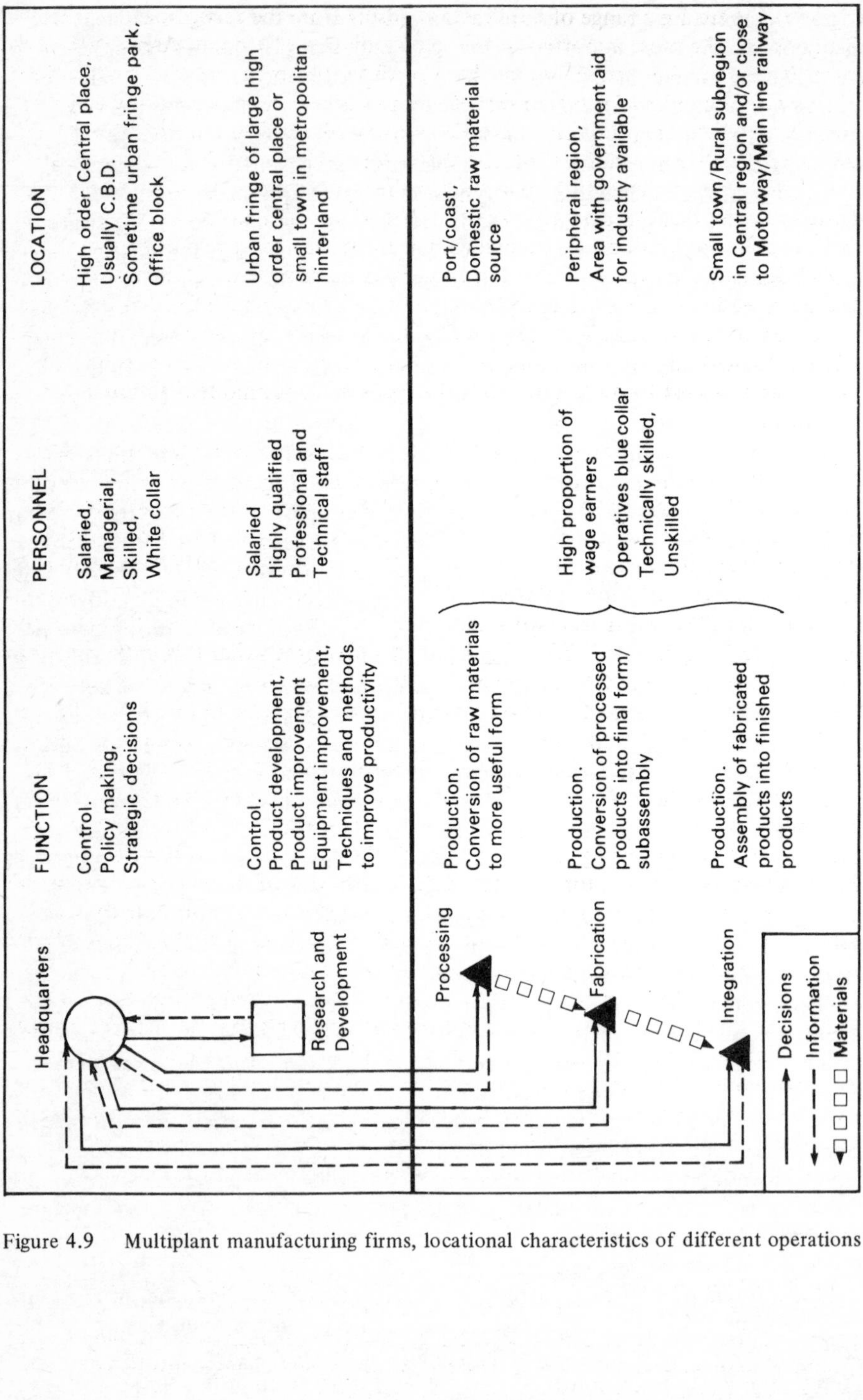

LOCATION

High order Central place,
Usually C.B.D.
Sometime urban fringe park,
Office block

Urban fringe of large high
order central place or
small town in metropolitan
hinterland

Port/coast,
Domestic raw material
source

Peripheral region,
Area with government aid
for industry available

Small town/Rural subregion
in Central region and/or close
to Motorway/Main line railway

PERSONNEL

Salaried,
Managerial,
Skilled,
White collar

Salaried
Highly qualified
Professional and
Technical staff

High proportion of
wage earners
Operatives blue collar
Technically skilled,
Unskilled

FUNCTION

Control.
Policy making,
Strategic decisions

Control.
Product development,
Product improvement
Equipment improvement,
Techniques and methods
to improve productivity

Production.
Conversion of raw materials
to more useful form

Production.
Conversion of processed
products into final form/
subassembly

Production.
Assembly of fabricated
products into finished
products

Headquarters

Research and
Development

Processing

Fabrication

Integration

Decisions
Information
Materials

Figure 4.9   Multiplant manufacturing firms, locational characteristics of different operations

(fig. 4.9). There are a range of implications arising from the recognition of these distinctions. The most important is the spatial division of labour. Areas, regions or towns having a higher proportion of the control functions of manufacturing industry will have a different social structure, with more workers in higher-income categories, than places which are primarily concerned with production functions. The nature and range of job opportunities will also differ for residents seeking local work in their home regions, depending upon the local manufacturing operations structure. There are two other important potential implications. The first is the suggestion that the main source of new entrepreneurs in the UK is that group of people with knowledge and experience of decision-taking and management. If such people are concentrated in certain areas, then those areas are likely to have a higher incidence of new entrepreneurial activity. Secondly, Watts (1981) suggests that where a head office is located distant from some of the plants, then it might show bias towards those plants nearest to it for new product expansion or for modernization investment.

The evidence available suggests that some of these features are now apparent in the UK. Thus of those UK manufacturing firms employing more than 5,000 people in 1975, 65% or more had head offices separate from their other operations. Most of these head offices were located in the major metropolitan areas. For example 93% of the separate head offices of firms employing 30,000 people or more were in fact located in central London (Watts 1981). A study of the headquarters locations of the leading 500 industrial companies in the UK in 1971–2 showed that 65% were in the SE region (Daniels 1975). Further evidence suggests that this increased in the subsequent five years (Goddard and Smith 1978). Examined from the production side, 86% of manufacturing employment on Merseyside and almost 60% of that in Scotland is in companies where the headquarters are in another region or country (Dicken and Lloyd 1981). The regional effects of these features in terms of differential occupational structure is much more difficult to establish, because of the nature of the occupation statistics available for the UK. Nevertheless, the evidence that is available tends to substantiate the existence of such differences. Frost and Spence (1981), for example, suggest that 'one of the important features of many of the Northern industrial and mining areas of the country was the over-representation of people occupationally classed as "labourers" within their industrial structures' (p. 94). Further support comes from a study of the regional consequences of the mergers and acquisitions by UK companies which have proceeded apace since 1960 (Leigh and North 1979). This showed that the process was leading to ultimate business control (and by implication more of the control jobs) becoming increasingly concentrated in the SE and London in particular, at the expense of the other regions in which were located the companies being merged or taken over. Clearly the geography of individual firms is a major element in the changing geography of manufacturing in the UK.

II.6 How Change has Occurred

The description of *what* has happened leads naturally to an analysis of *how* the spatial changes described have occurred. For this it is useful to identify two separate elements. The first is explicit spatial change, involving change in the numbers employed in a plant or in an area. The second is implicit change, involving qualitative changes in the manufacturing activity in a plant or area. This is usually but not necessarily accompanied by explicit change.

There are four basic ways in which explicit change in manufacturing employment can take place: (i) The opening or 'birth' of a new operating unit; (ii) expansion of an existing operating unit; (iii) contraction of an existing operating unit; and (iv) closure or 'death' of an operating unit.

The opening of a new operating unit may originate in several ways. It may be by a new firm first starting production or it may be by a firm operating elsewhere establishing a new plant. The latter includes those cases where the new plant is an additional operating unit, as well as cases where migration is incurred with closure of operations at one site and their transfer to a new site.

II.7   Explicit Change

(i)   Birth and Expansion

The most frequent source of firms entirely new to manufacturing is by individuals who have previously gained knowledge, skills and experience in a manufacturing industry establishing their own operations in that same industry. Not surprisingly such new firm formation is relatively high in industries characterized by small average plant size, where capital requirements are less (Swales 1979). Most such firms employ fewer than ten employees at their foundation and seldom grow to employ more than fifty people in their early years. They also have a relatively high death-rate and there has historically been a declining rate of creation of new firms in the UK. It is unlikely that this will change significantly despite increased emphasis on the encouragement of small businesses and of the indigenous growth of new firms under government policy since 1975. In the past the spatial distribution of new firms being formed has shown a marked concentration in the conurbations and especially in the W Midlands, NW and London. These are thought to be favoured by a wide diversity of manufacturing industry, a large number of manufacturing operations and a wide range of firm size, a large number of component suppliers and services, a choice of premises, a good supply of skilled adaptable labour, and good access to information and large local markets (Cameron 1980). More recently, however, the idea of the inner city being the major seed-bed of small firms has been replaced by the suggestion that the periphery of metropolitan areas is now a more important source of such activity (Danson, Lever and Malcom 1980).

A second source of new manufacturing enterprises, generating far fewer new manufacturing jobs in total, is the establishment of a manufacturing unit by a previously existing non-manufacturing firm. A simple example of this would be the opening of a factory to process and pack foodstuffs imported in bulk, by a major supermarket company. Backed by larger financial resources and a range of management experience, such new operations are normally larger from the beginning and are in many ways similar to branch plants opened by existing manufacturing firms.

Because of their small size and relatively high death-rate, births do not contribute a large proportion of new jobs in manufacturing. Their significance lies largely in their potential in some cases to grow into large employers, their contribution to diversification, and their likely increased importance in the 1980s as an indigenous source of manufacturing growth, during industrial depression when industrial movement has declined.

Most work on manufacturing change confirms that expansion of employment at existing manufacturing sites is the most important source of manufacturing growth in the UK. Evidence from a study of Berkshire, Buckinghamshire and Oxfordshire quoted by Keeble (1976) suggested that in that area, expansion accounted for 53% of growth. This is hardly surprising since, other things being equal, it is easier and often cheaper to expand existing operations than to move or to set up a branch operation. The direct impact of such expansion on the spatial distribution of industry is likely to be small. Indirectly it will cause change because of differences in industrial structure in different areas and through the internal geography of the firm, resulting in decisions on where to locate such expansion if a choice exists between various units of a multiplant firm.

(ii) Deaths and Contraction
Large-scale and widespread closure of manufacturing operations is a relatively recent phenomenon in the UK, gaining major significance for most areas only after the mid-1970s. Few studies of deaths have thus been carried out, but these suggest that this has been the most important source of decline in London and a major contributor to change in other conurbations (Gripaios 1977; Danson, Lever and Malcom 1980; Cameron 1980). In other areas and regions, until the end of the 1970s at least, more of the change was accounted for by structural decline and by differential growth than by deaths. Evidence on contraction is even less easy to obtain. Until 1979 closures and movement were much more important, with stable employment or expansion more frequent in surviving plants. The situation changed with the sudden increase in the rate of decline of manufacturing employment between 1979 and 1982. Since 1979 it is plant closures which have attracted most public attention. However, it is likely that reduction in the labour force at surviving plants will be shown to have made an even greater contribution to the declines when the necessary data becomes available.

(iii) Industrial Movement
The establishment of branch plants and to a much lesser extent the closure of operations at one site and their transfer to another site, have been an important element in industrial change in the UK since 1945. There are five phases which can be identified. Between 1945 and 1951 the shortage of new buildings led to many branch plants being set up in old premises and ex-war-production factories. Many of these were located in the peripheral regions of the west and north of the UK. In the 1950s, easing of building restrictions and the development of the New Towns led to shorter-distance movement of manufacturing firms from the conurbations to their outer metropolitan areas and few long-distance moves. In the early 1960s continuing overall national growth in manufacturing was coupled with the decline of heavy industries in the older industrial regions. This resulted in government regional policies which led to transfers and branch plants once more moving to the peripheral regions. From 1966 to 1972, the policies to help the older industrial areas suffering structural decline were strengthened and incentives to move increased. This resulted in a major flow of manufacturing to the Assisted Areas (AAs). From 1972 to 1979 major manufacturing contraction reduced the amount of movement, with short-distance moves once more becoming important. Since 1979 concern felt earlier about massive loss of manufacturing jobs from the conurbations led to attempts to help inner cities in particular and an emphasis on indigenous growth rather than movement. Statistics are not yet available for this

latest period, but table 4.18 shows the inter-regional moves which occurred between 1972 and 1977. Fig. 4.10 shows the amount and destination of moves from the SE and W Midlands, the two major originating regions during this period. The employment involved can be seen to be relatively small, though it is likely that the total will grow as the new plants develop and mature. It has been suggested that in practice the 'movers' can be divided into two groups (Keeble 1976), each with different characteristics. One group comprises the short-distance, usually intra-regional movers. These typically involve smaller plants, going to smaller towns, often complete transfers of operations concerned with making newer products with as yet unstandardized production techniques. They tend to employ a greater proportion of research staff and skilled workers in the fastest-growing industrial sectors. Most of this movement occurs within the central regions of the UK. Between 1966 and 1971 33% of all employment created by manufacturing movement was intra-regional (Keeble 1978).

TABLE 4.18

Openings of Manufacturing Units, UK Regions, 1972–7[*]

| | Source of units originating outside the region | | | |
| | From other UK regions | | From abroad | |
Region	Number of units[†]	Employment mid-1977 (000s)	Number of units[†]	Employment mid-1977 (000s)
North	67	6.7	21	1.4
Yorks. and Humber.	75	4.2	12	0.6
E Midlands	127	8.6	20	0.6
E Anglia	120	6.5	7	0.1
S East	43	1.9	60	4.0
S West	96	8.1	12	0.6
W Midlands	39	1.1	8	0.2
N West	67	3.9	19	0.8
Wales	105	7.0	23	1.6
Scotland	75	4.6	41	5.7
N Ireland	7	0.3	7	0.4
TOTAL	821	52.9	230	16.0

[*] units originating within each region are excluded
[†] surviving at the end of 1977

Source: Regional Trends (1981)

The second group is that involved with longer inter-regional moves, mostly to the AAs of the UK from the central regions, often of branch plants, larger on average in employment, using standardized techniques for mass-producing goods on assembly lines, employing a high proportion of unskilled or semi-skilled labour, often female. Most moves originating from abroad also fall into this group, and have been even more concentrated in the AAs of peripheral regions. Though recognition of the two groups is useful, it has been suggested that some intra-regional moves are simply

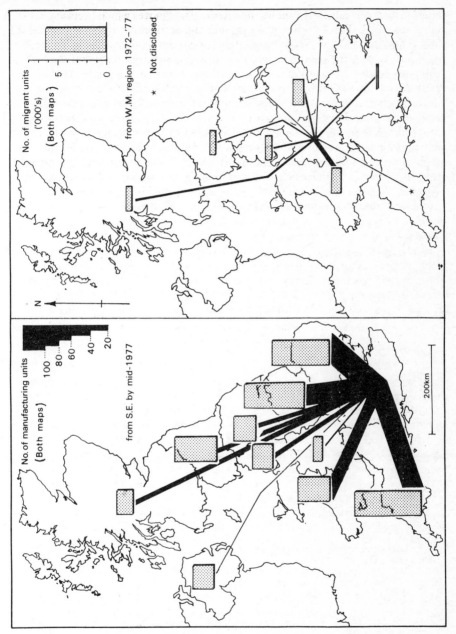

Figure 4.10   UK inter-regional manufacturing moves, originating in the SW and W Midlands regions, 1972–7. Data source: *Reg. Trends* (1981)

decentralization of the first kind to metropolitan satellites which are really extensions of the suburbs, while other moves are over longer distances (though still intra-regional) to small towns and the rural periphery of a region. There is some evidence, too, that the two types of regions compete with each other for some of the moves, so that there is some overlap in the groups (Sant, quoted by Townroe 1979).

As a result of studies of the 1966–71 period, Keeble (1978) concluded that industrial migration added to industrial decline in a few sub-regions, by far the most important of which were in the SE and W Midlands regions. Even so, the losses were only a small proportion of total job loss, around 10% at most. By contrast, the greater majority of sub-regions in the UK experienced net gains in manufacturing employment through industrial movement. Movement was particularly important in the peripheral sub-regions, over 40% of which had employment gains by move-ment greater than the amount of decline or growth of indigenous manufacturing (Keeble 1978). Though the amount of movement subsequently declined, it is unlikely that the general trends changed until after 1979, if then.

Finally, it must be remembered that estimates of the amount of employment generated by movement are likely to be too low. This is because some change allocated to indigenous industry may take place in firms which moved into an area before the beginning of the period being studied. Beyond that, the existing manufacturers may supply the needs of arrivals, expanding their employment as a result.

II.8 Implicit Change

Changes in the functions within an individual plant which constitute qualitative change may be very important to a particular area but are difficult to study. One indicator of such change is obtained by analysing floorspace statistics in con-junction with employment figures. This was done by Hamilton (1978) for the period 1964 to 1972. He revealed that except for London and SE Lancashire, the axial belt of the UK recorded very substantial increases in floorspace per manufacturing operative. Where this occurs it suggests considerable investment, modernization and in situ production expansion. In London, despite absolute declines in both employment and floorspace, there was a marked increase in floor-space per worker, suggesting continued innovation and higher labour productivity in the surviving industries. This contrasted with SE Lancashire, where the ratio remained virtually unchanged, indicating little capital intensification and invest-ment – a less healthy state. Sub-regional data showed that in the W Midlands, the NW, E Scotland and NE England, the largest increases in industrial floorspace per worker occurred in the greenfield zones between, or in the outer fringes of, the major urban areas. This indicated the attraction to such areas of space-consuming, modern, large-scale, assembly-line industries. The more rural sub-regions however, had only marginal growth in floorspace per worker, which is interpreted as the result of smaller, lighter, labour-intensive industry, moving out of traditional urban locations to these areas (Hamilton 1978).

Another way in which qualitative changes can occur without necessarily affecting employment numbers is through shifts in the nature of operations at plants. Opportunities for this are largely confined to multiplant firms. The most striking examples of such change come from the study of the effects of acquisition of one company by another. This has been a frequent occurrence in the UK since 1960. Such acquisition normally results in responsibility for long-term goals, investment planning, major capital investment and performance expectancy being withdrawn from the senior executives of the acquired company (Leigh and North 1978). In practice it was found that this led to the concentration of business control in the SE region as described earlier (Goddard and Smith 1978). Middle-management functions, essentially involving the implementation of top-level policy decided at headquarters, was usually left with the acquired company and so no spatial change in this occurred. It was also found that production normally expanded in acquired plants (Leigh and North 1978). Thus the net effect was overall expansion of employment at an acquired plant with growth of production functions masking loss of high-level executive and administrative responsibility or functions and of job opportunities at that level. In other multi-plant firms a study of a large sample revealed that alteration of the relative importance of different plants through time was usual, as a conscious decision about allocation of work. This tended to result in a spatial shift in production from inner city to outer city locations, or from larger to smaller towns. In some cases the premises left behind were then changed from production to non-production functions for the firms, by being used for research, offices or warehousing (Hamilton 1978). This, too, is how significant change has occurred to produce the contemporary patterns of manufacturing in the UK.

II.9 Explanation of the Patterns

Contemporary explanations of the spatial patterns and changes in the geography of manufacturing in the UK fall into three readily recognizable groups: those which see the external environment as exerting the main influence on the location of industry; those which see the internal environment of the firm and its operations as exerting the main influence on location; and those which seek alternative explanations based on explicitly ideological interpretations of society.

(i) The External Environment

The search for explanation in the external environment is a long tradition in geography. The classical location theories of people like Weber, Palander and Hoover aimed to show how spatial variability in the cost of such things as land, labour and capital, and the influence of transport costs, determined the locational choices of manufacturing industry. The basis of this kind of argument is that manufacturers will seek out, or be most successful at, locations where they can minimize the cost of the factors of production which they need. Studies have been made which demonstrate that there is such spatial variability in the cost of factors of production in the UK (Smith 1971). For transport it is obvious that added distance increases cost. However, Rawstron (1958) pointed out that because there are differences in cost does not mean that they influence location. They only become important in this context if the differences are sufficiently large to be significant in the total costs of production and distribution. He drew attention to the fact that for most manufacturing it is possible to identify the limits of an area within which production would be economically viable. Within these limits there is a wide choice of location for most industries, with difference in profits between the alternatives being relatively insignificant. In the case of transport costs, Gudgin

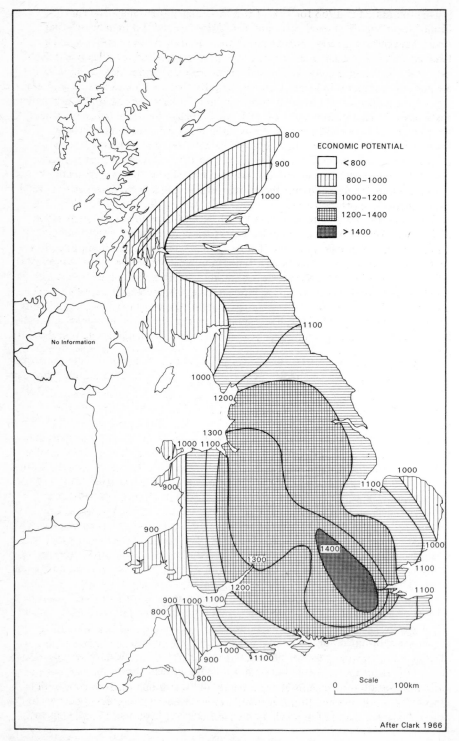

Figure 4.11   Economic potential, GB, 1960 (after Clark)

(1978) found that in 1968 for 75% of British industry the transport element formed less than 3% of total costs, and for 95% it formed less than 5% of total costs. Furthermore, a large proportion of these transport costs are likely to be fixed costs, such as loading and unloading and insurance, and less than half will vary with the distance goods are carried. Thus for many industries transport costs are not a *major* factor in location choice. Clearly there will be exceptions. Heavy weight-loss industries in particular need to minimize their raw-material transport costs, as in the case of iron and steel making. Similarly there are industries where the product has a low value per unit bulk, as in ready-mixed concrete, where transport costs bear heavily. But these can be considered as exceptions. The position now seems to have been reached, within the UK, where variations in the cost of factors of production and in transport costs need to be considered in reaching a location decision, but these variations are unlikely to determine the final choice made by most industries.

Two other external factors seem to have been of increasing importance in the period since 1965 in ways which differ from their earlier effects. These are market influences and external economies of scale. It has been suggested that under contemporary economic conditions a market location is now the 'norm' for modern industry. Locations other than near the market need to be explained by factors which prevent market location or by lower costs elsewhere which outweigh market attractions. Clark (1966) produced a map showing the geography of the market in Britain in 1960 (fig. 4.11). It is based on his concept of economic potential, which he defines as the sum of incomes in areas adjacent to a particular geographical point, divided by their distances from that point. The importance of proximity to market is not difficult to understand. A number of manufacturing industries are essentially consumer-oriented, either because of the perishability of their product, for example the making of fresh bread and the manufacture of local and regional newspapers, or because of the need for personal consumer contact, as in custom tailoring, or because of the bulk gains in manufacture or low value of the product, as in the example of soft drinks or made-up boxes. Though improvements in transport and the advantages of increased scale of operations have widened the locational choice of such industries, they still tend to be distributed roughly according to the distribution of population, with the largest number of employees where there is best access to the largest population concentrations and/or market potential. A further stimulus is growth of employment. This has occurred mainly in the service sector since 1965, and especially in larger cities, adding to their attractions for consumer-oriented industries. In this sense service-industry development can be thought of as stimulating manufacturing expansion. Before 1960 the effect of market attraction had been to ensure the maintenance of manufacturing in central cities and in inner city locations in many cases. Significant changes since then have contributed to the development of manufacturing in sub-regions around the periphery of the conurbations and in the more rural sub-regions, as described earlier. The most important single change has been the rise in importance of road transport. Manufacturing industry has turned increasingly from rail to road transport as the main method of moving materials to and from factories. At the same time the number of passenger cars on the roads has increased tremendously. The growth in the number of vehicles has outstripped improvements in the capacity of most urban roads to cope with them. The result is congestion, decreased average speeds and increased journey times. Locations within the previously urbanized areas have thus become less and less attractive. At the same time, the construction of the motorway system since 1960 has improved market access from peripheral locations close to the motorways. The attractions of such locations are further strengthened by their having wider labour catchment areas as a result of motorway availability. More and more workers travel to work by car, requiring car-parking space, often readily provided on extensive suburban or rural sites but not available at congested urban sites. Thus access to market is now better from a peripheral or rural location with proximity to a motorway, than from a city-centre location close to a rail depot where it was often best historically.

These new patterns have been reinforced by the effects of external economies of scale in manufacturing industry. For small factories there are external economies of scale to be obtained by clustering. In this way some of the services needed can be jointly financed, while others can be more easily provided. As important has been the fact that the development of clustered factories on estates makes industry more manageable for planners. Such estates are also cheaper to develop, an important consideration where publicly financed or privately financed estates are set up in advance of occupancy. Industrial estates became a familiar feature of the British industrial landscape after 1945, whereas previously they had been an exception. In the period up to 1965 it was the large industrial estates which appeared in largest numbers. These were located near large centres or at accessible journey-to-work points for sizeable numbers of people (Florence 1962). After 1965 it became much easier for Local Authorities to develop their own estates, and these tended to be very much smaller and more widely dispersed. The clustered estates, large and small, were generally built where land was available on the edges of urbanized areas with proximity to good roads or motorways. On these sites, too, have been located the wholesale distribution depots to which many manufacturers deliver and from which final distribution to the consumer takes place.

(ii)   The Internal Environment

Advocates of the importance of the internal environment of the firm in explaining industrial location argue that the external environment provides the conditions, but that the response to those conditions is determined by the internal nature and characteristics of the enterprise. They suggest that the same external environment will cause different responses by firms with differing internal characteristics. Hamilton (1967, 364; 1974, 32–41) has pointed out how locational decisions are affected by ownership, with individual and corporate ownership differing from each other and from state organizations in their location decisions. In particular, the private entrepreneur works within the context of satisfying his needs, usually from a single establishment. The corporation is generally aiming to optimize economic returns from a number of establishments. State organizations often have to operate within the constraint of contributing to national or regional economic needs as well as, or instead of, achieving economic returns from a particular operation. In 1945 the individual entrepreneur was common in UK manufacturing industry and many companies owned just one or two factories. Any one industry had a large number of controlling interests. This made agreement on rationalization and centralization of operations much more difficult. Individual entrepreneurs were frequently more concerned with protecting their interests as they perceived them, and the interests of their factory and workmen, than in any potential increase in economic returns. Subsequently the situation changed. Until the 1960s the changes were relatively small and mainly of two kinds. The first was state involvement: directly through nationalization, as in the steel industry, and indirectly by such means as allocation of defence contracts or state aid, as in aircraft production and shipbuilding. The second change was that much of the manufacturing growth was in new industries with strong corporate management. Multinational corporations became much more familiar in the UK and decisions were being taken on a large scale. Initially there was little geographical change as a result of these ownership and control developments. For the large new industries this was a time of expansion anyway, which limited the need for centralization. After 1960, however, there were obvious gains to be had by rationalization and concentration of production at a smaller number of factories. A spate of company mergers and amalgamations, and of large companies buying small companies, occurred and some small companies simply went out of business in face of strong competition. As a result many industries ended up with control centred in a small number of hands.

The need for such developments, to make industry more efficient and competitive, was recognized by the government in 1966, when they set up the Industrial Reorganization Corporation. Until it was abolished in 1971, this body gave financial aid to industries to encourage centralization and rationalization. Following the General Election of February 1974, public involvement in British industry once more increased. The *Industry Act* (1975) aimed to help regenerate British Industry by the development of new institutions. Thus the National Enterprise Board (1972) was set up to take the initiative in stimulating development in key sectors of the British economy, with the appropriate functions of the Board in Scotland and Wales carried out by the Scottish Development Agency (1975) and the Welsh Development Agency (1976). While similar to the Industrial Reorganization Corporation, the NEB can also take shareholdings in companies and has the power to initiate new ventures and to join with private companies in joint developments. It had vested in it existing government shareholdings in such companies as Rolls-Royce (1971) Ltd and Nuclear Enterprises Ltd. Under the *Industry Act*, public ownership was to be extended through community ownership of development land, the British National Oil Corporation and extension of public ownership in various sectors of British manufacturing. These developments of public ownership were severely limited following the election of a new government in 1979. Subsequent development was dominated by the further major contraction of manufacturing employment. This produced further rationalization, largely through a sharp rise in plant closures which accompanied deepening economic depression. The number of operating units in existing industries was reduced and production concentrated at a smaller number of factories.

A second important internal characteristic has been productivity, measured in terms of output per employee, which varies markedly from industry to industry. Smith (1949) pointed out that the further along the production chain an industry lay, the more labour-intensive it could be expected to be and the less important were raw materials in determining its location. He illustrated this point by showing that in 1935 the weight of materials used per operative per year was 1,762 tonnes in blast furnaces, 157 tonnes in steel-works and rolling mills, and only 9 tonnes in mechanical engineering shops (Smith 1949, 374). This still holds true for most manufacturing, with fewer people needed to manufacture a tonne of flour from wheat compared with the number needed to manufacture a tonne of bread from flour, or per tonne of nylon fibre compared with a tonne of nylon shirts.

Although the Census of Production no longer provides tonnage figures for various industries, some indication of the extent of these differences between heavy and light manufacturing can be gained by using instead the figures showing the value of gross output per employee (table 4.19). These show that growth in demand for consumer goods generates more employment per unit of output at the finishing end of industry than in the primary manufacturing stages. The geographical relevance of this is that the major concentrations of primary manufacturing industries in the UK were established early in the industrial revolution, and their location changed little before 1960. These palaeotechnic industries were mostly heavy weight-loss or bulk-reduction industries, and so were initially strongly attracted to those places which had available adequate supplies of raw materials and fuel and water. Thus primary iron and steel production was concentrated on the western and northern coalfields, textile-making located along the eastern and western flanks of the Pennines and in Scotland, brickmaking on the coalfields, and heavy chemicals were produced in the NE and Cheshire and linked with the coke and gas works on the coalfields. Most of these areas had previously been only sparsely inhabited and the new industries dominated the local economies (Rawstron

TABLE 4.19

Gross Output per Employee in Selected Industries, UK, 1974

	Gross output	Total employment	Gross output per employee	Region where this industry was largest % of manufacturing employment
	£ million	thousand	£ thousand	
Iron and steel (general)	3,474	242	14,355	Wales
Miscellaneous (non-electrical) machinery	665	88	7,557	E Anglia
General machinery engineering	1,070	171	6,257	South East
Grain milling	672	18	37,333	N Ireland
Bread and flour confectionery	813	140	5,807	N Ireland
Sugar (mainly refining)	392	13	30,154	*
Cocoa, chocolate and sugar confectionery	775	74	10,473	Yorks. and Humberside
Production of man-made fibres	715	45	15,889	*
Spinning and doubling on the cotton and flax systems	476	62	7,677	*
Overalls and men's shirts, underwear etc.	235	50	4,700	N Ireland
Paper and board	1,008	63	16,000	Scotland
Cardboard boxes, cartons and fibreboard packing cases	759	73	10,397	North West
Synthetic resins and plastics materials	1,192	52	22,923	North
Plastics products	1,048	121	8,661	E Midlands

*Not available

Source: *Census of Production* (HMSO 1974)

1964). Moreover, each region tended to specialize. Prior to 1945 while these developments were taking place there was little alteration in the distribution pattern of lighter manufacturing. This remained concentrated in central and southern lowland Britain, where it had been located previously, and where the largest concentrations of the population and hence of consumer demand remained. The only other manufacturing that was attracted to the heavy industrial areas was usually either directly dependent, such as textile-machinery manufacture in Lancashire and wagon works in Wales and Scotland, or served the local markets, making such things as confectionery or milk products. The survival of these patterns until 1945 influenced subsequent development. Productivity differences meant that increases in output generated most employment in the central and southern parts of the economy where the light manufacturing was concentrated. Much less employment generation accompanied increases in output in the peripheral regions, because of the dominance there of heavy industries with their higher gross output per man.

This was not the only way productivity made a contribution to the changing geography of manufacturing. Continuing improvements in manpower productivity have affected employment in the older heavy industries in particular. They suffered not only from having been developed much earlier, but also from the inadequate investment in modernization in the 1920s and 1930s. Thus they inherited per capita output rates well below what had been shown to be possible in other parts of the world. Newer industries were less affected, since they already incorporated much more advanced technology in their initial development, and so already had higher rates of output per man. All the heavy industries, however, both old and new, had higher manpower productivity figures than most light manufacturing. This meant that small percentage improvements in productivity in the heavy industries could cope with much larger increases in demand without increased employment than was the case in the rest of manufacturing. For most light manufacturing, rapid growth in demand contributed substantial growth in jobs. The effect of percentage productivity improvements in restricting employment growth were thus much greater in areas of heavy-industry concentration than in areas with concentrations of light manufacturing. In fact in some of the heavy industries the manpower productivity increases outstripped the rate of increase of demand for their products, so that they had to reduce employment even as production went up. Classic examples occurred in the S Wales steel industry. At Port Talbot, for example, steelmaking capacity was increased from 3.0 to 3.4 million ingot tonnes a year between 1968 and 1972, while the labourforce was reduced by over 30% from 18,000 to 12,500. Even in the newer heavy chemical industry, ICI doubled the value of its output at Billingham between 1946 and 1959, while reducing its labourforce from 15,000 to 14,800. A further effect of productivity differences was that where new primary processing industries were developed, their high productivities and capital-intensive nature meant that they required fewer employees. Though spectacular in terms of output or capital cost, such industrial developments generated fewer direct jobs in the peripheral regions, where they were often located, than the processing of their output generated in industries further along the production line towards the final consumer.

Finally, in the twenty years 1945—65 productivity differences between various industries contributed to the different rates of manufacturing employment growth of the various regions through the process of structural change. This was particularly true in the peripheral regions, where the decline in jobs was in such labour-intensive industries as shipbuilding, cotton and linen textiles. The new growth that did take place in these regions was frequently of capital-intensive industries which were the growth industries of the mid-twentieth century: steel strip mills and oil refineries in Wales and Scotland, synthetic textiles and petro-chemicals in Wales, electronics in Scotland, motor-vehicle industries in Wales and Scotland. As a result there were insufficient new jobs available to employ all the available labour. In Wales, for example, textile manufacture, mainly man-made fibres, which was expanding, had a net output per employee of £2,132, while railway carriages and wagon and train manufacture, which was contracting, had a net output per employee of only £1,380. Substantiating these comments are those statistics which indicate that, until the late 1960s, the peripheral regions of the UK had employment growth which was further behind the national average than their rate of growth of output. This showed that these regions were achieving a more rapid improvement of productivity than the country as a whole. Wales and N Ireland had above-average rates of productivity growth in the 1950s and 1960s; Scotland achieved improvements roughly equal to the UK average in the 1950s, but in the 1960s her annual growth of productivity was 3.6% compared with 3.1% for the nation as a whole (McCrone 1969, 160). In this situation these regions needed a higher rate of growth of *output* than the national average to achieve a rate of *employment* growth equal to the national average.

Until the Second World War, most new light manufacturing industry developed in the central regions of the UK and especially in and around the conurbations in those regions. In the years 1945–65, large numbers of new light industries also went to the older industrial regions, largely as a result of government policy. This industry was built to modern standards, usually with the latest equipment installed and used the most efficient production methods. By the 1965–82 period, therefore, the older industrial regions had a younger stock of modern light industry while the central regions tended to have older plants. While economic conditions were buoyant, both could survive. With the onset of economic depression in the 1970s, however, the newer best-practice plants, developed in the older industrial regions, were more likely to survive. It is likely that these differences were contributory to the differential declines described earlier. Despite the adverse economic conditions, even in the 1970s further improvements in efficiency were being achieved through new investment in existing plants. One indicator of this was the increase in floorspace per worker, analysed by Hamilton (1978). In restricted conurbation sites where expansion was difficult or impossible, the effect of such investment was to retain the same floorspace and thus reduce the labourforce. Restrictions on expansion in such locations, were added to by the difficulties in obtaining Industrial Development Certificates (IDCs). In the Development Areas and rural sub-regions of the UK, such physical restrictions on expansion seldom applied and IDCs were more readily obtained. Investment there usually resulted in expansion of floorspace, with the retention of the same number of staff or even expansion.

One important way in which the internal environment of manufacturing caused geographical change was through the improvement of internal economies of scale, especially in older industries. The inherited pattern of production in UK manufacturing in 1945 was essentially one of small-scale units. Even in iron and steel-making, no works had a capacity of more than one million ingot tonnes a year.

Textile manufacture was in a large number of small mills; although there were some large car works, most motorcar manufacture was in small factories, with output measured in hundreds rather than thousands of cars a year. In food production, for example, small family bakers still dominated bread output, and the few large breweries produced a small proportion of total output. One of the geographical implications of this state of affairs was that much more locational dispersion was possible. For a given output there were a large number of works and these could be, and usually were, widely dispersed. Being small there were a myriad places which had sufficient labour to meet their needs. Where such small factories employed several hundred people, they dominated the economy of the small places in which they were located.

Well before 1945 it had been recognized that there were economic advantages to be gained in many industries from large-scale operations. But achievement of these economies was usually by replacement of men by machines in order to obtain higher productivity, and usually also meant larger premises to cope with expanded output. Both required the investment of capital, which had been in short supply for much of the previous twenty-five years, and there were other inhibiting factors like the fragmented ownership discussed below. As a result, by 1945 all too few industries were taking advantage of the economies of scale thought to be available. Some increases in size of unit began to appear by 1955, but it was not until later that substantial changes occurred. This is brought out in table 4.20 where employment per establishment is plotted. In some cases growth was achieved by expanding output on existing sites, in others by building new green-field factories. Some industries had both. Until 1973, growth in the economy allowed these changes to be achieved by the large new units meeting the increased demand, while old factories continued in operation. In many cases, however, centralization occurred, with many smaller older units being closed down as output was concentrated in a few new larger factories, and this became more common when the economy stagnated after 1973. Classic examples occurred in the iron and steel and tinplate industries in S Wales (figs. 4.12a and b) (Humphrys 1972, 117–27). Some industries which were virtually new could start operating at the scale suited to contemporary conditions. This was particularly true of consumer-durable manufacture, such as the production of washing machines or television sets, and of such new industries as plastics and electronic equipment. The geographical effect of these changes was to reduce the total number of works needed for a given output. Where an old-established industry was involved this usually caused local changes only, though in some cases an entire industry was lost from a region. Output became concentrated into fewer but larger-scale production units. The effect of implementing changes to achieve these economies of scale normally meant increases in labour productivity, so that employment might be reduced even though output had increased. Good examples of these trends come from the flour-milling industry. Where an old geographical pattern has been modified, certain trends can be identified. Usually the larger newer works are located near a major urban centre, with the closures taking place in the smaller towns where the smaller, older works were located. Centralization has both geographical and economic connotations. Because of increasing scale of operations, the larger works or factories require better facilities for movement of materials and goods in bulk. They also need a large labour supply. This means locating in a large urban centre or at a point with a large enough journey-to-work hinterland to generate the quantity and quality of labour

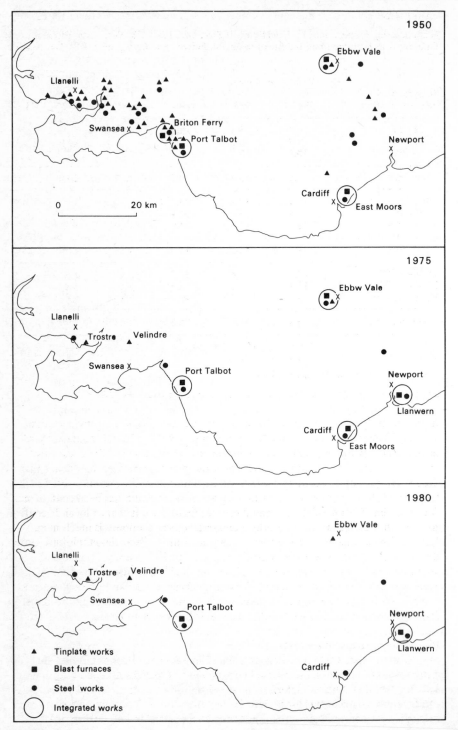

Figure 4.12a, b, c   S Wales. Iron, steel and tinplate industry, rationalization, 1950–80

TABLE 4.20

Manufacturing Employment by Establishment Size, UK, 1947–78: Percentage Distribution of Employees in Manufacturing Industries in Establishments Employing more than Ten Persons

Size-group of establishment	% total employees					
	1947	1955	1963	1968	1972	1978
11–24	4.0	3.4	4.8	4.4		
25–49	6.9	6.6	4.5		20.0	
50–99	10.5	9.7	8.2	11.3		
11–99	21.4	19.7	17.5	15.7	20.0	21.0
100–249	18.7	17.3	20.2*	37.0	32.2	
250–499	15.6	15.0	11.4			
500–999	13.9	14.6	14.0	14.0	14.9	
100–999	48.2	46.9	45.6	51.0	47.1	47.9
1,000–1,999	12.3	12.8	13.7	NA	NA	
2,000–4,999	11.4	12.3	13.2	NA	NA	
5,000 and over	6.7	8.3	10.0	NA	NA	
1,000 and over	30.4	33.4	36.0	33.3	32.9	31.1
	100.0	100.0	100.0	100.0	100.0	100.0

*Estimated, Census of Production, 1963

Source: Annual Abstracts of Statistics and Census of Production (HMSO)

required. In spatial terms the location requirements are now more specific and limiting. There are a smaller number of locations likely to be able to meet them; indeed many of the smaller, older centres do not meet these requirements. But extension of the journey to work, by use of the private motorcar, has meant that the former production centres could often be within travelling distance of the location of the large new works or factory where production has been centralized. A further implication of the increased economies of scale is that of local diversification. With the average size of works increasing, a local economy is much more likely to be dominated by an industry than previously. Factories employing more than 4,000–5,000 are now fairly commonplace. In 1978 nearly 7% of the employees in manufacturing were employed in establishments of over 5,000 employees. Two such factories could employ all the manufacturing workers in a town of 40,000 people, since the labourforce of such a town would be around 20,000 of whom roughly half could be expected to be in services.

(iii) Alternative Explanations

The final group of explanations rejects the dominant importance of either the external environment or the internal environment in explaining manufacturing location and distribution. Instead it is suggested that the patterns are the outcome of the nature of the capitalist society in the UK. One such alternative explanation interprets the capitalist mode of production in a particular way. A simplified description of this suggests that owners of capital invest in manufacturing by acquiring factories and equipment for production. They employ labour to use that equipment to manufacture goods. These are sold and the proceeds are used to cover the costs of production, including the payment of labour, and to yield surplus value in addition. This surplus value is available for investment to maintain and improve the capital equipment, to give a higher return to labour which created the wealth through production, and to provide higher profits to the owners of the invested capital. In such a simplified system, control is clearly in the hands of the owners of capital. Their aim is to maximize the surplus value which they can appropriate. They have a number of choices in what they do with the surplus value. It can be re-invested on the operations to provide the latest equipment and methods to maximize competitiveness and earnings. This normally leads to continual improvements in productivity and increased earnings by labour as well. For capitalists concerned with maximizing returns, such investment is only justified if the returns are as good as or greater than can be obtained from use of the surplus value for something else. This may not be in manufacturing at all, but in service activities or property. It may be profitable to continue to invest in existing manufacturing operations, but it may be *more* profitable to invest in something else. Failure to re-invest in manufacturing will cause the operations to deteriorate in productivity over time and eventually to become unprofitable. Thus in the UK, lower returns from much of manufacturing compared with alternative investment opportunities have led to insufficient investment and deteriorating competitiveness. This tends to have a spatial effect, since the oldest investment tends to be in the older declining industries and, for modern light industries, in those areas which acquired them first in the central regions and their conurbations. Beyond that, it is possible to realize assets by closure of manufacturing operations and selling the site, factory and equipment. It may be financially advantageous to owners of capital to do this even where an operation is profitable, if the capital gained in this way can be diverted to an alternative investment with a higher rate of return. This was a fairly common occurrence in major cities in the UK in the 1960s, when suitably located sites could be sold for high profits for conversion to alternative uses. In peripheral locations and rural sub-regions the sites were less valuable, but if a company rented a factory it could be advantageous to sell off the equipment to realize capital and simply relinquish the lease.

Carney, Lewis and Hudson (1979) used this kind of argument in an analysis of the origin of the industrial problems of the peripheral industrial regions of the UK. They suggested that these can be traced back to the actions of capitalist combines which dominated the economies of these regions at the beginning of this century. They claim that appropriation of surplus value for use elsewhere and failure to invest sufficiently to maintain the basic industries led inevitably to many of the economic problems these regions still suffer. They further suggested that owners of capital can maximize their return by taking advantage of government aid as far as possible. Hence the attraction of locations with public sector aid available, such as the Development Areas (DAs). Massey and Meegan (1979), in a study of the British electrical and electronics industries, showed how industrial restructuring produced significant geographical change. In particular Greater London, Birmingham, Liverpool and Manchester lost jobs, while DAs recorded gains. It might also be suggested that where a large multiplant company is involved, there is a preference for location in an area where the factory will be a major employer and/or ratepayer

(Lever 1979). This is because the company is more likely to be able to exert more influence and thus have more control over its external environment than in a major city. Without further substantive research, many of these alternative approaches to explanation of manufacturing location and distribution in the UK must remain controversial hypotheses.

III SERVICES

III.1 Significance

Since at least as early as 1950 the service sector in Britain (orders XVII–XVIV 1958 SIC; XX–XXVII 1968 SIC) has employed more people than primary production and manufacturing combined. Between 1950 and 1980 this dominance was strengthened as employment in services grew by 40% while that in manufacturing and in primary activities declined. Since employment in large part determines the location of the population, and most employment in Britain is in services, it follows that the pattern of service employment is today of fundamental importance in the human geography and planning of the country. This is most obvious in those areas where service employment *growth* is located, since this normally accompanies, or is caused by, population expansion. This in turn stimulates spatially associated economic, social and physical demands for such things as shops, schools and housing. Beyond this, the distribution of the service jobs has considerable significance for manufacturing. It was argued earlier that an important influence on the distribution of manufacturing, especially of light manufacturing, was the location of the market. When discussed in general terms, the market means purchasing power, which in turn goes with jobs. Since most people in Britain work in services, it follows that they are an important element in determining where the consumer market is, thus influencing the location of manufacturing. Here a precautionary note must be introduced since this is one of the situations where differences within the employment figures are significant. The majority of the workers in services are women, and much of the expansion that has taken place has occurred by an increase in female participation in the labourforce (table 4.21). The relevance of this is that wage rates in services in general are lower than in manufacturing or primary industries, and wage rates for females have tended to be lower than for males in Britain in the past (COI 1976, 337).

III.2 Flexibility of Location

Studies by economic geographers to explain these patterns of service location have been very limited in the past. One of the reasons for this was the false assumption, made not only by geographers but also by others such as economists and planners, that the location of services will coincide with the location of the primary and secondary industries, which directly and indirectly controls the demand for them. While there is some validity in this assumption at the national level, at the regional, and more particularly at the intra-regional level, there are too many exceptions involving a large number of employees for it to be even a working rule. In elaborating this it is necessary to distinguish clearly between ubiquitous and flexible services, a distinction which is fundamental to any understanding of the changes and trends in the geography of services in Britain.

TABLE 4.21

Increase in the Number of Employees, UK, 1950–75* (in thousands)

Employment sector	1950			1960			1970			1975		
	Men	Women	Total	Men	Women	Total	Men	Women	Total	Men	Women	Total
Primary	1,626	135	1,761	1,308	117	1,424	744	92	836	637	116	753
Manufacturing	5,677	2,872	8,549	6,013	2,933	8,947	6,274	2,802	9,075	5,262	2,226	7,488
Service	6,694	4,116	10,810	7,354	4,977	12,331	7,586	5,948	13,535	7,633	6,832	14,465
Grand total	13,997	7,123	21,120	14,675	8,027	22,702	14,604	8,842	23,446	13,532	9,174	22,706

* Because of changes in definition and methods of compilation, the figures for each sector are not strictly comparable over time and are given to indicate the main trends only.

Source: Dept of Employment

Ubiquitous services are those which depend upon direct consumer contact, and are, therefore, located within the immediate vicinity of the populations they serve. Good examples of ubiquitous services are general practitioners, hairdressers, opticians and laundrettes. Other things being equal, it can be expected that the distribution of these services will be closely correlated with the distribution of population. *Flexible* services on the other hand are those which do not need direct consumer contact, so that they are much more flexible in their choice of location. Examples of such services include head offices of building societies, national libraries, or electricity board headquarters. For these the choice of location is spatially circumscribed only by national or regional boundaries. The ubiquitous and flexible services thus described are, of course, the extremes of what in fact is a continuum grading from extreme flexibility. This continuum is best illustrated by reference to the education service in the UK. It is generally accepted that primary schools need to be located as close as possible to the homes of the children attending them. To minimize the movement of pupils, such schools are normally provided within the neighbourhood which they serve. At the next higher stage in education, junior comprehensive schools are fewer in number than the primary schools. They have larger enrolments and on average are further from pupils' homes, but still normally within the local community they serve. The senior comprehensive schools are fewer in number again, and so on average are still further away from pupils' homes, serving perhaps several communities. At the next level a further education college will usually have a much wider catchment area, and a college for the training of teachers will draw on a wider catchment still. Finally, a university or medical school can be built almost anywhere in the UK and will still attract students. In this context the university would seem to have complete flexibility in its choice of location. The example of the education service illustrates the whole range of location types in the services, from those governed by the need for close consumer contact, to those facing problems of having their location choice governed not so much by proximity to consumers as by other factors.

In practice this range of locational type is comparable with that found in manufacturing. Those manufacturing industries requiring close customer contact, such as jobbing printers, or which involve high bulk gain or whose products have high perishability, such as soft-drink manufacture or bread baking, have a ubiquitous distribution. At the other end of the range those industries involving high weight-loss or which use a high proportion of low-value raw materials, tend to locate at their raw material sources, or where the raw materials are imported, and are not governed by customer locations to the same degree, e.g. oil-refining, flour-milling or steel-making. It follows from this that far from the distribution of many services being controlled by the distribution of the population, they are much more akin to manufacturing in being influenced by other locational requirements.

In looking at the distribution of service employment in the UK, the distinction between ubiquitous and flexible services is important for two reasons. The first is that the flexible services tend to have grown more rapidly since 1960, and secondly, the degree of flexibility of most services has been increasing. The more rapid growth of the flexible services has been less significant in absolute numbers but nonetheless the trend was an important one.

III.3 Changing Location

With considerable freedom from locating close to consumers, much of the growth

of the most flexible services in fact took place in SE England, especially in and
around London (Manners 1963). By 1964, for example, of the 76 main government
research establishments 59 were in SE England (Hammond 1967). Government
office activities appeared to be even more attracted to the London region, with 71%
of all headquarters staff in the non-industrial Civil Service in SE England in 1972.
In those cases where there were constraints to locate within particular regions, then
the locations chosen were similar to the national pattern, that is, there was a marked
preference to be in or near the regional capital (Humphrys 1972, 138–50). Thus
half the 1961 office rateable value in England and Wales outside the SE, was located
in a handful of regional cities: Manchester, Birmingham, Liverpool, Leeds, Newcastle,
Bristol and Cardiff (Buswell and Lewis 1970). In the case of Scotland, Wales and N
Ireland the similarity to the national pattern was even greater, in that the capitals in
each case happen to be in the south-east of their territories. Although reasons can
be suggested for this uneven distribution, such as availability of better communications or supporting services, or that this allows central government offices to be
close together in the provincial capitals, none of these in the last resort is conclusive.
There is little evidence to suggest, for example, that the Aluminium Research
Association laboratories could not function just as successfully closer to major
aluminium-working centres in Scotland or Wales rather than in Oxford (Wright
1967). Similarly, the development of three university-level institutions in Cardiff –
the University College of S Wales and Monmouthshire, the University of Wales
Institute of Science and Technology, and the University of Wales School of
Medicine – was a matter of inertia and historical accident rather than positive
locational forces determining the choice (Coates and Rawstron 1971, 180).

While the increasing concentration of the growth of flexible services in the capital
cities in particular was bringing about changes in the distribution pattern, there
were other changes of equal importance that were making possible the rearrange-
ment of existing service provision. For many services there was an observable trend
towards increased flexibility in location. This had repercussions mostly at the intra-
regional rather than the inter-regional level, but it was nonetheless important
because of that. The main contributory factors to increasing flexibility were
changes in organization, increasing opportunities to take advantage of economies of
scale and the increasing mobility of the service consumers.

III.4 Organization and Control

Prior to 1945 many of the service industries were under the control of local government, or, in the commercial sector, were in the hands of a multitude of small
companies, or of individuals who had limited means at their disposal and limited
aims. Good examples of these conditions could be found in the environmental
services of gas, electricity and water, in personal services such as medicine and
education and in commercial services such as cinemas, retail distribution and dry-
cleaning. The effect of this kind of control was that services were very dispersed.
In the public sector, local authorities usually operated as if their areas were islands.
For example, each local authority that provided a gas-supply service in its area
would normally have a gas-making plant and a full range of necessary administrative
and maintenance staff (Ordnance Survey 1951). Similarly in the private sector
many grocers owned and operated just one shop, and would adapt and accept
reduced profits to stay in business at a place when commercial principles might

indicate that the location had outlived its usefulness. Many of the services then had an organization and a location pattern that had grown up in a previous period and was suited to earlier conditions.

III.5 Public-Sector Developments

The inhibiting influence of small-scale organization on change was drastically reduced after 1945. Major changes came about in several of the services through nationalization. In some cases the effect of this was to transfer a service from the private to the public sector, as happened with the railways. In other cases, where both local authorities and private companies were involved, such as gas and electricity distribution, nationalization imposed uniform public-sector control. The effect in either case was to replace diverse and variously organized systems of small-scale operations by large-scale integrated organization. The resulting centralization of control created the necessary conditions for rationalization to take place. The immediate spatial impact was in fact relatively limited. The lack of capital in a country still recovering from six years of war, and the need to gain operating experience, delayed change. The full effects did not really make themselves felt until after 1955, and it was only in the 1960s that the new patterns began to dominate. The basic change was that the newly nationalized services were no longer constrained by area or regional boundaries, imposed from outside, in their decisions on location of their activities. At the same time any duplication resulting from the previous multiplicity of ownership could be eliminated. Thus the gas and electricity boards were able to create their own patterns. They established their own regions, within each of which there was a central headquarters with a hierarchy of district and area offices below that. These replaced the mixture of local authority and private-undertaking offices which had existed previously in so many parts of Britain. The result of this rationalization process, however, was to reduce employment and to centralize activities in the most suitable locations, reducing the number of places from which services operated. In the health services the changes in the pattern of hospital provision were detailed in a Hospital Plan (NHS 1962). There the same trend was observable (fig. 4.13). The aim of the plan was to achieve uniformly adequate hospital provision over the whole of the UK, in place of the considerable variation in hospital-bed availability which had arisen prior to nationalization. The location of the new and replacement hospitals could now be determined, not as previously, on the basis of availability of local funds or adequacy of local organization but on the basis of proper distribution.

After 1945, partly as a result of nationalization and the extension of public ownership, and partly by expansion and extension of previously existing government services, public control of the service sector grew to substantial proportions. In 1975 of the total employment in services of 14.5m people, 6.3m were working in such public-sector services as gas, electricity and water supply, road and rail transport, health, education and government. Beyond this direct employment, indirect control was especially strong in the construction industry which in 1975 had a workforce of 1.3m. 45% of the construction industry output was for public authorities, and government decisions on such things as availability of housing improvement grants considerably influenced the demand for the services of small local building firms. The implications of such extensive public ownership and influence in the service sector is that the government now has considerable control

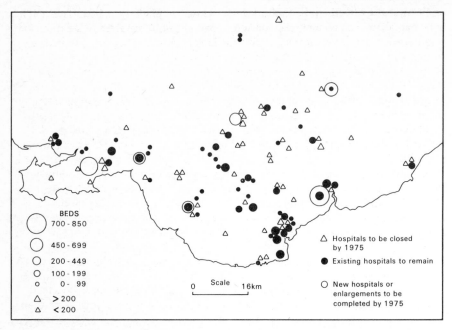

Figure 4.13   Plan for hospital development, industrial S Wales, 1961–80

over employment in services, and especially over its location, if it decides to exercise it. As a corollary, government, both local and national, had assumed considerable responsibility for ensuring a proper distribution pattern of service jobs and for the results of any changes initiated by policy decisions.

III.6 Private Ownership and Control

In the private sector similar trends are readily identifiable, though with greater multiplicity of ownership and considerable inertia the effects have generally been more limited. Most people are familiar with the changes which have occurred in the retail trade, especially in the ownership and organization of food and clothing shops (Hall, Knapp and Winsten 1961; Thorpe 1968). In most British town centres, locally owned foodshops have given way to those owned by large grocery chains, so that by 1975 just six major grocery chains accounted for one-third of the £7,500m spent in grocers. A similar process has taken place in men's tailors, women's clothing and shoe provision. As early as 1961 nearly one-half of all speciality shoe shops in Britain were multiples, with even higher proportions in men's outwear, retailing, and radio and television shops. Furniture, electrical appliances and stationers are other examples. The geographical effect is that the controlling companies maintain operations only where an adequate return is earned on the capital invested. If sales or earnings drop below what is considered acceptable, then a store is closed. This is in contrast with the small individual shopowner, who would often accept a lower income or make other adjustments to maintain his shop, since it is the only one he has (Scott 1970, 26). With larger organizations there is better chance, too, of locational investigation before a new store is opened, to ensure as far as possible that the right choice has been made (Scott 1970, 42). This again contrasts with the private shopowner, who is more likely to be influenced by personal rather than commercial considerations. Again the greater financial resources and better management make the larger organizations very competitive, so that they can often capture sales from small shopowners if they are in competition for a limited market. Finally, rationalization occurs not only as a result of the above trends but also through mergers and takeovers with one large organization combining with another. Where both have outlets close together in a shopping centre, there is a likelihood that only one will survive. Many of these developments in the private sector took place in the 1960s, which allowed rationalization and centralization to be taken advantage of to an increasing extent in the 1970s.

The service least affected by these tendencies was Construction. About 40% of the employees in this order are engaged in building maintenance, which offers little chance for rationalization and is ubiquitous in distribution. Moreover, nearly one-quarter of the 66,000 firms in this activity are one-man businesses. Roughly 20% of the 1.3m operatives are engaged by local authorities, which again limits rationalization. However, two relevant trends have become apparent. The first is the reduction of on-site work in new construction. This is especially noticeable in house-building, where increasingly such items as door, windows and even roof structures, plumbing items, and concrete, are delivered to the site having been manufactured elsewhere. While pre-fabrication of complete dwelling units has not yet become popular in the UK, pre-fabrication of many components for assembly and installation by construction workers on site is now commonplace. The second trend was the development of major companies operating nationally or internationally. By 1970 there were more than 220 firms with over 600 employees (COI 1976, 246). Many of these had developed permanent central offices where much of the preparation work, such as design and administration, could be centralized.

III.7 Increased Mobility

A factor affecting the location of services at the intra-regional level was the change in the field of transport. Public road transport in many areas was improved by the provision of faster and more comfortable services, while, prior to the oil price increases since 1973, the cost of travel became much less of a burden as average income per employee increased. Greater affluence over this same period also resulted in many more people having their own means of transport, in the form of a private car. This reduced the problems of distance quite considerably. Technical improvements both in vehicles and in road quality contributed to the same end. Empirical evidence for this, not surprisingly, suggests that households with cars tend to rely less on local centres, and travel greater distances to a wider variety of centres than households without cars (Scott 1970, 61).

The resulting greater mobility has received most attention because of the greater distances people were prepared to travel to work (ch. 2.IV.5), but there was an equally important impact on the journey to services. Because it became financially less of a burden and physically less of a strain, people not only could, but did, travel greater distances to obtain the services they required. This in turn relieved the services of the need to be within such close proximity of the population they aimed to serve, and allowed them much greater latitude in their choice of location. In this way many services have become more flexible in their location choice.

III.8 Economies of Scale

The changes in organization and transport discussed so far were important because they altered the basis on which locational decisions were made. Their greatest impact was probably achieved because they allowed advantage to be taken of the increasing economies of scale available in the service sector. When the distances people are prepared to travel are relatively short, then it is necessary to have a large number of service points close to the population being served. This was the position in the UK in the period before 1950. It was encouraged by the form of ownership and control, which favoured the retention of a wide distribution of service points in both the public and the private service sectors. But a wide distribution also meant small individual units, whether offices or shops. Changes in the constraints described above, however, made it possible to alter the pattern so that any one place served a much wider area. The advantage of this was that each operational unit could be larger, and through economies of scale, more economically efficient. Technological advance made such developments even more desirable. For example, the financial cost of providing expensive office or medical equipment can only be justified where there is sufficient demand to keep such equipment economically occupied. The greater the turnover of the office or hospital, the greater the demand is likely to be, while offices or hospitals with small turnovers might be below the threshold size at which investment in the facilities is considered justifiable. The effects of taking advantage of such economies of scale became increasingly apparent in the UK in the 1960s, although the process had begun much earlier. In the public services it could be seen in the 1961 Hospital Plan, where the underlying principle was one of closure of small hospitals and their replacement by fewer but larger hospitals at suitable central locations (fig. 4.13). Similarly in the gas and electricity services, administrative work was concentrated into fewer centres (fig. 4.14). In the case of these utilities the process proceeded by stages with the effects of the initial rationalization being relatively slight, but subsequent change was achieved by progressive increases in the size of the administrative areas and consequent reduction in their number, and in the number of area offices and of such things as stores and maintenance service depots.

The same trends were evident in the *transport services*, and even in railways which was one of the services to suffer major decline. The rationalization of the railways which took place after 1963 was based on the proposals in the Beeching Plan (Min. of Transport 1963). This had shown that 50% of the stations provided only 1% of the passenger receipts, and that there were many places where lines were unnecessarily duplicated. The proposed solution to the problem was the concentration of activities on the most-used facilities which could be shown to be paying their way. The effect of implementing this proposal was the withdrawal of services from areas which generated the lowest traffic income, generally areas with small dispersed populations, and improvement of services where traffic was greatest, usually between areas of dense population. Here again, even in decline, economies of scale played a major part in reforming the geographical pattern. Servicing, maintenance and goods depots were concentrated to achieve greater efficiency, and the number of passenger stations reduced, with consequent increasing intensity of use of those that remained.

In the private sector the largest employment group is Retail and Wholesale Distribution. This group employs one in five of all the employees in the service sector, and one in ten of the total insured labourforce. Scott commented on the

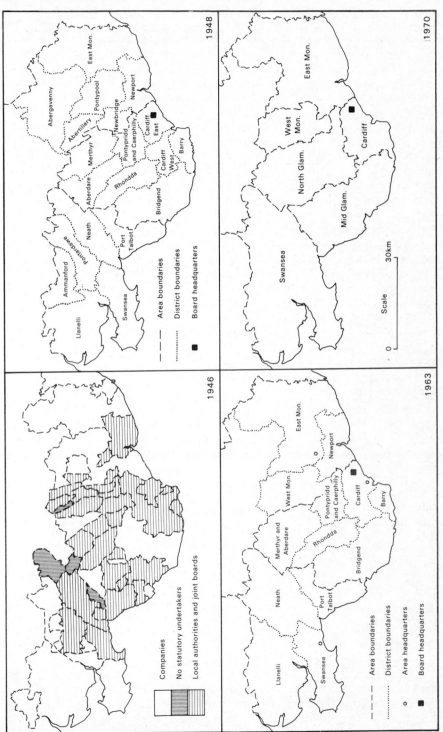

Figure 4.14   S Wales Electricity Board. Rationalization of administrative areas, industrial S Wales, 1946–70

'pronounced dis-economies of small-scale' in retailing (Scott 1970, 9). This was substantiated in the UK after 1960 by the rapid increase in the number of large stores for shopping and especially by the proliferation of supermarkets, defined as self-service shops with a minimum of $186m^2$ of selling area. There were 870 supermarkets in 1961. By 1971 the number had risen to 4,800 and they were handling nearly one-third of all retail food sales. At the same time all the major categories of shops in the clothing and footwear trades in the UK experienced decline in the number of separate establishments, largely owing to the growth of multiple ownership and the increasing size of stores. Similarly, in the grocery trade turnover expanded by 23.7% between 1961 and 1966, and by 37% between 1966 and 1971. Under previous conditions this expansion would have resulted in a proliferation of small shops with a dispersed pattern. What actually happened was that the number of establishments in the grocery trade fell by 15.9% in 1961–6, and by 12.8% in 1966–71. Turnover per establishment was rising rapidly during this time, going up from £15,016 in 1961 to £23,566 in 1966 and to £37,121 in 1971. Further development of these trends in the form of hypermarkets, defined as stores with over $4,645m^2$ selling area, has been inhibited by local authority refusal to grant planning permission for their construction. By the end of 1976 only four had been built in the UK, at Irlam, Lancashire, Eastleigh, Hampshire, Telford (Salop) and Caerphilly, Mid-Glamorgan, in contrast with the large numbers operating in France and Germany (Parker 1975). The fear is that such large developments would have a detrimental effect upon shopping facilities in their vicinity, but the continuing pressure of applications for planning permission for hypermarket construction (Dawson 1976) make it almost certain that they will become a more familiar part of the geography of retailing in future.

The geographical impact of these trends has been quite marked, though in some areas of the UK the effects in some services have been masked by the effects of the considerable local economic growth that has occurred. But basically there was a tendency for scale of operations to increase in all services. This happened either by increasing the average size of individual establishments, by closing small units and opening larger new ones as in the case of hospitals, schools and in the retail trade, or by increasing the size of existing individual establishments as happened with the universities. Most of these changes involve geographical change, either through the centralization of a scattered distribution of establishments into a smaller number of places, or by a certain limited number of places growing relatively faster than others causing redistribution. Whatever the method by which the changes occurred, a definite geographical trend can be identified. In general it is that the higher-order centres in any particular area or region tended to gain, while the losses were concentrated in the smaller centres which stagnated or declined.

This conforms with the hierarchy arrangement put forward in Christaller's *Central Place Theory* (Berry 1967, 59–73). The theory shows how, under idealized conditions, services in greatest day-to-day demand are located in the smallest service centres, which serve very limited surrounding market areas. Since everyone living in the theoretical landscape would need to be served by a centre, every part of the landscape would be in a market area. In an idealized landscape these market areas would be hexagon-shaped for maximum efficiency. The smallest service centres and their associated market areas or hinterlands would lie within the hinterland of a larger service centre, which would provide those services less frequently demanded: a specialized delicatessen shop rather than a general grocers, the area headquarters of a bank rather than a branch bank. Each higher-order centre would thus serve a wider area than the lower-order centres in its hinterland. These higher-order centres and their hinterlands would in turn lie within the hinterland of a still-higher-order centre providing services even less frequently demanded, or which control a number of lower-order services. This is where the wholesale grocer or the regional head-quarters of the bank would be located. There is, therefore, a hierarchy of service centres, with the next higher-order service centre having all the functions of the lower-order centres below it, but with additional superior functions which they do not have (Scott 1970, 16).

The relevance of this theory for the changing pattern of service employment in Britain is that the trends described have all tended to make the higher-order centres more attractive relative to the lower-order centres (Westaway 1974). Greater mobility and willingness to travel further has meant that services can locate further away from their customers. Changes in organization and control described earlier have allowed advantage to be taken of this much more readily, a trend encouraged by the economies of scale available when services are concentrated in fewer larger units. The underlying geographical trend has been a shift of service activity away from the smallest, lowest-order centres, to the smaller number of next-higher-order service centres. The latter have in this way grown at the expense of the former. These geographical shifts are most obvious in the public-sector services, where stronger central control has facilitated rationalization. The replacement of smaller hospitals by fewer larger units or the development of giant comprehensive schools in place of the much smaller secondary schools are good examples. In the private sector, the reduction in the number of small independent grocers, or of bread and confectionery shops, and their replacement by supermarkets, shows the same process at work. The effects of these trends are offset in some areas because growth of population or purchasing power may allow a service centre to maintain itself. The corollary is that the effects are best seen in areas where the population is in decline or static. In such areas the population declines are accelerated in the smaller places by the removal of service employment, which may be in small numbers in absolute terms but which made a significant contribution to the local economy.

III.9 Flexible Services Location

Having explained the geographical shifts which have occurred, it is also important to point out that for many of the more flexible services there seem to be no good economic or commercial reasons to justify the concentration of many of the jobs involved into the highest-order centres. Gottmann (1970) has suggested some factors which might explain the need for some services to cluster, but Rhodes and Khan (1971, 27) found among executives who were responsible for location decisions 'an obsession with psychological and environmental factors' at the expense of financial consideration. From the present state of knowledge in this field (Goddard 1975), there appear to be no good reasons why much of the routine clerical work involved with the accounting side of the electricity and gas boards, for example, could not be located elsewhere within the administrative boundaries of the areas they serve than in the largest city, which is where they are usually centred today. The location of the routine administration of county councils or national government departments could similarly be shifted. At the national level, recognition that this could be done, and needed to be done, arose mainly from the development of office space and employment in London (Daniels 1975). 80% of the office space in England and Wales for which planning permission was given between 1945 and 1962 was located in London (Wright 1967, 221). Moreover in the central areas of London, where more than half the employment increase in the conurbation was concentrated between 1945 and 1963, two-thirds of the increase occurred in office jobs, and these trends continued in the 1960s. Between 1964 and 1967 there was a net increase of 1.8 million m^2 of office floorspace in the SE planning region alone. This represented 56% of the total growth of office floorspace in England and Wales during that period (Daniels 1969). Westaway (1974) showed that head offices of the 1,000 largest companies in the UK are predominantly in London, and that between 1969 and 1972 the number of head offices in London increased by 30, while all other large cities recorded declines. Hall (1966) pointed out that projections for employment growth in the London region over the period 1961–81 showed that two-thirds, or about 750,000 jobs, would be in office employment. He further concluded that: 'The real answer to the question of London's future, then, hinges on the economics of office location'. Even in 1966 the SE region had 49% of the four million office-workers in England and Wales, as against only 36% of the economically-active population. This expansion was a major cause of the overgrowth of London and the SE region in the period up to 1970. It was clear that some of this office employment could be located elsewhere and still be economically viable, and so efforts were made to redistribute this growth. For the private sector the quasi-independent Location of Offices Bureau (1964) was established to persuade offices to move out of C London and Office Development Permits were introduced by the government to control new office building. This action resulted in some offices being dispersed, mainly to the outskirts of London or to other parts of SE England. Thus 84% of office moves organized by the LOB between 1967 and 1974 were within the SE region, though in the year ending March 1975 this figure had fallen to 70%. After 1979 the Conservative government required the LOB to give priority to the office requirements of the inner city.

In the public sector, the *Flemming Report* (1963, not published) suggested dispersal of some government work, and the *Hardman Report* (Civil Service Dept. 1973) made more detailed suggestions for various government departments. Acting on these recommendations, central government set an example by locating employment-generating office developments of their own in other regions. Amongst others, the National Savings Bank headquarters was located in Glasgow, the Business Statistics Office in Newport, Gwent, and the Driver and Vehicle Licensing Centre in Swansea, W Glamorgan. In addition, it was planned to move 31,000 central government jobs from the London area between 1975 and 1984. Since 1960 the possibilities of influencing the location of flexible service employment have been explored and the significance of such employment in planning regional development is now widely recognized. Though both the policies adopted and their effects have been criticized, by 1975 it was clear that the proper planning of the location of economic activity in the UK would in future result in more of the flexible service activities being distributed to the Development Areas, in the same way as the location of 'footloose' manufacturing industry had been influenced during the previous thirty years. What was also becoming apparent by the early 1980s, however, was that in the DAs these services were clustering in or near the largest centres, creating a concentrated decentralization pattern. This should make it easier for *regional* services to be shifted away from such centres, to help achieve the proper distribution of employment which is one of the aims of government regional policy. However, the onset of structural economic depression slowed these trends, even threatened to set them into reverse.

REFERENCES

The Power Industries

BRITISH GAS CORP. (1981) *Annual Rep. and Accounts 1980–1*, HMSO
CEGB (1981) *Statistical Yearbook*, London
DEPT ENERGY (1981) *Digest of Energy Statistics 1981*, HMSO
HAUSER, D P (1971) 'System Costs and the Location of New Generating Plants in England and Wales', *Trans. Inst. Br. Geogr.*, *54*, 101–21
HOUSE, J W and KNIGHT, E M (1967) *Pit Closure and the Community*, Newcastle upon Tyne
MANNERS, G (1971) *The Geography of Energy*, 2nd edn, London
          (1981) *Coal in Britain*, London
MARNELL, M J and HUMPHRYS, G (1965) 'Private Coal Mining in S Wales', *Geogrl Rev.*, *55*, 328–38
NORTH, J and SPOONER, D (1976) 'Yorkshire Coal Crop from Selby Farmland', *Geogrl Mag.*, *48*, 554–8
          (1978) 'The Geography of the Coal Industry in the UK in the 1970s: Changing Directions?', *Geojournal*, *2*, 3, 255–72
NCB (1975) *Annual Rep. and Accounts 1974–5*, vol. 1, HMSO
          (1981) *Annual Rep. and Accounts 1980–1*, HMSO
ODELL, P R (1979) 'North Sea Oil and Gas Resources: Their Implications for the Location of Industry in Western Europe', in HAMILTON, F E I (ed.) *Industrial Change*, London
ODELL, P R and ROSING, K E (1974) 'Weighing up the North Sea Wealth', *Geogrl Mag.*, *47*, 150–5
POSNER, M V (1973) *Fuel Policy: A Study in Applied Economics*, London
ROBINSON, C and MARSHALL, E (1981) *What Future for British Coal?*, London

Manufacturing Industry

BLOOMFIELD, G T (1981) 'The Changing Spatial Organisation of Multinational Corporations in the World Automotive Industry', in HAMILTON, F E I and LINGE, G J R (eds) *Spatial Analysis, Industry and the Industrial Environment, vol. 2 International Industrial Systems*, London, 357–94
CAMERON, G C (1980) 'Economies of the Conurbations' in CAMERON, G C (ed.) *The Future of the British Conurbations*, London, 54–71
CARNEY, J, LEWIS, J and HUDSON, R (1977) 'Coal Combines and Interregional Uneven Development in the UK', in MASSEY, D B and BATEY, P W J (eds) *Alternative Frameworks for Analysis*, London, 52–67
CLARK, C (1966) 'Industrial Location and Economic Potential', *Lloyds Bank Rev.*, *82*, 1–17
DANIELS, P W (1975) *Office Location: An Urban and Regional Study*, London
DANSON, M W, LEVER, W F and MALCOM, J F (1980) 'The Inner City Employment Problem in Great Britain, 1952–76: A Shift-Share Approach', *Urb. Stud.*, *17*, 193–210

DICKEN, P (1976)'The Multiplant Business Enterprise and Geographical Space:
    Some Issues in the Study of External Control and Regional Development', *Reg.
    Stud., 10*, 401–12
DICKEN, P and LLOYD, P E (1981) *Modern Western Society: A Geographical
    Perspective on Work, Home and Well-Being,* London
FLORENCE, P S (1962) *Post-war Investment, Location and Size of Plant,*
    Cambridge
FOTHERGILL, S and GUDGIN, G (1979) 'Regional Employment Change:
    A Subregional Explanation', *Progr. in Plann., 12* (3)
FROST, M and SPENCE, N (1981) 'Unemployment, Structural Economic Change
    and Public Policy in British Regions', *Progr. in Plann., 16* (1)
GODDARD, J B and SMITH, I J (1978) 'Changes in Corporate Control in the
    British Urban System 1972–77', *Environment and Planning A, 10,* 1073–84
GRIPAIOS, P (1977) 'The Closure of Firms in the Inner City: The South-east
    London Case 1970–75', *Reg. Stud., 11,* 1–6
GUDGIN, G (1978) *Industrial Location Processes and Regional Employment
    Growth,* Farnborough
HAMILTON, F E I (1967) 'Models of Industrial Location', in CHORLEY, R J and
    HAGGETT, P (eds) *Models in Geography,* London, 361–424
                (1974) *Spatial Perspectives on Industrial Organization and
    Decision Making,* London
                (1978) 'Aspects of Industrial Mobility in the British Economy',
    Reg. Stud., 12, 153–66
HAMILTON, F E I and LINGE, G J R (eds) (1979) *Spatial Analysis, Industry and
    the Industrial Environment, vol. 1 Industrial Systems,* London
                (1981) *Spatial Analysis, Industry and
    the Industrial Environment, vol. 2 International Industrial Systems,* London
HUMPHRYS, G (1972) *Industrial Britain: South Wales,* Newton Abbot
KEEBLE, D (1976) *Industrial Location and Planning in the United Kingdom,*
    London
                (1978) 'Industrial Migration in the United Kingdom in the 1960s', in
    HAMILTON, F E I (ed.) *Industrial Change: International Experience and Public
    Policy,* London
                (1980) 'Industrial Decline, Regional Policy and the Urban-rural
    Manufacturing Shift in the United Kingdom', *Environment and Planning A, 12,*
    945–62
LEIGH, R and NORTH, D J (1978) 'Regional Aspects of Acquisition Activity in
    British Manufacturing Activity', *Reg. Stud., 12,* 227–46
LEVER, W F (1979) 'Industry and Labour Markets in Great Britain', in
    HAMILTON, F E I and LINGE, G J R (eds) *Spatial Analysis Industry and the
    Industrial Environment, vol. 1 Industrial Systems,* London, 89–114
MASSEY, D and MEEGAN, R A (1979) 'The Geography of Industrial
    Reorganisation', *Progr. in Plann., 10,* 155–237
McCRONE, G (1969) *Regional Policy in Britain,* London
RAWSTRON, E M (1958) 'Three Principles of Industrial Location', *Trans. Inst. Br.
    Geogr., 25,* 132–42
                (1964) 'Industry', in WATSON, J W and SISSONS, J B (eds)
    The British Isles: A Systematic Geography, London, 297–318
SMITH, W (1949) *An Economic Geography of GB,* London
SMITH, D M (1971) *Industrial Location,* London
SWALES, J K (1979) 'Entrepreneurship and Regional Development: Implications
    for Regional Policy', in MACLENNAN, D and PARR, J B (eds) *Regional Policy:
    Past Experience and New Directions,* Oxford, 224–42

TOWNROE, P M (1979) *Industrial Movement: Experience in the US and the UK,* Farnborough
WATTS, H D (1978) 'Inter-organisational Relations and the Location of Industry', *Reg. Stud., 12,* 215–26
　　　　　　　(1980) *The Large Industrial Enterprise: Some Spatial Perspectives,* London
　　　　　　　(1981) *The Branch Plant Economy: A Study of External Control,* London

Services

BERRY, B J L (1967) *Geography of Market Centres and Retail Distribution,* Englewood Cliffs
BUSWELL, R J and LEWIS, E W (1970) 'The Geographical Distribution of Industrial Research Activity in the UK', *Reg. Stud., 4,* 297–306
COI (1976) *Britain 1976,* London
CIVIL SERV. DEPT (1973) *Dispersal of Government Work from London* (Hardman Report), Cmnd 5322, HMSO
COATES, B E and RAWSTRON, E M (1971) *Regional Variations in Britain,* London
DANIELS, P W (1969) 'Office Decentralisation from London: Policy and Practice', *Reg. Stud., 3,* 171–8
　　　　　　　(1975) *Offices: an Urban Regional Study,* Oxford
DAWSON, J A (1976) 'Lack of Decision Retards Retailing Investment', *Geogrl Mag. Lond., 48,* 759–60
GODDARD, J B (1975) *Office Location in Urban and Regional Development,* Oxford
GOTTMANN, J (1970) 'Urban Centrality and the Interweaving of Quaternary Activity', *Ekistics, 29,* 322–31
HALL, M, KNAPP, J and WINSTEN, C (1961) *Distribution in GB and N America,* Oxford
HALL, P G (1966) *World Cities,* London
HAMMOND, E (1967) 'Dispersal of Government Offices', *Urb. Stud., 4,* 258–75
HUMPHRYS, G (1972) *Industrial Britain: South Wales,* Newton Abbot
MANNERS, G (1963) 'Service Industries and Regional Economic Growth', *Tn Plann. Rev., 33,* 293–303
MINIST. TRANSPORT (1963) *The Reshaping of British Railways,* HMSO
NAT. HEALTH SERV. (1962) *A Hospital Plan for England and Wales,* London
ORDNANCE SURV. (1951) *Map of GB: Gas and Coke 1949,* 2 sheets, scale 1:625,000
PARKER, A J (1975) 'Hypermarkets: the Changing Pattern of Retailing', *Geogr., 60,* 120–4
RHODES, J and KHAN, A (1971) *Office Dispersal and Regional Policy,* Cambridge
SCOTT, P (1970) *Geography and Retailing,* London
THORPE, D (1968) 'The Main Shopping Centres of GB in 1961. Their Location and Structural Characteristics', *Urb. Stud., 5,* 165–206
WESTAWAY, J (1974) 'The Spatial Hierarchy of Business Organisations and its Implications for the British Urban System', *Reg. Stud., 8,* 145–55
WRIGHT, M (1967) 'Provincial Office Development', *Urb. Stud., 4,* 218–57

5

Transport

I INTRODUCTION: SOME THEORETICAL AND EMPIRICAL BACKGROUND

I.1 Transport Systems

A transport system is expected to facilitate the production process by moving goods to the right places at the right time and also to enable people to pursue complex patterns of daily and annual movement. The efficiency of a transport system cannot, however, be measured by the extent to which it satisfies all the wishes of its customers. It is not an infinite succession of magic carpets but is a complex of investments in a varied fleet of land, sea and air vehicles, the tracks over which they operate, the energy which keeps them moving and their terminals. Much of this investment, especially in track and terminal facilities, is very 'lumpy' – half a bridge is no use. Much transport equipment, especially new terminals and large vessels, takes several years to develop and build but is also expected to last or can be made to last for one or more decades. Transport systems therefore react rather slowly to changes in demand although some parts are more flexible than others. Vehicles are often more easily replaced or rebuilt than their track or termini: road transport is the most flexible of the modes in this respect.

Although the demand for transport is derived from perceived needs of other goods and services at the present moment (O'Sullivan 1980; Gwilliam and Mackie 1975; Thomson 1974), the supply of transport reflects the needs of several years ago. Our immediate demands must be satisfied in the short run by paying the price for operating the existing facilities plus the cost of investing in the new facilities we would like to have available. How much we can afford to invest in transport at any one time depends on what can be spared from other, equally urgent investment needs. An efficient transport system helps to deliver the goods but if it calls upon an inordinate share of the national resources of labour, energy, steel, etc. it will inhibit the production of the very goods it was designed to carry. The transport sector is allocated about 8–10% of national investment in many advanced countries at the present time and employs round about 5% of their industrial labourforce. There have, however, been short periods when the transport sector enjoyed much higher shares of national investment and resources. One of these was the 'Railway Mania' period of the 1840s in Britain, another occurred in many advanced countries during the 1960s associated with a rapid growth in the volume of road transport. The 1970s brought a sharp reminder that the oil upon which transport systems were increasingly relying was in limited supply in the long run and by no means evenly distributed around the world. The reaction to the oil crisis which began in 1973 was bound to be slow because of the long-term nature of most transport investment. During the 1970s, in Britain as elsewhere, transport investment was reduced to its normal share of the national output of goods and services. This was a decade when many expectations of a new geography of society based upon cheap transport were disappointed.

The present transport system is the result of a long evolution continually modified by changing demands and developing technology. It was an evolution with overlapping phases of dominance: of coastal shipping and inland waterways in the eighteenth century, of the railway throughout much of the nineteenth and of road transport in the third-quarter of the twentieth century. The accumulation of modes and networks with few attempts at conscious integration has been well documented (Smith 1949; Barker and Savage 1974; Dyos and Aldcroft 1969; Bagwell 1974). Road transport, for example, began its modern rise to dominance without major initial investment, but faced the major problems caused by high-density operation on a road network still largely attuned to a horse-and-carriage age.

The development of transport networks has been continuously influenced by considerations of physical environment, notably by relief (Appleton 1962). More important, however, have been the influences of *dimensions* and *insularity*, reflected primarily in the limitation of the distances over which the systems could develop. These characteristics impart to UK transport a measure of distinctiveness, especially by comparison with other European systems. The UK differs from mainland Europe in having invested more lavishly in transport during the nineteenth century and also in making much more intermittent investment during the twentieth century. Other European governments have generally accepted a greater responsibility for the formulation of transport policy, especially with regard to the railways and local public transport, and have pursued their policies more consistently.

When considering the influence of the UK transport system on the geography of the rest of the economy it is important to bear in mind that transport costs are now of limited importance for a growing majority of UK industries (Brown 1969). It has been estimated that the share of transport in the total cost of producing and distributing is 9% although there are very considerable variations according to the type of industry (Edwards and Bayliss 1971). It is broadly true that as the pace and level of economic development increase then transport costs become less important and concern for the quality of the service increases (Owen 1964). Certainly it is becoming more common to consider goods transport as the *logistic* or *physical distribution* aspect of an industrial activity rather than as a discrete element of the tertiary sector, and that transport costs will be subsumed within some form of the total cost concept. All these issues are reflected in the developing transport system of the UK and not least in the fact that it is clear that the larger portion of transport costs now relate to the movement of people and not of goods (Chisholm and Manners 1971, 240).

There has been a gradual change in emphasis in the forces moulding the transport system. Increasingly technological achievement has made it possible to overcome any physical environmental problems, but to do so at a cost. Thus in transport developments, as in so much of economic development, the point at issue is not whether it is technically possible but whether it is economically feasible. Moreover at the level of capital provision commonly required for transport development, economic feasibility tends to be interpreted largely in terms of whether the development is considered to be politically desirable. The same may be true of the maintenance, by subsidy, of existing facilities. The transport system thus tends to reflect the volume and nature of demand assessed in terms of the economic and technical characteristics of the available transport media, but viewed in the light of the existing socio-political order.

The considerations outlined above suggest that the impacts of change in the transport system on the geography of other sectors of the UK economy are ambivalent. In most years new investment represents a very small proportion of the stock of vehicles and fixed installations, and consists of the repair or replacement of equipment at the site of its existing operation. To this extent the transport system is a conservative factor in the geography of the UK. Few modern railway routes, for example, are less than one hundred years old and some of the earliest railway lines are still the most intensively used on the system. Exceptionally, however, a short burst of investment in a particular mode of transport may reduce the time and/or wear and tear spent in travel over wide areas and thus shrink the UK space. The motorway network of the 1960s and 1970s has achieved such a shrinkage and so have the development of domestic air-routes and fast 'inter-city' rail services between London and selected regional centres. The following pages will show that these developments have not benefitted the 'centre' at the expense of the 'periphery' as much as might have been feared. Nor have the major changes in the technology of sea transport (discussed in section V below) led to as high a concentration of seaborne cargo into a handful of ports as was once thought likely. Many interests work to preserve the existing geography of the UK, and we must consider political as well as economic and technical factors in any study of change and stability in the spatial layout of the UK transport system.

I.2   Transport Development, 1950–80

The last thirty years have seen major technical changes in several of the major modes of transport: changes in public attitudes to transport have been equally significant. There has been considerable discussion of the proper role of market forces and social objectives in determining the amount of investment to be allocated to competing transport modes, and there has also been increased emphasis on cooperation between them. As vehicles become more sophisticated and expensive and individual transport media more specialized, ideally they should cooperate to provide the most economical overall system. Such cooperation may be achieved through *coordination* – agreement between the media to improve interchanges and to eliminate duplicate services – or through *integration*, which involves the systematic replanning of the transport of an area or route so as to use each medium to best advantage. Integrated systems are often planned by teams responsible to the community rather than to an individual mode. Since coordination and integration are easier to plan than to achieve, theory is often many years in advance of practice. It is a further general characteristic of recent change that it has tended to an increased measure of concentration of activity within each mode, that is, to the more intensive use of some parts of the system. Also changed is the relative importance of the various modes within the total system.

The *change in demand* for transport was engendered by the continuation of the interwar trends resulting from the secular decline of heavy industry and the rise of consumer goods and service industries within a more prosperous and mobile society. Increased car ownership, in particular, placed sections of the system under severe strain, as for example the urban road network and the public transport services in both urban and rural areas. Indeed the increasing dominance of road transport is

TABLE 5.1

Estimates of Goods and Passenger Traffic, GB, 1960–80

Goods traffic	000,000,000 tonne-km			Per cent		
	1960	1970	1980	1960	1970	1980
Total land traffic	80	115	123	100	100	100
Road	48	85	96	60	74	78
Rail	30	27	18	38	23	15
Pipelines		3	10		3	8

Passenger traffic	000,000,000 passenger-km			Per cent		
	1960	1970	1980	1960	1970	1980
Total	255	408	528	100	100	100
Road						
Private transport	144	309	433	56	76	82
Public service vehicle	71	56	51	28	14	10
Rail	40	36	36	16	9	7
Air	–	2	2	–	–	1

Note: excludes traffic in N Ireland except air traffic to and from GB

Source: DoT (1981)

the most striking characteristic of the inland transport scene in the period since 1960.

Table 5.1 summarizes the changing volume of traffic and the changing relative importance of the different transport modes between 1960 and 1980. The substantial increase in the volume of land goods traffic was almost entirely carried by road, although pipelines trebled their modest throughput. The volume of rail freight traffic fell both absolutely and relatively as did railway passenger traffic. Public road transport showed an even larger absolute and relative decline, and passenger traffic in Britain, despite a small increase in air traffic, came to be almost completely dominated by the private car. Although the volume of coastal shipping traffic is no longer estimated in a manner enabling it to be included on Table 5.1, it is showing a declining trend from a peak of 25 billion tonne-km in 1966 to 20 in 1976. The canal and inland waterway network has been gradually reduced to 544 km of commercially used route, focussed on the Humber, lower Thames and the Manchester Ship Canal. These changes in the volume of traffic flowing through the British transport system form an essential background to a consideration of transport policies during the postwar years.

Changes in the volume of traffic have been accompanied by a number of technological changes. Merchant vessels (section VI.1 below) have increased in size and specialization, and there have been major changes in the layout of ports. The development of unit-load goods traffic has not only revolutionized the handling of almost all break-bulk freight in the ports, but has brought new traffic to the railways. It has also transgressed the divisions between the modes more effectively and to more lasting effect, than any previous change in transport technology. While the airways have greatly increased the capacity and speed of their craft, the railways replaced steam by diesel and electric traction, and began High Speed Train (HST) services on key routes in 1976. These changes have come about as a result of competition with road transport, which has taken an increasing share of the growing volume of traffic while merely improving the technology of the 1920s.

I.3   National Transport Policies
(for references to all Acts, see 'Public General Acts', pp. 505–7)

Transport is so all-pervading and the influences of transport are so widespread that 'almost every transport decision is a public issue' (Munby 1968). Moreover 'transport gives the government powers of positive planning unrivalled in any other field' (Patmore 1972, 50–61). British governments have generally been reluctant to use these powers, for transport policy may be highly controversial and difficult to implement because of the complex interaction of long-term and short-term patterns of demand and supply. Transport considerations play an essentially secondary role in that they facilitate but do not determine the sort of society we want to have. Transport policies have therefore seldom formed major planks in party political programmes: the Ministry of Transport is not regarded as a leading department of state and the Minister of Transport seldom sits in Cabinet. At the local level, transport issues loom larger: the transport policies of counties and districts are discussed in section III below.

Transport policies may be broadly classified as active or reactive, regulatory or developmental. An *active* policy seeks to reshape the transport system, or parts of it, to meet some ulterior objective such as the prestige of the state as identified by its rulers, social equity, economic efficiency or a reshaping of the links between central and peripheral regions. A *reactive* transport policy attempts to adjust the contemporary transport system to new demands or technological developments, and to maintain or re-establish a balance between competitive modes or routes. *Regulatory* policies are concerned with competition within the transport sector. They may also attempt to limit monopoly and to control the adverse side-effects of transport operations such as personal accidents, pollution and damage to the environment. *Developmental* policies are concerned with the introduction or major expansion of a specific transport mode or type of service.

Until the First World War, British governments were encouraged by their belief in the superiority of the market economy to follow reactive and regulatory transport policies and were enabled to do so by the availability of private capital for the transport sector. In the eighteenth century, the inter-city road network was largely rebuilt on a pay-as-you-go basis through Turnpike Trusts; later 4,700 km of canals were financed in a similar way. The early nineteenth century saw the construction of a comprehensive railway system by private capital at relatively high engineering standards in a remarkably short space of time. Acts were passed (notably Gladstone's *Railway Act* of 1844) to ensure high safety standards on the railways. The threat of national or regional railway monopoly was averted by legislation controlling railway charges and the acceptance of traffic, also by the refusal of successive Parliaments to allow regional mergers between the relatively small independent railway companies. The clause in the 1844 Act which forced the reluctant railway companies to provide low-fare services on all routes (the Parliamentary Trains) was an 'active' developmental policy of great social significance for it gave access to the railways to the whole population (not excluding the

Irish immigrants) both to seek work and for pleasure. Transport was no longer restricted to one or two social classes as it had been in the age of the coach. Later social transport policies provided government finance for the construction of roads, piers and even a railway in the peripheral Crofting Counties of Scotland and the Congested Districts on the west coast of Ireland.

British transport policies during the nineteenth century may be contrasted with those of European mainland countries where shortage of capital obliged most governments to take an active interest in the development of the railway system, and considerations of defence ensured continuing state supervision of most transport modes. In France, in particular, successive governments from the reign of Louis XIV to the presidency of Mitterand have regarded the active development of transport infrastructure as one of their major responsibilities.

The prospective growth of road transport led to the establishment of the *Ministry of Transport* in 1919 but interwar governments were unable to finance plans for a national reconstruction of the road network to carry new flows of freight and passenger traffic. Legislation was largely aimed, as Gwilliam (1964) has pointed out, at regulating the growing competition between road and railway transport and between private and public carriers. It was hoped that internal cross-subsidization would enable the individual transport modes to solve their own economic problems. After a period of government direction during the First World War, the railways were amalgamated into four companies, each of which operated in both heavily and lightly trafficked areas. A measure of competition was retained between the new companies on inter-city routes linking major regional centres. The bus industry was reorganized on the same general principle under the *Road Traffic Act* of 1930, with large regional bus companies covering a variety of services but protected from competition on their more profitable routes. No satisfactory solution was found for regulation of the growing competition between road and rail, largely because the type of services provided by each mode and their method of capitalization were so radically different. *Coordination* was considered by the *Royal Commission on Transport* (1930) but was only implemented, and then to a limited extent, in the *London Passenger Transport Board* of 1933.

The *Transport Act* (1947) was the first attempt at comprehensive legislation for the transport system. The newly created *British Transport Commission* (BTC) acquired all railways, inland waterways and road-haulage undertakings except those operating within 40 km of their base, or used by firms to carry their own products. The required provision of an adequate service envisaged the support of some unremunerative services by cross-subsidization (Gwilliam 1964). Transport undertakings were enabled to negotiate Treasury grants, although the level of this support has varied with government attitudes and the advances and recessions of the economy. The *Transport Act* (1953) removed road haulage from the BTC, with the exception of 7,000 lorries retained by British Road Services. In an attempt to bring a greater measure of competition to inland transport, the Act abolished some restrictive obligations on the railways. In the aftermath of the 1953 Act the Beeching proposals for withdrawal of unprofitable railway services were presented and were partially implemented during the early 1960s (MoT 1963B). Similarly, the *Civil Aviation (Licensing) Act* (1960) allowed the monopoly of British European Airways on major internal air-routes to be challenged. The *Transport Act* (1962) reorganized the nationalized undertakings and, while removing further restrictions from rail operation, also gave a measure of protection to coastal shipping from railway competition. The *Pipeline Act* (1962), on the other hand, treated pipelines as a natural monopoly, to be protected against duplication and excess capacity.

The rapid growth of road transport in the early 1960s, which was clearly forcing the railways and public road transport into retrenchment, led to increasing concern. The Labour government of 1964–70 produced a series of White Papers (MoT 1967A–D), followed by the *Transport Act* (1968) which represents the nearest approach to a comprehensive developmental and active transport policy ever produced by a British government. Alongside a road programme which offered a basic skeleton of motorway and other high-capacity roads for the whole UK, the Act proposed to retain the existing rail network and to subsidize 'socially necessary' services in both rural and urban areas. A quantity licensing provision, which was intended to direct all goods traffic over distances in excess of 160km and in vehicles of over 16 tonnes on to the railway, was never implemented. Other features of the Act included the integration of container traffic on road and rail in the National Freight Corporation (NFC) and the establishment of passenger transport authorities in the major conurbations.

The 1968 Act ushered in a period of substantial agreement on transport policy between the major political parties. This was associated with the view that, within the framework laid down by the 1968 Transport Act, customers should have a free choice of transport mode and that each mode or transport company should cover its costs in the medium and long term. The transport provisions of the *Local Government Act* (1972) and the *Railways Act* (1974) also attracted general inter-party political support. Indeed the *Railways Act* was drafted by the Conservatives and passed during the subsequent Labour administration as the fourth postwar attempt to secure a viable financial structure for British Rail. Gross national production was expanding and, as car ownership spread rapidly down the social scale, no major political party in Britain (or in any other democratic 'advanced' Western country for that matter) could deny to its people the opportunity to buy cars or fail to promise to build more roads upon which to drive them.

Another area of substantial agreement was enunciated both in a review of the economic objectives of the nationalized industries (Treasury Cmnd 3437, 1967) and in the Transport White Paper (DoT 1977A), where it was suggested that the price of a transport service should relate to the 'marginal social cost' of providing it – that is the cost of all the resources needed to supply additional units of that service. Transport economists have made considerable advances during the last thirty years in enumerating and assessing these costs. Substantial uniformity in methods of appraising investment had been achieved by the early 1970s. These methods are discussed in DoE 1976 (vol II Paper 5) and Starkie (1973, 1976; Heggie and Jones 1978; Dept Trade 1978). Briefly, *financial appraisal* based on the assessment of discounted cash flows is used where investments and returns can be expressed in monetary terms. This applies when considering railway inter-city passenger and inter-regional freight investment and also the operations of the *British Waterways Board*, the *National Bus Company* and the *National Freight Corporation*. Cost-benefit analysis is used where the values of time, peace and quiet, death by accident, or any other factors which have no money equivalent are being considered. It is therefore relevant to trunk and local road programmes, rural railway closures and the planning of journeys to work. Common evaluation by one or other of these methods facilitates submission of investment programmes from government departments, local authorities and nationalized transport industries to the Public Expenditure Survey Committee.

During the later 1970s, Britain's increasingly difficult economic situation encouraged polarization of suggested political remedies and an increasingly vocal criticism of the existing structure of society by articulate pressure groups. Both economic recession and the break-up of consensus attitudes affected transport policies. Four significant aspects of these changes are discussed below. Although each is treated separately here, there was a considerable measure of interaction between them.

First, the rapid expansion of road and air traffic received a sharp jolt in 1973 when the price of oil doubled and there were rapid increases in the running costs of cars and aircraft. This led to a downward revision in the forecasts of future traffic, making it much more difficult to assess the future demand for major transport investments. Secondly, the baleful inflation in British prices which developed after 1973 led governments to cut public spending on transport. The Channel Tunnel and the proposed seaport and airport at Maplin were the first casualties, but their cancellation in 1974 was soon followed by reductions in the length and capacity of the planned trunk-road network. Thirdly, the opportunities for replacing labour by capital investment in order to achieve market efficiency were developing rapidly in many sectors of the transport industry; containerization is a good example. Transport operators and governments alike hesitated to add too rapidly to the growing army of the unemployed and the introduction of new techniques was often resisted by trade unions for the same reason. Fourthly, social criteria for assessing transport investment were increasingly advocated (Indep. Commn on Transport 1974; Transport 2000 1976; DoE 1976; O'Sullivan 1980; Adams 1981). These included the special needs of elderly, poor or isolated members of the community, the saving of fossil and imported fuel, and the reduction of environmental pollution.

The activities of 'environmental' pressure groups became increasingly significant in many Western countries during the 1970s. There were growing fears that irreplaceable natural resources were being used up too rapidly in the developed world and that the atmosphere was being polluted by emissions from motor-vehicle and aircraft engines (ch. 3.V.2–3). Many people who were worried about global pollution were anxious to challenge the assumptions underlying the prediction of future traffic trends in the UK and, at local level, supported local interest groups concerned with the preservation of recreational activities (usually identified with the maintenance of existing land uses and landscapes) and of peace and quiet around their homes.

Local councillors soon became aware of these views. Successive Labour and Conservative governments were anxiously searching for the least objectionable public expenditure cuts and were ready to heed popular and academic criticisms of major transport investment programmes. Since these programmes depended upon sophisticated cost-benefit analyses for their justification, there were many disagreements as to which factors should be analysed and how much weight should be assigned to them (Gwilliam 1979; Starkie 1979). It is a fundamental difficulty of all forms of economic appraisal that some costs and benefits are much easier to quantify than others. Critics asserted that the easily quantifiable factors such as time savings of car drivers and air travellers had received too much attention while the discomforts which motorways and major airports impose on people living near them had not been given sufficient weight. Insofar as the wealthier social classes

made a disproportionate use of aeroplanes and cars, some major transport investments could be seen, by those minded to do so, as benefitting the rich at the
expense of the poor. Similar objections could be raised against railway investment
since both inter-city and commuter services carry a substantial proportion of
businessmen, and one-half the revenue from passenger fares is derived from the
richest fifth of the population.

In the face of these doubts and uncertainties the *Transport Act* (1978) retreated
from firm commitments to specific proposals such as the completion of the
national motorway/dual-carriageway net planned in the late 1960s. An increasing
proportion of the declining total investment in transport was assigned to the
railways. The effects of these policy changes were not necessarily immediate since
many major road projects were already under construction and a substantial
proportion of the trunk-road programme had been carried out. Policies on subsidies
to transport and on the operating relationships between the transport modes can be
implemented much more rapidly than infrastructural policies.

The real commitment of governments to their policies may be measured by their
expenditure programme. This information is brought together, in broad terms, in
the annual Public Expenditure Surveys and is also summarized in DoT (1981).
Expenditure on surface transport in GB, including the capital expenditure of the
nationalized transport industries, has more than kept pace with public expenditure
as a whole. In terms of constant prices, subsidies to surface transport in GB more
than doubled between 1968–9 and 1975–6, while investment in public transport
rose by 150%. Government investment in transport, measured at constant prices,
rose to a peak in the financial year 1975–6 and has subsequently shown a steady
decline. The planned expenditure for 1983–4 will be only 70% of the real value of
1975 expenditure.

It can be estimated from public expenditure figures that about one-third of
expenditure on surface transport is directed to inter-city and inter-regional transport
and the remainder to essentially local transport needs. As a proportion of total
expenditure, the trunk-road programme fell from 22% in 1970–1 to 16% in 1975–6
and is planned to fall to 14% in the mid-1980s, with an increasing proportion of the
trunk-roads budget being devoted to maintenance rather than new construction.
Investment in British Rail, on the other hand, plus central and local government
subsidies to rail, amounted to 13% of the public surface transport budget in 1970–1
and about 30% in 1981–2. The railways are currently carrying 8% of passenger km
and 18% of freight km and user expenditure on railways has fallen to a mere 4.5%
of the total user expenditure on surface transport. As these proportions are not
expected to alter much within the next few years, it is clear that current government
expenditure on the railways is related to factors other than their current economic
performance. Public expenditure on ports has fluctuated at around 2% of the
transport budget since the mid-1970s and is expected to rise to 3% in the early
1980s. Two-thirds of the local authority transport budget is spent on roads,
equally divided between maintenance and capital investment.

The adherence of the UK to the EEC in 1973 has had little effect on transport
policy to date. European Transport Commission policies have been regulatory
rather than innovative. The Commission attempts to harmonize the transport
regulations of member countries in order to remove obstacles to the free flow of
goods and passengers within the Common Market. British transport policies have
been more concerned with economic efficiency within the UK than with harmoniza-

tion with the European mainland (Despicht 1969; Gwilliam and Mackie 1975; Bird and Pollock 1978).

II   INLAND TRANSPORT BETWEEN CITIES AND REGIONS

II.1   Traffic Flows

Transport in the UK is characterized by short journeys. The majority of journeys are local, inter-city distances are short even by European standards, and few journeys to and from ports exceed 160 km. Of the 55.9 million inhabitants of the UK (1981), 32m (58%) live in the so-called axial belt 400 km long and 120 km broad, extending from Kent to Lancashire but occupying less than one-fifth of the UK land space. Fig. 5.1 gives a broad picture of freight movements by road (which account for 78% of all land freight movements) between the Standard Regions and an indication of the volume of road traffic circulating within Regions. This data (DoT 1979B) shows that the axial belt generates and receives 55% of the freight traffic. Thus it is not surprising to find that the mean freight-haul by road is 69 km and by rail 115 km. The average freight-haul on inland waterways is only 19 km.

Since 1973 there has been a slight fall in the amount of freight carried in GB and no significant increase in the volume of goods transported is expected (DoE 1976). In general terms, the traffic flows of the UK form three distinctive but inter-connected systems: *international* − the flow of raw materials and passengers from abroad and the return movements of passengers and manufactured products through the ports and airports; *inter-city* − the flow of freight and passengers between the major conurbations and regions within the UK; and *local* − movements of people and goods to and from work, school and shops, also the collection and distribution of freight within towns, between neighbouring towns and in rural areas.

The majority of traffic movements can be assigned to one of these broad categories (in fact the vast majority of movements are local) but the detailed picture contains many complications. Passengers and goods may pass from local origins to distant destinations without passing through regional interchange points or using major through-routeways. Seaports, which specialize in international traffic, also handle coal and oil products moving from one part of the UK to another. The transport system of N Ireland is a discrete sub-system of that of the UK, only making connection with British transport through sea and airports, but it has strong historical ties and land links with the transport system of the Irish Republic.

These and many other complexities do not invalidate a general analysis of UK traffic flows at international, inter-regional and local levels. The urbanization of the country has led to growing concentration of population in conurbations and large towns, separated by rural areas of much lower population density. Many of the changes in transport geography during the postwar period have resulted from increasing concentrations of traffic passing through a limited number of nodes. Each mode of transport has attempted to adjust to these developments but has been hampered by the legacy of its past, when traffic flows were more diffuse and did not fit so clearly into the broad flow systems described above. To change the pattern of the network has not only required capital investment beyond the resources of the transport industries themselves but has required changes of attitude among management, trade unions, government and the general public, the abandonment of

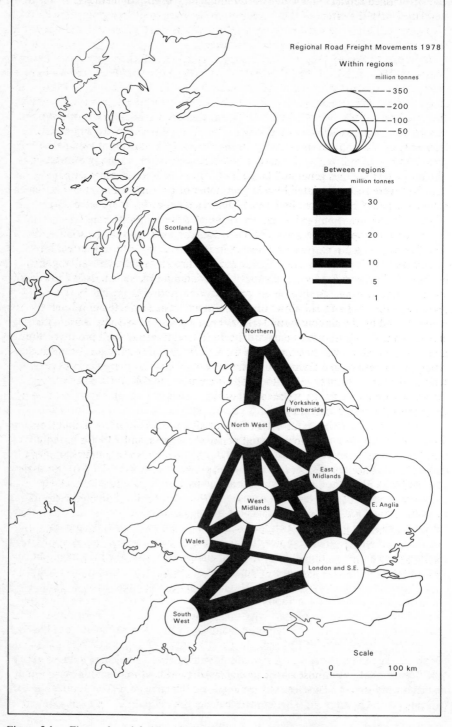

Figure 5.1   Flows of road freight within and between Standard Regions, 1978

long-established services and widespread redundancy in employment. This section is concerned with the effect of these changes on the pattern of transport networks, but continual reference must be made to the institutional frameworks and economic circumstances within which they have occurred.

The period from 1870 to 1950 was one of relative stability for transport networks within the UK. The roads had been asphalted in the early twentieth century but the pressures generated by the steady increase in road traffic had not yet led to major changes in route network. The density of the transport network was lowest in the uplands of the Atlantic Face of Britain where few canals were found and railways and some roads were single-track. The UK network was distinguished from that of European neighbours by its high capacity in regions of moderate population density 250–1, 300 per km^2 where most railways were double-tracked. The heavy traffic flows generated in areas of high population density within the axial belt were accommodated by a large number of alternative routes and nodes of medium capacity rather than by a few high capacity routes. There were only 57 km of high capacity inland waterway – the Manchester Ship Canal.

The Irish transport system evolved when the island was part of the UK but the establishment of a 1.6 metre gauge on the Irish railways in 1846 precluded the subsequent development of train ferries and the through-working of rail wagons between Ireland and Britain. The county boundaries which were hastily chosen in 1921 to form the boundary between the Irish Free State and the UK bore no relation to the road and rail networks of the island. The intricate net of country roads crossed by the sinuous boundary has been a source of political and military embarrassment to both governments. The 1921 Treaty would have preserved the unity of the Irish railway system under the jurisdiction of the Council of Ireland. Attempts to develop the Council were suspended in 1925 and rejected by the N Ireland electorate in 1973 (ch. 1.IV). The *Transport Act, N Ireland* (1948) contained provisions for the nationalization of the transport system similar to those of the British *Transport Act* (1947).

It is important to bear in mind that 27% of all journeys are made to and from work and school, 37% for shopping and personal business, and 23% for broadly social purposes, leaving only 12% of all trips as day-excursion or holiday journeys (DoT 1981). Therefore 52% of all journeys are of less than 3 km, 77% of less than 8 km and 90% under 16 km. Even day pleasure trips average only 34 km. Long journeys of over 40 km have declined since 1977 owing to the economic recession. In 1979, 42% of these 'long' journeys were business trips.

At all distances the car (including all employer's vehicles) is the most frequently used mode of transport. Buses are important in the 3–8 km range where they account for 28% of the journeys. The share of the train increases from 10% at 16 km to 42% for longer journeys of over 80 km, whereas long-distance coaches have only 6% of this traffic. Outside the commuter services 60% of train journeys are on business.

II.2   Trunk-Road Development

Modern road transport for passengers and freight began to develop after the First World War, satisfying almost all the new transport needs of the developing economy and capturing some traffic from the railways and inland waterways. The number of private cars reached 1m in 1930, 10m in 1967 and 15m in 1980. By this time, the roads were carrying 82% of the passenger km and 78% of the freight tonne km. Although the length of public road was increased by 8% between 1960 and 1980, British roads remain among the most crowded in the world.

During the 1950s the expectation of future traffic growth played a critical role in perception of the need for more roadspace to meet the expected traffic volumes of the future. Consumer expenditure on motoring rose from 2% of all consumer expenditure in 1949 to 8% in 1969, while expenditure on other forms of transport remained at 4% of total consumer expenditure. Planners asked themselves for how long this investment in private car transport could be sustained and how much traffic would have been generated before the use and ownership of motorcars levelled off.

While some forecasting models project the trend of past and present growth in vehicle numbers into the immediate future, others seek to identify the main factors which determine the level of car ownership (such as the size of the human population, distribution of incomes, GNP, costs of motoring, etc.) and estimate their incidence on car numbers in the future. Another method is to assume that, in common with other consumer durables, the number of cars will rise to reach a saturation level and will then virtually cease to grow. Analysis of the growth of car fleets in N America and W Europe suggests eventual saturation levels ranging from 0.25 cars per person (4 persons to the car) in inner cities, to 0.52 in the suburbs and 0.77 in other areas. Such levels would imply 21–28m cars in GB by year 2000 (Tanner 1977) but the date at which saturation levels might be reached is likely to be determined by the factors listed above. In 1980 there were 0.27 cars per person in the UK.

Twenty years ago, forecasters were predicting a more rapid rise in the car fleet. The Buchanan Report (Buchanan 1963), for instance, suggested a figure of 19m cars by 1980 (actual 15m) and 30m by 2000, when the car fleet would be approaching saturation point. Such predictions suggested an urgent need for a rapid expansion of the road network.

Roads of all types had, of course, been improved to higher capacity by widening and realignment wherever the increasing flow of traffic had created 'bottlenecks' in which the flow of traffic exceeded the capacity of the road to carry it except at greatly reduced speeds. County road authorities in particular have sought to eliminate the worst stretches of overcrowded road, which have high accident rates, but the removal of individual bottlenecks by road widening often merely created another bottleneck further along the road. This was particularly likely when expenditure on road-widening schemes did not keep up with the overall growth of traffic in the area.

Traffic was by no means spread evenly over the road network. In 1964, 1% of the total road length carried 25% of the traffic, with an average flow of 15,000 vehicles per day. A further 9% of the road length carried a further 40% of the traffic, but the remaining 35% of the traffic spread itself over 90% of the road mileage. The least used half of the road system was only carrying 500 vehicles per day, a flow well within the capacity of a two-lane road. In order to accommodate such concentrations of inter-city traffic, a network of trunk roads, under the direct responsibility of the Ministry of Transport, had been established in 1936. Trunk roads now account for 4% of the road network in GB and principal roads for a further 10%. In N Ireland 3% of the road network is classified as trunk and 7% as principal road.

The immediate postwar years were occupied in making up arrears of road maintenance and in improving roads at accident black spots. After improvements on the designated trunk routes during the early 1950s, the motorway-building programme began in 1957.

The motorways A motorway from London through Birmingham and Manchester to Liverpool had been suggested as early as 1924, in order to accommodate the rising flows of concentrated traffic. The first German motorway was constructed in 1928 but it was not until 1949 that the *Special Roads Act* established the legal framework for motorway building in Britain, and only in 1953 were the first short stretches of motorway opened. In 1957 the Transport Minister outlined a national motorway plan comprising 1,600 km of motorway and a further 1,600 km of dual carriageway route to be completed by the early 1970s. These routes were designed primarily for the benefit of internal freight traffic, linking the main industrial areas by the shortest feasible network. As pointed out by Appleton (1962), London was linked to four conurbations by only one motorway as far as Watford Gap, where the Leeds (M1) and Carlisle (M6) roads diverged. A similar situation had lasted on the railways only from 1847 to 1860.

An important feature of the road-construction programme was the replacement of estuarine ferries by bridges and tunnels. In a major bridge-building programme, from the Tamar Bridge in 1961 to the Humber Bridge in 1981, ten high-level bridges and four tunnels were built. Schemes for a barrage carrying a high-capacity road across Morecambe Bay, however, have been dropped in favour of the upgrading of road access to W Cumberland across the Lake District (A66).

As the tide of postwar prosperity and reconstruction began to ebb during the later 1950s, the 'depressed areas' of the 1930s began to re-emerge as shoals and islands of unemployment and deprivation in the economic geography of the country. Road schemes in these Development Areas, recommended in *White Papers*, including the *Hailsham Report* on the NE (Secretary of State 1963) and the equivalent study of C Scotland (Scottish Development Dept 1963), were accelerated. Later they were exempted from the capital-spending cuts of the late 1960s. Such road schemes were intended to facilitate the concentration of investment *within* Assisted Areas, alleviating unemployment by enabling longer journeys to work in the short term and the redistribution of population in the long term (Gwilliam 1964, 169–81).

Public investment In 1938–9 £10.3m was spent on new construction and major improvement of trunk and class I roads, and in 1947–8 £2.6m, only 4% of the total spending on public roads in GB in that year. From 1949–54 major improvement and new construction expenditure on trunk roads remained at just under £2m per annum but rose on class I roads to £4m. After 1954 expenditure on major improvement rose rapidly: on trunk roads to £12m in 1957, £32m in 1958, and £417m in 1973–4. By 1973 expenditure on new construction and major improvements represented 57% of the total expenditure on roads. The share of this expenditure devoted to trunk roads rose from 9% in 1938 to 26% in 1973. New construction included the extensive provision of dual carriageways between towns and the separation of fast and slow traffic on hills by the provision of three lanes.

The British motorway-building programme has been more modest than those of her European neighbours. In 1979 the UK had 2,485 km of motorway compared with 7,029 km in W Germany, 5,900 km in Italy and 4,603 km in France. In historical perspective the first 25 years of railway building (1830–55) produced 11,700 km of line.

Network planning While the first 1,600 km of motorway were under construction, new methods of trunk-route network planning were developed. The *National Motorway Plan* of the mid-1950s and the roads built in Development Areas in the early 1960s relied on rather generalized traffic data and on the belief that road construction is generally beneficial to industrial development. After the completion of the main section of the London to Birmingham motorway in 1959 it was possible to study the effects of the new trunk routes on traffic flows in their vicinity, and to begin to distinguish between the extent to which the motorway was catering for the general growth in traffic, generating new traffic and diverting traffic from pre-existing roads (Beesley, Coburn and Reynolds, 1959). The Ministry of Transport developed its research organization, collected more traffic data, began to use more sophisticated prediction models of car ownership and also took into account proposals of the regional Economic Planning Councils for the development of New Towns and the prospective location of other major traffic-generating installations, such as green-field industrial plant, seaports and airports. The benefits of each scheme, in terms of reduced vehicle costs, time savings and the avoidance of accidents are compared with the capital and maintenance costs over a period of 30 years. Systematic economic appraisal of costs and benefits was first introduced in 1963. This was formalized in 1967 and in 1973 replaced by a more sophisticated method of appraisal, called COBA, which was applied to the great majority of road schemes, excepting the smallest and the largest, during the remainder of the 1970s. Gwilliam and Mackie (1975) and DoT (1979A) describe transport planning criteria in more detail.

The new road plans were suggested in a Green Paper (MoT 1969A) and proposed in White Papers (MoT 1970; Scottish Office 1969; Welsh Office 1967). There was promise of a comprehensive national strategic network of roads which would eliminate congestion and make a major contribution to the planning of industrial and regional development and of the whole physical environment. The 1969 strategy routes gave a more even areal coverage of Britain but the 1970 proposals were more closely related to existing and prospective traffic flow, giving a more extensive network of high-capacity roads, i.e. 3,200 km of motorway and 2,400 km of dual carriageway by 1982, thus bringing every town of over 80,000 people within 16 km of a high-capacity road. By 1979 only six such towns (Aberdeen, Norwich, Grimsby and the resorts of Worthing, Brighton and Torbay) were more than 16 km from the high-capacity network.

By the late 1960s the detailed planning of high-capacity roads involved elaborate studies of the existing network and a degree of public participation. The planning process included: regional origin and destination surveys, extrapolated by forecasts of future traffic flow, studies seeking to accommodate the maximum satisfaction of road freight and passenger 'desire lines' with the minimum addition to the existing network, and evaluations of construction costs, compensation payments, and assessments of damage to the visual landscape. Final decisions on the route were taken after a public enquiry to which all interested groups and individuals were invited. This planning process is enlightened in that it brings the technical skills of planners and the democratic process into full play, but it cannot provide quick results.

The building of the high-capacity road network was the most important development in British transport infrastructure of the twentieth century. Like the building
of the inter-city rail network in the nineteenth century, however, it was a relatively
short-lived surge of transport investment. Each of the major trends underlying the
traffic forecasts which had made the motorway programme seem so urgent in the
late 1950s was reversed in the 1970s. The birth-rate fell to bare replacement levels,
GDP stagnated in real terms and the cost of petrol at the pumps rose from 7p per
litre in 1971 to 36p in 1981. Vehicle numbers, which had been forecast to reach
18m by 1970, achieved this level only in 1979. While the lorry fleet had greatly
increased its capacity by investing in larger vehicles, the growth in the numbers of
commercial vehicles was also much slower than had been predicted.

The nineteenth-century railways had faced a good deal of initial opposition from
among the literate and articulate groups of society but later came to be universally
recognized as beneficial. High-capacity roads, by contrast, experienced increasing
opposition as the network expanded. Motorways, which had looked so attractive
on the drawing boards of the 1960s, ran into local resistance when they came to be
actually built on their chosen sites. They were held to disrupt traditional patterns
of local movement, to scar the landscape and to create considerable noise and (it
was alleged) other forms of pollution largely for the benefit of strangers hurtling
past or above on their long-distance journeys.

Governments of both major political parties had based their transport policies
broadly on market forces, building roads to accommodate the rapidly increasing car
fleet of the British people and acquiescing in the consequent abandonment of public
transport services as passengers deserted them and revenues fell. There was indeed a
rapid increase in mobility as individuals transferred from public transport to private
cars, a move facilitated by the high level of company cars in Britain (Whitelegg
1981) during the 1950s and 1960s, and this process was expected to continue until
there was almost one car for every two people by the end of the century. During
the 1970s, however, there were fewer first-time buyers of cars and a significant
proportion of these lived in households which already owned a car. The number of
two- and three-car households grew but the percentage of one-car families remained
the same and the proportion of households without the regular use of car fell only
from 49% in 1969 to 42% in 1979. There were marked regional variations, from
33% of households with no car in SE England to 52% with no car in Scotland.
Hillman *et al* (1973) had pointed out that, in addition to households which could
not afford a car, there would always be a substantial number of people including
school children, young workers, the elderly and non-working mothers who lacked
the use of the family car during the working day. For these people the car did not
provide a substitute for public transport. As public transport declined through lack
of patronage, the increased mobility of the majority was being set in sharper
contrast to the decreasing mobility of the car-less population. In 1844, Gladstone's
Railway Act had opened railway travel, the universal transport of the time, to
virtually the whole population. It now began to look as if this process was being
reversed in the twentieth century by the growth of private motoring. How much
public investment should be devoted to increasing the comfort and quality of life of
the car-owning majority if this involved increasing deprivation for the car-less
minority?

While increased traffic may damage the environment through greater congestion
of the existing trunk network, new trunk roads can make drastic alterations in the

visual landscape and carve up formerly peaceful rural tracts (Sharp 1979). The solution to this dilemma of the 1970s was sought through more detailed and sophisticated planning, engineering design, and consultation, but each of these elements added significantly to the total cost of each road. The preservation and perhaps even the conservation of the British landscape during the last quarter of the twentieth century threatens to cost more than the British economy can afford.

By the late 1960s small groups of people who objected to motorways on either environmental or social grounds had begun to join forces. They could always rely on some local support, for few people viewed the prospect of a motorway coming close to their own home with equanimity. The objectors began to appear at planning enquiries to criticize not only the detailed line of local motorway proposals but also the national balance of investment in public and private transport and the reliability of current traffic forecasts. Local hostility to the routes of new roads grew rapidly during the early 1970s in volume, technical sophistication and legal expertise. Objectors also discovered that a measure of violent action during public enquiries attracted television cameras and thereby brought the progress of the national trunk-road plan to public attention. By 1976 several motorway enquiries were disrupted by objectors. When objectors gained the right to question the national trunk-road programme at local enquiries, planning procedures for specific routes were seriously delayed.

During the long gestation period of several high-capacity roads, reductions in finance for the road programme have so retarded schemes that they have been superseded by new evaluations of traffic need. Similarly, the arguments of pressure groups, even though failing to convince the minister making the final decision, have on occasion imposed such delays as have led to the indefinite postponement of the project. Changes of government in 1964, 1968 and 1974 provided the opportunity for reassessment of some projects but the differences in the road policies of the Conservative and Labour parties, when in office, should not be exaggerated. Each inherited a substantial commitment to road construction in progress and has followed policies very similar to those of other Western governments.

Finally, the increasing weakness of the British economy during the 1970s was exacerbated by the action of other oil-producing countries, who began to raise the price of petroleum in 1973. This drew dramatic attention to the dependence of the UK on oil imports at that time and provided justification for successive governments to make drastic cuts in the transport budget. They were increasingly receptive to social and economic arguments against the rapid completion of the original national trunk-road programme. The current road programme was cut four times in 1973–4, reducing its share in the total investment in transport from 48% in the early 1970s to 35% in plans for the mid-1970s. This was done by delaying the start of new road schemes rather than cancelling contracts for roadworks in progress. The annual construction of motorway, for instance, peaked at 400km in 1972 and fell irregularly to 70km in 1979. More detailed planning and consultation procedures and changes in the responsibility of local government for transport have emphasized tactical and regional considerations at the expense of strategic and national issues. Changes in the planning structure, financial stringencies, and a growth in the public awareness of social and environmental issues have all weakened the national drive to build new trunk roads. Major motorway schemes, such as the Manchester–Sheffield link, were abandoned or postponed indefinitely. The London Outer Ring road (M25) continues under construction.

large fleet of small goods wagons and passenger coaches. Between the 1920s and 1960s the railways lost their dominant position in passenger and freight transport to road vehicles but retained their pattern of services, their fleet of steam-engines, coaches and wagons and almost all their route network. During the last twenty years it has been increasingly accepted that railways have an important role to play in the transport system of the UK in three main areas: the long-distance movement of bulk freight; inter-city passenger traffic; and the journey to work in the larger conurbations.

Table 5.1 shows how the railway share of freight and passenger traffic has declined since 1960. The initial fall in traffic left the railways over-equipped and overmanned. With 80% of the total road and rail freight vehicle capacity, the railways were carrying 32% of the freight tonne-km in 1962 (Deakin and Seward 1969). However, Table 5.2 shows that track, stations, vehicles and workforce are now used much more efficiently. The economic and technical metamorphosis of British railways is more fully discussed in Aldcroft (1968); Dyos and Aldcroft (1969); Pollins (1971); Thomson and Hunter (1973); Barker and Savage (1974); Bagwell (1974); and Pryke and Dodgson (1976).

For successive railway administrations the overriding problems have been to pay wages and other current expenses while simultaneously finding capital for the further mechanization of the system: to develop a new railway while still operating an old one. Two aspects of subsidiary economic importance but considerable geographical interest, namely the diminishing size of the railway network and changes in accessibility brought about by new services, are illustrated in figs. 5.3 and 5.4.

The existence in Britain of a railway network of 32,000 km in 1950 can be explained by four main historical factors. First, was the real need during the nineteenth century for improved transport between coalfields, ports and factories, city centres and dormitory suburbs, and between the main population centres. Secondly, companies frequently built lines in anticipation of needs which were not subsequently justified by the traffic generated. Thirdly, the competitive structure of the railway industry in its early years led to duplication of routes in order to share potential traffic with rival companies or to forestall their access to particular markets. Fourthly, the technical advantages of the railway over other forms of transport for all purposes led to its ubiquitous coverage of the UK. The extensive use of small private wagons, especially the ten-ton coal wagon, required a high ratio of track to traffic, especially in the numerous marshalling yards.

The railways were providing a number of distinctive services which may be separated conceptually but share some of the same track and stations in actual operating practice. Modern railway terminology distinguishes *inter-city passenger*, *freight* and *parcels* services, which link the conurbations and the main regions of the country from *London and the SE*, and *rural* services. The railways of SE England are dominated by commuter services in and out of the main London termini and carry a relatively small quantity of freight. The conurbations outside London have urban railway services on a much smaller scale, often operated in association with the local Passenger Transport Executive. While on Clydeside, British Rail operate an electrified urban network, the Tyne and Wear PTE has converted former railway track into its own 'Metro' system on the pattern of those London Transport Executive underground services which extend as surface railways across the northern and western suburbs of the capital. Passenger services to remote

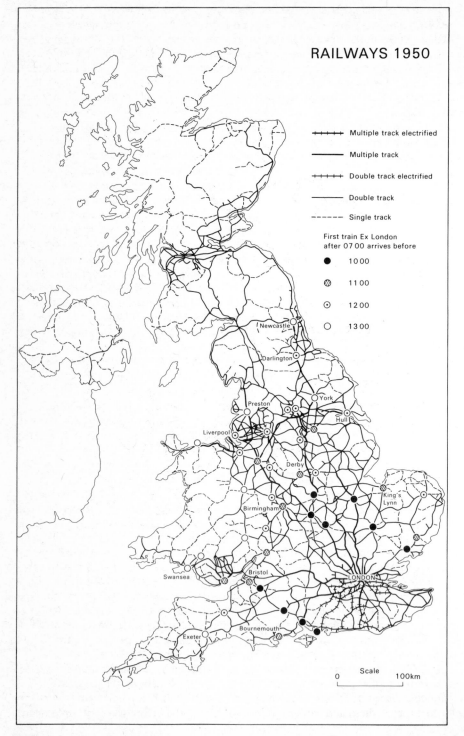

Figure 5.3   Railways, UK, 1950

'in conventional commercial terms there is no viable railway network and any significantly smaller network would require greater financial support than the present day railway.'

The *Railways Act* (1974) withdrew subsidies to specific services in favour of a general subsidy to the whole rail passenger operation, including those costs shared with freight transport, for a five-year period. Within this period further investment and reform of services was to take place while the network of routes was substantially maintained. Under this Act two-thirds of the total subsidies available for inland surface transport were given to British Rail by 1976. Although the railway carried only 8% of the total passenger mileage in Britain in 1974, passenger fares were only contributing about one-third of the factor cost of rail passenger transport. These large subsidies were not sufficient to prevent a rapid rise in passenger fares during the severe inflation of the mid-1970s which caused a slight decline in the patronage of inter-city routes.

Since the development of road transport during the 1920s the railways have found it difficult to attract new traffic or to benefit from changing patterns of industrial location (White 1978). Freight carried by the railways fell from 310m tonnes in 1928 to 153m tonnes in 1980 although tonne-kms did not fall so steeply. The railways found it less easy to retain the wagon-load traffic of small- and medium-sized manufacturers who often rated reliability, speed and security above cost of transport (Deakin and Seward 1969; Wallace 1974, 25–43). The decline in the production and use of coal and the rationalization of the steel industry have reduced the coal and ore traffic, both staples of railway freight transport. Coal traffic fell from 223m tonnes in 1913 (61% of tonnage forwarded) to 94m tonnes in 1980 (61% of tonnage forwarded). Other freight amounted to 141m tonnes in 1913 and 59m tonnes in 1980. Although steel traffic is declining, the railways have developed a significant traffic in petroleum products (14m tonnes) and building materials. Rail revenue is becoming increasingly dependent on a relatively small number of large firms, including nationalized industries and multinational corporations. In 1971 75% of railway freight revenue was derived from 300 customers, including 50% from only 30 firms (Pryke and Dodgson 1976).

The modernization of many main lines during the 1960s allowed British Rail to take the initiative in the land movement of the large modern *containers* which began to arrive at British ports, initially from America. The containers were loaded on to trains travelling at high speed on standard daily schedules. The first of these services was launched between London and Glasgow in 1959 and later 'Freightliner' services were extended to provincial centres (fig. 5.4) and to the new container berths at Felixstowe, Harwich, Tilbury, Fishguard and Holyhead. Inland customs depots were set up in each of the conurbations. Development was slower than had been hoped. Thomson and Hunter (1973) suggested that the efficiency of the rail freightliner only overtakes that of door-to-door road transport at about 240 km and that the economic collecting radius of a freightliner terminal is about 16 km. This puts only about 5% of all traffic within the freightliner range in Britain.

The railways partially replaced their declining coal traffic with oil products, whose traffic was doubled between 1963 and 1966, possibly forestalling a more extensive network of pipelines. The coal traffic itself was rationalized. Many power stations and steel works were adapted to take permanently coupled 'merry-go-round' trains operating from the larger collieries. The rail haul of domestic coal was concentrated at central depots. 'Company' trains provided regular transport between different branches of the same firms, notably the major car companies, or between producers and wholesalers, as in the case of whisky or beer. Accessibility to the dispersed factories of some firms has improved greatly since the 1950s and so have some long-distance services to ports. Inter-city passenger trains run faster and at more regular intervals. Further improvements in railway passenger speed were associated with the introduction of the 200 kmph High Speed Train (HST or Intercity 125) in 1976 which progressively linked London with the major provincial conurbations. The Advanced Passenger Train (APT), a lightweight train of radically new design with tilting suspension and a maximum speed of 250 kph, went into experimental service on the electrified line from London to Glasgow late in 1981. The Hovertrain, a tracked hovercraft, designed to link the conurbations on a new track at speeds of 400 kph during the 1990s, was cancelled in 1972. All these new trains were designed to compete against domestic air-routes for the business traveller, who provided 43% of railway passenger revenue (apart from commuter lines), the base load of demand which shapes the network of inter-city services.

A further move to replace ageing rolling stock and to modernize the railway was a proposed twenty-year programme of electrification which would result in 9,250 km of electrified route, on lines which now carry 83% of the passenger km and 68% of the freight tonne-km. Although the government refused to commit itself to a rolling programme of electrification on this scale, it appeared in 1981 to be prepared to approve schemes one by one and to raise the investment ceilings for British Rail as and when electrification schemes justified the investment.

The 1970s saw increasing contrasts between the commercial railway services which were profitable and which received considerable investment, and the social services which were maintained but hardly improved. In the context of falling revenue and ageing equipment it has been necessary to renegotiate the government subsidies to the railway system about every six years since 1968. The *Transport Act* (1968) stressed a market approach, requiring BR to balance revenues and cost 'taking one year with another'. Revenues included subsidies to specifically designated services which were seen as temporary measures. The *Railway Act* (1974), on the other hand, laid more emphasis on the social railway by supplying a block grant to BR (accounting for 26–30% of annual revenue) and requiring the company to maintain its passenger network and services at 1974 levels. This contribution was not sufficient for BR to replace as much obsolescent track and rolling stock as it would have liked.

In 1980 the revenue of BR was fairly well balanced with 25% from the national government (about half the proportionate contribution to revenue made to state railways on the European mainland), 5% from local authorities, 20% from freight, 20% from inter-city passenger services, 17% from services in London and the SE, and 6% from parcels services. While inter-city and London-area passenger services were able to make substantial contributions to indirect costs, fare revenue only covered 73% of direct costs on railway services run in conjunction with PTEs and only 58% on rural services (BRB 1981B).

The economic recession and associated strikes led to a significant decline in the volume of freight handled in 1979 and 1980. Iron and steel traffic fell by 50% and the general volume of freight by 13%. Even business travel on inter-city expresses was declining in 1981. The failure to maintain vehicles and track or to lay aside enough capital to renew them threatened a severe deterioration in rural railway services during the 1980s.

Even before the introduction of the HST, British railways were competing successfully with buses on the motorways and with domestic airlines over distances within the 160–640km range wherever rail speed had been increased through electrification or other modernization measures. The European railways have had similar success with Trans-European Express (TEE) services. Both British Rail and TEE services stood to benefit by linkage through a Channel Tunnel which would provide rail services between Manchester, Birmingham, London, Brussels and Paris at city-centre-to-city-centre timings shorter than the current journey times by air. The Dover Strait was first surveyed for a tunnel in 1836. Enabling bills for its construction were passed in 1875 but the project was stopped by the British government in 1882. A revival of interest in the late 1960s led to a new Anglo– French treaty (1973) for the joint construction of a rail tunnel from Folkestone to Calais. A new railway, built to the continental loading-gauge, was to link the Channel tunnel with west London. The project was, however, cancelled in 1974 as one of a series of cuts in public expenditure. The scheme was revived in the late 1970s in the form of a single tube carrying one railway track with a capacity of 60 trains per day in each direction. Road traffic would continue to use the ferries but it was expected that there would be some diversion of traffic from road to rail and considerably less environmental disturbance than with the larger, earlier scheme. It was also hoped that the scheme could be financed wholly by private capital. While this scheme found some favour with the British government, the French government continued to prefer a larger tunnel and a higher degree of state investment.

II.4   Inland Waterways

The inland waterways of the UK now perform a very limited transport function (below 0.1% of total UK freight tonne-km) with most of the commercial traffic on rivers where the navigable channel has been regulated and locked. It is no longer appropriate to identify an inland waterways *network* for traffic purposes rather a number of small separate sections, linked to major estuaries and acting as feeders to selected ports. The largest of these waterways is the Manchester Ship Canal, stretching for 57km from the Mersey estuary to Salford Docks in the centre of Greater Manchester. With a minimum depth of 8.5 metres to allow ocean-going vessels to reach the port of Manchester, this canal is of a totally different scale to all other inland waterways in Britain, is not administered by British Waterways and does not figure in tables 5.3 and 5.4.

The UK has never provided favourable conditions for the development of inland water transport. Even before the railway provided overwhelming competition, coastal shipping competed for trade between the many centres of population and industry which were located on tidewater. In most areas the relief of the country and the short distances between suppliers and markets limit the efficient operation of inland waterways. The piecemeal development of canals with varying widths and capacities, and with fragmented ownership, did not encourage the functioning of a network over the longest possible distances. There has also been a decline in demand for the type of services which the inland waterways can supply. Watts (1967) pointed out that it is not common in the UK for distances to be long enough and for vessels to be large enough to counteract the disadvantages of high terminal charges. The present commercially operated stretches of waterway are

those which are able to use the larger vessels and to do so with *direct* loading from
ship or factory, thus keeping terminal costs as low as possible. The traditional
categories of waterway are *narrow* and *wide* (or broad) but since 1965 the British
Waterways Board has recognized a threefold division into 'commercial waterways',
totalling about 547 km; 'cruising' waterways (1,770 km) for boating, fishing and
recreational uses; and 'remainder' waterways (970 km) which must be maintained
by the Waterways Board 'in the interests of public health, amenity and safety' — in
other words because they are an integral part of the local water network and
cannot economically be filled in. After long discussion, it was finally decided not
to include the British Waterways Board in the National Water Authority.

The commercial waterways, which handled 72% of the traffic in 1980, are: the
Weaver navigation, with its canal-side industry; the Lea navigation and the lower
Grand Union system, both concerned with distribution from the Port of London;
the Severn system linking the Port of Bristol with the W Midlands; and the most
extensive system, radiating from the Humber and including the Aire and Calder, the
Sheffield and the S Yorkshire canals where the main traffic is coal, together with
the Trent navigation from the sea to Nottingham, notably carrying petroleum
inland.

TABLE 5.3

Traffic, British Waterways Board, 1955–80

	million tonnes	million tonne-km	Percentage of traffic in 1980	tonnes	tonne-km
1955	10.7	300.2	Coal, coke etc.	40	26
1965	8.6	216.4	Bulk liquids	20	48
1975	4.2	73.7	General merchandise	40	26
1980	4.5	77.5		——	——
				100	100

Source: BWB, Annual Report 1980

TABLE 5.4

Average Length of Haul, BWB, 1964–74 (km)

	1964	1969	1974
Coal, coke and patent fuel	18	17	14
Liquids in bulk	38	29	24
General merchandize	25	20	19
All freight	25	21	19
Freight conveyed by BWB fleet	64	48	40

Source: DoE (1976)

Table 5.3 shows that bulk liquids dominate the traffic carried on the inland
waterways although providing only one-fifth of the tonnage. With the competition
of railway and road services, traffic on the inland waterways has declined steeply,

and the average length of haul has fallen. In this connection it is worth recalling that in 1955 the then average length of haul of 27 km was already regarded as too short for effective operation. By 1980, 70% of the expenditure of the Waterways Board (£33.2m) was financed through government grants-in-aid, 15% from commercial receipts and 6% from leisure traffic (BWB 1980).

The only major capital development now under way is the improvement of the Sheffield and S Yorkshire Navigation to allow 700-tonne barges to reach Mexborough and 400-tonne barges to reach Rotherham from the Humber estuary. This scheme, which began in 1979, is being funded by British Waterways, S Yorkshire County Council and the EEC.

II.5 Pipeline Development

Although an inconspicuous, indeed usually concealed, element of the transport system, pipelines have been extended rapidly in the last decade, mainly in relation to the transport of energy. The separateness and exclusiveness of the pipeline network is to some extent deceptive. From tanker to pipeline is clearly intermodal transport and there is competition between pipeline and coastal shipping and more directly between the pipeline and the railway. Pipelines undoubtedly have an increasing role in UK transport, but it must be noted that this is a role limited not only by the particular characteristics of the pipeline as a transport medium but also quite specifically limited by the size and shape of the country. The dimensions of the UK are such that the main asset of pipelines — bulk movement over long distances — cannot be fully exploited.

Pipelines are a restricted transport mode because of the rigidity of the route and the limited range of commodities which can be transported, mainly oil, gas and some solids as slurry. While able to handle greater gradients than any other transport mode, pipelines involve continuous movement at a constant rate and are invariably slow, perhaps 5–8 kmph. To operate effectively, pipelines need a persistent and high level of demand, for capital costs completely dominate the economics of pipeline transport and, with increased diameter, capacity increases at a faster rate than costs. Pipelines may be used for large volume storage and have a very low labour requirement. Their transport costs, where appropriate comparisons are possible, are usually regarded as equivalent to those of water transport and, in comparable situations, no more than one-quarter of the cost of rail transport. Pipelines may offer increasing competition to the railway in the movement of coal or ore as slurry, although the

TABLE 5.5

Pipelines: Oil and Petroleum, UK, 1964–80

Overland length of line, weight moved			
	1964	1970	1980
Length of line (km)*	819	1,702	3,416
Tonne-km moved (millions)	1,123	3,031	9,929

* these figures exclude pipelines of less than 25km, also North Sea crude oil and gas pipelines

Source: DoT (1981)

limited distances involved and the density of the present railway network may limit this development.

A remnant of the extensive wartime network to supply airfields is still in use but the effective present-day pipeline network is almost entirely a product of the 1960s. Developments after the *Pipeline Act* (1962), applicable to all pipelines over 16 km in length, took advantage of a much simplified, although still strictly controlled, procedure which previously required a private Bill in Parliament. There are three short stretches conveying gaseous oxygen and one moving chalk slurry for the Portland Cement Co. from Dunstable quarries to Rugby but most pipelines carry either oil products or gas. The first pipeline in the UK linked Finnart, a deepwater harbour on Loch Long, with Grangemouth refinery in 1951 (with a new pipe in 1969). In 1975 the same refinery was linked by 208 km of pipe to Cruden Bay, the landfall of the BP Forties field and also to the new Hound Point terminal on the Forth (figs. 4.4 and 5.6). Further lengths of crude-oil pipeline have been laid to feed refineries at Llandarcy (1960), Heysham (1967) and Stanlow (1977), where depth limitations prevent the use of large tankers. Overland crude-oil pipelines in 1980 had an aggregate length of 3,416 km. The development of North Sea oil, at distances of 160 km offshore, had added a new dimension of crude-oil pipelines with undersea pipes. Such pipelines, completed or well advanced, include in addition to the Forties to Cruden Bay link: Ekofisk (1975) to Teesside; Piper (1976) and Claymore to Flotta; and Brent and Ninian to Sullom Voe. The petroleum products pipelines, the main network, include stretches of the wartime network, notably, for example, the pipeline linking the Isle of Grain refinery to London Airport (Heathrow), and Stourport to Reading. The developments of the 1960s included the pipeline from Fawley to Staines and London Airport in 1963, the Thames and Mersey link with short Midlands offshoots completed in 1969, and the longest development (481 km) linking Milford Haven to Manchester, Birmingham and Nottingham (1973). Petrochemical feedstock pipelines linked Fawley to Severnside (1962) and interconnected two further main concentrations of the petrochemical industry, the Tees (Wilton), and Lancashire and Cheshire (Fleetwood, Partington, Runcorn and Stanlow) by 1968.

The first main length of the present natural-gas pipeline system was completed in 1962 from Canvey Island (Thames) to Leeds to carry Algerian methane gas brought as a refrigerated liquid by tanker. The situation was soon transformed by North Sea gas. In 1967 the West Sole well was linked to Easington (near Hull) and to Sheffield and the Leeds pipeline. The following year the Leman, Hewett and Indefatigable fields feeding to the coast at Bacton (Norfolk) were joined to the distribution grid at Rugby. The grid has spread into Wales, the South West peninsula and Scotland, where gas from the Frigg field (352 km NE of Aberdeen) is brought ashore at St Fergus near Peterhead. The dimensions over which pipelines can operate have been stretched into the North Sea by gas and by oil. It is possible, although unlikely, that the distance restraints of insularity could be removed by under-Channel links. Nonetheless pipelines are not without the potential to re-shape some economic distributions and could certainly do so to the detriment of industrial seaports, although perhaps in most instances the advantages of the coastal site would continue to prevail.

III LOCAL TRANSPORT

The growth in car ownership from one car per 21 people in 1951 to one per 4
people in 1974 has had an even greater impact on local than on inter-city transport.
Travel opportunities have been revolutionized for car owners and drivers, but only
58% of the households in Britain had the regular use of a car in 1979 and only 63%
of the adults had a driving licence. The remainder of the adults, and also older
children going to school, rely on public transport services which have been reduced
in speed and frequency as the private car fleet has grown, and can no longer operate
without a subsidy. The mobility gap between those who can drive whenever they
wish and people with limited or no access to cars is becoming steadily more
important as services concentrate (Mosely 1979). Schools, hospitals, administrative
offices and shopping centres are becoming larger and more widely spaced with
substantial potential economies of scale. The car owner can circulate freely
between these facilities and enjoy the benefits of centralization. People without a
car, or the exclusive use of one, may find access limited and time-consuming. Only
the most careful joint planning of the sites of new services and the public transport
network can reduce the mobility gap.

In town and country alike public transport services have been impelled into a
downward spiral during the 1960s and 1970s. As customers desert the buses and
local trains in order to travel in their private cars, the cost of the services must be
shared among the remaining passengers. The resulting rises in fares may well
discourage the remaining passengers from making some journeys. This leads to still
less economic running and to further fare rises. Since the prime costs – petrol and
wages – cannot be reduced by the operator, services tend to deteriorate slowly and
are eventually closed unless the rate- or tax-payer can be persuaded to fill the gap
between rising costs on one hand and revenues which are limited by what the
passengers are prepared to pay on the other. Table 5.1 shows a decline in passenger
km on bus services of 28% between 1960 and 1980 but there was a decline in
vehicle km of only 8% over this period. In fact the level of passenger fares on
public transport rose 20% higher than the general retail price index during the
1970s.

While district and county councils were enabled to subsidize public transport
services under the *Transport Act* (1968) and the *Local Govt Acts* (1972–3), not
all were willing to do so. The shire counties as a group were spending 91% of their
transport budgets on roads although, at the other extreme, S Yorkshire metropolitan county maintained passenger fares at the same monetary level after 1977
and the Greater London Council reduced fares by 25% in 1981, later denied by the
courts, in attempts to reverse the steady downward trend in passenger journeys.
When the Conservative government elected in 1979 brought local as well as national
public spending under increasingly severe control, the future of many local public
transport services looked uncertain.

III.1 The Coordination of Urban Transport Systems

Before the First World War the larger towns of the UK had municipal tramway
networks which were supplemented in the conurbations by local railway services.
London and Glasgow had underground railway systems as well. Between the wars
buses replaced trams and, outside London, fewer people used railways for short

journeys. In the large towns the dense network of the municipal services was heavily used and fares were low. Smaller towns were served by the regional bus companies established after the *Road Traffic Act* (1930). In these companies town fares subsidized rural routes.

These urban bus services attained their maximum development in 1953. In 1955 the estimated passenger kilometrage in private cars exceeded that in buses for the first time and from then onwards the speed, reliability and frequency of buses, and also the ratio of revenues to costs (of which wages comprised 71%), steadily declined. Fares rose faster than average prices. Between 1955 and 1980 passenger journeys on buses fell by 57% but vehicle km fell by only 19% and the number of vehicles by 4%. Calculations in the late 1960s (Hillman, Henderson and Whalley 1973) showed that even on short journeys of less than 6.5 km, door-to-door trips took twice as long by bus as by car and that bus-journey times lengthened by about one-fifth during the 1960s as a result of road congestion and one-man operation of buses.

As major traffic pressures built up during the late 1950s, plans were made for increased investment on urban roads. These included the construction of circumferential bypasses, the widening of radials and the diversion of traffic through residential streets (Mossé 1974). Forecasts suggested that increased traffic could be accommodated for several decades by road improvements, but traffic in GB grew much faster than had been foreseen and rapidly occupied the new roads to the limits of their design capacity. To accommodate further traffic growth it would have been necessary to build large-scale urban motorway networks on the N American model, but UK cities lacked the space and the resources for such schemes and their planners appreciated that motorways which are built to serve existing traffic also generate much new traffic as people adapt their lives to wider travel opportunities (Schaeffer and Sclar 1975). Towns sought to revalue their existing transport systems using concepts like total social cost (Foster 1975). An assessment of the total social cost of a traffic management scheme attempts to balance the obvious benefits to users against the often indirect damage to the interests of non-users and to the environment in general.

The *Buchanan Report* (Buchanan 1963) had considerable influence on urban planning in the UK. It proposed a sophisticated approach to urban traffic problems, related to the size of individual towns and the layout of their existing streets. Attention should be given to the 'primary distributors', major roads which carried traffic into and around towns, in the hope of creating pedestrian precincts and low-density traffic zones between them. Where the volume of traffic reached a point when the primary distributors and their extensive interchanges became so large as to dominate the visual environment and displace large numbers of dwelling houses, schemes for the restricting of traffic by limiting parking, licensing or road pricing should be considered. Accessibility must be balanced with environmental preservation when the environmental deterioration caused by enlarging the major roads was no longer acceptable. Public transport systems would then have to play an increasing part in moving people to work and to shop. The Report recommended planned coordination between transport systems, developed through the medium of a statutory development plan which took into account predictions of size and direction of traffic flows.

The expertise in the formulation of combined traffic and land-use surveys which had been accumulated in studies of the N American conurbations during the 1950s by several firms of international consultants, began to be applied to British cities, with the firm backing of the Ministry of Transport (DoE 1972; Starkie 1976). These surveys involved the recognition and analysis of traffic-flow systems and the motivations which lay behind them. They used newly developed computing techniques to design and to choose between complex solutions to the problems of future traffic movement. The separate planning of transport and land use was increasingly seen to be unproductive as highway engineers and town planners were drawn into closer association (Foster 1974, 166–91). In 1962 the *London Traffic Survey* was begun, developed under the GLC as a permanent *London Transportation Study* (GLC 1969; Collins and Pharaoh 1974; Foster, Bayliss and Blake 1970; Ridley and Tresidder 1970). Similar studies, supported financially by the MoT, began in the other conurbations and large towns in the UK in 1964. These studies are listed in Starkie (1973 and 1976). They depended on the extensive collection of data on the vehicular movement of people and goods. This data was analysed using traffic models and vehicle-growth forecasts in order to predict traffic growth and change over a period of ten to twenty years. Alternative strategies, with different combinations of new road building and public transport provision, could then be formulated and subjected to cost-benefit study (Solesbury and Townsend 1970; Wilson *et al* 1969). Traffic management is now seen as much in terms of protecting the existing urban environment as in circulating more cars through the streets.

The traffic studies, first published during the early 1970s, recommended considerable capital expenditure on new roads, but while the studies were being prepared the growth of traffic persuaded growing numbers of the articulate public to believe that investment in public transport would offer better relief from traffic congestion. As the first sections of urban motorway networks were being built and road costs and housing dislocation were much more apparent than the benefits of traffic relief, elected councillors and MPs were made aware of public disquiet. The government response (DoE 1972) was to extend compensation in the *Land Compensation Act* (1973). This measure increased the cost of new motorways and the likelihood of legal delays. New arrangements were also made for the consulta-tion of the public before motorway schemes were started (DoE 1973B); in 1975 the role of public enquiries was extended. This combination of rising costs, delays and the prospect of severe cuts in public expenditure led many towns to abandon large sections of their planned road network and face the prospect of increased traffic congestion during the 1980s.

The *Transport Act* (1968) introduced the first government grants for public transport and made provision for the establishment of Passenger Transport Executives (PTEs) in the conurbations. Under the *Local Government Act* (1972) metropolitan counties control transport in their areas, operating through PTEs. The national government gives substantial grants to the PTEs for infrastructure, railways, bus lanes and the building of transport interchanges so that all modes may be used in combination. Within overall spending limits, the metropolitan counties can choose the level of support they are prepared to give to British Rail services and can determine the fares. Outside the GLC area, services on about 1,600km of railway route, carrying about 8% of the railway passenger kilometrage, are subject to PTE policies. On Tyneside a new 54km 'Metro' light railway system opened in 1980–2, incorporating both underground lines and suburban surface railway lines which had first been electrified in 1907. Together with London Transport, PTEs

serve 37% of the UK population. In other towns, the shire county authorities are
required to develop public transport and may receive government grants for this
purpose.

Central government grants for specific transport projects and services were
replaced in 1975 by Transport Supplementary Grants and Rate Support Grants to
each county and Scottish region. For the first time the counties became responsible
for both land-use and transport planning and, until 1981, were able to decide on the
balance of expenditure between capital investment and subsidies to current
transport services within their areas. The size of the government grant to each
county depends on its population, existing commitments to transport and national
constraints on public spending.

The grants are awarded on the submission of an annual county Transport Policy
and Programme to the DoE. This programme must include a ten to fifteen-year
transport strategy which takes into account the plans of the DoE, the National Bus
Company, British Rail and other national operators for inter-city and rural
transport links within the county. County transport policy programmes must be
related to their structure plans but must also use nationally comparable methods of
policy analysis and evaluation. When awarding grants the government will naturally
look most favourably on county schemes which are aligned with current national
transport policies.

Within five years the interest of the local council in transport was thus expanded
from the ownership of a local bus service at most to responsibility for the planning
of a coordinated transport service and, in metropolitan counties, for the operation
of an integrated transport system. Local transport investment and expenditure,
predominantly urban, now accounts for 47% of the national transport budget.
Over two-thirds of the Transport Supplementary Grants for 1981−2 were awarded
to the metropolitan counties. This money was equally divided between investment
and the support of current services and between railway and bus transport. The
shire counties of England and Wales devoted 91% of their Transport Grants to
roads, fairly evenly dividing the funds between construction and maintenance.

It will be some years before the benefits of this radical reorganization will be
apparent, since it will be necessary to replace gradually the vehicles and interchanges inherited from the former separate transport organizations. The new
system should enable the costs and benefits of each service to be assessed as a basis
for a rational decision between alternative investment schemes.

There is considerable variation from town to town in the amount and kind of
transport investment which has actually taken place since 1955. Traffic-
management schemes are almost universal. The planning and building of a stretch
of urban motorway or a new railway/bus station may take ten years but planners,
politicians and the articulate public can change their minds within a matter of
months. The new enthusiasm for large investment in public transport systems which
replaced the desire for motorways unfortunately coincided with a national
economic crisis which led to the curtailing or postponement of many road and
passenger transport schemes.

With the largest population and most complex bus, railway and underground
system, London has the highest proportion (54%) of journeys to work on public
transport. Improved underground services include the Victoria line, the first new
underground line since 1907, planned in 1949 and opened in 1969; and the Fleet
line, approved in 1971 with a 100% government subsidy for its central London

traverse. At that time London Transport Executive planned to spend £500m at current prices on extending and renewing its underground railways and £200m on buses and their routeways. British Rail had a £220m investment plan to improve its surface commuter services up to 1980. These public transport services link the suburbs with the central shop and office areas. The number of journeys from one suburb to another by express buses, delivery vans and private cars grows as the city centre loses population and there is a limited decentralization of offices. To serve this traffic and to link the national motorways with the port and airports of London and the short sea crossings to Europe, three concentric motorway routes totalling 248 km were proposed in 1967. The cost of £850m would have roughly equalled the cost of investment proposals for public transport over the same period. The ringway proposals were based on detailed analysis of traffic flows and trends but met with mounting public opposition. In 1973 the London Labour Party carried out their election promise to abandon the scheme (Hall 1980). An orbital motorway, the M25, is now under construction about 10 km beyond the built-up area on the south side of Greater London. Efforts by a later Labour-controlled GLC to carry out election pledges to emulate most other large European cities in defraying most of the cost of provision of London bus and underground services from the rates rather than through passenger fares caused considerable controversy in 1981. As long as the GLC does not control the level of services and fares on the railway lines which cater for most of the longer public transport journeys in south and east London, it is difficult to establish an equitable basis by which the public transport system might be largely financed through local taxation.

Similar schemes on a smaller scale have been proposed and opposed in the other British conurbations. Differing approaches by local councils and their planners and traffic engineers, changes in political control and in the date of initial plans, are likely to bring about a situation in which the British conurbations will look less like each other as the century advances, as each imposes a different balance between private and public transport on an already varied urban or physical morphology. Thus Clydeside already had 32 km of motorway when the PTE was established but little road building has taken place in Edinburgh. In Newcastle the central area was replanned before the traffic and land-use study took place but the PTE was established before the urban motorway was built.

Almost all urban transport investment is restricted to transport modes which were invented by the end of the nineteenth century. Considerable experimentation in mini-vehicles for individuals, maxi-taxis available on request, moving pavements, light elevated busways and central control of traffic has not yet led to substantial provision of new vehicles or moving walkways.

III.2 The Changing Pattern of Rural Transport

Rural transport is defined here in its widest sense as local transport outside towns. The rural railways were built in the mid-nineteenth century and rural bus services established in the 1920s. Since that time, and most notably during the 1960s the growth of private car ownership created a situation where, as Robinson and Bamford (1978) point out, 'the overall level of transport availability in rural areas has never been so good as at the present time'. Together with public transport, cars provide a total supply of transport well in excess of the ability of rural populations to pay for it.

The rural transport situation varies with rural settlement geography and four characteristic patterns may be distinguished:

In areas within 80 km of conurbations with population densities of over 100 persons per km², in S England and in rural areas within 30 km of conurbations and coalfields in the rest of the UK, the rural population has been swelled by an adventitious population of retired people and commuters who own at least one car per family, who enjoy higher average incomes than those working in local agriculture and other rural industries, and wish to combine the advantages of rural life with access to urban facilities.

Prosperous agricultural areas with population densities of over 100 persons per km² and a village settlement pattern with most people living in communities of 3,000 or over. Many coalfield areas conform to this pattern. Such areas lent themselves to bus transport and had inherited rail services from the nineteenth century.

Areas of dispersed rural settlement in hamlets, as in SW England, the Welsh Borders and N Ireland, or in strings of valley-bottom houses separated by uninhabited interfluves as in C Wales or the Pennine Dales.

The NW Highlands and Islands of Scotland with a total population of 420,000 present the special problem of linear coastal settlements separated from each other by seas and from C Scotland by extensive tracts of uninhabited upland. There is a considerable literature on the transport problems of the NW Highlands (Scottish Dept Agriculture 1967; Knowles 1981; Turnock 1970; Scottish Office 1964; Thomson and Grimble 1968; O'Dell 1966). Since 1745 successive UK governments have provided, or paid for, roads, canals, harbours and railways in this area. Payments for postal services have effectively subsidized the operation of MacBraynes bus and steamship services. Air services to the islands have been cross-subsidized by British Airways.

The need for rural transport has grown steadily since the Second World War. As employment in agriculture and mining declined, the medium-sized towns increasingly supplied employment for rural inhabitants. Economies of scale in medicine and education favoured the development of the relatively large district general hospital of 800–1,000 beds and the secondary school of 500–1,000 pupils. Primary schools, maternity and geriatric hospitals are more frequently dispersed, but if the rural population wish to participate in rising national standards of living and welfare they are increasingly forced to travel to urban service centres in order to obtain these benefits. The introduction or retention of manufacturing or mining industry in rural areas has frequently required road improvements or the extension or maintenance of rail services.

The pattern of rural public transport from the 1920s to the 1950s was of road and railway passenger services supported by cross-subsidization from urban and inter-urban services. Many road freight services were provided by manufacturers operating their own vehicles under C licences or by wholesale and retail companies whose transport operations were inseparable from the rest of their business. The *Transport Act* (1947) enabled British Road Services to cross-subsidize rural routes if they so wished. Thus the supply of the commodity needs of the rural population, the sale of farm products and the movement of fertilizers could be accommodated in the private sector of the road transport system relatively easily. The pattern of bus routes about 1950 was analysed by Green (1950, 1951).

Car ownership is normally higher in rural than in other areas. In 1952, for

instance, when there were 16 people per private car in GB, there were 10–12 in the
counties of Mid-Wales, and in 1973 when there were 4.4 people to the car in GB,
the rural counties of Dyfed and Powys had 3.2. Swedish studies have suggested that
when car ownership passes the level of one car per 7 people, public transport begins
to have economic difficulties. This figure was reached in some rural areas in 1960,
in GB in 1963 and in N Ireland in 1965. Pilot studies of transport in rural areas of
Devon and W Suffolk (DoE 1971A and B) demonstrated the unsuitability of train
and bus services for meeting irregular and scattered demand. Only 3% of journeys
made by people who owned cars were on public transport; three-quarters of all
households had one car; in one-third of households at least two people had full use
of a car. As many journeys were made in the form of 'lifts' as on stage bus services.
The level of car ownership among men was double that for women, three times as
high among the upper two social classes as in the lowest two classes, and three times
as high among the under-45s as among the over-65s. The actual numbers of people
relying solely on public transport, non-driving mothers with young children, the
elderly and handicapped, had become relatively small, their needs being largely
catered for by lifts. Only 6% of all trips took place on public transport, including
7% of journeys to work and 13% of shopping trips. Half the population never used
public transport.

The concept of total social cost assumes that certain levels of welfare must be
available to all members of the rural community. It is then possible to consider to
what extent a concentration of transport on a limited number of routes or modes
will provide access to minimum welfare, or whether subsidies will be necessary in
order to maintain the rural population in their present geographical distribution.

The Devon and Suffolk studies showed that the purposes of rural journeys were
fairly evenly divided between shopping and business (25%), leisure (24%), work
(22%), and school (18%). The remainder of the journeys did not fit these
classifications but it seems apparent that between a half and three-quarters of
journeys are to a larger urban centre.

These findings clearly call into doubt the role of rural railway and conventional
bus services (Knowles 1978; Halsall and Turton 1979). Rural rail lines began to be
abandoned in the 1920s and by 1952 the Minister of Transport had announced that
railways were no longer obliged to retain uneconomic stations or branches; however,
the rate of closure up to 1962 was slow (Patmore 1966).

The publication of the *Beeching Report* (MoT 1963B) led to a notable public
outcry over the proposed closure of rural rail lines, although there were few
suggestions as to how the rural railway services might be made economically viable.
The subsequent closure of many lines took place under the provisions of the
Transport Act (1962) necessitating public enquiries, discussions with Transport
Users' Consultative Councils and, after the *Transport Act* (1968), with Regional
Economic Planning councils. Closures rose from a rate of 2% per annum of the
existing route km between 1958 and 1962, to 8% per annum between 1965 and
1968, but fell away to 2% per annum in 1969 and 1970. The route km had fallen
by 34% in nine years but remained half as large again as that recommended by the
1963 Report and four times as large as that recommended by the 1965 Report
(BRB 1965). Among railway lines to be maintained in the 1966 'Network for
Development' were included 'services which, although they may never pay their
way commercially, have an economic or a social value to the community as a whole
which outweighs their money costs. These include . . . some rural services where

alternatives would be impracticable or excessively costly' (MoT 1967A).

Although the 1963 Beeching proposal of 12,000 km and the 1965 proposal of 4,800 km was extended to 17,500 km in 1966, there are differences in the shape of the network. Several routes recommended for retention in 1963 have been closed while many recommended for closure have been retained. These variations show how appreciations of the relative value of specific railway lines have changed within the BR administration as its accounting procedures become more sophisticated, and they also show the effects of local pressure. Such services operate on about 8,000 km. Half the route km of British Rail, therefore, carried 6% of railway passenger km. The rural railway network has been broadly retained since 1968, but neither track nor vehicles have a indefinite life. By the early 1980s (Policy Stud. Inst. 1981) British Rail pointed out that there would need to be an expensive programme of capital renewal on the rural lines if they were to continue to function into the 1990s and that there was little prospect of finding the money for this investment from fare revenue or cross-subsidy.

The decline in profitability of rural bus services came later than that of the railways and was more complex in its effects. Besides the regional bus companies, formed under the *Road Traffic Act* (1930), there were a large number of small operators who provided stage carriage, coach and charter services between villages and market towns until the late 1950s. Television dealt a fatal blow to most of these local companies by reducing the demand for evening coach trips to urban cinemas, since contract work accounted for 50–65% of their gross revenue. The viability of small firms was further weakened by rising costs of petrol, replacement vehicles and more stringent safety standards. During the 1960s, as their urban routes became less economic, the regional bus companies found cross-subsidization of their rural routes less viable. They ceased to take over the routes of small operators when the latter suspended services and increasingly sought permission from the MoT to abandon routes or to reduce or 'rationalize' services.

The number of passenger journeys on rural buses fell from 6.0m in 1955 to 3.7m in 1970, by which time half the km run by the National Bus Company failed to cover costs. Rural bus services were particularly affected by inflation since wages formed up to 60% of operating costs and operational economies by the reduction in km or frequency of service may do nothing to lower wage, depreciation and terminal costs. On the Western National services, for instance, which cover a large sector of rural SW England, the number of passengers halved between 1955 and 1970, but the vehicle mileage only fell by 20% (DoE 1971A and B).

The National Bus Company and Scottish Bus Group, established under the *Transport Act* (1968) to run inter-urban rural services, saw their initial profits become a combined loss of £9.9m by 1970. In the same year the Highland, Island and coastal services of Caledonian MacBrayne lost £405,000. The National Bus Company therefore proposed withdrawal of unremunerative bus services unless local authorities were prepared to grant-aid them under the provisions of the 1968 Act. The government subsidizes fuel costs and contributes half of the cost of new buses.

The *Jack Committee* (MoT 1963A) considered that the concentration of school, post, parcels and other luggage transport on to one vehicle would offer only limited solutions in rural areas. Further studies produced little action until the amendment of the vehicle licensing regulations under the 1968 *Transport Act* enabled mini-buses to be run by private individuals for public carriage. Dial-a-bus schemes by which potential customers book seats on a vehicle or divert it from its standard route if they require a service are now in an experimental stage. Some rural communities own mini-buses which are operated by volunteer drivers as a social service.

The statutory obligation of local education authorities to provide bus or taxi services for children living more than two miles from a scheduled service to school was extended under the *Transport Act* (1968) to allow school buses, which already accounted for 60% of all bus journeys in the rural areas studied in 1971, to be used by other passengers. The Post Office may carry passengers on mail services and 160 such services are now in operation (Turnock 1977). Private hire operators may be allowed to pick up separate fares en route: works' contract buses were carrying 6% of journeys to work, as many as on public buses, in Devon and Suffolk (DoE 1971A and B).

Since 1968, railways have been the main beneficiaries of subsidy to rural transport. In 1970, for instance, £30m was paid to railways for services outside the conurbations, although they were estimated (RDC Assn 1971) to be carrying only 19% of the annual passenger mileage. Local buses only received £1m, shared by government and local authorities. The *Railways Act* (1974) replaced specific grants by a general grant to the railways, but it is government policy to maintain the present size of the network. Rural trains, which cost four to five times as much to run as rural buses, are thus preserved – the only element in the local transport system outside the financial responsibility of county authorities. It remains to be seen whether the different counties will feel able to increase subsidies to rural bus services and how they will weigh the needs of their rural populations against those of their urban populations in their transport policies. Although ways are now being sought, under the pressure of rising costs, to meet the need of those rural inhabitants without access to private car transport in one way or another, a strict operation of tests of economic viability at any time in the near future would virtually eliminate public rail and road transport services from the rural areas of the UK (Bracey 1970; Ramblers' Assn 1971; Clout 1972; Hibbs 1972; Whitby *et al* 1974; Pulling and Speakman 1974).

IV AIR TRANSPORT

IV.1 Traffic

This section concentrates on the role of air transport within the UK, including traffic to the Isle of Man and the Channel Islands. Internal air transport began on an experimental basis during the 1920s and the pattern of present services traces its origin to 1932. Dyos and Aldcroft (1969) give a history of interwar domestic aviation and show that almost all the routes in current use, with the exception of London–Manchester, were in operation before the Second World War, and that the number of passengers carried reached a peak of 161,000 in 1937.

Air services were fully resumed in 1946 and domestic passenger km doubled every four years from 1946 to 1974, when a small decline was registered as a result of the fuel crisis. Table 5.6 shows that over 7m passengers were carried and 2,770m passenger km were flown on domestic routes in 1980. The size of the UK tends to restrict the average length of flight, which was only 279 km. This distance is less than the most economic flying sector of most medium-range modern aircraft, and

TABLE 5.6

Air Traffic, UK, 1946 and 1980

Domestic flights	*1946*	*1980*
Aircraft km flown (million)	8.7	57.7
Passengers carried (million)	0.4	7.2
Passenger km (million)	48.4	2,770
Freight tonne-km (million)	0.1	7.1
Foreign flights (1979)		
Passengers carried (million)	0.2	41.6
% of total passengers	45	66
% Overseas journeys by air	*1960*	*1979*
Total	47	66
Irish Republic	34	46
Europe	46	60
N America	74	100
Other continents	47	100

Source: Ann. Abstract of Statistics, Transport Statistics GB 1970–80

contributes to the problems of air-passenger transport in competition with land transport in GB. The average distance between airports which serve the conurbations and major cities of the UK is 262 km and the average distance between adjacent major airports is only 160 km.

Fig. 5.5 shows the main domestic routes. Traffic between the four London airports of Heathrow, Gatwick, Luton and Stansted and the major regional capitals of Britain accounted for about half the domestic air traffic in 1980. Short sea crossings to Belfast, the Channel Islands and the Isle of Man represented a further third. The remainder included a small number of cross-country flights and the Highlands and Islands services in Scotland which link the Western Isles, Orkney and Shetland with Glasgow, Edinburgh and Aberdeen. The relatively heavy traffic to the Shetland airport of Sumburgh reflects the importance of the offshore oil industry in northern waters.

Of the 58m passengers using UK airports in 1979 42m were flying to or from foreign airports. Of passengers leaving the UK, 25% were bound for the adjacent countries of France, Germany, the Irish Republic and the Low Countries, 33% for more distant European countries (Spain, Greece, Italy, Switzerland and Scandinavia) and 16% for N America. Table 5.6 shows the extent to which air transport had captured the overseas traffic on these services. The growth in air freight transport since the Second World War has been twice as rapid as that of passenger traffic, and the growth of foreign freight traffic has been greater than that of domestic freight. London Heathrow is the third port of the UK in terms of the value of the goods which pass through it, although the volume of air freight remains relatively small. As specialized freight-carrying aircraft have increased in speed and capacity, containerization has been introduced using both standard boxes and the pallet-style *igloo* which is shaped to the cross-section of the fuselage for easy and efficient handling.

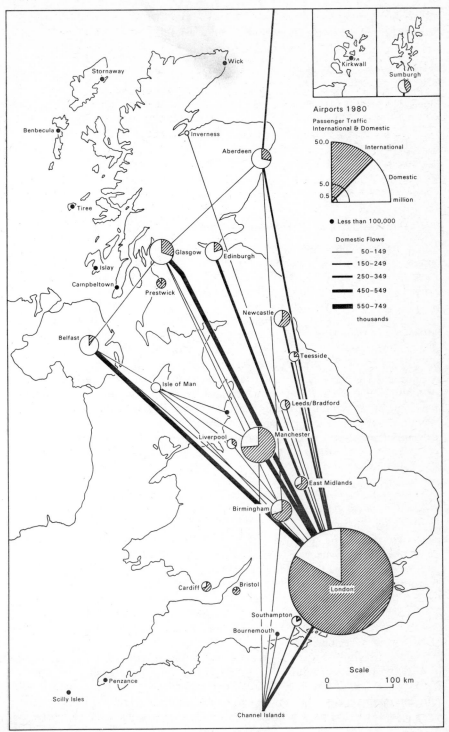

Figure 5.5   Airports and domestic air traffic, UK, 1980

TABLE 5.7

Terminal Passengers at Major UK Airports, 1980 (millions)

London airports	39.5	Sumburgh (Shetland)	0.6
Manchester	4.3	Prestwick	0.4
Glasgow	2.3	Liverpool	0.4
Birmingham	1.6	Leeds–Bradford	0.4
Belfast	1.5	Southampton	0.3
Aberdeen	1.4	Teesside	0.3
Edinburgh	1.1	Cardiff	0.3
Newcastle	0.9	Bristol	0.2
East Midlands	0.7		

Source: Civil Aviation Authority (1980)

IV.2 The Location and Development of Airports

Although several UK airports have the technical capability to handle the largest inter-continental aircraft, London dominates the international air traffic of the UK. There are only a small number of inter-continental scheduled flights from other airports and one-third of the domestic air-passenger traffic of the UK travels to or from foreign airports via London (Dept Trade 1975). The dominance of the London airports in UK air traffic depends on several factors. London is a world business centre, the largest British conurbation and the chief single focus of land communications in GB. In the early, formative years of air transport, London generated most of the official passenger and mail traffic which then formed a major component of airline business, and became the headquarters of the national and most of the charter and private airline companies. Although business passengers are not so numerous as leisure passengers, who comprise 75% of the passengers at the London airports, their journeys are not seasonal and form the base load of regular demand for air transport. Leisure travel, on the other hand, is expected to grow to 80% of the total of British traffic by the end of the century and will probably be dominated by foreign visitors. At the present time almost all foreign tourists visit London and 85% go nowhere else in Britain.

The *Roskill Report* (Dept of Trade and Industry 1971) on the third London Airport lists income, family composition and age as the chief factors affecting people's choice of air travel for holidays. Sealy (1967A and B) pointed out that the rapidly growing leisure air travel is strongly related to discretionary income, i.e. the amount of money available after basic needs for food, housing, clothing and taxation have been met. This discretionary income is higher in the SE and rises, as a proportion of total income, ahead of that of the other regions, so that apart from the fact that European travel is marginally cheaper from the SE than from more distant regions, the amount of money available for it is greater and therefore the SE generates more leisure travel. The proportion of retired people is also greater in the SE than in other regions.

London (Heathrow) was built as a national airport from 1943–54 and London (Gatwick) was developed after 1955 (Sealy 1955). The predicted increase in air traffic, when applied to contemporary routes in the late 1950s, suggested that a third international airport would be needed in SE England during the 1970s. The years since 1961 have been spent in a search for an agreed site for this airport.

Stansted, a former USAF base near Bishops Stortford and 58 km NE of London, was chosen in 1964 on relatively simple criteria but local opposition forced the government to appoint the Roskill Commission (Dept of Trade and Industry 1971). Although limited in its belief to the location of a third *London* airport the seven volumes of evidence and analysis include valuable cost-benefit studies (App. 15 and 20) and gravity models (App. 17–19). The government rejected the majority view of the Commission and chose a site at Maplin on the Essex coast in 1971. By 1974, however, the introduction of jumbo jets suggested that terminal rather than runway capacity would become the major constraint on traffic growth at Heathrow and Gatwick, and that the jumbos were likely to be less noisy than narrow-fuselage jets. At the same time, a sharp rise in the cost of aircraft fuel led to lower forecasts of future aircraft movements than those upon which the Roskill decisions were based. Since the current economic recession necessitated a drastic pruning of public expenditure, the government abandoned the Maplin project in 1974 (Adams 1971; Mishan 1970; Dept Trade 1978; Hall 1980).

The official view during the mid-1970s (Dept Trade 1975) was that a more even spread of demand at Gatwick and Luton, steeper increases in fuel costs and passenger fares and also a slower rate of growth in British incomes would enable an 'incremental' policy of progressive addition to the terminal facilities of the four London airports until the 1990s without massive expansion at any one of them or the diversion of traffic to provincial airports. By 1979, however, believing that Heathrow and Gatwick would reach their full passenger-handling capacity by 1988, the government decided that Stansted should take the bulk of the expected increase in passengers to SE England during the 1980s on its existing runway. A fourth terminal would be built at Heathrow but no second runway at Gatwick. Luton was to continue to handle the bulk of overseas charter flights. The final decision on the Stansted development, which went to its second public enquiry in 1981, was not expected until 1983.

The distribution pattern of provincial airports is inherited from the 1930s, when accessibility by surface transport was relatively restricted. Airports were then generally located within twenty to forty minutes of major railway stations by airport bus. The trunk-road network and faster inter-city rail services of the 1970s would, in theory, enable both current and potential traffic to be handled at a smaller number of airports, each large enough to attract a wider variety of services than are now operated. Many provincial airports are now eccentrically located in terms of the load centre of their present traffic, and in some cases their sites restrict present traffic or its predicted growth. Prestwick, for example is 45 km west of Glasgow airport and Edinburgh airport is only 65 km by motorway to the east. Similarly Liverpool airport is only 50 km west of Manchester airport and Leeds/ Bradford only 90 km to the north-east along the M62 motorway system. There is, however, an increasing differentiation of function between these neighbouring airports: in Scotland, for instance, Prestwick acts as the main gateway airport for N American services, while Glasgow and Edinburgh serve the West and East of central Scotland respectively for flights to Ireland, London and the European mainland.

A national airports plan was foreshadowed in 1945 but government policy (Sealy 1976, 40–54) has been to encourage local authorities to take the initiative in developing new airport facilities in their areas. Almost all provincial airports have required subsidies from their local authorities and most domestic air routes have been cross-subsidized from international services by air transport companies. Local authorities have lacked the resources to make investments in airports other than piecemeal improvements to satisfy conservative, short-run traffic forecasts. Few regional airports generate enough passengers from their own areas or attract sufficient passengers from other regions to support a wide range of services. Although half of the passengers between regional and foreign airports fly via London (DoT 1975), there is only limited demand for flights between specific regional and foreign destinations. It is difficult to see how the 80% of London-airport passengers with origins or destinations within SE England could be persuaded to use more distant provincial airports.

The widely held view that investment in airports and air services can play an important role in regional economic development was accepted by the *Edwards Committee* (Comm. of Inquiry into Civil Air Transport, 1969) although they called for further research into the matter. The government has admitted that too much attention may have been paid to the views of the air transport industry during the search for London's third airport in the 1960s. The British Airports Authority (which owns the London airports, except Luton, and the major Scottish airports) proposed to the Edwards Committee an hierarchical plan with regional implications. They suggested (a) that major international and domestic services should operate from London, Manchester and Glasgow; (b) that a further seven regional airports should have links to the major UK airports and to some European destinations. These airports have been allowed to invest in new terminal capacity during the squeeze on public expenditure in the early 1980s. (c) that six smaller provincial airports should have domestic feeder services and summer flights to Europe and the British islands; (d) that a larger number of local airports should be developed for business flights, small feeder services and air taxis. Such a policy might enable the major airports at least to reach viable thresholds for a range of international services as demand grows during the remainder of this century.

As the prospects for the development of short- or vertical take-off and landing aircraft (STOL or VTOL) appear to be small before the 1990s (DTI 1971, 18.5, 19), air routes within Britain may be subject to increased competition from high-speed trains. The numbers of passengers to Ireland and Europe may increase markedly, but in the absence to date of a national policy to meet the air-transport needs of the UK it is doubtful whether the degree of concentration of traffic at specific airports will be very different in the year 2000 from the pattern of the late 1930s. This is because investments have been made at each stage by a large number of authorities, each with relatively small resources in this, the most capital-intensive and centrally regulated of all transport modes.

V   SEA TRANSPORT

V.1   The Challenge of Change

The many changes in the transport industry which developed during the 1960s and were brought to fruition in the 1970s fundamentally affected the UK ports. Lying on the interface between both land and sea transport and domestic and international transport, the ports are influenced by every change in each of these sectors to some degree. What had been regarded as one of the basic functions of any port — the unloading of goods from road and rail onto the quayside and their reloading into a ship, or vice versa, was transformed by the unitization of what had been called break-bulk cargo, so that ports became merely the places on the coast where modular trays and boxes were lifted or driven directly from ships onto land vehicles or the other way round. Another basic port function, the landing of bulk cargoes for processing on the coast, was profoundly modified by a wave of investment which resulted in a major increase in the volume of bulk-cargo-carrying vessels and in the scale of the facilities required to receive them (Couper 1972). Finally, considerable changes in the pattern and direction of UK trade affected both bulk and unitized cargoes.

Most of the ports of the UK can trace a continuous evolution from the Middle Ages (Bird 1963). In the past they have been able, for the most part, to adapt to the changes in the nature, volume and direction of trade and to new types of land and sea transport. Changes in all these elements since the 1950s, however, have demanded an extraordinarily rapid reaction from the ports. The volume of imports and exports, for instance, had shown a steady increase since the 1820s (Mitchell and Deane 1971, 328), doubling roughly every twenty years until 1900 and then growing at a rather slower rate. The volume of British overseas trade fluctuated between the wars so that in the late 1940s it lay at about 490m tonnes, roughly the same level as in the early 1920s.

During the period 1960–79, when the physical *volume* of both imports and exports rose by 250%, the volume of food imports remained steady. The volume of imported raw materials, however, rose by 20% and of exported raw materials by 50%. The import of fuels rose rapidly, to reach a peak in 1974 at 50% above the 1960 volume. While fuel imports fell slowly thereafter as UK oil came on stream, the export of British fuel rose in compensation. The most striking change in commodity trade during the 1960s and 1970s, however, was the 500% increase in the volume of manufactured goods imported and the 240% increase in the volume of manufactured goods exported. The volume of trade in almost all these commodities between contiguous developed countries of the world rose much more rapidly than trade between the developed and underdeveloped countries. This process was assisted by the establishment of the EFTA and EEC trading blocks during the 1960s and by the accession of Britain and Ireland to the European Common Market in 1973.

In 1963, 48% of the *value* of UK trade was with countries lying outside Europe and N America. By 1979, trade with these more distant partners had fallen to 29% of the total value. Similarly the proportion of trade with N America fell from 16% in 1963 to 12% in 1979. It was displaced by trade with Scandinavia, Iberia, Switzerland and Austria, which rose from 11 to 16%, and by trade with the present member states of the EEC which rose from 25 to 42%. These changes not only represented a shift in trading partners but also a major growth of short-sea traffic.

Bearing in mind both the nature and the direction of trade, 43% of the value of UK trade in 1979 consisted in the exchange of manufactured products with other countries in W and N Europe, and a further 7% consisted of trade in fuels with the same areas. The value of the trade between the UK and the world beyond Europe and N America was 28% of the total, comprising 19% manufactured goods, 5% food and raw materials and 4% imported fuels.

These changes in the direction of UK trade have been accompanied by dramatic increases in the size of the largest vessels calling at UK ports, especially in the bulk trades. Although trade in manufactured goods has risen so markedly, the raw

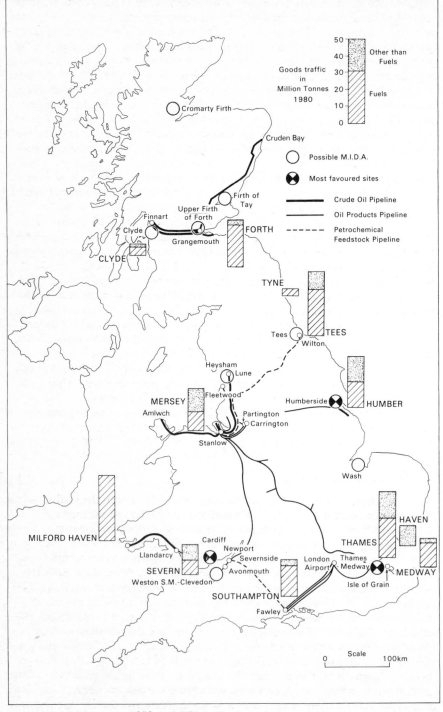

Figure 5.6   Major ports, 1979, and MIDA sites

materials out of which they are made are being carried for longer distances as the relatively rich virgin orefields and oilfields are being exploited across the world by Japanese, European and N American interests. As many of these trade flows are asymmetrical, with the probability of sailing one direction in ballast, there has been great pressure on ship designers to increase the capacity of vessels relative to their fuel consumption and the cost of manning them.

The outstanding technological developments in transport during the last twenty years have led to changes in the status and functions of ports. Further changes must ensue if the full advantages of modern transport are to be reaped. UK ports have not been noted for providing facilities in advance of demand during the recent past and this has sometimes led to criticism of port authorities as providing too little and too late.

In the past the high costs of inland transport and also the small size of vessels in use produced a dispersed pattern of ports. Recent developments in inland transport have allowed widespread accessibility and lower costs, so that, in theory, the possibilities of competition between ports are greatly enhanced (fig. 5.6). A dispersed pattern of ports would now be uneconomic and would inhibit ports from taking advantage of the technological possibilities of modern sea transport which has recently been the more compelling component of the sea and land transport relationship. However, while in the recent past it would seem that sea transport has been able, in some measure, to shape port developments and land transport networks to meet its needs, it is as well to remember that the volume of goods in foreign trade is only about 10% of the total goods moved in the UK and only 12% of container movements are destined for foreign trade. The needs of foreign trade are unlikely to dominate inland transport developments.

While there are important general economies related to size of vessel, the main concern in this present context is that increased size has made vessels more discriminating and demanding in terms of their depth requirements and the facilities they need (Hunter and Wilson 1969). Port costs in terms of dredging, facilities and installations rise with increasing ship size and may at some stage offset the economies of larger vessels.

V.2   Trade in Bulk Cargoes

The main changes in the bulk-cargo traffic of the UK have been the marked increase in volume carried from the late 1940s until the late 1970s and the increasing capacity of the specialized vessels in bulk trades. Both construction costs per tonne and operating costs per tonne decrease as the deadweight (dwt) of the vessel increases and operating costs do so at a faster rate, so that the largest vessels are most effectively and efficiently used over long distances. More specifically and in detail the advantages vary according to the type of vessel (Hallett and Randall 1970; McFadzean 1968; Hunter and Wilson 1969; Goss and Jones 1972; Hunter 1974). Oil tankers have demonstrated the most striking rise in total tonnage and in size of vessel. In 1950 only 5% of the world's tanker tonnage was of vessels over 20,000dwt, in 1969 more than 19% was of vessels of over 100,000dwt and by 1974 36% was of vessels of over 200,000dwt. Although some larger vessels are already in operation, it is doubtful if any main economies are to be gained by tankers of over 250,000dwt. In the case of specialized ore-carriers the main advantages have been reaped by the time the size of vessel has reached 90,000dwt and they may remain predominantly at about 100,000dwt although some combined-function carriers (especially the OBOs, Ore/Bulk/Oil) are operating at more than twice this size. In any event, apart from the economies of scale becoming less apparent after a certain point, there are other even less advantageous aspects of operating very large vessels which may curb the size to which they will commonly develop. Quite specifically in the case of oil-tankers the hazards of potential pollution and destructive explosions, although clearly not restricted to supertankers, are of greater impact the larger the vessel and the greater the capital risk. Doubts from these sources about supertankers are reinforced by the increased insurance premiums which have been charged following pollution claims and tanker explosions. For the tanker of 250,000dwt, insurance premiums form more than half the running costs.

The increase in tanker size has meant that fewer ports are involved in handling the imports of crude oil and more oil is being moved by pipeline. Four oil terminals, Forth (Hound Point 98ft, 30m depth), Clyde (Finnart, 95ft, 29m depth), Milford Haven (68–70ft; 20–21m depth) and Humber (Immingham 68ft, 20m depth), can handle tankers in the 250–275,000dwt range or above, fully laden. They were

TABLE 5.8

Major Bulk Cargoes, Leading GB Ports, 1979

Port	Total traffic (million tonnes)	Petroleum (million tonnes)	Petroleum as % of port	% of GB
London	40.2	23.2	58	10
Milford Haven	38.7	38.7	100	17
Tees	37.7	25.7	68	11
Southampton	21.8	18.2	83	8
Immingham	21.1	13.7	65	6
Shetland	20.4	20.6	100	9
Orkney	17.7	17.5	99	7
Medway	16.9	14.4	85	6
Liverpool	13.0	3.0	23	1
Manchester	11.0	7.2	65	3
Clyde	10.1	5.3	52	2
Total GB	376.8	234.0		80

Imports of ores and scrap

	(Million tonnes)	Ores % of port	of GB
Port Talbot	5.6	89	28
Tees	5.0	13	25
Immingham	5.0	24	25
Clyde	2.0	20	10
Liverpool	1.3	10	6
Others	1.3	–	6
Total GB	20.2		100

Source: National Ports Council, *Digest of Port Statistics* (1979)

joined in 1976 by the new Shell facility, a single buoy 3 kilometres off the north-west coast of Anglesey at Amlwch which is capable of handling a vessel of 700,000dwt. There are five other terminals (Thames, Southampton Water, Medway, Mersey and Tees) which offer depths of 45ft (13.7m) or over. It is a distinctive and important characteristic of oil cargoes that a variety of berthing systems, for example, using jetties or hose, may potentially be used. The Flotta (Orkney) terminal uses the deep water of the wartime anchorage of Scapa Flow to provide two single-point mooring towers (200,000dwt range) as well as a conventional berth for tankers and gas carriers. Oil is a significant cargo at most major UK ports. At some it comprises a high proportion of total trade: virtually 100% at Milford Haven, 77% on the Medway, 81% at Southampton. These three ports, together with London, handle 54% of the UK petroleum traffic.

Several new oil terminals have been developed at relatively isolated deep-water sites. The Finnart base on Loch Long, which is linked by pipeline to Grangemouth refinery on the Forth, was built between the wars. Postwar developments have been at Milford Haven, on a deep-water ria in SW Wales, which has become the second port of the UK in terms of tonnage handled. Oil began to flow to an oil base at Sullom Voe, on the Shetland main island 230km north of the Scottish mainland, in 1978. This port, which is able to handle vessels of up to 300,000dwt, takes oil from two pipelines from the Brent and Ninian oilfields respectively. Sullom Voe has a capacity of 1.4m barrels of oil per day and also facilities for separating out the associated gases. The oil and gas is then transferred by ship to British and Continental markets. About one-third of the seaborne oil movement to UK ports is in coastwise trade, a result of the transfer of crude stocks and of the distribution of refined products.

Iron-ore vessels are less demanding in terms of depth but they do require conventional berths with specialized handling equipment. Port Talbot with a tidal harbour (29ft, 8.8m, tidal range) is now able to handle vessels of more than 100,000dwt. Important additions to deep-water facilities have been made on the Humber (Immingham 1972, 65–70,000dwt); on the Tees (Redcar 1973, 120–150,000dwt) and on the Clyde (Hunterston 1977, over 130ft, 40m, depth, and potentially able to handle vessels of 350,000dwt). The 20.2m tonnes of ores and scrap imported in the foreign trade in 1979 showed a similar measure of port concentration to the petroleum traffic and indeed a more pronounced concentration if estuarial groupings are considered. Of the total imports, 64% was handled in the three estuaries (Severn, Tees and Clyde) associated with the steel industry and 28% of the total by Port Talbot. The ore trade is focused mainly on the leading industrial seaports, although it has been in the past, and is likely to be increasingly in the future, influenced by available depths of water and the available or projected handling facilities. The rapid rise in importance of Immingham as an ore importer is related to the expansion of the British Steel Corporation's activities at Scunthorpe (Anchor scheme).

None of the other bulk cargoes are of comparable volume or have shown a similar rate of increase in traffic in recent years. The coastwise coal trade of 5.2m tonnes in 1974 is very largely the lingering special relationship between the ports of NE England and the Thames. Coal has never regained its pre-Second World War importance in the foreign export trade and a volume of 4m tons in 1974 (mainly from Immingham and Swansea) was surpassed by exports of chemicals (6.1m tonnes – Tees, Liverpool, Manchester) and crude fertilizers and clay (5.1m tonnes –

Par). The most significant of the bulk imports were unmilled cereals (6.3m
tonnes – notably London and Liverpool); timber (5.9m tonnes – London and Hull)
and crude fertilizers and crude minerals (5.3m tonnes – Immingham and
Manchester). The remaining main bulk import trades were: coal with 3.7m tonnes
(especially at Teesport); pulp and waste paper (2.8m tonnes – London and
Manchester) and sugar (2.8m tonnes – London, Liverpool and Clyde). Most of such
bulk imports are related to industry within the ports.

V.3   Intermodal Transport

The last two decades have witnessed the unitization of the greater part of the
break-bulk traffic of the UK. Goods are no longer carried in a variety of bags,
bales, barrels and standards, each peculiar to its own trade, but are transported on
pallets or in containers of standard modular size. These may be assembled or
unpacked far inland from the ports themselves. Pallets and containers imply a
through transport system in which the role of the port is to ensure that the transfer
of the unit load from ship to shore or shore to ship is as expeditious as possible,
with tonnage per man-hour as the major criterion of its efficiency. Because the
unit-load concept is a through transport system it has required new investment in
road and rail vehicles as well as in ships, and in handling operations at the ports
most of all. No single one of these changes is fully effective or even profitable, in
many cases, unless it is accompanied by complementary new equipment throughout
the system. Unitization is most effective when cargo handling is mechanized from
the point at which it leaves the producer to its eventual arrival on the customers'
premises and when each unit load is kept together for as far as possible on the
journey. Effective container operation requires comparable facilities and access
inland for units loads at *both* ends of the trade route, and outstandingly it requires
a suitable *two-way flow* of cargo. At the present time about one-third of containers
are travelling empty. It has therefore been essential for each of the links in the total
transport chain to reorganize and re-equip its operations. The shipowners, port
authorities, road and railway operators, and the freight forwarders needed to
redirect their investment and labourforce in order to develop this new pattern of
international transport integration. The coordination of services has replaced the
former disjointed ship/road/rail operations of the break-bulk era.

An investigation of total transport costs for non-bulk cargoes from inland point
to inland point between N America and W Europe suggested that 62% of total cost
related to sea freight, of which about half was the cost of loading and discharging,
28% to inland freight and 10% to port charges and dues (OECD 1968). Containerization is already modifying this costing. It would appear that the ports have the
most to gain and certainly in the maritime section of the trade route the results of
unit-load operations can be pronounced. A considerable increase in tonnage can be
handled over a single berth. Although estimates vary, a total of about 100,000
tonnes per annum over the conventional berth is considered to be increased about
five times by roll-on operations and by at least ten times by full containerization
(Little 1967). It also follows that there is a considerable decrease in the number of
vessels required for a particular traffic, that there is a decline in the requirement for
port labour, that the costs of general cargo handling may well be decreased (and
reflected in lower charges at least on short sea routes where conference agreements
are not involved), and finally that a speedier and more efficient service will be

provided. In short, this is one of the best indications that merchant shipping has become, and seaports *must* become, increasingly capital-intensive. Although containerization has been widely developed it is not without opponents in some circumstances and certainly not without problems.

TABLE 5.9

Container and Roll-on Traffic, Leading GB Ports, 1969–79

Port	(000 loaded units) Foreign traffic 1969	1974	Million tonnes 1979
London	93	310	3.6
Dover	80	485	5.7
Southampton	52	296	3.9
Felixstowe	91	312	4.4
Liverpool	128	133	1.7
Hull	72	108	1.9
Others	432	996	20.5
Total GB	948	2,640	41.7

NB. Total goods is 'goods other than fuels' in foreign and coastwise trade.

Source: N Ports Council, *Digest of Port Statistics, vol. 1,* 1974, 1979

Unitization of cargo implies basically three types of unit. First is the container, a rectangular box 8ft high and 8ft wide, with a length of 20–40ft. Owing to their varying length, containers are often measured in terms of 20ft units. Apart from their shape, containers come in a considerable variety of types, firm or loose sided, with or without internal refrigeration, and so on. They need not be completely full, but stuffing (filling) or stripping (emptying) *en route* is avoided as far as possible. Many 40ft containers, however, can comply with the legal axle loads on British roads only when partly empty. Second is the pallet, a rigid tray of standard size upon which goods can be stacked and secured. Pallets lend themselves to smaller loads or to loads which may be aggregated or disaggregated in the course of the journey. They can be handled by fork-lift trucks as well as by cranes and may be carried inside containers. Palletization requires less costly equipment on both ship and berth. The costs of conversion from conventional operation to palletization are relatively small when compared with a fully containerized system and thus palletization may be preferable on lower-density routes and on shorter routes (Turner 1969). Moreover a greater proportion of general cargo can be palletized than containerized. An average load is pallet-sized (1–1.5 tonnes) and only 4% of non-bulk dry-cargo consignments weigh 10 tonnes or more (about 10 tonnes being the preferred full – 9 metre – container-load. The third type of unit load is the stack of timber or steel where the individual planks, tubes or bars are fastened together in standard units of length or weight.

The units are moved between ship and shore by either roll-on roll-off (ro-ro) or lift-on lift-off (li-lo) operations. In ro-ro operations, the load is either towed on board by a truck which then leaves the ship, or the lorry together with its load is

conveyed to the destination port in order to resume its land journey. Rail ferries
are also ro-ro operations. Lift-on lift-off involves either ship- or shore-based cranes
lifting the unit from ship to shore and may also require the containers to be stacked
at the port awaiting the arrival of the ship or the land vehicle. The land-based
cranes and the stacking areas comprise the major investments in unit-load facilities
for the port. Some berths and some vessels specialize exclusively on ro-ro or li-lo
traffic but there are many vessels, notably on short sea routes, adapted to carry
both types of traffic and common user terminals often find ro-ro and li-lo operations
complementary.

Containers can be and were carried on ships which had originally been designed for
break-bulk cargo but unitization is most economical when specially built container
ships are used. Many such container ships were built during the 1960s and it was
soon apparent that deep-sea traffic could be carried in very large vessels. All the
major deep-sea routes were converted to container operation by 1977 and few other
routes appear likely to repay the heavy initial investment. This has involved the
operation of a relatively small number of large, new vessels on regular runs between
a handful of ports in each continent. It is essential that these ships spend as much
of their working life as possible at sea and therefore have as few ports of call as
possible with the fastest possible turnround at these ports. Thus Tilbury has become
the port of call for the Australasian trade in the UK and Southampton for that with
S Africa. No such accord has yet been reached in respect of the much larger volume
of N American traffic for which several UK ports vie for trade. The involvement of
Felixstowe, Grangemouth, Greenock, Liverpool, Manchester, Southampton and
Tilbury in this traffic suggests a clear excess of tonnage and container-berth
capacity.

In short-sea traffic to the ports of Ireland, Scandinavia, Germany, the Low
Countries, France and Iberia, the speed of service is often paramount, for the
shipping line is often in competition with overland transport operators for part of
the journey. In order to combine frequent sailings with high load factors, the ships
are much smaller (often with a capacity of 150—200 20ft container units) and may
combine ro-ro and li-lo traffic.

One of the chief benefits of unitization is that the cargo can take advantage of
the most suitable transport mode at every stage of the journey. It is therefore
common to combine the advantages of short-sea and deep-sea operation through
'Feeder-relay' services which radiate from the few ports of call of the large deep-sea
container ships to the many ports which have berths for short-sea container ships.
This operation is profitable whenever the benefits a rapid turnround of full cargo on
the deep-sea vessel are not completely offset by the additional costs of operating a
fleet of much smaller feeder-relay vessels to collect and distribute the deep-sea
cargo to a wider group of ports. The east-coast ports of the UK from Grangemouth
to the Dover Strait are particularly well placed as outports for Rotterdam and, to a
lesser extent, Bremerhaven.

One of the important implications of unit-transport berths is that some of the
traditional functions in handling, sorting and distribution are lost to the port. It is
an essential characteristic of unit-load operation that the berth should be used for
trans-shipment only and that Inland Container Depots (ICDs) are established to
perform all other functions including Customs. Fifteen ICDs have been built and
operate on a 'common user' basis although in most instances involving British Rail.
There is no compelling reason why ICDs should be near the ports. It is in retrospect

perhaps unfortunate that two of the earliest and most publicized ICDs at Orsett (near Tilbury) and Aintree (Liverpool) should have been so near the port area in each case as to provoke industrial unrest by the apparent usurping of what is traditionally considered to be docker's work. Container bases serve a wide range of shipping lines, road-haulage firms and container operators, and can also be used as centres for the concentration and control of vehicles and containers as well as for the stuffing and stripping of unit loads.

Containerization has not only given reality to a through-transport system between sea and land transport but also has potentially made feasible a much greater integration between rail and road transport. Containers are not new to the railway but the main development followed the Beeching proposals with the formation of the Freightliner system. The first Freightliner ran from London to Glasgow in November 1965. The Freightliner system in external trade, linking the regions with Inland Container Depots (ICDs) and the ports, has been referred to earlier. A largely separate network, necessary as the ICDs involve HM Customs and the goods are in bond, handles inland trade with 23 Freightliner terminals sharing between them about 32 two-way services linking the main centres of population (Johnson, Garnett *et al* 1970). Road transport of containers is involved at the terminals and is directly in competition for container traffic over the shorter distances. Even in the limited period to date there has been some readjustment in the competitive relationship between rail and road, although Freightliner has not as yet developed as British Rail forecast. It clearly shares some of the same problems discussed in terms of maritime container routes. There is, however, some evidence of integration in, for example, the road hauliers' use of Freightliner for the trunk haul operation.

In very general terms, Freightliner services begin to show economies over container haulage by road at distances of 240–320km, which puts most of the economic core of the UK within the ambit of the road haulage (London to Stoke on Trent is 220km, to Preston is 300km). Services of less than 160km are, however, economic by rail for containers which are to be delivered to the cranes at dockside and when road collection or delivery is needed at only one end of the rail route. Services from London to Lancashire can be profitable because of the large markets at either end. The size of the train which can be filled regularly has a more significant effect on competition with road haulage than the actual length of haul since the cost of handling at terminals and road delivery/collection are relatively fixed irrespective of the distance of the main-line haul. When Freightliner services began in 1965, 40m tonnes of internal traffic were expected by 1973; in fact 6m tonnes was being carried in 1976. The traffic had only kept up with forecasts on journeys of over 500km: on journeys shorter than 320km, freightliner traffic came up to only 12% of the expected volume. Road gains were largely due to motorways and the increased payload of lorries; also speeds on the rail haul were only 2/3 of those Beeching predicted. Road hauliers have been able to be more flexible in their operations than British Rail since their vehicles have a shorter economic life. Inland clearance depots of all kinds only handle 11–12% of all the containers entering or leaving Great Britain.

The changeover from break-bulk to unitized transport systems has created great difficulties for British ports and has had important effects on their differing functions. Unitization is essentially a movement from specialized and sophisticated handling techniques to simple mechanized operation. The ports with the most highly specialized, elaborate and labour-intensive facilities during the 1950s have therefore found the changes most difficult to undertake. As mentioned above, both size of vessel and volume of cargo had increased very gradually over the preceding two centuries. Output per man had improved only marginally from 1895 to 1945 and the casual-labour system, which was originally adapted to the irregular arrival of sailing ships and to the difficulties of working in bad weather, was abandoned only in 1967. In fact, the time spent in unloading and checking the many small and varied packages in break-bulk cargo had been one of the major factors discouraging an increase in the capacity of merchant ships. Musclepower began to be replaced in the docks by the electric tractor during the 1920s but it was in the late 1940s that the quartet of pallet, fork-lift truck, mobile crane and tractor trailer began the main process of mechanization. The first ro-ro vessels, converted wartime landing craft, began operations on the short-ferry routes in 1947.

Shipowners took the initiative in proposing the parallel changes which introduced unitization in the ports of the world because of their pivotal position in the transport system and their capital resources. A major part of the working out of the system, however, and very often its chance of success, has rested with the land-based components. Unfortunately, the development of unit-load facilities took place in the piecemeal, unplanned and potentially wasteful fashion which has characterized so much of British transport history. There was very little government influence and no positive planning and control over the proliferation of unit-load facilities. The results of the various responses of the ports were impressive.

Although no deep-water berths for general cargo were built between the 1930s and the mid-1960s apart from Teesport, port authorities invested £400m between 1962 and 1976, largely borrowed from the state, and mostly directed to container facilities. 22 deep-sea container berths were constructed and 50 short-sea and 76 roll-on roll-off berths. As it became more apparent during the mid-1960s that most break-bulk cargo was eventually going to be unitized and that major trades were going to concentrate into one port only, the larger UK ports felt obliged to build short-term facilities for those trades which were moving into transition and also to offer more capacious facilities to potential future customers. Ports were trying at the same time to conserve their existing traffic in order to justify the large investments they were planning. The cheap inland distribution offered by containers was overturning existing port-hinterland relations and all ports felt the need to attract as much general traffic as possible in order to stay in operation, if they were not chosen as the UK base for one of the major overseas trades. This was the rationale behind the large, general container bases built by the Port of London at Tilbury and by the Mersey Docks and Harbours Board at Seaforth.

The high capital costs which were incurred during the late 1960s in building these terminals did not yield the short-term financial benefits which had been hoped, because the total traffic of the UK was not increasing as fast as the facilities designed to handle it. The transfer of traffic from break-bulk to unitized operation depressed the revenues per tonne obtained by ports at the very time when the ports were investing in new facilities, paying off a large section of their labourforce and witnessing a decreasing use of their older conventional berths. Competition from feeder-relay services from Rotterdam and other Continental ports put a ceiling on what could be charged for the use of the new container facilities. The growth of unit-cargo facilities was far removed from the theoretical concept of the way in which these new handling techniques should concentrate general cargo handling.

The diversity of uses possible with roll-on facilities and the moderate size of ships employed in trade with Europe have enabled a large number of ports to grow, and to do so without related investment proportionate to the amount of cargo handled, precisely because of the low-cost high-throughput possibilities of the system. The initial development and the widespread distribution were related mainly to the near-sea trade.

Some of the berths were used in more than one trade but only about 10% of the berths handled some deep-sea trade (comprising 24.2% of loaded units, foreign trade 1974). The largest number were concerned with the short-sea (17.6% of loaded units) and near-sea (58.2%) trades, and particularly with traffic to France, Belgium, Netherlands and W Germany. Coastwise movement of unit-loads has an important role in Scotland notably in the Highlands and Islands, and it is also a component of the strong flow, part coastwise and part foreign, across the Irish Sea (almost one quarter of the total loaded-units in foreign and coastwise trade). Of course not all of these berths were handling standard-sized containers with transporter cranes from cellular vessels. In 1975 the total unit-load capacity at British ports was 48.3m tonnes of which 12.4m were at deep-sea container berths, 11.9m at short-sea container berths and 19.5m at short-sea ro-ro berths. The current throughput was then 30m tonnes. There is also over-capacity all over western and northern Europe. Unitization involves the replacement of labour by capital. There were about 75,000 dockers at the end of the Second World War but numbers began to fall as mechanization was introduced. The decline in the labour-force was not brought about without industrial conflicts which temporarily damaged the capacity of some ports to compete for trade. By 1965 there were 64,000 dockers, 32,000 in 1975 and 27,000 in 1979.

By the late 1970s, the revolutionary impact of containerization had largely worked itself out. The world recession brought about an increase in competition on land and sea at a time when containers had captured much of the potential traffic on the long-distance routes. At the same time the sharp increase in the cost of oil towards the end of 1973 and the upsurge of labour costs in the industrialized countries tended to reinforce the advantages of unitized freight-handling methods. Container ships were more economical than conventional ships in terms of fuel economy per tonne of cargo carried. By 1975, however, the deepening world recession caused the first check in the world-wide growth of container operations.

Unitization not only replaced the cranes of a port. It also demanded a totally new layout of land and water space (Takel 1981). The rapid turnround of the vessels reduced the requirement for berthing space but the new large vessels engaged in the deep-sea trades needed deep water and good access to the berth. The prime requirement on land was stacking space for the containers, with enough clear ground to manoeuvre the straddle cranes, also for road and rail vehicles. Terminals need an additional area for manoeuvre equivalent to about 30% of their stacking space. A well-run terminal can handle 7,500–15,000 20ft container units per ha of stacked area per annum. A three-berth terminal could do with a 40ha site handling containers at a rate of 100,000 per annum per 10ha (= 400,000 20ft units per annum) on both ship and berth. There is, of course, no dispute that unit-load, of whatever kind, reduces handling costs and thus in respect of through-transport costs the greatest gains are achieved on short sea routes where terminal charges form a greater proportion of the total. It was on the short sea routes to Europe that the new techniques were first developed by UK shippers but they have had an increasingly widespread effect on the hierarchy and functions of UK ports and thus the location of unit-load facilities has been very important in the growth and development of ports within the last decade (McKinsey and Co. 1966; Little 1967).

It seems too often the case that an individual port development is viewed in relation to its investment profitability and too rarely placed in a context aimed at minimizing the costs of the complete door-to-door transport system for flows of imports and exports for *the country as a whole*. Again, while not gainsaying the necessity for a national approach, it is sometimes questioned whether this is strictly an economic issue at all. In unit-load traffic overall there are certain areas of concentration, for example, the importance of Dover in roll-on activity, but the six leading ports, each handling over 100,000 loaded units in 1974, handled only 60% of the traffic. The remaining 40% of the units, which in fact involved almost one-half of the tonnage of goods handled in unit load (15.2m tonnes from a total of 30.6m tonnes), were handled by no less than fifty-three ports (table 5.9).

Felixstowe has shown the most remarkable growth, to become one of the leading container ports of the UK by 1980. It lies opposite Harwich on the northern bank of the Stour–Orwell estuary, 200 km west of Rotterdam Europoort. However, the position of Felixstowe as one of the nearest UK ports to the main port of Europe has probably been of less significance to its rapid growth than a greenfield, non-traditional site and small initial labourforce. These enabled Felixstowe to remain aloof from the problems of labour redundancy which plagued older ports, and outside both the Dock Labour Scheme and the British Transport Docks Board organization.

V.4   Investment and Rationalization

If the ports of the UK are to take full advantage, both in cargo handling and in industrial investment, of the technological advances in maritime transport and also to compete more effectively with the ports of the NW coast of mainland Europe, then a rationalization of facilities is an urgent need (NPC 1974). Such a move raises difficult decisions of investment, of choice of sites and of integration. As in so much of UK transport, a more intense use and development of selected sections of the system is required.

The traditional problems of a port authority in seeking to initiate major capital schemes are markedly exacerbated by the present tempo of technological change in transport. A new vessel can be built within a year and the conversion of a vessel carried through in half this time. However, to plan, build and equip a dock may take at least three years. There is, moreover, the perpetual problem that the infrastructure of a port is much longer-lasting than the life of a merchant vessel. Major mechanical equipment such as cranes and loading bridges may be written-off within twenty-five years but for quay walls and port works a period of fifty years would be more normal. It is clearly unlikely that a period of fifty years' calm will be available to port authorities to accommodate this rate of depreciation. For both these reasons the port authority must not only attempt to forecast future developments but also provide a design which is sufficiently flexible to meet unforeseen circumstances.

It has been suggested above that the economics of operation of both bulk carriers and deep-sea container ships in the break-bulk trades demand the minimum number of ports of call. The very large investments required for the receipt and rapid turnround of these vessels strongly suggest that port facilities suitable to the new technology should be concentrated. Short-sea container traffic, with its smaller vessels, could operate from a wider range of ports but might well be able to take advantage of the investment in cranage and stacking area which is necessary for the deep-sea trades. Feeder-relay services, consisting of relatively small vessels ferrying containers to a larger pivot port which serves deep-sea trades, go some way towards adapting the historical legacy of our scattering of medium-sized and small ports to the needs of the new technology. Any dispassionate observer of the port scene around 1960 who could have foreseen the rapidity of technological change at sea, however, would surely have recommended a drastic concentration of investment. Indeed, the recommendations of the *Rochdale Report* (MoT 1962), McKinsey (1966, 1967) and Little (1967) all led in this direction. It was also clear to these observers that whereas the UK had about fifteen major ports, the North Sea and Channel coast of the mainland EEC had only nine equivalent ports serving a hinterland population twice the size. The postwar growth of Rotterdam in particular showed how an emergent pivot port could develop several individual initial advantages so that each served to bring about economies of scale for the others.

The ports were by no means dispassionate observers of their own fortunes. In the UK the largest ports were public trusts, deriving a large proportion of their investment income from revenues and with a statutory obligation to foster the trade of their area. Other ports were operated by the British Transport Docks Board, a nationalized industry, while yet others were private companies. There were also port installations under the ownership of nationalized and private industrial companies. On several estuaries there were a number of different and sometimes competing port operators in close juxtaposition. All these port operators had a direct interest in further expansion but few, if any, could command the investment capital to match the developments demanded by the rapid change in ship technology.

Although it could be argued that the physical and economic geography of the UK favours a dispersed rather than a concentrated pattern of ports and that the past success of our port and shipping industry owed a great deal to the vigorous and highly speculative acts of expansion carried out by our forefathers (Wilson 1965, 90), the influential Rochdale Committee of Inquiry into the major seaports of Great Britain (MoT 1962) saw a need not only for a more concentrated pattern of investment but for government help in funding major schemes. It regarded the lack of any central planning of port development in Britain as a fundamental defect in organization and proposed that a National Ports Authority should be established, to plan and supervise a programme of UK port development, with control over both port charges and major investment schemes. Although a National Ports Council was established in 1964, it was a much weaker body than the Rochdale Committee had envisaged, being financed by the ports themselves. The government retained power to withhold investment approval (under Section 9 of the *Harbours Act* (1964) for projects costing £500,000 (later £1,000,000) and over, so that the National Ports Council, as a client of the ports and a counsellor to the Ministry of Transport, found it difficult either to envisage or maintain a coherent plan. The Council has assisted in the amalgamation of port interests into a series of estuarine port authorities. It has also greatly improved the flow of statistical information about ports and has been deeply involved in the establishment of the new oil bases at Sullom Voe,

Scapa Flow and Cromarty Firth. Yet it has, not surprisingly, failed to reduce the chronic over-capacity of the older ports or to prevent an over-proliferation of modern container terminals around the coast. The individual ports are most unlikely to propose their own demise in the interests of nationwide rationalization and new investment proposals come to the Cabinet with short-term political implications as well as the long-term future of a national industry. The great political temptations to spread investment among the regions, even if this may result in national over-capacity, have been felt just as strongly in the transport industry as in steel and motor-vehicle production.

The majority of proposals for port development were approved as economically appropriate to individual ports. A proposal for major expansion at Portbury by the Port of Bristol was, however, refused on grounds of national over-capacity and the reasons for the minister's decision produced an interesting analysis of the wider implications of a development scheme at an individual port (MoT 1966B). The decision to abolish the National Ports Council in 1979 marked the temporary suspension of formal attempts at the central planning of the ports of the UK. The government, however, retained its control over major investments, loans to ports and certain senior appointments within the industry.

Britain's adherence to the EEC affected trade rather than investment in the ports, for EEC transport policy, such as it is, excludes ports, which remain under national jurisdiction (Powrie 1975; Bird and Pollock 1978). Many mainland European ports benefit from very high government investment for, in contrast to the Belgian and French governments' practice of paying respectively 100% and 80% of port infrastructure costs, the UK government's contribution has been limited to 20% of certain restricted types of port investment. This low level of direct government financial involvement has sometimes been considered a disadvantage of the UK ports compared to their continental rivals and notably, for example, with Antwerp and Rotterdam which have demonstrated so forcibly the benefits of a vigorous planned investment policy (Takel 1974; NPC 1976).

In some areas the commercial initiative of ports, rather than government action, has led to a more positive concentration of activity. This is seen clearly in the case of Southampton. Atlantic Container Lines' decision to base its transatlantic operations in the port, followed by Southampton's nomination by ACT, OCL and the Ben Line as the premier port for the Far East, its choice by the African Conference Lines and Elders' and Fyffes' decision to group all their banana and cargo operations in the port, are of major importance to the future development of Southampton. Similarly, a measure of increasing concentration has occured through British Rail's decision to concentrate its container movements to the continent through Harwich and those to Ireland through Holyhead. These commercial initiatives require, of course, the cooperation of the port authority and ultimately, as major finance is almost invariably involved, the imprimatur of public policy through the approval of the Minister of Transport.

Such changes in the relative status of ports reflect their reactions to new possibilities of growth and development. Thus the Tees, with developing chemical, steel and oil industries associated with major reclamation schemes, typifies the impact of the new industrial potential in ports. Felixstowe exemplifies the impact of the new transport technology in cargo-handling, having increased its trade from about 59,000 tonnes in the 1950s to 5m tonnes in 1979. The rate and diversity of growth in industrial port activities on Teesside in the last thirty years has certainly markedly changed the relative importance of the ports of NE England. The Tees has now outstripped all rivals. On the other hand, the growth of short-sea trading has revitalized some of the small ports of E Anglia, which have increased their proportionate share of UK foreign trade. The concentration of activity has been pursued more markedly in respect of bulk cargoes and industrial activity rather than unit-load handling. During the changeover to unit transport the flow of general cargo at the major terminals was particularly vulnerable to industrial disputes. This encouraged small ports which, without the bitter legacy of the past, may be well suited to the development of new patterns of trade and perhaps can operate without the burdens of the heavy costs of development land and of traffic congestion in the conurbations. Although outside the *National Dock Labour Scheme* they offer pay and conditions which are 'reasonably comparable'.

The changes in bulk handling and unit loading during the 1950s and 1960s left the traditional major ports with severe problems of excess area, obsolete facilities and surplus manpower. The UK ports as a whole could handle twice the tonnage which is actually traded. The trade of London, for instance, has fallen from 89m tonnes in 1960 to 40m in 1980 and the Port labourforce from 24,000 to 3,000. Within the port virtually all traffic has moved down-river to Tilbury and the port needed government aid to meet its financial problems during the late 1970s. Similarly the trade of Liverpool has fallen from 42m tonnes to 13m and the Portbury dock scheme at Bristol completed only in 1977 is being used far below its capacity.

One of the more successful applications of rationalization to the British ports industry since 1964 has been the amalgamation of ownership of port facilities on the major UK estuaries. Such amalgamations were recommended by the *Rochdale Report* (MoT 1962) and the National Ports Council. Between 1966 and 1968, reconstituted authorities on the Clyde, Tees and Forth assumed such comprehensive estuarial responsibilities and the new Port of Tyne Authority was a similar, although incomplete, reorganization (British Railways Board Dunston Staiths remained independent). In a more limited sense, in those areas where several major under-takings are operated by the British Transport Docks Board, e.g. the Severn, the Humber and Southampton Water, more formal and more positive cooperation has enhanced the estuarial focus. The Ministry of Transport working documents which served as a basis for consultation leading up to the White Paper, *The Reorganization of the Ports* (MoT 1969B), proposed the development of eight regional port authorities with wide independence, but these proposals were put aside at the change of government in 1970. A more comprehensive nationalization proposal, made in 1974, included all commercial ports. Many of the port authorities, for example the Public Trusts, would remain and merely be licensed by a National Ports Authority which would direct strategy. Given Britain's preoccupation with regional development since 1945, albeit with sporadic enthusiasm, it is strange that the ports have not played a more positive role. It has long seemed likely that the most appropriate development would be to create some formal link between the estuarial ports and the authorities concerned with regional development in their area. Under the *Local Govt Acts* (1972–3), transport planning became the responsibility of metropolitan and shire counties but this had no implications for the ownership or detailed control of port operations. Although the majority of estuaries were brought under single administrations, proposals to unite Bristol and Newport were never carried out, there is still divided responsibility on the Mersey and the Stour and Orwell estuaries (Haven ports) where Felixstowe remains private, and the other facilities are administered by the British Transport Docks Board.

Concern over the lack of investment in British ports was one of the reasons for the Rochdale Committee of Inquiry (MoT 1962). The Report stimulated the rate of investment: £20m was invested in 1964 and during the six years from 1965–70 a total of £245m was spent, of which about one-third was invested in the nationally owned ports. Although port-users have invested heavily in their own facilities, UK port investment as a whole has declined in real terms during the last decade and compares very unfavourably with expenditure in other areas of transport.

V.5   Seaports and Industry

The link between seaports and industrial development was forged in early medieval times in areas on or near the coalfields and was well established on many British estuaries by the mid-eighteenth century. The attractions of a port location include: the cheap assembly of varied raw materials, especially those of high bulk and low value per unit weight, which in the past were unable to stand the costs of inland transport; the ability to utilize direct water access as in shipbuilding and repairing, or merely in the shipment of the end product; the ability to develop associated industries, cognate or ancillary to the main undertakings, and thus contribute to the inter-related complex of industrial production which is characteristic of most major ports (Elliott 1962). There is no doubt, for example, that the greatly increased size of vessel markedly enhances the asset of low assembly costs for raw materials. Not all ports can take advantage of these possibilities since the requirements of such vessels are more exacting. Clearly physical environmental considerations have been reasserted in port growth and development, notably in the growth of industry within ports. Major modern industrial development in ports requires extensive areas of level land or alternatively the ability to reclaim such land. The handling of the massive bulk-carriers requires considerable depths of water, preferably at all states of the tide: deep water, in the right place, is one of the scarcest industrial resources.

Although the economic and technical changes of the period since 1945 have been conducive to major industrial development in seaport locations, it would appear that the attitude of British port authorities to industrial growth has not undergone an equally felicitous transformation. With the notable exception of the Manchester Ship Canal Co, no British major port has pursued industry in a methodical and sustained fashion. This lack of interest is the more surprising in view of the preoccupation with regional development since the war and the role which estuaries might play within this. Many British major ports are Trust ports (Adams 1973) in which the controlling bodies are dominated by port-users whose main concern has been to keep port changes low and uniform rather than to develop an adventurous and adaptable commercial policy. It is true that Continental rivals of the UK have been aided by local and central government subsidies, but they have also pursued much more enterprising and flexible development policies that very clearly demonstrate the new potential for industrial investment characteristic of port locations in recent years. The move of the iron and steel industry to the coast has been one of the most important changes in economic patterns in the UK within this century and, the development of the oil and petrochemical industries has markedly enhanced the significance of tide-water sites. Significantly perhaps, neither of these industries is inevitably tied to port locations. The fact that in the recent past they have been attracted overwhelmingly to coastal sites may serve to stress the particular contemporary assets offered by such locations. Moreover, these industries are of particular importance in that either or both may form the focus for an industrial complex of inter-related industries.

Major demands for large acreages of level land with deep-water access have been made by the oil industry. Direct water access is not inescapable for either refinery capacity or any associated petrochemical developments, but the balance of locational advantages has tended to retain such industrial growth on coastal locations, with notable concentrations on the Thames estuary, at Milford Haven and on Southampton Water. The location of oil resources has importantly influenced developments on the east coast of Great Britain in the recent past (fig. 4.3). The working of British Petroleum's Forties field, 177 km east of Aberdeen will, in time, increase considerably the throughput of the Grangemouth refinery to which oil is being sent by sea- and land-pipe, and a new *island* terminal has been constructed downstream of the Forth Bridges to handle the export of surplus crude and perhaps of petroleum products. The Philips Ekofisk petroleum field, on the Norwegian continental shelf but separated from the mainland by the major gash of the Norwegian Trench, is sending the oil westward by undersea pipeline to the Tees. It is estimated that this will more than double the crude oil (c. 15m tonnes) previously handled by Teesside refineries.

According to the extent of processing of petroleum feedstocks and natural gas, petrochemical production may take place within the refinery or on a separate, often adjacent site. The refinery might commonly produce raw materials (for example naphtha) and intermediates (for example propylene). Finished products such as plastics would be more commonly produced on a separate site and this need not be adjacent to the refinery. Petrochemical feedstock pipelines link ICI Wilton to Runcorn and the Stanlow refinery (125 km) with offshoots to Partington (near Manchester) and Fleetwood. Fawley is linked by a similar pipeline to the petrochemical developments at Severnside (70 km). Whether within refineries or not, petrochemical industries have in recent years made a major contribution to industrial investment in ports and have grown at an appreciably faster rate than the national economy. These are highly capital-intensive industries but nonetheless petrochemical development greatly increases employment as compared with the oil refinery alone.

The British steel industry has come to rely increasingly upon imported ores. Measured by iron content, imports comprised about 91% of the ores used in 1974 compared with about one-half in the immediate postwar years. Indeed total ore imports into the UK increased from 5m tonnes in 1945 to 21.7m tonnes in 1973. Since commonly more than half the cost of steel is accounted for by the delivered cost of production materials it is not surprising that there has been an increased emphasis upon seaport locations. The assets of such locations were enhanced by the increased size of ore-carrier developed although this was a development of which the British steel industry was very slow to take advantage. However, a programme of rationalization has concentrated production in modern Basic Oxygen Steelmaking (BOS) plants. Established coastal locations play a major part, notably S Wales (exemplified by the Llanwern works at Newport and the new dock and BOS developments at Port Talbot) and the S Teesside group (Lackenby, Redcar). Although the size of production unit involved may not seem to have fully exploited the advantages of bulk carriage, three new aluminium smelters came into production in 1970–1 at Holyhead (Rio Tinto Zinc), at Lynemouth near Blyth (Alcan) and at Invergordon (British Aluminium). Invergordon closed down early in 1982. Holyhead can handle vessels of 50,000dwt and the 22,500dwt possible at Blyth is quite adequate to the capacity of the nearby plant. The scale of vessel in use in recent years has also stimulated development in the handling of grain and in flour-milling, one of the range of food industries, sugar-refining is another, processing imported raw materials. Recent developments at London, Liverpool and Glasgow to handle the larger vessels of 50–60,000dwt which may now be used in the grain trade have reaffirmed flour-milling as a port activity and in the case of Tilbury have attracted one large new flour mill.

The MIDA concept The increase in size of bulk carriers, which began in the mid-1950s, encouraged planners to think in terms of extensive industrial estates based on seaborne materials, notably oil and ores. The first of these projects, at Botlek west of Rotterdam (1958), was soon followed by others in Japan and N America (Vigarié 1981). In 1967 the UK government commissioned an enquiry into sites suitable for maritime industrial development. This was not published but was broadly interpreted in the National Ports Council's *Progress Report* (1969); see also Preston and Rees (1970). The Report noted that size of ship and the extent to which direct water access is critical vary the particular requirements of specific industries. It is clear also that the search for potential industrial sites is made more difficult by the fact that most obvious sites are already in use while others are remote and/or have a high amenity value. It is suggested that MIDAs (Maritime Industrial Development Areas) would require first, to be near to deep water (now seen as 15–18.5m mean high water neaps without excessive dredging); secondly, to have a minimum of 2,200ha level land, although this may be obtainable if necessary by reclamation; and thirdly, to be near main population concentrations and have good transport links inland. Only three sites were considered to meet all these requirements: Humberside, Thames–Medway and Cardiff–Newport. Eight further sites met some of the requirements and were considered possible MIDAs: Cromarty Firth, Firth of Tay, Clyde Estuary, Upper Firth of Forth, Tees Estuary, Lune Estuary, The Wash and Weston Super Mare–Clevedon (fig. 5.6). Later, the National Ports Council (1973) suggested that the foreseeable demand for MIDAs could be accommodated at three sites: the Tees, Cromarty Firth and Clyde (Hunterston). No such developments have in fact taken place. As Hallett and Randall (1970, 108) concluded, decisions on the location of maritime industry have frequently been determined on too restricted a basis, frustrating the type of coordinated development which in the long run would be desirable from the viewpoint of both industrial efficiency and amenity.

There has also been opposition to MIDA-style development. The Murco refinery (1970) planned for Bishopton, 16km from Glasgow, was the first major economic development in Scotland to be rejected at the planning stage, mainly on the environmental argument of the potential threat of air pollution. Environmental pressure groups also succeeded in impeding but not preventing the commencement of an off-shore terminal and on-shore storage for oil on Anglesey to feed the large and expending refinery on the Mersey at Stanlow. The immediacy of the demand for oil-rig construction led to the development of limited and specialized MIDAs, on the Clyde and notably on the east coast of Britain at Nigg Bay (Easter Ross), Methil (Fife) and on the Tees. Such development proposals have often provoked environmentalist opposition, sometimes protracted and successful as at Drumbuie (Wester Ross). There are eleven sites in Scotland and there has been an increasingly formalized governmental aim of preventing widespread proliferation of sites, especially in areas of scenic interest. A government decision in 1976 to permit the development of a refinery at Nigg, contrary to the recommendation of the public enquiry, acknowledged the probable detrimental environmental effects but clearly saw the proposal as appropriate to the plan for Cromarty Firth to be an area of substantial industrial growth.

VI DEVELOPMENTS AND PROBLEMS

This chapter begins and ends with considerations of transport policy because ultimately the transport system reflects the demands of our economy and society. An ideal transport system would be *modern*, *efficient* and *comprehensive*, if we were to define efficiency in terms of carrying freight and facilitating passenger journeys at the lowest cost to total national resources, and comprehensiveness as providing an adequate service to all age-groups, to the rich and the poor, to inhabitants of remote places, under adverse weather conditions and during national crises. As these three goals are partially incompatible, policy makers have to look for compromise objectives which allow some progress towards one goal without deviating too far from the road to either of the others. It therefore is not surprising that the development of each transport mode over the last two decades has been complicated by changing objectives and constraints, and delayed by the unwilling-ness of national and local governments to come to firm, lasting decisions.

Many transport geographers recognize a series of stages in the historical develop-ment of transport systems. Mature economies are characterized by a stage of intensification in which urbanization and economies of scale in industrial produc-tion lead to a concentration of traffic onto those routes which link the main cities, centres of production and ports. Such routes are progressively upgraded to carry the increasing traffic. Intensification of this kind has been clearly evident in Britain since the 1950s within each mode (figs. 5.3 and 5.4) and along major axes such as London—West Midlands—Lancashire—Glasgow, now served by motorways, APT electric railway services and shuttle services by air. If not constrained by legislation or shortage of funds, the modernization of transport would, given the continued urbanization and suburbanization of Britain described in chapters 2 and 6, lead to economies of scale, provide larger vehicles on the more heavily used routes and lead to the general substitution of capital equipment for manpower. Transport policies which favour competition between transport modes also encourage the moderniza-tion of the more heavily used services, enabling customers to choose those which suit them best. Conservative and Labour governments alike have issued White Papers and Transport Acts which confirm that intermodal competition shall be the basis for transport policy in Britain. Governments have not only invested in motorway building but also in railway modernization and the expansion of airports which serve some of the same routes.

While supporting competition as a way towards modernization and efficiency, successive British governments have not lost sight of their other goal. The operation of market forces has not been allowed to reach the point where a mode which is losing traffic in a competitive struggle becomes so short of revenue that its services deteriorate and threaten to collapse. The railways have not been allowed to follow the inland waterways into oblivion. During the mid-1970s, for instance, restrictions on public spending led to large-scale deferments of the road programme but the share of capital investment and public spending allowed to the railways has been much larger than their share of current traffic. The financial restrictions which have been set on railway expenditure, coupled with the objectives laid down for the railways by the *Transport Act* (1968) and the *Railways Act* (1974), have led to the modernization of the more competitive inter-city services. The less directly competitive commuter and rural services have stagnated to the point where obsolescence of both track and rolling stock threatens a rapid decline in these services during the late 1980s.

Local transport, in fact, offers the greatest challenge to policies based on market pricing and consumer choice. One of the disadvantages of competition between transport modes is that it leads to over-capacity, as the customers spread themselves around the transport services on offer. In sparsely populated rural areas, competing services (and all public transport competes with the private car) can be remarkably wasteful and expensive to operate. Market forces are more likely to eliminate all public transport services than to favour one of the competitors. In conurbations the combined costs of providing public transport services, together with the roadspace and parking for private cars used in the daily journeys to and from work, can lead to totally unsatisfactory transport conditions for everybody (Thomson 1977).

Where competition fails, two policies are available: the enforced coordination of public transport services, or their total withdrawal in favour of private transport. The latter solution fails the test of comprehensive provision, while coordination may fail the test of efficiency in the narrow sense that a PTE may not be able to cover its costs from passenger revenues without raising them to a point where the service also ceases to be comprehensive. In so far as private car travellers do not pay the full social cost of their journeys at the time they travel, it does not seem wholly illogical to subsidize public transport riders. Britain has been more reluctant than her European neighbours to establish thoroughly coordinated urban transport systems or to ensure minimum public transport provision at reasonable cost in remote rural areas. The level of national and local financial support for public transport services is also among the lowest in Europe and transport policies in general, apart from a short period following the *Transport Act* (1968), have been more affected in Britain by the alternation of governments of different political persuasions. While there is some measure of agreement concerning the intermodal balance between road, rail and air on inter-city routes, there appears to be little public consensus on transport conditions in large cities and rural areas. Here the problem is the provision of sufficient long-term investment for public transport services where public propensity to travel is not sufficient to provide the necessary revenue, but where the ultimate costs to the community of discontinuing the service would be greater than subsidizing it.

REFERENCES

ADAMS, G (1973) *The Organisation of the British Port Transport Industry*, NPC, London
ADAMS, J G U (1971) 'London's Third Airport', *Geogrl J., 137*, 468–505
            (1981) *Transport Planning*, London

ALDCROFT, D H (1968) *British Railways in Transition,* London
APPLETON, J H (1962) *The Geography of Communications in GB,* London
BAGWELL, P S (1974) *The Transport Revolution from 1770,* London
BARKER, T C and SAVAGE, C I (1974) *An Economic History of Transport in Britain,* London
BEESLEY, M E, COBURN, T M and REYNOLDS, D J (1959) 'The London–Birmingham Motorway, Traffic and Economics', *Road Res. Lab. Tech. Pap. 40,* HMSO
BIRD, J H (1963) *The Major Seaports of the UK,* London
　　　(1969) 'Traffic Flows to and from British Seaports', *Geogr., 54,* 284–302
　　　(1971) *Seaports and Seaport Terminals,* London
BIRD, J H and POLLOCK, E E (1978) 'The Future of Seaports in the European Communities', *Geogrl J., 144,* 23–49
BRACEY, H E (1970) *People and the Countryside,* London
BRIT. RAILWAYS BD (1965) *The Development of the Major Railway Trunk Routes,* HMSO
　　　(1981A) *Passenger Timetable: Great Britain,* London
　　　(1981B) *Annual Report and Accounts,* London
BRIT. TRANSPORT COMMN (1955) *The Modernisation and Reequipment of British Railways,* HMSO
BRIT. WATERWAYS BD (1980) *Ann. Rep. and Accounts,* HMSO
BROWN, A J (1969) 'Regional Economics with Special Reference to the UK', *Econ. J., 79,* 759–96
BUCHANAN, C D (1963) *Traffic in Towns,* HMSO
CHISHOLM, M (1970) 'Forecasting the Generation of Freight Traffic in GB', in CHISHOLM, M *et al* (eds) *Regional Forecasting,* Colston Research Soc., *22,* 431–42
CHISHOLM, M and MANNERS, G (eds) (1971) *Spatial Policy Problems of the British Economy,* Cambridge
CLOUT, H D (1972) *Rural Geography – an Introductory Survey,* London
COLLINS, M F and PHARAOH, T M (1974) *Transport Organisation in a Great City – The Case of London,* London
COMM. INQUIRY INTO CIV. AIR TRANSPORT (1969) *British Air Transport in the Seventies* (Edwards Rept), Cmnd 4018, HMSO
COUNC. WALES and MON. (1972) *Report on the Rural Transport Problem in Wales,* Cmnd 1821, HMSO
COUPER, A D (1972) *The Geography of Sea Transport,* London
DEAKIN, R M and SEWARD, T (1969) 'Productivity in Transport', *Cambridge Dept Appl. Econ. Occ. Pap. 17,* Cambridge
DoE (1971A) *Study of Rural Transport in Devon,* HMSO
　　　(1971B) *Study of Rural Transport in W Suffolk,* HMSO
　　　(1972) *New Roads in Towns – Report of the Urban Motorways Committee,* HMSO
　　　(1973A) *Urban Transport Planning – Government Observations on the Second Report of the Expenditure Committee,* Cmnd 5366, HMSO
　　　(1973B) *Participation in Road Planning,* HMSO
　　　(1975) *National Travel Survey 1972–3,* HMSO
　　　(1976) *Transport Policy: Consultation Document,* 2 vols, HMSO
　　　(1981) *Transport Statistics Great Britain 1970–80,* HMSO
DEPT TRADE (1975) *Airport Strategy for GB:* Part 1 *The London Area;* Part 2 (1976) *The Regional Airports,* HMSO
　　　(1978) *Airports Policy,* Cmnd 7084, HMSO

DEPT TRADE and INDUSTRY (1971) *Rep. of the Commn on the Third London Airport* (Roskill Report), HMSO
DEPT TRANSPORT (1977A) *Transport Policy*, Cmnd 6836, HMSO
      (1977B) *The Role of British Rail in Public Transport*, Cmnd 7038, HMSO
      (1979A) *Report of the Advisory Committee on Trunk Road Assessment* (Leitch Report), HMSO
      (1979B) *The Transport of Goods by Road in GB*, HMSO
      (1981) *Passenger Transport Statistics 1970–80*, HMSO
DESPICHT, H (1969) *The Transport Policy of the European Communities*, London
DYOS, H J and ALDCROFT, D H (1969) *British Transport – an Economic Survey from the Seventeenth Century to the Twentieth*, Leicester
EDWARDS, S L and BAYLISS, B T (1971) *Operating Costs in Road Freight Transport*, HMSO
ELLIOTT, N R (1962) 'Tyneside, a Study in the Development of an Industrial Seaport', *Tijd. econ. soc. Geogr.*, *53*, 225–37 and 263–72
      (1966) 'The Functional Approach in Port Studies', in HOUSE, J W (ed.) *Northern Geographical Essays*, Univ. Newcastle upon Tyne, 102–18
FOSTER, C D (1974) 'Transport and the Urban Environment', in ROTHENBERG, J G and HEGGIE, I G *Transport and the Urban Environment*, London, 166–91
      (1975) *The Transport Problem*, London
FOSTER, C D, BAYLISS, B T and BLAKE, J L (1970) 'Comments on the London Transportation Study', *Reg. Stud.*, *4*, 63–83
FULLERTON, B (1975) *The Development of British Transport Networks*, Oxford
GOSS, R O and JONES, C D (1972) 'Economics of Size and Dry Bulk Carriers', *Govt Econ. Serv. Occ. Pap. 2*, London
GOVT N IRELAND (1963) *N Ireland Railways*, Cmnd 458, Belfast HMSO
GLC (1969) *Greater London Development Plan*, London
GREEN, F H W (1950) 'Urban Hinterlands in England and Wales – Analysis of Bus Services', *Geogrl J.*, *116*, 64–88
      (1951) 'Bus Services in the British Isles', *Geogrl Rev.*, *41*, 645–55
GWILLIAM, K M (1964) *Transport and Public Policy*, London
      (1979) 'Institutions and Objectives in Transport Policy', *J. Transport and Econ. Pol.*, *13*, 11–28
GWILLIAM, K M and MACKIE, P J (1975) *Economics and Transport Policy*, London
HALL, P (1980) *Great Planning Disasters*, London
HALLETT, G and RANDALL, P (1970) *Maritime Industry and Port Development in S Wales*, Univ. Coll. Cardiff
HALSALL, D A and TURTON, B J (eds) (1979) *Rural Transport Problems in Britain*, Inst. Br. Geogr. Transport Study Gp, Keele
HEGGIE, I G and JONES, P M (1978) 'Transport Themes, Economics and the Road Programme', in WILLIAMS, A F (ed.) *Transport and Public Policy*, Inst. Br. Geogr. Transport Study Gp, Birmingham
HIBBS, J (1972) 'Maintaining Transport in Rural Areas', *J. Transport and Econ. Policy*, *6*, 10–22
HILLMAN, M, HENDERSON, I and WHALLEY, A (1973) *Personal Mobility and Transport Policy*, London
HOUSE OF COMMONS SELECT COMM. ON NATIONALIZED INDUSTRIES (1977) *The Role of British Rail in Public Transport*
HUNTER, E and WILSON, T B (1969) 'The Increasing Size of Tankers, Bulk Carriers and Containerships with some Implications for Port Authorities', *Res.*

and Tech. Bull., NPC, 5, 180–224

HUNTER, T (1974) 'Recent Trends in Sizes and Dimensions of Tankers', *NPC Bulletin*, 6, 20–8

INDEPENDENT COMMN ON TRANSPORT (1974) *Changing Directions*, London

JOHNSON, K M, GARNETT, H C *et al* (1970) *Final Report on Containerisation*, Univ. Glasgow and Strathclyde

JURGENSON, H (1971) 'The Regional Impact of Port Investments and its Consideration in Port Investment Policy', in REGUL, R (ed.) *The Future of the European Ports*, Bruges, vol. 2, 576–602

KNOWLES, R D (1978) 'Options for Public Transport in Rural Areas', in WILLIAMS, A F (ed.) *Transport and Public Policy*, Inst. Br. Geogr. Transport Study Gp, Birmingham
            (1981) 'Island to Mainland Transport Development in Highland Areas', *Univ. Salford Discuss. P. in Geogr.*, *12*, Salford

LITTLE, A D (1967) *Containerisation on the North Atlantic: a Port to Port Analysis*, NPC, London
            (1970) *Transshipment in the Seventies – a Study of Container Transport*, NPC, London

McFADZEAN, F S (1968) 'The Economics of Large Tankers', *Strathclyde Lecture, March 1968*, Shell Int. Petroleum Co. Ltd, London

McKINSEY and CO. INC. (1966, 1967) *Containerisation: the Key to Low-Cost Transportation*, Rept to Brit. Transport Docks Bd, London

MINIST. TRANSPORT (1959) *Reappraisal of the Plan for the Modernisation and Reequipment of British Railways*, Cmnd 813, HMSO
            (1960) *Reorganisation of the Nationalised Transport Undertakings*, Cmnd 1248, HMSO
            (1961) *Report on Rural Bus Services*, HMSO
            (1962) *Report of the Committee of Inquiry into the Major Seaports of GB* (Rochdale Report), Cmnd 1824, HMSO
            (1963B) *The Reshaping of British Railways* (Beeching Report), HMSO
            (1966A) *Transport Policy*, Cmnd 3057, HMSO
            (1966B) *Portbury: Reasons for the Minister's Decision not to Authorise the Construction of a New Dock at Portbury, Bristol*, HMSO
            (1967A) *British Railways Network for Development*, HMSO
            (1967B) *Public Transport and Traffic*, Cmnd 3481, HMSO
            (1967C) *Railway Policy*, Cmnd 3439, HMSO
            (1967D) *The Transport of Freight*, Cmnd 3470, HMSO
            (1969A) *Roads for the Future, a New Interurban Plan*, HMSO
            (1969B) *The Reorganisation of the Ports*, Cmnd 3903, HMSO
            (1970) *Roads for the Future, the New Interurban Plan for England*, Cmnd 4369, HMSO

MISHAN, E J (1970) 'What is Wrong with Roskill?', *J. Transport and Econ. Policy*, *4*, 221–34

MITCHELL, B R and DEANE, P (1971) *Abstract of British Historical Statistics*, London

MOSELEY, M J (1979) *Accessibility – the Rural Challenge*, London

MOSSÉ, R (1974) 'An Introduction to Urban Transportation Problems', in ROTHENBERG, J G and HEGGIE, I G (eds) *Transport and the Urban Environment*, London

MUNBY, D L (ed.) (1968) *Transport – Selected Readings,* London
NAT. PORTS COUNC. (annually) *Digest of Port Statistics,* London
   (1969) *Port Progress Report,* London
   (1973) *Survey of Non-Scheme Ports and Wharves,* Final
Report, London
   (1974) *Comparison of the Costs of Continental and British
Ports,* London
   (1976) 'Port Perspectives 1976', *NPC Bull., 9*
O'DELL, A C (1966) 'Highlands and Islands Developments', *Scott. Geogr., Mag.,
82,* 8–16
OECD (1968) *Ocean Freight Rates as Part of Total Transport Costs,* HMSO
O'SULLIVAN, P (1978) 'Issues in Transportation', in DAVIES, R L and HALL, P
(eds) *Issues in Urban Society,* London
   (1980) *Transport Policy – an Interdisciplinary Approach,* London
OWEN, W (1964) *Strategy for Mobility,* The Brookings Institution, Washington
PATMORE, J A (1966) 'The Contraction of the Network of Railway Passenger
Services in England and Wales 1936–62', *Trans. Inst. Br. Geogr., 38,* 105–19
   (1972) 'New Directions for Transport', in CHISHOLM, M (ed.)
Resources for Britain's Future, London, 50–61
PINDER, D A and HOYLE, B S (1981) 'Cityports, Technologies and Development
Strategies', in HOYLE, B S and PINDER, D A (eds) *Cityport, Industrialization
and Regional Development,* Oxford
POLICY STUDIES INST. (1981) *The Future of Rural Railways,* London
POLLINS, H (1971) *Britain's Railways – an Industrial History,* Newton Abbot
POWRIE, P J (1975) 'The Community and the Ports', *NPC Bull., 7,* 3–17
PRESTON, M H and REES, R (1970) *Maritime Industrial Areas: a Preliminary
Report,* NPC, London
PRYKE, R J and DODGSON, J (1976) *The Rail Problem,* London
PUBL. GEN. ACTS, see list on pp. 505–7
PULLING, L and SPEAKMAN, C (1974) 'The Impact on Rural Life of Declining
Public Transport Services for Communities and Individuals', in INDEPENDENT
COMMN ON TRANSPORT *Changing Directions,* London
RAMBLERS ASSOCN (1971) *Rural Transport in Crisis,* London
RIDLEY, T M and TRESIDDER, T O (1970) 'The London Transportation Study
and Beyond', *Reg. Stud., 4,* 1, 63–83
ROBINSON, H and BAMFORD, C G (1978) *Geography of Transport,* Plymouth
ROYAL COMMN TRANSPORT (1930) *Final Report,* Cmnd 3751, HMSO
RURAL DISTRICT COUNC. ASSOCN (1971) *Rural Transport, What Future Now?,*
London
SCHAEFFER, K H and SCLAR, E (1975) *Access for All,* London
SCOTT. DEPT AGRIC. (1967) *Report of the Highland Transport Board on
Highland Transport Services,* Edinburgh HMSO
SCOTT. DEV. DEPT (1963) *Central Scotland, a Programme for Development and
Growth,* Cmnd 2188, Edinburgh HMSO
SCOTT. OFF. (1964) *A Programme of Highland Development,* Cmnd 7976,
Edinburgh HMSO
   (1969) *Scottish Roads in the 1970s,* Cmnd 3953, Edinburgh HMSO
SEALY, K R (1955) 'London's Airports and the Geography of Airport Location',
Geogr., 40, 255–65
   (1967A) 'Stansted and Airport Planning', *Geogrl J., 133,* 350–4
   (1967B) 'The Siting and Development of British Airports', *Geogrl J.,
133,* 148–78
   (1976) 'Airport Planning and Airport Strategy', *Theory and Practice
in Geography,* Oxford

SEC. STATE IND., TRADE and REG. DEV. (1963) *The North East: a Programme for Regional Development and Growth,* Cmnd 2206, HMSO
SHARP, C (1979) 'Environmental Impact of Transport and the Public Interest', *J. Transport and Econ. Pol., 13,* 88–102
SMITH, W (1949) *An Economic Geography of GB,* London
SOLESBURY, W and TOWNSEND, A (1970) 'Transportation Studies and British Planning Practice', *Tn Plann. Rev., 41,* 63–80
STARKIE, D N M (1973) 'Transportation Planning and Public Policy', in DIAMOND, D and McCLOUGHLIN, J B (eds) *Progress in Planning,* London, *1,* 313–91
            (1976) *Transportation Planning, Policy and Analysis,* Oxford
            (1979) 'Allocation of Investment to Interurban Road and Rail', *Reg. Stud., 13,* 3, 323–37
TAKEL, R E (1974) *Industrial Port Development,* Bristol
            (1981) 'The Spatial Demands of Ports and Related Industry and their Relationships with the Community', in HOYLE, B S and PINDER, D A (eds) *Cityport, Industrialization and Regional Development,* Oxford
TANNER, J C (1977) 'Car Ownership Trends and Forecasts', *Transport and Road Res. Lab., LR 799*
THOMSON, A W J and HUNTER, L C (1973) *The Nationalized Transport Industries,* London
THOMSON, D C and GRIMBLE, L (1968) *The Future of the Highlands,* London
THOMSON, J M (1974) *Modern Transport Economics,* London
            (1977) *Great Cities and their Traffic,* London
TRANSPORT 2000 (1976) *Transport Policy Tomorrow,* London
TREASURY (1967) *Nationalised Industries – a review of economic and financial objectives,* Cmnd 3437, HMSO
            (Annual) *Public Expenditure Surveys,* HMSO
TURNER, N I (1969) 'For and Against: Containers, Pallets and Roll-on, Roll-off', *Dock and Harbour Auth., 49,* 389–90
TURNOCK, D (1970) *Patterns of Highland Development,* London
            (1977) 'The Postbus – a New Element in Britain's Rural Transport', *Geogr., 62,* 112–8
VIGARIÉ, A (1981) 'Maritime Industrial Development Areas: Structural Evolution and Implications for Regional Development', in HOYLE, B S and PINDER, D A (eds) *Cityport, Industrialization and Regional Development,* Oxford
WALLACE, I (1974) 'The Relationship between Freight Transport Organisation and Industrial Linkage in Britain', *Trans. Inst. Br. Geogr., 62,* 25–43
WATTS, H D (1967) 'The Inland Waterways of the UK', *Econ. Geogr., 43,* 303–13
WELSH OFF. (1967) *Wales, The Way Ahead,* Cmnd 3334, Cardiff HMSO
WHITBY, M C *et al* (1974) *Rural Resource Development,* London
WHITE, H P (1978) 'Options for Inter-city Transport', in *Transport and Public Policy,* Inst. Br. Geogr. Transport Study Gp, Birmingham
WHITELEGG, J (1981) 'The Political Economy Approach – the Example of the Company Car', in *The Spirit and Purpose of Transport Geography,* Inst. Br. Geogr. Transport Geography Study Gp, Lancaster
WILSON, A G *et al* (1969) 'The Calibration and Testing of the SELNEC Transport Model', *Reg. Stud., 3,* 337–50
WILSON, G A (1965) 'The Effect on Land Transport Systems of Ports and Water Transport', *Dock and Harbour Auth., 46,* 537, 89–96

6

The Urban System

I INTRODUCTION

The UK is one of the most highly urbanized nations, in which the urban settlements collectively compose an extremely complex structure or system, in the sense that the hundreds of urban centres that comprise it are given a unity and coherence by their inter-connection and inter-dependence. This system of cities, towns and villages, because of its long settlement history, its rapid industrialization in the nineteenth century, and the massive impact of social, economic and technological change in the twentieth century, presents elements of both continuity and change. The social life of the nation is largely conducted through its urban centres, which are also the essential foci of its economic endeavours. Significant regional variations in the between-town comparisons or within-town differences, contribute a further element of diversity (Carter 1965; McWilliam 1975; Adams 1978). This great complexity and variety of the urban system creates considerable difficulty for any description and explanation.

The approach here is to stress the mechanisms or processes which, through time, have been responsible for creating the distribution of the varied towns and cities of today's urban system. This makes it possible to convey both a general under-standing and an explanation of particular cases. Most attention is given to large cities rather than small towns, since not only are the former socially and econo-mically dominant but they most appropriately typify the British urban system, dominated as it still is by the Victorian city created in the last century and some-what modified in this.

The city or town can be defined in two rather different ways. Physically an urban place means an area of buildings designed for specialized functions, while in a functional sense an urban place is one that performs urban activities, manufacturing, commerce and administration. The people who perform these activities are urban and the area in which they live as well as work would also be defined as urban in consequence. Until almost the end of the nineteenth century these two definitions, physical and functional, coincided; increasingly in modern times they do not. The distinction between settlement form and settlement function is reflected in this chapter in the separate accounts of urban structure (section II) and urban function (section III). Section IV discusses the way in which the UK, since 1945, has attempted to engineer urban change in the public interest to overcome particular problems, largely legacies from the nineteenth century.

I.1 Definitions

Urbanization is a multi-faceted phenomenon and it is difficult to give a concise definition of an urban place by a single criterion, in spite of the everyday use of terms such as metropolis, city or town. In the UK settlements called urban clearly possess all the significant physical and functional attributes regarded internationally as pertaining to an 'urban' place, and such a multi-criteria definition includes almost all the nucleated settlements. The seven criteria most used are (1) population size (exceeding a minimum usually of the order of 1,000 to 2,500) and population density (the minimum figure varies greatly because of the influence of arbitrary boundary definition); (2) marked spatial differentiation of land uses, giving rise to functional areas; (3) density of development, usually measured as a ratio between the floor-space provided in such buildings as houses, factories, offices, schools, etc. and their site area; (4) the great intensity of the network of purpose-built transport and communication facilities; (5) the occupational structure of the inhabitants, characterized by a few farmers, fishermen and foresters and a high proportion of service workers (normally in Britain the dominant group, and in many towns over 50% of the total workforce); (6) the existence of a legal or civic identity, usually conferring limited rights and responsibilities of administration and government; and (7) impersonal relationships characterizing much face-to-face contact of the inhabitants, e.g. people met at work are usually different from those met while engaged in other activities, and during each day everyone expects to have contact with many people who will be total strangers.

Faced with obvious measurement difficulties, boundary problems in applying these criteria and the near impossibility of combining them, official definitions, not surprisingly, have usually been based on criterion (6) which provides a precise limit, normally an administrative boundary. Though convenient to the data-gatherer, this practice creates major difficulties for the analysis and description of urban systems. The actual boundaries are not located consistently, frequently reflecting property boundaries fixed in the distant past, and thus making inter-urban comparisons (especially of density) very difficult to interpret. The boundary represents the granting of chartered rights by an often lengthy and cumbersome legal process, originally by the monarch or feudal lord in the Middle Ages or subsequently by Parliament, or its appointed agency such as the Local Boundary Commission of the 1950s. There is thus a marked tendency for the official designation and delimitation of a town to lag in time behind the actual physical reality. From the 1880s until the 1972 reform of local government (ch. 1.IV.3), the resistance by the largely rural counties to the areal extension of towns and cities resulted in large-scale under-bounding: that is, the administratively defined urban place was considerably smaller in extent than the actual pattern of 'bricks and mortar'. Population living in these physical extensions of the city, adjacent to but beyond the city limits, were not included in the population of the city, and, depending on the status of the administrative unit in which they lived, may not even have been included as urban population. This difficulty of under-bounding associated with the official definition can be seen from the fact that the rural districts of England and Wales increased in population in the decade 1961–71 seven times as fast as the urban areas. The explanation of this paradox is, of course, that rural districts were increasingly invaded by suburban development as the expansion of towns crossed administrative boundaries. The third major difficulty is that comparability through time is very difficult to establish because of the instability of the spatial units consequent on the slow but steady adaptation of boundaries, sometimes resulting in the disappearance or appearance of entire areas.

The radical nature of the reorganization of local government that was instituted in 1974 illustrates particularly well the limitations of using administrative areas to analyse the nature of population change. The data contained in table 6.1 has been specially provided by the 1981 census authorities to facilitate comparison with previous censuses. Of the 49m people recorded in the preliminary count as present on census night, in England and Wales, 77% (37.7m) were urban, a decrease of 1.9% over the decade, compared with an increase of 0.5% in the population as a whole. The 1961 urban population at 37.4m was almost exactly that in 1981. As a comparison with this official measure or urbanization it should be noted that less than 2% (1.7) of the employed population work in agriculture, fishing or forestry, which suggests an 'urban' workforce of 98% of the total.

TABLE 6.1

Urban Population, England and Wales, 1981

Type of District	No. of towns*	1981 Pop. (million)	% of total	Population change 1961–71	1971–81
Greater London	–	6.7	17.8	–6.8	–10.1
6 Metropolitan counties	185	10.5	27.9	–1.0	–5.4
Large cities	11	2.7	7.3	–1.5	–5.2
Small cities	19	1.6	4.3	+1.9	–3.6
Industrial districts	162	5.0	13.4	n.a.	n.a.
Wales and N England	93	2.6	6.9	+1.5	–1.2
Rest of England	69	2.4	6.5	+11.0	+4.2
New Towns	23	1.6	4.2	+28.5	+21.2
Resort and Seaside	84	2.5	6.5	+9.0	+2.7
Other	379	6.9	13.7	n.a.	n.a.
England and Wales	863	37.7	100.0	+2.9	–1.9

*i.e. urban administrative units prior to 1974 reorganization of local government

Source: OPCS (1981)

Below the national level, table 6.1 gives some indication of the wide variations in population trends between towns of different sizes and between different parts of the country. Between 1971 and 1981 the large cities show the fastest and largest declines, while the New Towns have the highest percentage increases (e.g. Washington 103, Milton Keynes 102, Runcorn 78, Redditch 63) together with the expanded towns (e.g. St Ives 72, Tamworth 60, Seaton Valley 44). However some small market towns in southern England also show rapid increases, as for example in Leighton Linslade (46), Witham (46), Guisborough (43), Royston (43), St Neots (39), Ashby de la Zouche (39) and Daventry (37).

There are two main ways of assessing the reality of urbanization in the UK: first, by the use of specific criteria to establish the extent of the *continuously built-up area* and, secondly, to attempt to establish a *functional* concept in contrast to this more obvious physical concept. Following suggestions by Geddes (1915) and later by Fawcett (1932), the 1951 Census of Population identified seven conurbations, which it defined in the following terms:

'a local authority should be considered for inclusion in a conurbation to whose focal centre it was strongly attached as a centre for work, shopping, higher education, sports or entertainment, and consideration should be given to population density' (GRO 1956).

Although based primarily on physical aspects, there is a clear attempt to recognize functional elements by the concern shown for ideas of association, interdependence and circulation, and, despite criticisms of the intuitive process of deciding which local authority areas to include (Self 1957; Carter 1972), they bear a close resemblance to the Metropolitan Counties established in 1974, which comprised 33% of the population of England and Wales in 1981. The English conurbations (as defined in 1971) lost population between 1961 and 1981 at an increasing rate (4.3% 1971–81, 8.1% 1971–81), and the total loss over the 20 years exceeded 2m people. London's loss alone amounted to almost 1.3m while W Yorkshire had the smallest loss, at just under 30,000 persons.

Metropolitan Areas

The functional definition of urban areas in Britain has not yet been formally accepted by the Census authorities (as it has in the USA), but all individual studies have in common an underlying *metropolitan* concept of urbanization. Economic activity is very heavily concentrated in a small number of large towns and cities which, as a consequence, exert a powerful influence on the daily pattern of life over a surrounding area extending well beyond their own administrative boundaries. Economic activity and the settlement pattern combine to create these concentrations of people, goods, information and movement, now found all over the industrial world. With only minor variation they are composed of an urban core with a high density of population, and especially of employment, surrounded by rings in which the density of population and employment decline with increasing distance from the core, until a wholly rural area is encountered. At this point the interest of the local population in the jobs, services and facilities of the now distant urban core is so low that no real relationship can be said to exist. Defined by this social and economic 'watershed' is an entity whose cohesion derives from the social and economic interaction that exists and operates within it. It is these city-focused areas to which the title city-region has been given by several authors (Diamond and Edwards 1975; R. Commn Local Govt 1969; Wise 1966).

The most thorough application of the concept in Britain is represented by the devising and delimitation of 'Standard Metropolitan Labour Areas' (SMLA) and 'Metropolitan Economic Labour Areas' (MELA) (Hall *et al* 1973) in a study of postwar urban growth in England and Wales. In this study, Hall translates the American Standard Metropolitan Statistical Area into a British setting, using census of population statistics because reasonably comparable data on residence, employment and journey to work are available over a long period. He argues:

'There is a certain logic in relying upon them: together, they present an integrated picture of the two most important within-place activities in most people's lives, in terms of the time devoted to them, together with a between-place function that relates them together. More than this, they focus on those relationships likely to be of great importance in the study of urban growth processes: the job, the home, and the journey between the two. If one is seeking a logically-based geographical framework for a functional urban area, within which to study the physical facts of urban growth, a metropolitan area defined in these terms seems the most promising one.'

Whatever their name — city-region, metropolitan region or SMLA — these areas are essentially employment cores and their commuting hinterlands. The major definitional difficulties associated with them are twofold: how should the core be defined — in land-use or employment terms, with a minimum density or not — and, secondly, what should be the cut-off value for the outer edge of the commuting zone? Hall's SMLAs extend outwards from the core, defined as a local authority with an employment density of over twelve employees per ha or a total employment of over 20,000, to include all areas from which more than 15% of the economically active population commute to the core. The employment core and commuting hinterland must have a total population of 70,000 persons or more. The fact that these statistical criteria must be applied to local authority areas to compile the SMLAs introduces an unavoidably capricious element; the overall similarity of the different investigations is revealed in table 6.2.

An accurate and standardized definition of urban places is ultimately linked to the spatial quality of the basic data. The replacement of the present highly variable system of local authority areas by standard quadrat units based on the national grid is being experimented with by the General Register Office, using 1971 census data. Meanwhile one must remain aware of the limitations of current data, and appreciate the range of scale at which the geographical analysis of urban Britain is conducted. Thus studies of physical urbanization based on land use can be either at the inter-urban scale, as in an analysis of the amount of urban land in each economic region, or at the intra-urban scale, as in a study of the internal differentiation of land uses in one city. Equally, studies of functional urbanization can be either inter-city in scale, as in regional migration analysis, or intra-city in scale, as in town traffic-flow studies. The fundamental geographical significance of this scale difference was captured in Berry's (1964) plea for 'geographers to examine each city as a system with a system of cities'.

TABLE 6.2

Some Metropolitan Definitions in England and Wales

Author and name	Date of definition data	No.	Largest (000s)		Smallest (000s)	
1. Schnore (Metropolitan Area)	1951	52	London	10,283	Gloucester	104
2. Hall et al (SMLA)	1966	100	London	9,157	Stafford	66
3. Drewett et al (SMLA)	1966	115	London*	8,837	Ellesmere Port*	62
4. Diamond (Metropolitan Region)	1966	50	London*	12,811	Carlisle*	101
5. Senior (City Region)	various	35†	London**	7,380	Carlisle**	157

* population at 1971
† Wales excluded
**population at 1969

Sources: 1 Econ. Geogr., (1962) 38, 215–33
2 The Containment of Urban England, vol I, 151
3 British Cities (1976), DoE
4 Business in Britain: a management planning atlas
5 Roy. Commn on Local Govt in England, vol II, Cmnd 4040, I

I.2 Urbanization in Britain

Both the sequence of events that comprise British urban history and the diverse topographical conditions, together with evolving social structure, through their endless interaction with each other create jointly a context which has given the process of urbanization its character in Britain. Whether the town arose or expanded, as elsewhere, to fulfil a defence role, a socio-political role in organizing society, a trade role or an industrial or mining role, it is the subtle and diverse influence of a combination of time, place, and culture that has fashioned the outcome at both the intra-urban and the inter-urban scales. Indeed, it is difficult to imagine in just how many different ways our island coastline, with its positive and negative aspects, and the domination in politics since Cromwell's time by the merchant class not the aristocracy, has influenced both the distribution of towns and their morphology. A different but vivid contemporary example is surely the immense effort made by civic authorities in Britain since 1955 to modernize their town centres (section IV) rather than follow the American example of abandoning them to decay as decentralization proceeds. The examples could be multiplied endlessly, since it would be no great exaggeration to say that the whole of the nation's history could be discovered from a careful investigation of the present urban system.

Even more than the countryside, towns present palimpsests which record the past activities of society in the contemporary scene. In any town with a long history an imprint is left on the urban morphology by the organization and aims of past society and the functioning of past technology. Often the successive phases of history result in concentric rings of development only partly obliterating the contribution of earlier periods. Saxon, if not Roman, sites, adapted to Norman usage and medieval growth, followed sometimes by eighteenth-century development in the grand manner and frequently by nineteenth-century factory-cum-housing development, ringed by interwar and postwar housing estates, tell a common story and describe a frequent pattern. Sometimes the evidence is clear in an entire district of a town, sometimes only faint traces remain in the survival of an individual building or in the alignment of the street pattern.

Just as form is a rough record of past activities at the intra-urban scale, so is the distribution of settlements a record at the inter-urban scale. The market squares in the frequent minor town centres on any main road in Lowland England are a forceful reminder that the last thing a medieval borough wanted was a by-pass. Without its castle towns and English bastides, Wales would be virtually devoid of urban centres, and in parts of C Scotland, Lancashire and Durham a very distinctive mining settlement pattern continues to exist after the end of local coal production. Not all towns can have their location accounted for in such practical terms: Harewood, Milton Abbas, Fochabers and Inverary are all where they are because their aristocratic founders wanted them there. Each replaced an older settlement that did not suit the owner's taste or fancy.

The early establishment of strong central government in England and Wales had particular significance in creating an urban personality so different from that of nearby France. It not only encouraged the establishment of towns but it discouraged the renewal of early medieval town walls, and many pre-Victorian towns which arose with the development of trade, handicraft industries or early mining were never walled. This allowed England to develop a low-density (usually two-storey) terrace or cottage housing style which has led today to the vast tracts of semi-detached suburban villas with garden plots at back and front, which Continental Europeans regard as quintessentially English. It was during the vast urban expansion in the mid-nineteenth century that this English trait became so obvious, in contrast to the Scottish fashion of building four-storey blocks of flats, still referred to today (in the original French) as tenements.

Two reasons help to explain why this accretionary characteristic developed so strongly in British towns. The durability of the urban fabric is not itself sufficient explanation, though clearly relevant; the more fundamental cause is the nature of private rights in property. At least since the Domesday Book, the thorough and accurate recording of the ownership of land has meant that property boundaries, once established, are extremely difficult to alter, and especially so if alteration of a street alignment is a likely consequence. Thus in the town centre, where economic pressure for change is often greatest, the town plan, because of the density of the street network, is most resistant to change. Buildings which can be adapted and even replaced entirely are less resistant to change, and land use (or more strictly floor use) is the most adaptable element in the townscape. Thus strong private rights in property have stimulated growth by peripheral expansion and have required Parliament's permission when exceptionally the society has wished to override these rights, as for railway construction or, after 1947, for comprehensive slum clearance. Nor should it be forgotten that the contemporary method for managing this balance between peripheral growth and internal restructuring, namely town planning, has elaborate legal and administrative procedures designed expressly to protect legitimate individual rights in property.

The second reason for the built-up area in both its functional organization and its physical townscape to become an accumulated record of social and economic development, is that any existing town has great attractions for new development because of its many existing facilities and services. Rather than start from scratch, advantage was usually taken of the nodality and the labour supply of a pre-existing settlement. Thus, given the very widespread distribution of towns throughout the UK by the end of the eighteenth century (including market towns, small industrial centres, fishing and commercial ports, coastal and inland spas), there was a strong tendency throughout the industrial revolution and since for factories and houses to be attached to existing towns, even if this profoundly altered their functional and morphological character. Only the street pattern indicates today where the pre-industrial town was located in Birmingham or Glasgow or Newcastle, which were all sizeable centres by 1750. The major exceptions to this general principle were towns located on new sites to serve as ports (e.g. Middlesbrough), mining settlements (e.g. Coatbridge) or resorts (e.g. Skegness); the pull of the natural resource to be exploited outweighed any disadvantages, and often the original layout was conceived and designed as a New Town (Bell and Bell 1972). It is interesting to note, however, that of the official New Towns started since 1946, only three (Aycliffe, Peterlee and Glenrothes) can really be regarded as 'green-field' sites with populations at the date of designation of less than 1,000, and that the most recent are more accurately described as town expansions (section IV, pp. 473–5).

The single most important conclusion from this discussion of the nature of urbanization in Britain is the great importance of past events for an explanation of the present situation. A graphic illustration of this was given when Sir Halford Mackinder (1919) said,

'There is one thing that can be said with certainty and it is that the geographical circumstances which in the past have conduced to the growth of the city, would not in this twentieth century suffice to create anew in this locality a great centre of activity, if for any reason, whether of military defeat or economic strife, Glasgow were now to cease to flourish.'

The numerous urban problems that claim so much attention and generate so much discussion today necessarily have their roots in the evolution of the urban system and owe their existence to an inheritance from the past. Further, all the possible solutions, social, economic, spatial or technological, or more likely some combination of these, must be compatible with the existing urban system, whose diversity, spatial spread and socio-economic importance is now the major influence on its own future development. Both change and resistance to change are simultaneously fundamental features of the British urban system.

I.3   An Overview

The urban population is resident in certainly more than 1,200 urban places in the UK, varying greatly in size and distributed in an irregular pattern, despite the existence of apparent similarity in some instances – Oxford and Cambridge, Southport and Eastbourne, Darlington and Crewe, Leicester and Nottingham, Ely and Wells. The average density of urban places is considerable; in 1981 it was 17 persons per hectare in England and Wales, and despite considerable reductions over earlier years the most striking feature remains the close association of high density with the largest urban places (c. 40 p.p. ha) and low urban densities with the smaller urban places (c. 10 p.p. ha).

There is a generally close network of centres and the actual distance between any centre and the nearest centre of equal or greater importance is usually not more than an hour or two's journey at the most. There are multiple, high-capacity connections between all the centres, road, rail and telecommunication links, and each town is therefore deeply embedded in the national system and is frequently, rapidly and substantially influenced by, and in turn influences, what happens in other towns. There is little isolation, and overwhelming integration in the British urban system. Although the townscape is dominated by Victorian and post-Victorian buildings, especially in the largest centres, there still remain hundreds of smaller towns with pre-Victorian elements which add significantly to their individuality (Clifton-Taylor 1978, 1981). Again, although very few inhabited areas are more than 30 km from a town of 10,000 persons or more, the vast majority of the nation's population live within 50 km of the dozen largest centres.

London is not only the capital, the largest and the most important centre of all, but has been the primate city for centuries. It is the only member of the British urban system which can truly be called a world metropolis, and while this brings benefit to the nation and to Londoners, there are immense problems of management and planning in maintaining the diverse facilities that will allow it to continue in this role. As an illustration, the Church authorities have recently sought professional advice to devise a pedestrian flow arrangement which can cope with the four million annual visitors that Westminster Abbey now attracts!

A list of major provincial centres always includes Birmingham, Manchester, Liverpool, Leeds, Glasgow and Newcastle upon Tyne, and many authorities have included Edinburgh, Bristol and Nottingham, and some Sheffield, Leicester, Belfast

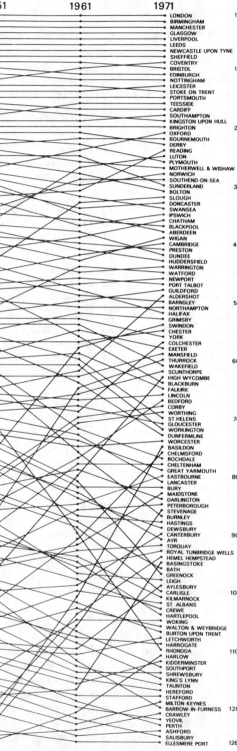

STANDARD METROPOLITAN LABOUR AREAS
1951   1961   1971

1951	1971
1 LONDON	LONDON 1
BIRMINGHAM	BIRMINGHAM
MANCHESTER	MANCHESTER
GLASGOW	GLASGOW
LIVERPOOL	LIVERPOOL
LEEDS	LEEDS
NEWCASTLE UPON TYNE	NEWCASTLE UPON TYNE
SHEFFIELD	SHEFFIELD
BRISTOL	COVENTRY
10 EDINBURGH	BRISTOL 10
NOTTINGHAM	EDINBURGH
COVENTRY	NOTTINGHAM
STOKE ON TRENT	LEICESTER
LEICESTER	STOKE ON TRENT
PORTSMOUTH	PORTSMOUTH
CARDIFF	TEESSIDE
KINGSTON UPON HULL	CARDIFF
TEESSIDE	SOUTHAMPTON
SOUTHAMPTON	KINGSTON UPON HULL
20 BRIGHTON	BRIGHTON 20
DERBY	OXFORD
PLYMOUTH	BOURNEMOUTH
BOURNEMOUTH	DERBY
MOTHERWELL & WISHAW	READING
SUNDERLAND	LUTON
BOLTON	PLYMOUTH
OXFORD	MOTHERWELL & WISHAW
NORWICH	NORWICH
SWANSEA	SOUTHEND-ON-SEA
30 ABERDEEN	SUNDERLAND 30
DONCASTER	BOLTON
READING	SLOUGH
IPSWICH	DONCASTER
SOUTHEND-ON-SEA	SWANSEA
BLACKPOOL	IPSWICH
LUTON	CHATHAM
DUNDEE	BLACKPOOL
HUDDERSFIELD	ABERDEEN
PRESTON	WIGAN
40 WIGAN	CAMBRIDGE 40
CHATHAM	PRESTON
WARRINGTON	DUNDEE
SLOUGH	HUDDERSFIELD
HALIFAX	WARRINGTON
CAMBRIDGE	WATFORD
BARNSLEY	NEWPORT
PORT TALBOT	PORT TALBOT
NEWPORT	GUILDFORD
BLACKBURN	ALDERSHOT
50 NORTHAMPTON	BARNSLEY 50
WATFORD	NORTHAMPTON
GUILDFORD	HALIFAX
YORK	GRIMSBY
WAKEFIELD	SWINDON
GRIMSBY	CHESTER
ST. HELENS	YORK
CHESTER	COLCHESTER
DUNFERMLINE	EXETER
EXETER	MANSFIELD
60 FALKIRK	THURROCK 60
WORKINGTON	WAKEFIELD
ROCHDALE	SCUNTHORPE
MANSFIELD	HIGH WYCOMBE
BURNLEY	BLACKBURN
ALDERSHOT	FALKIRK
LINCOLN	LINCOLN
COLCHESTER	BEDFORD
SCUNTHORPE	CORBY
GLOUCESTER	WORTHING
70 LANCASTER	ST HELENS 70
RHONDDA	GLOUCESTER
GREAT YARMOUTH	WORKINGTON
WORCESTER	DUNFERMLINE
GREENOCK	WORCESTER
BURY	BASILDON
SWINDON	CHELMSFORD
DEWSBURY	ROCHDALE
AYR	CHELTENHAM
HASTINGS	GREAT YARMOUTH
80 CORBY	EASTBOURNE 80
WORTHING	LANCASTER
DARLINGTON	BURY
BATH	MAIDSTONE
CARLISLE	DARLINGTON
BEDFORD	PETERBOROUGH
EASTBOURNE	STEVENAGE
THURROCK	BURNLEY
LEIGH	HASTINGS
CHELTENHAM	DEWSBURY
90 ROYAL TUNBRIDGE WELLS	CANTERBURY 90
HARTLEPOOL	AYR
KILMARNOCK	TORQUAY
PETERBOROUGH	ROYAL TUNBRIDGE WELLS
CREWE	HEMEL HEMPSTEAD
MAIDSTONE	BASINGSTOKE
TORQUAY	BATH
HIGH WYCOMBE	GREENOCK
BURTON UPON TRENT	LEIGH
SOUTHPORT	AYLESBURY
100 CANTERBURY	CARLISLE 100
BARROW-IN-FURNESS	KILMARNOCK
CHELMSFORD	ST. ALBANS
KING'S LYNN	CREWE
HARROGATE	HARTLEPOOL
ST. ALBANS	WOKING
TAUNTON	WALTON & WEYBRIDGE
WALTON & WEYBRIDGE	BURTON UPON TRENT
SHREWSBURY	LETCHWORTH
AYLESBURY	HARROGATE
110 LETCHWORTH	RHONDDA 110
HEREFORD	HARLOW
KIDDERMINSTER	KIDDERMINSTER
PERTH	SOUTHPORT
WOKING	SHREWSBURY
STAFFORD	KING'S LYNN
YEOVIL	TAUNTON
SALISBURY	HEREFORD
BASINGSTOKE	STAFFORD
MILTON KEYNES	MILTON KEYNES
120 HEMEL HEMPSTEAD	BARROW-IN-FURNESS 120
ASHFORD	CRAWLEY
BASILDON	YEOVIL
STEVENAGE	PERTH
ELLESMERE PORT	ASHFORD
CRAWLEY	SALISBURY
126 HARLOW	ELLESMERE PORT 126

Figure 6.2   Standard Metropolitan Labour Areas, UK, rank order, 1951–71
Source: as fig. 6.1

England and Wales

1	Aldershot
2	Ashford
3	Aylesbury
4	Barnsley
5	Barrow-in-Furness
6	Basildon
7	Basingstoke
8	Bath
9	Bedford
10	Birmingham
11	Blackburn
12	Blackpool
13	Bolton
14	Bournemouth
15	Brighton
16	Bristol
17	Burnley
18	Burton-on-Trent
19	Bury
20	Cambridge
21	Canterbury
22	Cardiff
23	Carlisle
24	Chatham
25	Chelmsford
26	Cheltenham
27	Chester
28	Colchester
29	Corby
30	Coventry
31	Crawley
32	Crewe
33	Darlington
34	Derby
35	Dewsbury
36	Doncaster
37	Eastbourne
38	Ellesmere Port
39	Exeter
40	Gloucester
41	Great Yarmouth
42	Grimsby
43	Guildford
44	Halifax
45	Harlow

46	Harrogate
47	Hartlepool
48	Hastings
49	Hemel Hempstead
50	Hereford
51	High Wycombe
52	Huddersfield
53	Hull
54	Ipswich
55	Kidderminster
56	King's Lynn
57	Lancaster
58	Leeds
59	Leicester
60	Leigh
61	Letchworth
62	Lincoln
63	Liverpool
64	London
65	Luton
66	Maidstone
67	Manchester
68	Mansfield
69	Milton Keynes
70	Newcastle
71	Newport
72	Northampton
73	Norwich
74	Nottingham
75	Oxford
76	Peterborough
77	Plymouth
78	Portsmouth
79	Port Talbot
80	Preston
81	Reading
82	Rhondda
83	Rochdale
84	St Albans
85	St Helens
86	Salisbury
87	Scunthorpe
88	Sheffield
89	Shrewsbury
90	Slough

91	Southampton
92	Southend
93	Southport
94	Stafford
95	Stevenage
96	Stoke
97	Sunderland
98	Swansea
99	Swindon
100	Taunton
101	Teesside
102	Thurrock
103	Torquay
104	Tunbridge Wells
105	Wakefield
106	Walton and Weybridge
107	Warrington
108	Watford
109	Wigan
110	Woking
111	Worcester
112	Workington
113	Worthing
114	Yeovil
115	York

Scotland

116	Aberdeen
117	Ayr
118	Dundee
119	Dunfermline
120	Edinburgh
121	Falkirk
122	Glasgow
123	Greenock
124	Kilmarnock
125	Motherwell
126	Perth

Northern Ireland

127	Belfast
128	Londonderry

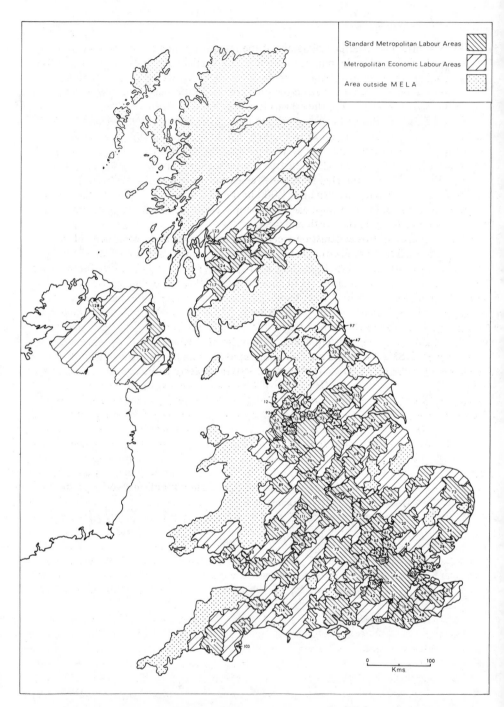

0   100
Kms.

Figure 6.1   Metropolitan structure, UK, 1971
Standard Metropolitan Labour Areas: 1 Aldershot, 2 . . . 128 Londonderry (see
table p. 435 for full list)
Source: British Cities: Urban Population and Employment Trends 1951–71,
1976 Res. Rep. *10,* DoE

and Cardiff. The different character of the regions dominated by these major cities is reflected clearly in the number, function and spatial pattern of the urban centres. Lancashire's cotton towns are never confused with the Black Country centres, which are as different again from the outer metropolitan area centres that ring London from Southend in the east to Reading and Guildford.

At the lower end of the size range are more than 300 towns with fewer than 10,000 persons which again show marked regional variations (Best and Rodgers 1973). Interestingly, although average population size was the same, the average urban area (housing, schools, industry, and public open space) is 29 ha per 1,000 people in centres in the Highland Zone (essentially north and west Britain), compared to as much as 39 ha per 1,000 in the Lowland Zone. Thus in the south and east of Britain on average each 100 people consume one ha more of urban land than people living in the north and west.

In the face of this contrast between world metropolis and overgrown village, the least misleading generalization is the Standard Metropolitan Labour Area. Fig. 6.1 shows the pattern of SMLAs in the UK, 128 in all in 1971, accounting for just over 80% of the total population. If the boundaries of these SMLAs are extended to include all local authority areas sending commuters to the 128 urban cores (thus forming what Hall calls MELAs), then some 97% of the UK population is included, and half of this was accounted for by the core areas. Some indication of the dynamism of this sub-system is indicated in fig. 6.2, which shows the changing order of all SMLAs ranked according to population in 1951, 1961 and 1971. The authors of the study note that 'the most striking feature is the continuity of change between the two decades' (DoE 1976).

Examination of the pattern of growth and decline in employment and population within these SMLAs led Hall to suggest a four-stage model of British urban development in which most centres are now in stage three, but a few of the bigger metropolitan areas have reached the later stage (Hall 1971). In the first stage, some time in the nineteenth century, both people and jobs concentrated in the cores of the metropolitan area; the ring was strictly non-existent, and the area later to be incorporated in the ring was rural, in both a functional and a physical sense, and it lost population to the town.

In the second stage, roughly 1900–50, because of greater mobility and the spread of home ownership, population began to migrate from the core to the sub-urban periphery. But the population of the core continued to rise, though at a slower rate than in the ring. Only in the biggest cities, before 1939, did slum clearance contribute to an actual decline in population in the core. Office and retail employment increased at the centre more rapidly than new factory building at the periphery.

In the third stage, typical of larger metropolitan areas since 1951 but above all since 1961, there was marked actual decline in population, largely arising from inner city redevelopment for commercial and slum-clearance purposes. Though there were continuing increases in office and other service employment at the core, these were outweighed by the effects of redevelopment and above all by the rapid growth of local service employment, plus perhaps some decentralized factory employment, in the suburbs.

The fourth stage was reached only by London in the 1960s and applies only to the very large metropolitan areas. In this stage, decentralization of both people and jobs continues a stage further; the metropolitan area as a whole tends to lose both

people and employment to other metropolitan areas. In the 1970s the other
conurbations appear to have followed London's lead (Cameron 1980).

  Although the situation is complex and still unclear, there is evidence that in the
UK, as elsewhere in Europe and in the USA, the 1970s saw not merely the final
stages of decentralization but the beginnings of 'counter-urbanization' (Fielding
1981). The rapid and real growth in population in medium- and small-sized towns
was not in the main due to the immigration of people and firms from nearby cities
and conurbations, but largely to new employment growth and its consequent
population effects. Instead of large cities having high net immigration as in the
nineteenth century, it is now the small towns that have high net immigration, thus
completely reversing the relationship between settlement size and migration.
Instead of urbanization, we now appear to be at the beginning of an era of counter-
urbanization in which problems of employment and population loss in the largest
cities are only partly offset by rapid growth (measured proportionally) in small and
medium-sized towns.

  This trend has great implications for many aspects of public policy, not least the
aims and methods of town and country planning. Established in 1947 largely to
tackle the problems resulting from urbanization, it has over the last thirty-five years
had an increasingly important impact both on the internal structure of the cities
and their functional roles. In a few cases the planning process has been directly
responsible for the growth of small towns but it cannot be held solely responsible
for the arrival of counter-urbanization. The search for an explanation of this
phenomena is the main research question in British urban geography of the 1980s.

II   INTERNAL URBAN STRUCTURE

Even small towns can have an elaborate and varied internal structure, as the studies
of Aberystwyth, Alnwick and St Albans (Carter 1958; Conzen 1960; Thurston 1953)
have clearly shown. In the larger cities where the effects of the patterning processes are often more evident because of their greater spatial extent, simple
descriptions of distinctive localities and activities have entered into everyday
language – docklands, west end, inner city, town centre, rush hour, bank holiday.
Varying combinations of three key components of the urban structure produce this
patterning (variously termed landscape region [Jones], urban region [Smailes],
townscape [Carter]), which geographers have attempted to identify in their studies.
These three principal components – (a) the town plan, including the street network
and property ownerships; (b) the actual buildings and other built structures, with
their varying ages, architectural styles and construction materials; and (c) the uses
to which the land and floor-space is put – possess many attributes. There is an
almost infinite number of possible ways of using them in combination to delimit
distinctive localities and rhythms within the built-up area that aid an understanding
of the way the city works. The numerous criteria reflect the subtlety and complexity of urban structure, which is further complicated by its atomistic and
dynamic nature. Every household, firm and organization has an impact on the
urban structure and although a change in an individual relationship frequently has
no significant effect, the consequences of multiple changes can be very dramatic, as,
for example, when all the bus drivers refuse to work or a major factory ceases
production. Infrequent and unwanted as these events are, they demonstrate clearly

the high degree of perpetual interdependence (or interaction) of people, structures and activities within the city. The internal structure of the city is thus a continually altering pageant with literally thousands of actors. Many of the interactions making up the almost endless chains of cause and effect that create and modify the urban structure are poorly understood at present, and consequently accounts of the internal structure of the British city can give only a rather limited, simplified and static picture of the reality. Here we examine first the kinds of process creating urban structure, and then describe the resulting patterns of land use.

II.1 Process

Although it is useful to regard the interactions that create urban structure in the UK as belonging to one of four major kinds of process – physical, economic, social (private), and community (public) – the reality is that at any point in time all the processes are at work. Their individual impacts, however, have not remained constant through time, and there seems considerable evidence to suggest that the 'community' process is perhaps now the dominant one; certainly it has never been as powerful in any previous era.

The **physical** process of urban growth can take three spatial forms, each of which has a clearly different impact on urban structure. It can give rise to peripheral expansion, and most commonly does. It can also give rise to infilling – that is, additional urban structure without expansion of the urban area as a whole. Thirdly, it can give rise to replacement – that is, demolition followed by new construction, which, depending on whether the density of development is greater or less than that it replaces, may or may not imply further expansion overall; or it may give rise to a combination of all three.

Although present in the Middle Ages, peripheral expansion was clearly secondary to infilling because the limited means of transport put a very high premium on accessibility to the market square. In this way the narrow street frontages with land extending back at right angles from the street gave rise to the burgage plot, whose outlines still dominate town plans dating from before about 1800. On this type of town plan (looking much like an urban version of open-field strips) the growth process (Conzen 1960) was one of steady infilling by 'backland' development. It was the combined effects of the rapid growth in population and the improvements in local transport that gave peripheral growth its great opportunity from the end of the eighteenth century. Except where physical conditions made it difficult or dangerous to do so, as on land along rivers liable to occasional flooding, expansion occurred in all directions around either the pre-existing settlement or the newly established mine, factory, mill or other place of employment.

The scale and nature of peripheral expansion since 1800 has been and remains the dominating element of the British townscape. Outward growth at a generally uneven rate helps to give British cities their characteristic concentric rings of distinctive development, especially clearly seen in the pattern of residential land use. So abrupt was the change from boom to slump in Victorian times and so lengthy the two world-war periods that between the end of one era of expansion and the beginning of the next some change in social attitudes, in transport technology or in building style arose to differentiate clearly the one from the other. In the nineteenth century it was the change in building materials (in Glasgow, for example, from grey carboniferous sandstone to pink old red sandstone in 1870, and to brick after 1900), coupled with the impact of bye-law regulations; in the twentieth century it has been more a product of fashion, of layout and house-type.

Two other characteristic features of the British townscape are associated with the process of peripheral growth. The distribution of institutional land uses such as cemeteries, convents and priories and later hospitals, universities and other land-extensive activities have been shown by Whitehand (1972) frequently to represent a relict fringe-belt marking a previous period of standstill in the expansion of the city. In this century the fringe-belt has achieved its ultimate form as the statutorily designated green-belt. In the outward spread of development a substantial number of villages and small towns have become engulfed, but because of their nodality and pre-existing functions have often developed as local service and community centres. Rasmussen (1951) regards this feature of urban structure as particularly English and has described it for the early growth of London:

> 'around every little village the buildings crystallized into a borough so that London became a greater and still greater accumulation of towns, an immense colony of dwellings where the people still live in their own houses in small communities with local government [he was writing in 1934], just as they had done in the middle ages'.

Very large tracts of British cities were built in a great hurry within a relatively few years, as was the case in all the industrial cities of the nineteenth century with only minor variations in timing, so that now, 120–150 years later, all these extensive areas require either rehabilitation or redevelopment. Thus a wave of slum clearance and redevelopment, begun in the mid-1950s, now characterizes much of the inner city but with very different layout, house-type and land use patterns (section IV.2). The replacement process has not been limited to public slum-clearance schemes, even though some of the earliest of these were in the 1870s in Glasgow and London, where overcrowding of the late medieval town produced a severe health hazard for the rest of the city's inhabitants. Redevelopment of individual plots has been and remains characteristic of town and city centres. The need for extensive, (i.e. multi-plot) replacement as a consequence of wartime bomb damage in Exeter, Coventry, Bristol, London and Plymouth provided an opportunity to restructure the street pattern and alter individual property owner-ships on a scale that normal urban growth and decay could never provide. The overall success of these early town-centre redevelopment schemes led to the idea being widely copied in hundreds of other towns and cities throughout the 1960s, spurred on as they were by increasing traffic congestion and the threat of major decentralization of retailing.

The **economic** process of urban growth refers to competition in the property market of different users for scarce space endowed with urban facilities. This is the arena in which decisions are reached over competition for urban space, thus uniting the physical and economic processes of growth. There is a strongly marked trend, dating from the early nineteenth century, for increasing public regulation of the operation of the property market, and in the period since 1945 there have been no less than three major pieces of legislation enacted by Labour governments (the most recent was the *Community Land Act* of 1975), and abolished by the succeeding Conservative government (Cullingworth 1981). It is not only the degree of regulation of the property market that influences the nature of change in cities, but even more important are the changing characteristics of the major actors involved. Thus the change from small speculative builders and the vast estates of the landed aristocracy that constituted the Victorian property market (Dyos 1968; Olsen 1973) to the present situation in which a majority of households are owner-occupiers has important implications for the nature of urban change (Ambrose and Colenutt 1975; Massey and Catalano 1978; Boddy 1980). Most owner-occupiers own their own homes only with the help of a building society mortgage, and coexist with large property development companies investing considerable sums for major pension funds. The evolution over time of the development industry is thus clearly reflected in the urban structure, in both urban morphology and urban function, although the spatial implications of the strategies adopted by private landlords, property investors, estate agents and transport managers interacting with local and even central government officials, are immensely difficult to ascertain for the reasons noted in the introduction to this section. The types of housing provided, the shifting balance between residential and commercial development, and the locations in which development occurs are all in large part an outcome of the working of the property market. It seems likely that the extension of owner occupation to lower income groups creates a new type of property-owning petty bourgeoisie who consequently resist environmental change, particularly if it might adversely affect the value of their property. Explaining the pattern of land values in American cities, Hurd (1924) described the process as one in which, 'since value depends on economic rent and rent on location, and location on convenience, and convenience on nearness, we may eliminate the intermediate steps and say that value depends on nearness'. Thus, it is argued that the use which can extract the greatest return from the site because of its particular nearness or accessibility requirements will become the occupier of the site, and in this process the city structure will evolve towards a most efficient land-use pattern. Although there are important reasons why towns in the UK responded to this free market process with less emphasis and in differing ways from towns in the USA, it nevertheless has had a major impact. The highest land values are associated with central areas and in particular with retailing and commercial offices, the former for accessibility to the customer potential of the metropolitan population and the latter requiring close proximity to other offices to facilitate the face-to-face contact which is such a feature of this activity (Goddard 1975). As a detailed study of land uses in central Glasgow in 1958 (Diamond 1962) has shown, however, the pattern of land uses seems remarkably finely adjusted to the pattern of accessibility created by mass public transport. In smaller centres where the railway did not arrive at the existing town centre (usually the medieval market-place), the new accessibility pattern often brought substantial changes in the distribution of activities within the town, even on occasions transferring the central area to the vicinity of the railway station.

The locational pattern of industry within British cities is also heavily influenced by the pattern of accessibility created for the movement of goods and raw materials. The ring of mixed industrial uses which typically surrounded the central area but has today often almost vanished as a result of post-1945 decentralization, acquired marked radial rather than zonal extensions, as first canals, then railways and then interwar major road improvements produced linear accessibility patterns. In London (fig. 6.5B), Birmingham (the Tame Valley), Glasgow (along the Forth–Clyde canal and river Clyde), Belfast and many other cities, these marked radial or sector patterns were reinforced by the influence of rivers, especially where these

could be modified to provide port functions. As the use of trucks and the ownership of cars has increased, the locational influence of accessibility has become more
diffuse. As a result other influences, often with greater social or cultural content,
have had greater impact. Thus, although the pattern of functional areas created in
the nineteenth century by the differing accessibility requirements of various urban
functions has lost its original rationale, the pattern is perpetuated by other location
factors. Inter-firm linkages, associated with component assembly manufacturing,
and the public control of industrial land use by the establishment of industrial
estates and the preparation of development plans under the 1947 *Town and
Country Planning Act* are probably the two most influential.

Households, firms and many other organizations make many of their locational
decisions in a manner in which individual taste, social custom and habit play a
major part, thus creating powerful **social** processes which give pattern to the urban
structure. Because many of these decisions are made almost intuitively, without
exhaustive analysis of the possible alternatives, they are difficult to trace by social
survey and consequently they tend to be inferred from maps showing uneven
distribution of the social characteristics of urban residents. Given that residential
land use is by far the largest single use of land in urban areas, these patterns often
tend to dominate geographical interpretations of urban structure. It is well to
remember, however, in a period of social mobility and considerable social change,
that the apparently orderly social geography displayed in the results of various
methods for delimiting urban sub-areas may result less from like individuals making
similar choices than from the nature of the census data commonly employed and
the aggregate scale of the analysis.

The patterning of residential areas by social choice seems to reflect three closely
interlocking aspects of people's life-style: the desire to have as neighbours people
with similar attitudes and behaviour; the attempt to choose a convenient location
for the household's major activities; and the ability to choose to live in a particular
type of dwelling associated with a particular kind of local environment. What
makes these aspirations so powerful in fashioning city structure is their high degree
of association. Income, occupation, education, social class of close relatives, household size and family stage have all been used as criteria to measure differentiation of
residential areas. Migration history, too, is an immensely powerful influence when
it results in a large minority group whose race, nationality or religion give it a social
distinctiveness. Social segregation is thus a multi-faceted phenomenon which
although present in all towns, can take different forms. The intensity of
segregation – a concept very difficult to establish quantitatively – varies through
time, not just with the degree of dynamism in the local economy, but also in times
of social stress when the clustering of the minority is accentuated in the search for a
sense of security, as events in Belfast and Londonderry in the 1970s tragically
demonstrated (Poole and Boal 1973).

Segregation in residential areas The spatial sorting of residential areas has now
been investigated in several studies in Britain by various forms of multi-variate
analysis, and sufficient similarity in the results suggests that three major dimensions
exist. The first, **socio-economic status**, is most obviously measured by occupation
or by what the census calls socio-economic group, which is a simplified classification
of occupations. Social status is a somewhat subtle attribute of people and in the
development of British society (Halsey 1972) has undergone change, particularly

since 1945. Robson (1975) has made the interesting suggestion that as the education, income, and occupation changes have led to a blurring of social distinctions
there has been as a consequence a tendency for social segregation to become more
marked. Certainly it is difficult to find the present-day equivalents of the
nineteenth-century examples of small-scale mixing of different social classes, as in
the mews flats that lay behind the grand terrace houses of the upper middle class.
A study of Crawley (Heraud 1968) showed that although the extent of social
segregation was less than in other towns, as might be expected from a balanced
population policy (section IV), there was clear evidence that 'a large number of
families move from district to district . . . thus Langley Green was developing into a
working class area and Tilgate was becoming predominantly middle class'. Heraud
emphasized that such segregation was occurring not only because of individual
choices made by those who moved, but by the change in Development Corporation
policy in the middle 1950s to allow substantial private housing development.
Further, middle-class families were over-represented in a growing movement to the
surrounding small towns and villages with a much more marked rural or countryside
atmosphere. In the early stages of such a trend − Pahl (1965) has described the
process in detail for Hertfordshire villages in the London green-belt − the result
must be a considerable decline in segregation as the newcomers mix with the
existing population.

More generally, sociological studies suggest that as greater income equality has
emerged between the manual and white-collar jobs and car ownership has as a
consequence become very widespread, general lifestyle differences have remained.
Type of leisure activities and degree of activity within the kinship network have
remained distinctive, and are strong determinants of the locational element in
residential site selection.

A second major dimension of social segregation in UK cities is associated with
the **age structure** of the population. While one expects very marked differences in
family size and household composition between one area and another in Belfast,
associated with market religious segregation (Jones 1960), or in cities with
substantial recent overseas migrants, it is rather more surprising that this feature of
segregation is in fact widespread in British towns. The study by Westergaard (1964)
of the outer suburbs of London revealed a pattern of age-structure types which are
widely typical. The explanation of such segregation is that at different stages of its
life-cycle a family or household has very different needs in size of dwelling (i.e.
number of rooms) and access to particular facilities. Families with young children
will value access to play-space, schools, clinics, swimming baths and so forth, and
single-person households will have an entirely different set of accessibility requirements. When this tendency is coupled with the uneven spatial distribution of house
sizes that exists in any town as a result of its social and economic history, the
patterning becomes comprehensible, especially where privately owned houses are
concerned. Since 1945, however, most local authority housing-allocation schemes
have used some kind of points system to give priority to families with children. In
Glasgow, for example, where such a scheme operates for a very large council-house
waiting list, the result has been that the percentage of families with children
increases progressively from the inner city through the interwar suburbs to a
maximum in the postwar municipal estates. Variations in the scale and age of the
municipal housing stock create variations between authorities, but, given the self-
contained nature of this stock as a housing market, extreme over- and under-

crowding are often found within public sector housing.

In an attempt to improve efficiency in the use of the stock of dwellings as well as to increase tenant satisfaction, authorities have arranged various schemes for the exchange of houses. A study (Bird and Whitbread 1975) of tenants' requests to be transferred showed that in Greater London and Newcastle upon Tyne about one in five tenants wished to transfer but that only 3% are moved each year. Although size, amenity and location were all reasons for tenants requesting a move, the result was 'queues of households for the dwellings with certain attractive features as well as queues to leave dwellings of less popular types (flats) or in less desirable locations'. Contrasting patterns of desired movement were revealed by the mapping of tenants' requests to move, with a strong decentralizing pattern in London compared with inter-suburban movement in Newcastle together with a noticeable backflow into the city centre (fig. 6.3). Yet the strong tendency for intra-urban migration to show a marked radial pattern, as described in Hoyt's well-known sector theory of urban growth, was evident and appears to be identical with the other examples of this process, including the movement of religious minorities (Jews in Belfast and Glasgow) and industries (in Greater London). The desire to retain reasonable access to employment, friends and relatives, which appears to explain this, underlines the powerful patterning influence of radial transport routes in large urban areas.

The outstanding example, however, of life-cycle influencing residential-site selection is the decision of elderly couples to move to a small house without stairs in a pleasant town beside the sea (fig. 6.3b). So powerful is this preference that it has created a recognizable inter-regional migration flow and produced a distinctive category of towns with very special social services and urban facilities (section III.3).

The third dimension consistently revealed in the analyses of urban structure in Britain is the nature of the **housing market** (table 2.19). Two features are of particular significance. The first is the virtual elimination of the private landlord and houses to rent, and the second the high degree of self-containment of the owner-occupied and public-rented sectors. The explanation for both these features lies in a complex social history (Cullingworth 1965; Donnison 1969), but their importance to urban structure in Britain is substantial in several ways (Pritchard 1976). Condition and amenity vary considerably between these types. Generally, public housing provides better physical amenities than do either privately rented or owner-occupied houses at comparable expenditure, and thus qualification for housing tenure by type rather than income is the determinant of housing standard. Consequently, once a household finds accommodation in a public sector dwelling, it is usually reluctant to change to another tenure type. The number of local authority houses per 100 persons is substantially higher in Scotland (53) than in England and Wales (28), where it does vary considerably between towns, e.g. Bournemouth (3), Sheffield (13). The filtering effect of new house construction is equally affected by this crucial public–private dichotomy. Since the local authorities responsible for the provision of public housing have to determine their policy in relation to the needs of their own area rather than some socio-geographic entity, such as the city region, there has been considerable impact on the distribution and density of housing which can be explained only in terms of the multitude of local authorities responsible for providing public sector houses. This inter-urban variety is being maintained, if not increased, by the varying response of local authorities to pressure by central government to persuade them to sell council

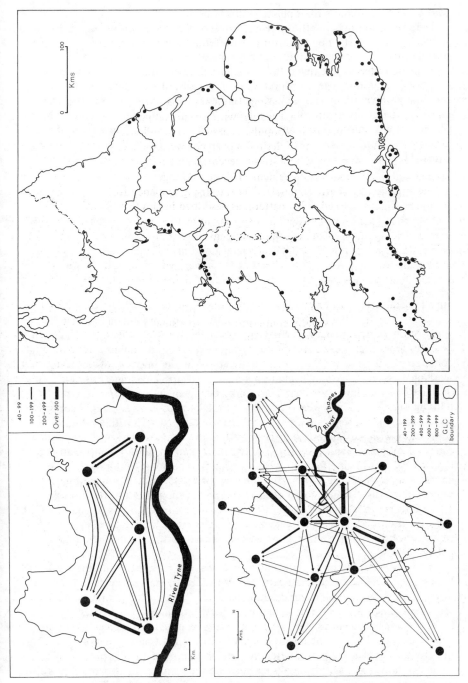

Figure 6.3   Residential migration: (A) Pattern of council house transfers in Newcastle upon Tyne and London; (B) Retirement towns in England and Wales (20% or more of population of pensionable age)

houses to sitting tenants wishing to buy.

The seven 'housing classes' that Rex (1968) sees as the outcome of political and market forces operating on an historically determined housing supply situation, are essentially a tenure and age-of-dwelling combination. The three ways of life that result he describes as 'the rich settle in the classy inner suburbs, the white-collar people aided by mortgages live further out in suburbs of semi-detached dwellings and finally, the working classes, having attained a measure of power in the town hall, have their own suburbs built for them'. Thus in competing for scarce housing people are distinguished from one another by their strength in the system of housing allocation – from the strongest (class 1) to the weakest (class 7), in the following terms:

Class 1   the owners of large houses in desirable areas
     2   the mortgage payers in the process of acquiring whole houses in desirable areas
     3   council tenants in council-built houses
     4   council tenants in slum houses awaiting demolition
     5   tenants of private house owners, usually in the inner city
     6   house-owners who must take in lodgers to meet loan repayments
     7   lodgers in rooms.

Such housing classes will also tend to have a 'definite territorial distribution in the city depending largely on the age and size of dwellings', as was confirmed in the study of Sparkbrook in Birmingham (Rex and Moore 1967). Clearly the hierarchy of status areas assumes that the owner-occupied house in the suburbs is an aspiration common to all groups. Areas of 'gentrification' or the invasion of traditional working-class areas by middle and upper income groups, as Hamnett's (1973) study of inner London shows, are characterized by Georgian and Victorian terraced housing of three storeys, adjacent to existing high-status areas and easily accessible to central London, so giving them a distinctive spatial pattern with a rationale fully compatible with Rex's thesis and reinforced by the vagaries of government policy over improvement grants (i.e. financial assistance to owners for the installation of basic amenities). This late 1960s phenomenon also demonstrates how the rules applied by the insurance companies, building societies, and local authorities in respect of housing finance to families, coupled with the pattern of the housing stock, affects the residential distribution of socio-economic groups (Williams 1976). Gentrification thus appears as the combined outcome of life-style preferences, character of the housing stock, occupational credit-worthiness and government policy.

The substantial immigration from West Africa, India, Pakistan and the West Indies during the late 1950s and early 1960s had led to marked concentrations of coloured population within some major cities (ch. 2.II.6). In addition to the socio-economic status and tenure factors in these circumstances, there is often a racial-prejudice element as well, which sharpens the pattern of segregation (Jones 1967; Hamnett 1976). The distinctive nature of the UK housing market is therefore a key element in understanding the patterning of the British city. While a system of housing classes distinguishes between the forms of consumption it is also important to note that local authorities, private landlords and building societies are all different types of property ownership, and council tenants, private tenants, lodgers and mortgagees are all constrained in their choice of where to live and in their capacity to adapt the dwelling. Nevertheless, the differences in location, behaviour and membership of the different housing classes is sufficiently great for this to be an important part of the explanation of the character of the UK city.

Public interest planning The fourth major process involved in structuring urban areas in the UK, with many distinctively British features, concerns the various constraints which are imposed on development or change in the name of the *community* for its supposed benefit. In the contemporary interventionist age the cumulative effect of such regulations and controls is enormous, and there are now so many different organizations involved in recommending, implementing or policing aspects of life in British towns that it is questionable if all are necessary. Fundamentally, the nature of the city itself has been the cause. Given the great density of people and structures and their need for common facilities and services, the community in all urban areas has throughout history imposed restrictions on the freedom of individuals, to prevent catastrophe or chaos. Conflagration and epidemic were the catastrophes most feared in the Middle Ages and led to early regulations about construction materials, disposal of waste and the establishment of special organizations such as the fire brigade or Dean of Guild. Pollution control through smoke-abatement zones or parking restrictions to keep traffic moving are not just twentieth-century ideas: both were tried in medieval London. Realistically, it has been noted that 'urban civilisation is a matter of discipline and drains'. Thus, while the positive externalities found in cities are often regarded as the major reason for urban growth, these have in fact been accompanied by negative externalities which require concerted public action if they are to be ameliorated. In Britain today, environmental regulations are devised and enforced by a considerable variety of official organizations and institutions, among which the local authority is the most influential. The Medical Officer of Health is responsible for declaring buildings unfit for habitation and so for identifying sub-standard housing; the Environmental Health Officer (in Scotland, the Sanitary Inspector) is responsible for ensuring the standard of hygiene throughout the food trade, including all who manufacture, distribute and retail food; the police are responsible for traffic control; and the city planning officer is responsible for creating plans which will lead to an improvement in the quality of life; as the chief planner for London put it, by 'promoting the desirable, assimilating the inevitable and forestalling the objectionable' (Collins 1951).

The powers of the town-planning authorities since 1947 typify best the way in which urban structure is extremely powerfully influenced by community needs and desires. Up to 1974 (1975 in Scotland) the County Boroughs and Counties were the planning authorities responsible for (a) making a Development Plan, essentially a map of the desired future land-use pattern, and for (b) granting or refusing planning permission largely according to whether or not the application conformed to the Development Plan. Thus it was hoped that by sanctioning only those kinds of change that were thought desirable from an overall community viewpoint it would be possible to achieve the greatest advantages and least inconvenience for both the individual and society as a whole. It would resolve conflicts over the use of land in an orderly manner and help to turn into physical reality the hopes of society for the kind of built environment it wanted. Simultaneously with the reorganization of local government, the major reforms contained in the 1968 *Town and Country Planning Act* (1969 in Scotland) were finally implemented, superseding the old-

style Development Plan by a new-style Structure Plan — a document setting out
broad policy concerned with social, economic and physical factors so far as they
are subject to town-planning control or influences — together with Local Plans of
various kinds. The evolution of the nature and method of British town planning
since 1947 is too large a topic to include here (Cullingworth 1974; Evans 1974;
Solesbury 1974), but the essential features that have influenced the urban system in
diverse and significant ways must be noted, despite the real and considerable
difficulties of any evaluation of the impact of town planning on urban structure
(Diamond 1975).

Unlike its predecessors the 1947 Act, which laid the foundation of town-planning
practice, was both spatially and functionally comprehensive in its coverage; the
entire country was covered and the definition of development was all-embracing:
'The carrying out of building, engineering, mining or other operation in, on, over or
under the land, or the making of any material change in the use of any building or
other land'. With such a wide definition it is not surprising that on average 400,000
planning applications were decided annually, and of these 38% were for residential
development, 14% for domestic garages, and 5% each for shops and factories, while
changes of use accounted for 12%. Refusals have averaged about 15% and
applicants appealed against the refusals in only one-quarter of the cases. As a
measure of total impact, however, these data are severely limited, since no one can
estimate the deterrent effect of the system in general and the publication of
Development Plans in particular. Despite the great powers of the town planners,
which have decisively influenced what kind of houses are available and in which
areas they are found, because the British planning system is fundamentally a
method of land-use control it is inevitably at the mercy of powerful social and
economic forces which operate indirectly on the land-use system. The plans that
town planners make are not all fulfilled, and, although the land owner as an
influence has greatly declined in significance, this does not by any means appear
true of the developer, as Marriott (1967) has shown for offices and Craven (1969)
for housing. Although the 'coal-face' of town planning is the local authority
planning department, it must be understood that a powerful, if delicate, control of
its activities is exercised by central government, which ensures that similar standards
apply throughout the UK. Especially significant in all kinds of public development
(schools, hospitals, libraries and leisure facilities, as well as roads, water supply and
sewage, and all local authority housing) are the various financial arrangements
between local and central government. As a consequence of the decline in the share
of local authority expenditure covered by rates, the central government's influence
has grown, and thus the level and volume of Treasury money made available
through ordinary housing subsidies, high flat subsidies, improvement grants,
transport subsidies and reclamation grants, etc., has increasingly influenced the kind
and rate of urban growth (Levin 1976).

Legislation between 1965 and 1979 tended to emphasize the role of plans, as the
policy element in administrative systems focused on the management of change,
and thus drew attention to the *aims* of town planning and consequently to the
significance of these goals for any explanation of the development of urban areas in
Britain over the last thirty years. An early aim of town planners was to create the
City Beautiful by achieving and maintaining a high standard of visual beauty.
Planning authorities in Britain have the right to refuse permission, for example, for
development (in the 1947 Act sense of the word) of a proposed commercial office

block that would spoil the skyline or obscure the silhouette of a famous historical building; or of a suburban house considered out of character with the neighbourhood; or of an application to alter the external appearance of an existing building which is judged to be an essential element in an architectural composition of historical importance and visual quality. The rationale for giving the community the right to impose its wishes in these various ways on individual members of society clearly stems from a belief that the quality of life in towns depends in part on a townscape that contributes visual satisfaction to its citizens.

Development control, however, has more than visual beauty as its aim. The health and safety of residents in a town is as much a conscious objective of town planners today as it was when cholera and tuberculosis were real threats. The City Safe and Convenient is today most vividly illustrated by the proposals planners produce to allow people as pedestrians to survive alongside the growing flood of vehicles. Whether it is a town-centre redevelopment scheme incorporating the segregation of pedestrians from vehicles by construction of a shopping precinct (only the twentieth-century version of the medieval market square), or a Radburn design for the layout of a new residential area, or the location of primary schools within a neighbourhood unit so that young children may reach school without crossing any main road, the objective is clearly safety for citizens in the same way as the daylight standards, sunlight standards, overcrowding standards and building codes, first used at the beginning of the century. During the 1950s, before traffic problems came to dominate the planning scene, an improvement to the health and safety of citizens was sought by detailed proposals concerning the future use of land in each part of the town. Planners sought to keep apart incompatible uses such as noxious industry and housing, and to structure the land-use pattern in such a way that environmental quality and convenience to local facilities, as well as health and safety, were all achieved to a higher standard. The clearest evidence of the impact of planning standards on the land-use pattern of cities is the fact that in the New Towns started in the 1950s, largely on green-field sites, the land-use map differed radically from that in existing towns.

During the 1960s national economic difficulties, very substantial demographic growth, and a deepening understanding of just how outworn and outmoded most of Britain's major industrial cities were, led to the development of a new emphasis in the work of town planners. Questions began to arise about the optimum size of a city, the most efficient use of scarce national resources for new schools, new sewage works and, most expensive of all, new high-capacity, high-speed urban roads. Threshold analysis (Hughes and Kozlowski 1968) was used to examine current and potential capacity for further expansion of existing settlements, and plans were produced based on the argument that it was more efficient to expand this settlement rather than that one. Plans appeared arguing that one spatial structure in the region rather than another was both more conducive to economic growth and minimized the cost of public sector infrastructure (such items as new airports, container depots and inter-city communications). Growth-points or growth-zones were designated and public sector investment of a wide variety, including notably several New Towns, was concentrated in a limited number of locations. The City Efficient ideal thus made an impact not only on the internal structure of the city but also at the regional scale, where it caused the rates of growth of towns to be different because planners seeking national efficiency influenced the spatial distribution of most government investment and even much private investment.

The fourth and final stage in the evolution of town-planning aims is currently proceeding, and therefore is not as clearly identified as the earlier stages. Town planning is increasingly being regarded not only as a method for improving the quality of life for all, but of doing so particularly for the less well-off and more disadvantaged groups. The City Just concept asks planners to realize that every plan changes the spatial distribution of facilities in towns and cities and asks them to ensure that those with poor housing, bad schools, little open space, no convenient shops, poor accessibility to employment opportunities, or some combination of these, are benefited more than others.

The distribution of the costs and benefits of particular planning policies falls unequally on different groups in the society. Public perception of this really seemed to grow out of the practice of building urban motorways through tracts of very poor quality housing because the land was least expensive in such areas. Whatever the benefits of such improvements are, they did not accrue to those people who had their homes demolished and thus were forced to change their place of residence, since they were overwhelmingly non-car owners. It may over-simplify a complex social change to say that this led in turn to an increasing demand by the public to be consulted about planning policies.

It is perhaps most important of all to realize that these stages in the evolution of town-planning aims have been additive, with each new aim complementing those already in use, rather than competing with them or being seen as a replacement or alternative. Thus the quality of life that town planners are seeking to realize will be found in the city that is at one and the same time beautiful, safe and convenient, efficient and just. This Utopia is not expected by the town planner to occur tomorrow, but it does define the direction in which he is seeking to go. It informs his choice of tools and helps to explain why, despite the mistakes, frustrations, delay and interference with private rights that are apparently an inseparable part of British planning, the activity continues. A discussion of the way in which these aims and methods of town planning have influenced the existing urban system is contained in section IV of this chapter.

Other kinds of organizations apart from governmental or quasi-governmental ones are also capable of influencing urban structure. In fact, interest groups of a great variety of kinds play roles of varying significance. It is curious, as Barker (1975) has commented, that 'just as British town and country planners had about finished establishing themselves as a proper profession, equipped to operate the world's most advanced system of statutory land-use controls for the benefit of all, the tendency for private citizens to form themselves into groups concerned with planning issues was also rising rapidly'. In addition, however, to over 1,100 amenity societies in 1974, there are others ranging from the local Chamber of Trade to the neighbourhood community action group and from tenants' associations to rate-payers' groups. How effectively they influence planning is really known only for a small number of case studies (Gregory 1971), but clearly the potential is substantial.

This review of the interacting processes that underlie the character of the British urban system reveals all too clearly an institutionally diverse and organizationally complex urban society and as a consequence how difficult is valid description and its explanation. It is not surprising therefore that some scholars have attempted to base their explanations on the type and behaviour of the institutions through which the social, economic, political and technological processes operate as urban-change agents. This 'managerialist' approach explains urban change by the actions of key persons in the institutional structure — referred to as 'gatekeepers or urban managers'. The identification of these key decision-makers and attempts to measure their value systems and discover their information systems have provided yet more evidence of the subtlety and complexity of cause and effect in the urban system (Robson 1975; Healey and Underwood 1978; Blowers 1980; Knox and Cullen 1981).

'Gatekeepers' include local authority housing officials, building society managers, solicitors, surveyors and estate agents, all of whom possess the keys necessary to unlock various 'gates' providing access to different types, ages, tenures and locations of housing. Central government decisions also complicate individual decision-making, for example by changing the legislation that determines the relationship between private landlords and their tenants, or by changing the levels of subsidy that accrue through tax relief to owner-occupiers, or through Exchequer Grants to local authorities and their tenants. Landowners, speculators and builders all play a part in regulating the supply of dwellings, and their decisions, too, will depend in part on central government policy. All these agencies, it is argued, play more important roles than do individual families in shaping the social geography of British cities.

II.2 Pattern

The above discussion of the various kinds of process which generate the internal structure of the city and give it a distinctive patterning suggests that although an endless variety of combinations will arise in different towns, there is nevertheless enough universality to allow the description of a typical or average case. Such an epitome is most unlikely ever to be found in reality but it provides a norm against which the actual pattern of existing cities may be viewed, to gain an understanding of deviations from a general theory as they develop under the time and space circumstances of particular places.

The British town or city can be thought of as possessing a particular pattern of internal structure resulting from the superimposition of *three patterned spaces* (fig. 6.4), themselves the result of a combination of processes. The 'physical space' pattern reveals the pre-Victorian nucleus surrounded by a continuous and compact ring of nineteenth-century development, itself surrounded by an even broader ring of twentieth-century expansion involving the engulfing of minor centres. The tendency to a star-shaped form was more pronounced at the end of the nineteenth century than now. Basically the pattern is distinctly zonal: the outcome of growth by peripheral expansion and economic competition for space, influenced by a radial transport network of limited density. The 'social space pattern' combines both zonal and sectoral patterns. The three sectors represent the status differences generated by social-class segregation, while the concentric zones indicate both the family-cycle process and the impact of the housing market with its tenure divisions. These are the three dimensions that have emerged most frequently and most strongly from the factorial ecology studies in Britain.

Several points can be noted. The inner zone of the high-status sector consists largely of privately rented housing in which elderly households of lower-middle-class status dominate (1). Students and young professionals also live here in small flats and 'bedsit' conversions. The main exception is a small area of privately owned houses (1a), a residential pocket of large Victorian or Edwardian terraces

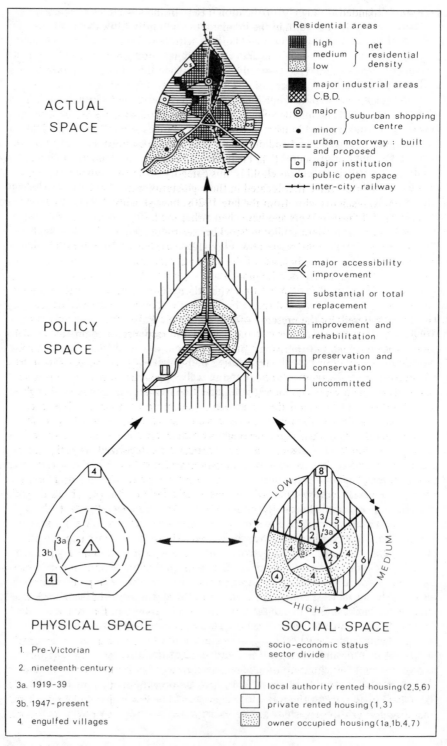

Figure 6.4   Internal structure of the British city

recently expanded through 'gentrification' (1b). In the low-status zone the privately rented houses contain the immigrant community (3a); the medium-status zone retains traditional working-class families with few children in houses nearing the end of their life (3). The remainder of the inner zone consists of redeveloped or rehabilitated slum areas (2). Council housing outside the inner zone is most widely distributed in the low-status sector occupying most of the middle (5) and outer zone (6), while in the inner zone high-rise flats have replaced Victorian working-class housing (2). The middle zone in the medium- and high-class sectors consists of interwar owner-occupied houses, in which most families are now without children (4). Postwar semi-detached and detached owner-occupied houses occupy the outer zone of the high-status sector (7). Professional people with young families and large mortgages are the typical household in this category. The two engulfed villages present a contrast, since that located in the high-status sector has been invaded by high-income residents who, from the late 1920s, have steadily displaced the original population of farm-workers and have then either modernized the old cottage-style buildings or built modern replics in 'stockbroker tudor' fashion. The low-status sector village (8) has a mixed pattern, since it has attracted both middle-income and working-class population because of the early railway connection to the city and the consequent industrial development.

Fig. 6.4 conveys the argument that while there is interaction between the patterns of physical and social space, both have their impact on the actual city structure 'filtered' by the presence of 'policy space'. Policy space represents the impact of the urban managers (i.e. the planners) in response to community politics. It is a curious blend of professional planners' ideology and the distribution of power among the main groups in the city. Thus a combination of the planners' wish to improve accessibility and reduce congestion, combined with pressure from car-owners and the business community, has resulted in policy proposals for a high-capacity inner ring road on the edge of the central business district linked to motorway-standard radial roads to connect the town to the region. Essentially planners attempt to manage the internal city system by influencing the rate of change (section II.1), and so the policy space can be categorized, as in fig. 6.4, in terms of the degree of change which the city has adopted as its policy and expressed in its statutory planning documents. Areas with change kept to the minimum possible, by strict preservation policies, include the urban fringe (with its designated green belt) and selected historic buildings in the town centre, either 'listed' individually or contained within a designated conservation area. Areas where radical change is being positively promoted include the city centre (e.g. a new shopping precinct by the local authority in partnership with commercial property developers), together with most of the area built in the nineteenth century where a programme of comprehensive redevelopment, already partly complete, will result in the disappearance of sub-standard houses and the typically mixed industrial and residential land use, and markedly improve public services, such as schools and parks. Surrounding the zone of radical and immediate change is an area proposed for gradual change, largely through a process of housing and local environmental improvement through the designation of General Improvement Areas and local plans involving only limited redevelopment. For a considerable portion of the city, mainly the areas developed since 1945, there are no firm policy proposals either to stimulate or to restrain changes, as there appear to be few major problems. A rather ad hoc approach to suggested changes in these areas is adopted, in which proposals

for the development of hypermarkets on the edge of the green belt will be refused
on the grounds that it is incompatible with green-belt purposes and likely to be
harmful to the existing pattern of shopping, especially the major new shopping
centre being built in the city centre. The possibility of establishing an industrial
estate on the site of the now-disused city refuse dump will, however, be investigated
with vigour, for although not an ideal site, it would, if successful, help to offset the
gradual decline in employment in the city's traditional industries. At the same time
it would improve the balance between jobs and residence within the city, which
until now has meant substantial commuting flows from the east and south through
the city centre to the employment concentrations in the north-east sector.

As a consequence of the combination of physical space with social space and the
superimposition of policy space on both, a generalized urban structure purporting
to be the typical British city emerges and is shown at the top of fig. 6.4 in terms of
major land-use categories. Even this simplified presentation underlies how varied
the internal structure of British cities can be, and why it is more helpful in
attempting to understand such variety and complexity to emphasize process rather
than pattern, function rather than form. Although a relationship always exists
between form and function, its precise nature is often forbiddingly difficult to
determine.

Characteristic features The British city clearly conforms to Dickinson's (1947)
dictum that the structure of the modern city tends to be a broad zonal arrangement
around the city centre, and this tendency although only one among several, is the
most important. Essentially, the concentric rings represent in plan a cone of
development whose peak is the city centre and from which the *density* declines
gradually as distance from the centre increases. Innumerable criteria have been used
in Britain to identify this basic structural feature: population density (with the
Central Business District devoid of residential population a volcano-like profile
emerges), floor-space density, land value, traffic-trip generation, employment
density, etc., all of them widely depicted in the basic urban geography textbooks
(fig. 6.4). More surprising and still largely unexplained, is the way in which the
density gradient appears in many other distributions of phenomena in the city.
Studies of medical geography in British cities (Bagley 1965; Castle and Gittus 1957)
have shown that infant mortality, schizophrenia and other illnesses often have this
pattern, and from other studies of educational attainment, fertility and even crime
(Davidson 1981) a broadly similar picture emerges. Understandably, it is difficult
to trace the complex associations involved, and even more difficult to begin to
identify cause. In his review of the relationships between housing, health and
environment in cities, Martin (1967) concluded that 'the evidence shows the clear
association of health with socio-economic conditions, overcrowding and air
pollution – when these are eliminated the influence of other factors is slight'.
Advances in medical treatment have eliminated some classical environmental diseases,
such as tuberculosis, but some commentators have remarked that others, such as
attempted suicide, appear to take their place. Even if the cause is not identified the
correlation in spatial distributions between bad health, poor housing, low educational attainment and other social pathologies suggests that there are still several
facets of city structure to be explored.

The density gradient in most British cities has been levelling off for several
decades as a consequence of both private decisions to migrate from the inner

higher-density zones to lower-density outer zones, and of public policies, especially those affecting the density of residential areas after redevelopment and those attempting to disperse industry away from locations close to the central area. In SE England this tendency for central densities to decline while the peripheral zones increase, extends to over 65 km round London.

The various aspects of London's urban structure shown in figs. 6.5 and 6.6 have been selected to show how the key features of British urban structure can be identified even in the capital. Figure 6.5B provides several illustrations of the way in which the zonal, radial and nucleated patterns predicted by the ecological theories of Burgess, Hoyt and Harris and Ullman are additive, as well as showing the degree to which functional areas show up at this scale of generalization. Note too the strong association between the industrial and the transport patterns, especially in the inner areas, and the very widespread distribution of all public buildings (including health and education), thus emphasizing their relationship to residential areas. Other patterns less obviously discernible are the major suburban centres with their commercial land-use concentration and some new largely fragmented fringe belts of open space, vacant land and institutions. The impact of government policy can be seen in the differential growth of suburban office and retail centres (fig. 6.6B) and to some extent in the decentralization of traditional wholesale markets. Reasonably typical of the British industrial city is the distribution of land use shown in table 6.3. This land-use budget, however, does not reveal that just over 20% of the GLC area is within the formally designated London green belt, and this accounts for almost 60% of the open areas. The table also shows the inner and outer contrast in land-use terms and indicates the effects of decline and decentralization on the land-use pattern.

Perhaps less typical of other British cities and towns because of its size and international fame, is London's central area (or CBD), which can be clearly

TABLE 6.3

Distribution of Land Uses in Greater London, 1966 and 1976 (%)

	1966		1976	
Use	Greater London	Inner London*	Greater London	Inner London*
Residential	33.4	36.3	34.2	35.0
Open areas	29.6	15.2	28.5	15.9
Roads	10.9	16.9	}15.8	}22.2
Transport	4.5	5.2		
Vacant	5.0	3.6	5.7	6.3
Industry and utilities	4.2	4.3	3.8	3.2
Shops and offices	3.2	5.7	3.8	6.3
Education	3.4	3.1	3.2	3.2
Other	5.8	9.7	5.0	7.9
	100.0	100.0	100.0	100.0
Thousand hectares	158	31	158	31

*Inner London is the area of the 13 boroughs in the Inner London Education Authority.

Source: GLC Land Use Survey (1966, 1976)

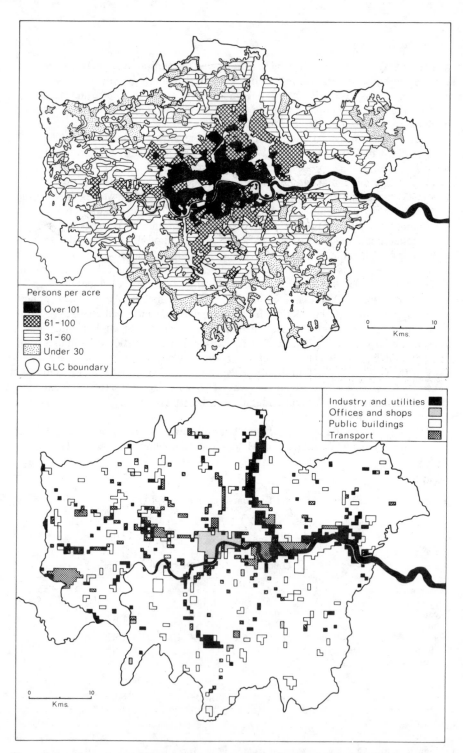

Persons per acre

- Over 101
- 61 – 100
- 31 – 60
- Under 30
- GLC boundary

0   10
Kms.

Industry and utilities
Offices and shops
Public buildings
Transport

0   10
Kms.

Figure 6.5   The patterns of land use in London: (A) Residential density; (B) Predominantly non-residential land use
Source: Rep. of Studies, GLC, 1969

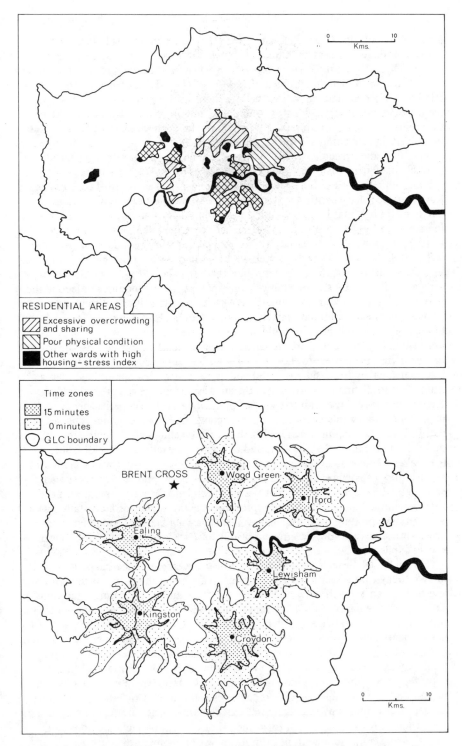

RESIDENTIAL AREAS

Excessive overcrowding and sharing

Poor physical condition

Other wards with high housing–stress index

Time zones

15 minutes

0 minutes

GLC boundary

BRENT CROSS

Wood Green

Ilford

Ealing

Lewisham

Kingston

Croydon

Figure 6.6   London: (A) Housing stress areas; (B) Accessibility to major shopping centres
Source: Rep. of Studies, GLC, 1969

distinguished on fig. 6.5B. Characteristically, it has an enormous imbalance between total residents (230,000 in 1971) and the total number of people at work (1,250,000 in 1971), thus generating the largest commuter flows in the country and a severe transport planning problem (Thomson 1977). The dominance of office, retailing, entertainment and government (administration) land uses, together with the presence of famous and historic buildings, notable public institutions like the University of London or museums, its major public open spaces, and even pockets of specialized residential use (including luxury hotels, student hostels, embassies, council flats and privately owned charity accommodation), gives it a powerfully distinct character of its own. The detailed studies of central areas throughout Britain (notably, for example, Glasgow (Diamond 1962) and Cardiff (Carter and Rowley 1966)) have confirmed what has been even more obvious in London (Goddard 1970), that there is an intricate patterning of functions associated with the great competition for land, and often very considerable levels of congestion. It has been shown how variations in the composition of office employment between different districts is closely associated with variations in the scale and type of retail shopping outside the primary retail zones. The boundary of London's CBD has been and still remains the location of many major planning inquiries reflecting the strength of land-use conflict in the traditional zone-in-transition. Birmingham, Glasgow and Manchester have largely completed their inner ring roads (fig. 6.4), but London no longer proposes to build one (Hart 1976).

Surrounding the central area of British cities is what has now come to be called the inner city, in contrast to the outer or suburban zone. As table 6.3 shows, there is proportionately less residential land and more road space than in the city as a whole, but its distinctive character in Britain arises from the age of the buildings, the mixture of land uses and the scale of population decline experienced since the mid-1950s. Today this zone consists of (a) completed slum-clearance schemes dating from 1955–65 in which up to 50% of the dwellings are in multi-story blocks of 15–20 floors in height, (b) scattered unused sites awaiting redevelopment, (c) pockets of densely developed housing often among multi-storeyed warehouses and factories decaying steadily as they await demolition prior to redevelopment, and (d) small patches of traditional Victorian residential development that have been rehabilitated – internally by improvement grants and environmentally by local authority expenditure on traffic management, parking facilities and open-space provision. Jones's (1960) description of this townscape (in Belfast) is no longer widely applicable.

The mixed land-use pattern is only part of the reason why the inner city is best known today for its bad housing conditions. The internal facilities of the houses and their external environment have been wholly outmoded by rising aspirations and modern standards. Coupled with the simple fact of age and lack of maintenance, this has created areas where the density of people per room exceeds one; where the net residential density usually exceeds 370 persons per ha; where the proportion of houses without baths, indoor toilets and hot running water exceeds 50% of the total; where the structural condition is such that a 10–20-year life is all that is expected; where the schools have inadequate play space; where public parks and playgrounds are very few; and where factories and traffic intrude noise, dirt and danger. It was these physical attributes that the urban renewal programmes of the 1960s and 1970s were intended to correct. In a context of declining household size, and substantial immigration from the New Commonwealth countries, the shortage of housing continued and the operation of the housing market led to severe housing stress in many inner city areas. High levels of multiple occupancy, measured by families sharing kitchens, often coincided with physically worn-out areas (fig. 6.6A). Not surprisingly, therefore, the inner city is also characterized by less social stability. In Inner London a survey showed that 20% of households were actively seeking to move, compared to 9% for London as a whole. The rising levels of unemployment in the 1970s have added to the problems of these areas and reinforced the tendency for a concentration of families with multiple deprivation characteristics to reside in the inner city (Hall 1981, 59).

It was this inner city zone that became the focus during the 1970s of increasing government attention (section IV), as physical deterioration, economic decline and social deprivation mounted despite the efforts of public policy-makers. Although it is true that serious street riots in 1981 occurred in classic inner city areas – Brixton and Hackney in London, Toxteth in Liverpool, St Paul's in Bristol and Moss Side in Manchester – there were many inner city areas that were not involved; Glasgow and Newcastle for example, and some riots were outside the inner city, Southall in London, for example. The report of the official inquiry by Lord Scarman concluded that, 'while the riots arose from a complex political, social and economic situation which is not special to Brixton, they were essentially an outburst of anger and resentment by young black people against the police'.

The outer or suburban zone is typically a contrast – lower net residential densities, a much more segregated land-use pattern and considerably more open space. The correlation between the decline in residential densities (fig. 6.5A) and the rise in levels of car-ownership expresses well the different life-style of this zone. In the case of London the inner suburbs are predominantly low status and have higher population densities, more overcrowding and more unfit housing than outer London suburbs (fig. 6.5A, 6.6A). The major exceptions are: the large local authority estates in outer London, built between 1919 and 1939 as a suburban solution to inner London housing problems, mainly occupied by unskilled and semi-skilled workers; the inner suburbs of Hampstead, Dulwich and Blackheath that have retained their high status; and areas like Camden Town, parts of Islington and Stockwell, that are regaining a professional middle-class population. Although there are contrasts between interwar and postwar development, between council houses and owner-occupied areas, these are clearly less significant than those between inner and outer metropolis. Almost without exception among urban studies, the division of the outer zone into sub-areas follows a sectoral pattern reflecting, especially in the conurbations, the fact that residents from one sector (e.g. south-east or north-west) rarely, if ever, visit the other sectors. Journeys to the centre for employment, shopping and entertainment are common, but lateral movement is both difficult and normally undesired. This is particularly well illustrated by the pattern of accessibility to major suburban shopping centres in London (fig. 6.6B) and is not only widely repeated in other cities but also sought by the planners to assist in the development of community and in the efficient provision of public services in urban areas where the residential densities are at their lowest.

Variations in site conditions are an important reason why the simplistic geometry of zones and sectors is not more obvious as a result of physical growth and functional change. Furthermore, the way in which topography has affected urban structure has altered through time, as changing technology has both created fresh problems and provided new opportunities. Thus London and Glasgow among many other cities grew up at convenient and feasible river crossing-points, which provided them with great nodality. As ship technology altered, both began to provide docks, and in Glasgow the River Clyde was deepened from an average of 2.4 metres in 1758 to 12.1m in 1958. In Manchester, where this was not possible, an artificial river was created. Subsequently, as the port function has migrated downstream to deeper water and modern facilities, these largely relict features have become obstacles to easy vehicular movement, necessitating an enormous investment in bridges and tunnels in the post-1945 era. The most striking case of the changing value of topography in the urban context are the defensive sites. Edinburgh and Stirling sited on dramatic 'crag and tail' formations, Durham and Shrewsbury within their incised meanders and Guildford on its ridge top commanding the gap, have all had their growth patterns very substantially influenced by conspicuous local relief. Although the impact of site is often regarded as most powerful in the earliest stages of town growth there are many examples of its continuing influence. The direction of spread of central business districts has often encountered the 'barrier' effect of a river and although the metropolitan accessibility of north Lambeth and Southwark in London, much of Gateshead in Newcastle, and the south bank of the Clyde in Glasgow, is as great as that on the immediately opposite bank, only fringe central areas have developed. In London this has allowed the planned development of a public entertainment complex, 'the South Bank', with amazing metropolitan centrality at relatively low cost.

Altitude in urban areas has frequently been associated with social status because of its amenity quality: the opportunity for views, greater freedom from pollution, and distance from railways and industrial land in the valley bottoms. Thus in the west-end residential area of Glasgow the existence of an irregular drumlin field has produced a parallel complex 'social topography'. On the top of each drumlin are large Victorian villas (often now converted to use as a specialized college or small private school) surrounded by fine terraces on the upper slopes (still occupied by the middle class) and in turn surrounded by intensive tenement development, with industry and transport in the intervening hollows and on the adjacent flood plain. There is thus a precise inverse relationship between altitude and net residential density. In York and Chester sentiment and the tourist value of the city walls reflect an indirect influence of topography, repeated in St Albans, where the combination of flood plain, Roman remains and cathedral has effectively blocked an entire quadrant of the town's site from urban encroachment. More obviously and more unusually the pattern of growth of Peterlee New Town is almost wholly related to the rate at which settlement and subsidence occur in areas recently mined for coal. These examples illustrate the role of site, but because its influence is always exerted through social and economic processes, making some possibilities attractive and others merely costly, it is easily included in a process-dominated explanation of city structure.

A possibly powerful cause of change in the urban structure in the future lies in the changing technology of the journey to work. Up to the present time the essential feature of the industrial city, as an agglomeration of economic activities with an internal highly-differentiated land-use pattern, has been closely related to the transport technology available and in particular to the mode of travel involved in the journey to work, which accounts for the majority of all trips made within urban areas (Thomson 1977). Two fundamental and new features of intra-urban travel are beginning to influence urban structure. First is the rise in real terms of the cost of petrol, and second is the rapid development of telecommunications enabling fast and reliable contact for voices and written material over large distances, thus replacing much of the need for travel and transportation. The significance of the volume, mode and length of intra-urban journeys for the structure of urban areas is difficult to exaggerate (Daniels and Warnes 1980), and consequently the interaction of public policy, private decisions and technological innovation in the near future will have major consequences for the future structure of urban areas in the UK.

III URBAN FUNCTIONS

The irregular distribution of towns and cities within Britain and their already noted diversity of size and internal structure is probably more closely related to their functional attributes than to any other possible cause. Despite this there has been little systematic analysis of the functional roles of the settlements comprising the urban system and their associated features. The present distribution of settlements of different size is the outcome of three major phases of urban growth (section I.2), each with a distinctive economic rationale, which has imparted massive change to the relative significance of individual settlements.

Before the industrial period (Dickinson 1947) the country was peppered with closely spaced small towns. Their genesis and growth, closely influenced by geographical and historical factors, derived from their capacity to serve as trading centres for the agricultural population living within a short radius around them. Poor transport confined their areas of influence, usually to within 6–8 km radius, the limits of a day's journey, there and back, for human beings and livestock on their own feet.

Bringing new sources of power and cheaper, more effective, transport, the industrial revolution led to the growth of much larger towns. Some, like Nottingham or Leicester, were old-established towns, able to take advantage of the new industrial processes. But many were a new kind of specialist industrial town: cotton and woollen textile towns in the Pennine foothills of Lancashire and Yorkshire; some Black Country centres turning out coal, brass and iron; places like Jarrow and Hebburn lining the Tyne, living by exporting coal and building ships. Such industrial towns had almost no connection with the rural populations around them. Hastily built, their housing usually of low standard, poorly provided with shops and urban amenities, they grew mainly by attracting rural migrants seeking employment. They had few services to offer people still living in the surrounding rural areas. Robson (1973, 38) has examined the pattern of growth in the nineteenth century and comments on the changes in rank order of the twenty-five largest towns in England and Wales as follows:

'London, the largest town in 1801, retained its rank throughout the whole period, Manchester and Salford, starting in the second rank, had fallen to third place by the end of the period at the expense of Liverpool which had moved from third to second. Birmingham retained its rank of fourth throughout the whole period. All of these larger places, indeed, show relatively little change in their rank orders over the whole period. On the other hand, with the smaller places there is a tendency for increasingly large fluctuations to occur at smaller city sizes. Some places move rapidly up the rank hierarchy: Exeter, for example, began at 20th position and had fallen to 65th by 1911, even though its fall was halted briefly in the period 1821—41. Other places show more fluctuating fortunes: Coventry, which began in 19th position, had fallen to 48th by 1881, but climbed back to 33rd by 1911.'

Over the last 30 years, too, there have been major variations in the economic fortunes of places within the urban system. These range from steady decline in Liverpool and Glasgow (Checkland 1981) to a more mixed experience in, for example, Leeds and Coventry (no longer the boom city with well above-national-average wage rates as in the 1960s, but currently with an above-national-average unemployment rate), to the select group who have maintained the strength of their local economies such as Leicester, Nottingham, Bristol, Southampton, Reading, Oxford and Luton. The fact that even in these towns the rate of population increase 1971—81 was well below that for the previous two decades shows how strongly national trends affect all settlements in the urban system, even the most successful. Despite this, the combination of structural decline in particular sectors of the economy (Section 4.II.2), the dispersal of population and industry from the large cities, and the growth of employment in services throughout the country have combined spectacularly to alter the functional rationale, and thus the socio-economic character and hierarchical status of many towns and cities in only the last three decades. The precise way in which these trends combine to affect the fortunes of particular places, and even particular groups within particular places (e.g. cotton-textile workers in Lancashire or car-workers in Coventry), is not well understood. To say that exogenous forces such as international competition (Japanese cars, Hong Kong textiles, German machine-tools), combine with secular trends born of technological change, as in the growth of information-based employment, and that both interact with domestic policies (e.g. a New Town programme or regional policy), and national institutional structures, gives only a hint of the complicated kind of explanation that is needed.

It is clear from the perspective of the early 1980s that 1950—70 was a period of growing metropolitan dominance (figs. 6.1 and 6.2). Particularly powerful in this metropolitanization of the urban system has been the increasing importance of service functions, both public and private sector, and their growing concentration in the largest cities. In two sectors — professional and scientific services and public administration — growth in the seven conurbations was particularly strong. However, by increasing service employment generally between 1961 and 1971 while population and manufacturing employment was actually declining, the relative growth of services was faster in the conurbations than elsewhere in the urban system (Cameron 1980, 64). The period 1945—75 is thus associated with problems of urban 'overgrowth', such as inflation of house prices and the physical problems of traffic congestion, which underlined the need for a policy of metropolitan decentralization. Recent research is, however, suggesting that past policy is a relatively minor cause of the uneven impact of the current economic recession because it sees changes in the mode of production, particularly the growth of multiplant, multinational companies (i.e. organizational change), new forms of the capital-labour conflict (i.e. increasing female labour and unionization), and technological innovation resulting from increasing international competition as more significant (Goddard 1975; Massey and Meegan 1978).

There is also clearly an intra-urban dimension to such changes, since past circumstances have combined to locate service employment and manufacturing employment in separate parts of the city, making different skills present in local labour markets within the same metropolitan area (Smart 1974). This had led to consideration of what steps can be taken to match the skills of those in the inner cities with the jobs that are available, and thus reduce the level of mismatch (i.e. imbalance) in the local labour market, as the Lambeth Inner Area Study (Shankland 1977) termed it. However, a detailed investigation of employment and work travel in five major cities concluded that intra- and inter-inner city diversity was the outstanding feature; thus, 'the features of residents and workplace characteristics differ significantly within and between cities, and the differing nature of the city structures themselves ensure that there are varied patterns of worktravel movement' (Frost and Spence 1981). However, the conclusion by the SSRC Inner Cities Working Party that, 'inner city areas can be best understood as phenomena resulting from underlying forces in the British economy and society including the international context, interacting with specific conditions prevailing in large urban areas to produce diverse outcomes, conventionally labelled the inner city problem' (Hall 1981) returns to the structural theme stressed by Massey and others, while at the same time noting the diversity of local outcomes.

III.1 Hinterlands

Although the essence of the modern town is that it provides specialized services, and the vast majority of the population of the UK live within easy access of a town, the territorial extent of the area over which specific towns exert their influence (i.e. the hinterland) is varied and notoriously difficult to delimit. Each centrally located facility, be it a department store, cinema or livestock market, has its own tributary area and the generalization of these to form a single hinterland must be highly subjective (Carter 1965, ch. 6). Consequently, studies examining the extent of urban spheres of influence have preferred to select a single criterion and apply it nationally, as was done in defining SMLAs. The first attempt to delimit such hinterland areas for the whole country (Green 1950) was a contribution to the new development plans under the 1947 Act. The allocation of land in town centres for commercial business and leisure uses could have been highly unrealistic without regard to the total populations using them. Green (1950) devised a method of analysing bus services in order to define urban centres and their hinterland areas. The existence of a bus route indicated a public demand, and the centres to which the routes led were those to which most people wished to go. Centres were defined as places with some 'magnetism' for buses, in that at least one service from smaller places terminated there, and in most cases it was easy to draw limits within which each centre was more accessible to the surrounding local population than any other centre. Green's published studies distinguished about 950 centres in GB each with a surrounding 'sphere of influence'. Such centres were the kind to which people would mostly go for weekly shopping and other frequently recurring needs. The growth of private car ownership and the associated decline of rural bus services since 1955 has not drastically altered the situation, since the same route network is used, and although a car journey is quicker the relative accessibility of one place to another remains the same.

Around all sizeable towns there is a rather sharp gradient from an inner zone, throughout which the town is unchallenged, to an outer zone within which the urban and rural inhabitants habitually use more than one centre to obtain a considerable range of services. Beyond this again there is often a fringe area within which some city centre services are used sometimes. Less important centres, however, have only small hinterland inner zones, or may lack them altogether, experiencing competition from other centres throughout their sphere of influence. It is within the conurbations, however, that the degree of overlapping of service centre hinterlands is most pronounced (Lomas 1964). Elsewhere the pattern is less complex and broadly approximates to the nested hierarchy predicted by central place theory. Several small towns with their limited hinterlands (e.g. Honiton, Chard, Bridgwater) lie within the larger hinterland of a more important town (Taunton), itself one of several such towns within the hinterland of an even more important place (Bristol).

Although the evidence is incomplete, it appears that for major shopping, entertainment and many professional services, the population has increasingly relied on the larger urban centres, which have as a consequence increased their dominance over their hinterlands. The growth of employment in city centres has heavily reinforced this trend. It is not surprising, therefore, that it was the emergence of these large, powerful community-of-interest areas, 'city regions' as they are often termed, that underlay much of the demand for local government reorganization in the 1960s (ch. 1.IV.3). This new scale of social organization was made possible by the motor vehicle, made necessary by the large threshold populations required by theatres, hospitals and other specialized services, and is defined by the distances people are prepared to travel by car, bus or works' coach in order to benefit from the wider choice of jobs, durable goods, entertainments and other services. According to Senior (Roy. Commn Local Govt 1969, II, 46), only one million people live in the peripheral parts of England still beyond the range of effective access to any centre offering city-level opportunities. Commuting hinterlands are discussed in ch. 2.IV.5.

III.2 Hierarchy

Almost as elusive to establish as the limits of an urban hinterland is the actual hierarchical rank of the urban centre containing the facilities and providing the services. Despite the real technical and data difficulties, urban centres in Britain certainly differ significantly in their importance (measured by many very different indices). Confirmation of this intuitive assessment abounds: almost all organizations and services covering the national territory show some hierarchical structuring, viz: universities/colleges/secondary schools/primary schools, or morning newspapers/evening papers/weekly newspapers, etc.

In the geographical literature the prevalence of retail-sales data to establish the hierarchy is more a reflection of data availability than anything else. Although the various studies are not strictly comparable, it is of interest to compare a sample, particularly for the top of the hierarchy, where the actual number of centres is not great. Table 6.4 shows that although there are the expected variations, the similarities are much more striking than the differences.

The dynamics of the urban system is a major reason for the differing results of the investigations. Some centres, such as the early postwar New Towns, are attracting services and functions and consequently climbing up the hierarchy, while others are making the opposite journey. Smith (1968) has examined the changes in

TABLE 6.4

Identification of the Urban Hierarchy in England, 1944–71

	1	2	3	4
Author	Smailes	Carruthers	Smith	Drewett *et al*
Date	1944	1961	1965	1971
No. of levels identified	6	3	4	n.a.
No. of centres in system	606	240	735	115
Top 15 centres in descending order of importance				
1	Manchester	Manchester	Manchester	Birmingham
2	Liverpool	Birmingham	Birmingham	Manchester
3	Birmingham	Liverpool	Liverpool	Liverpool
4	Newcastle	Leeds	Leeds	Leeds
5	Bristol	Newcastle	Newcastle	Newcastle
6	Leeds	Nottingham	Sheffield	Sheffield
7	Nottingham	Leicester	Bristol	Coventry
8	Sheffield	Sheffield	Nottingham	Bristol
9	Bradford	Bristol	Leicester	Nottingham
10	Hull	Hull	Hull	Leicester
11	Plymouth	Bradford	Southampton	Stoke
12	Southampton	Wolverhampton	Plymouth	Portsmouth
13	Leicester	Coventry	Coventry	Teesside
14	Norwich	Plymouth	Norwich	Southampton
15	Brighton (?)	Southampton	Bradford	Hull

The solid line indicates where each author identifies a major break in hierarchical status.

Sources:
Col. 1 Smailes, A E (1944) 'The Urban Hierarchy in England and Wales', *Geogr.*, *29*, 41–51.
 The rank orders are interpreted from the table given on p. 50.
Col. 2 Carruthers, W I (1967) 'Major Shopping Centres in England and Wales 1961', *Reg. Stud.*, *1*, 65–81.
Col. 3 Smith, R D P (1968) 'The Changing Urban Hierarchy', *Reg. Stud.*, *2*, 1–19
Col. 4 These SMLAs only in terms of their 1971 populations, are taken from fig. 6.2 for comparison purposes only.

status over the period 1938–65 in a study which uses over thirty-five indicators of status ranging from a principal orchestra (the rarest) to banks open daily (the most ubiquitous). Of his 606 centres he estimates that 138 show a rise in status and 78 a decline, corresponding broadly to what one would expect in a period of growing population. He found, however, considerable regional variations in the pattern of change: rises were concentrated in the SW, SE, E Anglia and the E Midlands, with the notable exception of most coastal centres which lost status. The NE and the W Riding contained a notable concentration of declining-status centres. Apart from the stability of most centres two further points of interest emerge. Where population was static or declining over a region, it was the larger centres that showed improvement, and where expanding regions established new small and medium-sized centres these generally looked very similar to the long-established centres of similar size. Recent studies, however, of the way businesses have been

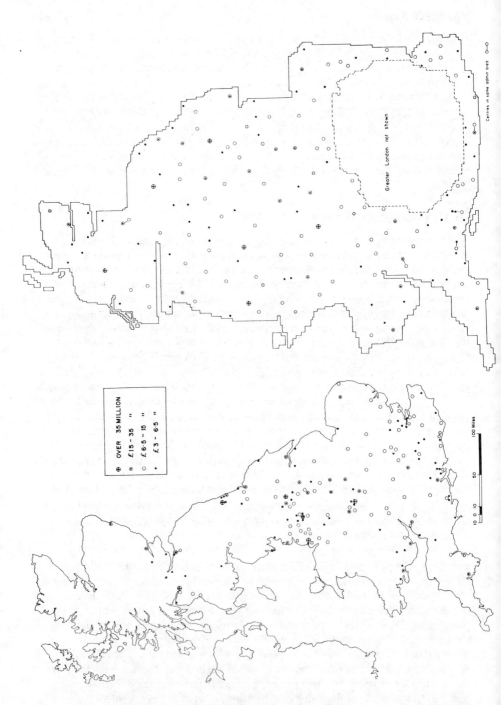

Figure 6.7   Shopping hierarchy, GB, 1961
The location of main shopping centres by volume of retail sales in 1961. Area in
the population cartogram is proportional to the number of people resident
Source: Urban Stud. (1968), *5,* 176—7

concentrating their head offices in major cities, so that the key control functions can have maximum accessibility to specialized information, suggest that the growing dominance of the high-order centre will continue unless public policies attempt to alter the trend (Westaway 1974).

Even if structural changes were not occurring and creating change in the urban system, reflected in changes in rank in the urban hierarchy, the movement of population itself would cause change, since many of the functions performed relate closely to size of hinterland population served. In a quite real sense each centre is competing with the other centres of similar rank for customers, and this process of spatial competition results in a remarkably even spread of centres (fig. 6.7, Thorpe 1968).

III.3 Classification

The functional role of a town or city is generally regarded as its single most significant attribute, capable not only of explaining why, where and when it was established and its subsequent history of growth and decline, but also its present socio-political structure. As Donnison and Soto (1980) point out, occupational structure goes further than anything else to explain other features of these towns and although every urban centre is in a very real sense unique, there are many similarities among urban centres over a wide range of attributes. Not surprisingly, this had led to attempts to classify centres in such a way as to maximize the homogeneity within each group and minimize the differences between the groups. The value of such a grouping procedure for public policy is clear. Many of the problems needing attention in Southport must have their identical counterparts in Eastbourne and, conversely, if it is true that Merseyside is the most distinctive of all provincial conurbations, then perhaps it merits special attention. It was this concern that underlaid Donnison's study which sought to discover which towns provide a good life for their inhabitants and how manual workers in general, and the less skilled and more vulnerable people (elderly) in particular, fare in towns of different kinds. Comparison between these studies is further complicated by the different time-periods involved — Moser and Scott using mainly 1951 census data, while Armen uses 1966 and Donnison and Soto 1971 — and methodological differences. Nevertheless, there are striking similarities between the categorizations produced.

There are two important general points to remember when examining city classifications in Britain. First, much of the economic activity of any city is identical with that in all other cities in the national system; for example, almost all the local public and private services. Then ideally any comparative approach should exclude these common elements. More often than not data difficulties prevent this, and the distinctions between city types are as a consequence somewhat blurred. The second issue is more specifically British. Because of the highly integrated character of the British urban system, it is somewhat unreal to think of each town having its own mini-version of the national economy. What is required conceptually is data on the volume, value and direction of the goods and services imported and exported by each urban centre or city region. In the absence of this kind of data such studies as exist have used a very wide range of characteristics in the hope that some will act as proxies for the non-existent data. Thus Moser and Scott (1961) used 57 variables to classify 155 local authority areas in England and

Wales into 14 categories, while Armen (1972) used 130 variables to classify 100 cities in England and Wales into 23 categories, and Donnison and Soto (1980) use 40 variables to classify 154 local authority areas in Britain into 13 clusters.

Moser and Scott study local authority areas with populations greater than 50,000 in 1951, with variables arranged in eight groups: population size and structure (7), population change (8), housing and households (15), economic (10), social class (10), voting behaviour (7), health (7) and education (2). Because many of the towns had similar rank in the array on each of several different criteria, principal-components analysis was employed to discover how much variation could be explained by a small number of basic dimensions. The results were remarkable: only four dimensions accounted for over 60% of the co-variance of the variables. The four dimensions were labelled as: social class, growth patterns 1931–51, growth patterns 1951–8, and overcrowding. The towns were then classified by a grouping technique applied to their position in the 'space' defined by the four major dimensions. Subsequently, Andrews (1971) has revised the classification. Most of the fourteen clusters can be labelled by economic descriptions. Thus a group (cluster 8) comprising Worthing, Hove, Hastings, Eastbourne, Bournemouth, Torquay, Harrogate and Brighton, are clearly 'resorts'. Another group – Liverpool, Newcastle upon Tyne, Gateshead, South Shields and Sunderland – are port and industrial centres in NE England (except Liverpool). The other clusters can be similarly labelled, but with more difficulty.

Armen's variables for towns with a population over 50,000 were selected to reflect people characteristics, place characteristics and activity characteristics, as of 1966. He produced an hierarchical classification in which 3 basic types divide into 8 sub-groups and these into 23 clusters. Again, functional labels fit the groupings at all three levels.

100 Cities

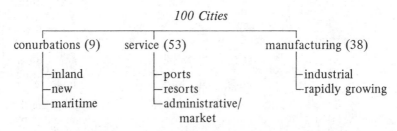

One cluster within the industrial sub-group is composed of Preston, Doncaster, Rugby, Darlington, Crewe, Swindon, all 'railway' towns. Another cluster within the administrative/market centre sub-group is composed of Exeter, Carlisle, Worcester, Peterborough, Chelmsford, Shrewsbury, St Albans, Guildford, Chester and York – all market and cathedral towns. In this classification Eastbourne, Southport, Hastings/Bexhill and Worthing form a 'coastal retirement' cluster, while Harrogate is grouped with Windsor/Slough, Tunbridge Wells and Maidstone as 'inland retirement' centres. Since Armen uses the continuously built-up area to define his centres, Gateshead is included within Tyneside, a maritime conurbation; while Sunderland is found with Swansea, Hull, Barrow-in-Furness and the Hartlepools as a 'medium port'. Encouragingly, the highest within-cluster similarity is found in the group composed of Basildon, Hemel Hempstead, Harlow, Crawley and Stevenage, all New Towns near London with very similar starting dates in the early 1950s. The use of a wide range of variables has the advantage of allowing similarity in many different aspects to influence the grouping procedures, which in turn makes for better descriptions. The 'ports' sub-group, for example, are similar to one another in the predominance of unskilled labour in their workforce, the high rate of unemployment, high density of population, poor housing, presence of consulates, hotels and boarding houses, dancing and night clubs, cinema and bingo halls, slipper baths and betting offices, pubs, cafes and a host of other characteristics. Surprises are possible too: Portsmouth and Yarmouth in the same cluster as Bournemouth and Brighton, and Bath in the same one as Reading.

These earlier studies are broadly confirmed by the most recent and methodologically sophisticated exercise by Donnison and Soto (1980), whose purpose was to identify which types of town develop and distribute economic and social opportunities (i.e. the Good City). In the light of this it was hoped that appropriate town planning and social policies could be formulated to remedy defects in other types of town. Again social status and industrial structure emerge as the two main dimensions, which results in two main groups of clusters: the white-collar towns and the broadly working-class towns. Towns with a high proportion of non-manual workers tend also to have low proportions of all the more vulnerable groups, except old-age pensioners. They have fewer people under 25 and fewer large families, one-parent families and sick people. These towns also tend to have a high concentration of service industries and government employment, and fewer workers in manufacturing and mining. They also have characteristics associated with high income and status such as advanced education, good housing, low unemployment, high car-ownership and self-employment. Their higher reliance on travel to work by car suggests that many of these towns are some distance from the main centres of work, and their residents traverse a larger labour-market area. They live in these more prosperous towns, but they may work elsewhere. However the occupations which distinguish towns do not simply provide a contrast between towns for manual and non-manual workers. There are sex differences too. There is a marked absence of women workers in both the professional and the skilled manual groups: women are more highly concentrated in the lower halves of manual and of non-manual work.

The resulting classification (table 6.5) comprises 13 clusters constituting 7 families, which in turn can be grouped into the two main types. Donnison and Soto find that, overwhelmingly, the best places to live are the growing ones that depend on service industry (of both the private and public variety) and on the newer forms of manufacturing. That is true for everyone, but it is especially true for manual workers in general and for the unskilled ones in particular. In such places they are more likely to have a job, own a car, have better housing and see their children doing well in school. Other vulnerable groups – women workers and single parents – also seem to do better. Thus they conclude: 'The growing prosperous city, the city which is kindest to its more vulnerable citizens and the city which distributes its opportunities more equally than most can all be the same place'.

In contrast, there is a Bad City. It consists primarily of the declining cities of the conurbations. Like the Good Cities, these Bad Cities also have concentrations of manual workers in general, and unskilled and semi-skilled manual workers in particular. But because their basic industries are declining, everyone loses ground: the skilled men lose opportunities for better jobs and higher earnings, and in turn they displace unskilled men into unemployment. Overall, then, such places have

TABLE 6.5

Functional Urban* Types, GB, 1971

Family	Cluster	Number of settlements	Most typical settlement
A. *Non-manual group*			
1	London	2	London
2	Regional service centres	16	Bristol, Cardiff
3	Resorts	10	Bournemouth, Thanet
4 {	Residential suburbs	10	Chertsey, Solihull
	New industrial	12	Worcester, Pudsey
	New Towns	10	Stevenage, East Kilbride
B. *Manual-group*			
5 {	Welsh mining towns	3	Rhondda, Aberdare
	Engineering towns	19	Doncaster, Stockport
	Textile towns	16	Bolton, Oldham
	Growing engineering towns	14	Swindon, Gloucester
	Heavy engineering towns	22	Walsall, Wigan
6	Inner conurbations	14	Manchester, Nottingham
7	Central Scotland	6	Glasgow, Paisley

*the 154 urban areas were defined on the basis of parliamentary constituencies

Source: Donnison and Soto (1980)

high rates of male unemployment. Women do better because they take new unskilled or semi-skilled jobs in service and other non-manual occupations – though these may not pay very well. Such towns also show low levels of educational attainment, which is most noticeable for the children of the less skilled. If this is a consequence of a lack of incentive due to declining economic opportunity then, as Donnison says, 'a town's educational attainment and its social composition may be more the effects than the causes of economic growth and urban development' (Donnison and Soto 1980, 155). If there is a single category which provides a clue to policy, Donnison believes it is cluster 10 (growing engineering), which includes towns of diversified industrial structure ranging from Stretford, Teesside and Ormskirk in the north, to Rochester, Gloucester, Slough, Luton and Thurrock in the south and includes Grimsby, Peterborough and Coventry in midland England. Just what the experience of these towns has been since 1971 as national economic difficulties have increased is one of the fascinating questions to be answered by analysis of the 1981 data (Fothergill and Gudgin 1982).

IV   PLANNING AND THE URBAN SYSTEM

Town and regional planning in Britain has had an extensive and pervasive influence on the nature of the urban system. Although the roots of planning go back to the early years of this century there is little doubt that the passing of the *Town and Country Planning Act* (1947) led to a level of town-planning activity that unquestionably justifies its inclusion among the major influences on the British settlement pattern. To the traditional geographical factors of site, situation, morphology and function, used in urban geography, must now be added town planning. Indeed, since the impact of town planning on the pattern and functioning of towns in Britain has been cumulative, the total effect, after thirty years of intensive professional activity, is now very substantial indeed. Perhaps it is because it has been a gradual and cumulative process that it has tended to be overlooked; not until 1973 was the first major assessment of this era of 'town planning control' published by a geographer (Hall *et al* 1973). Since then there have been several studies evaluating the impact of town and country planning at the national scale, for example Mellor (1977), Mackay and Cox (1979) and Ravetz (1980), and a great many in the form of local case-studies which examine the way in which, and the extent to which, town planning has affected the geography of particular places. These studies are by economists, sociologists and political scientists as well as geographers, and some focus on a particular theme — transport planning, slum clearance, new towns — rather than attempt a more comprehensive approach. The findings reported are far from unanimous in many respects, but unquestionably each author demonstrates that planning has had an extensive and pervasive influence, though the extent and distribution of the resulting benefits, and disbenefits, are much more disputed. It is something of a challenge to the orthodox view that planning, by emphasizing progressive and redistributive goals, by its explicit attachment to participatory democracy and through its potential for furthering economic well-being, is a fundamental part of modern society in a welfare democracy, that McAuslan (1980) concludes his evaluation with the view that planning law and procedure are inherently biased towards the maintenance of vested interests.

After the Second World War there was not only widespread agreement about planners' aims but also the opportunity of reconstruction in the extensively war-damaged cities, such as Coventry, Plymouth, Clydebank, Bristol and London. This combination of general purpose and specific opportunity provided an early test for the newly passed planning legislation, which by demonstrating the applicability of its methods, helped it gain general acceptance from the population. The early New Towns and the reconstruction schemes together provided a powerful example to planners working in the major conurbations as to the kind of new urban development that was possible. For ten years after the war the impact was mainly visible in the character of the major peripheral extensions undertaken by the largest urban authorities, such as Birmingham, Liverpool and Glasgow. After 1955, when the central government began to encourage local authorities to undertake large-scale slum clearance, the same ideology influenced the character of the redevelopment schemes.

Perhaps the most significant impact of the 1947 Act on the urban structure of Britain has, however, not been through positive proposals for change, but through the operation of the development control responsibilities of local planning authorities. In essence the 1947 Act permitted no development, defined in a very comprehensive way, without permission from the local planning authority, and, as was pointed out in section II, this involved the handling of hundreds of thousands of development applications from both large and small land and property owners. Just how much contribution to the visual quality, safety and convenience, efficiency and social justice of our cities today has been imparted by this control process is impossible to say in precise terms. No one doubts that were it not for development control, the green belts round the major cities would have long since disappeared, but in the complex environment of an existing city the overall impact over a period of years is beyond the possibility of careful measurement. Its potential effect is, however, surely enormous, for it applies not only to minor changes in land use, as from garden use to garage, but also to a major urban improvement, such as converting a now unused railway station into a major new commercial centre with offices, shops and entertainment facilities. In addition to the actual applications accepted, modified or refused, there must also remain an unknown number of applicants who were deterred from making an application, largely because they judged it would not prove acceptable. Although, therefore, no measurement of the impact of development control on the structure of the British city is possible, its cumulative effect over the years since 1947 must be very considerable. The evidence of the case-studies suggests that in locational terms the major effects have been felt in the restraint of piecemeal rural housing, adaptation of the older urban stock and on the location of factories, especially backyard-businesses. Thus it is clear that any comprehensive assessment of the impact of planning on the urban system must include both the negative and the positive mechanisms.

Before examining the three types of impact of major significance to the urban system, one overriding general characteristic must be noted. The essential mechanism of the British planning system is control of land use or floor use. This is clearly a sensible choice for a country which introduced planning only after a period of rapid urbanization and when facing a period of much more modest growth, requiring substantial restructuring of the existing urban fabric. Because of this essentially physical basis, however, the process of town and country planning is frequently at the mercy of strong social and economic forces, which operate indirectly on the land-use pattern. The changes in the social and economic structure of Britain since 1945, such as the population boom in the 1960s; the greatly increased number of households reflecting earlier marriage and smaller families; the increased participation of women in the labourforce; the rise in real income and associated shifts in aspiration (e.g. the fantastic growth in the demand for leisure facilities); and the accompanying technological changes, especially in transport, have combined to change dramatically the context in which planning operates. Early postwar planning was based largely on the Abercrombie model: an approximately circular shape with concentric rings of development, including the green belt as a limit to suburban sprawl. This physical design was matched by a social policy born of the English view that big cities are bad. A near-universal aim was the dispersal of people, to be achieved through density control in the centre and the creation of new or expanded satellite settlements beyond the green belt. Conservation groups, agriculture and the slum dweller appeared as joint beneficiaries, forming a powerful consensus.

The postwar years saw planning strongly affect the course of urban development as the professionals produced statutorily backed plans for the whole country. Legislation provided power for their implementation. But since the mid-1950s social and economic change has quickened, and this has itself considerably affected urban growth and structure. Important shifts in ideology have also occurred, as reflected in the growth of home ownership and the recurring debate on the taxation of development values, which have substantially affected the strength of planning in the property market (section II.1) and thus the capacity of the local planning authority to implement its plans (Diamond 1979). Clear evidence of such a shift is revealed in the date of designation of the New Towns (fig. 6.8), which with the notable exception of Cumbernauld fall into two brief periods, 1946–51 and 1961–70.

As the second phase of New Town building began in the 1960s and slum clearance rose to a steady 70,000 dwellings a year, city centre redevelopment boomed and major traffic planning schemes involving expensive urban motorways were planned. Then, just as economic and demographic growth slackened in the late 1960s massive institutional change (reorganization of local government) and radically new methods (structure and local planning) were imposed on planning. By the middle 1970s much seemed to be wrong and considerable doubt and disillusion settled on the profession. The Abercrombie model no longer seemed appropriate but no alternative emerged to replace it (Donnison 1972); two-tier local government made the implementation of plans more difficult; the public participation procedures adopted in the light of the Skeffington Committee's recommendations failed to win back public confidence in planning; and as public expenditure failed to match the planner's proposals, housing stress and traffic congestion continued to plague the big cities in particular. As slow economic growth turned into economic decline, the New Town programme was curtailed and then halted, inner cities became a focus of central government attention (Lawless 1981). With the arrival of the 1979 Conservative government, a major relaxation of land-use controls was initiated and economic revival was made the main and almost the only objective of planning policy, as expressed in government proposals for Urban Development Corporations in the London and Liverpool docklands and for twelve enterprise zones in England. These zones not exceeding 500 acres will benefit from tax exemptions and almost no planning controls in an attempt 'to bring new life back to areas of economic dereliction'.

Against this background it seems sensible to examine the impact of planning under three major headings: (a) urban form (the general structure of urban areas); (b) urban renewal (the changing internal structure); and (c) settlement strategies (the location, size and role of urban centres), each an area of considerable debate and effort within planning in the period since 1955.

IV.1 Urban Form

The general character of British industrial towns has felt the impact of planners seeking the goals discussed in section II.1 in two main ways: through their efforts to reduce densities, and their attempts to rationalize the land-use pattern. In both of these objectives the efforts of the planners have been paralleled by similar market trends occasioned by the weakening ties between home and workplace, and changing patterns of industrial location. Nevertheless, some idea of the likely extent of the planning influence can be obtained from examining the intentions of the planners. Table 6.6 compares the actual (1955) land-use budget in a sample of existing towns with the proposals for the New Towns. It clearly shows the extent to which planners were hoping to reduce the overall average density, by 4 ha for every 1,000 of the urban population in existing towns. The early New Town planners were aiming at a lower density (23.2 compared to 21.6 ha per 1,000 population), which by the early 1960s had fallen even further, as the later New Town master plans show. In 1970 the Milton Keynes master plan was advocating 35.4 ha per 1,000 people, an increase in space of over 100% on the actual situation in 1955. 70% of the increased land need for existing towns is accounted for by residential and educational space, clearly revealing the planners' social aims. A comparison of the proposals for existing cities with those for the later New Towns shows that of the overall increase in land need in the New Towns of 2.9 ha per 1,000 people, 1.8 ha is accounted for by residential and open-space use and a further 1.1 ha by industrial use, suggesting that public policy rather than market trends is the major influence. Another sample survey, again in 1955, but of 185 small towns with an average population of 30,000, revealed an existing overall density of 29 ha per 1,000 people and proposals by their planning authorities to increase this to 32.5 ha when the development plan is fulfilled. This makes an interesting comparison with the plan for Milton Keynes, which could thus be fairly described as a major new city (target population 250,000), planned at an average density somewhat lower than that proposed for much smaller towns fifteen years earlier.

TABLE 6.6

Urban Land Use Budgets: Actual and Planned

	ha per 1,000 population					
	Residential	Industrial	Educational	Open Space	Other	Total
Existing large towns[1]	7.7	1.4	0.4	3.2	4.6	17.4
Proposed large towns[2]	9.5	2.3	1.4	4.2	4.6	21.6
Early new towns[2]	11.7	2.3	2.0	4.4	3.0	23.2
Later new towns[3]	8.7	3.4	2.0	6.9	3.6	24.5
Milton Keynes	16.1	3.2	1.4	4.8	9.7	35.4

[1] A sample of 79 towns whose average size was 160,000
[2] The first 12 New Towns in England and Wales — see fig. 6.8
[3] Includes Livingston, Redditch, Runcorn, Skelmersdale, Washington and expansions of Basildon, Stevenage, Cumbernauld and Glenrothes

Sources: Best, R (1964) *Land for New Towns*; Llewelyn-Davies *et al* (1970) *The Plan for Milton Keynes,* p. 22; and *Rep. of the Minist. of Housing and Local Govt 1958* (1959), Cmnd 737, HMSO, App. XII.

Although the distinctive urban structure of the green-field New Towns are a remarkably direct illustration of the impact of planning ideals on urban forms (Derbyshire 1967), the same influence operates on existing city structure, though understandably in a slower and more complicated manner, as a result of the normal market in land from which the New Towns are excluded by legislation. Diversity of urban form, however, exists even among the new towns. Champion (1970) comments:

'neither individually nor collectively are the new towns following a consistent density policy. Instead, the space standards for each use would seem to be selected independently on their own merits in relation to overall town design and to special features of the site. Thus the high average densities proposed for new housing at Cumbernauld, Newton Aycliffe, Runcorn, and Skelmersdale reflect the importance attached to pedestrian accessibility to service centres and parkland. With open space, the differences between towns derive largely from the very unequal land provision for informal recreation and visual amenity, which in its turn seems to depend on the strength of local pressures on rural land resources and on the availability of physically suitable land.'

The explanation of this diversity is partly revealed in fig. 6.8, which shows that the New Towns may be grouped into two main categories according to their date of designation. Between 1946 and 1950 fourteen were started, mostly on 'green-field' sites and with target populations which even by 1974 did not exceed 100,000. Between 1961 and 1970 another fourteen were started, mostly with substantial populations living within the designated area at the time of designation and with target populations often over 200,000, and in the largest, central Lancashire, approximately 430,000. This contrast between the 1950s and the 1960s reflects the major change in the mix of goals the planners sought (section II.1), as they adapted to the changing social and economic context in which they had to work.

In the 1950s considerations of social balance, community participation and proximity to work led to the adoption of the guidance of the Reith Committee on New Towns (1946), so that very similar urban forms emerged for all the New Towns. A town centre surrounded by four or five physically separate neighbourhood units and usually two or three peripheral industrial estates were the basic components. The major peripheral expansions of the conurbation cities (often similar in scale to a New Town) and the GLC's out-county estates had a similar physical form, and in them the major commercial focus was often termed a township centre. By the mid-1960s, these plans were being criticized as inflexible, over-centralized, and with too rigidly segregated concentrations of different activities. The new plans spoke of choice, flexibility, efficiency and mobility as the important objectives, and in contrast to the earlier period a variety of urban forms was proposed.

Rationalization of the land use pattern became a matter of traffic planning, the dispersal of high-intensity, trip-generating activities replacing the segregation of land uses for social and environmental purposes. It was the steep rise in family car ownership that was, of course, mainly responsible. The new plans had to provide for the impact not only on the physical fabric but, equally important, on the changing social habits. Buchanan's (1963) concept of a hierarchy of road networks (primary district and local distributors, and access roads) forms the framework for all the post-Cumbernauld New Town master plans. It was elaborated fully in his study in 1967 for the progressive development on a 'directional grid' of both Portsmouth and Southampton to create a new Solent City of 1,750,000. The most important routes would connect to the national road grid; at right angles to them other routes would connect to the most important structural elements within the city region; again at right angles, lesser routes would connect communities of 90,000 people. The next series would be local distributors, followed by smaller community routes leading into residential areas, and eventually a system of footpaths. Within the hierarchy of the six major types of routeways there would be many different modes of transport. Principles of separation, free flow and linkage between the different zones of activity would be adopted in a logical manner, from the most important roads down the chain to the security of the footpath for the mother walking with her child to school and local shop. His urban facilities are grouped on alternative routes which he calls 'spines of activity'.

In the existing cities, where adaptation of the existing street pattern is both costly and very slow, decentralization of some central area functions was

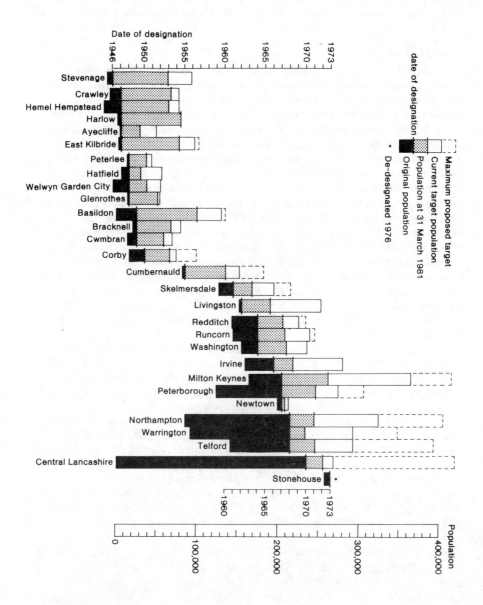

Figure 6.8   New Towns

increasingly adopted as a policy to help overcome congestion and peak-hour chaos. Typical was the suggestion in the *Greater London Development Plan* (1969) that six of the larger suburban centres (Croydon, Ealing, Ilford, Kingston, Lewisham and Wood Green) should be designated as major strategic centres to cater for substantial expansion of their shopping, office, entertainment and public-transport interchange functions and so take pressure off the Central Business District (fig. 6.5A).

IV.2 Urban Renewal

While the New Town planners were more or less successfully inventing the city of the future, the vast majority of planning effort has gone into the herculean task of upgrading and restructuring the existing urban centres, particularly the conurbations with their massive environmental problems. Although individual property and land owners have participated extensively in urban renewal in a general sense (although always with permission of the local planning authority), it is the major improvement schemes initiated by the local authority that have had the most visible effect on the internal geography of the city.

Until the mid-1950s policy was directed to providing additional houses, schools and factories by peripheral expansion. Outside war damage reconstruction schemes, renewal was primarily by small-scale clearance but increasingly this piecemeal approach proved inadequate. A comprehensive approach aimed at improving all aspects of the urban fabric proved inadequate. It involved not only replacement of slum houses, but selective rehabilitation and conservation, a clean-air programme, remodelling of the street pattern, drastic alteration to the shopping facilities, new educational and recreational facilities and concern for local employment opportunities. Essentially this was a campaign to provide twentieth-century facilities in our nineteenth-century cities. While recognizing the need to accommodate some market trends (e.g. providing shops that would be rented by private traders), all the major decisions affecting these policies were made by the local planning authority albeit with the necessity for central government approval. The location, size and timing of redevelopment, as well as the mix and intensity of replacement land uses, can be understood only in the light of local planning policy within a broad national context of recommended standards (such as net residential density, etc.) and subsidies (such as the clearance grant, high flat subsidy, improvement grant, etc.).

The 1947 Act had acknowledged the necessity for tackling redevelopment comprehensively in order to overcome the difficulty of the multiplicity of ownerships and the physical limitations of out-of-date street patterns, by empowering local authorities to define as an

> 'area of comprehensive development' 'any area which in the opinion of the local planning authority should be developed or redeveloped as a whole, for any one or more of the following purposes, that is to say, for the purpose of dealing satisfactorily with extensive war damage or conditions of bad layout or obsolete development, or for the purpose of providing for the relocation of population or industry or the replacement of open space in the course of development or redevelopment of any other area or for any other purpose specified in the plan'.

This legislation and the accompanying powers for compulsory purchase have provided the basis for the designation of thousands of CDAs (Comprehensive Development Areas) in British cities, ranging from schemes covering 526 ha in

Stepney-Poplar to as small as 4 ha or even less. Though the CDA plan is promoted by the local planning authority, it need not itself undertake the actual development.

In those CDAs involving city centre land and activities, the local authority usually enters into partnership with a private development company, which obtains a long-term lease on the site from the local authority, which remains landlord, and the developer then builds the offices and shops while the local authority undertakes the road improvements, new bus station, etc. In the middle 1960s there were over 400 town or city centre redevelopment schemes either approved or waiting approval from the minister. An (unpublished) survey in 1976 revealed that 128 central area shopping precincts had opened since 1955 or were under construction in England and Wales. Typically, they were between 2 and 6 ha in size and contained between 28,000 m^2 (e.g. Butts Centre, Reading) and 54,000 m^2 (e.g. Victoria Centre, Nottingham) of commercial floorspace. Guidance provided by the then Ministry (Housing and Local Govt 1963) gives some idea of likely spatial and functional effects of these schemes. The town centre map, showing in outline the local authority's proposals for the future development of the town centre, was to be based on research which paid attention to:

Land use: density and amount of floorspace.
Property values: with particular attention to the comparative costs of acquisition in different parts of the town centre, and sites whose values could be significantly increased by redevelopment or improvement.
Town character: distinguishing features and buildings worth preserving, needing improvement, and ripe for development.
Pedestrian movement: main pedestrian flows and meeting places within the centre, with reference to congestion, adequacy of pavements, safety and conflict with vehicular traffic.
Vehicular movement: volume and direction of flow at different times, origin and destination; service access; public transport.
Parking: amount, location, duration and trends, related as far as possible to particular parts and functions of the town centre.

A further inescapable conclusion is that some of the changes in the urban hierarchy must owe their existence to the energy and initiative of local planning departments as much as to inherent advantages derived from an historical role.

Extensive areas of mixed housing, industrial and commercial development of mid- or late-Victorian age, have been demolished in the inner area of British cities under the CDA procedure since 1955 (fig. 6.9). The scale of activity can be judged from the results now visible in Newcastle, Sheffield, Liverpool and so on. In Glasgow, a 1957 plan identified twenty-nine CDAs with an average density at the time of 990 persons per ha of housing land, and involving one-third of the city's housing stock and approximately 300,000 persons. Clearly, redevelopment on this scale presents both opportunities and problems, each with considerable significance for the geography of the city. To set against the undeniable benefits of improved housing and environmental conditions such as safety, more open space, and car-parking provision, are costs of various kinds.

First, uncertainty and then dislocation, which may particularly affect the small business man. Social disorganization can occur as family and neighbour relationships are irreparably broken, and economic relationships, too, are severed; employers lose their workers, shopkeepers see the numbers of their customers

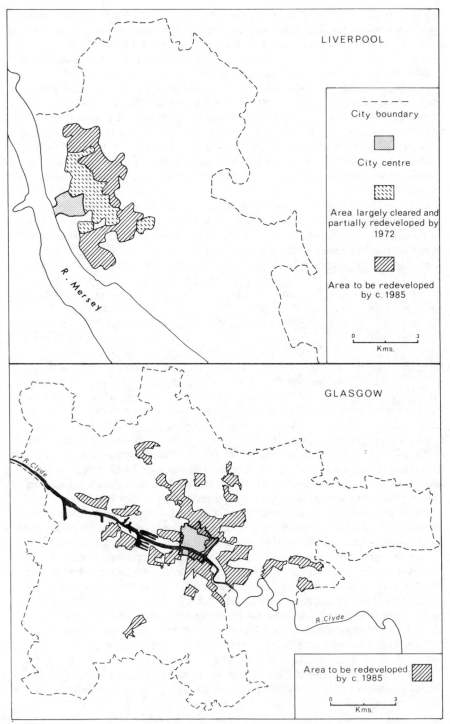

Figure 6.9   Comprehensive redevelopment: Liverpool and Glasgow
Source: City Planning Depts, Liverpool and Glasgow

decline rapidly. Cheap industrial premises, which the inner city has traditionally provided, vanish, and new firms may have greatly increased difficulty in getting established. Some of these problems have been ameliorated by public policy, such as the attempt by Glasgow and Birmingham to provide new low-cost premises for small firms with extensive inter-firm linkages.

The dominating outcome is the drop in density of population, and the decline in the intensity of development generally. In Birmingham the first three postwar schemes yielded a 30% overspill and in Glasgow 60%, despite redevelopment at a net residential density of 370 persons per ha. The land uses which consistently increased their share of the total were school and public open space. The new residential areas incorporate the neighbourhood design principle, involving the provision of local facilities and some variant of the Radburn principle of pedestrian/vehicle segregation.

Even if there had been pressure for neither commercial expansion nor slum clearance, the impact of the car would still have made comprehensive development an essential tool for urban renewal. The fact is, however, that many CDAs have been designed to achieve all three purposes simultaneously — commercial expansion, slum clearance and replacement, and improved accessibility. The problem of actually accommodating the car in a physical fabric largely built to accommodate public transport has influenced the form of redevelopment in two major ways in addition to the decentralization policies already referred to. In his *Traffic in Towns* (1963) Buchanan linked his concept of a hierarchy of roads to that of environmental areas. These were not 'precincts', in the sense of freedom from traffic; rather they were the rooms of a town, 'areas or groups of buildings and other development in which daily life is carried on, and where, as a consequence, it is logical that the maintenance of a good environment is of great importance'. These areas may be busy, of mixed uses, and very different environmental standards might obtain, but the basic idea for traffic flow was exclusion of extraneous traffic, 'no drifts of traffic filtering through without business in the area'. Almost every town and city, too, now shows some attempt to segregate pedestrians and vehicles — in the major shopping areas by closing streets or constructing precincts, and even by multi-level development, as in the Bull Ring in Birmingham; and increasingly in new residential development. Since the early 1970s planning policy has been striving to link these physical improvements with improved public transport services (ch. 5.III.1).

Public policy initiatives designed to facilitate urban renewal are not limited to the three discussed here, though they are the major ones from a geographical standpoint. A fuller account would have to include the now much wider range of interventionist policies involved. These would include the planning authorities' powers to designate a General Improvement Area within which the aim is to help and persuade owners to improve their properties and the external environment with financial assistance, the Community Development Projects sponsored by the Home Office urban programme and the Educational Priority Areas of the Dept of Education, and most importantly, Housing Action Areas designated by local authorities in areas of multiple deprivation in order to raise housing quality and remove the underlying causes of housing stress (Short and Bassett 1981). Physical change was no longer seen as the only way to restructure our cities; what the Dept of Environment (1973; 1977) called the 'total approach' is more eloquently put by Donnison (1972, 24):

'It would help people if the rungs in the ladders of opportunity were set close to each other, economically, spatially and culturally. People move most easily to a *slightly* more expensive house, *close* to their previous home. More important still, the different ladders which people mount must be set close to each other: it will be easier to get that more expensive house if there are better paid jobs within reach, and easier to get the jobs if there are opportunities for a better education and further training. Conversely, it will be easier for people to stick at their education (or persuade their children to do so) if it promises a better job, it will be easier to stick at the job if it offers more money, and the money will be worth more if it could secure a better home for the worker – or something else which his family really wants.'

The theme of the Inner Area Studies, that inter-related social and economic problems (poor housing conditions, limited employment opportunities, strained race relations) needed a less fragmented government response, was incorporated into government policy and legislation with remarkable speed. The *Inner Urban Areas Act* (1978) established a new set of administrative arrangements to 'secure a more unified approach to urban problems' and to focus more resources on 'the inner areas of some of the big cities because of the scale and intensity of their problems and the rapidity of run-down in population and employment'. In practice, the Labour government established seven inner-city partnerships – in Manchester/Salford, Liverpool, Newcastle/Gateshead, Birmingham and three in London: Docklands, Lambeth, Hackney/Islington – in which local and central government programmes are coordinated and leavened by a generous helping of public consultation, and fifteen Programme Authorities, with lesser powers mainly in provincial cities such as Leeds, Wolverhampton, Hull and Sunderland. As an example, the Lambeth partnership committees include representatives from central government departments, from the regional health and education authorities, from the Greater London Council (GLC) and from the local borough. These committees have the task of preparing and implementing inner-area programmes. The Conservative government has continued this approach, and matched it with its deregulation, market-oriented ideology through the introduction of enterprise zones and urban development corporations (see p. 473).

There can be no easy answer to the question, how far have the inner city areas been changed by this large, lengthy and varied bundle of programmes? Substantial and even dramatic change would have occurred in response to radically altered locational values (Cameron 1980, 63; Kennett and Hall 1981), whatever the public policy mix, as events in US cities show. A realistic answer must therefore include an assessment of the extent to which circumstances would have been different (worse) without these policy initiatives which have focussed attention on, and spent modest sums in, the inner cities without creating a major impact, though Hall (1981, 110) considers that the initiatives since 1977 – the Partnerships, Programmes, the extended Urban Programme, the UDCs – 'promise much more, and they may yet, despite all difficulties – deliver'. The crucial element here is an appreciation that area-based policies, of which the inner city has seen a remarkable profusion in the last 15 years, cannot succeed without clear national, people-based policies for poverty, housing, employment and discrimination, in effect a strongly redistributive approach. Given this, then action within particular areas should concentrate on what is most effectively achieved at a local level – new and improved housing, schools, bus services, shopping and community facilities and, importantly, local support for community enterprise.

IV.3 Settlement Strategies

'While the most difficult part of the planning problem will always lie in the continuous process of up-grading and restructuring of our existing cities, the big question is — what form do we attempt to give to our growing city regions, subject as they are to massive population growth and to structural diffusion?' (James 1967). This challenge of physical planning became from 1960 onwards increasingly involved with economic (resource-allocation and development) issues and led to a revival of government interest in regional planning which has had considerable effect on the national urban system (Bourne 1975). Regional planning is the focus of two rather different but closely related functions, both aimed at increasing the national welfare. The first is a mainly economic exercise concerned with the broad distribution of the nation's resources, including population, which seeks both efficient allocation and reduced regional disparities. In contrast, the second function is the devising and implementing of regional strategies for physical develop- ment to ensure an efficient and convenient settlement pattern, and is consequently mainly concerned with land use needs and locational appraisal. Clearly, the two are closely related — the *inter*-regional balance being influenced by and influencing the *infra*-regional pattern. Thus New Towns and expanded towns appear in this dual role, as instruments both for implementing a regional strategy and for influencing the balance of social and economic opportunity between regions (Diamond 1972).

Since the revival of government interest in regional planning in 1964, it has had an increasingly close relationship with the urban system. This has arisen as it was appreciated that the social aims being sought through a programme of planned dispersal involving overspill from the conurbations to new and expanded towns, could also be a major tool in achieving important economic goals (Farmer and Smith 1975).

In almost all aspects of new town development, the 1960s contrast markedly with the earlier period (ch. 2.IV.6). Indeed it is those aspects which differ most — purpose, size and location — that have the closest connection with regional planning. During the 1960s half of the newly designated New Towns were located in the development areas, the conurbations in the North West and W Midlands were provided with 'overspill' New Towns, and the scale and phasing of the New Town programme in the South East was discussed in the light of its possible effects on other aspects of the government's then reviving regional policies. The average target population was increased substantially as the social and economic consequences of a 60,000 target population came to be appreciated and because several of the designated sites included well-established towns. Five of the New Towns had populations in excess of 70,000 (C Lancashire, Northampton, Peterborough, Telford, Warrington) when designated, and these, together with Milton Keynes, all had original target populations for the early 1990s of 200,000 or more (fig. 6.8).

The development of these changes can be observed: from the designation of Skelmersdale as the first 'overspill' New Town for Liverpool in 1961, which was granted DA status although located outside the officially defined development area; through the discussion stimulated by the publication of the government's appraisal of population growth in the South East and its proposals for three new cities and six major expansions; to the 1970 designation of an area (C Lancashire New Town) including nearly 250,000 persons in Preston, Leyland and Chorley (target population, 430,000 by year 2000, now reduced to 270,000).

Among the causes of the government's revived interest in regional planning was paradoxically the experience of most of the first wave of New Towns. Glenrothes is probably the most striking instance, located as it was in a rather remote place, 48 km from Edinburgh and 40 km from Dundee by road and ferry across the Firths, solely to be close to the proposed new colliery. Just as Glenrothes began in 1958 to develop as an industrial growth-point with the attraction of an American electronics firm, so the industrial success (in spite of rather than because of regional planning) of many of the early New Towns drew attention to their potential as a likely effective tool for implementing regional policy.

Like Glenrothes, the other early New Towns could offer a quality of local environment, physically and socially, coupled with improving communications and a growing local labour supply, that gave promise of employment growth. This success was especially marked in Scotland and the North East where the almost full employment of E Kilbride, Cumbernauld, Glenrothes and Aycliffe contrasted with the dismal situation in other parts of these regions. The industrial success demonstrated the feasibility of an urban growth-point strategy, and its ability to establish self-sustaining centres of economic growth, while minimizing public-sector infrastructure costs (especially new and improved transport facilities), providing as wide a choice of opportunities as possible, given the rising threshold levels of viability for most service industries, and continuing the overspill programme.

The strategy, however, also revealed a possible conflict between the 'overspill' and 'growth-point' or 'counter magnet' roles. The former emphasizes quick action, often therefore necessarily close to the congested metropolis with the possibility of commuting, while the latter requires a balanced development at a greater distance from the metropolis. No greater contrast with the first wave exists than in the discussion of local labour markets, for as *The Strategic Plan for the South East* (SE Jt Planning Team 1970) showed, this problem, if not fully resolved, was examined and not ignored, as was the case in the 1950s.

Hall *et al* (1973) have described five case-studies of the interaction between urban development and regional planning and, in explaining the marked differences between them, suggests that local government arrangements were a crucial factor. In C Scotland the relationship between regional planning and urban policy is in its most advanced form. The severity of the challenge of the social and urban problems, as well as the regional economic difficulties, generated this level of response, greatly aided by the existence of effective administrative devolution in the form of the Scottish Office (Lyddon 1971).

After designating the only New Town to be built in the UK between 1951 and 1960, Cumbernauld (1955), with the novel arrangement that 80% of its immigrant population must come from the city of Glasgow, the Secretary of State proceeded to designate Livingston in 1961. This proposal contained a number of noteworthy innovations of significance to regional planning and economic development.

Although essentially an 'overspill' New Town for Glasgow the location chosen was considerably nearer to Edinburgh than to Glasgow. Thus for the first time overspill was being used to achieve a redistribution of population not merely within, but *between* major city regions. It had growth-point and rehabilitation aims as well, however, as the draft designation order points out:

'a New Town here would offer the possibility not merely of helping solve Glasgow's housing problem but also of using "overspill" constructively to create a new focus of industrial activity in the central belt of Scotland, linking the West with the centres of expansion in the Forth Basin, and at the same time revitalising with modern industries an area hitherto over-dependent on coal and shale'.

Clearly, Telford is a direct descendant of these ideas.

It was recognized that the development of Livingston and the surrounding small towns as a growth-point would require an attempt to identify its particular economic strengths and weaknesses, and thus the designation order referred to 'a comprehensive regional scheme of development'. The resulting *Lothians Regional Survey and Plan* (Robertson *et al* 1966) included economic analysis of the labour market, public sector investment, industrial prospects, etc., as well as what would today be called a sub-regional structure plan. One consequence was the government's ready acceptance that the target population of the New Town should be increased from 70,000 to 100,000 and that of the whole sub-region to 250,000 because of the marked economic and social advantages expected to accrue from this increased scale of development.

The *White Paper* (Scottish Devel. Dept 1963) extended these ideas to the entire area from Dundee to Ayr, a distance of almost 160 km. In addition to a framework of transport and infrastructure, including new motorways, airport and port development, railway modernization and a water grid, it identified eight growth-points, of which four were existing New Town sites and a fifth, Irvine, was proposed and later designated (in 1966). The Grangemouth—Falkirk area, also identified as a growth point, was already a town-expansion scheme (Robertson *et al* 1968). This total effort of planned intervention included comprehensive redevelopment, town expansion, the establishment of four new universities (making seven in all in C Scotland), the operation of growth-area working parties jointly manned by local and central government officials, and the improvement of regional industrial incentives (e.g. the granting of SDA status to Livingston and Glenrothes New Towns). This action is effecting a remarkable redistribution of the population, restructuring of the economic base, and reconstruction of its largely outworn infrastructure. The economic and social advantages originally sought within a concentrated high-density city are now being sought within a broad urbanized zone extending for 160 km; economies of scale and linkage, pools of skilled labour, proximity to large consumer markets, choice in educational, technical, and vocational opportunities, can, it is believed, be more efficiently provided in this polynucleated urban form not fundamentally very different from Ebenezer Howard's (1898) idea of 'social cities'. He proposed multi-centred city regions with 250,000 people in each.

The future settlement pattern in C Scotland is no longer obscure, but is beginning to emerge from planned development and even to dominate the regional landscape. It is now clear that a series of decisions concerning the location, sequence and scale of New Town development will make the whole pattern of life in C Scotland radically different from that in the period 1945—65. In essence it can be described as the planned integration of three city regions, those of Glasgow, Edinburgh and Dundee. Although a large extension of the built-up area has been required, this has been done in such a manner that it enhances the prospects of future economic growth and ensures a satisfactory quality of local environment.

This clearly meets the aims of both the intra- and the inter-regional facets of regional planning.

Nor is the Scottish case unique. Broadly similar changes in the location and roles of towns under the impact of regional planning are emerging in the NW, with three new towns between Manchester and Liverpool, and in the NE. In Co. Durham, in addition to the development of New Towns the planners have attempted since the mid-1950s to rationalize the entire settlement system by providing a detailed classification of all existing settlements in terms of their growth potential. The six types of settlement are those where: (1) major expansion is expected; (2) further development should be limited to what is appropriate to the settlement's character but will be considerable; (3) some development will occur but should be limited in scale; (4) no great changes are expected and any development should be closely related to the present size, character and function of the settlement; (5) no development should be allowed, but settlement will long continue to exist; and (6) no new development is allowed to occur and clearance of old houses is proceeding rapidly. It must be said, however, that the designation of a village for 'no development' inevitably produced the strongest possible local political reaction, one of the earliest and most positive indications of public interest in planning.

To conclude. Planning in the UK and its complex relationship with growth and change in the urban system reflects three fundamental dimensions. Based on the concept of the nationalization of the development of land without nationalization of the ownership of land, it also has to operate in a mixed economy with considerable diversity within both the public and private sector. The major consequence of this diversity is the complexity of the organizational arrangements for urban and regional planning. In this context the saga of the location of London's third airport provides a sad insight. Associated with this combination of a comprehensive land-use orientation, the maintenance of private rights in property and the evolving nature of the mixed economy, are the central-local relationships that determine the way in which governmental responsibility is shared. This context helps to explain why planning is often a largely invisible bureaucratic process, interwoven with other causes and effects in the urban system, somewhat slow-moving in realizing its aims and with a flexible attitude to them. It also helps to explain why the level of political debate often obscures the underlying consensus (Hebbert 1981) and it reinforces the view that without an understanding and assessment of the planning system, a large and increasing part of the explanation why our cities are what they are today, and will become tomorrow, is missing.

REFERENCES

ADAMS, I H (1978) *The Making of Urban Scotland*, London
AMBROSE, P and COLENUTT, B (1975) *The Property Machine*, Harmondsworth
ANDREWS, H F (1971) 'A Cluster Analysis of British Towns', *Urb. Stud.*, 8, 271–84
ARMEN, G (1972) 'A Classification of Cities and City Regions in England and Wales, 1966', *Reg. Stud.*, 6, 149–82
BAGLEY, C (1965) 'Juvenile Delinquency in Exeter: an Ecological and Comparative Study', *Urb. Stud.*, 2, 33–50
BARKER, A (1975) 'Studying Amenity Societies', *Tn Cntry Plann.*, 43, 302–4
BELL, C and BELL, R (1972) *City Fathers*, Harmondsworth

BERRY, B J L (1964) 'Cities as Systems within Systems of Cities', *Pap. Reg. Sci. Assocn, 13,* 147–63

BEST, R H and RODGERS, A W (1973) *The Urban Countryside,* London

BIRD, H and WHITBREAD, M (1975) 'Council House Transfers and Exchanges', *New Society, 33,* 671, 359–61

BLOWERS, A (1980) *The Limits of Power,* Oxford

BODDY, M (1980) *The Building Societies,* London

BOURNE, L S (1975) *Urban Systems: Strategies for Regulation,* Oxford

BUCHANAN, C D (1963) *Traffic in Towns,* HMSO

CAMERON, G C (1980) *The Future of the British Conurbations,* London

CARTER, H (1958) 'Aberystwyth: the Modern Development of a Medieval Castle Town in Wales', *Trans. Inst. Br. Geogr., 25,* 239–53

            (1965) *The Towns of Wales,* Cardiff

            (1972) *The Study of Urban Geography,* London

CARTER, H and ROWLEY, G (1966) 'The Central Business District of Cardiff', *Trans. Inst. Br. Geogr., 38,* 119–34

CASTLE, I M and GITTUS, E (1957) 'The Distribution of Social Defects in Liverpool', *Sociol. Rev., 5,* 43–64

CHAMPION, A G (1970) 'Recent Trends in New Town Densities', *Tn Cntry Plann., 38,* 5, 252–4

CHECKLAND, S G (1981) *The Upas Tree,* 2nd edn, Glasgow

CLIFTON-TAYLOR, A (1978) *Six English Towns,* London

               (1981) *Six More English Towns,* London

COLLINS, B J (1951) *Development Plans Explained,* HMSO

CONZEN, M R G (1960) 'Alnwick, Northumberland: A Study in Town Plan Analysis', *Inst. Br. Geogr. Publ. 27,* London

CRAVEN, E (1969) 'Private Residential Expansion in Kent', *Urb. Stud., 6,* 1–16

CULLINGWORTH, J B (1965) *English Housing Trends,* London

                (1974) *Town and Country Planning in Britain,* London

                (1981) *Land Values, Compensation and Betterment,* London

DANIELS, P W and WARNES, A M (1980) *Movement in Cities,* London

DAVIDSON, R N (1981) *Crime and Environment,* London

DERBYSHIRE, A (1967) 'New town plans: a critical review', *J. Roy. Inst. Brit. Arch.,* 430–40

DoE (1973) *Making Towns Better: The Sunderland Study; the Rotherham Study; the Oldham Study,* HMSO

      (1976) 'British Cities: Urban Population and Employment Trends 1951–71', *Res. Rep. 10,* HMSO

      (1977) *Inner Area Studies: Liverpool, Birmingham and Lambeth,* HMSO

DIAMOND, D R (1962) 'The Central Business District of Glasgow', in NORBURG, K (ed.) *Proc. IGU Symp. in Urban Geogr., Lund 1960,* Gleerup, Lund

              (1972) 'New Towns in their Regional Context', in EVANS, H (ed.) *New Towns: The British Experience,* London, 54–65

              (1975) 'Planning the Urban Environment', *Geogr., 60,* 189–93

              (1979) 'Aims and Implementation in British Urban and Regional Planning', *Geoforum, 10,* 275–82

DIAMOND, D R and EDWARDS, R (1975) *Business in Britain: a Management Planning Atlas,* London

DICKINSON, R E (1947) *City, Region and Regionalism,* London

DONNISON, D V (1969) *The Government of Housing,* Harmondsworth

              (1972) 'Ideas for Town Planners', *Three Banks Rev., 96,* 3–27

DONNISON, D and SOTO, P (1980) *The Good City*, London
DYOS, H J (1968) 'The Speculative Builders and Developers of Victorian London',
    Victorian Stud., 9
EVANS, H (1974) *The New Citizen's Guide to Town and Country Planning*, for
    TCPA, London
FARMER, E and SMITH, R (1975) 'Overspill Theory: a Metropolitan Case Study',
    Urb. Stud., 12, 151–68
FAWCETT, C B (1932) 'Distribution of the Urban Population in GB', *Geogrl J., 79*,
    100–16
FIELDING, A J (1981) *Counter Urbanisation in Western Europe*, Oxford
FOTHERGILL, S and GUDGIN, G (1982) *Unequal Growth: Urban and Regional
    Employment Change in the UK*, London
FROST, M and SPENCE, N (1981) 'Employment and Worktravel in a Selection of
    English Inner Cities', *Geoforum, 12*, 107–60
GEDDES, P (1915) *Cities in Evolution*, London
GEN. REGISTER OFF. (1956) *Census 1951, England and Wales: Report on Greater
    London and Five Other Conurbations*, HMSO
GODDARD, J B (1970) 'Functional Regions within the City Centre', *Trans. Inst.
    Br. Geogr., 49*, 161–82
                 (1975) 'Office Location in Urban and Regional Development',
    Theory and Practice in Geography, Oxford
GLC (1969) *Greater London Development Plan*, London
GREEN, F H W (1950) 'Urban Hinterlands in England and Wales: An Analysis of
    Bus Services', *Geogrl J., 116*, 64–88
GREGORY, R (1971) *The Price of Amenity*, London
HALL, P G (1971) 'The Spatial Structure of Metropolitan England and Wales', in
    CHISHOLM, M and MANNERS, G (eds) *Spatial Policy Problems of the British
    Economy*, Cambridge, 96–125
HALL, P G *et al* (1973) *The Containment of Urban England*, 2 vols, London.
    For problems of definition see particularly vol. 1, 42–68 and 117–40
HALL, P (ed.) (1981) *The Inner City in Context*, London
HALSEY, A H (ed.) (1972) *Trends in British Society since 1900*, London
HAMNETT, C (1973) 'Improvement Grants as an Indicator of Gentrification in
    Inner London', *Area, 5*, 252–61
                 (1976) 'Social Change and Social Segregation in Inner London,
    1961–1971', *Urb. Stud., 13*, 261–71
HART, D A (1976) *Strategic Planning in London*, Oxford
HEALEY, P and UNDERWOOD, J (1978) 'Professional Ideals and Planning
    Practice', *Progress in Planning, 9*, 73–127, Oxford
HEBBERT, M (1981) 'The Land Debate and the Planning System', *Town and
    Country Planning, 50*, 22–3
HERAUD, B J (1968) 'Social Class and the New Towns', *Urb. Stud., 5*, 33–58
HOWARD, E (1898) *Garden Cities of Tomorrow, a Peaceful Path to Real Reform*,
    London
HUGHES, A J and KOZLOWSKI, J (1968) 'Threshold Analysis – an Economic
    Tool for Town and Regional Planning', *Urb. Stud., 5*, 132–43
HURD, R M (1924) *Principles of City Land Values*, New York
JAMES, J R (1967) 'A Strategic View of Planning', *J. Roy. Inst. Brit. Arch.*,
    419–29
JONES, A (1960) *A Social Geography of Belfast*, London
JONES, P N (1967) *The Segregation of Immigrant Communities in the City of
    Birmingham 1961*, Hull
KENNETT, S and HALL, P (1981) 'The Inner City in Spatial Perspective', in
    HALL, P (ed.) *The Inner City in Context*, London, 9–51

KNOX, P and CULLEN, J (1981) 'Planners as Urban Managers: an Exploration of
the Attitudes and Self-Images of Senior British Planners', *Environment and
Planning, 13*, 7, 885—99
LAWLESS, P (1981) *Britain's Inner Cities*, London
LEVIN, P H (1976) *Government and the Planning Process*, London
LOMAS, G (1964) 'Population Changes and Functional Regions', *J. Tn Plann. Inst.,
London, 50*, 21—31
LYDDON, D (1971) 'Regional planning in Scotland: an interim assessment',
J. Roy. Town Planning Inst., 57, 300—3
McAUSLAN, P (1980) *The Ideologies of Planning Law*, Oxford
MACKAY, D H and COX, A W (1979) *The Politics of Urban Change*, London
McWILLIAM, C (1975) *Scottish Townscape*, London
MARRIOTT, O (1967) *The Property Boom*, London
MARTIN, A E (1967) 'Environment, Housing and Health', *Urb. Stud., 4*, 1—21
MASSEY, D and MEEGAN, R A (1978) 'Industrial Restructuring Versus the
Cities', *Urb. Stud., 15*, 273—88
MASSEY, D and CATALANO, A (1978) *Capital and Land*, London
MELLOR, J R (1977) *Urban Sociology in an Urbanised Society*, London
MIN. HOUSING and LOCAL GOVT and MIN. of TRANSPORT (1963) *Town
Centres: Current Practice*, HMSO
MOSER, G A and SCOTT, W (1961) *British Towns: a Statistical Study of their
Social and Economic Differences*, Edinburgh
OLSEN, D J (1973) 'House upon House: estate development in London and
Sheffield', in DYOS, H J and WOLFF, M (eds) *The Victorian City*, vol. 2,
London, 333—57
OPCS (1981) *Census 1981, Preliminary Report for Towns*, London
PAHL, R E (1965) *Urbs in Rure*, London
POOLE, M A and BOAL, F W (1973) 'Religious Residential Segregation in Belfast
in mid-1969: a Multi-level Analysis', in CLARK, B D and GLEAVE, M B (eds)
Social Patterns in Cities, Inst. Br. Geogr., London
PRITCHARD, R M (1976) *Housing and the Spatial Structure of the City*,
Cambridge
RASMUSSEN, S E (1951) *Towns and Buildings*, Liverpool
RAVETZ, A (1980) *Remaking Cities*, London
REX, J A (1968) 'The Sociology of a Zone of Transition', in PAHL, R E (ed.)
Readings in Urban Sociology, Oxford, 211—31
REX, J A and MOORE, R (1967) *Race, Community and Conflict*, London
ROBERTSON, D J, JOHNSON-MARSHALL, P E A and MATTHEW, Sir R H
(1966) *Lothians. Regional Survey and Plan*, 2 vols, Edinburgh HMSO
(1968) *Grangemouth/Falkirk Regional Survey and Plan*, 2 vols, Edinburgh HMSO
ROBSON, B T (1973) *Urban Growth: an Approach*, London
            (1975) 'Urban Social Areas', *Theory and Practice in Geography*,
Oxford
ROYAL COMMN LOCAL GOVT 1966—9 (1969) Vol. II, *Memorandum of Dissent
(D. Senior)*, Cmnd 4040, HMSO
SCOTTISH DEVELOPMENT DEPT (1963) *Central Scotland: a Programme for
Development and Growth*, Cmnd 2188, Edinburgh HMSO
SELF, P J O (1957) *Cities in Flood*, London
SHANKLAND, G (1977) *Inner London: Policies for Dispersal and Balance: Final
Report of the Lambeth Inner Area Study*, London
SHORT, J R and BASSETT, K A (1981) 'Housing Policy and the Inner City in the
1970s', *Trans. Inst. Br. Geogr., New Ser., 6*, 293—312
SMART, M W (1974) 'Labour Market Areas: Uses and Definition', *Progress in
Planning, 2*, 239—55

SMITH, R D P (1968) 'The Changing Urban Hierarchy', *Reg. Stud.*, 2, 1–19
SOLESBURY, W (1974) *Policy in Urban Planning*, Oxford
SE JOINT PLANNING TEAM (1970) *Strategic Plan for the SE*, HMSO
THOMSON, J M (1977) *Great Cities and their Traffic*, London
THORPE, D (1968) 'The Main Shopping Centres of GB in 1961. Their Location
    and Structural Characteristics', *Urb. Stud.*, 5, 165–206
THURSTON, H S (1953) 'The Urban Regions of St Albans', *Trans. Inst. Br. Geogr.*,
    19, 107–21
WESTAWAY, J (1974) 'The Spatial Hierarchy of Business Organisations and its
    Implications for the British Urban System', *Reg. Stud.*, 8, 145–55
WESTERGAARD, J H (1964) 'The Structure of Greater London', in CENTRE FOR
    URBAN STUD. *London: Aspects of Change*, London
WHITEHAND, J W R (1972) 'Building Cycles and the Spatial Pattern of Urban
    Growth', *Trans. Inst. Br. Geogr.*, *56*, 39–56
WILLIAMS, P R (1976) 'The Role of Institutions in the Inner London Housing
    Market: the Case of Islington', *Trans. Inst. Br. Geogr.*, New Ser. 1, 72–82
WISE, M J (1966) 'The City Region', *Advmt Sci.*, 23, 571–4

7

In Conclusion

I AN ASSESSMENT

This geographical interpretation of the economic, social or political conditions
affecting and affected by the UK space has been concerned with the changing
balance of forces, the spectrum of trends, the ensuing problems, and the shifting
public and private policy mix over more than three decades. Even in terms of
public policy, overall coherence of spatial objectives has been lacking and much has
been piecemeal in character. Indeed, public recognition of the importance of a
spatial perspective in national affairs has been both tardy and grudging, a situation
scarcely helped by the lack of sophistication in regional or other spatial methods in
social science. With supreme irony, as the methods and techniques became refined,
the political commitment to spatial planning faded even faster. It would thus be
crying in the wilderness, at the moment, to advocate clearer and more comprehensive spatial management objectives, to be implemented through the regional and/or
urban networks. Certainly, there is no optimal geographic solution to the arrangement of the UK space-economy, but given the innate diversity, there is everything
to be said for respecting and enhancing such a richness. Indeed, in a democratic
society, voices are likely to become increasingly powerful in claims for spatial/
regional, as well as for social, justice and authority. Furthermore, decentralization
of powers and decisions may well contain one of the keys to the hitherto elusive
problem of growth without disabling inflation in the contemporary UK. It is to be
hoped that the abrupt end to regional planning in 1979 may thus be no more than a
passing phase, if this country is to return to prosperity and, at the same time,
strengthen social harmony by the end of the century.

   The economic and social record of the UK since 1945 has been steady rather
than spectacular, lacking in 'economic miracles', but with general forward momentum until the early 1970s, albeit by any criterion somewhat slow and irregular. By
the time of entry to the EEC, the UK had achieved a major postwar transformation,
including a redefined and reduced world role. Unfortunately, assumption of a
supranational EEC role coincided with the first oil crisis of 1973–4, followed by
further violent petroleum price escalations in the late 1970s. As with all Western
industrial economies, the UK is in the grip of the powerful externalities which are
presently reshaping world economic geography. It is this irrevocable shift which
will set a binding and limiting framework to what domestic UK planning can
achieve, no matter what the political complexions of governments or their attitudes
to a spatial dimension in policy.

   Confident forward projections for the UK space are hard to justify, except in
very general terms, in face of the complexities and uncertainties of both the
immediate and the longer-term future. Furthermore, the ability to predict ahead
varies with the discipline. Reliable manpower forecasts rarely go beyond a few

years, land allocations in physical planning up to fifteen years, and broad regional strategies, until discontinued for the 1980s, set up speculative options to the end of the century. Predictions will also be conditioned by political beliefs and intentions, by an assessment of the likely and desirable courses of change in economy and society, as well as in political organization and structure.

Balance of forces At the base of all forecasting, in the light of the evidence of this book, lies the prime need to *evaluate and rank the forces which are tending to polarize, centralize or concentrate, on the one hand, and those which are tending in the opposite direction to disaggregate, disperse or breakdown concentration or congestion.* During the era of economic growth of the 1950s and 1960s the aggregating forces were strongly and increasingly apparent, notably in the range of market forces leading to concentration at fewer, larger sites in energy output; manufacturing or commercial plants or firms; transport nodes; major recreation centres; or water-storage sites. To these forces were to be added the centralizing tendencies in government, banking, insurance and finance, in the search for administrative efficiency or convenience. Spatially interpreted, these forces tended to the strengthening of the centre against the periphery, of more affluent against less prosperous regions.

On the other side of the argument, and together these forces may ultimately prove to be decisive, must be listed the desirability of greater regional balance in the economy and society of the UK, for the satisfaction of component national and regional aspirations, but also from the commonsense points of view of reducing congestion in growth regions, diminishing the sources of inflationary pressure there and spreading social justice and better prospects for economic growth throughout the UK space. Regional policies by successive UK governments recognized the validity of this thinking, but the means provided have never permitted the desirable ends to be realized. Keeble's (1976) postulation of a 'periphery-centre' reversal of the traditional centripetal polarization in UK industrial location trends seems to have been set into reverse by the adverse trends of the early 1980s.

The early 1980s Since the first edition of this book (1973), economic prospects for the UK have deteriorated sharply. Though the causes of this deep-seated recession are variously attributed, and externalities have been powerful, the roots lie surely within the economy, society and polity of the UK. The pursuit of a sustainable momentum of economic growth at full potential rate without an unacceptable level of inflation or serious damage to the balance of payments, has been the theoretical cornerstone of national investment strategy for the past three decades. Only thus could higher living standards, fuller and better social provision, and the promotion of full employment be both attained and maintained. In no other way might social justice be advanced for deprived groups, but also for localities, cities and regions in the UK space.

By any objective assessment the truth is that economic growth during the 1970s was slow overall (Beckerman 1979), fitful in its incidence and, by 1975, dramatically in secular reverse. The spatial impact has been uneven, but to the traditional structural and locational problems of the Assisted Areas have now been added the sharp deterioration in social conditions in many inner cities, and the emergence of nationwide serious pockets of unemployment, even in hitherto affluent regions of Britain. Coventry and inner London vie with Gateshead,

Lanarkshire and Belfast for the sympathy of the nation, and for priority aid from governments. British Leyland, Chrysler (UK) and Rolls-Royce have been recent supplicants for public largesse, even more than the traditionally depressed textile or shipbuilding firms.

Diagnosis of our many ills indicts countless culprits: governments, for their inability to manage the national economy, and their lack of a clear, coherent and inter-related public investment strategy, whose priorities might match the capacity of the nation to finance them adequately in time and in place; entrepreneurs, for their unwillingness to invest, modernize, rationalize, and for inefficiencies of management; organized labour, for its traditional attitudes, practices and low productivity; the general public, for its false priorities within savings and consumption, and for an ingrained demand for greater welfare and a fuller 'social wage' than the flagging Gross Domestic Product can reasonably provide.

Prescriptions for the patient are equally legion, from the doctrinaire to the pragmatic, from the grand design to the empirical, from the moral to the political. It is becoming increasingly clear that there can be no single universal 'solution' to our national problems, to be planned for, optimized, promoted and monitored until realized. Indeed, the growing revulsion against most forms of planning is disturbing to those who see the greatest need as the creation of ever more complex and sophisticated operational models to programme and control our collective futures. In the undoubted diversity in human conditions and aspirations in the UK lies both the greatest constraint for the planner, and yet, at the same time, the greatest potential for generating and accommodating to change. In all this the geographer has a distinctive role in the assessment and interpretation of the variegated urban and regional kaleidoscope of modern Britain.

II   THE REGIONAL PROBLEM

Speaking of the regional *problem* rather than accentuating regional *potential* is a fair comment on a state of affairs which has persisted in spite of almost five decades of varied government aid policies. Regional problems are common to all developed economies. Indeed, according to radical theorists (Carney *et al* 1980, 21), such problems are 'a permanent and necessary feature of accumulation in late capitalism'. Their origins lie in the fundamental inequalities of resource endowment, including natural and human resources, together with the attributes of location. Such seemingly inexorable geographical logic has been modified through time by changing technology, variations in investment, supply and demand and by changing public policies for spatial management. Resources have been revalued and fresh, mobile resources may have been introduced, intermittently, but some of the underlying realities have proved remarkably enduring.

Since the economic depression of the early 1930s, governments have been persistently and increasingly involved in policies of economic and social aid for regions, successively defined as Distressed, Development or Assisted Areas (ch. 1.III). Though the policy mix has been varied through almost five decades and measures have rarely been consistently implemented, there has been general political assent to the promotion of full employment, the pursuit of greater equality in living standards, growth prospects, and betterment of the 'living environment'; reduction in the levels of inter-regional net migration has been an additional, ambivalent, purpose on occasion. Progress towards all of these objectives can be demonstrated, for some areas and at certain periods. What is not clear is how and when, if at all, the objectives may be finally achieved and what part public policy (whether UK or EEC) must continue to play, for how long, and at what cost? More specifically, to what extent is the attempt to solve problems at the *regional* scale likely to be, or already in effect is, at the expense of aggregate national well-being?

These questions have not been answered effectively in either public or academic debate, and it is not hard to see why. It is difficult enough to trace the multiplier effects of particular ministerial policies at the regional level, even more to evaluate what might have happened without such policies, or by a different mix in time and space. It is virtually in the realms of pure conjecture what might have been the outcome of different policies. Indeed, the most important question of all may be what effect certain public policies can have, in any case, upon a complex market situation in which externalities seem to be increasingly dominant. No one has ventured to look so far ahead as to envisage a time when regional policies may no longer be necessary, given the eventual achievement of sufficient equality between British regions. Perhaps this is because, like the poor, regions will always be with us. Their built-in geographical diversities can be modified but not fundamentally changed, and the pursuit of equality is really the never-ending quest for equity, or social justice, not so easily, if ever, satisfied.

In the mid-1970s the *regional debate* (ch. 1.III) became more sharply polarized, among both academics and public policy managers. There is, moreover, a burgeoning political dimension to the debate, among nationalists and regionalists at home and among the nation-states at the level of the EEC. Not surprisingly, the mainsprings of difference are between those living and working in the Assisted Areas and those in more affluent regions. A second major distinction is between those who are insistent upon the economic logic behind policies and their impact, and those who are prepared to weight social-benefit variables elastically, even electorally. Ironically, the most reliable assessment of regional policy prospects at the present is that characteristically Scottish verdict – 'not proven'. Furthermore, and paradoxically at a time when theoreticians are proclaiming, ever more stridently, that the regional problem is but the varied expression of a national problem, the groundswell of political opinion in the 1970s became increasingly insistent upon devolution and decentralization, upon regional control over regional destinies (ch. I.IV). In the event, devolution was side-tracked, regional aspirations weakened by the demise of regional strategic planning on abolition of the Regional EPCs (1979). Radical thinkers (Carney *et al* 1980, 21) interpret the entanglement of the state in regional problems as a prime cause of their deterioration. Given the overall failure of state intervention to solve regional problems, the rise of political ferment at less than national level was an inevitable outcome. So too was the stifling of such opposition, in the interests of the state seeking to sustain central power against the periphery. The dissolution of regional policy in the UK and the negative response of government to the aspirations of regions was not dictated by the restrictive conditions of a UK siege-economy. Indeed, in an economic situation of no less gravity, the Mitterand government in France (Philipponneau 1981) gave a first priority to the processes of decentralizing power to the regions and, at the same time, gave notice of an intention to promulgate a statute for safeguarding minority languages.

It would be optimistic to assume that UK policy will be conditioned by recogni-

tion of the merits in those of our Continental neighbours. The course of EEC
regional development policy confirms such a view. The Regional Development
Fund of the EEC is only supplementary to national measures, not a first step in the
direction of markedly different market policies. Though new categories of region
for EEC aid were defined (Commn European Communities 1975), the authority to
use EEC grants remains firmly in the hands of national member governments, an
intention espoused by both Labour and Conservatives at Westminster.

III   POPULATION TRENDS AND PROSPECTS

The stagnation and possible fall in population numbers expected from pre-1939
trends, especially the level of births, did not transpire (ch. 2). Higher birth-rates
than were anticipated prevailed from the mid-1950s to the late 1960s, due in part
to earlier and more universal marriage and to increased illegitimacy rates, together
with a further reduction in general and infant mortality. Reflected in a gradual
increase in expectation of life, these have led to higher natural growth rates in the
1950s and 1960s than were forecast by the *Royal Commission on Population*
(1949). Net immigration gains from overseas in the late 1950s and early 1960s,
together with the natural increase from this relatively youthful population, further
assisted a steady increase in numbers in the UK. Estimation of future population
levels on the basis of past and current trends is a hazardous business for they
depend on assumptions which may be quickly invalidated by changing social and
economic circumstances. Successive revisions of population estimates for 1990 led
to estimates varying between 53m (based on 1955 assumptions) and 67m (1964-
based), differences due largely to alternative assumptions concerning birth-rate and
to a period of migrational gain.

While all estimates from the mid-1950s predicted growth into the 1990s, the
downturn in births of the 1970s sharply changed this trend and actually led to a fall
in natural increase in 1976 and 1977, the first since civil records were started in
1837. Hence the relatively modest growth-rates of some 0.7% per annum predicted
by the 'moderate' 1968-based estimate fell to less than 0.2% per annum by the
1974-based projection. Allowing for additional births resulting from the large
cohorts of the early 1960s, the 1979-based projections (which assume an average
net migrational loss of 30,000 per annum) think that an average annual growth of
0.21% is likely to continue in the 1980s and 1990s (fig. 7.1). Even such a modest
rate of increase would produce 59.56m people in the UK as against the 1980 mid-
year estimate of 55.95m (census 1981, 55.68m).

Many now challenge the capacity or desirability of growth in such a populous
and, in some urbanized regions, already over-crowded country. In the late 1960s,
the debate was joined over what might be an optimum population for the UK, a
debate which reflects a growing awareness of the significance of population trends
and distribution for all aspects of national life – demographic (Population
Investigation Commn 1970), social, economic and environmental (Taylor 1970).

An optimum population is not capable of a single, precise definition since it
depends upon many variables, each of which is dynamic: population, resources,
land, the level of expectations, and consumption. The first official investigation
considered these problems in an appropriately wide context, and gathered evidence
from a very wide range of viewpoints (House of Commons 1971), but did not

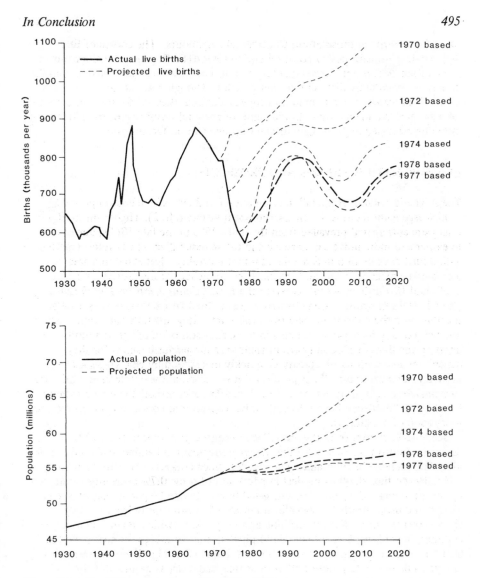

Figure 7.1   Population projections, UK, 1970–2020

emerge with any general consensus, though it did make a number of recommendations which amounted to a possible population policy for the UK and provided for
periodic reviews of the demographic situation (OPCS 1978).

It would be foolish to speculate over precise future population totals in view of
the fluctuating trends in population of the last thirty years. This underlines the
need for flexibility in economic and social policies related to population. But it *is*
possible to indicate the sort of problems which must be taken into account in any
analysis of the spatial and environmental implications of population. In terms of
food and natural resources the UK would certainly be regarded as over-populated

already, if we depended upon indigenous supplies alone, for we support only two-thirds of our present population. Indeed a suggested maximum of 40m people, made some years ago by the then President of the British Association (Hutchinson 1966), is not unrealistic in this context. However, neither on the basis of present population trends, nor of any envisaged, is such a target likely to provide the basis of a practical policy, at least in the foreseeable future though increased efficiency of farming has made us more self-sufficient.

Population is potentially an economic asset, arguably the most important which the UK, as a technologically-advanced society, possesses. Over the past two centuries a numerous, vigorous and inventive people have proved capable of enlarging the economic capacity and population potential of our islands at a rising standard of living for an increasing proportion of our people. They may be capable of doing so into the future, though decreasing demand for manpower, in terms of numbers as against skills, has already been reflected in growing unemployment in the past few years and sheds doubt on our capacity to absorb the larger potential labourforce of the 1980s. Policies to mobilize their potential skills must be vigorously pursued.

One of the most powerful factors behind the growing concern over population growth in the UK, as in other parts of the developed world, has been an increased awareness of the enormous environmental impact of a large and closely packed population in a modern industrial and urbanized society. Pressures on basic resources such as land and water, as well as on food and raw materials, are reflected in growing demands from recreation, waste disposal, both human (sewage) and non-recoverable (such as plastics or poisonous chemicals), and via pollution of air, water and land (ch. 3.V), though such environmental problems are being actively tackled.

While undoubtedly many such difficulties are due to misuse of the environment and past irresponsibility by industry, commerce and private individuals, they are exacerbated by population numbers and concentrations. Loss of land to building and communications is not likely to pose insurmountable problems over the next thirty years, not least because of the slowing down in housing and road-building programmes, but it will undoubtedly add to pressures which are already severe in some large urban areas. One way of helping to ease such problems could be a more positive approach to the problem of urban decay, with its associated complex problems of social and economic blight.

Seen thus, one critical aspect of UK population problems, now and in the future, is that concerning regional distribution and trends. The UK could, perhaps, have accommodated the population of up to 80m forecast in the mid-1960s for the second quarter of next century. The present slow growth-rates will probably produce 59–60m people by the first decade of the twenty-first century. Yet even such modest growth will require a more satisfactory regional and intra-regional balance of population in relation to land, resources and communications than that of the present day. Population policy should be seen not as a separate part of national planning but rather a key aspect for regional planning policy. Any major problem of regional planning today illustrates this point: the dispersal of homes and people farther from cities into the rural periphery with accompanying disposal of jobs in both industry and services; the provision of adequate transportation; access to land for recreation; environmental control and restoration.

Regional changes over the next decade are unlikely to differ fundamentally from those of the 1970s (fig. 2.4). The largest projected increases for 1979–91 are in

E Anglia (10.7%), the SW (6.1%) and the E Midlands (4.4%), with small increases in Yorkshire and Humberside (1.2%), the W Midlands (1.3%) and the SE (2.5%), though Greater London's population is expected to fall by 338,000 (5.6%). The fastest growth is likely to be in the non-metropolitan counties, especially in the southern parts of the country, while continuing New Town development at Telford (Shropshire), Milton Keynes (Buckinghamshire) and Northampton will be reflected in high rates of increase in their respective counties. But metropolitan counties are likely to continue to decline, W Yorkshire alone excepted. The decline of S Wales is likely to continue, but retirement migration to N Wales and the recent population recovery of parts of Mid Wales may give a relatively large increase (4%) to the principality. Scotland's continuing decline is largely due to a projected fall of over 10% in Greater Glasgow (GRO 1980) but apart from the Borders and Tayside, all other regions are expected to continue their recent growth, though the high increases projected for Grampian and, especially, Shetland will rely heavily on oil-related development. Despite its continuing economic and political problems, N Ireland's relatively high natural increase will probably produce growth of some 4.5%, 1979–91.

Relocation of city populations over more extensive regions may well continue. If not controlled, this trend could put continuing pressure on both the environmentally vulnerable areas between large cities, especially between Greater London and the W Midlands, and on the cities themselves. Especially in the conurbations, investment in urban renewal could be an act of population policy as well as of economic, social and regional planning. But to retain population and redress the imbalance of the last sixty years, capital will be needed to remedy the many deficiencies in housing, education and amenities – social as well as physical – in the inner city and in the older industrial regions.

If we do not fully utilize the resources of the whole of our islands, even modest population increases will inevitably bring greater and perhaps intolerable economic and social pressures. In recommending that a special government office should be set up to deal with these problems, a Select Committee (House of Commons 1971) urged that it should take account not only of population but also of 'such major issues as food supplies, natural resources, economic growth and the environment'. In appointing in December 1973 a minister with special responsibility for population questions, government showed itself responsive to such advice. However, as birthrate has continued to fall in the 1970s, so the concern for population policy seems to have diminished. The anti-natalist policy implicit in the two Private Members' Bills which led to the *Family Planning Act* (1967) and the *Abortion Act* (1967) before the declining births of the 1970s, was probably less effective in reducing births in the 1970s than more effective contraception and economic decline. The question has been asked whether they might be replaced by pro-natalist policies in the 1980s (Brooks 1975; Buxton and Craven 1976). Despite a considerable increase in the numbers of women of marriageable age in the 1980s, a product of the 'baby boom' of the early-to-mid 1960s, the situation in which in many households the wife is the principal wage-earner or where both husband and wife are in work, the changed role and status of women in society and a growing concern for the state of the economy and its impact on families, may all contribute to smaller families and fewer births in the late 1980s and nineties than were forecast a few years ago. Such rapid changes in population structure and trends call for greater flexibility in social and economic policy, and in public investment, a question considered in a government Central Policy Review Staff report (Cabinet Office 1975).

While recent population forecasts might seem to deny it, the UK undoubtedly has a population/resources problem. The current economic crisis and the failure to absorb a growing population of working age in the workforce will be a key issue in the social, economic and regional geography of the UK in the late twentieth century. The deterioration in the UK's economic situation in the 1970s is bound to slow down the rate of change over the next twenty or thirty years. Population numbers are already adjusting to the changed situation and we seem set for a period of slow or little natural change. But regional and local imbalances, both economic and social, still exist and are reflected in many aspects of population behaviour. Despite the shortage of public funds, it is important that flexible and effective policies designed to alleviate inequalities within the UK population should continue to receive attention.

IV   ENVIRONMENT AND LAND USE

Environmental management will become increasingly important as pressures for space increase with the need to optimize the available resources in the interests of all land users. The apparent conflicts between these users are no doubt a result of lack of liaison hitherto rather than intention, and can only be adequately resolved by adopting conservation or management policies which take all potential users into consideration. While short-term decisions may be satisfactorily made by subjective means, in the long term it would appear necessary to have complex models where evaluation of land-use policies can be fully tested. For this, continued data collection and research into the relationships between land use and environment is an urgent need. However, there is clearly a dilemma, for land use requires field observation and is therefore both costly and slow, and the more detail required the longer it will take. Stamp's land-use survey was kept simple and was thus completed within a short time. The more detailed second land-use survey is of necessity a much slower operation and its value as an inventory on which to base planning decisions is thereby greatly reduced, particularly on a regional or national scale.

Land classifications have a similar problem but the complexity of the environment makes it essential for the classification to consider the potential user of the map so that no universally satisfactory classification can be produced. Because of the variety of users, more classifications are needed in the future, a task facilitated by data storage and retrieval systems, though the problem of interpretation of environmental factors for specific purposes remains. Modelling of land-use systems, at present being developed for uplands where the conflicts between agriculture, forest, urban water-supply and recreation are relatively simple, must be extended to include the much more complex problems of the heavily populated lowlands.

Many aspects of *measurement of the physical environment* can be improved and in particular, the closing of the wide gap between the macro-climatic scale of standard meteorological records, which exist over a long period of time, and the micro-climates which so clearly affect human activity. The development of studies of local climates must again be problem-orientated. This, however, involves the isolation of the parameters important to production, particularly the commercial yields and potentials of living things such as agricultural plants and forest trees.

Equally important to production are the physical conditions permitting work to be carried out, e.g. in certain farming operations water may be critical, or in building operations wind and temperature could be limiting. The accurate prediction of these conditions will enable industry or agriculture to project production and to make more efficient use of human resources. However this will only be possible by improvements in the long term forecasting of these parameters.

Environmental pollution will change in its nature and effects so that continual monitoring is necessary. Water pollution and land pollution is a matter for river-basin management and can be more effectively controlled under the administrative reorganization carried through in 1974 in England and Wales. Conservation must imply continuance, though not necessarily maximization of production, rather than just preservation, so that here too industrial and agricultural land use must be evaluated in terms of the long-term effects on the environment. On occasion there may be a major conflict between the desire to attract industry (or allow it to grow) and priorities in conservation. Studies of industrial and urban pollution must not remain a UK problem in isolation. Entry into Europe brought with it an opportunity to achieve a measure of environmental control over the atmosphere and the seas of Europe, notably the North Sea, which could not be envisaged before.

It is as yet too early to state with confidence that environmental constraints will eventually set limits to economic growth, but it is already clear that increasing numbers of citizens are prepared to evaluate, take into account, and then give precedence to environmental implications arising from excessive preoccupation with growth.

V   DISTRIBUTION OF ECONOMIC ACTIVITY

It is becoming increasingly apparent that the evolution of the economic patterns in the UK since 1945 fall into three main periods: 1945–60, 1960–73 and post-1973.

The period **1945–60** was essentially one of adjustment following the disruption of the Second World War (Chisholm 1974). Maximization of production was at a premium and some of the growth in employment that resulted was diverted to the DAs by government action. However, by the end of this period the distribution of economic activity remained familiar. Traditional industries such as cotton in Lancashire, wool in Yorkshire, shipbuilding in N Ireland and coal and steel in S Wales and the North East, had further declined but still dominated those regions to a surprising extent. In the service sector the foundations for subsequent change had been laid by centralization of control, through nationalization of electricity and gas distribution, health and transport, but by 1960 shortages of capital for the necessary investment limited the geographical impact. Personal mobility was still restricted by low private car ownership rates which inhibited the locational flexibility of services and to a lesser extent manufacturing.

1960–73 This situation changed in the period 1960–73, when the factors described in chapter 4 were most influential in the evolution of the economic geography of the UK. The structure of the economy altered substantially, with dramatic declines in the importance of the traditional 'heavy' industries, including coal-mining, textiles, shipbuilding, metal-making, and a substantial increase in the proportion of the labour force in services. There was continued centralization of control in industry, allowing rationalization and increasing size of units to achieve economies of scale. The effective economic distance between major centres was reduced, through road-transport improvement in particular. All these tended to increase the attractions of market locations at the national and regional levels, a trend only partly modified by government action, which influenced some of the more flexible manufacturing and service activities to expand in the DAs. Within individual regions the same trends, and especially the growth of private car ownership and affluence, allowed greater flexibility of locational choice, with manufacturing and services now able to disperse farther out from main centres. As the traditional industries declined, in regions of former dominance they lost their premier positions to growing light industries, especially engineering, which was attracted to the DAs by regional incentives. The effect of this restructuring, in reducing regional differences, was reflected in the convergence of regional percentage unemployment figures after 1970. By the end of the period a new geographical pattern had emerged, substantially different from the inherited patterns still apparent in 1960. Natural gas and oil became more important than coal in the energy patterns, services location became an important determinant of the distribution of the market, influencing local and regional market-oriented manufacturing if not that serving national markets, while individual factories became larger and smaller factories clustered together on industrial estates. Decanting of manufacturing, and later services, employment from the larger cities to the urban periphery or to the DAs, created problems for the inner city. This period then was one of major changes in the economic geography of the UK.

The considerable developments of the two periods prior to 1973 were facilitated by, and dependent upon, continuing overall growth. The population expanded much more than had been anticipated, and the needs of those born in the 'baby boom' of the late 1940s (ch. 2.I) influenced market demand in the UK right through to their maturity in the late 1960s. Many industries and almost all services planned their developments to meet continued increases in demand. At the same time the government was concerned with controlling growth, guiding it away from overgrowth areas into areas of need as recommended by the *Barlow Commission Report* (R. Commn Indus. Popul. 1940). Even in 1970 the economic sections of regional plans were still concerned with influencing the location of expected growth to achieve desired spatial distributions (ch. 1.V). At the national scale, development of the estuarine areas of Humberside, Severnside and Tayside, and of New Towns and even of a New City at Milton Keynes to cope with projected population growth, were expected to have a major impact on the distribution of economic activity in the UK.

1973 onwards It is the change from this state of actual and anticipated growth, to a situation of actual non-growth, that distinguishes the third period which began in 1973. Information about this changed situation is still becoming available and too short a time has elapsed for the implications to be properly evaluated or for the duration of the non-growth situation to be predicted. What evidence there is, however, does give some basis for comment (Eversley 1975). The number of people in employment has fallen since 1973 and unemployment has risen massively. Public investment has been postponed and plans revised. With the market stagnant, private investment in manufacturing and office development has markedly declined. Contributing to this non-growth state was the rise in oil prices, following the action of the Middle East producers in 1973. This had the effect of increasing the cost of transport, reversing the trend of the 1960s. Birth-rates have continued to fall, and by 1975 were barely keeping pace with deaths and net emigration from England and Wales. Demand for major development in the estuarine areas to cope with major national population growth to the end of the century has evaporated, while New Towns have had to re-examine their position. Present trends indicate that some of the proposals which emerged in response to anticipated growth were as much as decades premature. In the new circumstances the amount of change to be expected in the distribution of economic activity in the UK is very much less than occurred in the 1960s, since lack of investment will severely limit alteration of patterns of activity.

The most obvious exception is the development of the North Sea oil resources. Much of the impact so far has been concentrated in E Scotland, with industrial C Scotland also benefiting (Dept of Industry 1975A). Industrial development in the form of petrochemical plants is expected to be located mainly in NE England and E Scotland. Elsewhere what changes do occur will continue the trends described in chapter 4, though clearly at a very much slower rate. Improved efficiency will remain at a premium, with rationalization and economies of scale still being one source of improvement, thus continuing to alter distribution patterns. One difference from the earlier periods, however, is likely to be in the field of government distribution of industry policies (Chisholm 1976). In order to achieve stated aims it will no longer be possible to divert *some* of the growth occurring in one region to another so that both grow — as was attempted in the past. In a situation of national non-growth, one region can grow only if another is in decline. Redistribution to prevent decline will be possible only by taking away any growth which one region might have had and transferring it to a region where contraction is occurring. Such a policy, which requires fossilization of the distribution of economic activity, is unlikely to be acceptable politically. Moreover, parts of former source areas of growth, such as the W Midlands and the SE, have already begun pressing their own cases for help (Falk and Martinos 1975). The best example is the inner cities from which industries have moved elsewhere, especially to the metropolitan fringes. Their economic decline has left local problems equal in some cases to those more familiar from the DAs (Gripaios 1976). In the new situation intra-regional problems such as this are expected to attract far more attention, and to influence government action on the distribution of economic activity as much as on inter-regional problems.

These comments leave little doubt that the considerable changes in the patterns of economic activity within the UK space between 1945 and 1973 (ch. 4) were much greater than the differences which can be expected to occur in the foreseeable future. The Victorian mould of Britain's economy and geography, which survived to 1945 and to a considerable extent even to 1960, was at last structurally adapted to the needs of the late twentieth century. The long term effects of sustained recession are unpredictable, so that the changes now likely are expected at most to consolidate and further develop the patterns which have emerged. These will be modified by the development of offshore fuel resources and in the longer term by changes in government policies influencing the distribution of economic activity.

VI   TRANSPORT

The rising curve of inland transport activity, increasingly dominated by road traffic, showed signs of levelling during the 1970s. At sea, the traditional network of ships and ports inherited from the nineteenth century, was largely replaced by container and bulk-cargo vessels and their respective port facilities.

The prospects for UK transport in the remainder of the twentieth century are not easily assessed for they depend on both economic and political developments. The volume of future transport will depend on whether the British economy declines, stagnates or regains the growth levels of the 1960s. In each of these scenarios political decisions will have to be taken on whether to expand, retain or reduce the present level of inter-city, urban and rural public transport. Public transport services in their present form will not survive without substantial investment and, in the areas of rural and urban transport, a system of charges which reflects the relative total costs of public and private transport to the community.

There are other choices to be made in transport policy. The desirability of long-term structure plans to which new investment may be related as opportunity arises has long been accepted at the county level, although interference in such plans by national governments in the perceived interests of their short-term policies has increased in recent years. At the beginning of the 1970s there were signs of a consensus on a national transport structure plan which would identify the main corridors of inter-city movement, along which the different transport modes might well compete, and the locations of major ports, their associated industrial zones and the airports for international traffic. The trunk road/motorway plans of the late 1960s and the MIDA proposals were tentative moves in this direction. By the late 1970s, however, both major political parties, faced with marked differences of interest among their supporters and by strenuous local objections to the specific locations of component motorways and airports, disavowed national structure planning in favour of more general intermodal competition.

The failure of the political parties to espouse long-term transport policies, both in government and in opposition, is one of the reasons for the remarkable failure to bring several transport debates to conclusion. The long-running saga of the Third London Airport began in 1961 and arguments on the desirability or otherwise of *social* railway services have continued since the publication of the *Beeching Report* (1963). The Channel Tunnel project has a much longer history. Continued uncertainty about Britain's future in the Common Market influences investment in ports and ferry services and indirectly affects the future volume of overseas trade and the level of industrial output. The pursuit of short-term policies and political expedients in the transport field by successive Conservative and Labour administrations created uncertainty about the prospects of specific transport services and has reinforced the understandable reluctance of the transport workforce to move from labour-intensive to capital-intensive methods of operation.

It is a depressing paradox of late-twentieth-century Britain that, while immense strides have been made in the collection and scientific analysis of transport data during the past 25 years and in the greater understanding of the interaction between engineering, economic and social aspects of transport services by a whole new generation of transport planners and traffic managers, the policies of successive governments have been characterized by short-term perspectives and rapidly diverging dogma. As long as transport issues are presented to the public through the simplistic and misleading iconography of Beeching axes and juggernauts, there is little prospect of popular understanding of the complexities of transport policy. Until the UK finds a better solution than hitherto to the problem of democratic guidance of technically sophisticated sectors of the economy like transport, little progress can be made towards designing transport services which reflect the present and projected needs of the national economy and its regional components.

VII THE URBAN SYSTEM

Any forecast of probable changes in the British urban system over the next twenty or so years is more than usually difficult to make in the early 1980s. Substantial uncertainty surrounds several of the major influences. Official population forecasts now predict a net addition substantially less than that forecast in the late 1960s (section 7.III). The rapid and substantial increase in the real cost of petrol is beginning to alter mobility patterns and if it continues commuting and leisure may be substantially affected. In contrast to these trends, which would tend to slow down the rate of decentralization, there are others which might accelerate it. New and improving telecommunications technology could make dispersal more possible, while the pressure from families in the inner-city areas of the conurbations for more space and improved living conditions will see traditional physical planning policies continued, favouring further decentralization. In political terms, however, the problems of the inner cities (not least those of C London) led in 1976 to pressures for reversal of the decentralization policies for overspill which had characterized spatial planning since 1945. At the same time, the programmes for New Town expansion came under equally critical review.

The scale and the strength of the decentralization pressure in individual towns, cities and SMLAs will depend to a large degree on the regional economic dimension. New cores for emerging metropolitan areas will arise, if employment decentralization from the conurbations continues despite the national economic difficulties. Increasing metropolitanization of free-standing towns will occur in some localities in response to changing economic opportunities, as North Sea oil has already demonstrated in Scotland. Regional policy and transportation investment will continue to remain significant background influences under the control of central government. In general the role of cities in steering the pattern of regional growth and decline seems likely to obtain greater recognition and consequently regional policy will probably come to have a more explicitly urban character.

It is possible therefore that the period 1975–2000 will not see changes in the British urban system as great as those in the period 1950–75. Almost certainly the city-region or metropolitan area will continue to be the dominant settlement type. By the year 2000, however, continued expansion among the adjacent and over-lapping metropolitan areas from Southampton and Southend to Lancaster and Leeds, whether planned as in the case of Northampton, Milton Keynes, Warrington and Swindon, for example, or otherwise, will have begun to create a megalopolitan structure in which the complexity of inter-city and intra-city movements makes the definition of individual metropolitan areas less useful. The outstanding feature of this highly interlocked urban system will be the intensity and diversity of the communication channels for people, goods, and particularly information (Cowan *et al* 1969).

Both the major urbanized zones beyond this megalopolitan heartland, the North East and C Scotland will also be characterized by megalopolitan features, as the planned integration of the city regions (Glasgow–Edinburgh–Dundee and Newcastle–Teesside) is achieved. Elsewhere, rural zones providing essentially either recreation or agriculture will exist with minor centres and the exceptional free-standing city region, e.g. Aberdeen and Plymouth.

The most uncertain question of all is whether local, regional, and national planning processes are capable of managing the continuing evolution of the urban system in a fashion that brings widespread public support. Without a deep and continuing commitment to intervention in the public interest, the influencing of the diverse private interests in a populous, developed and metropolitanized nation is impossible.

VIII A FINAL NOTE

A postscript of the early 1980s must necessarily be bleakly less optimistic than one of even a few years ago (Hudson Institute 1974). Preoccupation with serious and deepseated structural economic problems in the UK halted, indeed reversed, the dramatic trends of growth and change since 1945 (Leicester 1972). The problems endemic in slow growth or in the steady-state society require sensitive planning measures, the more difficult in that they must now also carry conviction with sectional interests, as well as with the public. The continuing distribution, or redistribution, of national wealth among classes and regions is central to public policies, but to be implemented needs sufficient sustained economic growth. Whether to promote growth, to stabilize, or to accept a measured decline, the mobilization of regional and national support on the grand scale is an urgent task. The verdict of this book is that such a mobilization is technically and geographically feasible and it is little short of disastrous that the regional voice has been muted. Careful public management and monitoring of the economy will continue to be essential, but such deliberate public intervention should take more fully into account for the future the variegated characteristics, the many constraints, but especially the infinitely greater potentials which have been shown to be inherent in the complex geographical character of the UK space.

REFERENCES

BECKERMAN, W (ed.) (1979) *Slow Growth in Britain,* Oxford
BROOKS, E (1973) *This Crowded Kingdom: An Essay on Population Pressure,* London
BUXTON, M and CRAVEN, E (eds) (1976) *The Uncertain Future,* Centre for Stud. in Soc. Pol., London
CABINET OFF., CENT. POLICY REV. STAFF (1975) *Joint Framework for Social Policies,* HMSO
CAMPBELL, R (1979) 'Population Projections: English Regions and Counties, *Popul. Trends, 16,* 17–21
CARNEY, J, HUDSON, R and LEWIS, J (1980) *Regions in Crisis: New Perspectives in European Regional Theory,* London

CHISHOLM, M D I (1974) 'Regional Policies for the 1970s', *Geogrl J.*, *140*, 215–31
        (1976) 'Regional Policies in an Era of Slow Population Growth
and Higher Unemployment', *Reg. Stud.*, *10*, 201–13
COMMN EUROPEAN COMMUNITIES (1975) *General Regional Aid Systems*,
COM (75) 77, Brussels
COWAN, P *et al* (1969) 'Developing Patterns of Urbanisation', *Urb. Stud.*, *6*,
279–453
DEPT INDUSTRY (1975A) 'Oil-related Developments in Scotland', *Scott. Econ.
Bull.*, *7*, 8–13
        (1975B) *Airport Strategy for Great Britain*. Pt. 1 *The London
Area. A Consultation Document*, HMSO
EVERSLEY, D (1975) *Planning without Growth*, London
FALK, N and MARTINOS, H (1975) *Inner City*, London
GRIPAIOS, C (1976) 'A new Employment Policy for London?', *Nat. West. Bank Q.
Rev.*, August, 37–45
GRO (Scotland) (1980) *Projected Home Populations of Scotland by Area* (1979
based)
HOUSE OF COMMONS (1971) 'Population of the UK', *First Report of the Select
Comm. on Sci. and Technol.*, HMSO
HUDSON INST. (1974) *The UK in 1980?*, London
HUTCHINSON, Sir J (1966) 'Land and Human Populations', *Advmt Sci.*, *23*, 111,
241–54
KEEBLE, D (1976) *Industrial Location and Planning in the UK*, London
LEICESTER, C (1972) *Britain 2001 AD*, HMSO
LLOYD, T I (1955) 'Potentialities of the British Railway System as a Reserve
Roadway System', *Proc. Inst. Civil Engrs*, 4, 1, 732–88
MIN. of TRANSPORT (1963) *The Reshaping of British Railways* (Beeching
Report), HMSO
OPCS (1978) *Demographic Review: a Report on Population in Great Britain, 1977*,
HMSO, series DR, No. 1
PHLIPPONNEAU, M (1981) *Décentralisation et Régionalisation*, Paris
POPULATION INVESTIGATION COMMN LSE (1970) *Towards a Population
Policy for the UK*, London
PUBL. GEN. ACTS, see list below
ROY. COMMN DISTRIBUTION OF THE INDUS. POPULATION (1940) (Barlow)
Rep., Cmnd 6153, HMSO
ROY. COMMN POPULATION (1949) *Rep.*, Cmnd 7695, HMSO
TAYLOR, L R (ed.) (1970) 'The Optimum Population for Britain', *Inst. Biol.
Symp.*, *19*, London

PUBLIC GENERAL ACTS

(1844)   Railway Regulation, Ch. 85
(1888)   Local Government, Ch. 41
(1894)   Local Government, Ch. 73
(1919)   Forestry, Ch. 58
(1920)   Government of Ireland, Ch. 67
(1930)   Road Traffic, Ch. 43
(1933)   Road and Rail, Ch. 53
(1936)   Trunk Roads, Ch. 5
(1945)   Distribution of Industry, Ch. 36

Index